African American Biographies

*This book is dedicated
to my mother,
Helen M. Johnson Hawkins*

African American Biographies

Profiles of 558 Current Men and Women

by

Walter L. Hawkins

McFarland & Company, Inc., Publishers
Jefferson, North Carolina, and London

Acknowledgments

I should like to express my appreciation to Brenda Procter for her administrative assistance, Sharon Crittendon and JoAnn Campbell for their technical assistance, and Clarence Green, Jr., for his assistance and technical advice in the photographic area. I am grateful to the many persons who performed valuable services in the preparation of this book.

I wish to express my appreciation to NASA, the United States Air Force, the United States Army, the United States Navy, and the White House staff for the assistance rendered.

British Library Cataloguing-in-Publication data are available

Library of Congress Cataloguing-in-Publication Data

Hawkins, Walter L. (Walter Lee), 1949–
    African American biographies : profiles of 558 current men and women / by Walter L. Hawkins.
      p.   cm.
    Includes index.
    ISBN 0-89950-664-X (lib. bdg. : 50# alk. paper) ∞
    1. Afro-Americans—Biography—Dictionaries.   I. Title.
E185.96.H38   1992
920'.009296073—dc20
[B]   91-50938
                                           CIP

Manufactured in the United States of America

McFarland & Company, Inc., Publishers
  Box 611, Jefferson, North Carolina 28640

Contents

Foreword

This book provides profiles of 558 of the nation's most notable black Americans. The entries are arranged alphabetically with all individuals meeting two general criteria for inclusion. First, they were born or spent their childhood years in the United States. (A few exceptions were made when foreign-born figures resided most of their adult lives in the United States.) Second, they must have played an important role in the development of African American children, by serving as a role model. Anyone who died in the year 1968 (the year of the assassination of Martin Luther King, Jr.) or before is not included.

The standards used to measure contribution and accomplishment include membership in professional and community organizations; notable athletic achievements and records; career successes; national, state, city or community leadership; being the first African American in a profession, field, or position; major honors or Olympic medals, or selection to any hall of fame.

African American Biographies provides the reference librarian, the student, or any researcher with brief, objective, accurate, and well-researched biographical articles about living and deceased (marked with a †) African Americans. Some of the names are familiar, but I also expect that you will meet several men and women whose names are not well known, but whose accomplishments are obviously deserving of recognition.

This book does not attempt to chronicle the full range of African American contributions in the United States. Instead its intent is to identify those individuals who have served as role models and insure that their achievements are noted and recorded historically, to be made readily available for generations to follow.

African American Biographies

AARON, HENRY LOUIS, was born February 5, 1934, in Mobile, Alabama, to Estella and Herbert Aaron. He married the former Billye Suber Williams, and he has six children: Hank, Larry, Gail, Gary, Dorenda and Ceci. He attended Central High School in Mobile, and attended Josephine Allen Institute in 1951. Aaron's first baseball team was a sand-lot outfit named the Pritchett Athletics. The Indianapolis Clowns, a Negro League team, signed up Aaron in 1952.

Aaron came to the Milwaukee Braves' attention through a postscript in a letter from Syd Pollock, owner of the Clowns. "We've got an eighteen-year-old shortstop batting cleanup for us," Pollock wrote. The Braves bought Aaron from the Clowns on June 12, 1952. The Braves sent Aaron to Eau Claire, Wisconsin, in the Class C Northern League. There he played shortstop, batted .336, and was voted Rookie of the Year. The following season he played second base with Jacksonville, Florida, in the Class A South Atlantic (Sally) League. During the winter before the 1954 season Aaron was sent to Puerto Rico to learn the art of playing the outfield. He reported to the Braves for spring training in 1954. He led the National League in homers, with 44 home runs and 132 runs batted in. Home run number 43 came on the night of September 24, 1957, in the 11th inning of a game with the second-place Cardinals. The four-bagger broke a 2-2 tie, clinched the National League flag for the Braves and sent the "Beer City" residents into a frenzied celebration. Hank continued his heroics against the New York Yankees in the seven-game World Series which the Braves won by a 4-3 margin. Aaron battered Yankees pitching at a .393 clip. His 11 hits included three home runs. Aaron was able to become the all-time home run champ by sustaining a relatively unspectacular but remarkably consistent career. He was never hurt badly enough to be out of the lineup for an extended period of time. He was not a particularly aggressive baserunner, so his legs suffered little wear and tear. He averaged 33 home runs a year, and drove in more than 100 runs 15 times, including a record 13 seasons in a row. He was an All-Star in each of the 23 seasons he played.

On April 8, 1974, he completed baseball's most memorable moment by hitting the 715th home run of his career in a game against the Los Angeles Dodgers. In 1975, Aaron returned to Milwaukee and concluded his career as a designated hitter for the Brewers. He hit 22 homers in the American League and finished with 755, and 3,600 hits. Aaron's unparalleled career is an American legend. In 1976, Aaron returned to Atlanta as director of player personnel for the Braves farm system. In 1979, he was named vice

1

president and director of player development for the Atlanta Braves. At that time he was the only black executive serving a major league baseball team.

―――――――

ABDUL-JABBAR, KAREEM, was born April 16, 1947, Ferdinand Lewis Alcindor, Jr., in New York, New York, the son of Ferdinand and Cora Alcindor. He attended St. Jude's elementary school in Inwood. He won his first medals and trophies for Little League baseball, ice skating, and swimming. The secondary school he attended was Power Memorial Academy, a Roman Catholic institution on the west side of Manhattan run by Irish Christian Brothers. In his sophomore year, 1962–1963, he averaged 19 points a game. Power Memorial was undefeated in 27 games and won the New York City Catholic High School basketball championship. In 1963–1964, Alcindor's junior year, he averaged 26 points and 18 rebounds a game, and Power Memorial won all 27 of its games and again captured the Catholic High School championship. By his senior year he was averaging 33 points a game and Power Memorial won its third consecutive championship. Alcindor set a New York City high school scoring record, with his career total of 2,067 points.

More than 100 colleges and universities made him scholarship offers; he chose the University of California at Los Angeles on the recommendation of Ralph Bunche, the United Nations under-secretary. He enrolled at UCLA in 1965. While there he was named Player of the Year in 1967 and 1969 and first team consensus All-American in 1967, 1968 and 1969. He was a member of NCAA Championship teams, 1967, 1968 and 1969, and was named NCAA Tournament most outstanding player, 1967, 1968 and 1969.

He began his pro-basketball career with Milwaukee on April 2, 1969. This was the era of the Black Panthers, Black Muslims, the death of Dr. Martin Luther King and ghetto riots. It was a time when Cassius Clay changed his name to Muhammad Ali and refused to go to war, a decision that so outraged the sports establishment that it cost him the heavyweight title. This was a year after two black American athletes had raised their fists in protest in the 1968 Olympics, the same Olympic games Alcindor decided not to play. In 1971, he declared his religious conversion by changing his name to Kareem Abdul-Jabbar, which means noble, powerful servant. In 1970, he appeared in the NBA's All-Star game as a rookie, and Abdul-Jabbar was named Rookie of the Year. On December 10, 1971, he scored a career high 55 points in a game against Boston. Also in 1971, he was named Most Valuable Player, named to the All-NBA First Team, led the league in scoring, and named Playoff MVP. In 1972, he was again named Most Valuable Player, chosen for the All-NBA First Team, and led the league in scoring. In 1973, Abdul-Jabbar was again named to the All-NBA First Team. In 1974, for the fourth straight year, he was named to the All-NBA First Team, and won his third Most Valuable Player award. On June 16, 1975, he was traded to the Los Angeles Lakers. On December 14, 1975, he grabbed a career high 34 rebounds in a game against the Detroit Pistons. Also in 1975, Abdul-Jabbar led the league in blocked shots.

In 1976 as a Laker, he was named Most Valuable Player, chosen for the All-NBA First Team, and led the league in both rebounding and blocked shots. On December 4, 1977, he began a string of 787 consecutive games with 10 or more points scored. In 1977, Abdul-Jabbar was also named Most Valuable Player, chosen for the All-NBA First Team, and led the league in field-goal percentage. In 1979, he led the league in blocked shots. In 1980, Abdul-Jabbar was named Most Valuable Player, chosen for the All-NBA First Team, led the league in blocked shots, named to the NBA's 35th Anniversary All-Time Team, and was a member of the Championship Team. In 1981, he was named to the All-NBA First Team and in 1982 he was a member of the Championship Team. In 1984, he was named to the All-NBA First Team and that year he passed Wilt Chamberlain on the all-time scoring list. In 1985, he was named Playoff Most Valuable Player, and was a member of the Championship Team. In 1986, he was named to the All-NBA First Team. In 1987, he was a member of the Championship Team, and on December 2, 1987, he ended his string of 787 consecutive games with 10 or more points scored.

In 1988, Abdul-Jabbar was a member of his last Championship Team, and on December 16, 1988, he played in his 1,500th game. Entering 1989 postseason competition, he held playoff records for most points (5,595), seasons (18), games played (222), minutes played (8,500), field goals attempted (4,275), field goals made (2,288), personal fouls (754) and blocked shots (465). On February 5, 1989, he scored his 38,000th point. On February 12, 1989, he appeared in his 18th all-star game. On April 16, 1989, he became the only 42-year-old ever to play in the NBA. He holds All-Star Game records for most points (251), games played (19), and field goals made (105).

Abdul-Jabbar's achievements, NBA regular-season record: Points—38,387; Seasons—20; Games—1,560; Minutes played—57,446; Most field goals made—15,837; Most field goals attempted—28,307; Most blocked shots—3,189; Most personal fouls—4,657. He retired in 1989. After 20 professional campaigns, Kareem Abdul-Jabbar had played his last regular season game. He may be the best player in pro-basketball history.

Certainly, a case can be made in his favor. Any time such a player leaves, the game itself can't ever be quite the same. By playing so long at such an elite level, he has given fans a sharp picture of what can be produced by truly remarkable athletic ability combined with iron determination. There has never been anyone quite like him before, not even Wilt Chamberlain or Bill Russell. And there is no heir apparent waiting to replace him. Abdul-Jabbar showed that a player could have magnificent individual statistics and still be such a significant team player that he can retire with six championship rings. Chamberlain had magnificent individual statistics, but titles eluded him most of his career. Russell played on 11 championship teams, but his statistics never came close to matching those of Kareem.

ABERCRUMBIE, P. ERIC, a native of Falmouth, Kentucky, is married to the former Claudia M. Colvard. They have two children, Paul Eric and Erica Marie. A graduate of Covington Holmes High School in 1966, in Falmouth, he received his B.A. in sociology and his M.A. in counseling from Eastern Kentucky University and a Ph.D. in the Interdisciplinary Studies Program from the University of Cincinnati. His academic and professional expertise has been focused on issues concerning black males in America. Also, he is the originator of the Black Man Think Tank which has received national acclaim. Abercrumbie is highly recognized in his works with cultural diversity. He has served as a racial/human relations consultant to corporations, community groups, and educational systems. P. Eric Abercrumbie served as director of ethnic programs, and services and adjunct assistant professor in the Department of African American Studies at the Evening College and the College of Arts and Sciences respectively, at the University of Cincinnati. In 1978 and 1980, he was named by the United States Jaycees as one of the Outstanding Community Leaders of the World. In 1986 and 1987, he was elected to Who's Who Among Black Americans. He was named an honorary member of the Golden Key National Honor Society. Also in 1987, Abercrumbie was named by the United States Peace Corps as the Black Educator of the Year, and by the YMCA of Greater Cincinnati as a Black Achiever.

In 1988, he was recognized by the University of Cincinnati Racial Awareness Pilot Project as one of ten distinguished faculty members who promote racial and cultural diversity and he was recognized as the University of Cincinnati United Black Faculty Member for a quarter. He served on the Executive Committee of the Greater Cincinnati Martin Luther King, Jr., Coalition, and as a head basketball coach for the BON-PAD Athletic Association.

---

†ABERNATHY, RALPH DAVID, was born March 11, 1926, in Marengo County, Alabama. He married the former Juanita Odessa Jones and they have four children: Juandalynn Ralpheda, Donzaleigh Avis, Ralph David, III and Kwane Lithuli. He received a B.S. degree from Alabama State University in 1950. He received a master's degree in sociology from Atlanta University in 1951. At the age of 22, he was ordained a Baptist minister, and became pastor of the First Baptist Church in Montgomery, Alabama, where he became a close associate of Dr. Martin Luther King, Jr. They worked side-by-side in the Montgomery bus boycott starting in late 1955, and early in 1957. In 1957, King, Abernathy and several other black clergymen formed the Southern Christian Leadership Conference, Abernathy first serving as financial secretary-treasurer, King as president. As an associate of King, Abernathy was committed to nonviolence. At Dr. King's urging, the Rev. Abernathy followed by his side to Atlanta, becoming pastor

of West Hunter Street Baptist Church in 1961. It was also in 1961 when Abernathy and King arrived in Montgomery to help Freedom Riders test rulings against non-discriminatory transportation.

For 13 turbulent years, from December 1955 until Dr. King's assassination in April 1968, Abernathy was constantly at his side during the civil rights revolution. Abernathy and King were jailed together 17 times, including the time in Birmingham when Dr. King wrote his famous "Letter from the Birmingham jail" in 1963. Abernathy was a few feet away when Dr. King was shot down in Memphis in 1968. He succeeded King as president of the Southern Christian Leadership Conference (SCLC). In 1973, he resigned as SCLC president, but associates persuaded him to stay. He quit again in 1977, this time for good. Abernathy had experienced a series of setbacks in the 1980s: a stroke in January 1983, a by-pass operation for a blocked cerebral artery in March 1983, and an apparent second stroke in June 1986. In 1990, he released his book, *And the Walls Came Tumbling Down,* an autobiography. Abernathy died of cardiac arrest April 17, 1990. He had been the pastor of West Hunter Street Baptist Church for 29 years. On April 28, 1991, about 200 supporters, friends and family attended the unveiling of Ralph David Abernathy Boulevard in Atlanta, Georgia. The street dead-ends at Martin Luther King, Jr., Drive, giving the Rev. Abernathy a place next to his partner in the struggle for justice and equal rights.

ADAMS-ENDER, CLARA LEACH, was born on July 11, 1939, in Willow Springs, North Carolina. She received a B.S. degree from North Carolina Agricultural and Technical State University, and received a Master of Science degree in Medical Surgical Nursing from the University of Minnesota.

From August 1961 to October 1961, she was a student at the United States Army Nurse Corps Orientation Course, at Brooke Army Medical Center at Fort Sam Houston, Texas. From October 1961 to May 1963, she served as staff nurse in the Recovery and Intensive Care Unit at Walson Army Hospital at Fort Dix, New Jersey, as a first lieutenant. From May 1963 to June 1964, she

served as a staff nurse in the 121st Evacuation Hospital, with the United States Army in the Pacific. From July 1964 to December 1964, she was a student at the United States Army Nurse Corps Officer Advanced Course, at Fort Sam Houston in Texas. She was promoted to the rank of captain on September 17, 1964.

From December 1964 to August 1967, she served as a medical-surgical nursing instructor and later chief of the Ward Training Section of the Nursing Science Branch, at Fort Sam Houston. From September 1967 to June 1969, she was a student at the University of Minnesota in Minneapolis. From June 1969 to July 1972, she served as a medical-

surgical nurse instructor, later as assistant professor, at Walter Reed Army Institute of Nursing in Washington, D.C. She was promoted to the rank of major on February 23, 1968. From July 1972 to May 1974, she was the education coordinator at Walter Reed Institute of Nursing, Walter Reed Army Medical Center. From May 1974 to May 1975, she served as the assistant chief of the Department of Nursing at the United States Army Medical Activity at Fort Meade, Maryland. She was promoted to lieutenant colonel on May 7, 1975. From June 1975 to June 1976, she was a student at the United States Army Command and General Staff College at Fort Leavenworth, Kansas. From June 1976 to June 1978, she served as the inspector general at the Headquarters of the United States Army Health Services Command at Fort Sam Houston, Texas. From June 1978 to July 1981, she served as the assistant chief and later as chief of the Department of Nursing at the 97th General Hospital, United States Army in Europe. She was promoted to the rank of colonel on July 10, 1979.

From July 1981 to May 1984, she served as chief of nurse recruiting at the United States Army Recruiting Command, Fort Sheridan, Illinois. From May 1984 to August 1987, she served as chief of the Department of Nursing at Walter Reed Army Medical Center. In August of 1987, she was assigned as a special assistant to the chief of Army Nurse Corps, Office of the Surgeon General, at Falls Church, Virginia. In September 1987, she was promoted to the rank of brigadier general, and assigned as chief of the Army Nurse Corps, Office of the Surgeon General, Falls Church, Virginia. She has received numerous awards and decorations which include: the Legion of Merit; Meritorious Service Medal (with 3 oak leaf clusters); the Army Commendation Medal; the Expert Field Medical Badge; and the Army Staff Identification Badge.

ADRINE, RONALD B., was born and raised in Greater Cleveland. He spent his childhood in the Glenville area and his adolescence in Shaker Heights. He attended Parkwood Elementary School, Patrick Henry and Woodbury junior

high schools, and Shaker Heights Senior High School, graduating in 1965. He matriculated for one year at Wittenberg University in Springfield, Ohio, before transferring to Fisk University in Nashville, Tennessee, in 1966. Upon his graduation from Fisk University in 1969 with a B.A. degree in history, he was chosen for the Ohio Bell Telephone Company's Management Development Program. In the fall of the same year he entered the night program at Cleveland State University's Cleveland-Marshall College of Law. In 1973, he completed his course of study and was awarded a juris doctorate degree. In July of 1973, he took the Ohio Bar Examination and in November of that year was admitted to the practice of law in Ohio.

In June of 1974, he left the telephone company and took a position as assistant prosecuting attorney in the Criminal Trial Division of the Cuyahoga County Prosecuting Attorney's Office. He remained with that office

from June of 1974 until January of 1977, when he entered private practice with his father, Russell T. Adrine, forming the firm of Adrine and Adrine. In June of 1978, he was given the opportunity to join the legal staff of the Dr. Martin Luther King, Jr., Task Force of the United States House of Representatives' Select Committee on Assassinations. At the conclusion of the Committee's mandate, he returned to Cleveland and re-entered private practice with his father. In November of 1981, he was elected to the position on the bench of the Cleveland Municipal Court.

Judge Adrine has been active in both professional and civic organizations in the community. He is the founder and a past president of the Norman S. Minor Bar Association, the largest association of black attorneys in Ohio. He was also a member of the Ohio State, Cuyahoga and federal bar associations and the District of Columbia Bar Association. He had served as a member of the Governor's Task Force on Family Violence and was appointed to Ohio's Victim Assistance Advisory Board by Attorney General Anthony J. Celebrezze, Jr. The Judge was selected for inclusion in the pages of *Who's Who in the Law; Who's Who in the Midwest;* and *Who's Who Among Black Americans.*

ALEXANDER, AVERY C., was born in Houma, Louisiana, in Terrebonne Parish to Abner and Lena Taplett Alexander who were sharecroppers on a sugar cane plantation. The oldest living of seven brothers and sisters, he was married to the late Pansy Garrett; they had one daughter. He came to New Orleans in 1927 and attended Thomy Lafon Elementary School and Gilbert Academy. He completed high school in 1939. He attended Xavier University, Leland College, Southern University, Tulane University, Union Baptist Theological Seminary and the University of New Orleans. Alexander worked as a laborer and longshoreman and attended school at night. He has been a Baptist minister and the state representative for the people of Legislative District 93.

Alexander became a member of the NAACP and has been active in the labor movement on the waterfront. At a time when it was almost impossible for a black to register to vote — they were ridden down by white policemen on horseback in New Orleans; in other places in Louisiana they were jailed, beaten and killed for attempting to register — he traveled throughout the state participating in black voter registration drives. He was chased out of many little towns. He was the past president of the Consumers League of Greater New Orleans, the organization which spearheaded the consumer movements that pressured white business establishments to hire blacks in department stores on Canal Street and throughout the city and in supermarkets like Schwegmann, Winn Dixie and A&P in positions above the broom and mop level. It also forced beer and soft drink manufacturers and distributors to upgrade black employees from their position of helpers to salesmen-drivers, which tripled their incomes. Under the threat of boycott, it forced New Orleans Public Service, Inc., to hire black bus drivers for the first time in history. Under the threat of successful boycott activities, banks and other financial institutions and many other businesses that had previously excluded blacks from clerical, managerial and executive positions began to hire them in those positions.

Alexander was in the march from Selma to Montgomery, Alabama, with the late Dr. Martin Luther King, Jr. He was in the march from Memphis to Jackson with Dr. King. He was in the first march on Washington and the second march on Washington in 1963 when Dr. King made his famous prediction in the "I Have a Dream" speech. He was involved with Dr. King in Birmingham after four little black girls were bombed and killed in Sunday School and King wrote his "Letter from a Birmingham Jail." Alexander helped to integrate segregated lunch counters throughout the city of New Orleans. While attempting to integrate the eating facilities at City Hall, he was arrested and dragged by his heels up a flight of stairs and thrown into a patrol wagon. He was a real estate broker and insurance agent, and managed the Longshoreman Welfare and the Monarch (now Universal) Life Insurance Company. Alexander is a former member of the Democratic State Central Committee and the Orleans Parish Democratic Executive Committee. He was a delegate to the Democratic National Convention in 1972 in Miami, Florida, and in New York in 1980. He is president of Brothers Improvement Association.

———

†ALEXANDER, CLIFFORD LEOPOLD, JR., was born on September 21, 1933, in New York, New York. He received a B.A. degree in American government from Harvard University, graduating cum laude in 1955. He received an LL.B. degree from Yale Law School in 1958. He then enlisted in the 369th Field Artillery Battalion of the New York National Guard, and after the completion of a six-month tour of active duty as a private at Fort Dix, New Jersey, in February 1959, he worked for two years as an assistant to the district attorney of New York County. In 1961, he became executive director of the Manhattanville–Hamilton Grange Neighborhood Conservation Project on New York City's Upper West Side. In 1962, he served as Program and Executive Director of Harlem Youth Opportunities Unlimited (HARYOU). In 1963, he devoted himself full time to private law practice in midtown Manhattan. later in 1963, he went to Washington to work for the administration of then — President John F.

Kennedy. He joined the staff of the National Security Council where his main responsibility was to keep track of cable reports about Asia, particularly Vietnam.

On June 18, 1964, he was appointed to the White House staff by President Lyndon B. Johnson. He first served as a deputy special assistant for personnel and administration. In 1965, he was named an associate special counsel, and in 1966, deputy special consultant. In 1967, President Johnson made him his personal consultant on civil rights problems. In 1967, President Johnson appointed Alexander chairman of the Equal Employment Opportunities Commission (EEOC). He took office on August 4, 1967. He was the first black to serve as chairman. In 1969, he left the EEOC and became a partner in the law firm of Arnold & Porter. He remained with Arnold & Porter until January 1976, when he joined another noted Washington, D.C., law firm. On January 19, 1977, President Jimmy Carter appointed Alexander as Secretary of the Army, the first black to serve in that position. At the time Alexander took office, the department's budget amounted to $28.8 billion and its personnel included some 370,000 civilian employees in addition to the 1,300,000 Army regulars, reservists, and National Guardsmen.

ALI, MUHAMMAD, was born January 17, 1942, in Louisville, Kentucky. He was born Cassius Marcellus Clay, Jr., the son of Cassius Clay, Sr., and Odessa "Bird" Clay. He married four times, to Sonji Ray, Belinda, Veronica, and his present wife, Yolanda. He has eight children: Laila, Hana, Maryum, Muhammad, Jamilah, Rasheda, Miya and Kaliah. When Cassius was 12, his $60 bicycle was stolen. He reported the theft to the police and encountered policeman Joe Martin, who was active in the Golden Gloves program. Martin told him he had better

learn to fight so he could protect his property. Soon Cassius and his younger brother Rudy (Rachman Ali) were hanging around Martin's gym, learning to box. Young Cassius was noted as a prodigious eater, pretty good rock fighter and dead-eye marble shooter, who also found time for such teenage athletic activities as softball, basketball and touch football. His part-time jobs included babysitting, working with Rudy at a local rollerskating rink and light maintenance work at Nazareth College (now Elizabeth Spaulding College).

As an amateur boxer Clay compiled a 100-8 ring record en route to a berth on the 1960 United States Olympic team. He attended DuValle Junior High and Central High School in Louisville. He appeared regularly on "Tomorrow's Champions," a weekly televised boxing program in Louisville in the late 1950s. He became the national Golden Gloves champion in the light-heavyweight division in 1959, and again in 1960. He went to the Olympic trials in San Francisco in 1960 and earned the right to represent the United States in the light-heavyweight division in the Rome Olympics. John F. Kennedy was campaigning for the presidency when Cassius returned triumphant from the Olympic Games. Shortly after he got home, a group of 11 white millionaires from Louisville, men known as captains of Kentucky industry, signed the Olympic gold medal winner to a lucrative contract as soon as he announced his intention to turn professional. He turned pro and had 19 victories in almost 40 months, then the unbeaten kid fought Sonny Liston for the championship. An 8 to 1 underdog, the screaming Clay predicted he would win in the eighth. But Liston quit early just to spoil his prediction.

Clay's victory pumped life into the dead boxing game. He was called "The Louisville Lip" and became an international hero. He was only 22 and all the world lay before him. But at the same time he buried the name of his birth,

Cassius Marcellus Clay, Jr., and announcing his conversion to Islam, became Muhammad Ali. When Ali's contract with the Louisville group expired in 1966, Ali signed with Herbert Muhammad, the son of Elijah Muhammad, founder of the Black Muslim movement. Ali had earned $2.3 million during his six years with the Louisville Sponsoring Group. He would win twice that amount in the first six fights Herbert Muhammad set up for him. Taking a 40 percent cut of his fighter's earnings, Muhammad engineered colossal financial deals built on the premise that Muhammad Ali was the most popular performing athlete the sports world had ever seen. Exploiting Ali's planetary appeal, Herbert Muhammad masterminded a series of sporting coups by getting independent governments, rather than ordinary promoters or sports arenas, to sponsor prize fights. "Invite Muhammad Ali to fight," Herbert Muhammad said, "and your country will share the world spotlight." Zaire, Malaysia and the Philippines took him up on it, each hosting and footing the bills on multimillion-dollar boxing extravaganzas. Egypt, Saudi Arabia, Iran, Santo Domingo and Haiti tried to get in on the action.

On April 28, 1966, the day Ali refused induction into the Army, the New York Boxing Commission rescinded his license to engage in prize fights in New York and the World Boxing Association declared he was no longer heavyweight champion of the world. Ali had refused to be inducted on the grounds that he was a Muslim minister. In 1967, in the midst of the war in Vietnam, he was convicted of draft evasion and the boxing commissions did what no fighter had been able to do — they stripped Ali of his title. From April 1967 to October 1970, he fought a legal battle during his exile, one that exhausted his savings. He appealed his draft conviction to the Supreme Court of the United States. On June 20, 1970, the Court ruled

unanimously that the once and future champion qualified as a conscientious objector. He had, evidently, proved that he was a certifiable man of conscience. The stage was set for Ali's return to the ring, and it was Georgia's black state Senator Leroy R. Johnson that staged Ali's comeback bout against boxer Jerry Quarry on October 26, 1970. The exile had robbed him of three precious years in his mid–20s, when an athlete's body is as good as it ever will be. But Ali went on to become the greatest fighter in any weight. Any man who could come back the way Ali did had everything. He had the body, the physical being. He had the reach with a left that could keep an opponent off all night. He had the most extraordinary foot speed for a heavyweight, and the same speed in his hands.

In his last fight, Ali looked respectable from the opening bell, but failed to come out for the 11th round. For the record, the fight was designated as a knockout in the 11th round. That decision was made by WBC president Jose Sulaiman afterward. Drawing from a record live gate of 25,000, Ali received a guaranteed $8 million, while Holmes, Ali's one-time sparring partner, received $6 million. Muhammad Ali has had many honorary degrees conferred upon him, including one doctoral citation from Ortanez University in Malina. In November 1990, Ali went to Baghdad, Iraq, and after a few days met with Iraqi President Saddam Hussein. On December 4, 1990, he returned to the United States with 15 freed Americans.

ALLEN, CAROLYN W., was born in Cleveland, Ohio. She was raised in Glenville and graduated from John Hay High School in 1965. She attended Central State University where she received her Bachelor's Degree in 1969, and received her Doctorate of Law from Case Western Reserve University in 1972. Married to Robert L. Allen, with two children, Tiffany and Cicely. Ms. Allen is an active member of Mt. Olive Baptist Church on Cleveland's East Side.

After her admission to the bar, Allen started her career in Columbus, Ohio, where she served briefly with the Department of Housing and Urban Development. She entered the private practice of law from 1973 to 1975 and developed expertise in civil rights litigation. Allen left the practice of law to become executive director of the Legal Aid Society of Columbus where she was responsible for providing legal services to the indigent in Columbus. She also served on the Franklin County Public Defender Commission where she was instrumental in setting policy for the new public defender services for Franklin County. Upon her return to Cleveland in 1978, she was appointed by then–U.S. Attorney James R. Williams to an assistant U.S. attorney's position with the U.S. Attorney's office of the northern district of Ohio. There she handled a variety of litigation in the federal district courts.

She remained with the U.S. Attorney's Office for 11 years until 1990 when she was appointed to the position of Director of Public Safety of the city of Cleveland by Mayor Michael R. White. Her duties entailed serving as the executive head of the police, fire, emergency medical service, traffic engineering, and city kennels. The make up of her department consists of 3,300 city employees.

ALLEN, DEBORAH, was born January 16, 1950, in Houston, Texas. She is the third of the four children of Andrew Allen and Vivian (Ayers) Allen. She married Norman Nixon and has two children: Vivian Nichole and Norman, Jr. She received a Bachelor of fine arts degree, cum laude, from Howard University, Washington, D.C., in 1971. Allen began taking dance lessons at the age of three, training at the Ballet Nacional de Mexico, and was admitted to the Houston Foundation for Ballet at the age of 14. She was given a full scholarship, becoming the only black in the company. She was refused admission to the North Carolina School of the Arts, despite being asked to demonstrate technique to the other auditioners, because, according to the dance director, she was "built wrong."

After this stinging blow, she stopped dancing for a year. She enrolled at Howard University in Washington, D.C., where she began studying Greek classics, speech, and theater arts. While she was at Howard University, choreographer Mike Malone was able to get her in his dance troupe and give her a part in his production of *The Music Man*. She also danced with student groups at Howard, studied at the National Ballet School, and headed the dance department at what is now the Duke Ellington School of the Performing Arts. In 1971, she headed for New York where the choreographer Louis Johnson cast her as a dancer in a musical *Purlie*. In 1973, she was cast in a Broadway musical *Raisin*. After leaving the cast of *Raisin* in 1975, Allen began landing television jobs, first in commercials. Her first variety series was a comedy called *3 Girls 3*. In 1977, she appeared as Ben Vereen's dancing partner in the television special "Stompin'." In 1979, she was seen in the theater, on television, and in the movies. In February she starred in *The Next Generation;* in March she replaced Charlene Woodard in *Ain't Misbehavin'*. In 1980, she was in Broadway's *West Side Story;* in 1981, she took a role in the movie *Ragtime;* in 1981, she also won a role in NBC's adaptation of *Fame*. The show won five Emmy awards; Allen won one for best choreography.

In 1984, Allen was named one of *Fame*'s producers, and she directed several of its episodes. On October 23,

1983, in a made-for-television movie, *Women of San Quentin*, Allen played a tough prison guard. In 1984, she co-wrote, choreographed, and performed in "Dancin' in the Wings," a one-hour television special. In 1986, she was cast in Richard Pryor's movie *Jo Jo Dancer*, and back on Broadway in *Sweet Charity*. By 1991, Debbie Allen, the singer, dancer, actor, choreorapher, created lots of excitement as director of the hit TV series *A Different World* on NBC. She has directed episodes of *The Fresh Prince of Bel-Air, Family Ties*, and *Quantum Leap*.

ALLEN, NIATHAN, a native of Walton County, Georgia, attended the Newark, New Jersey, public schools. He earned his Ph.D. in interdisciplinary studies at the University of Cincinnati (where he served as a business officer), an M.S.W. from Atlanta University, and a B.A. from Johnson C. Smith University where he excelled as an athlete-scholar and graduated cum laude. Allen is an Aspen Institute fellow; a New York Community Trust scholar; and a graduate of the Federal Executive Institute in Charlottesville, Virginia. He was the first black to serve as executive director of the famous Henry Street Settlement House, one of the nation's oldest, largest, and best known agencies on New York's historic lower east side.

As one sensitive to the importance of how a social service agency was perceived in its community, and particularly among centers of influence and affluence, Allen set about building bridges to those individuals and organizations that an agency needs to benefit itself by being visible in the community by positive interaction with funding sources and by constant participation in selected meetings on local, state and national issues. It is precisely this outreach and intellectual vigor that caught the attention and in-

terest of the Massachusetts governor who appointed Allen chairman of the Citizens Advisory Committee for the Boston state hospital site. He developed and implemented a training and strategy center which analyzed the impact of proposed federal and social legislation on local communities adjacent to the Cathedral Church of St. John the Divine in New York, where he served as deputy to the dean. Allen also served as campaign coordinator for former state Senator H. Carl McCall of New York, who later became America's deputy ambassador to the United Nations. He went on to serve as special assistant for public policy to state Senator William F. Bowen, the former chairman of the Ohio Senate Finance Committee, and received two special resolutions drafted in his honor by the Ohio and Massachusetts senates. Allen is a former chairperson of the executive director's council of the United Neighborhood Houses of New York. While he was in the Justice Department, Allen was cited by the attorney general for sustained superior performance.

Dr. Allen has published numerous articles on urban and municipal issues, and he is listed in editions of *Outstanding Young Men in America, Community Leaders* and *Noteworthy Americans*, and at the International Biographical Center (Cambridge, England). He has served on the Boys Harbor board of directors in New York City and the executive committee of the Governor's Community Development Coordinated Council; he has been a member of the executive committee of the Greater Boston Civil Rights Coalition; and he functions as board treasurer of the Harvard Street Community Health Center. His major concerns and commitments are in educating youth, particularly student athletes.

ALLEN, ROBERT LEE. The Allen family resides in the Betholite community where Bob is a deacon of Betholite Church, chairman of the deacon board, a Sunday school teacher, and church treasurer. He is married to Helen Savage of Magnolia. The parents of five children — Katrina, Gina, Alfred, Eric and Kevin — and six grandchildren. Allen graduated from the public school of Cocoa, Florida, and the Mount Nebo High School of Cocoa, and completed nearly all requirements for an associate degree in business administration at James Sprunt Technical College, Kenansville, North Carolina. He is a retired petty officer of the U.S. Naval Reserve. He is very active in community affairs.

Some of his activities include serving on the advisory council of Rose Hill Magnolia Elementary School, as past treasurer of Rose Hill Magnolia P.T.O. serving for two years; as a board member of General Electric Co. credit union, as a past member of the Duplin County Planning Board, and as an active member of the NAACP. He attained a 32nd Degree in the Scottish Rite Free Masonry. He was supervisor at Eastern Airlines, Kennedy Airport, and manager of Horn and Hardart Retail Company. He was elected in November 1988 as Duplin County Commissioner of District 6. Allen served on the board of directors of the Neuse River Council of Government, was chairman of the Neuse River Council of Government's Area Agency on Aging (AAA), a member of the Water Commission of Duplin County. He has received several awards and certificates: in 1975, he was selected for the G. E. Phillipe Award, Peer Review Award, N. C. State University, Raleigh, N.C.

ALLEN, ROY L., II. A native of Savannah, Georgia, Allen married the former Leilani Pa'Alan; they have one son, Roy L. Allen, III. A graduate of Benedictine Military School, Allen received his B.A. degree in philosophy (cum laude) from Howard University in Washington, D.C., and his master's of public administration from the University of Georgia with a concentration in state and local government. He received his legal training from the University of Connecticut School of Law in West Hartford, Connecticut, and did additional graduate study at the University of Hartford in Yale University. He has been a practicing attorney and the owner and senior member of the law firm of Allen & Perry with offices in Savannah and Atlanta. The firm recently entered into a joint venture with the law firm of Arrington & Hollowell, specializing in municipal bonds and finance law.

His professional memberships include the Georgia Bar Association, the American Bar Association, the Georgia Association of Criminal Defense Lawyers, and the Georgia Trial Lawyers Association. He has been a member of St. Benedict's Catholic Church where he served on the Holy Name Society, as well as a member of the Knights of Columbus, and has also been chairman of the school board for St. Vincent's

Academy. He has been active in several fund-raising and development drives for the Catholic Diocese of Savannah and has had public and private audience with Pope John Paul II in May of 1984 and August 1987.

In 1980, he was elected to the Chatham County Commission, and prior to serving his full term, he was elected to the Georgia House of Representatives in 1982. As a member of the Georgia House he had served on the powerful Appropriations Committee as well as the powerful tax-writing panel, the Ways and Means Committee, and was also a permanent subcommittee chairman on criminal law and procedure on the House Judiciary Committee. He was elected to the state senate and began his term of service in January 1991. Allen is an author of legislation on teenage unemployment, drug trafficking, deferred taxation, public transportation, crimes against children, insurance fraud and crimes against senior citizens.

AMBROSE, HENRIETTA, has been married to Walter L. Ambrose, Sr., for 42 years and has three children and six grandchildren. She is a lifetime resident of Webster Groves, Missouri, and an active volunteer in church, community, and cultural organizations. Prior to being appointed to the Webster Groves City Council in 1986, Ambrose worked for the federal government and retired in 1985 after 30 years of service. She ran for the Webster Groves City Council in 1988. In October 1987, Ambrose organized the North Webster Neighborhood Coalition. The purpose of this organization was to provide an effective means through which the people in the area could work together to maintain and improve social, educational and economic conditions of the area. Further, she served as liaison between the citizens of this area and official government agencies of Webster Groves and St. Louis County. She is treasurer of the Missouri Humanities Council Board and former member of the legislative committee of this board. Chairman of the subsidy committee of the Interfaith Housing Board of St. Louis.

In 1989, she was appointed by Secretary of State Roy Blunt to the board of directors of the Friends of the Missouri Archives and served as chairman of the planning committee. Also appointed to serve as a trustee of the State Historical Society of Missouri. Ambrose is a member of the Webster Groves Historical Society and served as president of the society from 1983–85. As chairman of the society's black history committee, she presided over the mounting of a photographic exhibition of over 200 pictures on "Black History in Webster Groves." The University of Missouri Press at Columbia will soon publish a book entitled *A History of Black Families in Webster Groves.*

AMOS, ARCHIE L., JR., is married, and the father of two children. He graduated from the State University of New York at Buffalo with a B.A. degree in urban studies while serving as the coordinator for the university district's neighborhood revitalization program. In 1979, he began a career as a professional firefighter while simultaneously teaching for the Buffalo Public School system at West Hertle Middle School. He was a member of the New York State Division for Youth in 1982; Board President of Youth Developmental Center #6, 1985 to present. Elected in 1985 to the Office of Council member for the university district for the City of Buffalo Common Council. He was re-elected in 1987 and 1989. Amos has held two positions since 1979 as city representative for the City of Buffalo and since 1986 has served as fireman for the Common Council Fire Department.

Prior positions include: coordinator for all software programs, city of Buffalo; supervisor for supply room, city of Buffalo; foreman, Iron Workers Local; licensed insurance underwriter in life and health insurance for Equitable Life; and laborer for Bethlehem Steel. The recipient of several awards which include the Distinguished Alumni Award in 1986 and 1987 from the State University of New York at Buffalo; Man of the Year Award from the University Democratic Club; participation awards from St. Joseph's Roman Catholic School and from the Brain Injured of Erie County; achievement recognition award from the Buffalo Common Council; and the President's Award from the New York State Division for Youth. His professional affiliations have been numerous.

ANDERSON, EUGENE, was born in Diffee, Georgia, on March 9, 1944, one of 11 children. He graduated from Douglass High School in 1962 and entered the military immediately after graduation. While in the Army, he served as a personnel specialist with the 101st Airborne Division at Fort Campbell, Kentucky, during the Vietnam Era. Senator Anderson and his wife Jewel have three children and one grandchild. A resident of Wichita since 1965, he was elected to the Kansas House of Representatives in 1972 and again in 1974, serving in that position for four years. He later joined the staff of United States Congressman Dan Glickman, where he served as a district aide until 1978. Upon leaving Congressman Glicksman's employment, he became a brakeman/switchman for the Atchison-Topeka and Santa Fe Railway Company where he worked for nine years.

In 1979, Governor John Carlin appointed Anderson chairman of the state Civil Rights Commission where he served for four years. In 1984, the voters of the 29th senatorial district elected him to the position of state senator. He was elected to that position again in 1988 and presently serves in that capacity. Senator Anderson serves on the National Conference of State Legislatures, is ranking minority member of the Federal and State Affairs Committee, and is a member of the Public Health and Welfare Committee, the Financial Institutions and Insurance Committee, the Educational Planning Committee and the National Confer-

ence of Legislature's Education and Job Training Committee. He is also a member of the National Business League, a past president of the Optimist Club of Northeast Wichita and a past treasurer of the state Democratic Party.

ANTHONY, CLARENCE E., is a graduate of Palm Beach Community College, Lake Worth, Florida; pre-law major, 1979; B.A. degree, Florida Atlantic University, Boca Raton, Florida, social science, 1981; master's in public administration, Florida Atlantic University, Boca Raton, 1982; post-graduate studies, Florida Atlantic University. A lifetime resident of Palm Beach County, specifically Belle Glade and South Bay, Florida, Anthony was elected mayor of the city of South Bay. Prior to becoming mayor, he was president of C. E. Anthony & Associates, Inc.; director of the Palm Beach County Board of Commissioners; administrative assistant to Commissioner Ken Adams, District V; Planner, Palm Beach Council; regional planner, Treasure Coast Regional Planning Council; research assistant, South Florida Water Management District (Internship); adjunct professor, Florida Atlantic University, Nova University, Palm Beach Community College, and Florida Memorial College; appointed member, Palm Beach County Planning Council; Chairman, Florida League of Cities board of directors; chairman, directions committee, Palm Beach County Municipal League (PBCML); chairman, PBCML nominations committee; member, 1985 and 1986 growth management directions committee for Palm Beach County; participant, C-51 Growth Management Conference (January 1985).

The recipient of many honors: South Florida Business Journal 1990 Up & Comer's Award; Florida Jaycees 1989-1990 Mayor of the Year for the state of Florida; *Ebony* Magazine Future Leader; McKnight Foundation Black Doctoral Fellowship; FAU Distinguished Alumnus Award; Palm Beach Community College Distinguished Alumnus Award; *Outstanding Young Men in America; Outstanding Community Leaders of America;* Environmental Growth Management Graduate Fellowship. Mr. Anthony's professional affiliations have included: Suncoast Chamber of Commerce board of directors; member, Economic Council of Palm Beach County; Florida League of Cities board of directors and executive committee; National League of Cities Human Development Steering Committee; member, Leadership Palm Beach County; Florida Atlantic University Institute of Government board of directors; member, board of directors, Palm Beach County Minority Cultural Consortium; chair, Tri-City League of Cities; member, Omega Psi Phi Fraternity; member and Chapter Services Director, Gold Coast Chapter of American Society for Training & Development.

ARNOLD, WALLACE CORNELIUS, was born July 27, 1938, in Washington, D.C. He received a B.S. degree in industrial education from Hampton Institute and an M.A. in personnel management and administration from

George Washington University. He received an ROTC commission to 2nd lieutenant in May 1961. From May 1961 to September 1961, he was a student in the air defense artillery officers basic course at the United States Army Air Defense School, Fort Bliss, Texas. From September 1961 to November 1962, he was a platoon leader in the 2nd Battalion of the 71st Air Defense Artillery in Korea. From November 1962 to August 1964, he served as Assistant S-4 of the 35th Air Defense Artillery Brigade at Fort Meade, Maryland. From August 1964 to January 1966, he was the Commander of H Battery of the 35th Air Defense Artillery Brigade. From February 1966 to September 1966, he was a student in the artillery officers advanced course at the United States Army Air Defense School at Fort Bliss, Texas. From October 1966 to January 1968, he served as brigade personnel officer at headquarters of the 30th Air Defense Artillery Brigade, in Okinawa. From January 1968 to March 1969, he was assigned as the S-3 of the 8th Battalion, 3rd Air Defense Artillery, in Okinawa. He was promoted to the grade of major on February 26, 1968.

From March 1969 to June 1969, he was a student at the United States Army Institute for Military Assistance, Fort Bragg, North Carolina. From July 1969 to July 1970, he served as the Chief of Psychological Operations Division, G-5, at headquarters of the XXIV Corps in Vietnam. From July 1970 to June 1971, he was a student in the United States Army Command and General Staff College, Fort Leavenworth, Kansas. From June 1971 to May 1972, he served as Chief of the Air Defense Artillery Section at the Air Space Control Element of the 6th Battalion, 68th Air Defense Artillery, at Fort Bliss, Texas. From May 1972 to October 1974, he served as a personnel management officer for the Air Defense Artillery Branch, Officer Personnel Directorate, United States Army Military Personnel Center, in Alexandria, Virginia. From December 1974 to July 1976, he was the commander of the 3rd Battalion, 61st Air Defense Artillery, 3rd Armored Division, United States Army, in Europe. He was promoted to the grade of lieutenant colonel on June 1, 1974. From August 1976 to July 1977, he was a student at the Naval War College at Newport, Rhode Island. From July 1977 to June 1979, he served as a computer systems software and analysis officer, Functional Systems Division, Office of the Assistant Chief of Staff for Automation and Communications, United States Army, in Washington, D.C.

From June 1979 to June 1981, Arnold was a military assistant in the Office of the Undersecretary of the Army, in Washington, D.C. He was promoted to the grade of colonel on August 1, 1980. From June 1981 to April 1982, he served as inspector general for VII Corps, United States Army, in Europe. From April 1982 to November 1984, he was the commander of the 69th Air Defense Artillery Brigade, 32nd Army Air Defense Command, United States Army, in Europe. From November 1984 to June 1987, Arnold served as director of personnel, J-1/inspector general, United States European Command. He was promoted to the one-star grade of brigadier general on August 1, 1985. From June 1987 to May 1990, he was the commanding general of the First Reserve Officer Training Corps Region, Fort Bragg, North Carolina.

He was promoted to the two-star grade of major general on October 18, 1989. In May 1990, he was assigned as commanding general of the United States Army Reserve Officer Training Corps Cadet Command at Fort Monroe, Virginia.

He has received numerous awards and decorations, including the Defense Superior Service Medal, the Legion of Merit (with oak leaf cluster), the Bronze Star Medal (with oak leaf cluster), the Meritorious Service Medal (with four-oak cluster), Army Commendation Medal (with oak leaf cluster), and the Parachutist Badge.

ARRINGTON, MARVIN S., was born in Atlanta, Georgia, a product of Atlanta's public housing. He is married to Marilyn and the father of two children, Marvin, Jr., and Michelle. He is a graduate of Clark College and the Emory University School of Law. He received his doctor of laws degree after having been one of the two blacks to integrate the law school. Arrington studied as an International Business Fellow at the London School of Business. He also taught on the graduate level at the Atlanta University School of Social Work and is one of the most well-known and highly respected trial and municipal bond attorneys in the South, having been recognized as one of the 25 top attorneys in Atlanta. Arrington was president of the Atlanta City Council and is a practicing attorney and senior partner in the law firm Arrington & Horne. Having distinguished himself while serving for 12 years in various capacities on the Board of Alderman/Atlanta City Council, he was elected president of the council in 1980 to complete the unexpired term of his predecessor. He then was elected to a full four-year term as council president in 1981, and reelected in 1985.

During his extensive public service career, and especially since becoming council president, Arrington has sought to assure open-minded, comprehensive and broad-based consideration of complex and often competing public policy issues. But he is probably most often characterized by his energy, hard work and strong preference for action. He has established a strong public policy record on issues affecting Atlanta's economic climate, including leadership initiatives aimed at revitalizing Auburn Avenue. But strengthening public safety throughout the city and the training, educating and motivating of Atlanta's youth and illiterate adults have also

have also been high priorities. In his capacity as council president, Arrington repeatedly has acted to encourage social responsibility for all Atlantans and contributed to the overall health and progress of the city. His long record of commitment and accomplishment have earned him numerous professional and civic awards, along with carrying out many other commitments to public service.

ARRINGTON, RICHARD, JR., was born October 19, 1934, in Livingston, Alabama, the older of two sons born to sharecroppers Richard and Ernestine Arrington. Married to the former Rachel Reynolds of Montgomery; they have seven children: Anthony, Kenneth, Kevin, Angela, Patrick, Erika Lynn, and Matthew Richard. He graduated from Fairfield public schools in Alabama. Richard's training in higher education was in the fields of biology and biochemistry. He received an A.B. degree from Miles College, a master's degree from the University of Detroit, and a Ph.D. degree from the University of Oklahoma. In 1966, he served as professor of biology at Miles College. He also served for four years as academic dean at Miles College. In June 1970, he assumed the position of executive director of the Alabama Center for Higher Education, an organization of the eight black senior colleges in Alabama. In November 1971 and 1975, he was elected to four-year terms on the Birmingham City Council.

He served on the board of directors of a large number of community service organizations. Included among these were the executive boards of the Boy Scouts of America, the Salvation Army, Goodwill Industries, the Birmingham Urban League, and Positive Maturity (Aging). He was chairman of the board of Positive Maturity, Alabama Goodwill Industries and the Birmingham Urban League. Served as chairman of the local United Negro

College Fund Campaign on several occasions and on the executive committee of the Democratic Party at the county and state levels. He was also a member of the board of trustees for Alabama State University. He has received academic honors as an outstanding student and in the last two years has been given more than 25 awards for outstanding community service.

In 1979, with about 10 percent of the city's white voters crossing the color line, Richard Arrington defeated a white opponent to become the first black mayor of Birmingham, Alabama. Arrington, a two-term city council member, swapped the lead several times during the counting process with attorney Frank Parsons, a conservative who was making his first bid for public office. Arrington joined Ernest Morial of New Orleans and Maynard Jackson of Atlanta as black mayors of major Southern cities. In 1991, Arrington was still serving as mayor of Birmingham. He adopted a citywide hiring policy that increased the black representation on both the fire and police departments. During his tenure, Arrington's sensitivity and intelligence have helped him appeal to the black and white communities.

ARTHUR, GEORGE K., is a native and lifelong resident of Buffalo, New York. Married to Frances Bivens Arthur, they have three children: Hugh, Janice and George K. Jr. Arthur was educated at P.S. #32, Seneca Vocational High School, Millard Fillmore College and Empire State College, with a B.A. in political science. He served in the U.S. Army for two years, and is a member of First Shiloh Baptist Church. Arthur served as president of the Buffalo Common Council. Arthur carved out a distinguished career as a public official beginning with his election to the Erie County Board of Supervisors in 1963. Arthur had served as Ellicott district councilman and councilman-at-

large before being elected to his post as president of the Buffalo Common Council in 1983.

Arthur has been a consistent and articulate spokesperson for Buffalo's most underserved people, the poor and the elderly. He has championed excellence in education, neighborhood revitalization and improved housing for all citizens. He is indeed a man with a plan. George's interest in the community of Buffalo transcends politics; he has actively served in a variety of social and civic action organizations. Among these are the Ellicott Neighborhood Advisory Council (former chairman); Federation of Block Clubs; Black Leadership Forum; Council #82 AFSCUME. He was on the boards of Kleinhans Music Hall; Buffalo Philharmonic; the Better Business Bureau and the NAACP.

ARTISON, RICHARD E., was born in Omaha, Nebraska, in 1933. Married and the father of three children. Received B.A. degree from Drake University, Des Moines, Iowa, with majors in sociology and psychology. Attended

Graduate School of Business and Public Administration, Cornell University, Ithaca, New York, under a fellowship in 1973-1974, completing the Education for Public Management Program, with emphasis in industrial and labor relations. Attended numerous schools, seminars, career development and in-service training sessions in areas of law enforcement and management. August 1983 to date, sheriff of Milwaukee County, responsible for the operations of the second-largest law enforcement agency in the state of Wisconsin.

Prior to this position Artison was a special agent in the U.S. Army Counterintelligence Corps, Detroit Regional Office, 1955-1958, with an honorable discharge; beat patrolman and detective on Omaha, Nebraska, police department, 1958-1962, where he served on robbery and homicide squads and received two commendations; criminal investigator and special agent, U.S. Treasury Department, alcohol, tobacco and tax division in Virginia, Illinois, Missouri and Wisconsin, 1963-1965; community relations specialist, Milwaukee Fire and Police Commission, 1967-1968; 1968-1983, U.S. Treasury Department, U.S. Secret Service, various positions held in Milwaukee, Los Angeles and Washington, D.C. He was special agent in charge of the Milwaukee office of Secret Service from October 1974 to August 1983. He was assigned to protect every president and vice president from 1965 to 1983 and all major presidential and vice presidential candidates during the 1968, 1972, 1976 and 1980 campaigns. He lectured on various criminal justice subjects at Marquette University, University of Wisconsin-Milwaukee Area Technical College, University of Wisconsin-Platteville, Los Angeles Police and sheriff's departments training academies. Artison has made numerous local radio and television appearances.

The recipient of numerous awards: U.S. Treasury Department High Quality Award for solving a $4 1/2 million counterfeit money operation in Los Angeles which resulted in 175 indictments; Albert Gallatin Award for Public Service granted by U.S. Treasury Department; Special Service Award from Frontiers International for fundraising efforts resulting in placement of a bust of Duke Ellington in the Performing Arts Center, Milwaukee; Award for Exemplary Achievement in Law Enforcement from Kappa Alpha Psi Fraternity; Excellence Award for Achievement and Civic Participation from the Wisconsin Association for

Sickle Cell Anemia; Gavel Award from Allied Council of Senior Citizens of Wisconsin for efforts to improve community relations; Law Enforcement Commendation Medal from the Wisconsin Society of the Sons of the American Revolution; 1985-1990 Career Youth Development Image awards; Mary Church Terrell Club Award for Community Services; IBA Humanities Award; Fourth District Wisconsin American Legion Law and Order Award; State of Wisconsin American Legion Outstanding Police Officer Award; Father of the Year

Award from Children's Outing Society; Professional Service Recognition Award from the Wisconsin Chapter of National Black Alcoholism Council; Wisconsin Governor's Conference on Crime Prevention Award for Outstanding Dedication and Commitment in Crime Prevention; Milwaukee Police Department-Northwest Training Center Anti-Drug Award and Fifth District American Legion Civic Award.

Memberships in numerous organizations include: past president of the Badger State Sheriff's Association; past president of the Federal Official's Association of Milwaukee; charter member of the Federal Criminal Investigators' Association, Milwaukee Chapter; past vice-president and executive board member of Milwaukee Club of Frontiers International; member of Milwaukee County Law Enforcement Executive's Association; executive board member, Milwaukee County Council, Boy Scouts of America; board of trustees, Boys & Girls Club of Greater Milwaukee; board of directors, American Red Cross; advisory board, Children's Outing Association; Wisconsin Attorney General's Law Enforcement Advisory Committee; president and charter member, Wisconsin chapter, National Organization of Black Law Enforcement Executives (NOBLE), 1990; president, Friends of School of Education, University of Wisconsin-Milwaukee and School of Social Welfare Community Advisory Board, University of Wisconsin-Milwaukee.

ASHE, ARTHUR, JR., was born July 10, 1943, in Richmond, Virginia, the son of Arthur Ashe, Sr., and Mattie (Cummingham) Ashe. He has a younger brother, John. He married Jeanne Marie Moutoussamy, and they have a daughter, Camera Elizabeth. In 1958, at age 14, he entered the junior national tennis championships and reached the semifinals in the under–15 division. He won the junior singles title in 1960 and re-tained it in 1961. After he became junior indoor singles champion, Richard Hudlin, a tennis official in St. Louis, Missouri, offered to coach Ashe. He accepted the invitation and moved to St. Louis after completing his junior year at Walker High School in Richmond. In St. Louis he lived with the Hudlin family and completed his secondary schooling at Sumner High School.

In 1962, he ranked fifth among U.S. junior players. After his graduation from Sumner High, he accepted a tennis scholarship at UCLA. In 1963, he was ranked 18th in the senior men's amateur division and was named to the Davis Cup team. The only Davis Cup match he played that year was in the American Zone final against Venezuela, and he won it in straight sets. In 1965, he was ranked third, and he won the Queensland championships at Brisbane, beating Emerson in five sets. In June 1966, he graduated from UCLA with a degree in business administration. After graduation he spent six weeks in a Reserve Officers Training Corps encampment, where he was rated second in his platoon for overall achievement. Ashe's military service was from 1967 to 1969; he attained the rank of first lieutenant. In 1975 at the Wimbledon Singles Championship he became the first and only black to win that championship.

In 1981, he became the first black to be named captain of the U.S. Davis Cup Team, a position he held until 1985. During that time the team won the international competition in his first year, 1981. Ashe is the only black American to serve as captain of the team. In the 1960s and 1970s, Ashe had to be determined and concentrate on his goals, which was hard to do in the predominantly white world of tennis. Playing at Forest Hills, Long Island, and other places where the only other black he would see was a waiter or locker room attendant, Ashe stated, "The American tennis community, and white society in general, is afraid that if we get our foot in the door, we'll do in tennis what we've done in basketball — take over." To the black youth of America, Ashe stated, "We have been on the same roads, sports and entertainment, too long. We need to pull over, fill up at the library, and speed away to Congress and the Supreme Court, the unions and the business world." He was retained by Coca-Cola and hired by Philip Morris to work for its Clark Gum as a promoter. He also worked for ABC-TV as a sports commentator. He is also an author and consultant.

ATKINS, FREDD GLOSSIE, was born June 19, 1952, and is married to Luethel and the father of five children: Nilaja, Amina, Baraka, Dumaka and

Zakia. He graduated from Sarasota High School, 1970; Manatee Junior College, Bradenton, Florida, 1979, receiving an A.A. degree in social welfare; and attended the University of South Florida (1 semester away from a B.S. degree in interdisciplinary social science). Was elected city commissioner in April 1988. His prior positions include: counselor for the State of Florida Health & Rehabilitation, 1975–1978 and to date; assistant program coordinator for the Manatee County Community Mental Health Center, 1979; legal researcher (part-time) for Lipman & Weisberg, attorneys at law, 1980; counselor for the Youth Offender Program, 1980–1981; substitute teacher for the Sarasota County School Board, 1981–1983; counselor/teacher for the City of Sarasota Parks and Recreation Department, Newtown Community Center in 1982–1985; director of marketing for Genus Enterprises, Inc., 1985–1987; and vice president of group sales for Central Life Insurance Company of Florida, 1988–1989.

Atkins' awards and honors include: Outstanding Floridians by the Florida State Jaycees, 1989; Grand Master Achievement Award, 1988; Interdenominational Ministerial Alliance-First Annual Human Rights and Achievement Award, 1988; NAACP Achievement Award, 1988; Islamic Center Award for Outstanding Community Service, 1988; Special Recognition Award for Founding Father and President, Newtown Little league, 1988; Community Achievement Award-Heritage Foundation of Sarasota, 1988; serves as Second Vice President of the Florida Black Caucus Local Elected Officials, Inc.; appointed by the governor to serve as a member of the Affordable Housing Study Commission in July 1987; Lower West Coast Blood Bank Award of Merit, 1986; Kappa Alpha Psi Political Academic Award, 1985; Spokes People-Outstanding Spokesperson, 1985; Outstanding Sports Writer, by the Northside County Businessmen's Association, 1984; Martin Luther King, Jr., certificate of service to youth, by the North County Civic League; certificate of service to community youth by the Bulletin; Jimmy Walker Cultural Achievement Award for outstanding contributions to youth, by the heritage Foundation and Board of Directors-Opportunity Industrial Council (OIC).

AUSTIN, RICHARD H., was born in Alabama, the son of an itinerant coal miner. When Austin was 11, his father died and the family moved to Detroit where he continues to reside. Austin worked his way through school to help his mother support the family, which included two brothers. His scholastic achievements and ability as a high school track star won him a scholarship to Wayne University, but family circumstances forced the young man to abandon his scholarship. During the day, he sold and repaired shoes and kept books in a shoe store. At night, he studied accounting at the Detroit Institute of Technology. Richard earned a B.A. in business administration from the Detroit Institute of Technology. In 1941, he became a certified public accountant (Michigan's First Black CPA). He was senior partner of Austin, Washington & Davenport, certified public accountants, specializing as a business management and tax consultant to publishers, hospitals, physicians, insurance companies and government.

Over the years, he helped organize a number of other businesses, philanthropic foundations and civic organizations. He continued to serve as an officer and director of several small business corporations. Richard's accounting office, established in 1942, served clients in Michigan, Illinois and Kentucky. For a quarter of a century, it was the only provider in Michigan of professional experience enabling young black college graduates to qualify for CPA exams. The prestigious national accounting firms operating in Michigan at the time did not employ blacks on their professional staffs. In 1961, Austin began his public service career as an elected delegate to the Michigan Constitutional Convention. In 1966, he was elected Wayne County auditor. He has served on numerous state and local government commissions and study groups; had articles published on taxation, legislative apportionment, voter registration and traffic safety; and has served as a member of the advisory group to the U.S. commissioner of internal revenue.

In 1970, Richard Austin was the first black person elected in the United States to the statewide post of secretary of state. He was re-elected four times, enjoying wide margins of victory. In the last two re-election bids, he received 68 percent of the vote, carried 81 of Michigan's 83 counties, and was returned to office by a margin of over 1 million votes. In 1982 and 1986, he received the highest percentage of votes among all candidates for statewide office, earning him the title of Michigan's most popular elected official. He is currently the longest serving black statewide elected official in the United States. Secretary Austin is a member of numerous organizations. He has received many special awards, including honorary degrees and distinguished citizen awards.

Some of these include Outstanding Alumnus of the Detroit Institute of Technology, Liberty Bell Award, Michigan Association of CPAs' Distinguished Achievement Award, Builder of Detroit Award, Silver Antelope Award from the Boy Scouts of America and numerous awards for promotion of traffic safety in Michigan. In 1984, Austin was named Distinguished Professional of the Year by the Michigan Association of Professionals and received the AAA Steering Wheel safety recognition award and the Champion of Safety Award from the Michigan Safety Conference. For several years, he was included among *Ebony* magazine's 100 Most Influential Blacks. In 1985, he was named one of ten Michiganians of the Year by the *Detroit News* and received an honorary doctor of laws degree from Michigan State University of Detroit and the Distinguished Service and Leadership in the Public Sector Award from the Michigan State Chamber of Commerce. He received an honorary doctor of public service degree from Northern Michigan University in 1989. As secretary of state, he is second in succession to the governor and heads a department with over 2,000 employees and 186 branch offices. He is Michigan's driver and motor vehicle administrator and chief official in charge of elections and historic preservation. His administration has been highly acclaimed for operational innovation and efficiency, friendly and convenient service, encouragement of greater citizen involvement in the political process and sincere devotion to highway safety.

His many accomplishments and innovations have included purchase of license plates by mail, voter registration in branch offices (first in the nation to combine driver licensing and voter registration), staggered vehicle registration by birthday, driver license renewal every four years instead of three, driver license renewal by mail and

and driver improvement programs focusing on the young driver. As chairman of the Michigan State Safety Commission, Austin has been a key spokesman for the traffic safety community in its efforts to develop a comprehensive and effective traffic safety approach in Michigan. He led the fight to retain Michigan's motorcycle helmet law. He was a key advocate of Michigan's child restraint law. He has supported stiffer penalties for drinking drivers. And he successfully led a 14-year effort to enact a safety belt law.

---

†**BAILEY, PEARL MAE**, was born on March 29, 1918, in Newport News, Virginia, the youngest of four children of the Rev. Joseph James Bailey and Ella Mae Bailey. She and her husband, Louis Bellson, Jr., had two adopted children: a son, Tony, and a daughter, DeeDee. Her parents were divorced when she was a child, and her mother later married Walter Robinson. At 4 Pearl Bailey moved to Washington, D.C., with her family. Later she lived with her mother and stepfather in Philadelphia, where she attended the Joseph Singerly School and William Penn High School. Her early ambition was to become a schoolteacher. Her introduction to show business came in 1933, when at 15 she entered the amateur night contest at the Pearl Theater in Philadelphia, where her song and dance routine won her first prize. She dropped out of school to become an entertainer after winning another amateur contest, this time at the famous Apollo Theater in New York's Harlem. Developing her vocal talents, she appeared in nightclubs and theaters in Washington, Baltimore and Philadelphia. During World War II she toured with USO troupes from coast to coast.

Pearl Bailey made her bow as soloist at a major New York nightclub about 1944, when she was featured at the Village Vanguard. In 1945, Ms.

Bailey was asked by Cab Calloway to appear in his show at the Strand Theater. She remained with Calloway on a 3-week tour and on a 16-week run at the Zanzibar nightclub on Broadway. During the early 1950s, Ms. Bailey kept busy making solo appearances in theaters and night clubs throughout the United States. In 1956, she appeared in the Paramount comedy *That Certain Feeling*. In 1957, she was one of the featured entertainers at the festivities following President Dwight D. Eisenhower's second inauguration. In 1958, she was W. C. Handy's Aunt Hagar in *St. Louis Blues*, Paramount's film biography of the blues composer. In a 1959 MGM film, she appeared as Maria, the cookshop woman in *Porgy and Bess*. In 1960, she appeared in a supporting role in her next motion picture *All the Fine Young Cannibals*. In 1966, she made her first concert appearance at Philharmonic Hall in New York's Lincoln Center. In the summer of 1967, she played the starring role in *Call Me Madam* at Melodyland in Berkeley, California. On November 12, 1967, she opened in *Hello, Dolly!* at the St. James Theater in New York City. In the presentations on April 21, 1968, of the 22nd annual Antoinette Perry (Tony) awards of the American Theater Wing for distinguished achievement in the New York theater during the 1967–1968 season, Pearl Bailey received a special award for her performance in *Hello, Dolly!*

Among her other honors were designation as Entertainer of the Year, 1967; the March of Dimes annual award for 1968; and the USO Woman of the Year award for 1969. In 1978, she decided to enroll at Georgetown University, where she had received an honorary doctorate degree. She majored in theology. An avid book reader, she also wrote some books, including *Raw Pearl*, published in 1968; *Between You and Me*; and *Hurry Up America & Spit*. Former President Richard Nixon presented her with an official ambassador certificate, appointing her ambassador of love to the entire world. She was a special delegate to the United Nations under the Ford, Reagan and Bush administrations.

BARANCO, GREGORY T., was born March 10, 1948, and raised in Baton Rouge, Louisiana. He is married to attorney Juanita Powell Baranco, and the father of four. A 1970 graduate of Southern University with a B.S. degree in business administration. During a summer internship at the Dearborn Stamping Plant at the Ford Motor Company, Gregory first decided to become an automobile dealer. He joined Audubon Ford in October 1969 and became, at age 23, one of its youngest salesmen to be promoted into management. In 1978, less than ten years after his decision to become an automobile dealer, Baranco founded his own dealership. This teacher who set such a fine example for those students is also president of Baranco Pontiac GMC Truck,

Inc., in Decatur, Georgia; Baranco Lincoln-Mercury in Duluth, Georgia, and Tallahassee Acura in Tallahassee, Florida.

Based on new car sales, Baranco Pontiac has historically ranked in the top three among 137 Pontiac dealers in metropolitan Atlanta. Under his direction the dealerships have doubled their volume of new and used car sales. This dramatic growth and the resulting strong financial position of the dealerships have enabled Baranco to create over 200 jobs in the Atlanta area. Moreover, his businesses have improved and expanded to include new buildings and facilities, further contributing to the economic growth of the area. Factory and consumer groups alike applaud Baranco's commitment to developing the type of quality leadership and concern which was epitomized by the Baranco dealerships. On the basis of sales, service and customer satisfaction, this dynamic businessman has been cited as a master dealer, and his Pontiac operation holds the distinction of being a Five Star Service Award Winner. The dealerships receive letters of appreciation and commendation daily from their customers. The Baranco popularity is further attested to by the approximately 3,000 people who attend the free annual Halloween carnival hosted by Baranco.

Baranco's status as an outstanding businessman is enhanced by his reputation as a leader in both his field and his community. He was recognized as the Outdoor Advertising Dealer of the Year in 1978. Baranco has served as president of the Metro Atlanta Automobile Dealer Association and several times as chairman of the Atlanta International Auto Show. Other leadership activities include serving as director of the Junior League of Atlanta and the Dekalb County Chamber of Commerce, and as a director of the League of Minority Auto Dealers. Baranco has received numerous awards and citations

in recognition of his outstanding ability. Every year since 1980, his Pontiac dealership has been named one of *Black Enterprise* magazine's top 100 businesses. He has also been recognized as *Time* magazine's Businessman of the Year. Additional awards received by Baranco include Minority Supplier of the Year, the Masters Competition Award, the W. E. Hoglund Award for Sales, and the J. M. Losh Award for Sales.

Despite the long hours involved in running several successful businesses, Gregory Baranco believes in the importance of community participation. A long list of civic activities backs up Baranco's philosophy and emphasizes further his leadership ability. Baranco has served on the boards of the Atlanta Business League and the President's Council of Spelman College. He has received awards for his outstanding contributions to the following organizations: the Metropolitan Atlanta Red Cross, the Dekalb Council for the Arts, the United Negro College Fund, and the Georgia Association of Minority Entrepreneurs. Baranco participated in the donation of an automobile to St. Joseph's Children's Hospital and has provided an automobile and personnel to assist in the driver's education program of Dekalb County. In educational activities, Baranco has served as faculty adviser for the General Motors Dealer Academy and has been a guest lecturer at the University of Alabama and at numerous schools and businesses throughout the Atlanta area. He is associated with the Dekalb Community College Fund and Junior Achievement's Project Business. He is active in his church and in numerous charitable fund-raising activities.

BARHAM, SADIE G. A native of Jackson, Tennessee. She moved to Grand Rapids, Michigan in 1948 and to Jackson, Michigan in 1958 where she was a resident for 32 years. She is married to Ex Rhodes Barham, a city commissioner, and is the mother of three children: June, Gaylon and Jacquelyn and the grandmother of eight. Barham's educational background includes: B.A. degree from Calvin College, Grand Rapids, and M.A. degree from the University of Michigan, Ann Arbor. She worked as an educator for 27 years as a schoolteacher, guidance counselor, secretary and vice president for Jackson Public School system until she was elected as Jackson County Board of Commissioners 3rd district commissioner in 1984. Active in community affairs as well as church activities. Two of her children are teachers in the Jackson Public School system.

Barham has received many honors and awards, some of which include the Martin Luther King, Jr. Humanitarian Award; Susan B. Anthony Award for Community Service (Y-Center); Education Service Award (Ministers' Wives and Widows); Appreciation Award (Bilingual State and Federal Programs); Appreciation of Service Award (Jackson Public Schools Board of Education); Distinguished Service Award (Michigan Association of School Boards); Recognition Award (Superintendent of Jackson Public Schools); Christian Service Award (Community Afterglow); Feminist Award (Human Relations Commission); Certificate of Appreciation (Human Relations Commission); Community Service Award (Negro Business and Professional Women); Humanitarian Award (Lane College, Jackson, Tennessee); Recognition Award (State Prison of Southern Michigan), and Ebony Award (Community AME Church). She has been active in numerous civic, social, church, business and community organizations.

BARNES, GEORGE H., SR., was born and reared in and around the city of Wabbaseka, Arkansas. He was the fourth son, and fifth child of 12 children. Most of his childhood was spent on the farm where his father worked to support his family. Barnes attended school in the Wabbaseka School District. He graduated from the former J. S. Walker High School in 1968. He is married to Earnestine Shelton and has four children: George Jr., Rayford, Michelle, and Earnest. During the early years of his marriage Barnes lived in Chicago and supported his wife and small son by working for the Zenith Corporation. The family later moved back to Wabbaseka, and Barnes attended Arkansas Baptist College where he studied theology and divinity. He preached his first sermon at his home church. He was later elected pastor of Union Valley Missionary Baptist Church, where he has been pastor for the past 14 years.

Barnes has held many other positions since he graduated: housing inspector, farm supervisor, and painter for Riceland Food until he was injured in 1971 and was no longer able to do the job effectively. He has served on many community and political committees: eight years as alderman for the city of Wabbaseka, Boy Scout master, Jefferson Comprehensive Care Board, Housing Resource Board. He is the founder and president of the Wabbaseka Council of Human Resources and chairman of the small cities and advisory council for the state of Arkansas with the Arkansas Municipal League. He served as president of the Southeast Arkansas Regional Planning Commission. Barnes also has served as president of the Arkansas Black Mayors Association and as mayor of Wabbaseka. He has received many community service awards.

BARNES, THOMAS V., is married to Frances J. Barnes, with whom he has one child, Paul M., and two grandsons. He graduated from Roosevelt High School in 1954. In 1958, he received a B.S. degree from Purdue University.

He received a J.D. law degree from De-Paul University in 1972 and graduated from the United States Army Command & General Staff College in 1970. Barnes retired from the United States Army Reserves as a colonel, and served as a staff judge advocate. He also served as a civilian aide to the secretary of the Army. Past occupations include three elected terms as assessor, Calumet township; private attorney; member of Tolleston Community Council, 1980–1981; laborer in the Inland Steel Company; and caseworker for the Department of Public Welfare. He was admitted to practice for the Supreme Court, state of Indiana, the United States District Court, Northern and Southern Districts of Indiana, the United States Court of Appeals, and the United States Military Court of Appeals. He was elected mayor of Gary, Indiana, in November 1990. He has been involved in numerous organizations such as NAACP (life member), James G. Kimbrough Law Association (founding member), reserve officers and Share Food Gary (Honorary Director & Former Legal Advisor).

BARRETT, JACQUELYN HAR-RISON, was born on November 4, 1950, in Charlotte, North Carolina, to Cornelius and Ocie Perry Harrison. She is married with two children and is a 1968 graduate of Harding High School. Her graduating class was the first to enter high school under an order to desegregate the Charlotte public school system. In 1972, she graduated from Beaver College in Glenside, Pennsylvania, with a B.A. degree in sociology, concentrating in criminology. The experience of attending a women's college instilled in her the confidence to tackle issues and areas traditionally thought of as male dominated. She was admitted to Atlanta University (now Clark-Atlanta University) on a full scholarship to continue work in the field of sociology, graduating in 1973 with a master's degree again concentrating in criminology.

After working for a time as an adult basic education teacher with the Atlanta Board of Education, Barrett went to work as a criminal justice planner for the cities of East Point, College Park and Hapeville, Georgia. Her responsibilities included writing and managing criminal justice grants, compiling crime statistics, monitoring the municipal courts, and serving as municipal liaison with various state agencies. In 1976, she accepted a curriculum specialist position with the Georgia Peace Officer Standards and Training Council (POST). Here she researched and wrote basic and advanced curriculum guides for peace officers throughout the state of Georgia. An early assignment was to construct the first mandate school for newly elected sheriffs. She designed the first communication/dispatcher course and the first basic and advanced arson investigator courses. Barrett has always added interpersonal relations units to courses she designs. Her thinking is that if race relations — and by extension the reduction of brutality by police officers against black citizens —

was to improve, it would be in part because of better understanding and exposure through the training process. As director of the research division and the training standards division and as assistant to the executive director, she came to specialize in developing management training courses for chiefs and sheriffs and in training instructors to work in the regional and departmental police academies.

She left POST to work as chief administrative officer for Georgia's first elected black sheriff, Richard B. Lankford. This assignment gave her the opportunity to work with an agency under court order to improve conditions at the county jail, and to work closely with attorneys for both sides, a federal court monitor, county commissioners, and federal judges. Barrett made significant improvements to living and confinement conditions at the jail. Because of her extensive knowledge of law enforcement training, she transferred within county government and assumed the responsibilities of director. For her work in the area of law enforcement training, Barrett has received the Pioneer in Law Enforcement Award from the National Organization of Black Law Enforcement Executives (NOBLE), Georgia chapter.

BARRETT, STEVE A., was born July 26, 1952. Married to Evelyn Barrett of the Opa-locka police department since 1975 and is the father of three children: Steven Jr., Ceira and Eric. He attended Madison High School, Madison, Florida, 1971; Miami Dade Community College (courses taken in criminology), 1973; Miami Jackson Senior High Adult Education Program (earned a certificate in cosmetology), 1982–1984. In 1989, he was elected vice mayor of the city of Opa-locka. Prior to becoming vice mayor he was commissioner for the city of Opa-locka, beginning a four-year term in 1988.

Since 1988, he has been owner and president of SECE, Inc.; from 1984 until 1989, he was part owner and president

of B&R Manufacturing; 1981–1983, owner of Bolts Bookstore; 1978–1980, owner of Car Wash Service; 1973–1984, warehouse manager of Grand Union Food Chain; 1971–1973, manager of frozen food section at Winn Dixie supermarket.

Barrett's special interest is working with the young people of Opa-locka and the business community throughout Dade County. He received the Opa-locka Humanitarian Award in 1987. He has been an active member of the Church of Christ "Written in Heaven" for the past 12 years. Community activities include serving on the Optimist Club board of directors, the Miami Dade Chamber of Commerce board, Opa-locka Zoning Board of Appeals, Opa-locka Code Enforcement Board, Opa-locka Recreational Activities Advisory Board, Opa-locka Charter Board. His future goals are to continue manufacturing quality hair care products for the black community with a major distribution throughout the United States. He is also working toward a quality independent janitorial service.

BATHER, PAUL, is married to Coretta Waddell, and is the father of twins, Omar and Amir. Bather concentrated in accounting and law while obtaining his M.B.A. from the University of Louisville School of Business in 1980. He earned a master's degree in social work from the City University of New York in 1970 and a liberal arts degree from Fairfield University (Connecticut) in 1968. As part of his continuing education requirements, he attended accounting and legal seminars sponsored by the American Management Association and the Finance Executives Institute. Bather was elected to his third term as 12th ward alderman in November 1990. He served as chairman of the economic development committee and was a member of the appropriations and budget committee. Paul had worked closely with Louisville Mayor Jerry Abramson to move the city of Louisville forward by creating jobs and improving the overall quality of life.

Bather was employed as vice president and general manager of WJYL Radio (101.7 FM) for two years. During his tenure, WJYL became the number one urban station and expanded its audience to reach virtually all segments of the Louisville market. Bather was responsible for management, budgeting, marketing and ensuring a strong commitment to community service. Prior to working at WJYL, he was the associate director of the University of Louisville's Urban Research Institute. He wrote a business plan to secure university sponsorship of the *Journal of Urban Affairs* from the Urban Affairs Association. He also directed the development and implementation of a computerized accounting information system. His responsibilities included management, accounting budgeting, personnel, computers, word processing, and internal control. As treasurer of Jefferson County government for five years, he was responsible for receipts and disbursements from a budget of $82 million. He was also charged with overall responsibility for cash management, capital budgeting, audits, investments and financial planning. His innovative policies earned the county over $10 million in investment income. Bather also served as executive director of the Kentucky Association of United Way for two years. He coordinated the government relations, fundraising and public affairs functions of the agency in Kentucky. Through his efforts, the United Way raised over $15 million annually.

Bather has a proven record of leadership for the citizens of Louisville and Jefferson County. Rated as one of the "86 People to Watch" by *Louisville* magazine in 1986, he had established himself as an experienced elected official with creative solutions to complex problems that had confronted his community. He was recognized as the National Alumnus of the Year by the American Center for International Leadership in 1986. He was selected to be a U.S. representative in an American-Soviet leadership exchange that included meetings in Moscow, Leningrad, and Alma Ata, U.S.S.R. He also served as host of a Hungarian delegation that visited Louisville in 1986, and in 1987 he was selected to serve as U.S. representative to a leadership exchange that met in Mexico City and Cocavoc, Mexico.

BECTON, JULIUS W., JR., was born June 29, 1926, in Bryn Mawr, Pennsylvania; married the former Louise Thornton, with whom he has five children: Shirley, Karen, Joyce, Renee and Wesley. They also have six grandchildren. Becton's public service career includes two key federal positions after nearly 40 years of active commissioned service in the U.S. Army, during which he rose to the rank of lieutenant general. He is the first graduate of Prairie View A&M University to attain star rank in the military. In November 1989, the Texas A&M University System Board of Regents unanimously elected him president of Prairie View A&M University. After receiving his B.S. degree in mathematics from Prairie View A&M University in 1960, he earned his M.A. degree in economics from the University of Maryland in 1967. He is also a graduate of top military schools, including the U.S. Army Command and General Staff College, the Houston-Tillotson College in Austin and Muhlenberg College in Pennsylvania.

Becton enlisted in the U.S. Army in July 1944 and graduated from Officer's Candidate School in 1945. A veteran of World War II and the Korean and Vietnam conflicts, he has served in various positions at scores of posts in this country. Overseas duties have carried him to Germany, the Philippines, France, the Southwest Pacific, Korea, and Japan. His active duty assignments have included deputy commanding general, U.S. Army Training and Doctrine Command; commander, VII U.S. Corps in Germany; and commander, 1st Cavalry Division. He served 22 months as director of the Office of U.S. Foreign Disaster Assistance before being nominated by then-president Ronald Reagan and confirmed by the Senate as director of the Federal Emergency Management Agency, a position he held for nearly four years before moving into the private sector. Prior to his acceptance of the position of president of Prairie View A&M University, he served as chief operating officer for American Coastal Industries.

President Becton has also been asked by the U.S. government to serve as chairman of a new select group of the Senior Civil Emergency Planning Committee of NATO in Brussels, Belgium. The native of Bryn Mawr, Pennsylvania, serves as secretary on the World Board of Governors for the United Services Organization (USO). He is 1st vice president of the U.S. Armor Association and a member of the Federal Emergency Management Agency advisory board, the board of trustees for Valley Forge Military Academy and Junior College, and the defense Equal Opportunity Management Institute Board of Visitors. He has been listed in several Who's Who directories and was named by *Ebony* magazine several times as "One of the 100 Most Influential Blacks in America." He has been awarded the Distinguished Service Award (Federal Emergency Management Agency); Distinguished Knight (Gold), Order of St. George; and Honorary Colonel, 17th Cavalry Regiment.

BELAFONTE, HARRY, was born March 1, 1927, in New York City. He was named Harold George Belafonte, Jr., by his parents, Harold George and Melvine (Love) Belafonte. He and his wife, Julie, have two children, David and Gina. He has two daughters, Adrienne and Shari, by a previous marriage. When Harry was eight years old, the family moved to Mrs. Belafonte's old home in Jamaica. Five years later, they returned to New York where Harry attended St. Thomas the Apostle (parochial) School. He later attended George Washington High School for two years. He left school in 1944 to enlist in the United States Navy.

Returning to civilian life at the age of 19, he got a job as a maintenance worker in an apartment house. One of the tenants gave him two tickets, as a tip, for *Home Is the Hunter*, an American Negro Theater production. It was the first legitimate show Harry had ever seen and the beginning of his ambition to be an actor. He enrolled under the G.I. Bill at Erwin Piscator's Dramatic Workshop but was unable to get an acting job. In order to earn a living he accepted employment in New York's garment district pushing a dress cart. The owner of the Royal Roost, a Broadway jazz club, gave Harry an audition to sing, signed him for a two-week engagement, then extended it to 20 weeks. He was booked for a national tour, and he spent two years singing popular songs in night clubs throughout the United States. He signed a contract with RCA, which launched him as a recording star. He then starred in two films, *Bright Road* and *Carmen Jones*, followed by *Island in the Sun* in 1957. He starred in three of his own HarBel film productions, *The World, the Flesh and the Devil, Odds Against Tomorrow* and *The Angel Levine*, and co-starred with Sidney Poitier in *Buck and the Preacher* in 1972. He starred in the Broadway production *Three for Tonight*.

In 1965, he marched from Selma to Montgomery, Alabama, with Dr. Martin Luther King, Jr. He was the first entertainer to be named cultural adviser to the Peace Corps by President John F. Kennedy. He has served as the goodwill ambassador for the United Nation's Childrens Fund (UNICEF). He

became the prime minister of hope, with a mission to end world starvation and sickness, to mobilize world support for the plight of child survival. He was the mastermind behind and spokesperson for USA for Africa, serving as its vice president. In addition, Belafonte participated in the homeless awareness vigil Hands Across America and sang on the star-studded "We Are the World" record that raised funds for famine victims throughout central Africa and drought victims in Ethiopia. In 1990, he was the recipient of the Nelson Mandela Courage Award. The award was sponsored by TransAfrica Forum, a group that lobbies on behalf of Africa and the Caribbean.

BELL, WILLIAM V., was born January 3, 1941, in Washington, D.C. He is married and the father of four children.

Bell was educated in the public schools of Winston-Salem, North Carolina. In 1961, he received a B.S. in electrical engineering from Howard University, Washington, D.C.; in 1968, an M.S. in electrical engineering from New York University, New York, New York. He served in the United States Army Signal Corps as a first lieutenant, 1961–1963. Bell was elected to the Durham Board of County Commissioners, Durham, North Carolina, in 1972 and served as chairman from 1982 until 1991. From 1968 to 1991, Bell was senior engineer for IBM Corporation, Research Triangle Park, North Carolina.

He is the recipient of many community awards: the North Carolina Outstanding Leadership Award, 1980, presented by Governor James B. Hunt, Jr.; 1985 Outstanding Alumnus Award, presented by the Howard University Club of Research Triangle; and the 1988 Howard University Distinguished Alumni Achievement Award in Engineering and Public Service, awarded by the Howard University Board of Trustees. His community and professional affiliations include the North Carolina Association of County Officials; the board of trustees of the North Carolina School of Science & Mathematics; the board of directors of the Greater Durham Chamber of Commerce; the board of directors of the Durham County Hospital Corporation; and the board of directors of the Fund for the Advancement of Science & Mathematics Education in North Carolina.

BELTON, SHARON SAYLES, is married to Steven Belton, with whom she has three children. Belton is a native Minnesotan. She attended Minneapolis Central High School and Macalester College in St. Paul. After college, Sharon worked as a parole officer for the Minnesota Department of Corrections. In her next career move, she developed innovative projects for the state as assistant director of the Minnesota Program for Victims of Sexual Assault. While serving her third term on the Minneapolis City Council, where she represented the residents of the 8th Ward in south Minneapolis, her city council committee assignments were the following: zoning and planning committee; community development, health, environment and human development; and the executive committee. She also represents the city on the Board of Estimates and Taxation, the Heritage Board, and the Minneapolis Youth Coordinating Board. She was chosen by her colleagues as president of the city council. Belton is deeply committed to civil and human rights and has initiated changes in the policies of the city of Minneapolis in this area. She was instrumental in the selection of a minority-owned firm as subcontractor for the new convention center.

In addition, Sharon has worked with the Minnesota Minority Lawyers Association to ensure the participation of their members in contracts for city legal services. She is proud to have authored the resolution passed by the city council mandating the divestment of city funds in South Africa. Sharon has extensive volunteer experience. Over the past 17 years she has served on many national, state and local organizations including the following: president for five years of the Harriet Tubman Shelter for Battered Women; vice president and president of the National Coalition Against Sexual Assault; Metropolitan Task Force on Developmental Disabilities, for four years; board member for Minneapolis Youth Diversion Program, Minnesota Women Elected Officials, Children's Theater and Turning Point, a program for black chemically dependent persons. She received three awards in recognition of her advocacy for individuals from the community.

BENHAM, ROBERT, is married to the former Nell Dodson, with whom he has two sons: Corey Brevard and Austin Tyler. He was an honor graduate of Tuskeegee Institute, where he received a B.S. degree in political science. He furthered his education at Harvard University, and later received a juris doctor degree from the Lumpkin School of Law at the University of Georgia. He received a master of laws degree from the University of Virginia.

He is also a graduate of the Trail Lawyers Institute. He holds membership in numerous professional organizations, including eight national, state and local bar associations, the American Judicature Society, the Lawyer's Club of Atlanta, the National Criminal Justice Association, the Georgia Bar Foundation, the Georgia Legal History Foundation (Trustee), and Scribes— The American Society of Writers on Legal Subjects. A former vice president of the Georgia Conference of Black Lawyers, a former board member of the Federal Defender Program, and a former member of the American Trial Lawyers.

Benham is a former chairman of the Governor's Commission on Drug Awareness & Prevention, a member of the State Bar Task Force on the Involvement of Women and Minorities in the Professional, a member of the Georgia Commission on Children and Youth, a member of the Commission to Protect the Public and the Lawyer through a Disciplinary Process that is Prompt and Just, and a member of the advisory committee of the Center for the Study of the Black Male. He has held numerous civic positions, including board chairman of the Coosa Valley Area Planning & Development Commission, and board member of the Cartersville-Bartow County Chamber of Commerce, the Bartow County Development Authority, and the Wheeler-Noble Hill Foundation. A Mason, a Shriner and an Elk, Benham has also served as a Sunday school superintendent and deacon and board member of the Mt. Olive Baptist Church. Judge Benham was appointed to the Court of Appeals in 1984, and his subsequent statewide election represented the first time that a black person had held a statewide position in Georgia in the 20th century. Judge Benham was appointed to the Supreme Court of Georgia in 1989 and elected to a full term on that court in 1990.

BERRY, EUGENE DWIGHT, was born December 3, 1952, in Kendall, Florida, to Eugene B. and Carolyn Dorsett Berry. He has been a resident of the Homestead and Florida City, Florida, area for the past 37 years. He attended A. L. Lewis Elementary School, for kindergarten through sixth grade, West Homestead Junior High for seventh and eighth grades, Mays Senior High for ninth through eleventh grades. When the school was phased out as a senior high school, his senior year was completed at South Dade Senior High, where he was the first black quarterback on the football team and finished June 11, 1970. He attended Morristown College in Morristown, Tennessee, for one year and returned home. Berry married his high school sweetheart, Cathy Eppinger, in 1973. They have two daughters, Lenita Renne and Angela Eureka.

He was employed by Florida Power and Light Company at its Turkey Point Nuclear Power Plant since 1973 and held the title of mechanical commissioner in Florida City because he wanted a hand in helping the people of his community. In 1986, he beat the former mayor in a runoff election, which was the beginning of his political career. As a new commissioner he wanted to make an impact, so he chose parks and recreation, an area that needed some leadership. The first thing he did was to set goals for the department; to have lights installed on most useful parks in the city, this park had been without lights for some 12 years; to provide more activities for the kids; give the citizens someone they could trust and believe in; to come out and support their kids in the activities that were planned for them; to see the kids and parents take pride in what they had accomplished and to reduce crime between the ages of 7 and 16.

In January 1990, Berry was elected to a second term in office due to the hard work that had been done the past four years. In May 1990, the switch for a $140,000 lighting project was turned on. The city had five football and cheerleading teams in the greater Miami Pop Warner football league and had won five championships and three runners-up. There were four basketball and baseball teams in the Dade County Youth Leagues. The people had someone they could come to when they had problems, the parents' support had increased 100 percent, the overall improvement of the parks had given the kids and parents a sense of ownership in their community, and the kids' crime rate was down to nothing. Berry believes that none of the goals would have been possible without city officials, the kids, and the citizens of the Homestead and Florida City area.

BETHEA, JULIANNE, Received a B.S. degree in zoology from Howard University in 1969. She received an associate of arts degree in nursing from Prince Georges Community College in 1972. In 1979, she received a B.S. degree in nursing from Howard University. She graduated from Marymount University and received an M.S. in nursing administration. After graduating from Howard University in 1969, she served as a substitute teacher for the D.C. schools, working in elementary, junior and senior high school, where she taught math and science. After receiving her associate degree in nursing in 1972, she joined the nursing staff of Providence Hospital in Washington, D.C. Bethea worked as a charge nurse, with medical-surgical, in the medical intensive care and coronary care unit. In 1975, she served as a community health nurse, primary nurse, and terminally ill project nurse for the Visiting Nurses Association of Washington, D.C.

In 1980, Bethea joined the D.C. General Hospital as a nurse facilitator/educator for the federally funded senior care program. In 1982, she worked for Kaiser Permanente as an advice nurse. Bethea left Kaiser in late 1982 to join the staff of the Veteran's Administration Medical Center, where she worked from 1982 to 1989 as a staff nurse in the medical intensive care unit and outpatient clinic department. She also served on the nursing standards committee as a tutor for partners in the adopt-a-school program, assisted in interpreting for deaf employees, and was a CPR instructor. She was elected as a city council member for two terms, serving as mayor pro tem and mayor for the town of Colmar Manor from 1985 to 1989. In 1989, after receiving her master's degree, she joined the staff of Walter Reed Army Medical Center, as a clinical nurse for the Kyle Metabolic Endocrine unit, where she stayed until 1990. She accepted the position of clinical nursing instructor for second-year nursing students in medical-surgical nursing at Anne Arundel Community College in 1989. Bethea has served with numerous community, professional organizations, including the American Nurses Association, the American Public Health Association, American Red Cross, and the Prince Georges County Economic and Development Commission.

BIRCKHEAD, FANNIE W., is married to Lewis C. Birckhead, Sr. and the mother of two daughters, Janeen and Nicolle. Attended Worcester High School in Snow Hill, Maryland; received college credits from University of Maryland, Eastern Shore, in Early Childhood; and earned certification from Geriatric Nursing and Cosmetology. Birckhead was the first council member elected from the Western District, of Snow Hill, Maryland. While in office she assisted in a number of changes in which the mayor and council had been influential. A new housing subdivision was under way and an apartment project for the elderly was in the planning stages. She was the treasurer for the Worcester County Extension Advisory Council.

Birckhead first became interested in city government when a friend ran for the city council and she worked as a poll watcher later. Prior positions included the following: substitute teacher at Worcester County Board of Education; Avon representative; seasonal employee for the Department of Transportation, Ocean City, Maryland, and notary public. She has held memberships in many groups: The House of Ruth; Snow Hill Citizens for Decent Housing (Secretary); Worcester County NAACP; Greater Salisbury Leadership; Extension Advisory Council (Treasurer); Snow Hill High School advisory board; Shore Up/Head Start (Worcester County Representative);

Adult Chapter of American Field Service; Ebenezer United Methodist Church; and Sunshine Fund (treasurer). She has also served in a myriad of school and civic committees and organizations.

BISHOP, LOUISE WILLIAMS, was born in Cairo, Georgia, and is the mother of four children: Todd James, Tabb Jody, Tamika Joy, and James Alburn Bishop, Jr. A graduate of West Philadelphia High School, Bishop received her degree in communications and radio broadcasting from the American Foundation of Dramatic Arts. Bishop was elected to the Pennsylvania House of Representatives in 1988 to begin her first term as a state legislator. She is an ordained Baptist Evangelist minister and has a 30-year career that spans the Philadelphia airwaves as a radio personality. She was the first evangelist ordained by the Pennsylvania Baptist Association in 1978. She served her ministry with the message of God's saving grace and has conducted revivals throughout the East Coast.

Her radio career began on WHAT until she began hosting her own program on WDAS-AM and FM, where she was a host and gospel programmer of "The Louise Williams Show" on WDAS-AM. Bishop was appointed by House Speaker James J. Manderino to the following House committee assignments for the 173rd legislative session: State Government, Urban Affairs and Youth and Aging. She was secretary for the Pennsylvania Legislative Black Caucus. For her commitment and dedication, Bishop has been honored with the following awards: Philadelphia Mayor's Council on Youth Opportunity Outstanding Citizen Award; City Council of Philadelphia Citation of Merit; Outstanding Woman Award, Bright Hope Baptist Church; Richard Allen Award (highest African Methodist Episcopal Church award); Mother of the Year Award, Pin Memorial Baptist Church; Missionary Baptist Pastors Conference Community Service Award; Women Preachers of the Year, Ministers Conference; Philadelphia Mass Choir of the James Cleveland Workshop of America Community Service Award; *Philadelphia Tribune* Achievement Award; Outstanding Radio Personality awards by CBS Records, Philadelphia Record Promoters and Gamble & Huff; Woman of the Year Award, Operation Push/Jesse Jackson; Thomas A. Edison Home and School Association Community Award; The Voice of Fellowship, United Holy Church of America; and Pennsylvania State Choir. She has memberships in numerous community and national organizations.

BLACK, CHARLIE J., was born April 19, 1934, in Beatrice, Alabama. Black and his wife Lola have two children, Lisa Yvonne and La Sonja Ann. He received a B.S. degree in education from Alabama State University in 1956. In 1978, he received an M.B.P.A. from Southeastern Univer-

sity and from 1979 to 1980 he earned 12 semester hours for doctoral work in high education administration from Catholic University of America. From 1956 to 1958, he worked as a band director for R. R. Moton High School. From 1958 to 1962, he worked as a band director and math teacher at Harrison High School. In 1962, he worked for a year as a math teacher in the Atlanta public schools before accepting in 1963 a job as a cartographer for Aero Chart & Info Center. In 1965, he was hired as an educational adviser for the United States Army Education Center.

In 1966, Black returned to the classroom as a math teacher for the St. Louis public schools. Later that year he accepted a job as an educational specialist for the United States Navy Publication Division. In 1972, he was licensed by Equitable Life Assurance Company as an insurance representative. From 1973 to 1975, he served as district manager for Southern Aid Life Insurance Company. In 1976, he again returned to the classroom as a math teacher for the Washington, D.C., public schools. Then, in 1981, he became a math teacher for the Montgomery County public schools. Since 1984, he has served as publisher/editor for *The Washington Provider*. Black is also a columnist whose "Upward Mobility" column has been read by city, state and national officials for the past 16 years. He is the author of "Meeting the Mathematical Needs of Students in a Georgia Secondary School." He served as president of the Brightwood Community Association for five years and was chairman of the Civil Protection Committee for the D.C. Federation of Civic Associations for six years. He has served in five councils of the Boy Scouts of America and as explorer adviser in West Point, Georgia. He was a founder of the Georgia Avenue Corridor Community Development Corporation.

BLACK, DON G., a native of Chicago, Illinois, attended Roosevelt University in Chicago, Sinclair Community College, and Wright State University in Dayton, Ohio. He began his career in communications as a market research technician at Monsanto Research Corporation in the late 1960s. Black's experience in both the public and private sectors included managing and directing public relations departments in a health care facility and a federally funded three-county training facility. Understanding that an American dream of enterprise is to strive toward participation in that dream as a business person, in 1970 Don Black founded a multifaceted communications and photographic firm under the name of Don Black Associates Inc. This was the beginning of a 20-year career to date of self-employment enterprise.

In late 1977, Black dissolved Don Black Associates, Inc. in order to establish with two partners from Columbus and Cleveland, Ohio, what was known as Multi-Western Public Relations/Marketing, Inc. This firm was established to provide a broad-based communications agency to tap many of the region's communications businesses, particularly as they related to minority emphasis and target marketing. In 1983, the partnership was dissolved and Don Black became the sole owner of MW. Even though Multi-Western was a Dayton, Ohio, communications firm, Black's involvement in national business and civic and community relations as well as organizational communications is well documented. His clients have included national organizations such as the National Business League, National Council of Churches, N.Y.; National United Methodist Volunteer Services, N.Y.; and the Ohio Governors Conference to name a few. His public relations expertise has assisted nationally recognized individuals such as NBC's Clifton Davis, 5th Dimension, New

York's CEBA Awards, Ashford & Simpson, Motown Industries, and many other recognized events and individuals.

Black believes that public relations have no bounds or limits to tell the story of a client. When working with a diverse client base, it is important to obtain a working knowledge that transcends many bounds. Black's clients have come from industry, small business, financial institutions (banks, S&Ls, MESBIC), health care, religion, educational institutions, media (radio & television), the arts and city, county and state governments. Understanding that public relations is a "planned effort to influence opinion through exceptional two-way communications" means working from both ends of the spectrum to achieve results. Mr. Black has been cited with several awards and citations: NBL President's award, Martin Luther King, Coordination Award, CEBA Award of Excellence, U.S. Air Force Community Affairs Award, Outstanding Young Men in America Award, and several others.

Black's community involvement has been vast. Among his many involvements have been serving as a member of the Governor's Task Force on Minority Business; as two-term president of the Dayton NBL chapter; as president of the Ohio Association of Black Marketing Advertisement and Public Relations Agencies; as a board member of Dayton's SCLC chapters, NBL chapters, Goodwill Industries BAC, and the Urban League Council; and as citywide MLK Holiday Celebration coordinator, as well as several other task forces and committees. His special recognitions include: 1990 special feature "Discover Dayton Magazine," Who's Who Among Black Americans, Who's Who Among Communicators, Outstanding Leader Dayton Registry, and Outstanding Young Men in America.

Action oriented is the best way to describe Don G. Black. With over

20 years of hands-on experience in the field of communications, it is no wonder the he was known as a leader in the field. In the early 1970s he spent many hours via telephone and often in person with his hero, noted author D. Park Gibson, learning about the idea of black consumerism and the black marketplace. The idea of public relations centers on positioning, understanding how to utilize media, a people-to-people strategy and the art of market development. Understanding and practicing this phase of communication makes Don G. Black the expert.

BLACKWOOD, RONALD A., was born in Kingston, Jamaica. Has one daughter, Helen Marie, with his wife Ann. Blackwood attended Elizabeth Seton College and received a B.B.A. in management from Iona College. He became the 18th mayor of Mount Vernon, New York, and the first elected black mayor in the history of New York on January 25, 1985. He served as acting mayor in 1976 and was a member of the Mount Vernon City Council for 15 years, serving as president four times. Mayor Blackwood was also a member of the Westchester County Board of Supervisors from 1968 to 1969 and is a past president of the New York State Association of City Councils. On November 3, 1987, he was re-elected to a full four-year term as mayor of Mount Vernon. As chief executive of the city of Mount Vernon, Blackwood served as chairman of the Board of Estimate and Contract, and the urban renewal and Industrial Development Agencies.

During his tenure as mayor he has taken bold action to fight drugs and crime by establishing the Mayor's Task Force on Drugs, Crime and Blight. He added new police and fire personnel, ensuring a full complement for both departments; lowered the tax rate while improving city services; developed in-

novative programs to provide affordable housing for Mount Vernon families; attracted millions of dollars in state, federal and private investment to improve housing citywide; initiated an extensive beautification program in Mount Vernon, the first ever citywide; developed economic initiative plan to create new jobs; established the 21st Century Committee to address critical issues of Mount Vernon's future; and launched the most ambitious recycling effort in the history of Mount Vernon.

Mayor Blackwood has received special recognition from the United States Department of Housing and Urban Development for outstanding achievements in promoting minority business enterprise. He is a member of various community and national organizations.

BLAIR, FRED, was born August 25, 1940, in Corsicana, Texas. He is married to Evelyn N. Blair, with whom he has four children: Fred Jr., Sandra, Reginald and Tiffany. Blair attended El Centro Junior College. He was elected to

the Texas House of Representatives District 110 in November 1986. Since 1968, Blair has been engaged in a general real estate practice under the name of Fred L. Blair Real Estate Company, located in Dallas, Texas. He specializes in sales, management and appraisal of all types of real estate property. Prior positions included being elected to the Dallas City Council, 1980–1984; deputy mayor pro tem of the council, 1980–1983, and mayor pro tem of the council, 1983–1984. He has served on several legislative committees: Human Services, Urban Affairs, Legislative Black Caucus; Affordable Housing Task Force; Ad Hoc Committee on Minority Health Care; Special Advisory Committee on Bishop College; Council on Minority Health Affairs (chairman); Council of State Governments Committee on Suggested State Legislation; Special Advisory Committee on the Creation and Expansion of Minority and Women-Owned Business Ownership Opportunities.

He is the recipient of numerous awards: Boy Scouts of America Certificate of Appreciation, 1970; U.S. Postal Service, Southern Region Employee and Labor Relations, Certificate of Appreciation, 1973; Dallas Association of Real Estate Brokers, Inc. Outstanding Service, 1974; Dallas City Planning Commission Certificate of Appreciation, 1975–1977; Dallas Black Chamber of Commerce Community Service Award, 1975; National Association of Real Estate Brokers, Inc. Realtor of the Year, 1976; Dallas Chamber of Commerce Leadership Dallas Certificate Award, 1976; National Association Real Estate Brokers, Inc. Bicentennial Award, 1976; State of Texas House of Representatives Certificate of Citation, 1976; Texas Real Estate Association Recognition Award as president, 1976–1978; Dallas Black Chamber of Commerce, 1977; Carver Heights Baptist Church Certificate of Appreciation, 1980; The Methodist Men of St. Luke Community United Methodist Church, 1980; Drug Enforcement Administration Certificate of Appreciation, 1981; Dallas Police and Fire Pension Fund of Trustees Certificate of Appreciation, May 1981; Omega Psi Phi Fraternity, Inc., Theta Alpha Chapter, Citizen of the Year, 1980.

Also, Budge Equal Employment Opportunities Award, July 1981; Honorary Citizenship Award, Fort Worth, Texas, 1981; CB Club of America, Dallas Chapter, 1981; Friendly Ladies Social & Charity Club Outstanding Service Award, 1981–1982; Boy Scouts of America Appreciation Award, 1982; Dallas Black Chamber of Commerce Leadership Award, 1982; Dallas Association of Real Estate Brokers Realtor of the Year, 1982; Dallas Association of Black Social Workers Special Award, 1982; Progressive Beau Monde League Award of Excellence, 1983; National Association of Real Estate Brokers H. M. Michaux, Sr., Realtor Award, Aug. 12, 1986; Dallas Association of Real Estate Brokers A. Maceo Smith Award, June 1987; NAACP Juanita Craft Political Award, 1987; Top Ladies of Distinction (Certificate of Appreciation), 1988; and Burl's Award (Certificate of Appreciation), 1988. His professional affiliations have included the National Association of Real Estate Brokers, Inc. (past vice president); Texas Association of Real Estate Brokers, Inc. (past chairman of the board); Dallas Association of Real Estate Brokers, Inc. (past president); Real Estate Management Brokers Institute; Dallas Black Chamber of Commerce (past 1st vice president); and Dallas County Coalition of Black Democrats.

BLAKE, RICHARD, was born at home in Cocoa, Florida, the son of Virgil and Bertha Black, the seventh of ten children. He is the father of three children, Mike, Sheralyn, and Mark.

He attended Monroe Elementary and Monroe High schools and was valedictorian of the 1951 graduating class. After graduating from Monroe High, Dick continued his education, entering Claflin University in Orangeburg, South Carolina, on a full athletic scholarship. While at Claflin, he was a three-year letterman in football, basketball and baseball. During his senior year he was named an All American in football and was captain of the basketball team. He graduated from Claflin on May 24, 1955, with a B.S. degree in physical education and science. In 1961, he received his master's degree in administration and supervision from Columbia University, New York. Blake is presently enrolled in the doctoral program at the University of Florida, Gainesville.

Blake began his teaching career upon returning to his "roots" to teach math and general science at Monroe High School. While at Monroe, he served as dean of students and guidance counselor in addition to his teaching assignment. He remained at Monroe until 1967 when he transferred to Cocoa High School where he taught physical education. When the new Cocoa High School opened in 1970, he was appointed assistant principal at the new school and continued in that capacity until 1978 when he was named principal of Cocoa High School.

Blake is an active community affairs member of the board of trustees of Wuestoff Memorial Hospital in Rockledge, a member of the Civilian-Military Human Relations Council, a member of the Elks Indian River Lodge #692, president of the Cape Coast Conference, and has served as trustee at the Metropolitan Missionary Baptist Church. He is an active supporter of Little League baseball, Miss America softball, and Midget League football and a member of the Kiwanis Club of Cocoa and Omega Psi Phi fraternity, which honored him in 1976 as Outstanding Educator of the Year. He received a similar honor from the Cocoa Jaycees in 1971. He was the first African American elected as a member of the Rockledge City Council in 1976 and served as chairman of the council in 1983 and 1984. In his last two elections he ran unopposed.

BLUDSON-FRANCIS, VERNETT, was born February 18, 1951, in New York City. She has one son, Robert, Jr., with husband Robert. She holds a B.S. and master's degree in public administration, both from NYU's School of Business and Public Administration. Bludson-Francis has been vice president of Citibank, N.A., and director of the bank's Minority/Women's Vendor Program, which coordinates institutional purchases of products and services from minority- and women-owned firms nationwide. Bludson-Francis began her banking career in 1973 at Morgan Guaranty Trust Company. She joined Citibank in 1975 and, through her development and implementation of the bank's institutional procurement policies, increased Citi-

bank's expenditures with qualified minority vendors more than tenfold in ten years.

Citibank's Minority Vendor Program became a model for other major corporations instituting their own minority purchasing programs. In 1988, through Bludson-Francis' efforts, the MVP evolved into the Minority/Women's Vendor Program, offering women business enterprises, as well as minority entrepreneurs, access to the bank's bidding process. In 1989 Citibank dollars with women- and minority-owned businesses exceeded $20 million. Public recognition of Bludson-Francis and her program has been extensive. In both 1982 and 1983, Citibank's MVP received the National Minority Business Council's (NMBC's) "Outstanding Corporate Support" award. Bludson-Francis was named one of Citibank's Black Achievers in 1984. In 1985, she received the National Urban Affairs Council's (NUAC's) Those Who Make a Difference Award, and was designated by the U.S. Department of Commerce MBDA's regional office as Minority Advocate of the

Year. At the same time, Citibank was recognized nationally by the MBDA for its outstanding efforts in minority business enterprise development. The bank, also in 1985, received a Helping Hand award in the corporate buyer classification from the vendor input committee of the NY/NJ Minority Purchasing Council (MPC). In 1986, 1987, and 1988, Citibank received Helping Hand recognition in all three award classifications — corporate, corporate buyer, and minority vendor coordinator, and in 1989, once again, took corporate and minority vendor coordinator Helping Hand trophies.

Bludson-Francis was honored in 1986 with the National Council of Negro Women's Mary McLeod Bethune Award for minority business enterprise development. In 1987, she was further recognized with the Banker of the Year award from the Urban Bankers Coalition (UBC), Inc.; the Woman of the Year award from the Harlem YMCA; and the Cecelia Cabiness Saunders Award, given by the New Harlem YMCA. In 1988, she was named one of America's Top 100 Black Business & Professional Women by *Dollars & Sense* magazine; and in 1989 she was inducted into the National Association of Negro Business & Professional Women's (NANBPW's) Black Women's Corporate Hall of Fame, and recognized by *Black Opinion* magazine as one of its 1989 Black Achievers. She was honored by the Association of Minority Enterprise of New York with its Outstanding Service award, and she was listed in *Who's Who Among Black Americans*, *Who's Who in U.S. Executives*, and *The World Who's Who of Women*.

Active in many support groups, Bludson-Francis has served as vice chair on the board of directors of the NY/NJ MPC; as a member of the advisory council of the NMBC; as financial secretary on the board of managers of the Harlem YMCA; as a member of the corporate boards of the Association of

Minority Enterprises of N.Y. and the Caribbean-American Chamber of Commerce and Industry; and as a member of the boards of Associated Black Charities, Harlem-Dowling Westside Center, and YW-YMCA Day Care, Inc. She is a member of the Edges Group, Coalition of 100 Black Women, National Forum for Black Public Administrators, NAACP, UBC, NUAC, Black Achievers in Industry Alumni Association, Images-Wall Street Chapter, Cornell University's Cooperative Extension Program, NANBPW, the National Association of Women Business Owners, and the N.Y.S. Department of Economic Development/Minority and Women's Business Division.

BLUFORD, GUION STEWART, JR., was born November 22, 1942, in Philadelphia, Pennsylvania. The oldest of three brothers, he married the former Linda Tull of Philadelphia and they have two sons, Guion Stewart, III, and James Trevor. As a young boy Bluford had a paper route and was a Boy Scout, attaining the rank of Eagle Scout. Fascinated from an early age by aviation, Bluford was determined to

understand the dynamics of flight. In junior high school his interest was focused on science and mathematics, and by the time he entered high school he had declared his intention to become an aerospace engineer. At the same time he was fascinated with the military. He graduated from Overbrook Senior High School in Philadelphia in 1960. He received a B.S. degree in aerospace engineering from Pennsylvania State University in 1964; an M.S. degree with distinction in aerospace engineering from the Air Force Institute of Technology in 1974; a Ph.D. in aerospace engineering with a minor in laser physics from the Air Force Institute of Technology in 1978; and an M.B.A. from the University of Houston, Clear Lake, in 1987.

Bluford attended pilot training at Williams Air Force Base, Arizona, and received his pilot wings in January 1965. He then went to F-4C combat crew training in Arizona and Florida and was assigned to the 557th Tactical Fighter Squadron, Cam Ranh Bay, Vietnam. He flew 144 combat missions, 65 of which were over North Vietnam. In July 1967, he was assigned to the 3630th Flying Training Wing, Sheppard Air Force Base, Texas, as a T-38A instructor pilot. He served as a standardization/evaluation officer and as an assistant flight commander. In early 1971, he attended Squadron Officers School and returned as an executive support officer to the deputy commander of operations and as school secretary for the wing. In 1974, he was assigned to the Air Force Flight Dynamics Laboratory at Wright-Patterson Air Force Base, Ohio, as a staff development engineer. He served as deputy for advanced concepts for the Aeromechanics Division and as branch chief of the Aerodynamics and Airframe Branch in the laboratory.

Bluford has written and presented several scientific papers in the area of computational fluid dynamics. He has logged over 4,800 hours jet flight time in the T-33, T-37, T-38, F-4C, U-2/ TR-1, and F-5A/B, including 1,300 hours as a T-38 instructor pilot. He also has an FAA commercial pilot license. Bluford became a NASA astronaut in August 1979. His assignments have included working with the remote manipulator system, Spacelab-3 experiments, Shuttle systems, Shuttle Avionics Integration Laboratory (SAIL), and the Flight Systems Laboratory (FSL). Bluford first served as a mission specialist on STS-8, which was launched from Kennedy Space Center, Florida, on August 30, 1983. He was accompanied by Capt. Richard H.Truly (spacecraft commander), Cmdr. Daniel C. Brandenstein (pilot), and fellow mission specialists Lt. Cmdr. Dale A. Gardner and Dr. William E. Thornton. This was the third flight for the shuttle *Challenger* and the first mission with a night launch and night landing. During the mission, the STS-8 crew deployed the Indian National Satellite (INSAT-1B), operated the Canadian-built Remote Manipulator System (RMS) with the Payload Flight Test Article (PFTA), operated the Continuous Flow Electrophoresis System (CFES) with live cell samples, conducted medical measurements to understand biophysiological effects of space flight and activated various earth resources and space science experiments along with four Getaway Special canisters. STS-8 completed 98 orbits of the Earth in 145 hours before landing at Edwards Air Force Base, California, on September 5, 1983.

Bluford was next a mission specialist on STS 61-A, the German D-1 Spacelab mission, which was launched from Kennedy Space Center, Florida, on October 30, 1985, aboard the *Challenger*. This was the largest crew to fly to date and included Henry W. Hartsfield (spacecraft commander); Col. Steven R. Nagel (pilot); fellow mission specialists Col. James F. Buchli and Dr. Bonnie J. Dunbar; and three payload specialists, Dr. Ernst Messer-

schmid (Germany), Dr. Reinhard Furrer (Germany), and Dr. Wubbo J. Ockels (Holland). This was the first dedicated Spacelab mission under the direction of the German Aerospace Research Establishment (DFVLR) and the first U. S. mission in which payload was transferred to a foreign country (German Space Operations Center, Oberpfaffenhofen, Germany). During the mission, the Global Low Orbiting Message Relay Satellite (GLOMR) was deployed from a Getaway Special (GAS) container, and 76 experiments were performed in Spacelab in such fields as fluid physics, materials processing, life sciences, and navigation. The experimental test facilities used included melting, solidification and crystal growing furnaces; facilities for the observation of fluid physics phenomena; chambers to provide specific environmental conditions for biological samples; and a vestibular sled. After completing 111 orbits of the Earth in 169 hours, Challenger landed at Edwards Air Force Base, California, on November 6, 1985. With the completion of this flight Bluford had logged a total of 314 hours in space. In 1987, he served as astronaut office point of contact for generic Spacelab issues and external tank issues, including payload development, hazard analysis, crew interface issues and design certification.

BOGLE, DICK, was born in Portland, Oregon, and has lived there all his life. A fourth-generation Oregonian, Bogle and his wife Nola have five children: Ericka, Tiffany, Richard, Richelle and Renita. He was elected to the Portland City Council in December 1984, and was elected to a second four-year term in the May 1988 primary election. He currently serves as commissioner of public safety. His portfolio of assignments includes Bureau of Fire, Rescue and Emergency Services, Bureau of Buildings, Bureau of Emergency Communications, Bureau

BOLDEN, CHARLES F., JR., was born August 19, 1946, in Columbia, South Carolina, to Mrs. Ethel M. Bolden. He is married to the former Alexis (Jackie) Walker of Columbia, South Carolina, with whom he has two children, Anthony Che, and Kelly M. He graduated from C. A. Johnson High School in 1964; received a B.S. degree in electrical science from the United States Naval Academy in 1968 and an M.S. in systems management from the University of Southern California in 1978. Bolden accepted a commission as a 2nd lieutenant in the U.S. Marine Corps following graduation from the United States Naval Academy in 1968. He underwent flight training at Pensacola, Florida, Meridian, Mississippi, and Kingsville, Texas, before being designated a naval aviator in May 1970. He flew more than 100 sorties into North and South Vietnam, Laos and Cambodia in the A-6A Intruder, while assigned to VMA (AW)-533 at Nam Phong, Thailand, June 1972–June 1973. Upon returning to the United States, Bolden began a two-year tour as a Marine Corps officer selection officer and recruiting officer in Los Angeles,

of Licenses, Bureau of Purchases and Stores, Interstate Firehouse Cultural Center (IFCC), and various boards of appeal (Building Code, Electrical Code, Heating and Ventilation, Housing Code, Plumbing Code, Advisory Board of Special Inspections, Noise Review Board).

In addition, Bogle has served as council liaison to the Fire Code Board of Appeals, Central Coordination Budget Advisory Committees, EMS Policy Board, and Model Cities Economic Development Trust Fund. He has been a member of the human development policy committee of the National League of Cities. Bogle sees his life as one dedicated to public service. He served for eight and a half years (1959–1968) as a Portland police officer. He spent 15 years (1968–1983) as news anchor and reporter for KATU-TV and hosted various radio and television talk shows. He served for two years (1983–1984) as executive assistant to former city commissioner Mildred Schwab.

California, followed by three years in various assignments at the Marine Corps Air Station, El Toro, California.

In June 1979, he graduated from the U.S. Naval Test Pilot School at Patuxent River, Maryland, and was assigned to the Naval Air Test Center's Systems Engineering and Strick Aircraft Test Directorates. While there, he served as an ordnance test pilot and flew numerous test projects in the 6-E, EA-6B, and A-7C/E airplanes. He has logged more than 5,000 hours of flying time. Selected by NASA in May 1980, Bolden became an astronaut in August 1981, qualified for assignment as a pilot on future space shuttle flight crews. His technical assignments to date include: Astronaut Office safety officer, technical assistant to the director of the Johnson Space Center, Astronaut Office liaison to the safety, reliability and quality assurance directorates of the Marshall Space Flight Center, and the Kennedy Space Center, Chief of the Safety Division at JSC, and lead Astronaut for Vehicle Test and Checkout at the Kennedy Space Center.

On his first mission Bolden was pilot on the crew of STS-61C which launched from the Kennedy Space Center, Florida, on January 12, 1986. During the six-day flight of *Columbia* the crew deployed the SATCOM KU satellite and conducted experiments in astrophysics and materials processing. STS-61C made a successful night landing at Edwards Air Force Base, California, on January 18, 1986. With the completion of his first space flight Bolden logged 146 hours in space. More recently, Bolden was pilot on the crew of STS-31, which was launched aboard space shuttle *Discovery*, on April 24, 1990, from the Kennedy Space Center. During this five-day mission, crew members deployed the Hubble Space Telescope and conducted a variety of middeck experiments. They also utilized a variety of cameras, including both the IMAX in-cabin and cargo bay cameras, for earth observations from

their record-setting altitude of 380 miles. Following 75 orbits of the earth in 121 hours, STS-31 *Discovery* landed at Edwards Air Force Base on April 29, 1990. With the completion of his second mission, Bolden had logged a total of 267 hours in space. Col. Bolden commanded the crew of STS-45. The mission was scheduled for launch in April 1991, aboard the space shuttle *Columbia*, and was dedicated to studying atmospheric phenomena.

Bolden is a member of the Marine Corps Association, the Montford Point Marine Association and the United States Naval Institute; a lifetime member of the Naval Academy Alumni Association, the University of Southern California General Alumni Association and Omega Psi Phi Fraternity; a recipient of the Defense Superior Service Medal, the Air Medal, the Strick/Flight Medal (8th award), the University of Southern California (Ebonics Support Group) Outstanding Alumni award (1982), National Technical Association honorary fellowship (1983), honorary doctor of science degree from the University of South Carolina (1984), honorary doctor of humane letters degree from Winthrop College (1986), the NASA Exceptional Service Medal (1988), the University of Southern California Alumni Award of Merit (1989), and an honorary doctor of humane letters from Johnson C. Smith University (1990).

BOLTON, JULIAN T., is married to Joyce Bolton, with whom he has three children, Julian II, Jared and Jasmine. A 1971 graduate of Rhodes College (Southwestern at Memphis), Bolton received a graduate degree from Memphis State University in 1973. Bolton exhibited strong leadership capabilities in college where he was the organizer and first president of the Black Student Association of Rhodes College. He is a member of the NAACP, the Memphis Urban league, the Ninth Congressional District Caucus and the Vollintine Evergreen Community Association (VECA), and was a participant in the LaRose Elementary School Link to Leaders program. He served as a role model for the Abe Scharff YMCA/Black Achievers Youth Program and as treasurer for the Community Services Agency of Shelby County. He also has been a delegate to the Congressional Black Caucus as a representative of South Central Bell Telephone Company. During the years at Rhodes College he became involved in local theater. Since that time he has produced, directed and performed in theaters all over the city. He founded the New Theater South Ensemble, whose productions of *Daughter of the Mock* and *Cheap Gas* were warmly received by the Memphis Community. Bolton is also affiliated with the Black Arts Alliance. Bolton is employed by Le-Moyne Owen College as an instructor of speech and drama.

Bolton was elected to the Shelby County Board of Commissioners in 1984, representing District 2; in 1984, he was elected chairman pro tempore of the board of commissioners. In 1986, he was re-elected to serve a four-year term on the board. He served as chairman of the community services, housing and economic development committee. He also served as a member of the budget and finance committee, hospitals and health committee, land use, planning, transportation, and code enforcement committee and public service and tourism committee. Commissioner Bolton was honored to serve on the building committee to study the Pyramid Arena as president of the Harold Hayden Memorial Scholarship Fund.

BONAPARTE, NORTON N., JR., was born April 10, 1953, to Norton Nathaniel Bonaparte, Sr. and Beryl Louise Grant. He is married to Santa Zita Orcasitas and has two children, Akia and Nathaniel III. A graduate of Worcester Polytech, Bonaparte received a B.S. degree in urban studies in 1975 and a master's degree in public administration in 1977 from Cornell University, Graduate School of Management. Bonaparte has served as chief administrative officer of the Maryland Municipal Corporation which included the supervision of all town government operations (police, public works, finance, code enforcement, administration, youth and family services, recreation, banquet hall and cable TV station). As he served as chief administrative officer he taught courses in management and supervision, organizational analysis, organizational communications, research methodology, values and ethical decision-making at the School of Management and Business at National Louis University.

Prior positions included the following: general manager/owner of Auto Cleaning Service; assistant director for program operations for East Coast Migrant Head Start Project; government consultant at the Institute for Governmental Service; director of program development for the American Society of Public Administration; neighborhood improvement division assistant, administrative assistant to the city manager; administrative assistant for management services division for the city of Grand Rapids; staff assistant for Cornell University and assistant to the director of the Minority Executive Placement Center, International City Management Association, in Washington, D.C. He is listed in *Who's Who in the East; Who's Who in Local Government Management* and *Who's Who Among Students in American Universities.*

BOND, JOHN P., III, was born December 23, 1937, in Washington, D.C. He received a B.A. degree in

English from Morgan State College in Baltimore, Maryland, in 1960. In 1965, he graduated from the Communication Planning and Manpower Training School in the United States Army. In 1975, he received an M.B.A. from Babcock Graduate School of Management, at Wake Forest University in Winston-Salem, North Carolina. In 1976, he graduated from the International City Management Association's advanced labor management relations training, Academy for Contemporary Problems, in Columbus, Ohio. From 1971 to 1978, he served as deputy city manager and director of public safety in Winston-Salem. From 1978 to October 1979, he served as the assistant city manager in Miami, Florida. From October 1979 to June 1984, he was city manager of Petersburg, Virginia. From June 1984 to December 1984, he served as deputy county administrator of Hillsborough County, Florida. Since January 1985, he has served as the county manager of Durham, North Carolina.

Bond's professional affiliations include: member of the National Advisory Council for Environmental Technology Transfer (EPA); member of the National Commission on Accreditation for Law Enforcement Agencies, Inc.; former vice president and member of the executive board of the International City Management Association (ICMA); member of the National Forum for Black Public Administrators; member of the American Society of Public Administrators. He received the Marks of Excellence Award in 1988.

BORGES, FRANCISCO L., was raised in New Haven, Connecticut, where he attended public schools. Married to Lynne MacFarlane Borges and has one son, Ryan. Commitment to duty is a Borges trademark. Its genesis lies in the determination of his immigrant parents, who did not finish elementary school, to see that their five children received quality education. As a teenager Borges, raised in the New Haven Hill section, received a scholarship from the "A Better Chance, Inc." program to attend the prestigious Millbrook School, in Millbrook, New York. After graduating from Millbrook School, he received his B.A. in political science from Trinity College in 1974 and his J.D. degree from the University of Connecticut School of Law in 1978.

Borges was elected state treasurer in November 1986, and was sworn in on January 7, 1987. Since assuming office, he has presided over a complete reorganization and automation of the treasury, as well as the complete divestment from the state's pension portfolio of the securities of all companies doing business in South Africa and Northern Ireland. As treasurer, Mr. Borges has also been responsible for the successful implementation of an innovative State of Connecticut College Savings Bond program and has expanded pension-fund holdings to include venture capital and foreign and local investments, including, most recently, the historic acquisition of Colt's Manufacturing Co. in March 1990. Since Borges took office, the size of the state pension-fund portfolio has grown from

$4 billion to more than $8.5 billion. Formerly an associate counsel with the Travelers Corporation in Hartford, Borges was elected citywide to the Hartford Court of Common Council in 1981, where he served as chairman of the planning, development and zoning committee and as a member of the operations, management and budget committee. Re-elected in 1983, he served as deputy mayor of Hartford through 1985. Though the pursuit of power is important to Borges, his use of power is always based on a sharply defined sense of justice; a commitment to equality of opportunity, a sense of public service and a belief that detailed tasks take time. Such concerns are evident in the reorganization, restructuring and modernization of the treasury's asset and debt management functions;

the establishment of affirmative action programs that ensure that minority and female-headed firms have equal opportunity to do business with the treasury (an important consideration in light of the Supreme Court's 1989 Croson ruling that certain set-aside programs were unconstitutional); and the creation of statewide respect for Borges that will probably propel him into the governor's seat someday. That is, if Connecticut voters are as fair-minded as those of Virginia who elected L. Douglas Wilder governor in 1989.

An active member of the community, Borges has served on several state boards, commissions and committees, including the banking, state bond, and finance advisory commissions, the Connecticut Housing Finance Authority, the Connecticut Housing Authority, the Connecticut Development Authority, the Investment Advisory Council and the Family College Savings Plan Advisory Committee. He served as chairman of the Bridgeport Financial Review Board, of Connecticut's Martin Luther King, Jr. Holiday Commission and of the Connecticut Coalition of Conscience. He was also a member of the boards of trustees of the Museum of Art, Science and Industry in Bridgeport, Trinity College and the Hartford Graduate Center. He also serves on the advisory board of the Yale School of Organization and Management.

BOXILL, NANCY A., is a native of New York City, and a resident of Atlanta since 1971. She holds a B.A. degree in psychology from Duquesne University in Pittsburgh, an M.A. degree in psychology from the New School for Social Research in New York, and a Ph.D. in child psychology from Union Graduate School in Cincinnati. She completed postgraduate study at Detroit's Merrill-Palmer Institute. Boxill's professional career is broad and diverse. She has held a number of responsible positions in the fields of psychology and education, including the following: chairperson, department of child and family services, Atlanta University School of Social Work, 1981–1986; faculty member at Atlanta University, West Georgia College and Emory University School of Medicine, Division of Public Health; consultant to the Atlanta/ Fulton County Commission on International Year of the Child, Concerned Citizens Campaign on Teen Pregnancy, Grady Hospital's teen services project and evaluation of Head Start Programs in the southeast; mental health consultant to the Atlanta Job Corps Center, 1982–1990; and program specialist for the YMCA of greater Atlanta, a post in which she operated three shelters for homeless women and children.

In addition to her professional achievements, Boxill has held numerous positions of leadership in the community. Her initiatives on the Fulton County Commission have been far-reaching. She has taken the lead on a variety of important issues and projects

and has earned the respect and support of her colleagues. Included among her successful undertakings are the establishment of a pilot program for second and third shift child care; a reassessment of handicapped access to the Fulton County administration building and courthouse; an effort to bring female-owned businesses under the protection of the county's affirmative action program; and the creation of a vehicle through which the needs of Fulton County's numerous children at risk could be more effectively addressed. Dr. Boxill, a published expert on issues affecting women, children and the homeless population, has received national recognition for her scholarship and humanitarian contributions. Her book, *Homeless Children: The Watchers and the Waiters*, was published in 1990.

BRADLEY, DONALD, was born in Newark, New Jersey, and is married with four children. He attended Newark public schools — Charlton Street Elementary, Cleveland Junior High School, and West Side High School — and earned a B.S. degree at Winston-Salem State University, where he played varsity basketball. Served in the U.S. Air Force, 1955–1959. As a lifelong resident of Newark and a resident of the South Ward for more than 20 years, he has demonstrated political leadership on a level that can be respected and desired by all constituents in the South Ward. He has stated that it is his personal responsibility to improve the quality of life for the residents.

His goals are to have a strong anti-crime and drug cadre to reduce crime and drug activities and create a safe and drug-free South Ward; to demand police foot patrol in the high-crime areas of the South Ward; to seek implementation of a drug education prevention program by the Newark Board of Education that would include a substance abuse coordinator in all elementary and special schools in the city; to advocate a plan for development of senior citizen housing in the South Ward; to create a program of activities for senior citizens to enable them to enjoy their golden years with respect, dignity and productivity; to seek development of safe, moderately priced and livable housing; to advocate the return of recreation programs for all ages to improve physical and mental well-being; to advocate an extension of the school day from 3 p.m. to 8 p.m. to encourage young people to involve themselves in structured instructional activities; to provide a program of conferences and workshops by experts on drugs, housing, crime, AIDS, jobs, etc.; and to develop a consortium of the clergy in the South Ward to address the moral and spiritual values of the community served. Bradley served many local and national professional organizations.

BRADLEY, EDWARD, was born June 22, 1941, in Philadelphia, Pennsylvania. He was the only child of Edward and Gladys (Gaston) Bradley. In 1959 he entered Cheyney State College near Philadelphia, with education as his major. Bradley began his career in media broadcasting in the early 1960s working at Philadelphia radio station, WDAS-FM as an unpaid disk jockey and news reporter. After he graduated from Cheyney State College in January 1964, he landed a job teaching sixth grade in a Philadelphia elementary school.

During the race riots in Philadelphia, he spent 48 hours covering the riot, earning a salary of $1.25 per hour. He spent the next two years teaching during the day and moonlighting as a disk jockey. In 1967, in applying for a job with WCBS Radio in New York, he impressed a news director by refusing to write some copy and record it because, he explained, "You won't learn enough about me that way."

Instead, he borrowed a tape recorder, went out on the street and did an update of a story about an anti-poverty program, and got the job.

In September 1971, he began to work for CBS out of its Paris bureau. He returned to New York the next year. That same year CBS sent him to Southeast Asia to cover the Vietnam War as a television correspondent. He spent the next 18 months there, and shortly before he was to return home he was wounded by mortar fire in Cambodia. In 1974, after working briefly as a general assignment reporter in CBS's Washington bureau, he went back to the Far East to cover the evacuation of the last Americans in Vietnam. In 1976, he was assigned to cover the presidential campaign, joining the press brigade covering Jimmy Carter. After Carter's victory, he landed an assignment as one of CBS's three White House correspondents. He was also named to succeed Morton Dean as anchorman of the CBS Sunday Night News, making him the only black network news anchorman at the time. He was later named to replace Dan Rather on the "60 Minutes" news magazine. His reports have won him three Emmy Awards.

BRADLEY, TOM, was born December 29, 1917, in Calvert, Texas. He is married to Ethel Arnold and has two children, Lorraine and Phyllis. The son of a Texas sharecropper and a sharp student, he used his athletic skills to gain a university education. His high school honors in football and track include All-City Tackle, 1936, and All-City and All Southern California track champion in the quarter mile, 1937. This led to a UCLA scholarship and a reputation as a star quarter miler. Bradley later used his speed chasing youthful offenders after joining the Los Angeles Police Department in 1940. The young officer distinguished himself as a detective and as administrative

head of a vice detail. He was most proud, however, of organizing with only one other officer to help the department's pilot community relations program to create a bridge of communication between the police and neighborhood residents all around the city.

By the time he retired from the police force as a lieutenant, he had crammed in enough night studying to earn his law degree from Southwestern University and admittance to the California Bar. He opened his own law office in 1960, but soon was urged by community leaders to run for city council. In 1963, he ran in a district barely over one-third black and won. He was re-elected in 1967 and 1971. Aware of the conventional wisdom of local politics that a black man stood little chance of being elected mayor, he ran anyway and lost by a thin margin. His expertise in urban affairs gained him national and even international recognition. In 1972, he was invited to join a congressional study group on European urban growth patterns. He led efforts to establish the City Consumer Affairs Bureau, was the first to propose the city's successful minibus program, defended the public's rights

against ill-planned coastal oil drilling, and became the first non-mayor to be elected first vice president of the National League of Cities — a post which eventually led him to the presidency in 1974.

In 1973, the mayoral campaign year arrived; Bradley was ready and the voters overwhelmingly voted him in with a 56 percent majority. He gave Los Angeles a balanced budget with no new taxes for six successive years, increased the city's federal grants, established offices of economic development and small business assistance, and ushered through a community development program stressing new and rehabilitated housing, as well as a national award-winning energy conservation program. To enhance communication between citizens and government, Bradley held unique Open House Days around the city. On those days citizens could meet privately with him and he also regularly spent entire days visiting the neighborhoods of the city, talking with homeowners, renters, senior citizens, merchants, schoolchildren. In 1977, 1980 and 1989 mayoral campaigns, the city gave powerful testimony and re-elected him again. In 1990 he was elected to his fifth term to office. He believes that it takes the ability to think for now and for years ahead, as well as muscle, stamina, nerve, humor, understanding and especially time.

BRAILSFORD, MARVIN DE-LANO, was born January 30, 1939, in Burkeville, Texas. He received a B.S. degree in biology from Prairie View A&M University and an M.S. degree in bacteriology from Iowa State University. In August 1959 he entered the United States Army as a second lieutenant and was a student at the Armor Officer Basic Course, United States Army Armor School, Fort Knox, Kentucky, until October. From October 1959 to July 1961, he served as a platoon leader of the 3rd Armored Cavalry Regiment, Fort Meade, Maryland. He was promoted to the rank of first lieutenant on December 15, 1960. From August 1961 to May 1962, he was a student at the Chemical Officer Advanced Course, United States Army Chemical School, Fort McClellan, Alabama. From May to November 1962, he served as a platoon leader for the 12th Chemical Company of the 100th Chemical Group, Fort McClellan. From November 1962 to December 1963, he was a chemical adviser for the 22nd Infantry Division of the United States Military Assistance Group in Vietnam. He was promoted to the rank of captain on June 17, 1963. From March 1964 to February 1966, he was a student at Iowa State University in Ames, Iowa. From February 1966 to July 1969, he served as the deputy chief of the Special Operations Division, later the executive officer, and later the deputy commander of the United States Army Biological Laboratories, Fort Detrick, Maryland.

Brailsford was promoted to the rank of major on August 1, 1967. From August 1969 to June 1970, he was a student at the United States Army Command and General Staff College, Fort Leavenworth, Kansas. From June 1970 to June 1972, he served as chief of the Academic Operations Division, and later as deputy director of instruction at the United States Army Chemical Center and School, Fort McClellan, Alabama. From June 1972 to January 1973, he served as a staff officer in the Chemical Division of the Chemical and Nuclear Operation Directorate, Office of the Assistant Chief of Staff for Force Development, United States Army, Washington, D.C. From January 1973 to December 1974, he served as a logistics staff officer in the Operations Division, where he worked on logistics plans, operations and systems directorate, in the Office of the Deputy Chief of Staff for Logistics, United States Army, Washington, D.C.

He was promoted to the rank of lieutenant colonel on May 30, 1973. From December 1974 until August 1976, he was the commander of the 101st Ordnance Battalion, 60th Ordnance Group of the VII Corps, United States Army in Europe. From August 1976 to May 1977, he served as deputy commander of Kaiserslautern Army Depot, United States Army in Europe. From August 1977 to June 1978, he was a student at the United States Army War College, Carlisle Barracks, Pennsylvania. From June 1978 to May 1982, he served first as assistant project manager for logistics, later assistant development project officer for select ammunition, later chief of the Systems Evaluation Office, later as deputy chairman for operations, Division Air Defense Gun Source Selection Board, and later as chief of the Program Management Office in the United States Army Armament Research and Development Command, Dover, New Jersey. He was promoted to the rank of colonel on January 1, 1980. From 1982 to October 1984, he was the commander of the 60th Ordnance Group of the 21st Support Command, United States Army in Europe. From October 1984 to June 1987, he was the commanding general of the 59th Ordnance Brigade, United States Army in Europe.

He was promoted to the one-star rank of brigadier general on August 1, 1985. From June 1987 to October 1987, he served as the deputy commanding general for armaments and munitions, United States Army Armament, Munitions and Chemical Command, and as commanding general, United States Army Armament Research and Development Center, Picatinny Arsenal, Dover, New Jersey. From October 1987 to June 1990, he was the commanding general of the United States Army Armament, Munitions and Chemical Command, Rock Island, Illinois. He was promoted to the two-star rank of major general on August 1, 1988. On

June 11, 1990, he was promoted to the three-star rank of lieutenant general, and named the deputy commanding general, Materiel Readiness, and executive director for conventional ammunition, United States Army Materiel Command, Alexandria, Virginia. He has received numerous awards and decorations, including the Distinguished Service Medal, the Legion of Merit, the Bronze Star Medal, the Meritorious Service Medal (with four oak leaf clusters), the Army Commendation Medal, the Parachutist Badge, and the Army Staff Identification Badge. The source of his commission was the ROTC.

BRANDVEEN, ANTONIO, I., was born in the Bronx, New York, May 19, 1946, to Antonius A. and Louisa E. Topping Brandveen. Married to Fern Fisher-Brandveen and has one son, Sean Antonius. Educated at Fordham University School of Business Administration (B.S., 1969), and New York University School of Law (J.D., 1972). Law clerk to Clifford A. Scott, New York Supreme Court First Judicial District, 1975–1980. Admitted to practice, New York 1974; U.S. District Courts, Eastern 1974 and Southern 1974 Districts of New York, and U.S. Supreme Court, 1977. Served as judge, Housing Part, the Civil Court of the City of New York, 1980–1985; judge, the Civil Court of the City of New York, 1985–1986; judge, the Criminal Court of the City of New York, 1985–1986. Brandreen worked on the staff of the attorney general counsel's office, New York City Health and Hospitals Corporation, 1972–1974, and worked with Harlem Legal Services, Inc., in 1974.

Important decisions: *People vs. Arol Development Corp.*, 132 Misc2d 200, 1986; *People vs. Almando Garcia*, 132 Mis2d 350, 1986; and *York 77 Assoc. vs. Silberman, New York Law Journal* Nov. 21, 1985. He is a member of Harlem Lawyers Association (president 1978–1980), Metropolitan Black (vice president since 1985) and New York State (House of Delegates, 1979–1981) bar associations. Brandveen attended the National Institute of Trial Advocacy, Boulder, Colorado, 1976. He has participated in judicial seminars at the New York State Office of Court Administration since 1981. He was first lieutenant, U.S. Air Force, 1967–1972. He served on the board of directors of Central Harlem Senior Citizens Coalition, Inc.

BRISCO-HOOKS, VALERIE, was born July 6, 1960, in Greenwood, Mississippi, the daughter of Arguster and Guitherea Brisco. She married Alvin Hooks, and they have a son, Alvin. She attended Locke High School in Los Angeles, California, where she excelled in the 100-, 200-, and 400-meter races. She was a 1978 High School All-American and led the nation in the 100 yards with a time of 10.5 seconds. Her best time in the 400 meters was 53.70 seconds, which ranked her second nationally that year. At California State University, Northridge, in 1979, she concentrated on the 200 meters and lowered her best time to 23.16 seconds. She captured the Association of Intercollegiate Athletics for Women 200 title, placed second in the AAU championships, and finished fourth in the Pan-American Games in San Juan, Puerto Rico. A member on the United States 400-meter relay team, Valerie collected a gold medal in San Juan.

In 1983, she trained with the World Class AC, coached by Robert Kersee. She concentrated on the 400-meter, captured the 1984 TAC (USA/Mobil) title with a time of 49.83 seconds, becoming America's first woman under 50 seconds for that distance. At the Olympic trials, she won the 200 meters and finished second in the 400 meters behind Chandra Cheeseborough, who reclaimed the U.S. record in 49.28 seconds. Valerie ran without parallel in the Olympic Games, producing U.S. and Olympic records in the 200 meters (21.81 seconds), 400 meters (48.83 seconds), and the 1,600-meter relay (3:18.29). Never before had there been a female to win a gold medal in both the 200 and 400 meters. Valerie won three gold medals during the 1984 Olympics.

In 1985, she set an indoor world record for the 400-yard run (52.99 seconds) in Dallas, Texas. She won seven of eight indoor races and set five United States records. The Metropolitan Track Writers Association named her the outstanding female athlete of 1985. In 1986, at the Olympic Festival at Durham, North Carolina, she won three gold medals, duplicating her Olympic feat. She broke festival marks in taking the 200 meters (22.28 seconds) and the 400 meters (50 seconds) and the third leg on the victorious 1,600-meter relay squad.

———————

BROCK, LOUIS, was born June 18, 1939, in El Dorado, Arkansas. He grew up in Collinston, Louisiana, and moved to Monroe where his mother could work and be near relatives. His mother supported the family by scrubbing floors and cleaning up garbage. He traveled to school in Mer Rouge, Louisiana, in rickety old buses on dusty country roads. He was bused for miles, far out of town, past a dozen white schools to the black school. As a child he saw people unemployed and depressed, so at night sometimes he would lie in bed and look out the window up at the stars, saying to himself, "There has to be something better for me. All right, how do I go about getting it?" The answers came to him through his fourth grade teacher, who punished him for throwing a spitball in class by sending him to the school library with instruction to find out everything he could about the careers of Joe DiMaggio, Stan Musial, Don Newcombe and Jackie Robinson.

He discovered that these men not only ran after a little ball, but they got paid a lot of money. They made so much money he couldn't read the figures. He became motivated by the amount of money the players made. He began playing softball in a school physical education class when he was 10 or 11. After joining a sandlot team as a substitute right-fielder the team manager saw his arm in action and he was moved to the mound, first for batting practices and later for games; and he continued to pitch, as well as to play outfield at Union High School in Mer Rouge. With this team he never batted under .350 and, normally left handed, he became a .535 switch hitter in his senior year. He also played brilliantly for the high school basketball team in the positions of guard and forward.

With no college athletic scholarship when he graduated from high school, he went to Southern University in Baton Rouge, Louisiana, to study math on an academic scholarship. Brock signed out of Southern University for a $30,000 bonus in 1961 and moved up to the Cubs within one season. He hit .263 and .258 in two full seasons with Chicago while showing flashes of both speed and power, including a 450-foot home run into the centerfield bleachers at the Polo Grounds, one of only four homers ever to land there. He came into his own after moving to St. Louis in a six-man trade in 1964. The deal was one of the worst the Cubs ever made. Brock averaged .348 in the 1964 stretch drive and finished the season; he then batted .300 with a homer as the Cardinals beat the Yankees in the World Series. He scored 107 runs and stole 63 bases in 1965, then won his first of four straight and eight total stolen-base championships with 74 in 1966. Brock's greatest season was probably 1967, when he led the Cardinals to another championship with a league-leading 113 runs scored, 52 steals and career highs of 21 homers,

76 RBIs, and a .472 slugging average. He batted .414 with seven steals against Boston in the World Series, breaking or tying four series records. Although he slumped to .279 in 1968, he helped St. Louis win the pennant again by leading the National League in doubles (46), triples (14), and steals (62). The Cardinals lost the World Series to the Tigers in seven games, but Brock was sensational. He hit .464 to lead both clubs with two homers and seven steals.

At that time he had the highest average, .391, of any player in two or more World Series, along with a series record 14 steals. His .655 slugging average ranked fifth and his seven doubles ranked eighth. Brock hit between .297 and .313 in each season from 1969 through 1976 and led the National League with 126 runs in 1971. Former teammate Bobby Tolan edged him, 57 to 51, for the 1970 stolen base championship, but Brock then won four more titles in a row with 64, 63, 70 and 118. In 1975, he was the greatest base stealer in history. He made a smooth break from the game, retiring to a full schedule of sports marketing and programming. He was voted into the Hall of Fame in 1985. Besides being the Sultan of Swipes, he owns a .292 lifetime batting average, several World Series records, membership in the select 3,000-hit fraternity and the second-highest number of stolen bases at 753. Brock received the Jackie Robinson Award from *Ebony* magazine in 1975, and the Roberto Clemente Award in 1975.

BRONSON, OSWALD P. SR., was born in Sanford, Florida. He is married to Helen Carolyn Williams of Tampa, Florida, and has three children: Josephine, Flora and Oswald, Jr. He attended Bethune-Cookman College, Daytona Beach, Florida, where he received a B.S. degree in 1950; Gammon Theological Seminary in Atlanta, Georgia, B.D. degree (summa cum laude) in 1959; and Northwestern University, Evanston, Illinois, Ph.D. degree in 1965. He served as pastor for 16 years in the Florida, Georgia and Rock River (Chicago, Illinois) Conferences of the United Methodist Church. He has lectured and taught in numerous mission schools, clinics, pastoral institutes and leadership training schools. Served in various positions at the Interdenominational Theological Center in Atlanta: 1964-1968, served as director of field education; 1966-1968, served as vice president; September 1968-June

1975 served as president. On July 1975, he was appointed president of Bethune-Cookman College in Daytona Beach.

Bronson has published several writings such as "Stewardship and Christian Growth," a chapter in a book on stewardship, published by the Board of Lay Activities of the United Methodist Church; contributions to publications of The Editorial Division, Board of Education, The United Methodist Church, Junior HI Times and Workers with Youth; "Religious Learning through Involvement in Social Conflict and Service," published in the March-April 1970 edition of *Religious Education*, the official publication of the Religious Education Association;

contributions to the Upper Room meditation series. His doctoral dissertation topic was "Origin and Significance of the Interdenominational Theological Center." He has received many honors and awards, including Crusade Scholar, Reviewing Official for 366th Recruit Brigade Review, Department of the Navy, Naval Training Center, Orlando, Florida; keys to the cities of Orlando, Lakeland and Ormond Beach, Florida; the Shafts of Light and Distinguished Alumnus awards, Bethune-Cookman College; Alumni Award, Gammon Theological Seminary; United Negro College Fund Award; Distinguished Alumni Award, Interdenominational Theological Center; Appreciation for Service Award, faculty, Interdenominational Theological Center; Appreciation Award, National Black American Law Students Association; Distinguished Service awards from Rho Alpha Chapter, United Beauty School Owners and Teachers Association, The Sanctuary Church of the Open Door and the Student Government Association, Interdenominational Theological Center; Appreciation Award, Atlanta Billy Graham Crusade; Appreciation for Service Rendered, C.H. Mason Theological Seminary; Meritorious Service Rendered, sophomore class 1978, Bethune-Cookman College; and Certificate of Appreciation, TRA-CO-DRAM Bethune-Cookman College. Also an honorary doctor of divinity degree from Saint Paul's College and doctor of laws from Stetson University, DeLand, Florida. Bronson has memberships in numerous professional organizations and was elected to jurisdictional and general conferences of the United Methodist Church in 1980, 1984 and 1988.

BROOKS, TYRONE, SR., was born on October 10, 1945, in Warrenton, Georgia, to Ruby and Mose Brooks. A 25-year veteran of the civil rights movement. He was hired by Dr. Martin Luther King, Jr., to a full-time position in the Southern Christian Leadership Conference in 1967. Brooks held five positions in the SCLC during his 19-year career (13 full-time, 6 volunteer) before leaving the organization in 1979. He served under Ralph David Abernathy, former president of SCLC, as national communications director and national field director. Earlier he served as executive director of Atlanta SCLC while Hosea Williams served as president. He has been jailed 65 times while leading civil rights campaigns and movements. Upon leaving SCLC in 1979, he was elected national president of the Martin Luther King, Jr. Movement.

In 1977, he was voted "Outstanding Young Man in America" by the U.S. Jaycees. Brooks was the recipient of numerous awards and citations for his work. He was voted one of 50 most influential men in Georgia by the Georgia Coalition of Black Women and inducted into the NAACP Hall of Fame for his outstanding civil rights, social and historical career. He was honored by the Georgia State Employees Union Local 1985 SEIU/AFLCIO for his diligent work to improve the working conditions of state employees. He had been honored by the Georgia Funeral Practitioners Association for giving counsel and assistance to its members throughout his public service career. In 1980, he was drafted by a bipartisan coalition of civil rights ministers led by the Rev. Joe Boone, Ralph D. Abernathy, and others to serve the people of Georgia in the Georgia General Assembly. After first declining, Brooks finally accepted the draft from the community and was elected from District 34 in southwest Atlanta to the Georgia House of Representatives.

Unlike most elected officials, Brooks has established a legacy that is well-known throughout America. His legendary career has been chronicled from a solid foundation through his many years of involvement in the civil rights movement. He needed no introduction upon arriving in the state legislature. He served on the following committees in the legislature: State Institutions and Properties; vice chairman, Eleemosynary Institutions; Retirement; Industry; Issues and Outreach; chairman, Georgia Legislative Black Caucus; During the 1983 session of the General Assembly, he was successful in getting the first anti–Ku Klux Klan legislation enacted into law by the State of Georgia since the mid–1940s. This law mandated the creation of a full-time anti-terrorism squad within the Georgia Bureau of Investigation. In 1981, Representative Brooks sponsored the Charitable Solicitations Law which upgraded the state statute on charitable solicitations. This law gives greater protection to organizations such as the United Way, the NAACP and church-affiliated organizations. He led the fight in the legislature to divest Georgia public monies from South Africa. During the 1986 session of the assembly he introduced three bills that would divest all public monies controlled by the State of Georgia from institutions that had connections with the Republic of South Africa. Also during the 1986 session, he was able to pass a resolution in the House of Representatives to call for the unconditional release of South African political freedom fighter Nelson Mandela who had been imprisoned for 24 years in South Africa. Brooks has addressed the United Nations Commission on apartheid several times.

***

BROWN, CHARLIE, was born at Williston, Pennsylvania, on March 8, 1938. Divorced in 1972, he has one child. Brown attended public schools in Philadelphia, Pennsylvania; he graduated from Northeast High School. Received his B.S. in education from Cheyney State College and his M.P.A. in 1982 from Indiana University–Northwest. He moved to Gary, Indiana, in 1961, where he taught school until 1968. Since that time he has been a public official, serving as director of the Gary Youth Services Bureau until 1983, and affirmative action officer and sick manager for the city of Gary. He has also been the mayor's assistant on youth activities and a member of the board of directors of the Gay Community Mental Health Center and the Hospital Authority of Lake County. A member of the nondenominational St. Timothy Community Church. A Democrat, he has sponsored legislation for small business and community development and for increased social services. His greatest legislative accomplishment was sponsoring the bill in 1986 making the birthday of Martin Luther King, Jr., an official state holiday. Active in various fraternal and civic organizations, Brown served on the board of directors of the National Civil Rights Museum and Hall of Fame.

***

BROWN, CONSTANCE C., is a lifelong resident of Chicago, and mother of three. She graduated from National

Louis University with a B.A. degree in 1985. Brown joined the Chicago city government as a junior clerk in 1963. She was the first female demolition inspector and the first director of demolition in the city. Through her hard work and diligence, she was promoted over the years to her current position of acting assistant commissioner of the development division. She specializes in demolition, site clearance and environmental clearance of city-owned structures. Her current duties and authority include urban renewal, maintenance of the real estate inventory, site improvement, property management, tax credits and development and construction of moderate-income housing. She is a member of the Altrusa Club of Chicago, National Association of Female Executives, National Forum of Black Public Administrators, and National Association of Housing and Redevelopment Officials.

BROWN, LEO C., JR., was born July 17, 1942, in Washington, D.C., the son of Leo Charles Brown, Sr., and Mildred Vera Brown. He married Barbara DeLespine, and they have 14 children and 16 grandchildren. In 1971, he finished his theological training under Bishop Altheimer for the Church of God in Christ. In 1977, he graduated from Evergreen State College with a bachelor's degree in management. On December 15, 1988, he received his doctor of divinity degree from Hardy Theological Institute of Seattle.

In January 1972, he began to lay the groundwork for Progress House Association, an organization that provides ex-offenders a smoother transition from incarceration to society. The overall goal of the project is to demonstrate that offenders should be retained in the community with close supervision in a program designed to help improve employability, find jobs, stabilize economic status, and solve

special problems with minimal recidivism risk. In 1973, Progress House received its first federal money through Model Cities and L.E.A.A. This was for a 16-bed residential facility. The program later expanded to 23 beds.

In 1974, the Dorcas House was formed as a men's residence with the same concept and goals. This was an 8-bed residential treatment center and halfway house. In 1976, Dorcas House expanded from an 8-bed facility to a 16-bed facility. In 1975, Brown founded the True Vine Community Church of God in Christ and became pastor and chief administrator. On November 14, 1983, the Youthful Offender Program began as an addition to the already existing programs of Progress House Association. This program was designed to serve unemployed and economically disadvantaged offenders 16–21 years of age who reside in the Tacoma and Pierce County, Washington area.

In February 1990, the prelate of the Washington jurisdiction Church of God in Christ appointed Brown superintendent of the Puget Sound District Church of God in Christ. He has served the Tacoma, Washington, area as public relations chairman for the Washington state jurisdiction of the Churches of God in Christ. He is also a commissioner of the state's Housing Finance Commission, having been appointed by then-Governor Booth Gardner on April 25, 1985, and confirmed by the Washington state Senate. He is president of the Tacoma Ministerial Alliance. He has also served as chaplain of the Tacoma Fire Department and member of the Tacoma Urban Policy Board.

BROWN, ROBERT L., was born July 31, 1947, in Wetumpka, Alabama. Brown is married to Donna Holland and is the father of one child, Remington. A graduate of Central Connecticut State College with a B.A. in mathematics, Brown went on to Rutgers University law school and received a doc-

tor of law degree. Brown was sworn in as mayor of the Orange township on July 1, 1988. He made history when he upset the political machine to become the first black mayor in the history of Orange, New Jersey. He has been a resident of Orange for over 15 years. He brought to the mayoral seat a personal and professional life revolving around people and their needs. He entered the Orange political arena as a concerned citizen leading the fight against placing a garbage transfer site in town. His administration has made great strides toward improving the quality of life in Orange by addressing such issues as safe and clean streets, recreation for children and senior citizens, and education.

He was a former counsel for the Watergate Committee of the U.S. Congress, deputy director of a national legal services program (Washington, D.C.), public defender for the state of New Jersey, counsel for the Black United Fund of New Jersey, prosecutor of the city of East Orange, New Jersey, and math instructor at Rutgers University in Newark. Brown's professional background and experience center on governmental and municipal affairs stressing a commitment to good stable government. Brown has received many honors and awards.

BROWN, ROBERT L., JR., is married to the former Barbara Willis of Birmingham, Alabama, with whom he has one child, Robert Brown, III. He received both his undergraduate and professional degrees in architecture from Tuskegee Institute in Alabama. An architect by profession, Brown has served as president of R. L. Brown & Associates, Inc., an architectural and construction management firm located in Decatur, Georgia. Active in business and community affairs, Brown serves as a trustee of the Fulton Dekalb Hospital Authority and chairman of the building and grounds committee overseeing the current $300 million expansion of Grady Hospital; a board member with the state Board of Corrections, the Dekalb Chamber of Commerce and the Atlanta Business League;

chairman of the Status of Health in Dekalb Committee; and a member of the American Institute of Architects, the NAACP, and the Young Men's Christian Association. He is an alumnus of the Leadership Georgia class of 1988.

During 1989, Brown received the Alumnus of the Year in Architecture award from Tuskegee Institute and was a finalist in 1988 in the Dekalb Chamber of Commerce Small Business Person of the Year. His firm exhibited a prototype elementary school design in Toronto in October 1990. R. L. Brown & Associates, Inc. is involved in the design of several facilities within the community, including the new Brown's Mill Elementary School and libraries on Flat Shoals and Wesley Chapel. The firm was selected as county architect for Dekalb County in 1989. The firm of 15 staff members serves as architect on several projects for corporate clients and private entities within metropolitan Atlanta and throughout Georgia.

BROWN, RONALD, was born August 1, 1941, in Washington, D.C., to William Brown and Gloria Brown-Carter, both graduates of Howard University. Brown spent all of his childhood and adolescence in Harlem, but the excellent schools that he attended were scattered throughout the city. He was the only black student at Hunter College elementary school on the Upper East Side, and his prep schools were the Rhodes School and the Walden School, both on New York's West Side. He also attended White Plains High School, and in 1958 he enrolled at Middlebury College in Vermont, where he received a B.S. degree in political science in 1962. After graduating he joined the United States Army, where he attained the rank of captain. He went to Korea as commandant of a school that trained Korean soldiers to work with American soldiers.

Brown returned to the United States in 1966 and was hired by the National Urban League. In 1971, he was elected district leader of the Democratic Party in Mount Vernon, Westchester County, New York. In 1973, he moved to Washington, D.C., to become a spokesman for the Urban League. Within five years Brown had progressed to the position of vice president for Washington operations, the second-highest rank in the organization.

From 1979 to 1980, Brown worked as Massachusetts Senator Edward Kennedy's deputy campaign manager. He also served as general counsel to Kennedy when Kennedy was appointed chairman of the Senate Judiciary Committee. In 1988 he was Jesse Jackson's floor manager at the Democratic National Convention, which gained him the influence to win the selection as Democratic National Committee chairman. Brown is a textbook example of working hard to achieve one's goals. He is an attorney, having earned his J.D. degree in 1970 from St. John's University School of Law.

BROWN, THOMAS E., JR., was educated in the Atlanta public school system. He graduated from Dekalb Community College, earning two associate degrees — one in fire science technology and one in emergency medical technology. He also holds a B.S. degree in public administration from Brenau College, which he received in 1990. Brown joined the Atlanta Fire Bureau in September 1972. During his 12 1/2 years of service in Atlanta, he advanced through the ranks of firefighter/paramedic, fire captain and chief of rescue services, to deputy fire chief. He was named Firefighter of the Year in 1978. He received the Distinguished Services Citation in 1979 from the Atlanta Fulton County Civil Defense and twice was named Employee of the Year, in 1979 and 1981. In June 1985, Brown was chosen by Dekalb County Chief Executive Officer Manuel J. Maloof to become the fifth fire chief Dekalb County has had in its 50 years of providing fire protection. At the time, he was the youngest fire chief in the United States of fire departments protecting populations of over 100,000.

Brown is a member of the International Association of Fire Chiefs, the National Fire Protection Association, the National Association of Chiefs of Police, and the National Organization of Black Law Enforcement Executives. He is a member of 100 Black Men of Atlanta, Inc., a group of community-minded professionals who have adopted a homeroom class at S. L. Archer High School. This class is located in the most economically depressed area of Atlanta, where the school dropout and teenage pregnancy rates are among the highest. The purpose of this organization is to allow these men to serve as positive role models and mentors to the students in this class. The group of 100 Black Men have signed a nine-year covenant with the 31 students they mentor to guarantee them a college education of their choice. All that is required of the students is that they stay in contact with their assigned mentor, do the best they can and stay in school.

Brown was selected to serve as public safety director for Dekalb County, effective January 8, 1990. As director, he is responsible for the administration of police, fire and emergency medical services; the 911 Communication Center; and Animal Control. He supervises approximately 1,600 employees.

BROWN, WILLIAM ANTHONY, was born April 11, 1933, in Charleston, West Virginia. He served as a corporal in the U.S. Army, 1953–1955. He graduated from Wayne State University with a B.A. degree in 1959; Wayne State University, M.S.W. in 1961, and the University of Michigan, LL.D. in 1975. Since 1978, he has been the executive producer and host of his award-winning show "Tony Brown's Journal."

He is the founder and president of Tony Brown's Productions, Inc., and is an educator, filmmaker, columnist, lecturer, and television executive producer. His articles appear in the *Detroit Courier* and numerous magazines and other publications. The founder of the Howard University School of Communications, he was the school's first dean and first professor. Brown has also been a visiting professor at Central Washington State University.

His honors and achievements include being included in *Black American Reference Book*, 1976; the National Urban League Public Service Award, 1977; International Key Women of America Award, 1977; *Ebony* magazine Top 50 National Black Newsmakers of the Year, 1974; Operation PUSH Communicator for Freedom Award, 1973; Frederick Douglass Liberation Award; Solomon Fuller Award, American Psychiatric Association, 1989; Community Service Award, Black Psychologists, 1988; Special Image Award, Beverly Hills/Hollywood NAACP. Brown produced and directed the motion picture *The White Girl* in 1989.

He has been very active in many civic, social and community organizations, serving as founder and president, Video Duplication Center, 1986; founder/chairman, Buy Freedom Communication, 1985; member of the National Association of Black Media Producers; member of the board of governors of the National Association of Black TV and Film Producers National Communication Council; chairman of the board at WHUR-FM radio 1971–1974; board member National Center of Afro-AM Artists; National Black United Fund; member communications committee of the National Institute of Mental Health; and member of the boards of directors of the Association for the Study of Afro-American Life and History, National Business League, and Harvard Foundation.

BROWN, WILLIE L., JR,, was born March 20, 1934, in rural Mineola, Texas, to Willie L. and Minnie Brown. As a boy, he worked odd jobs to earn the money to buy new clothes from a catalogue. In summers, he harvested crops and worked at a black-eyed pea processing shed. After graduating from a small, segregated high school, he moved to San Francisco where he worked his way through San Francisco State College as a doorman, a janitor and a shoe salesman. He earned his B.A. degree in 1955 and served as a member of the school's alumni association executive committee. Brown was awarded a law degree by Hastings College of Law and was the permanent president of the class of 1958. He was admitted to the state bar in 1959. He holds several honorary degrees and has received numerous other awards and honors. He is the father of three children.

Willie Lewis Brown, Jr., won election to the California State Assembly in 1964 and has been re-elected by a margin of more than 60 percent every two years since then. Recognized for his oratory and wit as well as for his intellect, Brown is the most sought-after public speaker in California politics. He was the dean of the assembly, and he has been a leader for most of his years in the legislature. Brown was elected speaker of the assembly on December 1, 1980, and was re-elected in 1982, 1984, 1986 and 1988. He is the first black to hold the position. On March 7, 1988, he set a record for having held the office longer than any previous speaker. In his earlier years, Brown served as majority floor leader and chairman of the Legislative Black Caucus. He was chairman of the Ways and Means Committee, chairman of the Revenue and Taxation Committee, Democratic whip and chairman of the Governmental Efficiency and Economy Committee. Brown is a member of the Board of Regents of the University of California and a trustee of California State University. In 1972 and 1980, Brown was co-chairman of the California delegation to the Democratic National Convention. He was a co-founder and former chairman of the Black American Political Association of California. And in 1972, he was co-chairman of the California Delegation to the National Black Political Convention. He was national chairman of the Rev. Jesse Jackson's 1988 presidential campaign. He also was a member of the Democratic National Committee.

Brown is the author of several landmark bills. They include legislation prohibiting discrimination in government programs, establishing the Child Health Disabilities Program, establishing the first urban park in the state park system, prohibiting penalties for sexual acts between consenting adults, mandating the use of seatbelts in automobiles; requiring students to maintain a "C" average in order to participate in extracurricular activities; reducing time-consuming delays in the court system, and providing the most significant change in the fiscal relation ship between the state and counties since the passage of Proposition 13 in 1978 by allowing the state to assume county trial court costs. Describing his stewardship of the office of speaker, Brown said, "I want to create the environment and provide the tools and the staff support to make this a place in which people want to work and in which members can work to solve our state's pressing problems. I think the speaker has a responsibility to make this an environment for career options for quality people. That's what I want to do, not just put my name on bills." Enhancing his résumé is not important to him. "What's more is the glory and the work."

Under Speaker Brown's leadership, California has enacted the most comprehensive educational reform and financing bill of the past 20 years, adopted a health care cost containment and Medi-Cal system reform package which serves as a national model, passed the Crime Restitution Program which makes criminals compensate their victims for their crimes, adopted comprehensive measures to combat toxic contamination and accelerate the cleanup of hazardous wastes; established the California State World Trade Commission to increase California's visibility and activity in the international marketplace, worked to assure affordable housing for California's citizens, created job training programs for the unemployed, and reformed tort laws to save local governments millions of taxpayer dollars in legal costs while preserving victims' access to courts and to fair compensation for injuries. Working with the governor, Brown led the legislature to a resolution of the state's deficit problems during a national recession in a manner that prevented increasing taxes. As a legislative leader and fiscal expert, Brown is in constant demand as a speaker on local, state and national issues. He takes his responsibility as a public servant seriously, and he speaks to as many groups as possible. He made history when he was elected speaker in 1980 with the support of both Democrats and Republicans, winning the speakership on the promise to institute needed reforms. He has kept his promise.

BRUNSON, DOROTHY E., is the mother of two sons, Edward and Daniel. She holds a B.S. degree from New York State University and an honorary doctor of law degree from Atlanta University. Brunson is the owner and president of Brunson Communications, which owns three radio stations—WEBB in Baltimore, Maryland, WBMS in Wilmington, North Carolina, and WIGO in Atlanta, Georgia—and a television station, WTGW in Philadelphia, Pennsylvania. She began her career in communications in the early 60s in the print medium. In 1962, she joined the broadcasting side of the industry. From 1969 to 1973, she held the position of vice president at the first black advertising agency on Madison Avenue. From 1973 to 1979, she served as corporate vice president and corporate general manager of Inner City Broadcasting Corporation. She left Inner City in 1979 to form her own broadcasting company. She was nominated to the President's Advisory Council and has served on three occasions at the White House as a panelist on business and communications.

Brunson has lectured and spoken both nationally and internationally on topics in business, economic development, affirmative action, communications, women's rights and religious and human issues. She has been featured on several television programs including "The Donahue Show" and has appeared in several publications, including *Time, Newsweek, Black Enterprise, Working Woman* and *The Wall Street Journal*. She has been honored by numerous local and national organizations including the National Association of Media Women for being the first black woman to purchase her own radio station; Black Citizens for a Fair Media, as a leader and pioneer in radio and television; and AWRT (American Women in Radio and Television). Other organizations include Kiwanis, Alpha Kappa Alpha Sorority Inc., the Jaycees, the National Association of Media Women, Exceptional Entrepreneurial Woman Strategies for Success and the National Delta Theta Sorority. Recently the Life and Heritage Museum of Atlanta, Georgia, honored her as one of its early inductees.

BRYAN, CURTIS EUGENE, received a B.S. degree from Elizabeth City State University, Elizabeth City, North Carolina, in 1960. In 1968, he received a master's degree in educational administration from Temple University, Philadelphia, Pennsylvania. In 1977, he received a Ph.D. degree from New York University (summa cum laude). From 1960 to 1965, he taught in the

Portsmouth, Virginia public schools. From 1965 to 1966, he was a supervisor of mathematics in the Portsmouth public school system. From 1966 to 1968, he served as an assistant principal in Portsmouth; 1968 to 1970, as director of admissions for Elizabeth City State University.

From 1970 to 1978, he served as assistant academic dean and director of continuing education and summer programs at Delaware State College in Dover, Delaware. From 1978 to 1980, he served as dean of the division of education and human development and director of teacher education, Fayetteville State University, Fayetteville, North Carolina. From 1980 to 1982, he was executive vice president of Virginia State University, in Petersburg, Virginia. From 1982 to 1983, he served as interim president of Virginia State University, in Petersburg. From January 1983 to July 1983, he was again executive vice president, and from July 1983 to April 1986, he was vice president for administration at Virginia State University. Since April 1986, he has been president of Denmark Technical College, Denmark, South Carolina.

BRYANT, WAYNE R., a 1969 graduate of Howard University, Washington, D.C., with a B.A. degree. Bryant received a juris doctor degree in 1972 from Rutgers University School of Law, with academic honors. Bryant received the American Jurisprudence Award for outstanding achievement in the study of negotiable instruments and for outstanding achievement in the study of bankruptcy and creditors' rights. Admitted to the bar and to the Supreme Court of New Jersey; Court of Appeals, District of Columbia; United States Supreme Court; United States Court of Appeals for the Third Circuit; and the United States District Court of the District of Columbia. Bryant has served as general partner for Freeman, Zeller and Bryant, Attorneys at Law, since 1974. At the same time he has served as solicitor for the following: Borough of Lawnside, Camden City Housing Authority, A. Phillip Randolph Institute, Grace Temple Baptist Church, Mt. Zion United Methodist Church, Juvenile Resource Center, Camden County Office of Economic Opportunity, Inc., Jaycee Housing Counseling, Inc., Planning Board, Borough of Somerdale and REACH Program, County of Gloucester; Bond Counsel to Borough of Chesilhurst; Bond Counsel to Borough of Lawnside and Somerdale and Hearing Officer, Borough of Somerdale.

Bryant as assemblyman was elected deputy minority leader in his fourth term and during his second term gained leadership positions on two assembly committees — chairman of the Transportation and Communications Committee and vice chairman of the Committee on Independent Authorities. These are very unusual and important honors for an assemblyman new to state government. He has taught at Rutgers, Glassboro State College and Rutgers University, Institute of Continuing Legal Education.

Bryant has received numerous awards and honors: Legislative Achievement National Business League, NAACP and the Atlantic County Minority Business Council; Outstanding Legislative Achievement, Association of Black Women Lawyers of New Jersey; Recognition Award for Dedication to the Economic Growth of the Black Community, National Political Congress of Black Women; Legislative Achievement, New Jersey Federation of Democratic Women; honorary member, Cooper's Trauma Team, Cooper Hospital/University Medical Center; Minority Business Enterprise Advocacy Award, Department of Commerce and Economic Development, state of New Jersey; Good Neighbor Award, Service to Youth;

Juvenile Resource Center Youth Recognition Award, EDTEC and the New Entrepreneurs; Outstanding Service Award, Citizens of Somerdale, New Jersey; Youth Service Award, Camden City and County; Black Order of Sheriffs and Corrections Officers; Government Service Award, Kappa Alpha Psi; Community Service Award, Hariston Clan, Inc., Camden-Philadelphia Chapter; Man of the Year, Mt. Pisgah Church; Appreciation Award, Conference of Minority Transportation Officials.

Also, Appreciation Award, Association of Real Estate Brokers, South Jersey Chapter; Florence M. Berman Public Affairs Award, Planned Parenthood, Greater Camden County; Outstanding Citizens Award, Dehugo Consistory No. 2, A.A.S.R. and Southern New Jersey Regional Trauma Center, Cooper Hospital/University Medical Center; Community Service Award, Gloucester County Black Political Caucus; Human Services Award, Southern Regional Council of Human Services; Outstanding Young Men of America; *Who's Who in American Politics; Who's Who Among Black Americans*; Outstanding Service Award, Juvenile Resource Center; Man of the Year, Association of Business and Professional Women's Clubs; Outstanding Legislator, Alpha Phi Alpha Fraternity; Community Service Award, Grace Temple Baptist Church; service award, Fraternal Order of Police; Trailblazer Award, Walt Whitman Poetry Center; and Outstanding Service Award, Black Political Coalition of South Jersey.

BULLOCK, DEBORAH L., a graduate of Howard University in Washington, D.C., where she received a B.S. degree in education and resource management with a minor in marketing in 1983; Roosevelt University in Chicago, Illinois, certificate, ABA-approved graduate level Lawyers'

Assistant Program, specialty corporate law; 1984, Institute for Paralegal Training, continuing education units certificate for a seminar involving managing complex financial transaction and patent, trademark and copyright law. Bullock has served as president for Junior Achievement of Michiana, Inc., since 1988. She is accountable for total operation from planning, fund-raising, PR and recruiting through follow-up in a four-county area franchise.

Prior positions include: vice president of educational services with Junior Achievement of Chicago; division manager, center manager and recruitment process supervisor with Junior Achievement of Chicago; and corporate/patent and trademark paralegal with Winston and Strawn. Bullock has received many honors and achievements. She was a 1990 member of the National African-American Task Force of Junior Achievement. In 1990 she was selected for the World Who's Who of Women. In 1989 she was chosen as one of the Outstanding Young Women of

America. She was also selected by *Dollars & Sense* magazine in 1988 as one of Chicago's Up and Coming Business & Professional Women. Bullock was a member of the National Women's Task Force of Junior Achievement, 1986–1987.

BURKE, WILLIAM A., was born May 13, 1939, in Zanesville, Ohio. Burke and wife Yvonne have two children, Autumn and Christine. He is a 1961 graduate of Miami University, with a B.S. degree; attended Boston University, 1963–1964, and Harvard University, 1963–1964; received a doctorate in education from the University of Massachusetts in 1977. He has served as president of the Los Angeles Marathon since 1984, and as chairman of the board for Genesis International. Prior positions include XXIII Olympiad tennis commissioner, where he organized and administered the planning of the tennis event representing 35 nations in the 1984 Olympic Games; member of the board of directors for the Southern California Tennis Association (SCTA), honorary consul general for the Republic of Mali; and president of World Mining Development Co., Inc., where he supervised planning construction of mining concession in Mali.

Burke has served as president of the California Wildlife Conservation Board, the California Fish and Game Commission, and Bently International Trading Company. During his presidency Bently accomplished the development of a full-scale mining concession out of dense jungle, which involved extensive building, development of an industrial park, a housing development for 500 employees, hospital facilities, a processing plant, storage yards and construction of concrete dams for hydroelectric power.

Burke was also president of the American Health Care Delivery Corp.

from 1972–1974; president of Batik Wine and Spirits, 1969–1972; deputy for a Los Angeles city councilman, 1966–1969; director of legislative radio and television activities for the California state legislature, 1965–1966; officer, United States Air Force, deputy commander of armed forces; Korean Network and 5th Air Force tennis champion, 1961–1965; and a member of the Miami University varsity tennis team, 1958–1961.

He has received many awards: L.A. Media Women; Democratic County Central Committee; state of California Assembly Resolution; Meritorious Service Award, city of Los Angeles; Green Power Foundation; Los Angeles City Council Resolution; alternate delegate to the Democratic National Convention; certificate of A.U.S. Citation of Honor California Senate; Alpha Epsilon Rho (national radio and television honorary fraternity).

BURKE, YVONNE BRATHWAITE, was born October 5, 1932, in Los Angeles, California, the only child of James T. Watson and Lola (Moore) Watson. At the urging of her elementary school principal, who found her an exceptionally bright child, she was transferred from public school to a model school affiliated with the University of Southern California where she was the only black pupil and was occasionally the target of racist taunts. At the Manual Art High School she became vice president of the student body. Yvonne enrolled at the University of California at Berkeley in 1949. In her junior year she transferred to UCLA.

After graduating from UCLA in 1953 with a B.A. degree in political science, she entered the University of Southern California School of Law. In 1956, she received her J.D. degree, graduating in the top third of her class. She was admitted to the California bar the same year and entered private law practice, specializing in civil, probate, and real estate law. In 1957, Yvonne married Louis Brathwaite, a mathematician. Seven years later they were divorced.

She first became interested in the possibility of running for public office while working as a volunteer for the reelection of President Lyndon B. Johnson in 1964. In June 1966, she defeated six male opponents in the primary to win the Democratic nomination to the California General Assembly from the 63rd district. She won that election and was regularly returned to the General Assembly by her constituency. In 1972, she decided to run for the U.S. House of Representatives when a court-ordered reapportionment of California created a new and largely black congressional district in southwest Los Angeles, including Watts. In a five-way race, she got 54 percent of the total votes cast to win the nomination. On June 14, a few days after the primary, she married William A. Burke, a Los Angeles businessman. On November 7, 1972, she pulled more than 73 percent of the vote, handily defeating her Republican opponent. She was returned to Congress by an equally decisive margin on November 5, 1974.

BURRIS, ROLAND W., was born and raised in Centralia, a small town in southern Illinois. He earned a bachelor's degree at Southern Illinois University at Carbondale and a law degree at Howard University in Washington, D.C. Burris and his wife Berlean, associate provost for campus operations and director of the Chicago campus of the National College of Education, reside in Chicago. They are the parents of two adult children. Burris was elected Illinois comptroller in 1978, and served three terms as the state's chief fiscal control officer. After graduating from Southern Illinois University

in Carbondale, he studied at the University of Hamburg, Germany, as an exchange student before going to Howard. He has served as vice president of the Continental Illinois National Bank; from 1973 to 1977, in the governor's cabinet as the director of the Department of General Services; and as national executive director of Operation PUSH. Burris writes 15 million checks annually, oversees the expenditure of $90 million daily, and each month issues reports on the state's financial condition detailing the spending of public funds.

In recognition of his work, Burris has received numerous awards for significant improvements in financial services. He is listed in *Who's Who in America*, *Who's Who in Government*, and *Who's Who in Law*, and *Ebony* magazine named him one of "The 100 Most Influential Black Americans." Burris has been elected by his colleagues to serve as president of the National Association of State Auditors, Comptrollers and Treasurers; as president of the National State Comptrollers' Association; and to the board of directors of the Government Finance Officers Association of the United States and Canada. From 1985 to 1989, he served as vice chairman of the Democratic National Committee. In November 1990, Burris captured 72 percent of the vote in Chicago to become the first black state attorney general in the United States.

Throughout the history of the United States, African-Americans have aspired to law schools and top positions in the legal profession. Most black lawyers with political ambitions are Democrats. But until this election, no black Democrat had ever been elected attorney general of any state in the nation. Burris broke that barrier November 6, 1990, in Illinois. He took office January 14, 1991, as the 39th attorney general of Illinois. At that time Burris became the senior constitutional state official in Illinois and its highest ranking Democrat. The only higher ranking black state official in the United States is L. Douglas Wilder, governor of Virginia.

BURRUS, CLARK, born in Chicago, Burrus has one son, James, with his wife Lucille. He is a graduate of Englewood High School where he was active in football, track and basketball. At Texas State University he was a halfback on the varsity football team, and in 1949 he was one of three athletes honored by the governor of Texas for outstanding scholarship. Burrus received his master's degree in public administration with honors and his B.S. degree in accounting from Roosevelt University. Burrus, a senior vice president in the North American Banking Group, is head of the health, education, municipalities and services department. The division reports to Burrus who is responsible for providing traditional commercial banking services to health

care, higher education, government and cultural institution markets, in addition to marketing such tax-exempt investment banking transactions as managing underwriter services for negotiated bond and note sales, financial advisory and agent services for negotiated bond and note sales, and financial advisory and agent services for privately placed offerings. The group serves large government, corporate and institutional customers in these markets throughout the nation.

Burrus joined the First National Bank of Chicago in 1979 as a senior vice president in the asset and liability management department, where he was responsible for strategic planning and new product development. He was a member of the bank's senior vice presidents council, and a vice president and board member of the First National Bank Foundation. He also served on the foundation's contribution committee. Before joining the First National Bank of Chicago, Burrus was employed by the city of Chicago. He served under mayors Martin Kennelley, Richard J. Daley, Michael Bilandic and Jane Byrne. In 1973, he was named city comptroller by the late Mayor Daley. As the chief fiscal officer of the city, the comptroller heads the department of finance, which includes the offices of city comptroller, city treasurer, and department of revenue. During Burrus' tenure as chief fiscal officer, the city achieved its first double-A bond rating and its first Certificate of Conformance in Accounting. Burrus was the architect of the first low-interest-rate mortgage revenue bond program issued in the United States.

He also served as a trustee of five public pension funds: president of the Police Pension Fund, vice president of the Laborers' Annuity and Pension Fund and Municipal Employees Pension Fund, chairman of the Investment Committee of the Fireman's Pension Fund, and member of the Chicago Teachers Pension Fund. A board member of the Regional Transportation Authority, Burrus served as chairman of the legislative affairs committee and as a member of the chairman's coordinating committee and the ad hoc committee for mobility limited. Burrus has also served on several boards and commissions. He has published several articles: "Minorities in Public Finance," published in *Government* magazine in 1982; "Issues Concerning the Financing of Mortgages with Tax Exempt Bonds," published in 1979; and the Tri-National Research Project sponsored by the Republic of West Germany, published in 1979.

BUSH, STEPHANIE R., was educated in the New Jersey school system; spent her college summers working in the East Orange Drug Abuse Program and in the departments of Welfare and Recreation. While attending American University for her juris doctorate, Bush worked for the Department of the Army at the Pentagon where she was awarded a Certificate of Appreciation for her dedication in that position. Now a second-term legislator, Bush was first sworn into the New Jersey assembly on January 12, 1988. During her freshman year, Bush had more action taken on her bills than any of her other first-term colleagues. She has sponsored well over 200 pieces of legislation, co-sponsored 61, and had over 40 bills released from various assembly committees. More than 30 of those bills passed the assembly and 8 are now laws, including the Temporary Family Leave Bill, the Increase in Minimum Wage Bill, and the Women's Demonstration Resource Center Bill which provides certain services to Hispanic women, as well as others. Another 28 are awaiting consideration. Bush's primary focus remains on issues that affect the poor, the elderly, the homeless, children, women and minorities.

She is also especially concerned with the housing problems faced by residents of New Jersey.

Bush, a graduate of American University Law School, serves as the assembly Democratic majority whip, is chairperson of the Senior Citizen Committee, vice chairperson of the Financial Institutions Committee and vice chairperson of the New Jersey Commission on Criminal Disposition while also serving as chairperson of the Committee on Alternatives to Incarceration. She is also a member of the board of trustees of East Orange General Hospital. Assemblywoman Bush has served as an attorney for the East Orange Board of Adjustment and Planning Board while maintaining a private practice, the Law Offices of Stephanie R. Bush, P.C. Bush has been a practicing attorney since 1978. While licensed to practice in Pennsylvania as well as New Jersey, she chose New Jersey where her expertise in the area of law can bolster her efforts to make a difference in the lives of the people of her home state. Her efforts toward making a difference have not gone unrecognized.

As an attorney and an assemblywoman, Bush has received many accolades and honors, including the Southeastern Chester County Black and Professional Women's Achievement Award, the Garnett's Achievement Award, and the city of East Orange's Achievement Award. She has been asked to speak at numerous schools and colleges and before such prestigious organizations as the National Organization for Women, the New Jersey Black Issues Convention and the National Political Congress of Black Women. She is a member of the National Bar Association and has served as president of the Association of Black Women Lawyers of New Jersey. Bush has maintained her membership with the American Trial Lawyers Association and has been listed in *Who's Who in America*.

BUSKEY, JAMES E., is a graduate of the Mobile County public school system in Alabama. Buskey received a B.S. degree from Alabama State College, Montgomery, Alabama; a master's degree from the University of North Carolina, Chapel Hill; educational specialist, University of Colorado. From 1976 to date, Buskey has served in the Alabama House of Representatives. He has served as chairman of the Alabama Legislative Black Caucus, 1986–1990, and was a member of the State Democratic Executive Committee, 1986–1990. Prior positions include an assistant principalship in the Mobile public schools and, since 1987, the principalship of E. S. Chastang Middle School. Buskey's committee assignments have been Rules, Insurance, Public Utilities & Transportation, N.C.S.L., National Energy Commission. His professional organizations include Omega Psi Phi fraternity; Commonwealth National Bank (organizer and director), and Franklin Primary Health Center (organizer and director).

BUTLER, JERRY, was born December 8, 1939, in Mississippi. He and his wife Annette have twin sons, Randy and Tony. He attended Washburn High School on the near North Side of Chicago. Being a realist has been one of the key ingredients in Butler's survivalist outlook over the years, since the age of 14 when, as the eldest son of four children, he provided much of the support for his widowed mother, Arvelia. "Those definitely were the lean years," he said, recalling how he worked odd jobs to support the family. During that time he also managed to attend Washburn High, where he not only starred in basketball but also studied to become a cook. And had it not been for the success of "For Your Precious Love," the first of many million-selling recordings that Butler would either write or perform, he more than likely would have become a professional chef. "Cooking was my first love," said Butler, who often gives dinner parties and invites close friends and relatives just to find an excuse to cook. "Cooking is like performing," he said.

Butler is by most accounts a perfectionist, yet he does not exactly see himself that way. "I'm from the old school," he said. "I believe that anything that's worth doing is worth doing well. I don't deal in half truths; I go all out for the things I believe in." That is clearly evident in the tireless efforts he has put forth over the years for such causes as fighting drug addiction and illiteracy, and in behalf of civil rights and health care. Butler became involved in the civil rights movement right at the start of his career in 1958, when he and some of his fellow entertainers were consistently denied hotel rooms and restaurant service in the South. Butler contributed to the movement by donating his time and talents to a variety of causes including fund-raisers for the Southern Christian Leadership Council (SCLC), Operation Breadbasket, the NAACP, CORE and the United Negro College Fund (UNCF), to name but a few. As the pace of the movement quickened and the national focus shifted, he directed more of his energies to the economic and political arenas, participating in campaigns both locally and nationally. He has been active in three presidential campaigns and the congressional races of five states. The results of his financial support and physical labors bore fruit in the election of several prominent politicians, including the mayors of such major urban areas as Chicago, Detroit and Washington, D.C.

Butler has enjoyed over 30 years as an entertainer, songwriter and composer. He has won a Clio, two Billboard awards, was nominated for three Grammy awards and has sold over 30 million records, with eight of his records going gold. His compositions have been recorded by such greats as Aretha Franklin, Tina Turner, Earl Grant, Otis Redding, Isaac Hayes, Joe Cocker, The Supremes, Dusty Springfield, Liberace, and Elvis Presley. The Songwriters Workshop, which was a joint venture between Butler Music Publishing and Chappel Music Co., exposed the talents of LTD, Thelma Houston, Brenda Lee Eager, Freddie Perrin, Skip Scarborough, Jeffrey Osbourne, Chuck Jackson, and Natalie Cole, to name a few. Jerry has performed in some of the world's greatest showrooms and theaters: Caesars Palace, the Copacabana, the Apollo, Wintergarden, Greek Theatre, Carter Barron, the Fairmont, Latin Casino, and the Regal. He has toured London, Amsterdam, Lisbon and the Caribbean. Though invited to perform in South Africa, he has declined due to the apartheid system.

Over his career, Butler has made guest appearances on various television shows: "The Ed Sullivan Show," "American Bandstand," "The Merv Griffin Show," "The Mike Douglas Show," "Soul Train," the "CBS Morning News," and the "Today Show." Additionally, he has hosted a great many programs ranging from beauty pageants to a documentary tribute to the late Dr. Martin Luther King, Jr. As a testament to Butler's special interest in youth, the Chicago public schools presented him with the Valuable Asset Award for Volunteerism in Education. Additionally, Shaw University gave him a special recognition for his generous financial support, and he received the President's Award from the National Academy of Recording Arts and Sciences for his achievements as a politician, businessman and humanitarian.

In spite of the uncertain economic climate in recent years, Butler has demonstrated an uncanny ability as an independent businessman. After starting a small beer distributorship in 1973 and selling it five years later at a significant profit, he envisioned a new market

and an expanded product line. He has since formed Iceman Beverage Company, a G. Hieleman distributorship located in Chicago, distributing beer, wine and mineral water.

The year 1985 marked another change in Butler's life. After 11 months of arduous campaigning, he was elected to the board of commissioners of Cook County, the largest county in Illinois. This body is charged with the task of overseeing the county hospitals, forest preserves, schools, jails and finances. Taking his campaign to the streets, Butler emerged as a top votegetter in that race, second only to the board president. He hasn't ruled out recording again but for now he is avidly pursuing his second career as a politician. Although "Only the Strong Survive," one of his two million-sellers, is his highest rated song, Butler considers his unsuccessful 1958 recording "For Your Precious Love," to be his first. Some of his other top songs are "What's the Use of Breaking Up," "Hey Western Union Man," "Make It Easy on Yourself," "Moon River," "Never Give You Up," and "Find Another Girl." In 1991, Butler was still a member of the Cook County Board of Commissioners.

BYRD, MELVIN LEON, was born November 1, 1935, in Suffolk, Virginia. He received a B.A. degree in accounting from Howard University, and an M.B.A. from Babson College. From February 1959 to March 1959, he was a student at the Infantry Officer Basic Course, United States Army Infantry School, Fort Benning, Georgia. From March 1959 to September 1959, he was an administration officer for the United States Army Garrison, Camp Drum, New York. From September 1959 to November 1961, he served as a platoon leader for the 5th Ordnance Company, Aberdeen Proving Ground, Maryland, with duty station Camp Drum. He was promoted to the rank of first lieutenant on November 26, 1960. From December 1961 to May 1963, he was the repair parts supply officer for Company B, 801st Maintenance Battalion, 101st Airborne Division, Fort Campbell, Kentucky.

On May 27, 1963, he was promoted to the rank of captain. From June 1963 to October 1964, he served as an ordnance adviser with the military adviser group of the United States Army Element in Iran. From October 1964 to March 1965, he was a student at the Ordnance Officer Advanced Course, United States Army Ordnance Center and School, Aberdeen Proving Ground, Maryland. From March 1965 to May 1966, he was an ordnance adviser with the United States Military Assistance Command in Vietnam. From May 1966 to November 1967, he was the chief of welding, metal body division, and maintenance officer, United States Army Ordnance Center and School, Aberdeen Proving Ground. On June 20, 1967, he was promoted to the rank of major. From November 1967 to September 1968, he served as a civilian affairs officer with the 199th Brigade, United States Army, in Vietnam. From September 1968 to June 1969, he was the executive officer of the 7th Combat Support Battalion, 199th Infantry Bridge, United States Army, in Vietnam. From June 1969 to July 1972, he was chief of the Maintenance Management Branch, United States Army Quartermaster School, Fort Lee, Virginia. From July 1971 to June 1973, he was a student at the Marine Corps Command and Staff College, Quantico, Virginia.

From June 1973 to December 1974, he was a student at Babson College, Babson Park, Massachusetts. From December 1974 to July 1976, he served as a logistics staff officer in the Materiel Management Division, Office of the Deputy Chief of Staff for Logistics, United States Army, Washington, D.C. From September 1976 to September 1977, he was the commander of

the 702nd Maintenance Battalion of the 2nd Infantry Division, United States Army, in Korea. From September 1977 to July 1979, he served as an inspector general in the Assistance Division, United States Army Inspector General Agency, in Washington, D.C. On September 30, 1979, he was promoted to the rank of lieutenant colonel. From July 1979 to June 1980, he was a student at the United States Army War College, Carlisle Barracks, Pennsylvania.

From June 1980 to January 1981, he served as the deputy director for Joint Actions, Plans, Force Structure and Systems Directorate, Office of the Deputy Chief of Staff for Logistics, United States Army, Washington, D.C. He was promoted to the rank of colonel on July 1, 1980. From March 1981 to June 1983, he was the commander of Division Support Command, 82d Airborne Division, Fort Bragg, North Carolina. From June 1983 to July 1986, he was the commander of the United States Army Electronics Materiel Readiness Activity, Vint Hill Farms Station, Warrenton, Virginia. From July 1986 to July 1988, he was the commanding general, United States Army Materiel Command, in Europe. He was promoted to the one-star rank of brigadier general on October 1, 1986. He has received numerous decorations, badges and awards.

BYRD, PHILLIP EUGENE, was born December 9, 1942. He is married and is the father of one child. He is a graduate of Ball State University, Muncie, Indiana, with a B.S. degree in education, 1967; Indiana University, South Bend, Indiana, with an M.S. in education, 1972; National School of Commercial Lending, University of Oklahoma, Norman, Oklahoma, 1976; Stonier Graduate School of Banking, Rutgers University, New Brunswick, New Jersey, 1978; and postgraduate classes in accounting at Indiana

University, South Bend. Byrd has served as executive vice president and chief administrative officer for Indiana Society Bank in South Bend since 1990.

Prior to this position he was a teacher for South Bend Community School Corporation, 1967–1970; associate director for the Urban League of South Bend and St. Joseph County, 1970–1971; executive director of Youth Development and Delinquency Prevention Program for Urban Coalition of St. Joseph County, 1971–1973; management trainee, 1973–1974; credit analyst, 1973–1974; assistant cashier and junior commercial loan officer, 1974–1976, managing a commercial loan portfolio of approximately $15 million; assistant vice president commercial loan officer, 1976–1978, managing a commercial loan portfolio of approximately $35 million; vice president and corporate banking officer, 1978–1987, managing three commercial lenders and a commercial loan portfolio of approximately $85 million; senior vice president and senior lending officer, 1987–1990, managing the corporate lending function of the bank, which included a portfolio of approximately $275 million, and supervising the ten commercial lenders and the credit and operation function of the bank; senior vice president and senior credit officer, January 1990–July 1990, supervising and managing credit quality of the bank, including the management of commercial loan operations, credit and loan analysis and the supervision of loan work outs and loan reviews.

CADORIA, SHERIAN GRACE, was born on January 26, 1940, in Marksville, Louisiana. She received a B.S. degree in business education from Southern University A&M College, and an M.A. degree from the University of Oklahoma. She received a commission by direct appointment, and from January 1962 to May 1963, she was a platoon officer for Company B, Women's Army Corps Training Battalion, Fort McClellan, Alabama. From June 1963 to May 1965, she served as executive officer, WAC Company, and assistant adjutant, United States Army Communications Zone, in Europe. From June 1965 to July 1966, she served as adjutant of special troops, United States Army Quartermaster Center, Fort Lee, Virginia. She was promoted to the rank of captain on May 17, 1965.

From July 1966 to December 1966, she was a student at the Adjutant General School, Fort Benjamin Harrison, Indiana. From January 1967 to December 1967, she was the administrative officer in the Provost Marshal's Office, United States Army, in Vietnam. From January 1968 to October 1969, she served as the protocol officer in Qui Nhon Support Command, in Vietnam. She was promoted to the rank of major August 1, 1968. From November 1969 to July 1970, she served as chief of the Personnel Division/Adjutant, United States Army Ordnance Center and School, Aberdeen Proving Ground, Maryland. From July 1970 to June 1971, she was a student at the United States Army Command and General Staff College, Fort Leavenworth, Kansas.

From June 1971 to June 1973, she was an instructor at the Officer Education and Training Branch, United States Army Women's Army Corps Center and School, Fort McClellan, Alabama. From June 1973 to June 1975, she served as a personnel management officer, later executive officer, Women's Army Corps Branch, Officer Personnel Directorate, United States Army Military Personnel Center, Alexandria, Virginia. From June 1975 to December 1976, she served as a personnel staff officer with the Law Enforcement Division, Human Resources Development Directorate, Office of the Deputy Chief of staff for Personnel, United States Army, Washington, D.C. On July 1,

1976, she was promoted to the rank of lieutenant colonel. From December 1976 to July 1978, she was the commander of the Student Battalion, Training brigade, United States Army Military Police School, Fort McClellan. From July 1978 to June 1979, she was a student at the United States Army War College, Carlisle Barracks, Pennsylvania.

From June 1979 to May 1982, she served as a special assistant to the provost marshal, later chief, of Physical Security Division, Office of the Provost Marshal, United States Army in Europe and Seventh Army. On September 1, 1980, she was promoted to the rank of colonel. From May 1982 to July 1984, she was the commander of the First Region, United States Army Criminal Investigation Command, Fort George C. Meade, Maryland. From July 1984 to July 1985, she served as chief of the Law Enforcement Division, Human Resource Development Directorate, Office of the Deputy Chief of Staff for Personnel, United States Army, Washington, D.C. From August 1985 to September 1987, she served as director for manpower and personnel, J-1, Organization of the Joint Chiefs of Staff, in Washington, D.C. On October 1, 1985, she was promoted to the one-star rank of brigadier general. In September 1987, she was assigned as the deputy commanding general, Total Army Personnel Command, Alexandria, Virginia. She has received numerous decorations and badges including the Defense Superior Service Medal, the Legion of Merit, the Bronze Star Medal (with two oak leaf clusters), the Meritorious Service Medal (with oak leaf cluster), the Air Medal, the Army Commendation Medal (with three oak leaf clusters), and the Joint Chiefs of Staff Identification Badge.

CANNON, JAMES F., a graduate of McClain High School in Greenfield, Ohio, in 1949; attended several other institutions including Youngstown University in Youngstown, Ohio; University of Omaha, Omaha, Nebraska; San Jose City College, San Jose, California; University of Maryland, European Division; Wright State University in Dayton, Ohio (graduated magna cum laude with a B.A. degree in sociology and an M.S. degree in social and applied economics); University of Dayton School of Law in Dayton; Ohio Judicial College in Columbus, and the National Judicial College in Reno, Nevada. Cannon has served as a judge for the Dayton Municipal Court since 1987.

Prior positions included private law practice, hearing officer for the Dayton human relations counsel; hearing officer for labor disputes, Comprehensive Employment and Training Act (CETA) Program, for the city of Dayton; assistant county prosecutor for Montgomery County, representing the state of Ohio in criminal cases; hearing officer, Dayton city prosecutor's office, and night prosecutor's program; city of Dayton, division of youth and manpower; graduate assistant, economics department, Wright State University; non-commissioned officer in charge of postal operations, U.S. Air Force, Vietnam Military District; USAF postal inspector, postal finance supervisor, chief clerk, and sergeant of the guard.

Cannon is a member of the Dayton Bar Association, the American Bar Association, the Ohio State Bar Association, the National Bar Association, the Thurgood Marshall Law Society, the American Judicature Society, the board of trustees of the Buckeye Trails Girl Scout Council, and American Legion Post 776. He is a life member of the Wright State Alumni Association and the Air Force Sergeants Association.

CAREY, HOWARD H., a 1957 graduate of Morehouse College, Atlanta,

Georgia, with a B.A. degree in sociology; received an M.S.W. degree from Atlanta University in 1963 and a Ph.D. degree in 1977 from the United States International University, San Diego, California, in leadership and human behavior with special emphasis in urban development. Since 1989 he has been an instructor in the San Diego State University School of Social Work in San Diego, California, and since 1972 he has served as president and CEO of the Neighborhood House Association in San Diego, California. As president and CEO he is responsible for the total operations of the 27 agency programs, supervising of approximately 400 employees, administering a budget in excess of $10 million, representing the agency in a variety of situations and other functions related to the overall successful administration of the agency.

Carey's prior positions included field instructor for graduate social work training and coordinator and instructor for urban quarter field experience, Wooster College, Wooster, Ohio; acting executive director and program director for Neighborhood House Association; program development specialist for the Economic Opportunity Commission of San Diego, Inc.; field instructor for San Diego State University School of Social Work in San Diego, California; and associate director of the San Diego Urban League. His professional memberships include Alpha Phi fraternity; Alpha Kappa Delta honorary sociological society; National Association of Social Workers Certified by the Academy of Certified Social Workers; and the Association of Black Social Workers, Harambee Grand Boule Sigma Pi Phi fraternity.

CARSON, JULIA M. PORTER, was born July 8, 1938, the daughter of Clifford and Velma Porter. Although born in Louisville, Kentucky, she in sists that she was almost a Hoosier: "My mother was en route to Indianapolis. I just didn't want to wait till the end of the ride." Carson attended the Indianapolis public schools, graduating from Crispus Attucks High School. She has attended Indiana Central Business College and Indiana University-Purdue University, Indianapolis, and is finishing a political science degree through St. Mary-of-the-Woods College. Divorced and the mother of two children, she worked for ten years for the United Auto Workers before joining the staff of U.S. Congressman Andrew Jacobs, Jr. She served Jacobs both in Washington and as director of his Indianapolis office.

It was this experience plus her strong commitment to civil rights that convinced her in 1972 to run for the state house of representatives. As a lawmaker she has sponsored legislation for penal and welfare reform, for improved housing, and for the elimination of racial and sexual discrimination. As a Democrat she has held every position from precinct committeewoman to member of the national committee. Since 1973, she has been employed as a public affairs consultant for Cummings Engine Company. In 1985, she opened a women's clothing store in Indianapolis. She is a Missionary Baptist and a member or trustee of numerous political and community organizations. Carson shares with Katie Hall the distinction of being the first African Americans to serve in the Indiana Senate.

CARTER, ANNETTE, a graduate of Academy High School in Troy, Alabama, attended the University of Connecticut in 1970. She has served as state representative of the Hartford 7th Assembly District and as a community organizer for the Capitol Region Conference of Churches since 1975. Prior positions include teller for the Society for Savings Bank; consultant for South

Arsenal Development; house mother for Amstead House for Girls; director of personnel, community organizer, and community trainer for Model Neighborhood Incorporated; and director of summer program/field worker for Community Renewal Team.

Carter has received many honors and awards: Certificate of Appreciation, United States Department of Commerce, Bureau of the Census; Housing Now, Inc., appreciation of the Involvement Services and Cooperation; Outstanding Woman of the Year Award in Hartford; state of Connecticut House of Representatives Resolution No. 577, introduced by Representative Milner, 7th Assembly District, recognition of being named Outstanding Woman of the Year in Hartford, and for the many contributions to the city of Hartford and to the state of Connecticut; appointed by the Governor of Connecticut as a public member of the Board of Examiners of Hypertrichologists to serve at the pleasure of the governor; had charge over Governor Grasso's North Hartford campaign headquarters; member of the Emanuel staff of Professional Associates of the U.S.; Leader of the Month Award, sponsored by WKND Radio and Connecticut Mutual Life Insurance Company; volunteer recognition for outstanding achievements for Break Through for the Aged; first runner-up for scholarship fund-raising presented by the Church of the Good Shepherd; certificate of appreciation for outstanding contribution to the city of Hartford; and Camping Family of the Year Award, from Springfield, Massachusetts. Carter's professional community and civic affiliations are numerous.

CARTER, MARGARET L., was born in Shreveport, Louisiana. She is a mother who raised nine children, five of her own and four from her husband's previous marriage. Carter graduated as high school salutatorian and spent two years at Grambling State University on a music scholarship. She received a B.A. degree from Portland Community College, and a master's in educational psychology from Oregon State University (Corvallis). While at Grambling State University, she played the piano and sang gospel music semi-professionally. Later, marriage and divorce would leave Margaret with five children to raise on her own, and bring her face to face with poverty.

In 1967, she left Louisiana to travel west to Oregon with nothing but her children and a strong work ethic. Carter went on to be awarded a graduate degree at Portland Community College while raising her children. Bringing up nine youngsters in her busy northeast Portland home, mostly as a single mother, is the accomplishment that gives her the most pride. Carter worked as a teacher's aide in Portland public schools but went on to a master's degree and a job at Portland Community College as a counselor. She also serves as director of a musical group, "The Joyful Sound."

In 1984 Carter, who had never run for any public office, sought an Oregon legislative seat and became the first African American in the Oregon Legislative Assembly. She was re-elected in 1986, 1988 and 1990. Since 1984, Ms. Carter has received over 80 percent of the popular vote in each general election and, in 1990, for the first time ran unopposed in the primary and general election.

Carter has been commended by the state's largest newspaper, the *Oregonian*, for unifying District 18. Only about 8 percent of Portland's population is black, and Carter has won the Democratic primaries and general elections with the support of whites, including statewide business leaders. As co-chair of the Joint Trade and Economic Development Committee, she has effectively used her position to improve conditions for citizens in her urban Portland district, being the driving force behind the Workforce 2000 Act to improve industrial training and job skills, bring advanced technology centers into communities and enhance the Public School Partnership Program. The creation of the state's first Urban Enterprise Zone, a permanent Head Start and the Youth Conservation Corps are examples of her efforts. Carter was the chief sponsor of Oregon's model South Africa Divestiture Act and of the Dr. Martin Luther King, Jr. State Holiday Act. Through hard work, and a deep spiritual commitment, Margaret Carter has emerged as one of the most successful legislators in the history of North-Northeast Portland.

CARTER, VIC, a native of Radford, Virginia, Vic resides in Dekalb County with his wife Jan, a teacher in the Dekalb County School System, and their two children. Carter graduated with honors from Morehead State University at Morehead, Kentucky, with a degree in journalism. In 1989, students at the Henry Grady School of Journalism at the University of Georgia named Vic Carter Journalist of the Year. Carter is one of Atlanta's most recognizable television news anchors and reporters. He is the host of Channel 2's "Good Morning Georgia." Each day metro Atlantans start their day with Vic as he anchors the 5:30 and 6:30 a.m. newscasts.

He came to WSB-TV in 1982 and has since covered a wide range of local, national and international stories. His experiences cover all of Georgia, most of the United States, and six foreign countries. Prior to his assignment with WSB-TV, Carter worked as a reporter for WRAL-TV in Raleigh, North Carolina. He began his career in 1978 at WSET-TV in Lynchburg, Virginia. His work has been recognized with some of broadcasting's most coveted national and local awards—among them, the Peabody Award given by the George Foster Peabody Society of the University of Georgia and the Gavel Award from the Atlanta Bar Association and the Atlanta Press Club. Carter has also received awards from the National and Atlanta Associations of Black Journalists and the RadioTelevision News Directors Association of the Carolinas.

Carter is currently the chairman of the Atlanta Association of Black Journalists and is a member of the national association as well. He has served on the board of governors for the Atlanta chapter of the National Academy of Arts and Sciences and the Society of Professional Journalists, Sigma Delta Chi. He is also an active member of Alpha Phi Alpha Fraternity and 100 Black Men of Atlanta. He takes his community and civic obligations seriously. He was named Big Brother of the Year for Dekalb County for 1989. He also gives his support to Georgia Special Olympics and the Clothe-a-Child program at the Carrie Steele Pitts Home, and is an active member of Friendship Baptist Church.

CARY, WILLIAM STERLING, born in Plainfield, New Jersey, he graduated from Morehouse College in Atlanta, Georgia, and from Union Theological Seminary in New York City. He is married to the former Marie B. Phillips of Pittsburgh, Pennsylvania. The Carys have four children and two grandchildren. Cary has served as conference minister of the Illinois Conference of the United Church of Christ since 1975. In this capacity, he is the chief administrative officer of a state religious body of 575 ministers in full standing and 327 local churches with approximately 118,000 members. Cary's career has involved responsibilities at the local, regional and national levels of church life. From 1953 to 1955, Cary served as minister of the Interdenominational Church of the Open Door in Brooklyn, New York, and from 1958 to 1968, he served as minister of Grace Congregational Church in New York City. Before coming to Illinois, Cary was chief executive of the Metropolitan and Suffolk associations of the New York Conference of the United Church of Christ. He held this position from 1968 to 1975.

In 1972, Cary became the first member of the United Church of Christ and the first black to serve as president of the National Council of Churches of Christ, the nation's largest ecumenical body with 33 Protestant, Orthodox and Anglican communions. In this capacity for the next three years, he traveled widely in the United States and abroad as chief spokesperson for American Protestantism. From 1975 to 1980, his responsibilities also included serving as a member of the governing board, National Council of Churches; member of United Church of Christ Representative to Consultation on Church Union; vice chairperson of Council of United Church of Christ Commission for Racial Justice; and member of the governing bodies of the Council for Christian Social Action and the United Church of Christ Office of Communication. Cary was appointed by President Ford to the 17-member Task Force on Vietnamese Refugee Relocation.

He has served on the board of a number of civil rights agencies, including the NAACP and the Urban league. He has served as chairperson of the Council of Religious Leaders of Metropolitan Chicago from 1986 to 1988 and continues as a member of that council. He has served as a member of the board of trustees of the Chicago Theological Seminary and is a former member of the Church World Service Board. Cary holds several honorary degrees and is listed in *Who's Who in America*, *Who's Who in Religion*, *Who's Who in the Midwest*, and *Two Thousand Notable Americans*. He has been cited by *Ebony* Magazine in 1974 and 1975 as one of the 100 most influential blacks in America, and has received numerous plaques and awards from organizations throughout the country.

CHAMBERS, LAWRENCE CLEVELAND, was born June 10, 1929, in Bedford, Virginia. He entered the United States Naval Academy as a midshipman on June 30, 1948. On June 6, 1952, he was promoted to ensign and from June 1952 to November 1952, he was assigned to the USS *Columbus* (CA-74). From November 1952 to October 1953, he was a student at NABTC, NAS, in Pensacola, Florida. From October 1953 to March 1954, he was a student at NAAS, in Kingsville, Texas. He was designated a Naval Aviator (HTA) on June 9, 1954. From March 1954 to June 1954, he was a student at NABTC, NAS, Pensacola. From June 1954 to June 1955, he served in Air Anti-Submarine Squadron 37. From June 1955 to April 1957, he was assigned to Attack Squadron 215. On July 1, 1956, he was promoted to the rank of lieutenant. From April 1957 to August 1959, he was a student at the Naval Postgraduate School, Monterey, California. From

August 1959 to September 1960, he was a student at the NROTC Unit at Stanford University, Stanford, California. From September 1960 to July 1961, he was assigned to the Attack Squadron 125. From July 1961 to December 1963, he was assigned to Attack Squadron 22 (OIC, Det. Romeo).

On September 1, 1961, he was promoted to the grade of lieutenant commander. From December 1963 to January 1967, he served as assistant curricula officer in the aeronautical engineering programs at the Naval Postgraduate School, Monterey. He was promoted to the grade of commander on July 1, 1966. From January 1967 to August 1968, he served on the *USS Ranger* (CVA-34) (CIC Off.). From August 1968 to November 1971, he served as a PCO of Attack Squadron 67, later as commander of Attack Squadron 67, then as commander of Attack Squadron 15. He was then assigned to the *USS Oriskany* (CVA-34) (AIR Off.). From November 1971 to June 1973, he served as the deputy project manager at A-73 Project Office, Naval Air Systems Command. He was promoted to the grade of captain on July 1, 1972. From June 1973 to January 1975, he was the commander of the *USS White Plains* (AFS-4). From January 1975 to December 1976, he was the commander of the *USS Midway* (CVA-41).

In December 1976, he was designated rear admiral while serving in billets commensurate with that grade. From December 1976 to November 1978, he was appointed assistant chief of naval personnel for enlisted personnel development and distribution, Bureau of Naval Personnel. On August 1, 1977, he was promoted to the grade of rear admiral. From November 1978 to April 1979, he served as chief of naval personnel, Naval Military Personnel Command. From April 1979 to August 1979, he was a student in the Senior Officers Ships Materiel Readiness Course,

Idaho falls, Idaho. From August 1979 to May 1981, he was the commander of Carrier Group Three. From May 1981 to March 1, 1984, he served as deputy commander for ASW at Naval Air System Command. He has received numerous medals and awards including the Bronze Star Medal, the Meritorious Service Medal; the China Service Medal and the Vietnam Service Medal with three bronze stars.

CHANDLER, ALLEN E., was born September 16, 1935, in Hagerstown, Maryland. He married the former Barbara Hardiman, and they are the parents of three children. Their oldest son, Allen, is deceased. Their second son, Rodney, is a UH-1 (Huey gunship) pilot with Troop D, 104th Armored Cavalry Squadron, PAARNG. Their youngest son, Roderick, is a pre-law student. Chandler graduated from North Street High School in Hagerstown, Maryland, in 1953. he began his military career as a private on May 18, 1955, in the United States Army Reserve. He continued his enlisted service until he was commissioned on June 3, 1957. He is a distinguished military graduate of the ROTC program and the recipient of a B.S. degree, summa cum laude, in chemistry from Morgan State College, Baltimore, Maryland.

Chandler served as a supervisory nurse with the 30th General Hospital from October 15, 1957, to June 13, 1959, while attending Jefferson Medical College in Philadelphia, Pennsylvania. He was promoted to first lieutenant, Medical Service Corps on June 5, 1959 while serving with the 361st General Hospital. Chandler received his doctorate in medicine in 1961, graduating with honors from Jefferson Medical College. He served a rotating internship at the Fitzgerald Mercy Hospital, Darby, Pennsylvania, during 1961 and 1962 and completed a pediatric residency at Jefferson Medical College from June 1962 through May 1964. Militarily, he served on active duty as the chief of the pediatric department, General Leonard Wood Army Hospital, Fort Leonard Wood, Missouri, from 1964 through 1966. He performed this duty as a captain, Medical Corps. He was certified by the American Board of Pediatrics, 1966.

Chandler joined the Pennsylvania Army National Guard on September 14, 1976, as the chief of medical services for the 108th Combat Support Hospital. He was promoted to lieutenant colonel on March 10, 1977. He assumed command of the 108th Combat Support Hospital on October 1, 1977. He took a reorganized unit that had formerly been a field artillery battalion and developed it into a high priority hospital. Chandler completed the Army Medical Department Command and General Staff College on April 4, 1980. He was promoted to the rank of colonel on May 13, 1980. He continued his service as the commander of the 108th Combat Hospital. Until his selection as the state surgeon, Headquarters, State Area Command,

Pennsylvania, Chandler was responsible for developing of medical plans, policies and training utilizing all medical assets of the state, both military and domestic. He also served as the FUSA adviser to the National Guard Bureau Surgeon from 1984 to 1988.

He was assigned as the assistant adjutant general in July 1987 and promoted to his current grade on March 24, 1988. In this capacity, his duties include supervision of personnel, logistics, maintenance, medical, chaplain, judge advocate, provost marshal, safety and selective service activities. He is a medical doctor of pediatrics in private practice in Philadelphia. He is also the senior pediatrician in the Philadelphia health department and the medical director of the Childhood Lead Poisoning Program of Philadelphia and has years of experience in the area of heavy metal intoxication. He develops, manages and monitors all programs that affect the health of all children in Philadelphia from birth to 18 years of age. He directly supervises

45 board-certified pediatricians and four senior pediatric consultants in a program which functions with a budget of $7.5 million and has over 300,000 patient visits per year.

Academically, Chandler has served on the professorial staff of Thomas Jefferson University since 1964. In addition, he served as a member of the admissions committee there from 1971 to 1979. From 1972 to 1978, he was the director of minority admissions at Jefferson Medical College. On March 24, 1988, Chandler's promotion to the one-star rank of brigadier general made him the first African American to hold that position in the Pennsylvania Army National Guard at Fort Indiantown Gap, Pennsylvania. Brigadier General Allen E. Chandler serves as assistant adjutant general, Headquarters, State Area Command.

CHARLES, RAY (ROBINSON), was born on September 23, 1930, in Albany (Dogherty Co.), Georgia, the first of three children of Bailey and Aretha Robinson. He and his wife,

Della have three children: Ray Jr., David and Robert. He was born Ray Charles Robinson but later dropped the last name to avoid confusion with the boxing champion of the same name. Ray Charles was not born blind, only poor. He hit the road early, at about three months, when the Robinsons moved across the border to Greenville, Florida. It was the height of the Depression years and the Robinsons had started out poor. "You hear folks talking about being poor," Charles recounts. "Even compared to other blacks ... we were on the bottom of the ladder looking up at everyone else. Nothing below us except the ground." When Ray was age 5 and his brother George was age 4, Ray watched his brother drown in a tub of water used to wash clothes. Ray tried to pull him out, but he was too heavy for the 5-year-old.

By age 7, Ray was legally blind due to possible glaucoma and was sent to a state school for the blind in St. Augustine, Florida. Toward the end of his first term, his right eye was in constant pain and had to be removed. At the racially segregated school, Ray learned to read in Braille, took formal piano lessons (he'd been playing informally since age 4) and learned to play the clarinet and to memorize music, often as many as 2,000 bars at a time. Ray recalled, "The kids come from all over the state and go to the school to live. If you went home—say, Christmastime or Easter, your parents had to pay for the ticket home. I had my parents until I was 15, but we didn't have the money, so I missed going home for the holidays. I had to stay at school, which was a hurtin' feeling. The whole school was damn near empty except for a few of us kids who couldn't afford to go home. I would spend this time in the piano room without havin' any trouble. This campus I'm speaking of had what they called the colored side and the white side. The only time you went on the 'white side' was if you got sick, because that's where the hospital was. Now this was a blind school. The kids were blind. The piano room was on the white side, and I liked playing the piano, but I couldn't always use it — except on the holidays, when everybody was gone. So it worked out a little bit."

After his mother died, Charles decided to quit the St. Augustine school for the blind. He was 15 and on his own. To support himself, he started traveling with hillbilly and rhythm and blues bands around the South, playing piano, saxophone and clarinet. He also wrote music, having taught himself to compose in Braille or by dictating songs and arrangements to a sighted musician. The road to greatness was hard; in fact, while earning his dues around and about Florida, Charles almost starved at times, hanging out at various musicians' locals, picking up gigs when he could. He began to build himself a solo act, imitating Nat King Cole. When he knew it was time to head on, he asked a friend to find him the farthest point from Florida on a map of the continental United States. It was Seattle, Washington, the turning point for Ray Charles.

In Seattle he became a minor celebrity in local clubs. There he met an even younger musician, Quincy Jones, whom he took under his wing, marking the beginning of an intertwining of two musical lifetimes. While in Seattle, Charles formed the McSon Trio, the first black band to have its own television show in the American Northwest. He toured for about a year with Lowell Fulsom's band. Charles stayed with his original record company, Swing Time, until 1952, when his contract was bought by Atlantic. His music had found a largely black audience until Atlantic released "I Got a Woman" (1955), a smash hit and the first of his distinctive recordings to cross over and reach a nonblack audience. It was the beginning of a star career that would produce such hits as "Crying Time," "I

Can't Stop Loving You," "Busted," "Drown in My Own Tears," "Hit the Road Jack," "Ruby," "What'd I Say," "Unchain My Heart," and "America the Beautiful." In 1959, he recorded his greatest hit, "Georgia on My Mind," which became the official song of the state of Georgia in 1979.

In 1963, Ray Charles starred in his first feature film, *Ballad in Blue*. In 1980, he was a featured star of the film *The Blues Brothers*. In 1988, he appeared in the feature *Limit Up* . . . playing God. In recognition of both his artistic and humanitarian achievements, Charles received a star on Hollywood Boulevard's "Walk of Fame" December 6, 1981. In 1983, he was once again nominated for a Grammy for his single "Born to Love Me," his first nomination ever in the "Best Country Vocal Performance, Male" category. To date Charles has won a total of ten Grammy awards, the most recent in 1975. Also in 1983, he was honored by the NAACP's Image Awards as recipient of its Hall of Fame Award. He also received an award that year at the NAACP's televised ceremonies for Best R&B Male Vocalist.

In 1984, Ray Charles was hired by the Committee to Re-Elect the President to perform at the Republican National Convention. His televised rendition of "America the Beautiful," first recorded on the ABC Records label on his "A Message to the People" LP, was both inspirational and electrifying. In 1986, his collaboration with Billy Joel on "Baby Grand" reached the top ten on the pop charts. Also in November of 1986, he was honored by the French government when he was made a Commander of Fine Arts and Letters, the second time Charles had been selected for a distinguished honor by the Republic of France. In 1988, Charles appeared for the first time with the New York City Ballet, which choreographed dances to some of his classics. Joining Charles in playing for the engagement were members of his original band, Hank Crawford, Leroy Cooper, and David "Fat Man" Newman. The date was such a success that it was repeated in 1989 for a sold-out audience.

In January 1988, Ray Charles received the highest award that can be given by the National Academy of Recording Arts and Sciences, its Lifetime Achievement Award. Charles accepted the special Grammy at a ceremony that was televised over CBS-TV. In 1989, Charles had a #1 single, "Ellie My Love," in Japan, recorded for exclusive release there. He received the Japanese equivalent of a gold record, signifying over 2 million in sales. In April of 1990, Ray Charles received an honorary doctorate of fine arts from the University of South Florida in Tampa. It was an emotional moment for Charles, who began his years as a professional musician in the Tampa area. In 1990, Ray Charles was recording exclusively for Warner Bros. Records.

In January of 1991, Ray Charles played Carnegie Hall, after which he said: "It is truly like you've gotten to the golden gates of heaven. Once you play Carnegie Hall, in my opinion, you have made it, because you don't get into Carnegie Hall unless you are somebody." "What's beautiful to me about America — and it sounds corny — is the freedom. Not the freedom to walk out that door, but to say anything you want and go anywhere you want. I was reared in a small town, dirt poor, blind, you name it. And yet, here I am today. I find that great. I know there has to be something great about my country when other people in other countries are willing to die to try and get here. I think you can overcome any obstacle in this country. It may be a little harder for you than someone else; like when Jackie Robinson got into baseball [as the first black player in the major leagues]. He couldn't just be an average second baseman, 'cause there were plenty of them around. He had

to be better than what was already there. So sometimes you have to be a little bit better, but that's all right too." Like Ol' Man River, he just keeps rolling along and honors and adulation keep coming his way.

CHESTER, LEMUEL DARNELL, JR., of Cambridge, Maryland; married to LaVon C. Chester, with six children. Chester has been a one-man army fighting poverty in Dorchester County, Maryland, doing what he can to give hope to less fortunate members of his community. In 1975, he received the Harriet Tubman Award, from the Dorchester chapter of the NAACP. In 1978, he received the Volunteer of the Year Award from the Black Culture Committee of Cambridge, Maryland. In 1979, he received President Jimmy Carter's People Program Award for his community service. In 1984, he was named Volunteer of the Month for Dorchester County, and was Channel 11 (WBAL, Baltimore) Man of the Year, receiving the Jefferson Award. In 1987, he was selected for Representative Roy Dyson's National Selection Committee to choose candidates for the Naval Academy; he was the only black on the committee of eight. Also in 1987, he served as a member of the governing board of directors of the Dorchester Community Development Corporation.

It was in 1987 that Chester became the first elected black official on the eastern shore of Maryland. As a county commissioner he was not only a politician but also an addictions counselor for the Dorchester County health department. He is a lifetime member of the NAACP. He belongs to both the Harriet Tubman Association, which holds Dorchester's annual Harriet Tubman Day honoring the famous abolitionist, and the Harriet Tubman Coalition, which works to educate young people about their local and national heritage.

Besides working in those organizations, Chester and his wife LaVone annually serve Thanksgiving and Christmas dinner in their home to approximately 150 needy people. As a member of the Dorchester Volunteer Group, Inc., Chester has planned cultural trips for community youth to museums, colleges and ball games. He is a member of Club Jazz, which hosts a Halloween and Easter program for hundreds of minority children. To get out of poverty and then come back to help others requires a great deal of willpower and determination, something Dorchester County Commissioner Lemuel Darnell Chester never seems to lack. He works to help the area's needy, particularly children in trouble. In 1979, he was recognized by the Maryland Department of Juvenile Services for community service to juveniles.

CHISHOLM, SHIRLEY ANITA, was born November 30, 1924, in the Bedford-Stuyvesant section of Brooklyn, New York. She is the daughter of Charles Christopher and Ruby (Seale) St. Hill. She graduated from a girls' high school in Brooklyn, and in 1946 received a B.A. degree cum laude at Brooklyn College. She also received an M.A. degree in elementary education from Columbia University. During the 1950s she served as director of the Friends Day Nursery in Brownsville, New York, and the Hamilton-Madison Child Care Center in Lower Manhattan. From 1959 to 1964, she was an educational consultant in the division of day care of New York City's Bureau of Child Welfare.

In 1964, she campaigned for the New York State Assembly. Her victory at the polls in 1964 made her the first black woman from Brooklyn to serve in the Assembly. On November 5, 1968, she was elected to the United States House of Representatives. Chisholm defeated James Farmer, the former chairman of CORE (Congress of Racial Equality), who had a national reputation in civil rights activity. Her win made her the first black woman ever elected to the United States House of Representatives. She served in the House of Representatives from 1968 to 1983. In 1972, she made an unsuccessful run for the presidency of the United States. Although she lost, she had established another first for a black woman.

CHRISTIAN, SHERIDAN M., was born December 4, 1933, in Smithfield, Ohio. He was educated in the Smithfield school system and graduated from high school in 1952. He married the former Sandra Hampton in 1953, at which time he changed his residence to Steubenville, Ohio. He is the father of three sons and two daughters and is a veteran of the U.S. Navy. He was the first black mechanic and lieutenant on the Steubenville Fire Department. He is presently employed as a production clerk at Weirton Steel Corp., the largest employee-owned steel mill in the country. He was elected January 1, 1990, as chairman of the Brooke, Hancock, Jefferson County Metropolitan Planning Commission of Ohio and West Virginia.

Christian is the past vice chairman of Black Elected Democrats of Ohio, Steubenville Chapter. He relocated August 26, 1976, to his hometown of Smithfield and was appointed to the Smithfield Council, September 1980. He was elected to the council in 1983 and served three years as council president. He filled the unexpired term as mayor from September 1987 to January 1988. Christian was elected as mayor in January 1988 for a four-year term.

CLARK, MICHAEL A., a graduate of the University of North Carolina at Chapel Hill with a B.A. degree in political science in 1975, received an M.S. degree in public administration from the University of Oregon in 1982. He has served as an analyst in the debt management division, Oregon State Treasury, in Salem, Oregon, since 1983. In this position he performs complex analyses and reviews of laws and financing alternatives. He also writes administrative rules, provides technical assistance to municipal and state agencies, recommends appropriate policy to decision-makers, and writes and edits periodicals, official statements and reports. He reports to the manager of the debt management division and the deputy state treasurer. Prior positions include: job service representative in the employment division, Department of Human Resources, state of Oregon, Springfield; analyst for the city of Roseburg, Oregon, where he developed comprehensive policies for managing the city's equipment fund, including data gathering for a management information system, and engineered a computer-based fixed assets accounting system; analyst with Benton County, Corvallis, Oregon, where he prepared and administered the county budget, coordinated grant applications and was on the citizen advisory committees.

Clark worked as an intern for the city of Roseburg, Oregon, where he researched special projects and prepared a revenue bond prospectus for a multi-level parking garage. He was a graduate teaching fellow at the School of Community Service and Public Affairs, University of Oregon. In this position he provided academic advising to undergraduates to facilitate their admission to and success in the school. He served as an adviser in the Educational Opportunities Program at Central Washington University in Ellensburg, Washington. In this position he recruited, made admissions decisions and taught. His emphasis was on service to non-white and non-traditional students. Clark traveled statewide and served as liaison to the black community. He has been involved as a member in the following organizations: Oregon Commission on Black Affairs; board of commissioners, River Road Water District, Eugene, Oregon (elected to four-year term in 1983 and re-elected in 1987); Joint Cities/County Revenue Sharing Task Force (Eugene representative); Lane County, Oregon, Reapportionment Task Force; Lane Community College Vocational Education Advisory Committee, 1986–1989; Oregon Chapter, American Society for Public Administration, 1987–1989; and Oregon Assembly for Black Affairs. He is a lifetime member of the Academy for Political Science and the NAACP.

CLAY, RUDOLPH, is married to Christine Clay (Swan) and has one son, Rudolph, Jr. He served as Indiana state senator from 1972 to 1976. In September 1973, without regard for his personal safety, Clay entered the Indiana State Prison by the authority of the governor, quenched a riot and thereby negotiated the release of all hostages. In 1974, he was responsible for implementing the hiring of minority Indiana state troopers by instituting $100,000 from the state budget to be used for the recruiting of minorities. From 1978 to 1984, he served as Lake County councilman; then as Lake County Recorder, 1984–1986; then as Lake County commissioner, becoming president of the commission. He was president of the board of Lake County Job Training Corporation, 1989–1991.

Clay led the fight for a veterans' outpatient clinic to be located in northwest Indiana. He helped to pass legislation requiring utility companies to return deposits to customers without request. Clay obtained $50,000 to purchase oxygen masks for Gary, Indiana, firefighters. His professional memberships include the following associations: American Legion, Gary Branch of the NAACP, Israel CME Baptist Church/Steward Board, National Association of County Officials and the

National Association of Black County Officials.

CLAYTON, XERNONA, was born August 30, 1930, in Muskogee, Oklahoma. She is the daughter of the Rev. and Mrs. James Brewster. She married Paul Brady. Clayton received a B.S. degree from Tennessee State University. Graduating with honors, she received several scholarships for graduate study, one of which was to the University of Chicago. She taught in the public schools of Chicago and Los Angeles prior to moving to Atlanta where she accepted a position with the Southern Christian Leadership Conference and worked closely with the late Dr. Martin Luther King, Jr. Clayton also traveled extensively with Coretta Scott King on the nationwide tours.

Dedicated to promoting racial understanding, Xernona Clayton has been a leader in civic projects and civil rights activities for several years. In 1966, she coordinated the activities of Atlanta's black doctors in a project called Doctors' Committee for Implementation, which resulted in the desegregation of all hospital facilities in Atlanta. This project served as a model and a pilot for other states throughout the country and received national honor from the National Medical Association for its impact. Her persistent fight against prejudice and bigotry was never more apparent than in 1968, when the grand dragon of the Ku Klux Klan denounced the Klan and credited Xernona's influence with the change. Clayton was the nationally acclaimed host of "The Xernona Clayton Show," a regular feature on WAGA-TV, CBS affiliate in Atlanta. Beginning her broadcast career in 1967, she became the South's first black person to have her own television show.

In 1979, she joined the SuperStation (TBS), as a part-time documentary specials producer and has served Turner Broadcasting System in a number of capacities over the years. She began hosting "Open Up," a public affairs program, in January 1981 and became the weekly program's full-time host/producer in November of the same year. In 1982, Clayton was named coordinator of minority affairs and served as the company's liaison with the minority communities and organizations. During her years in the public affairs department, she created numerous award-winning productions. Previously, she was vice president of public affairs for TBS SuperStation. She is assistant corporate vice president for urban affairs with Turner Broadcasting System, Inc. In this position, she serves as liaison between the corporation (which comprises TBS SuperStation, TNT, Atlanta Braves, CNN, Atlanta Hawks, and Headline News) and civic groups in Atlanta across the country. Her responsibilities include monitoring corporate philanthropic contributions, developing and maintaining communication with community groups and enhancing the corporate image in communities around the nation where Turner Broadcasting has operations.

She also assists the vice president of personnel in implementing and developing corporate affirmative action programs. She counsels employees in career guidance and coordinates the resolution of employee concerns and counsels with department heads in matters of employees' interests. She also develops programs to highlight employee accomplishments and profiles employees' career positions in publications. As a corporate executive, Clayton is one of the highest-ranking female employees in Turner Broadcasting System. Xernona Clayton's list of community service and volunteer work is extensive. She serves on the boards of the Martin Luther King Center, the Atlanta Urban League and Southwest Community Hospital, and is serving a third term as chairman of the board of the National Association for Sickle Cell Disease, Inc. She is a member of the National Issues Forum of the Jimmy Carter Presidential Library.

Clayton has also been a guest lecturer at Harvard University's Institute of Politics for the Kennedy School of Government. As governor of Georgia, former President Jimmy Carter appointed her to the Motion Picture and Television Commission for the state of Georgia, making her the first woman and the first black to serve on the initial Board. She is the first woman and first black to serve as commissioner of the three-member board of review, the appellate board for unemployment compensation. She is the recipient of numerous media awards and has been honored worldwide for her contributions to humanity by receiving the Trailblazer Award (she was its first recipient), the Superior Television Programming Award, the President's Award from the National Conference of Mayors, the Pioneer in Media Award, the Kizzy Award, and an Emmy award from the National Association of Television Arts and Sciences for juvenile justice documentary. She

has also been named Communications Woman of the Year, Black Georgian of the Year, and Media Woman of the Year.

CLEAVER, EMANUEL, II, was born in Waxahachie, Texas. He and wife Dianne have four children: Evan, twins Emanuel III and Emiel, and Marissa. He is a graduate of Booker T. Washington High School in Wichita Falls, Texas; undergraduate at Prairie View A&M College, Prairie View, Texas; received a master's degree at Saint Paul School of Theology, Kansas City, Missouri; and pursued a doctorate in social ethics at Saint Paul School of Theology. He has served as pastor of Saint James Paseo United Methodist Church and mayor pro tem of Kansas City, Missouri. As pastor of the Saint James Paseo United Methodist Church in Kansas City, which has been recognized by the bishop of the Missouri Area of the United Methodist Church for the largest growth of any church since 1985, the Rev. Cleaver's messages can be heard each Sunday at 2 p.m. over radio KCXL-AM presenting the theological side of his double occupation.

Cleaver served three terms as 5th District city councilman and is a former chairman of the city council plans and zoning committee. He was a guest at the White House of President Jimmy Carter in 1977. He participated in the Selma March and the March on Washington. He is a lecturer and speaker in demand throughout the nation and speaks annually to more than 100 churches, schools, civic and social organizations and seminars. Cleaver has appeared on the NBC "Today Show," the "Oprah Winfrey Show," the "McNeil/Lehrer Report," "Nightline" and "Good Morning, America." He served as chairman of the Heartland Committee which was organized to lure the 1988 Democratic Convention to Kansas City. He helped introduce municipal legislation which declared a city holiday for Dr. Martin Luther King, Jr.

His honors include *Who's Who Among Black Americans*, 1985; 1971 Centurions Leadership Award; the William Yates Distinguished Service Medallion, the highest non-academic award of William Jewell College, 1987; 1987 Centurions Leadership Award; and honorary doctorate of divinity, Baker University, 1988. His professional affiliations include board of directors for DeLaSalle Education Center; chairman, city council policy and rules committee; chairman, legislative committee; mid-central regional vice president, Southern Christian Leadership Conference (SCLC); president, board of trustees, Leon Jordan Scholarship Fund, Council on Finance, United Methodist Conference; board of directors and former chairman of the board, Freedom, Incorporated, a highly touted political organization; Alpha Phi Alpha Fraternity, Inc.

CLEMENT, JOSEPHINE DOBBS, a native of Atlanta, Georgia, she is a graduate of Spelman College and holds a master's degree from Columbia University in New York. She has taught at colleges in Georgia and at North Carolina Central University in Durham. Her husband is William A. Clement, retired executive vice president of the North Carolina Mutual Life Insurance Company, past chairman of the Raleigh-Durham Airport Authority, and past grand master of the Prince Hall Masons of North Carolina. The Clements are the parents of six adult children and belong to the White Rock Baptist Church where Mrs. Clement is assistant teacher of the Susie V. Norfleet Bible Class. Her former activities include membership on the Durham City-County Charter Commission (1971–1974); membership on the Durham City Board of Education (1973–1983), serving as chairperson for

five years; and service as co-chairperson for the Durham County for Jim Hunt campaigns in 1980 and 1984. Current boards include the Durham County Board of County Commissioners, Mechanics & Farmers Bank, Shaw University, the Z. Smith Reynolds Foundation, the Duke University Hospital Board, Durham County Board of Social Services, and the Board of Visitors (School of Arts and Sciences), Wake Forest University.

She is a member of several fraternal, civic, and political organizations including the Durham Committee on the Affairs of Black People, Delta Sigma Theta Sorority, Inc., and the NAACP. Clement has been named Outstanding Den Mother by the Boy Scouts, Woman of the Year (Southern Area) by Links, Inc., Outstanding Board Member for 1983 by the North Carolina School Boards Association, and Mother of the Year for 1986 by the Durham Merchants Association. She was awarded an honorary doctor of laws degree from Shaw University in 1986. She and her husband were honored jointly by the NAACP in 1980. In 1988 she was a YWCA Woman of Achievement Silver Medallion winner.

COBB, JEWEL PLUMMER, was born January 17, 1924, in Chicago, Illinois. She is the daughter of Frank V. Plummer and Carriebel Cole Plummer. She is divorced from Roy Cobb, with whom she had one child, Jonathan Cobb. She received a B.A. degree from Talladega College, Talladega, Alabama, in 1944. She received an M.S. degree from New York University in 1947, and received her Ph.D. there in 1950. From 1955 to 1956, she served as an instructor at New York University, and was an assistant professor there from 1956 to 1960. She also served as a visiting lecturer at Hunter College, from 1956 to 1957.

From 1960 to 1969, Cobb served as a biology professor at Sarah Lawrence College in Bronxville, New York. In 1969, she became a dean and professor of biology at Rutgers University, Douglass College, New Brunswick, New Jersey. In 1981, Cobb became president of California State University at Fullerton. Cobb has performed extensive studies of pigment cells in the hope of solving some of the mysteries of cancer. She has sparked students' curiosity in biology, anatomy and zoology, and has encouraged many women and minorities to pursue science. A member of numerous educational and civic organizations, she has also received numerous honors.

COFFEY, VERNON CORNELIUS, JR., was born June 1, 1928, in Kansas City, Kansas. He is married to the former Sarah Grigsby, and is the father of three children: Karen, Vernon III and Craig. He graduated from Sumner High School in Kansas City in 1946 and attended the University of Iowa at Iowa City, Iowa, and the University of Kansas City. He was drafted into the Army in 1952. After completing basic training in Schofield Barracks, Hawaii, he remained at Schofield Barracks as an instructor and cadre until he entered Officers' Candidate School at Fort Benning, Georgia, in October 1952. He graduated from Officers' Candidate School as a distinguished graduate and was commissioned as a second lieutenant in the infantry upon graduation on April 17, 1953. After commissioning, he remained at Fort Benning to receive parachute training, after which he was awarded the Parachutist Badge. Assigned to the 504th Airborne Infantry Regiment of the 82nd Airborne Division at Fort Bragg, North Carolina, he served as platoon leader, company executive officer, company commander, and battalion S-4.

In August 1955, he was assigned to the 32nd Infantry Regiment of the 7th Infantry Division in Korea, where he performed duties as company executive officer, company commander and assistant battalion operations officer. Upon returning to the States, he attended the Army Ranger School at Fort Benning and graduated with honors. He then became a Ranger instructor with the Jungle and Amphibious Committee at Eglin Air Force Base, Florida, and at the Fort Benning Ranger Committee. In September 1959, he attended the Infantry Officer's Advanced Class at Fort Benning, then attended the French Language Course in July 1960 at the Army Language School, Monterey, California. Assigned in January 1961 to the Orleans Area Command of the United States Army Communications Zone, Europe, he served as company commander and Assistant S-4, Services.

In June 1964, he returned to the States to attend the United States Army Command and General Staff College at Fort Leavenworth, Kansas. Upon graduation from Command and General Staff College, he attended St. Benedict's

College at Atchison, Kansas, where he graduated magna cum laude and received a B.S. degree in business administration in January 1966. In January 1966, he was assigned to the staff communications division of the Office of the Chief of Staff, Army, where he served as assistant branch chief and branch chief until his departure in February 1968 for Vietnam. He reported for duty as Deputy Chief of Staff, G-4 with the 1st Infantry Division and on May 1968, he assumed command of the 228th Infantry, "The Black Lions," of the 1st Infantry Division. He served as battalion commander until November 1968, after which he became executive officer of the 3rd Brigade of the 1st Infantry Division and served in this position until his return to the States. Lieutenant Colonel Coffey has been Assistant Military Aide to the president since December 1968. He preceded President Nixon to Communist China to assist in arranging security measures for the historic visit.

COGGS, G. SPENCER. In his fourth term in the Wisconsin State Assembly, Spencer Coggs has retained his post as chairman of the Committee on Urban and Local Affairs. He has also retained his post as majority caucus vice chair, one of four leadership positions in the majority Democratic State Assembly. Rep Coggs continues to serve as a member of the committees on Rules, Colleges and Universities and Children and Human Services, the Legislative Council's American Indian Study Committee, and the Select Committee on the Future of the University of Wisconsin System. He has also been appointed to the newly created Committee on Urban Education. Spencer is a member of the National Conference of State Legislatures (NCSL) and the National Black Caucus of State Legislators (NBCSL), and serves as a member on the Education Committee

the State-Federal Assembly. The State-Federal Assembly is the NCSL organizational arm which discusses national issues of importance to states. It also develops policy resolutions and strategies to guide the conference's efforts before Congress, the White House and various federal agencies.

As Chairman of the Legislative Council's Peace Officer Study Committee, Coggs forwarded and passed legislation relating to police use of force and statewide uniform procedures for citizens' complaints (WI Act 131). Rep. Coggs also authored WI Act 319, amendment to the Wisconsin Fair Housing Law which gives the state stronger enforcement powers. Additionally, Spencer has sponsored or co-sponsored major legislation concerning minority business certification (S.A. to SB 650), fair pharmaceutical services for HMOs (AB 179), authorization for the fire and police commission to set rules for fire and police departments (A.A. SB 56), and various other legislative initiatives to improve conditions for residents and businesses in Milwaukee and the state. Spencer's extensive community involvements include membership on the Milwaukee Urban League's Health and Human Services Resource Panel, the Northwest-side Community Development Advisory Committee, and UW-System President Kenneth Shaw's Community Leadership Committee.

COGGS-JONES, ELIZABETH, was elected 10th District supervisor in 1988 and is now serving her first term on the county board. Her previous elected office was as Milwaukee County Democratic Committeewoman of the 6th Aldermanic District. She was born in Milwaukee December 2, 1956. She graduated from Urban Day School and attended Messmer High School before transferring to Lincoln High School where she graduated in 1974. She attended the University of Wisconsin-Milwaukee and is an alumna of Future Milwaukee. The daughter of Isaac N. Coggs, she is the first African American elected to the Milwaukee County Board in 1964. Her mother, Marcia P.

Coggs, was the first African American woman elected to the Wisconsin State Legislature. Coggs-Jones and her husband Wendell have three daughters: Priscilla, Chloe and Devona.

She has a lifetime involvement in the Milwaukee community. She is a former secretary for the NAACP membership committee. She was vice president of the Harambee Ombudsman Project, Inc. board and a member of the Children's Outing Association, the Inner City Arts Council, the Governor's Advisory Board on Bicycle Safety and the ESHAC, Inc. board. She is presently a member of Cross Lutheran Church and its social ministry committee. She also serves on the advisory board of the Welfare Alternative Project, the Downtown Child Care Development Advisory Committee, TEACH Advisory Council, Preschool to 5th Grade Advisory Council, Parents of Brown Street School Academy, North Division Neighborhood Ujima Housing Co-operative Team, Waico Advisory Council, Habitat for Humanity honorary committee for Carter Project, social development commission of the Community Relations, and Fighting Back Citizens Drug Task Force.

COLE, JOHNNETTA BETSCH, was born October 19, 1936, in Jacksonville, Florida. She is the mother of three children: David, Aaron and Che. She has a B.A. degree from Oberlin and M.A. and Ph.D. degrees in anthropology from Northwestern University. She was associate provost for undergraduate education at the University of Massachusetts, where she taught anthropology and African-American studies. She was also a professor of anthropology at Hunter College and a member of the graduate faculty of the City University of New York, where she directed the Latin American and Caribbean studies program. Other universities in which she has taught are Washington State University, and the University of California at Los Angeles, Williams, and Oberlin.

In 1987, Cole was named president of Spelman College, becoming the first black woman to hold this powerful educational leadership position. Cole reaches out to thousands of young black women scholars, molding future leaders. Knowing that academia cannot thrive on tradition alone, she has been a lightning rod in encouraging increased contributions to the endowments of Spelman. On the day she was inaugurated as the first black woman president in the school's 107-year history, she was presented with an unprecedented $20 million donation from Bill Cosby and his wife Camille. In 1990, Coca-Cola Enterprises announced that its board of directors had been expanded to 13 members, and by a unanimous election, Cole joined Coca-Cola's board of directors.

COLEMAN, ERIC D., graduated from the Pomfret School and Columbia College of Columbia University. He received his J.D. degree from the University of Connecticut School of Law in 1977. Coleman is a member of the American Bar Association, Connecticut Bar Association, Hartford County Bar Association, National Bar Association and the George Crawford Law Association. He is married to the former Pamela Lynette Greene, with whom he has three children: Trevonn, Lamar and Erica. They make their home in Bloomfield, Connecticut. Coleman is an attorney engaged in the general practice of law, having been admitted to practice in Connecticut in May 1978 and admitted to practice in the federal district court in February 1979. Prior to establishing his own law practice he worked as a consultant for Aetna Life and Casualty, as an attorney for the Connecticut Division of Public Defender Services, and as an attorney for Neighborhood Legal Services.

Since 1983, Coleman has been state representative for the 1st Assembly District in Connecticut. He has served as a member of the Appropriations Committee, a ranking member of the Regulation and Protection Appropriations Subcommittee, deputy ranking member of the Planning and Development Committee, and a member of the Special Committee of Inquiry into Intelligence and Criminal Investigations in Connecticut. He is currently a member of the Judiciary Committee and the Insurance and Real Estate Committee. Additionally, he is chairman of the Connecticut Legislative Black and Puerto Rican Caucus and the Minority Business Enterprise Review Committee and an assistant majority leader in the House of Representatives. He is also a member of the National Conference of State Legislatures and the National Black Caucus of State Legislators.

During his legislative career, Rep. Coleman has sponsored legislation improving Connecticut's minority business set-aside program, establishing a mutual housing program in Connecticut and prohibiting hate crimes in Connecticut. He is very active in the community; additionally, he has served on several boards as a director or a trustee. These include Neighborhood Legal Services, Inc.; Bloomfield access television station; Mutual Housing Association of Greater Hartford; North Hartford Senior Citizens Center; Hartford Community Mental Health Center; Humanidad, Inc.; Pomfret School; the San Juan Center; and Tobacco Valley YMCA.

COLEMAN, LYNN CARNELL, was born May 23, 1954. She is married, and the mother of one child. She is a graduate of Washington High School in South Bend, Indiana, 1972; attended Indiana University, South Bend, completing course work in the School of Public and Environmental Affairs, 1975–1976; and graduated from the Indiana Law Enforcement Academy, Plainfield in 1978. Coleman has served with the South Bend police department since 1977 and has been promoted to coordinator of the juvenile aid bureau.

Prior positions include working for the South Bend Housing Authority; supervising summer youth employment for the city of South Bend; and comprehensive employment training, general labor and operating forklift for AM General Corporation. She has received many awards: Youth Commitment Award, Certificate of Appreciation, Role Model Award, Outstanding Police Officer, Community Service Award, Office of the Year, Outstanding Citizenship Award, Minority Policeman Service Award and Mayoral Commendation. Her professional affiliations are numerous.

COLLINS, CARDISS, was born in St. Louis, Missouri, September 24, 1931, and moved to Detroit at the age of 10. After graduating from the Detroit High School of Commerce, she chose the road of higher academic achievement and relocated to Chicago to attend Northwestern University. With a keen interest in politics, Collins established herself in the city's political machine and became committeewoman of the city's 24th Ward Regular Democratic Organization. She became heavily involved in the campaigns of her late husband, U.S. Rep. George Collins, who served as a Chicago alderman and committeeman. Congresswoman Collins was first elected to Congress in 1973 in a special election to fill her husband's vacant seat after he was killed in a plane crash. During the special election she won more than 85 percent of the vote to retain her seat. This victory marked her first run for public office and continued a strong hold in her district to capture a decisive block of votes for re-election.

Running unopposed in the 1988 congressional election highlighted the fact that the Collins' popularity is a result of hard work and dedication to the interests of her district, which is 68

percent black. She is a member of the House Energy and Commerce Committee and serves on the subcommittees on Health and the Environment, Oversight and Investigations and Telecommunications and Finance. In addition, she chairs the Government Operations Subcommittee on Government Activities and Transportation (GAT) and serves on the House Select Committee on Narcotics Abuse and Control. Collins, who remains the only black woman in Congress, is guided by a deep sense of commitment. For more than 17 years, she has served as a major power broker on Capitol Hill for the people of the 7th Congressional District of Illinois and the nation. Her leadership on important social, political and economic issues has earned her a reputation as an effective policymaker.

In the development of her legislative agenda, Collins has spent a significant amount of time on the following issues: comprehensive federal child care program, access to minorities in the communications arena, problems black broadcasters face in securing advertising revenues, consumer protection, requiring full disclosure of service charges by banks, prohibiting electric and natural gas utilities from terminating service during winter months, prohibiting the disclosure of personal information by creditors, Medicaid, infant mortality, health insurance, alcohol and drug abuse and the effectiveness of security at domestic and international airports.

As a trailblazer during much of her term in office, Collins is recognized as a first in her field. She was the first woman to chair the Congressional Black Caucus (1978–1980), the first woman and the first black to chair the Manpower and Housing Subcommittee of the House Government Operations Committee, and the first black and the first woman to hold a Democratic leadership position (whip-at-large) in the House of Representatives. She is a member of the Friendship Baptist Church of Chicago, the Alfred Street Baptist Church of Alexandria, Virginia, NAACP, the Chicago Urban league, LINKS, the Coalition of 100 Black Women, the Black Women's Agenda, the National Council of Negro Women, the National Council of Negro Women, Alpha Kappa Alpha Sorority and Alpha Gamma Phi. She has received honorary degrees from Barber-Scotia College, Spelman College and Winston-Salem State University.

COLLINS, MARVA DELORES, was born August 31, 1936, in Monroeville, Alabama, some 70 miles north of Mobile. She is the daughter of Henry and Bessie (Nettles) Knight. She began her formal education at Bethlehem Academy in Monroeville and completed her secondary education at Eschambia County Training School in Atmore graduating in 1953. She obtained her B.A. degree in secretarial science in 1957. She returned to Alabama and took a job teaching typing, shorthand, bookkeeping and business law at Monroe County Training School in June 1957. In 1959, she moved to Chicago and went to work as a medical secretary at Mount Sinai Hospital. On September 2, 1960, she married Clarence Collins.

In 1961, she decided to reenter the teaching profession, so she entered the Chicago school system as a substitute teacher. Her first students were second-graders at Calhoun South Elementary School. She quit her job with the city schools in September 1975, and with $5,000 in retirement money began what was at first called the Daniel Hale Williams Westside Preparatory School in the basement of Daniel Hale Williams University. Her first class consisted of her daughter and three neighborhood children. In 1979, she had some 30 children from an all-black, poverty-level apartment community.

Another 400 children were on a waiting list.

Her curriculum is tailored to produce a special kind of education, as flexible as it is traditional, as sophisticated as basic. Like most educators, Collins bases her teaching on reading skills. "If you can't read, you can't do anything else," she said. "I can't see why society finds this so difficult to understand. Just about all learning branches from that skill, and almost every profession today demands exactness." Collins teaches exactness; children are drilled on vocabulary and multiplication tables. They are required to read one book every two weeks, memorize one poem a week, and write a composition each day on a topic she chooses. The news media referred to her as a "miracle worker" and a "superteacher." Cicely Tyson portrayed her in a television film drama, *The Marva Collins Story*. She has been offered a succession of prestigious jobs, including that of United States secretary of education.

CONLEY, KARYNE JONES, a graduate of Sam Houston High School, she received her bachelor's degree in political science from Clark Atlanta University, and her master's degree in public affairs and urban management from Northern Illinois University. She is married to Judge Jim Conley, an attorney and Justice of the Peace for Precinct 4 of Bexar County, and is the proud mother of four children: James, Jason, John and Karyne Jalon. Conley is a fourth-generation San Antonian and the state representative of District 120 representing East Bexar County and San Antonio.

Rep. Conley has a very diverse background. Her involvement in issues related to education, the arts, human services, economic development, civil rights and politics has been intensive. She has served on numerous boards and advisory committees, including

the board of directors of Communities in Schools, a dropout prevention program; Community Alliance for Traffic Safety a program that assists in the prevention of DWI offenses (tri-chair); executive committee of San Antonio Fighting Back, a drug abuse prevention program; Parents Anonymous, an assistance and counseling program for abusive parents; and the board of trustees of Incarnate Word College.

Her professional background includes having served as congressional aide to Rep. Andrew Young of Georgia. When Andrew Young was appointed by President Jimmy Carter as ambassador to the United Nations, Conley became his public affairs officer at the United States Mission to the United Nations. Upon returning to San Antonio, she held positions as director of the Carver Cultural Center, grantwriter for the University of Texas Institute of Texan Cultures and program developer for continuing education at San Antonio College. Before her election in 1988 to the Texas Legislature, she was a professor of Texas politics and American government at San Antonio College. In 1989, she was sworn in as a state representative. She has served on the State, Federal and International Relations Committee and the Judiciary Committee.

Conely has received numerous honors and awards for her community service. She was selected as the 1989 Outstanding Young San Antonian by the San Antonio Jaycees. She was inducted into the San Antonio Women's Hall of Fame and named 1989 Democrat of the Year. She is an alumna of the Greater Chamber of Commerce Leadership San Antonio Program. After her first term in office, she was named by *Texas Monthly* magazine as one of its Rookies of the Year.

CONYERS, JOHN, JR. Conyers was educated in Detroit's public school system and earned his bachelor's and doctor of law degrees at Wayne State University. He has received many awards for leadership, including a Southern Christian Leadership Conference leadership award presented to him by Dr. Martin Luther King, Jr.,

and honorary degrees from numerous colleges and universities. During his 24 years in Congress, social justice and economic opportunity have become focal points of Rep. Conyers' accomplishments. He introduced in the 100th Congress legislation on voter registration, alcohol warning labeling, social security, public housing, civic and constitutional rights, small business, family farmers, voter rights, education, economic and community development, foreign affairs, defense contracting and procurement, and criminal justice.

Conyers authored and spearheaded the drive for passage of the Dr. Martin Luther King, Jr. holiday bill, which was signed into law on November 2, 1983. He is also one of the founders of the Congessional Black Caucus and a principal architect of its annual alternative federal budget. He offered the first nuclear freeze amendment on the House floor, and his amendment prohibiting the export of nuclear-related materials, technology, equipment, information, and personnel to South Africa became a part of the House-approved Anti-Apartheid Act. In addition, Conyers was a principal sponsor of the Humphrey-Hawkins Full Employment Act, which was enacted in 1978, and has authored a wide range of full-employment legislation, including legislation to create additional jobs through shorter work weeks and the elimination of compulsory overtime.

He has recently authored legislation that would prevent utilities from shutting off gas and electric service in households during the winter months when health can be threatened. In his Judiciary Committee role, Conyers has conducted hearings in several cities on policy violence, racially motivated violence, sentencing, white collar crime, grand jury reform, and other criminal justice matters. His legislation to provide literacy and vocational training in correctional institutions has been incorporated into two major educational bills. A Detroit Democrat, Conyers was elected in 1988 to his 13th term in the House of Representatives, winning 91 percent of the vote in Michigan's 1st Congressional District. He is chairman of the Government Operations Committee, and is a senior member of the Judiciary Committee, where he sits on the Judiciary Subcommittee on Civil and Constitutional Rights. He is also a member of the House Small Business Committee and the Speaker's Task Force on Minority Set-Asides.

Conyers is also recognized as a major figure in Congress in policy concerning the death penalty. He has conducted hearings on race and fairness in administering the death penalty, and he authored the Supreme Court amicus brief for the Congressional Black Caucus in its major case on racism in capital punishment. He is also a critical figure in maintaining the strong federal anti-fraud statute, known as RICO, which protects consumers and small business investors. Conyers has written numerous articles which have been published in national newspapers, magazines and books. He also maintains an active speaking agenda throughout the country.

COSBY, WILLIAM HENRY (BILL), JR., was born July 12, 1937, in Philadelphia, Pennsylvania, the son of William Henry and Anna Pearl Cosby. He and his two younger brothers grew up in all-black housing projects. He was a student at the Germantown High School for Gifted Students. While there he was captain of the track and football teams and played basketball and baseball. He dropped out of school in tenth grade and enlisted in the United States Navy. During his four years of service, he earned his G.E.D. and learned physical therapy. After completing his military service in 1961, he enrolled at Temple University in Philadelphia. His career as a professional comedian started during his sophomore year, when he took a job at a local bar as a bartender and comedian.

In 1965, he appeared on the "Tonight Show with Johnny Carson," which led to his first acting assignment. Television producer and former actor Sheldon Leonard saw Cosby on the show and, impressed by his personality and talent, gave him a screen test for a part in the upcoming NBC-TV adventure-espionage series "I Spy." He was cast in the role of Alexander Scott, which had not been conceived for a black actor. It was a popular series from its premiere on September 15, 1965 to September 2, 1968.

He received a bachelor's degree in sociology from Temple University and a master's degree and a doctorate in education from the University of Massachusetts. Cosby has recorded 18 comedy albums and three musical LPs which sold more than 12 million copies, won eight Grammy awards for comedy albums, collected three Emmy awards, starred in six television shows and eight movies, and created one of the most successful family shows in the history of television: "The Cosby Show." Since its premiere in 1984, "The Cosby Show" has been the top family show through 1991, taking NBC to the tops in the ratings of network television. In 1988, the show went into syndication for $500 million. In the show Cosby takes the role of Cliff Huxtable, an obstetrician/gynecologist whose wife Claire (portrayed by Phylicia Allen-Rashad) is a lawyer. He is also father to the five Huxtable children, four girls and one boy. He has starred in such films as *Uptown Saturday Night* and *Let's Do It Again* with actor Sidney Poitier. In 1990, he starred in *Ghost Dad*, playing Elliot Hopper, an overworked widower with three kids who dies and returns as a ghost.

During the 1980s, Bill Cosby and his wife Camille (whom he married in 1964) donated $20 million to Atlanta's

Spelman College, $1.5 million to Meharry Medical College in Nashville, $1.5 million to Bethune-Cookman College, $1.3 million to Fisk University and $425,000 to Central State University in Cleveland. His books *Fatherhood, Time Flies,* and *Love and Marriage,* each broke publishing industry records. He also is a product spokesman for several major companies, including General Foods, Kodak and Shearson Lehman Hutton. Through it all, Cosby has established a winning formula for health and wealth: Live, laugh, and learn, and sign your own checks.

COTTRELL, COMER J., JR., was born December 7, 1931, in Mobile, Alabama. He married Isabell Paulding, and their children are Renee Brown and

Aaron Comer, III. He was educated at Mobile Catholic grade and secondary schools, and at the University of Detroit, Michigan. He entered active military service in the United States Air Force, where at the age of 18 he became a staff sergeant and acting 1st sergeant. He later became a PX manager and

instructor at the United States Armed Forces Institute. He served his overseas duty in Okinawa from 1949 to 1953. From 1954 to 1956, he was employed by the United States Postal Service; from 1954 to 1958, he was also a partner in Cottrell-Wright Agency; from 1958 to 1964, he was a partner in Mil-Com Publications Co. From 1964 to 1969, he was a division manager with Sears and Roebuck. Since 1970 Cottrell has been chairman and president of Pro-Line Corporation, a maker of ethnic health and beauty aids. Cottrell founded the corporation with $600 and a borrowed typewriter. It is now the largest black-owned business in the Southwestern United States, fourth largest manufacturer of ethnic health and beauty aids, and 19th largest black-owned corporation in the United States with over $36 million in sales in 1989.

COUSINS, WILLIAM, JR., entered the University of Illinois in 1945 and graduated in 1948 with honors in political science and with an ROTC commission. He received his LL.B. degree from Harvard Law School in 1951 and was admitted to the bar in 1953 after a two-year interval of service in the U.S. Army as an infantry platoon leader in Korea. A graduate of the Army Command and General Staff School, he retired in 1976 from the Army Reserve Corps as lieutenant colonel in the Judge Advocate General Corps. He taught a litigation strategy and technique course at DePaul Law School as a part-time faculty member from 1981 to 1984. In the summer of 1987, he was a faculty adviser at the National Judicial College.

His legal career includes a period of four years as an attorney with the Chicago Title and Trust Company, four years as an assistant state's attorney, and over 15 years in private practice. One of his clients was the village of Phoenix, Illinois. He was appointed a member of the executive committee of Illinois Judicial Conference by the Illinois Supreme Court in December 1983, re-appointed as a member in 1986, and re-appointed as a member and as chairman of the Illinois Judicial Conference in December 1989. He has served as treasurer and also as chairman of the Illinois Judicial Council.

Before his election as a judge, he was active politically. He was an alderman for the 8th Ward, Chicago, from 1967 to 1976, a delegate to the Democratic National Convention in 1972, a former vice president of Independent Voters of Illinois, and a former board member of Americans for Democratic Action. He is a member of the Chicago, Cook County, Illinois, American and National bar associations. He is a past member of the board of directors of the Cook County Bar Association, the Illinois Judges Association, and the Illinois Judicial Council. He received the Edward N. Wright Award from the Cook County Bar Association (CCBA) in 1968 for "excelling as a lawyer in politics." Another recognition, the William R. Ming Award, also from the CCBA in 1974, cited him for his spirit of dedication as an attorney to the cause of his clients.

In 1980 and again in 1988, he was honored as Judge of the Year by the Balsa Chapter of John Marshall Law Students. In 1985, he was the recipient of the Thurgood Marshall Award from the Balsa Chapter of Students at IIT Chicago-Kent College of Law. In October 1987, the *Illinois Bar Journal* published an article written by him entitled "A Judge's View of Judicial Selection Plans." He was elected to the Circuit Court of Cook County in November 1976, and was retained in November 1982 and 1988. From December 6, 1976, to January 1983, and from June 14, 1984, to 1991, he was assigned to the Criminal Division, Circuit Court of Cook County. From 1983 to 1984, he was assigned to the personal injury jury, 1st Municipal Division, and to law jury between January 1984 and June 1984. Active in numerous civic and religious affairs, he served as president of the Chatham-Avalon Park Community Council, 1962–1965. He is also a former member of the executive council of the United Church of Christ and the board of PUSH.

COWINGS, JOHN SHERMAN, Was born August 11, 1943, in New York City. He received a B.A. degree in civil government from New York University, and an M.B.A. from Golden Gate University. He entered the United States Army with an ROTC commission of 2nd lieutenant in November 1965. From November 1965 to January 1966, he was a student in the Ordnance Officer Basic Course at the United States Army Ordnance School, Aberdeen Proving Ground, Maryland. From January 1966 to March 1967, he was a platoon leader in Company C, later Company D, of the 702nd Maintenance Battalion, 2nd Infantry Division, United States Army, in

Korea. From August 1967 to September 1968, he served as the shop officer, later acting commander, of Company C, and later as commander of Company D, 701st Maintenance Battalion, in Vietnam. From October 1968 to September 1969, he was a student in the Ordnance Officer Advanced Course, United States Army Ordnance School, Aberdeen Proving Ground.

He was promoted to the rank of captain on February 7, 1968. From September 1969 to April 1971, he was the commander of the maintenance company, General Support Group, Fort Ord, California. From April 1971 to May 1972, he served as a special assistant to the commanding general, United States Army Combat Development Experimentation Command, Fort Ord. From May 1972 to September 1975, he was a student at Golden Gate University, San Francisco, California. From September 1973 to June 1975, he served as the historical officer, later student, at the United States Army Command and General Staff College, Fort Leavenworth, Kansas. He was promoted to the grade of major on June 5, 1975. From June 1975 to June 1977, he served as a research and development coordinator, United States Army Institute for the Behavioral and Social Sciences, Far East Field Unit, in Korea. From June 1977 to September 1978, he served as a staff officer, Manpower Coordination Branch, Allocation and Documents Division, Office of the Deputy Chief of Staff for Personnel, United States Army, Washington, D.C.

From October 1978 to October 1979, he served as the executive officer, Office of the Director of Manpower, Plans and Budget, Office of the Deputy Chief of Staff for Personnel, United States Army, Washington, D.C. He was promoted to the grade of lieutenant colonel on August 12, 1979. From November 1979 to May 1982, he was commander of the 708th Maintenance Battalion, 8th Infantry Division (Mechanized), United States Army in Europe. From June 1982 to June 1983, he served as a logistics staff officer and North Atlantic Treaty Organization team chief, Office of the Deputy Chief of Staff for Logistics, United States Army, in Washington, D.C. From June 1983 to June 1984, he was a student at the Industrial College of the Armed Forces, Fort Lesley J. McNair, Washington, D.C.

From July 1984 to June 1985, he served as director of the Maintenance Directorate, United States Army Munitions and Chemical Command, Rock Island, Illinois. He was promoted to the grade of colonel on October 1, 1985. From June 1986 to June 1988, he served as commander of Rock Island Arsenal, Rock Island. From July 1988 to September 1989, he served as chief of staff, Tank-Automotive Command, Warren, Michigan. He was promoted to the one-star grade of brigadier general in October 1989. He was then assigned as the commanding general of the 3rd Support Command (Corps), United States Army in Europe, and Seventh Army. He has received numerous awards and decorations including the Legion of Merit (with oak leaf cluster), Army Commendation Medal (with two oak leaf clusters), Meritorious Service Medal (with six oak leaf clusters) and the Bronze Star Medal.

COX, KEVIN, is a 1968 graduate of Bishop McGuiness High School. He received his bachelor's degree in political science from Florida A&M University (1972), and a master's degree in public administration from the University of Georgia (1974). He was selected as one of the Outstanding Young Men of America in 1979 by the U.S. Jaycees, and in 1981 he was named Citizen of the Year by the Oklahoma City Set Club. Cox is married to the former Carlise Ann Washington, a special education teacher in the Oklahoma

City public schools. A lifetime resident of Oklahoma City, he has participated in a broad range of activities affecting District 97, the black community, Oklahoma City, and the state of Oklahoma.

Cox is very active in a wide range of community activities. He is an usher of St. John Baptist Church; a life member of Kappa Alpha Psi Fraternity (1980–1983); a former member of the Urban League Board of Directors; a board of management member of the Eastside YMCA, which named him Outstanding Lay Worker in 1977; a life member of the NAACP and a charter member of the Citizens Actions Council; a member of the Oklahoma City All-Sports Activities Association; a member of the Amateur Softball Association; a certified referee for football, basketball, and softball; and a certified lifeguard. Cox's motto is, "I'm a workhorse and not a showhorse!"

CRAIG, ROGER, was born July 10, 1960 in Preston, Mississippi. Craig and wife Vernessia have three children: Damesha, Rometra and Rogdrick. A graduate of Davenport (Iowa) Central High, where he was a football, wrestling and track star. He finished his college career as the Cornhuskers' fourth all-time leading rusher with 2,446 yards while playing fullback and tailback. He scored 26 touchdowns and spent most of his career as a backup to Jarvis Redwine and Heisman Trophy-winner Mike Rozier. He ran hurdles on the track team and earned his degree in criminal justice in 1983. A constant, relentless player, Craig is described by teammates as having the heart of a lion. He gained the majority of yardage after breaking tackles among all-time NFL leaders for receptions by a running back.

A superbly conditioned athlete, he played every game of his professional career. He was a second-round pick, 49th overall and the sixth running back, taken behind Eric Dickerson. He set a team rookie record with 12 touchdowns (8 rushing 4 receiving) and 72 points scored. His 725 rushing yards were the third highest total ever for a 49er rookie, bettered only by Vic Washington's 811 (1971) and Ken Willard's 778 (1965). In the 1984 season he was a team leader with 71 receptions and 10 touchdowns. He set 135 total yards in 38–16 Super Bowl win against Miami. In 1985 he was the only player in NFL history to surpass 1,000 yards rushing and 1,000 yards receiving in a single season. He had 1,050 rushing and 1,016 receiving, and his 2,066 combined yards established a team record for a total rushing and receiving yards. He set the NFL record for running backs with 92 receptions, and won the team's Len Eshmont Award given annually to the most courageous and inspirational player.

In 1988, he set a team record with 1,502 rushing yards and was tied for NFL leadership with Herschel Walker in total offense with 2,036 yards. He set a career high with 190 rushing yards against the L.A. Rams, was NFC Offensive Player of the Week for Week 7 and surpassed 1,000 rushing yards for the year at Phoenix. He served on numerous charitable groups during off season.

He began his career as a model with Macy's department stores in 1968 and received his first acting opportunity when he appeared with O. J. Simpson on HBO's "1st and 10" series during the 1989 off season. He co-starred in his first movie, *Dark Obsessions*, playing a detective in a 1990 off-season project, along with teammates Keana Turner, Ronnie Lott, Eric Wright, and former 49er Carlton Williamson. Craig operates the Sports City Cafe, a restaurant in Cupertino, California. He has been an international representative for Mizuno sports apparel and has done national print and television advertising for NFL Properties, the merchandising wing of the league. As spokesman for "Powerburst" energy drink, he co-hosted Pacific Sportsman's Activities, a syndicated television broadcast which premiered highlights of various sports. He has also been featured twice weekly with sports commentary on KNTV-TV. Craig served as chairman and rode lead bike in the 1990 Great San Francisco Bike Adventure which benefited American Youth Hostels, an organization that provides low-rent boarding for youth traveling in the U.S.A. Craig holds Super Bowl Records for most touchdowns in a game (tied with Jerry Rice); most points scored in a game (18, tied with Jerry Rice); most pass receptions in career (20); most points in career (24, tied with Jerry Rice); and most touchdowns in career (4, tied with Jerry Rice and Franco Harris).

CRAWFORD, WILLIAM A., is now in his seventh term in the Indiana House of Representatives. He was born January 28, 1936, in Indianapolis, the son of Kenneth C. and Essie L. Crouch Crawford. He was educated in the local public schools and high schools. He has also taken college work and special courses in data processing. After high school he served in the U.S. Navy. He is married to Lennie M. Crawford; the couple has four children. Crawford is a member of St. Johns Missionary Baptist Church, where he was employed as a youth coordinator from 1972 to 1978. Prior to that time he was a postal clerk and community organizer. Since 1978 he has been executive director of the Indiana Christian Leadership Conference.

A Democrat in politics, he was administrative assistant in 1978 to the Marion County clerk. He is a member of the Urban League, the NAACP, TransAfrica, the Southern Christian Leadership Conference, and the Free South Africa Movement. Crawford also was an organizer of the Indiana Black Expo. As a legislator he has concentrated on areas of special concern with constituents, such as housing, criminal justice, education neighborhood assistance, health care, taxation and economic development.

CROCKETT, GEORGE W., JR., is a Democrat from Detroit, Michigan. Crockett was born in Jacksonville, Florida, on August 10, 1909. He was educated in the Jacksonville public school system and graduated from Stanton High School in 1927. He received his B.A. degree from Morehouse College in Atlanta, Georgia, in 1931, where he now serves on the board of trustees. In 1934, he graduated from the University of Michigan's law school with his J.D. degree. While at the University of Michigan, Crockett met and married the late Ethelene Jones Crockett, M.D., with whom he had three children: Elizabeth Ann Hicks, George W. III, and Ethelene Crockett Jones. In 1980, Crockett married the former Harriette Clark, M.D., of Washington, D.C.

Crockett began his legal practice

in Jacksonville after being admitted to the Florida bar in 1934. In 1935, he was admitted to the West Virginia bar, in 1940 to the U.S. Supreme Court bar, and in 1944 to the Michigan bar. In 1939, he was appointed to become the first black lawyer with the U.S. Department of Labor. He later became the senior attorney and the department specialist on employee lawsuits under the Fair Labor Standards Act. In 1943, with the formation of the nation's Fair Employment Practices Commission, President Roosevelt called upon George Crockett to be one of its first hearing examiners. In 1944, Crockett founded and was Director of the International United Auto Workers Fair Employment Practices Department. He remained with the UAW serving as general counsel and administrative assistant to the international secretary-treasurer until 1946. From 1946 until 1966, when Crockett was elected judge of Recorders Court in Detroit, he was in private practice as a senior partner in one of the nation's first interracial law firms, Goodman, Crockett, Eden and Robb.

In 1972 Crockett was elected to a second six-year term on the Recorders Court and in 1974 was elected presiding judge. Following his retirement from that court, he served as a visiting judge for the Michigan Court of Appeals. In 1980, he served as acting corporation counsel for the city of Detroit. Throughout Crockett's career as a lawyer, civil rights activist and judge he has found time to lend his support to several community and professional organizations such as the judicial council of the National Bar Association (he was founder and first chairman), the NAACP, Kappa Alpha Psi fraternity, National Conference for Black Lawyers friends and founders committee, and Hartford Baptist Church, Detroit.

On November 4, 1980, Crockett was elected to the U.S. House of Representatives. He was sworn in on November 12 to fill the vacancy created by the resignation of Charles C. Diggs, Jr. At the same time Crockett was elected to the 97th Congress. In November 1982, he was re-elected to the 98th Congress; in 1984, re-elected to the 99th Congress; and in 1986, re-elected to the historic 100th Congress. As a member of the U.S. House of Representatives, Crockett serves on the following committees: Committee on Foreign Affairs, where he serves as chairman on the Western Hemisphere Affairs Subcomittee and ranking majority member on the Subcommittee on Africa; Committee on the Judiciary, Subcommittee on Crime, Courts, Civil Liberties and the Administration of Justice; and the Select Committee on Aging, Subcommittee on Retirement Income and Employment.

CROMARTIE, EUGENE RUFUS, was born October 3, 1936, in Wabasso, Florida. He received a B.S. degree in social science from Florida A&M University and an M.S. degree in education/guidance and counseling from the University of Dayton. He received an ROTC Commission to the rank of 2nd lieutenant on June 3, 1957. He was promoted to the rank of 1st lieutenant on January 14, 1959. On January 15, 1962, he was promoted to the rank of captain. On September 21, 1966, he was promoted to the rank of major. From June 1971 to November 1972, he served as chief of the Elective Branch, Office of the Director of Graduate Studies and Research, United States Army Command and General Staff College, Fort Leavenworth, Kansas. He was promoted to the grade of lieutenant colonel on August 9, 1971. From December 1972 to July 1974, he was the commander of the 503rd Military Police Battalion, Fort Bragg, North Carolina. From July 1974 to June 1975, he was appointed provost marshal, 82nd Airborne Division, Fort Bragg.

From June 1975 to July 1976, he served as the personnel management officer, Assignments Branch, Lieutenant Colonels Division, Officer Personnel Management Directorate, United States Army Military Personnel Center, Alexandria, Virginia. From August 1976 to June 1977, he was a student at the National War College, Fort Lesley J. McNair, Washington, D.C. From June 1977 to May 1978, he served as a special assistant to the commanding general, United States Army Criminal Investigation Command, Falls Church, Virginia. He was promoted to the grade of colonel on August 5, 1977. From June 1978 to November 1979, he was the commander of the First Region, United States Army Criminal Investigation Command, Fort Meade, Maryland. From January 1980 to October 1983, he first served as deputy provost marshal, then as provost marshal of the United States Army in Europe and the Seventh Army. He was promoted to the grade of brigadier general in April 1982. In November 1983, he was promoted to the two-star grade of major general and then was

assigned as commanding general, United States Criminal Investigation Command, Falls Church, Virginia. He has received numerous awards and decorations including the Bronze Star Medal (with oak leaf cluster), the Meritorious Service Medal (with two oak leaf clusters), the Army Commendation Medal (with oak leaf cluster) and the Parachutist Badge.

CUNNINGHAM, RANDALL, was born March 27, 1963, in Santa Barbara, California. He is the youngest of the four sons of Samuel and Mabel Cunningham. Each of the Cunningham boys attended college on a football scholarship, with the oldest, Sam, and Randall going on to become stars in the NFL. Sam was a fullback while at the University of Southern California (USC) and the New England Patriots of the National Football League. Randall maintained a solid B average and was a star at track, in which he recorded a six-foot, ten-inch high jump, as well as football. In his senior year he received scholarship offers from several universities but chose to enroll at the University of Nevada at Las Vegas (UNLV). His first year at UNLV proved an extremely difficult one. His mother died of cancer, and football was a big disappointment. The coach who had recruited him left and was replaced by a coach who favored the running game.

To make matters worse, Cunningham performed miserably during the 1982 spring practice sessions. He became the fourth-string quarterback behind a senior and two juniors. But in his sophomore year, Randall became starting quarterback. At about the time that Cunningham was taking command of the Runnin' Rebels' offense, his father died unexpectedly. A devastated Randall found the sudden grievous loss of both parents very painful, and he turned to religion. On the field of play, Cunningham was a sensation in his first year as a starter. He passed for 2,847 yards, including 26 touchdowns and only 12 interceptions.

Over the next two years, he compiled passing numbers on the way to becoming the third player, after John Elway and Doug Flutie, to pass for more than 2,500 yards in three straight seasons. His overall completion percentage of 58.1 and his 614 completions established passing marks for the PCAA. Yet the only All-America recognition he received was as a punter, and he was never a contender for the Heisman Trophy. At the 1985 NFL draft, he was passed over by every team in the NFL on the first round. On the second round the Philadelphia Eagles made him the 37th college prospect to be selected overall. In the summer of 1985, Cunningham joined the Eagles. After two years of carefully nurturing Cunningham, the Eagles turned him loose on the rest of the NFL, and the multitalented quarterback promptly became a defender's worst nightmare. Defensive linemen lost considerable wind trying to chase Cunningham down, and cornerbacks covered long distances to chase down his majestic passes.

Randall is a talent, a great natural athlete and a great leader on the field; he runs, kicks (he's the Eagles' backup punter), passes, and decimates NFL defenses. In 1987, his first full season as a starter, he was selected as first alternate to the NFC with a QB passer rating of 83.0 and had a string of 118 straight passes without an interception. In 1988, he capped an outstanding season by being selected as the starting quarterback in the AFC-NFC Pro Bowl and was MVP in that game. He also received the Bert Bell award as the NFL player of the year from the Maxwell Football Club, and NFC player of the year honors from the Washington Touchdown Club. He became the first quarterback to lead his team in rushing yards two straight years since the Packers' Robin Rote (1951–1952). In 1989, he posted numbers similar to those of his spectacular 1988 campaign, but with a defense that kept opponents off the scoreboard and a more balanced attack on offense, Cunningham's uncanny knack for late-game heroics was not needed as often in 1989 as in the past. Cunningham, for the fourth straight year, was the leading rusher among quarterbacks and became the first quarterback in modern NFL history to lead his team in rushing for three consecutive years.

He had the best passing game of his career at Washington, where he orchestrated a victory by bringing the Eagles from as many as 20 points behind with career-high figures for yards (447 — an Eagles record), completions (34), and TDs (5), including three in the fourth quarter en route to Miller Lite NFL and NFC offensive player of the week honors. In 1990, Cunningham once more led his team in rushing and accounted overall for more than 80 percent of the Eagles' offensive yardage. Again his team finished second in the NFC East behind the New York Giants. Cunningham became one of the wealthiest athletes in the world in September 1989, when he signed a five-year contract with the Eagles worth $17 million.

CUNNINGHAM, WILLIAM "PETE", a native of Union County, North Carolina, and a retired veteran of the United States Navy. He has been president of HKL, Inc., and the Excelsior Club, and is an investor in commercial real estate ventures. From 1973 to 1984, he was president of Hatchett & Cunningham Associates, Inc., a leader in the placement of minority and female candidates with many of the nation's largest companies, and he is a former director of minority recruiting for Charleston-based RLS Associates. Cunningham attended Perry's Business College, Florida State University Extension, and is an alumnus of Johnson C. Smith University where, since 1988, he has served as a member of the JCSU Board of Visitors. He is also a former vice president, administrative dean, and instructor at the Southeastern Business College in Charleston, South Carolina.

Cunningham has been a member of the N.C. House of Representatives and has worked diligently to make life better for the citizens of North Carolina. His efforts have been to improve services for senior citizens, to provide more affordable housing, to increase teacher pay, and to help find solutions to mounting crime problems and viable alternatives to the growing prison population. He believes that legislators must initiate steps to clean up and protect the environment and natural resources. He lists other concerns as drugs, school dropouts, education, economic development, prenatal care, political redistricting and the growing need for child care services for parents who want to work but cannot afford day care for their children.

Cunningham is a teacher, administrator, churchman, businessman, and civic leader. He was the first president of the Charlotte Business League, an organization designed to support and aid in the development of minority businesses. In 1975, he was honored by being listed in the inaugural edition *Who's Who Among Black Americans*, and from 1978 to 1984, he was listed in *Who's Who in Black Corporate America*. He is also a past member of the executive committee of Durham College, past president of the Charleston Retired Veterans Association, and a past member of the Johnson C. Smith University Alumni Association.

Cunningham is currently chairman of the board of trustees of Parkwood Institutional CME Church and a member of Compassion World Vision, the Christian Children's Fund; the Lions Club; the United Negro College Fund; Johnson C. Smith University 100 Club; American Legion Post 212; United States Navy Fleet Reserve

Association. He is also a board member of the Anita Stroud Foundation. As a North Carolina representative, Cunningham has served on the following House committees: Aging, Corrections, Finance, Human Resources, Housing, Insurance, Mental Health, and Veterans' Affairs.

CURRIE, JACKIE L., a wife and mother of four sons, Currie was elected a Wayne County commissioner in November 1974, and took office January 1, 1975. A Democrat, she represents District 4 which encompasses about 150,000 residents of downtown Detroit. Throughout metropolitan Detroit, no public official is better known or more respected than Commissioner Currie for her interest in senior citizen affairs, juvenile correction programs, indigent health care and public safety. On the county commission, she is chair of the public safety and judiciary committee, vice chair of the committee on administration and rules, vice chair of the committee on roads, airports and public services, and a member of the

committee of the whole, committee on economic development and a special committee on senior citizen affairs.

She is also chair of the Wayne County Community Corrections Advisory Board, a member of the justice and public safety steering committee on the National Association of Counties operating from Washington, D.C., and a member of the Manpower Advisory Council. Currie is a member of some 40 other civic and community organizations. She founded the Cultural Enrichment Program for inner-city students and is a member of the boards of directors of SHARE HOUSE, Detroit Central City Community Health, Inc., Detroit East, Inc., and Project C.H.I.L.D. She is vice chair of the Poly Johnson Cancer Foundation. Currie is further employed as counselor and community services coordinator for Wayne State University, her alma mater, and she is pursuing a master's degree in social work from the University of Michigan. In addition, she has studied at Mercy College, Wayne County Community College, and AM&N College in Pine Bluff, Arkansas, her native state. Currie is also active in sorority affairs supporting student scholarships, and in local and national black women's political leadership organizations.

CURRY, ANNA ANTHONY, was born in Baltimore and graduated from Dunbar High School and Morgan State College (now University). Curry received her M.L.S. from Atlanta University in 1959, and later that year began her career as the young adult librarian at the Enoch Pratt Free Library's Pennsylvania Avenue Branch. Subsequently she served as head of the Central Library Young Adult Department, branch librarian and regional librarian. In 1976, Curry became the assistant director of the Pratt Library. She was appointed director in 1981, becoming the first black woman to hold that position. As director of the Pratt Library, Curry's accomplishments include obtaining the $1 million National Endowment for the Humanities Challenge Grant which launched a major capital campaign, administering the renovation of the Pratt Central Library and working with the library staff and board to develop a long-range strategic plan for the 1990s. Key initiatives of that recently implemented plan are the school/library partnership and the opening of a Lifelong Learning Library at the Broadway Branch.

As director she has appeared before the Maryland General Assembly and Baltimore City Council seeking increased financial support for public libraries, as well as equity in public access to books and information. Curry has served on the governing council of the American Library Association and is a member of ALA's Black Caucus and Public Library Association. She is also a member of the International Association of Metropolitan Libraries and is the legislative officer of the Maryland Library Association. Curry is a member of the Heritage United Church of Christ, and her community activities include service on the board of Tissue Banks International and the United Way management resources committee.

DAVIE, FRANK, was born in Madera, California, a farming community. He and his wife Barbara have two children, Michael and Kameron. He attended Cal Poly (California Polytechnical University, San Luis Obispo), then transferred to a college in Fresno. He eventually moved to Los Angeles, California. He worked in sales—first for a pharmaceutical company, then for a company that dealt with water treatment. There he gained some knowledge of chemicals and chemical applications through those jobs. The curl trend in the hair care market was already established by the late 1970s, but Davie looked at the trend and noticed a gap with the products then on the market. Cremes and lotions were available, but Davie had a better idea. In 1979, he created a gel, which he later called Worlds of Curls Gel Curl Activator. Worlds of Curls was founded in 1979; with the "original gel" in demand, WOC had ten employees on staff by 1980.

Operating from a garage, the company took the hair care industry by surprise with the introduction of the gel curl activator. By late 1980, Worlds of Curls had moved into a 5,000-square-foot office building located in Los Angeles. In 1982, expansion brought about a relocation to a 26,000-square-foot manufacturing plant in Compton, California. In 1989, Worlds of Curls Products, Inc., celebrated its 10th anniversary at the new corporate world headquarters in Compton, a facility of about 160,000 square feet, conveniently nestled in Compton's exclusive indus-

trial area. As stated by Davie, president and CEO of Worlds of Curls Products, Inc., "The mission of WOC is to serve the needs of black consumers by providing the best possible products and service to the community and offer financial assistance to deserving high school graduates."

On July 16, 1989, Worlds of Curls Products, Inc., held its Fifth Annual Scholarship Awards Program. Davie handed out $27,000 in scholarships to 27 of the best and brightest students from Los Angeles and surrounding school districts. He also contributed to PUSH, the NAACP, the United Negro College Fund, and many black churches. In December 1989, Davie received an award for his community service and support at Kids Against Drugs awards dinner.

DAVIS, BENJAMIN OLIVER, JR., was born December 18, 1912, in Washington, D.C. His parents were Brigadier General Benjamin O. Davis, Sr., U.S. Army Retired, and Sadie Overton Davis. He graduated from Central High School in Cleveland, Ohio, in 1929, then attended Western Reserve University in Cleveland and later the University of Chicago. He entered the United States Military Academy at West Point, New York, in July 1932 and graduated in June of 1936, with a commission as a 2nd lieutenant of infantry. In June 1937, after a year as commander of an infantry company at Fort Benning, Georgia, he entered the Infantry School there and a year later graduated and assumed duties as professor of military science at Tuskegee Institute, Tuskegee, Alabama. In May 1941, he entered Advanced Flying School at nearby Tuskegee Army Air Base. He received his pilot wings in March 1942.

Davis transferred to the Air Corps in May 1942. As commander of the 99th Fighter Squadron at Tuskegee Army Air Base, he moved with his unit to North Africa in April 1943, and later to Sicily. He returned to the United States in October 1943 and assumed command of the 33rd Fighter Group at Selfridge Field, Michigan. He returned with the group to Italy two months later. In 1945, he returned to the United States to command the 477th Composite Group at Godman Field, Kentucky, and later assumed command of the field. In March 1946, he went to Lockbourne Army Air Base, Ohio, as commander of the base. In July 1947, he became the commander of the 332d Fighter Wing there. In 1949, Davis went to the Air War College at Maxwell Air Force Base, Alabama. After graduation, he was assigned to the deputy chief of staff, Operations, Headquarters United States Air Force, Washington, D.C.

Davis served in various capacities with the headquarters until July 1953, when he went to the advanced jet fighter gunnery school at Nellis Air Force Base, Nevada. In November 1953, he assumed duties as commander of the 51st Fighter Interceptor Wing, Far East Air Forces (FEAF), Korea. He served as director of operations and training at FEAF Headquarters, Tokyo, from 1954 until 1955, when he assumed the position of vice commander, Air Task Force 13 (Provisional), Taipei, Formosa. In April 1957, General Davis arrived at Ramstein, Germany, as chief of staff, Twelfth Air Force. He was transferred to Waco, Texas. In December 1957, he assumed new duties as deputy chief of staff for Operations, Headquarters USAFE, Wiesbaden, Germany.

In July 1961, he returned to the United States and Headquarters United States Air Force where he served as the director of manpower and organization, deputy chief of staff for programs and requirements. In February 1965, he was assigned as assistant deputy chief of staff, programs and requirements. He remained in that position until his assignment as chief of staff for the

United Nations Command and United States Forces in Korea in April 1965. He assumed command of the Thirteenth Air Force at Clark Air base in the Republic of the Philippines in August 1967. He was assigned as deputy commander in chief, United States Strike Command, with headquarters at Mac-Dill Air Force Base, Florida. He had additional duty as commander in chief, Middle East, Southern Asia and Africa.

Davis was the second black U.S. general, and the first black Air Force general. He was also the first black American to obtain the three-star rank of lieutenant general. He retired from active duty February 1, 1970, and was appointed by the president of the United States to serve as assistant secretary of the United States Department of Transportation. He has also served as director of public safety for the city of Cleveland, Ohio.

DAVIS, JAMES K. Jim and his wife, Glenda, are from Florence, South Carolina. They have two children, James III and Jacquelynn. Davis holds a bachelor's degree from Claflin College in Orangeburg, South Carolina (graduated June 1962), and a master's degree from the Georgia Institute of Technology in Atlanta, Georgia (graduated December 1975). In addition, he was a graduate of the Harvard University Advanced Management Program, Boston, Massachusetts (graduated November 1989). He is vice president for corporate relations for Georgia Power Company. Prior to serving in this capacity, he was the director, corporate relations; manager of community development, assistant to the president; community development representative; and employee relations counselor for the company. Along with his responsibilities in corporate relations, Davis was on the generation plant evaluation committee. As a member of this committee, he made monthly visits to generating plants to evaluate production and performance standards and conduct EEO quarterly meetings for managers.

Davis has been actively involved in a leadership capacity in numerous local and statewide organizations. He chaired and or served on the executive committees of Atlanta Southside Economic Summit, board member; Butler Street YMCA, board member; Atlanta Area Council of Boy Scouts of America, board member; founder, Georgia Association of Black Elected Officials Corporate Roundtable; National Conference of Black Mayors Task Force, member; Georgia Tech College of Management Alumni Advisory Committee, board member; Foxhead Development Corporation, chairman of the board, Southeastern Electric Exchange Advisory Committee, advisory board member; American Association of Blacks in Energy, board member; Atlanta Urban League, board member; United Negro College Fund Telethon chairman since 1986; Southern Christian Leadership Conference (Policy Committee), board of directors; Renaissance Capital Corporation, board of directors (a Minority Enterprise Small Business Investment Corporation [MESBIC]).

Davis has also served as chairman of the Minority Contractor/Vendor Program at Georgia Power Company; NAACP (first vice president, Atlanta Branch, and member of the National Energy Committee); City of Atlanta Older Atlantans Task Force, board of directors; 100 Black Men of Atlanta, member; Mayor's Task Force on Public Education, board of directors; Gammon Theological Seminary, board of trustees; Georgia Department of Human resources, board of directors; Leadership Georgia Alumni, 1974; Leadership Atlanta alumni, 1977; member of Ben Hill United Methodist Church. Davis has been named in *Who's Who in American Colleges and Universities* and Outstanding Young Men in America. Most recently, he was honored by Southern Bell for his outstanding service to Atlanta and the black community. For this honor, he was recognized in Southern Bell's 1986–1987 Calendar of Atlanta Black History, and for corporate achievement, an honor received from the Equitable Life Assurance Society of the United States.

DAVIS, L. CLIFFORD, born in Wilton, Arkansas, October 12, 1925. He is married to the daughter of a Methodist minister and they have two adult daughters. He is a graduate of Philander Smith College, a Methodist-related college in Little Rock. He pursued graduate study at Atlanta University and earned his J.D. degree at Howard University Law School, Washington, D.C. He has been active in the Fort Worth community for over 35 years, with political, economic and social welfare programs for communities. His involvements include the YMCA, Camp Fire, Precinct Workers Council, the Black Chamber of Commerce and the NAACP.

Davis' record of involvement with the church is outstanding. He has been a Sunday school teacher, steward, two separate rotations as chair of the Administrative Board, a member of the finance committee, and served as chair of trustees. He has served by appointment or election of city, county and state government; and by appointment and by election as a criminal district judge in Tarrant County. He is active as a visiting judge in the judicial region.

DAVIS, MONIQUE D., is a graduate of Chicago State University, B.A. degree in elementary education, 1967, and master's degree in guidance and counseling, 1974; DePaul University, graduate studies in administration; University of Illinois, community organization development, and National

College of Education, organization and administration. Davis has served as Chicago Board of Education coordinator of educational service center #6 since 1986 to date, and state representative for the 36th District (second term) to date. As state representative he was chief sponsor of legislation that prohibits the sale of drug paraphernalia. He co-sponsored legislation in the area of fairness in the judiciary, and is a requested speaker on issues such as school reform, chemical warfare, infant mortality, drug abuse, women's rights, child care and minority issues. He coordinated the 21st Ward for the election of Mayor Harold Washington, 1983.

As a legislator, Davis served on various committees including: Elementary Secondary Education, Public Utilities, Consumer Protection, and was vice chairperson of Reform Implementation Committee. Prior positions include: Teacher at Gresham Elementary School, 1968–1986, and instructor for GED, Chicago State University, 1976–1984. He has sponsored reading, math, and tennis classes for adults and children during the summer months of 1989, and solicited volunteer teachers to assist with tutoring and classes. He held a community forum on crime and drugs in the community, where he addressed over 100 participants. He also hosted regular weekly meetings to inform residents of the content of newly passed school reform legislation. In addition, he spoke to numerous community-sponsored meetings informing participants on school reform and what it means to the community. He was a sponsor of a Health Seminar at Olive Harvey College and was the recipient of many honors and awards.

DAVIS, PHILLIP SAMUEL, was born November 15, 1953, in Hartford, Connecticut. A graduate of Northwest Catholic High School in Hartford in 1971, Davis received a Martin Luther King, Jr., scholarship to Providence College in Providence, Rhode Island, where he received his B.S. degree in social work, minor in mathematics, in 1975. While attending Providence College he was nominated by Senator Abraham Ribicoff to the United States Military Academy at West Point, New York. At that time, he was the first African American from the State of Connecticut to be nominated and to attend West Point. He later decided that his mission in life was to help others. Thereafter, he resigned the academy and returned to college where he worked for the Poor People's Federation in Hartford.

Davis received his master's degree from Boston University in 1977, in social work, with honors and a master's in Afro-American studies, and in 1980 he received his J.D. degree from Boston College Law School. While working toward his law degree at Boston College, he had the unique opportunity of working with the Secretary of Education for the State of Massachusetts as an administrative assistant. In addition, he went on to serve as a legal intern with United States Attorney Richard Blumenthal during his law studies at Boston College. He also had the distinct and rewarding experience of clerking with United States Magistrate Owen Eagan in Hartford.

Davis was hired by the state attorney's office in Dade County, Florida, where he worked with that office for two and one-half years, ending his work as an assistant state attorney for Dade County in 1983. He resigned his position and set up his own private practice in the heart of Overtown. He was trying to assist those individuals who were unable to afford efficient legal services. His practice consisted of both criminal and civil litigation with an emphasis toward criminal defense and appellate work. The practice thrived and became one which was both local and national in scope. He handled matters before several courts in several states, more specifically, Tucson, Arizona; Washington, D.C.; the Commonwealth of Pennsylvania; and in the United States District Court in Hartford.

In 1987, Davis embarked upon his lifetime goal of becoming a judicial officer and began his campaign in the fall of that year, working earnestly and with dedication toward achieving that hallmark. On November 8, 1988, he was elected to the Circuit Court of Dade County as a circuit court judge. He received over 185,000 coalition votes of the various community groups in Dade County, which was known for its quad-ethnic environment made up of blacks, whites, Hispanics, and Haitians. His accomplishment of becoming Dade County's first elected black circuit court judge gave tribute to the fact that opportunity taken advantage of, honestly and morally, can serve to give immeasurable rewards both for an individual and for his community. This idea was one which he tries to instill in young offenders who appear before him while going through the judicial system. A difficult task, but one which

he felt he was slowly but surely accomplishing. His involvement included: visiting the Department of Corrections Basic Training Program (Boot Camp); with the Positive Program (a program designed to bring a positive message to youth gangs); and working within the One Church/One Child Program (a program placing black children with adoptive families) proves his commitment and dedication to the citizens of Dade County.

DAVIS, WALTER JACKSON, JR., was born on August 1, 1936, in Winston-Salem, North Carolina. He married the former Constance P. Surles

of Pensacola, Florida, and they have two daughters, Sharon P. Davis Clayton and Kimberly D. Davis. He received a B.S. degree in electrical engineering from Ohio State University in 1959, and an M.S. in aeroelectronics from the Naval Postgraduate School, Monterey, in 1967. On August 1, 1959, he was commissioned an ensign in the United States Naval

Reserve. From August 1959 to December 1960, he was a student at NABTC NAS in Pensacola, Florida. From June 1960 to December 1960, he was a student at NAAS at Kingsville, Texas. He was promoted to the rank of lieutenant (junior grade) on December 3, 1960. On December 19, 1960, he was designated naval aviator (HTA).

From December 1960 to October 1961, he was assigned to Fighter Squadron 121 (DUINS); to Fighter Squadron 53 from October 1961 to March 1962; to Fighter Squadron 143 from March 1962 to July 1964. On October 15, 1963, he was augmented in the United States Navy. From July 1964 to June 1967, he was a student at the Naval Postgraduate School, Monterey. From June 1967 to May 1970, Davis was first assigned to Fighter Squadron 121 (DUINS) and later as the assistant operation officer/maintenance officer, with Fighter Squadron 143. He was promoted to the grade of lieutenant commander on May 1, 1968. From May 1970 to February 1971, he attended the Naval Test Pilot School, NATC Patuxent River (project officer). From February 1971 to July 1973, he was appointed project officer of the Weapons Systems Test Division, NATC Patuxent River. From July 1973 to July 1974, he was a student at the Naval War College (DUINS). He was promoted to the grade of commander on July 1, 1973. From July 1974 to May 1977, he was first assigned to Fighter Squadron 121 (DUINS), then as deputy commander (XO) of Fighter Squadron 114, later as commander of Fighter Squadron 114.

From May 1977 to February 1979, he was appointed assistant project manager for the F-14s at the Naval Air Systems Command Headquarters. From February 1979 to June 1979, he was a student at the Surface Warfare Officer's School Command, Newport (DUINS). From June 1979 to December 1980, he was assigned as the deputy commander (XO) of the USS *Kitty Hawk* (CV-63). He was promoted to

the grade of captain on July 1, 1980. From December 1980 to May 1981, he was appointed chief of naval personnel (DUINS). From May 1981 to December 1981, he served as Staff, COMNAV-SURFPAC (DUINS). In May 1981, he was the commander of USS *Sacramento* (AOE 1).

From August 1984 to June 1985, he was a student at the Industrial College of the Armed Forces (DUINS). From June 1985 to May 1987, he was the commander of the USS *Ranger* (CV-61). In August 1988, he was appointed commandant of the Naval District in Washington. He was promoted to the grade of rear admiral (lower half), on December 1, 1988. He has received numerous awards and medals which include: the Legion of Merit; the Meritorious Service Medal; the Air Medal with numeral "10"; Navy Commendation Medal with Combat "V"; the Sea Service Deployment Ribbon with one Bronze Star; Vietnam Service Medal with one silver and one Bronze Star.

DAVIS-HARRIS, JEANNETTE G., is a graduate of the University of Massachusetts, Amherst, Massachusetts, where she received a B.S. degree in bacteriology, minor concentration in public health, in 1972, and Ed.D. and M.Ed. degrees concentrating in international education and anthropology, in 1974; and the School of Law, Western New England College, Springfield, Massachusetts, in 1988. Since 1978, Harris has been employed by the Massachusetts Department of Education, Western Massachusetts Regional Education Center, Chicopee. The center serves school districts throughout the western Massachusetts counties, interfacing with community organizations and corporations, addressing health education and human service issues and emphasizing collaboration between community and educational institutions. She is responsible for the administration of varied state and federal grants, the monitoring and enforcement of state regulations, the management of complaints, the provision of technical assistance in proposal writing/program development and the interpretation educational laws. She also facilitates the education department arm of the Governor's Alliance Against Drugs.

In 1987, she initiated the Health-Related Professionals, an association for professional networking offering specialized seminars (including issues on AIDS, human sexuality, drugs and alcohol, stress and genetic disorders) focused on the comprehensive nature of health education. This four-county association has gained statewide recognition. From 1969 to 1978, as chairperson of the Classical High School social studies department in Springfield, Massachusetts, Davis-Harris introduced a new program in African American studies. She designed implementation and monitoring of instructional content, learning materials and department objectives. As

department head and instructor, her duties further included writing grants, evaluating federal and state programs and serving as critic-teacher for college-level training programs. She also designed and implemented a series of African American courses at several institutions of higher education in western Massachusetts.

Prior positions included bacteriologist in charge at the Lahey Clinic, Boston, where she supervised and performed laboratory procedures, trained laboratory personnel, and conducted specialized research in bone histology, and medical missionary in Bolahun, Liberia. She is the author or co-author of several texts. Davis-Harris received the Community Service Award from the Brethren, Springfield, in 1985; is listed in Marquis' *Who's Who in the East* and in *Who's Who in the World;* and is affiliated with many professional organizations.

DAVISON, FREDERIC ELLIS, was born September 28, 1917, the son of Albert Charles Davison and Sue (Bright) Davison. He married the former Jean E. Brown and they have four children, Jean M., Andrea S., Dayle A., and Carla M. He is a native of Washington, D.C., and attended the all-black Dunbar High School there. He earned membership in the National Honor Society. After graduating from Dunbar in 1934, he entered Howard University where he starred in track. He received a B.S. degree from Howard cum laude in 1938, and his M.S. degree there two years later. Having completed ROTC training, he was commissioned a lieutenant in the United States Army Reserve in 1939. He was ordered to active duty in 1941, a few months before America entered World War II.

During the war, in the rank of captain, he led the all-black B Company, 371st Infantry, 92nd Division, in fighting up from Sicily, through Italy. Between 1947, when he was training an

ROTC unit at South Carolina Agricultural and Mechanical College, and the early 1950s, when he was a battalion operations officer in Germany, the United States Army gradually rid itself of segregation. In 1954, Davison entered the Command and General Staff College at Fort Leavenworth, Kansas. In 1957, after a stint as a personnel management officer in Washington, he was promoted to the rank of lieutenant colonel, and then, in 1959, was sent to Korea as chief of GI personnel services with the Eighth Army. Back in the United States, he enrolled at the Army War College, in 1962 to 1963, and received an M.A. degree in international affairs at George Washington University, in 1963. During the following two years he was in charge of manpower and reserve matters at the Pentagon.

From 1965 to 1967, he commanded the Third Training Brigade at Fort Bliss, Texas. At his own request, Davison was sent to Vietnam in November 1967 as deputy commander of the 199th Light Infantry Brigade which was deployed in the defense perimeter around Saigon. When the North Vietnamese and National Liberation Front demonstrated their military and popular power in the astounding Tet offensive of February 1968, the brigade's commander was absent. Davison led the defense of the United States base at Long Binh in such close rapport with the men under him that they continued to treat him as their de facto leader even after their commander returned.

In August 1968, Davison, then a full colonel, was made brigade commander, and the following month General Creighton W. Abrams, the United States commander in South Vietnam, pinned the silver stars of a brigadier general on his collar in a promotion ceremony at Binh Chanh. From September 1971 to May 1972, he was deputy chief of staff for United States Army personnel in Europe. Meanwhile in April 1971, he was promoted to the rank of major general. Davison returned to his native city to take command of the Military District of Washington on November 12, 1973. He retired in 1974.

DEIZ, MERCEDES F., was born in December 1917, in New York City. She married Carl H. Deiz and is the mother of three children, Bill, Karen and Gilbert and has seven grandchildren. A

graduate of Hunter College, New York, she received a J.D. degree from Northwestern College of Law, Portland, Oregon, in 1959. A permanent Oregon resident since 1948, Deiz has served as judge of the Circuit Court of Oregon from 1973 to date (4th six-year term). Prior positions include: judge of the District Court of Oregon, 1970–1972; administrative law judge with Oregon Workmen's Compensation Board, 1968–1970; trial lawyer, general practice of law, Portland, 1960–1968 (admitted to practice before the courts of the State of Oregon, the Federal

Federal District Court, the U.S. Court of Appeals, and the Supreme Court of the United States); legal secretary, Portland, 1954–1958; law library assistant, Bonneville Power Administration, Portland, 1949–1953, with earlier employment in New York.

She is the recipient of many honors and awards: the first black elected to remunerative office in the state of Oregon; first black woman judge in the entire Pacific Northwest; Woman of Accomplishment, 1969; honorary member of the Oregon United Nations Association; Urban League award: Devotion to League's Concept of Equality, 1977; listed in various "Who's Who" publications; "Mothers of Achievement" and selected by *Willamette Week* (local newspaper) as one of the ten most influential blacks in this area.

DELLUMS, RONALD V., was born in Oakland, California, November 24, 1935. He is married to the former Leola (Roscoe) Higgs. They are the parents of three children, Brandy, Eric and Piper, and reside in Washington,

D.C. He spent two years in the United States Marine Corps before acquiring a B.A. degree from San Francisco State College, and an M.S.W. degree from the University of California at Berkeley. He also holds an honorary LL.B. degree from Wilberforce University in Ohio. Dellums is the U.S. Representative for California's Eighth Congressional District, which includes parts of Alameda and Contra Costa counties. He was the first member of his Congressional Class (of 1970) to be elected to the chair of a full committee of the House of Representatives. He was also the chairman of the D.C. Subcommittee on Fiscal Affairs and Health, a member of the House Armed Services Committee, where he served on the Research and Development Subcommittee, and also chaired the Armed Services Committee Panel dealing with the problems of the Island of Vieques.

A manpower specialist, he served as a psychiatric social worker for the California Department of Mental Hygiene (1962–1965), program director of the Bayview Community Center (1964–1965), and associate director of the Concentrated Employment Program of the San Francisco Economic Opportunity Council (1967–1968). Prior to going to Congress in 1971, he served on the Berkeley City Council from 1967 to 1971. He was employed as a senior consultant for Social Dynamics, Inc., a Berkeley-based enterprise which developed manpower and community organization programs on a nationwide basis. He was also a lecturer at San Francisco State College and at the Graduate School of Social Work at the University of California at Berkeley.

Dellums' first priority upon entering Congress was ending the war in Indochina, which he characterized as "illegal, immoral and insane adventurism." His major goal remained the termination of America's all-too-ready reliance on brutality and force to accomplish its objectives overseas and at home. He believed that militarism, the mentality that was so afraid of life that it seeks to control it through death, was the basic cause of his failures at home and abroad. He felt that the size of the military budget and the power it gives to the Pentagon is still the basic challenge of contemporary politics. He had become the principal leader in the House in the struggle for a significant reduction in our overseas military manpower. He argued that this voracious appetite for the taxpayers' dollar was threatening to starve the civilian component of government resources, both human and fiscal. He strongly believed that effective answers to these problems can only come from people working together around their concrete interests. Only this kind of true "Coalition Politics" would have the necessary staying power and the realism to turn the country in a new and more constructive direction. When people begin to realize how and why they are being victimized and manipulated, then they will be able to join together and form the basis for a new political and social majority, regardless of race or economic status.

In Dellums' view, Congress was not the only place where this new coalition would evolve. Still, he felt that the Congress had an important role to play. In his efforts to jolt the House of Representatives from its moribund institutionalism, he conducted three extra-official hearings on major problems that regular House committees refused to handle. The first of these hearings was an investigation into United States war crimes in Vietnam (April 1971). The other two hearings were held in conjunction with the Congressional Black Caucus. They included an examination of racism in the military (November 1971) and of governmental lawlessness and bureaucratic indifference (June 1972). All of these hearings produced major legislative proposals. The War Crimes hearings produced repeated demand for thorough

investigations of United States government conduct during the Indochina War. The "Racism in the Military" hearings produced bills to reform the system of military justice, and to end discrimination based on discharge status, among other measures. From the Governmental Lawlessness hearings came the Bureaucratic Accountability Act, to strengthen Congressional oversight capacity, and to give the ordinary citizen the legal tools needed to force the bureaucracy to adhere to the law.

In the 96th Congress Rep. Dellums re-introduced his comprehensive Health Care bill. In his view, health is one of the most important domestic reforms since uncertainty and skyrocketing expenses had made disease, and the threat of illness and disease for any duration, a major cause of anxiety and insecurity for all Americans. He feels strongly that a higher standard of living, as measured in material possessions, is meaningless if we cannot live in a society that protects the health of all its people. Other important legislation which he sponsored includes: the World Peace Tax Fund, the Adequate Income Act, the Omnibus Penal Reform Act, the Omnibus Intelligence Community Reorganization and Reform Act, and a number of bills dealing with women's rights, the plight of senior citizens, the critical problem of youth unemployment, and other areas of major social and political concern.

DELPIT, JOSEPH A., was born January 9, 1940, in Baton Rouge, Louisiana. He is the son of Edmae Delpit Butler and the late Thomas H. Delpit. He is married to the former Precious Robinson and has five children, Joseph, Jr., Thomas, Deidre, Desiree and Derrick, and four grandchildren, Jhaune, Douglas, Reginald and Dexter. He attended elementary school at St. Francis Xavier and graduated from McKinley

Senior High School. Also, he attended Southern University in Baton Rouge, where he received credits in business administration, and foods and nutrition. He has also received certificates for participation in numerous business and community development seminars around the nation.

Since 1959, Delpit has owned and operated the Chicken Shack, a restaurant started by his father in 1935 with only 34 cents capital. He, along with his wife, has expanded and added five new locations. He is now president of Chicken Shack Systems, Inc., a fast-growing fast food chain. Other business interests include: president of Lettsworth Oilfield Services, Inc., and president of D&W Health Services Inc. He serves as consultant for local, state and federal agencies and also business organizations. He is the first black councilman to serve the city of Baton Rouge. He also served briefly as mayor pro tempore. He was re-elected to a second term on the council with a first primary victory. While on the council, he was elected chairman of the executive committee, and the governor appointed him to the Greater Baton Rouge Port Commission.

In November 1975, he was elected state representative of District 67 in the first primary, and served on the Municipal and Parochial Affairs Committee, Agriculture Committee and Appropriations Committee. In April 1980, Rep. Delpit was sworn in for a second term as the representative from District 67, East Baton Rouge Parish, after a first primary victory in the October 1979 primary election. In 1983, he was unopposed for an unprecedented third term as the state representative for District 67. On March 12, 1984, he was elected speaker pro tempore of the Louisiana House of Representatives, making him the highest-ranking black elected official since Reconstruction and the first black to hold this office. He was re-elected to his fourth term as District 67 representative in 1987. Also,

Rep. Delpit served as Master of Ceremonies at the 1972 and 1984 Inauguration of Governor Edwin W. Edwards. Presently, he serves on the House Education Committee and House Labor and Industrial Relations Committee.

———————

DEMERSON, ELISHA L., born March 11, 1951, is married has three children. Demerson, educated at Palo Duro High School, Amarillo, Texas and West Texas State University, Canyon, Texas, received a B.A. in physics and has 24 credit hours toward a master of engineering technology, at West Texas State University. Demerson was elected county judge, Potter County, Amarillo, in 1987; county commissioner, Potter County, Amarillo, 1979–1986; senior scientist, Pantex Plant, Amarillo, 1975–1976; management trainee program, 1974–1976.

Demerson has been honored by *Who's Who in Law Enforcement,* 1990; Texas Association of Student Special Services Program's Outstanding

Outstanding Achievement Award, 1988, 1989, Austin; Southwest Association of Special Services' Outstanding Achievement Award, 1988, New Orleans; Leadership Amarillo, Class of 1988; Outstanding Young Man of America Award, 1987, 1988; Palo Duro High School "Dons' Hall of Fame," 1987; and Personalities of the South Award, 1979. Demerson is involved in numerous political, civic, social and religious activities.

DEVARD-KEMP, JEAN, was born in Jacksonville, Florida, and received a B.S. degree in elementary education/psychology from Voorhees College, an M.S. in special education/reading from South Carolina State College, an education specialist certificate in special education/reading from the University of Connecticut and a Ph.D. degree in education psychology/child development from the University of Connecticut. DeVard-Kemp was appointed in 1988 to serve as Georgia's first assistant commissioner in the Department of Technical and Adult Education for Adult Literacy Programs. In this position, she manages and oversees all aspects of the adult literacy programs. This program defines the service delivery areas at all levels of adult literacy, develops long- and short-range plans for meeting the literacy needs of Georgia adult population.

DeVard-Kemp brings to this position over 30 years of advance training and experience in promoting the growth and development of children and adults through increasingly responsible positions. Her range of experience began with public school teaching, counseling, management and supervision, college professor, education administration, and program director in the public and private nonprofit sectors at local, state and national levels. She served a Fulbright-Hayes Fellow at Stella Maris College, Madras, India; program development intern at the University of Puerto Rico; and Bureau of Education for the Handicapped and Disadvantaged Fellow at South Carolina State College.

Additional study by DeVard-Kemp was done at the University of Michigan's Research and Development Program, Council for Exceptional Children Leadership on Individualized Educational Program Planning, Albuquerque, New Mexico, and Council for Exceptional Children Training Institute on Career Education, St. Louis, Missouri. She has been an active participant in many community service organizations in Atlanta. She is a member of Alpha Kappa Alpha Sorority, Inc., Phi Delta Kappa Honor Society, Council for Exceptional Children, Association of Children with Learning Disabilities, and served as a Department of Education national grants and proposal reader.

DINKINS, DAVID N., was born in Trenton, New Jersey, and raised in Trenton and New York City. He is married to Joyce Dinkins and is the father of two children, David, Jr., and Donna, and has one grandson, Jamal. He graduated from Brooklyn Law School in 1956, and was engaged in the private practice of law from 1956 to 1975. He received his B.A. degree in mathematics from Howard University in 1950. He is a veteran of the U.S. Marine Corps. On January 1,

1990, he was elected as the 106th mayor of the city of New York, a job often referred to as the second most challenging in the nation. His election in November 1989, marked the first time in New York City's 365-year history that an African American had been chosen to serve as the city's chief executive officer.

As mayor, Dinkins represents a city of more than seven million residents. He manages a budget that for 1990 exceeded $26 billion, one of the largest governmental budgets in the world. He oversees an organization of more than 250,000 employees and is responsible for more than 40 agencies. He appoints the city's members of the Board of Education, the boards of the City University of New York, the Health and Hospital Corporation, the Metropolitan Transportation Authority, and numerous other city agencies, councils and advisory boards.

Prior to his taking office as mayor, Dinkins served a four-year term as the Manhattan Borough president. He used the position to address problems in education, to promote economic development, and to assist homeless people and those with AIDS. He also concentrated attention on the need for pre-natal and early childhood health care, on the rights of people with disabilities, and on the desire for racial and religious tolerance. The *New York Times* said in its editorial endorsement of Dinkins that "his instinct is to unify." The newspaper wrote, "This decency can help the city confront its biggest problems: a sagging economy and tension between the races." The *Daily News* said, "It is in the vital intangibles — personal style, warmth, generosity of spirit, magnetism — that Dinkins stands out. He exhibits a natural, innate sense of fairness and compassion. There is in David Dinkins a deeply rooted civility that is the essence of effective and humane leadership." The *New York Post* agreed, "David Dinkins is a conciliator

and a healer," the editorial said. "The ascendancy of David Dinkins has had a civilizing influence on political discourse in this volatile city." *New York Newsday* offered a similar observation, "David Dinkins is the man for these times . . . His years of experience with urban social issues — from AIDS to housing to education — combined with his sensitivity to the problems of race and class provide him with a consensus-building capability that will stand him in good stead as mayor."

By emphasizing coalition-building, Dinkins has been a voice of clarity and perception in matters of human and civil rights, speaking out forcefully for the rights of Soviet Jews and Black South Africans. His commitment to the struggle against apartheid has placed him at the center of efforts to combat South Africa's intolerable legal structure. He has led the fight for disinvestment by municipal agencies and private companies that conduct business in South Africa. He is also a strong supporter of Israel; he has often declared that any resolution for the Middle East must be acceptable to Israel, and that he believes in Israel's right to live in safety and security.

Before becoming Manhattan Borough president, Dinkins served as a state assemblyman in 1966, where he helped create the Search for Education, Elevation and Knowledge (SEEK) program which provides low-income students with grants and other forms of assistance to increase their ability to succeed in higher education; as president of the Board of Elections from 1972 to 1973, where he established guidelines that encouraged voter registration; and as city clerk of New York from 1975 to 1985.

DIXON, IRMA MUSE, is a graduate of Walter L. Cohen Senior High School in New Orleans, Louisiana. Dixon received a certificate of completion from the University of Houston,

Texas, Hotel Motel training School in 1974, and completed undergraduate studies at Southern University of New Orleans, receiving a B.A. degree in sociology in 1976. She received an M.S.W. from Tulane University School of Social Work in New Orleans in 1979. She attended Harvard University, John F. Kennedy School of Government program for Senior Executives in State and Local Government. In 1986, she attended Tulane University, University College, for real estate appraising.

Dixon has served as state representative for District 95 from 1988 to date. She has been appointed to many committees: Ways and Means; House and Governmental Affairs; Municipal, Parochial and Cultural Affairs, and House Executive Committee. Prior positions include: director of the City of New Orleans Department of Property Management; director of the City of New Orleans Department of Recreation; Private Sector Initiative Title VII Project for the City of New Orleans, Office of Employment Training and Development, bureau chief of Management Services; director of City of Kenner, Louisiana, Department of Development; assistant to coordinator/planner for the City of Kenner, Department of Community Development; director/social worker for TCA Children Development Center, Total Community Action, Inc., New Orleans; and bell captain for the Fairmont Hotel, New Orleans.

Dixon is the recipient of many awards: Alliance for Good Government Legislator of the Year Award; State Treasurer Award in recognition of Outstanding Service to Louisiana Department Treasury; Earhart/Tulane Corridor Association 1989 Leadership Award; National Black Caucus of the State Legislators Presidents Award; Louisiana Association of Educators/National Education Association Legislative Honor Roll Award; Urban League of Greater New Orleans Award of Outstanding Service and Common Cause Award for Distiguished Public Service.

DIXON, JULIAN C., was born in Washington, D.C., is married to the former Betty Lee of Los Angeles, and is the father of one son, Cary Gordon Dixon. He was elected to the U.S. House of Representatives in 1978 and served his six terms in Congress, representing California's 28th Congressional District. The 28th Congressional

District of California encompasses the Los Angeles areas of Crenshaw, Ladera Heights, Westchester, and Pico Union. It also included Culver City, Marina del Rey, Playa del Rey, and parts of Inglewood. Dixon served on the powerful House Appropriations Committee which recommended funding for all federal programs. He was chairman of the Appropriations Subcommittee on the District of Columbia, and was a member of the Subcommittee on Defense, which helped set national defense priorities, and military construction. He was California's only member of the Defense Subcommittee.

Since 1985, he has served as chairman of the House Committee on Standards of Official Conduct, known as the Ethics Committee. This panel enforced the House of Representatives Code of Conduct and the Ethics in Government Act of 1978 by investigating alleged misconduct by members of Congress. It also advised members and their staffs on the appropriateness of their professional conduct. He served on the Appropriations Subcommittee on Foreign Operations. In 1983, he wrote the first economic sanctions law against South Africa, and in 1987 he authored an urgent appropriations bill to provide humanitarian aid to South Africa, the world's poorest region. He has also been instrumental in gaining increased development assistance for Africa, disaster assistance for Jamaica, and scholarships for disadvantaged South African students.

Dixon has worked hard to maintain our nation's commitment to civil rights for all Americans. He led the fight to preserve the independence of the U.S. Civil Rights Commission after attempts were made in the 1980s to undermine it. He was a co-sponsor of every major civil rights initiative in recent years. Since 1983, Mr. Dixon has been instrumental in securing federal funds for construction of the Los Angeles Metro rail project, the subway designed to address traffic and pollution problems of Los Angeles County. He has also helped win federal funds for noise abatement in Inglewood.

Dixon has been recognized for his leadership on issues related to mass transit, low- and moderate-income housing, education, and health care for senior citizens. In 1985, Politics in America named him one of the twelve Unsung Heroes in Congress in acknowledgment of his ability to garner support for his legislative agenda. His voting record has received 100 percent ratings from senior citizen, educational, civil rights, labor and environmental organizations. His effectiveness as a legislator and commitment to justice has earned him honors and awards from numerous civic groups. Dixon serves as president of the Congressional Black Caucus Foundation, a non-profit institution engaged in public policy analysis which encourages minority participation in the legislative process. During the 98th Congress, he served as chairman of the Congressional Black Caucus, and in 1984 he served as chairman of the Standing Committee on Rules for the Democratic National Convention. Before entering Congress, he served six years in the California state assembly, and was chairman of the Assembly Democratic Caucus.

DIXON, SHARON PRATT, was born January 30, 1944, in Washington, D.C. She is divorced and the mother of two daughters, Aimee and Drew. She attended District of Columbia public schools and graduated with honors from Roosevelt High School in 1961. She furthered her education at Howard University, earning a B.A. with honors in political science in 1965, then a J.D. from the university's law school in 1968. She then used her new legal talents advocating the rights of children and their families. She sacrificed the early part of her career to assist her ex-husband, Arrington L. Dixon, through Washington politics to a failed run for the school board and a successful term on the city council.

In 1972, as an instructor at the Antioch School of Law, she inspired in students the value of public service. Her growing reputation as an advocate for D.C. residents prompted former House Speaker Thomas (Tip) O'Neill to appoint her vice chairperson of the D.C. Law Revision Commission. In her new position, she helped transfer the District's Criminal Code authority from Congress to the D.C. Council.

In the mid-70s, Dixon joined the General Counsel's Office of the Potomac Electric Power Company (Pepco) and, in 1983, became the first African American woman ever to become vice president of the company. As vice president of consumer affairs and, then, public policy, she launched a series of unprecedented services, both financial and operational, that eased the burdens for low- and fixed-income residents. She also decentralized Pepco and brought jobs to the community by providing satellite branches of Pepco throughout city neighborhoods. A widely respected leader in the Democratic Party, she was the first African American and first woman to become treasurer of the Democratic National Committee. She served four consecutive terms on the committee and held a seat on its executive committee.

In 1990, Dixon joined the relatively short list of women who head state or local governments, the first black woman to have been elected to run such a large city, when she defied great odds on November 6, 1990, to become the first female leader of the nation's capital and first native to serve as mayor of Washington, D.C. Her unprecedented mayoral victory followed more than 20 years of community involvement and activism in local and national politics. Proclaiming "Yes, We Will," she promised District residents an "honest deal" and vowed to restore the city to greatness and improve the quality of life for all.

Upon taking office, Dixon immediately sought economic recovery for the financially burdened District. She called for agencies to reduce spending and redirect resources to the improvement of city services. She challenged and won from the private sector — the city's largest employer — a pledge to get involved. Her message,

considered wise and prudent by the U.S. Congress, led to Mayor Dixon again defying great odds and winning $100 million in Congressional emergency-funding support for fiscal year 1991. She is the daughter of a retired Superior Court judge, a member of the Legal Aid Society, Howard University's Board of Trustees, the D.C. Chapter of the NAACP, and the United Negro College Fund.

DORSETT, KATTIE GRAYS, was born July 8, 1932, in Shaw, Mississippi. She is married to Warren G. Dorsett and the mother of one child, Valerie. She is a graduate of Alcorn State University in Mississippi where she received a B.A. degree and continued her education at Indiana University, Bloomington, where she received an M.S. degree in business. She then relocated to Greensboro to accept a professorship at North Carolina A&T State University in the School of Business and Economics. She later attained an Ed.D. degree from the University of North Carolina, Greensboro, in curriculum and instruction. In 1987, she retired from North Carolina A&T after 32 years of service. Dorsett has committed herself to the economic and overall enhancement of the Guilford County area through her professional teaching career and strong community involvement.

With a teaching background in business management, she recognized the need for minority economic development and representation within Guilford County. She has served on the Guilford County Board of County Commissioners, 1986 to date, and councilwoman for the city of Greensboro, 1983–1986. During her first term as county commissioner, she spearheaded such projects as the Minority and Women Business Enterprise Program; the expansion of the Parks and Recreation Commission to broaden minority representation; and the implementation of policies allowing greater diversity on county boards and commissions. She was the first African American woman elected to the council.

Dorsett received numerous honors which include: the Sojourner Truth Award for community service, presented by the National Association of Negro Business and Professional Women in 1986, Outstanding Alumna Award–National Association for Equal Opportunity in Higher Education in 1987, Bennett College Community Leadership Recognition in 1988, and Woman of the Year, from the Greensboro Branch NAACP in 1989. Her former associations include membership on the Mayor's Task Force on Substance Abuse, the Governor's Council on Sickle Cell Syndrome, the United Ways of North Carolina and of Greater Greensboro and the Governor's North Carolina Assembly on Women in the Economy.

DORSEY, IVORY. She is the president/owner of Golden Eagle Business Services, Inc., an Atlanta-based

training and consulting firm. The firm specializes in the areas of sales, management, customer service and motivational training programs. It is most noted for the customized approach to training and the authenticity of the approach to sensitive areas such as team-building and awareness training. When offering training sessions to clients, the response has been tremendous and clients describe Dorsey as not only a practitioner but a role model as well. Her background includes 10 years with Xerox Corporation in Houston and Dallas, Texas, as well as Atlanta. This high performance career includes customer education, field sales, field sales management, and retail store general management. Dorsey has won numerous awards in sales and management with Xerox where she was a consistent overachiever.

Prior to Xerox Corporation, Dorsey was a business education teacher in Milwaukee, Wisconsin, a private secretary for Ethyl Corporation in Houston, and simultaneously a part-time instructor for the Houston Community College system. Since moving to Atlanta in 1979, she has served as a part-time instructor for Georgia State University. After a powerful history of work experience, in 1984 she launched Golden Eagle Business Services, Inc., a natural evolution. In this capacity she serves a diverse clientele including Fortune 500 companies, progressive medium and small companies, government entities and various businesses and organizations, gaining rave reviews for effectiveness.

Dorsey can be found on the public speaking circuit frequently and is often described as the "highlight" of business affairs because of her experience and down-to-earth style combined with her versatility as she identifies with both the corporate as well as the business community. An active leader in numerous professional organizations, she served as an appointed vice chairwoman in the governor's Small and

Minority Business Advisory Committee, recruiting chairwoman for Sales and Marketing executives of Atlanta, co-chair for membership for Women Business Owners, co-chair for Tradeshow '89 for the Atlanta Chamber of Commerce, and an active member of the National/Georgia Speakers Association and other professional and business associations.

Dorsey was voted the grand winner in the consultant's category by corporate buyer of the Georgia Minority Supplier Developpment Council, 1989. She is recognized as one of the top 10 women of achievement in Cobb County, Georgia, by the Cobb County YWCA Tribute to Women in Business and Industry 1989. In 1990, she became a graduate of Leadership Atlanta, and in 1991, served as president-elect of the Atlanta Chapter American Society for Training and Development (ASTD) and was active in other professional and business associations. Her personal philosophy is drawn from her business philosophy and is stated simply: "People function with either an 'Eagle' mentality or a 'Buzzard' mentality—the difference is waiting or working."

DUCKETT, KAREN, I., resides in Atlanta, Georgia with husband Wardell Duckett and children Chioke, Shani and Makiri. She is a graduate of Woodrow Wilson College of Law, J.D.; Occidental College/Yale University, M.A. degree in urban studies, 1981; and Ohio University, Athens, Ohio, B.A. degree in fine arts, School of Architecture, 1969. She is president of Duckett and Associates, Inc. with 22 years of design and facility planning experience, developing projects for both public and private sectors.

Duckett's career has provided her the opportunity to work with such ergonomic pioneers as Quikbourner, Herman Miller, and Lawrence Halprin and Associates, Inc. Her planning and design experience from concept to move-in has included multimillion dollar office projects, medical facilities from hospitals to clinics, and the planning and design of a law enforcement and judicial facilities. As president of Duckett and Associates, she is responsible for the management and contracting activities of the firm. She is also directly involved in the development of facility programming, site planning, space planning, and design concept development in a majority of the firm's projects. Further, she reviews the firm's projects for interior compliance with handicapped and life safety codes.

Prior to establishing the firm in 1985, Duckett operated as an independent consultant for eight years in the areas of project management, facility programming and interior design. During this period she designed over 750,000 sq. ft. of office space for such clients as the Coca-Cola USA Headquarters building, and Employees Center Southwest Hospital Professional office building along with 150,000 sq. ft. of offices for various institutional clients (city of Atlanta

Public Schools, Atlanta University, etc.).

As an administrator in the Department of Community and Human Development for the city of Atlanta, Duckett managed and directed a number of major multi-use projects for the city. Part of her responsibilities included administering a $47 million capital improvements/redevelopment program budget. Her public administration experience provides the firm with exceptional understanding of the issues confronting public sector and institutional design stations. She has served as corporate space planner and director of the Rochester Design Office for Xerox Corporation. She directed space plans and designs for over 100 projects, working with budgets ranging from $30,000 to $7 million. She established the Corporate Standards Program and developed the first facility space/workstation analysis in conjunction with Herman Miller.

DYMALLY, MERVYN M., was born May 12, 1926, in Cedros, Trinidad. He is the son of Hamid Dymally and Andreid Richardson. He married the former Alice M. Gueno, and they have two children, Mark and Lynn. He received a B.A. degree from California State University, Los Angeles, a master's in government from California State University, Sacramento, and a Ph.D. in human behavior from the United States International University, San Diego. From 1955 to 1961, he taught mentally retarded children in Los Angeles city schools. From 1961 to 1962, he was a coordinator in the California Disaster Office. In 1962, he was elected to the California Assembly.

Dymally served in the assembly until 1967, when he was elected to the California Senate. He was the first black ever elected to the California senate. He remained until 1975, when he was elected lieutenant governor of California. Dymally was the first black man to serve as lieutenant governor of California. He served four years as lieutenant governor, then in 1979, he became president of Mervyn M. Dymally Company, Inc. In 1980, he was elected to the United States House of Representatives. He has received numerous honorary degrees, awards and citations. He is a member of numerous civic and political organizations which include: the NAACP, the Urban League, and the Congressional Black Caucus.

EARLY, NORMAN S., JR., was born November 14, 1945, in Washington, D.C. He married Adriana Scott Early and is the father of one son, Norman Ali. He received his primary and secondary education from the District's public school system, and a B.A. degree in government from the American University in Washington, where he was elected student body president and was the recipient of the Stafford H. Cassell award as outstanding senior. He earned his law degree from the University of Illinois College of Law, at Champaign-Urbana where he was also recognized as Outstanding Graduating Senior. On January 31, 1983, Early was appointed Denver district attorney by Governor Richard D. Lamm.

In November 1984, he was elected to a full four-year term and re-elected in November 1988. Prior to his appointment, he served for 10 years as chief deputy district attorney to District Attorney Dale Tooley. As chief deputy, he had supervisory responsibility over a felony courtroom and personally tried 12 to 15 cases a year ranging from fraud to murder. In addition, he was the developer of the District Attorney's Victim/Witness Assistance Project, the Drug Education Program, It's Just Not Worth It (Drinking and Driving) Program, and others.

Early received awards including: the National Black Prosecutors Distinguished Service Award (1986), the United States Department of Justice Award for Outstanding Service on Behalf of Victims of Crime (1987), National Organization of Black Law Enforcement Executives' Award of Appreciation (1987), the Distinguished Faculty Award of the National College of District Attorneys (1980), Kops 'n Kids Leadership Award (1988), Award for Outstanding Leadership as a Division Chair in the United Way Campaign (1986), the Kempe Center Award for his work in the field of child abuse (1988), the 1988 Lubavitch Shem Tov Award, the 1988 Award of Appreciation from King Baptist Church for his work with Colorado's youth, and the American Legion Certificate of Appreciation (1989). These are just some of the awards presented to Early for his contributions to the community and the criminal justice system.

Early was the founder and first president of the National Black Prosecutors Association. He is the current president of the Colorado District Attorney's Council. He served as president of the board of the National organization for Victim Assistance and as a member of the board of the National District Attorney's Association. He was a founding member of the Sam Cary Bar Association. He also sat on the board of directors of the Model Constitutional Convention, Freedom's Foundation at Valley Forge, I Have a Dream Foundation, Salvation Army-Capital Campaign, Crimestoppers, Channel Six, Family Focus, Justice Assistance Act (Division of the Department of Criminal Justice), Arthritis Foundation, and Sportswomen of Colorado, to mention a few. He is a member of Slippers and Sliders Ski Club, Colorado Unity, Colorado Black Elected Officials, Denver Partners, Inc., NAACP, and Colorado Black Women for Political Action.

EBBESEN, SAMUEL EMANUEL, was born on September 15, 1938, in Saint Croix, Virgin Islands. He received a B.S. degree in political science from the City College of New York, and a master's in public administration from

Auburn University. He enlisted in the Army in September 1961 and was assigned as a platoon leader in Company D, 1st Training Regiment, Fort Dix, New Jersey. He went on to serve the Army in numerous assignments which include: March 1963, commander of Company F, 1st Training Regiment, Fort Dix; July 1965, commander of Headquarters Company, 1st Battalion, 15th Infantry, 3rd Infantry Division, United States Army in Europe; in 1969, the headquarters commandant of the 4th Infantry Division, United States Army in Vietnam. In August 1971, he was a student at the Command and General Staff College, Fort Leavenworth, Kansas.

In July 1977, Ebbesen was assigned as the commander of the 2d Battalion of the 32d Infantry, 7th Infantry Division, Fort Ord, California; in May 1983, he served as commander of the 1st Brigade of the 101st Airborne Division (Air Assault), Fort Campbell, Kentucky; by April 1990, he had been promoted to the rank of major general

and assigned as the commanding general of the 6th Infantry Division (Light), Fort Wainwright, Alaska. He has received numerous medals and badges which include: the Legion of Merit (with 3 oak leaf clusters); the Bronze Star medal with "V" device; the Air Medal; Combat Infantryman Badge; Parachutist Badge; and the Air Assault Badge.

EDELMAN, MARIAN WRIGHT, was born June 6, 1939, in Bennettsville, South Carolina. She is married to Peter Benjamin Edelman and is the mother of three sons, Joshua, Jonah and Ezra. She is a graduate of Spelman College, Atlanta, Georgia, where she received a B.A. degree (junior year University of Geneva, Switzerland), 1960; LL.B. from Yale Law School, 1963. Since June 1973, she has served as president of the Children's Defense Fund.

Prior positions include: 1971–1973, director, Center for Law and Education, Harvard University; 1968–1973, field foundation fellow and partner, Washington Research Project of the Southern Center for Public Policy (a public interest law firm and the parent body of the Children's Defense Fund); summer 1968, Congressional and Federal Agency Liaison, Poor People's Campaign; 1964–1968, director of NAACP Legal Defense and Educational Fund, Inc., Jackson, Mississippi; and 1963–1964, staff attorney, NAACP Legal Defense and Educational Fund, Inc., New York. She has traveled extensively and written for numerous publications. She was the principal author for: *Children Out of School in America* (1974); *School Suspensions: Are They Helping Children?* (1975); *Portrait of Inequality: Black and White Children in America* (1980); *Families in Peril: An Agenda for Social Change*, Harvard University Press (1987), and over 11 published articles and papers. She is the recipient of over 45 honorary degrees.

Her many awards include: Merrill Scholarship for a year's study at the Universities of Paris and Geneva, Switzerland; *Who's Who in American Colleges and Universities*; valedictorian, college graduating class; John Hay Whitney Fellowship, Yale Law School; *Mademoiselle* magazine award as one of the four most exciting young women in America; Outstanding Young Women of America; honorary fellow, University of Pennsylvania Law School; Louise Waterman Wise Award; *Time* magazine list of 200 Young American Leaders; Presidential Citation, American Public Health Association; Outstanding Leadership Award of National Alliance of Black School Educators; Distinguished Service Award of National Association of Black Women Attorneys; National Award of Merit of National Council on Crime and Delinquency; Washingtonian of the Year; Whitney M. Young Memorial Award (Washington Urban League); *Black Enterprise* magazine Professional Achievement Award.

Additionally, she was awarded the National Women's Political Caucus/Black Caucus Outstanding Leadership Achievement Award; National Hookup of Black Women's Outstanding Community Service Award; Big Sisters' Woman of the Year Award; American Academy of Pedodontics, Award of Recognition; honorary membership, Delta Sigma Theta Sorority; Rockefeller Public Service Award; Gertrude Zimand Award (National Child Labor Committee); Florina Lasker Award (New York Civil Liberties Union); Anne Roe Award (Harvard University Graduate School of Education); Roy Wilkins Civil Rights Award (NAACP Image awards); Women's Legal Defense Fund Award; Hubert H. Humphrey Award (Leadership Conference on Civil Rights); MacArthur Foundation Prize Fellow; Grenville Clark Prize, Dartmouth College; Compostela Award (the Cathedral of St. James); A. Philip Randolph Award (the National Urban Coalition); the William P. Dawson Award (the Congressional Black Caucus); the Trumpeter Award (National Consumer League); Colleague, St. John the Divine; Catherine Dunfey Award: New England Circle; honorary membership, American Society of Dentistry for Children; Albert Schweitzer Humanitarian Prize, Johns Hopkins University; Radcliffe Medal; the AFL-CIO Award; honorable membership, Phi Beta Kappa Honor Society (University of South Carolina Law Center); and the Fordham Stein Prize.

Edelman's professional organizational affiliations include member of: District of Columbia Bar, State of Mississippi Bar, and Commonwealth of Massachusetts Bar. Board memberships include: Spelman College Board of Trustees, Yale University Corporation (1971–1977), Carnegie Council on Children (1972–1977), Aetna Life and Casualty Foundation, Center on Budget and Policy Priorities, Citizens for Constitutional Concerns (People for the American Way), Council on Foreign Relations, Joint Center for Political and Economic Studies, March of Dimes, NAACP Legal Defense and Educational Fund, Inc., U.S. Committee for UNICEF, Robin Hood Foundation, and the Aaron Diamond Foundation.

EDMONDS, ALBERT J., was born January 17, 1942, in Columbus, Georgia. He married the former Jacquelyn Y. McDaniel of Biloxi, Mississippi. They have three daughters, Gia, Sheri and Alicia. He graduated from Spencer High School in Columbus, in 1960; received a B.S. degree in chemistry from Morris Brown College, in Atlanta, in 1964; and received an M.A. degree in counseling psychology from Hampton Institute in 1969. He graduated from the Air War College as a distinguished graduate in 1980 and completed the National Security program for senior officials at Harvard University in 1987. He entered the Air Force in August 1964 and was commissioned upon graduation from Officer Training School at Lackland Air Force Base, Texas, in November 1964.

After completing the basic communications-electronics course at Keesler Air Force Base, Mississippi, in February 1966, he was assigned as a data systems officer to the Tactical Communications Area at Langley Air Force Base in Virginia. In February 1969, he was assigned to Pacific Communications Area, Hickam Air Force Base, Hawaii. While there he served successively as an inspection team chief in the Office of the Inspector General; contributing editor on Project Corona Harvest; and director of emergency mission support. He later served as chief of operations for the 2083rd Communications Squadron (Provisional) at Takhli Royal Thai Air Force base, Thailand. He was assigned to Air Force Headquarters, in May 1973, as an action

officer in the Directorate of Command, Control and Communications where he was responsible for managing air communications programs in the Continental United States, Alaska, Canada, South America, Greenland and Iceland.

In June 1975, Edmonds was assigned to the Defense Communications Agency and headed the Commercial Communications Policy office. In this capacity he was responsible for establishing Department of Defense policies for the acquisition of long-line communications and overseeing the procurement activities of the office. He was assigned to Anderson Air Force Base in Guam, in 1977, as director of communications-electronics for Strategic Air Command's 3rd Air Division and as commander of the 27th Communications Squadron. After completing Air War College in June 1980, he returned to Air Force Headquarters as chief of the Joint Matters Group, Directorate of Command, Control and Telecommunications, Office of the Deputy Chief of Staff, Plans and Operations.

From June 1, 1983 to June 14, 1983, he served as director of plans and programs for the Assistant Chief of Staff for Information Systems. He was assigned to Headquarters Tactical Air Command, Langley Air Force Base, as assistant deputy chief of staff for communications and electronics, and vice commander, Tactical Communications Division. In January 1985, he became deputy chief of staff for communications-computer systems, Tactical Air Command, Headquarters; and commander, Tactical Communications Division, Air Force Communications Command, Langley. In July 1988, he became director of command and control, Communications and Computer Systems Directorate, United States Center Command, MacDill Air Force Base, Florida.

Edmonds was promoted to the rank of brigadier general July 1, 1988.

In May 1989, he assumed the command responsibility for United States Military and Security interests in a 19-country area in the Persian Gulf, Horn of Africa and Southwest Asia. His military decorations and awards include: the Defense Distinguished Service Medal; Legion of Merit; Meritorious Service Medal with two oak clusters; and the Air Force Commendation Medal with three oak leaf clusters.

EDMONDS, NORMAN DOUGLAS, was born September 16, 1938, in Suffield, Connecticut. He is the father of three children, Jeremy, Suzanne, and Andrea. He received a B.S. degree from the University of Connecticut in 1960. From 1961 to 1969, he worked for the Travelers Insurance Co. In 1967, Edmonds became the first black corporate officer with Travelers, in corporate management services and planning and then as director of marketing for life, health and financial services activities. In 1977, he became the first black chief elected official in the state of Connecticut, when he was elected chief of the Board of Selectmen of the town of Tolland.

Edmonds also serves as a member of the board of directors of the University of Connecticut Alumni Association. Since 1979, he has served as assistant vice president and later second vice president of the Phoenix Mutual Life Insurance Company. He has received numerous awards and achievements which include: a member of the New England Championship Soccer Team in 1959, and the All New England Soccer Team, 1959–1960, and the distinguished service award of Greater Hartford Jaycees.

EDWARDS, AL, is a native Houstonian, married to Lana and the father of three children, Albert, II, Jason and Alana. He received his B.S. from Texas Southern University; certified in cor-

rective therapy, Tuskegee Institute; graduate work at the University of Houston; and student of Houston Bible Institute, 1988. He was elected to the House of Representatives in 1978, served on Intergovernmental Affairs and Human Services committees and on the Interim Select Committee on State Employee Productivity; elected to 67th Texas Legislature, House of Representatives, and served on Intergovernmental Affairs and Transportation committees and chaired the Interim Joint Committee to Study Rail Passenger Service in Texas. Elected to the 68th Texas Legislature, House of Representatives, currently serving on Urban Affairs Committee; vice chair of the Transportation Committee and was re-elected to sixth term in 1988.

Edwards was responsible for the passage of H.B. 1016 which made Emancipation Day, Juneteenth, June 19th, an official state holiday commemorating the day the slaves in Texas actually were freed. He is Texas' leading advocate of improved passenger train service and introduced a number of bills and resolutions to that end. Some of his interests are: trans-

transportation, energy, senior citizen issues, health services, business and finance, educational and employment issues. He carried a bill to restore prayer in the schools.

Edwards has been involved as Texas chairman of Jesse Jackson campaigns, 1984 and 1988; Texas co-chairman of the National Democratic Convention; Texas chairman of the Rainbow Coalition; elected member of the National Democratic Committee; vice president of PUSH International Trade Bureau; founder of Juneteenth, U.S.A.; founder and president of the Turkey Day Classic; founder and president of Operation Justus; chairman of the Texas delegation for Jesse Jackson to the National Convention in Atlanta, and a strong advocate and supporter of Lynell Mattox.

EDWARDS, LINDA A., is a 1979 graduate of Susquehanna University in Selinsgrove, Pennsylvania, with a B.A.

degree in English. Edwards was a working journalist from 1979 to 1984, first at WJLA-TV in Washington, D.C., as a writer and associate producer of the 5:30 p.m. newscast, then as a writer at WTOP-AM, Washington, for the morning drive newscasts. Formerly manager of broadcast news services for the Chemical Manufacturers Association, she is the new executive director of the National Association of Black Journalists. She assumed her new post on September 10, 1990, succeeding Carl E. Morris, Sr., NABJ's executive director since April 1987.

Edwards joined the Washington, D.C.-based Chemical Manufacturers Association in 1984 to write and produce the group's syndicated radio series, "The Report." During her tenure, the broadcast grew from a monthly to a daily show and the number of radio stations using the show increased from 800 to 3,000. She was promoted to manager of the association's broadcast news services in 1987, overseeing both radio and television production for the association. Her duties also included conducting media training for staff and member company representatives, testimony and speech training, and serving as the CMA representative on several industry coalitions.

Edwards has written free-lance pieces for the *Washington Post* and the *Washington Informer*, and wrote a monthly social and food column for the now-defunct, Baltimore-based magazine *Metropolitan*. A member of NABJ and its Washington, D.C. affiliate chapter for nearly a decade, she also is a member of the Radio-Television News Directors Association and Women in Communications, Inc. Thomas Morgan, III, NABJ president, said: "Linda Edwards comes to NABJ as we prepare to enter our next stage of development. The NABJ board of directors is excited about Ms. Edwards' long time commitment to goals of the organization and the enthusiasm she shows for the challenges ahead. We believe that her professional management skills, new ideas and energy will serve the organization well in the years ahead."

ELLER, CARL, a native of Winston-Salem, North Carolina, has made his home in Minneapolis, Minnesota, with his wife, Mahogany, and their three children, Regis, Holiday and Cinder. Mahogany Eller is president of a national speakers bureau, Positively Speaking, representing many celebrities and professional athletes on the lecture circuit. Carl Eller was a two-way starter playing both offense and defense and twice won All-American honors at the University of Minnesota. He was drafted by the Minnesota Vikings on the first round in 1964. A familiar name in American sports history, his illustrious 15-year career with the Minnesota Vikings' famed "Purple People Eaters" includes Rookie of the Year, the League's Most Valuable Lineman twice, All-Pro five times, All-NFC five times, six Pro Bowls, nine Conference Championships, four Super Bowls, and two NFL Hall of Fame nominations. He is the Vikings' record holder with 134 career sacks, 23 opponent fumble recoveries and nine blocked kicks, as well as 766 solo tackles and 202 assists for 968 total tackles.

In 1985, he was named to the Vikings' Silver Anniversary All-Time Team. In 1989, he was named to the Minnesota Sports Hall of Fame. Today Eller is a certified chemical dependency counselor and executive director of Triumph Life Center, a drug and alcohol treatment facility in Minneapolis and St. Paul. As a consultant to the National Football League on matters of drug and alcohol abuse, he helped start the Chemical Dependency Awareness and Training Program for the NFL and 28 member teams.

Eller has also worked with professional hockey, basketball and baseball teams. He is the executive director for the United States Athletes Association (USAA), a national network of students organized to promote positive, chemical-free lifestyles. He has traveled with former First Lady Nancy Reagan assisting with her drug abuse program and has testified before special committees of the United States Senate and the United States House of Representatives. He has appeared frequently on national television and radio. Eller is also a contributing editor for *Alcoholism and Addiction* magazine. He maintains an active schedule on the lecture circuit speaking to Fortune 500 companies, the Million Dollar Round Table, sports organizations, colleges and universities, professional and community groups across the United States and abroad.

ELLISON, CARL, was born March 20, 1951. He is a graduate of Central High School, South Bend, Indiana, 1969, and received his B.A. degree in English and black studies from the University of Notre Dame, 1973. Ellison has served as assistant vice president of Memorial Hospital in South Bend from 1987 to date. He is responsible for the Community Affairs Office, where he functions as the primary administration liaison with the Memorial Hospital Auxiliary.

Ellison's prior positions include: interim president and chief executive officer, Urban League of South Bend and St. Joseph County; assistant vice president for Memorial Hospital and Memorial Health System, Inc.; planning director, Memorial Hospital; deputy associate administrator for minority small business for the U.S. Small Business Administration, Washington, D.C.; executive director, Department of Redevelopment, South Bend; executive director, Community Development Program; executive director, ACTION, Inc.; deputy director, Community Development Program; administrative assistant to the director of Human Resources Economic Development, and housing coordinator, Model Cities Program, South Bend. His professional, community and civic affiliations are many.

ENGLISH, CLARENCE R., was born in the Hickory Hill Community of Morrilton, Arkansas, and is a lifelong resident of Menifee, Conway County, Arkansas. He studied auto mechanics at the 3M Company for 25 years, operating a bus line at one time. He is married to Alpha Taley English, a Spelman graduate. Seven children were born to this union, only five of whom survived; all received college training.

English was elected mayor of Menifee in 1979 and re-elected in 1983. Since becoming mayor, he has obtained a grant for improvement of Menifee City Park, purchased land and built a fairly well-equipped City Hall with a full-time clerk, built a Senior Citizen Center with much effort on the part of citizens and supporters, and constructed natural gas lines for patrons who formerly used butane. In 1985, he also secured a water grant and loan for $591,000; work is now in progress. At present, besides mayoral duties, English serves as Bible School teacher, a member of the executive committee of the Arkansas Municipal League, a member of the NAACP, and an active member of the Black Mayors Conference of Arkansas. He was re-elected in 1987.

ERVING, JULIUS WINFIELD, II (DR.), was born on February 22, 1950, in Roosevelt, New York. He and his wife Turquoise have four children, Cheo, Jay, Jazmin and Cory. He graduated from Roosevelt High School in New York and studied at the University of Massachusetts until the spring of 1971, his junior year.

Erving, his younger brother Marvin, and older sister Alexis, were abandoned by their father in 1955, leaving their mother Callie Mae Erving (since remarried, now Callie M. Lindsey) to raise her children alone living in low-income housing and working as a domestic servant. Despite his hardships, Erving emerged as a basketball player of rare ability and assurance. In his junior year at the University of Massachusetts (where he earned the nickname of "Dr. J"), he averaged 26.9 points and 19.5 rebounds per game. In 1971, he left school to play in the old American Basketball Association.

At first, there was talk he might turn pro and play for the ABA team on Long Island, the New York Nets, but the Nets didn't offer Erving a contract; he turned pro anyway, signing with the Virginia Squires. He played for the Virginia Squires for the next two years, becoming the star of that team. He only appeared on national television twice during this time, thereby not getting the public recognition deserved. After two years with Virginia, he was traded to the New York Nets. He led the Nets to two ABA titles in both 1974 and 1976. He was the ABA MVP in the years 1974 and 1976 and the co–MVP in 1975.

Erving was traded from the Nets to the Philadelphia 76ers in 1976. At that time the ABA and the National Basketball Association had just merged, and Erving was the star of the Nets, the defending ABA champs. He played in the 1977 All-Star game and was named the game's MVP. In 1979, he appeared in a film "The Fish That Saved Pittsburgh." In 1981, he became the first "small man" since Oscar Robertson to be named the NBA's MVP. On May 31, 1983, in the Forum in Inglewood, California, Erving and the 76ers won the NBA's World Championship and he received his first Championship Ring.

In 1984, "Dr. J" won the NBA's first Gatorade Slam-Dunk Championship. He played in 16 consecutive All-Star games and by 1988, had become the third-leading scorer in pro-basketball history. In 1985, Erving and Bruce Llevellyn acquired the Philadelphia Coca-Bottling Company. They made it not only one of the largest Coca-Cola bottling operations, but also one of the country's largest black-owned firms. He is president of the Erving Group, Inc., and co-owner of WKBW television station in Buffalo, New York. He is noted nationally for his volunteer and community service work, particularly with inner city youths. In December of 1990, Erving turned businessman and was named to the Clark Atlanta University Board of Trustees.

ESCOTT-RUSSELL SUNDRA E., was born February 21, 1954, in Birmingham, Alabama, the seventh of 13 children to the Rev. and Mrs. Wedzell Escott, Sr. She is married to David Russell. She is an honor graduate from Alabama State University, with a B.S. degree in business education/mass communication, secondary education certificate, 1977; honorary doctorate of law degree from Faith College, Birmingham, 1984; and M.B.A. from Troy State University, 1986. Her career includes a position with the governor of the state of Alabama as an administrative assistant, 1976–1980; self-employed Fashion Boutique, 1976–1980; owner of Financial Association, Inc., since 1979; A.L. Williams Marketing Firm, service president, since 1980; and Alabama state representative to date.

Escott was the recipient of many honors and achievements including Board of Trustees Israel Methodist Church 1980, Who's Who Outstanding Women of Alabama 1980, 1982, 1983, and 1984, President's Council A.L. Williams Marketing Firm 1984 and 1985. Her affiliations include memberships with: Alabama legislative black caucus, Alabama House of Representatives, National Order of Women Legislators, Metropolitan Democratic Women Organization; Delta Sigma Theta National Service Sorority; president and founder of Financial Associates — an insurance and real estate investment firm; twice selected as one of the ten most outstanding young women of America and Alabama; National Sales Director, A.L. Williams Marketing Firm; member of New Israel Historical Church.

FARRAKHAN, LOUIS, was born May 11, 1933, in New York City as Louis Eugene Walcott. His mother was from the Bahamas, and his father, who died when Louis was three, was born in Jamaica. Farrakhan was brought up in St. Cyprian's Episcopal Church on Tremont Street in Boston and became a scholar, athlete and accomplished musician. In the late 1940s he was one of the first blacks to appear on Ted Mack's television show, "The Original Amateur Hour." He graduated with honors from Boston English High School. He was in the school orchestra and a member of the 1950 state championship track team. After graduation he enrolled in predominantly black Winston–Salem State Teacher's College in North Carolina. When his wife and childhood sweetheart, Betsy, became pregnant with the first of their nine children at the end of his junior year, he dropped out of college and embarked on a career in Boston as a professional entertainer.

It was while entertaining as Calypso Gene and the Charmer in 1952 that he first met Malcolm X. Three years later, while performing in Chicago, he was invited to the Nation of Islam's Savior Day service, which featured a speech by the Honorable Elijah Muhammad. He joined the Nation of Islam on the spot. Back in Boston, Farrakhan advanced quickly: he was appointed captain of the Roxbury temple's Fruit of Islam paramilitary security force, and by 1956, just one year after joining the organization then known as the Black Muslims, he became minister of the mosque, a position he held until 1965. He wrote the Nation of Islam's first song, "A White Man's Heaven Is a Black Man's Hell," as well as its first play, Orgena ("A Negro" spelled backward).

When Malcolm X was assassinated on February 21, 1965 (after repudiating the black supremist teachings of Elijah Muhammad), Minister Louis X, as Farrakhan was called,

replaced him as head of the high-profile Harlem mosque. When Elijah Muhammad died in 1975 without a will, leaving some of his 21 children and his followers squabbling for more than a decade over an estate valued at up to $20 million, many expected the charismatic Farrakhan to succeed him. But the Nation of Islam hierarchy passed over Farrakhan, selecting one of Elijah's sons, Warith Deen Muhammad. Warith, or W. Deen as he was sometimes called, repudiated his father's black supremacy teachings, relaxed or abolished many of the strict dress codes, moved the organization toward orthodoxy and declared that contrary to his father's teachings, W. D. Fard, the person who helped Elijah start the Nation of Islam, was not God reincarnated.

Farrakhan worked with Warith for two years, spent almost a year outside of the organization and, in 1978, resurfaced to form a splinter group that revived Elijah Muhammad's original teachings and the organization's old name, the Nation of Islam. Warith's group, known as the American Muslim Mission, disbanded in 1985.

FAUNTROY, WALTER E., a native of Washington, D.C., Congressman Fauntroy was educated at Dunbar High School, Virginia Union University where he graduated cum laude in 1955, and at Yale University Divinity School where he earned his B.D. degree in 1958. He began his public career in 1959 as pastor of the church of his childhood—New Bethel Baptist Church—where he continues to serve as pastor. Fauntroy is married to the former Dorothy Simms of Petersburg, Virginia. They have one son, Marvin Keith, born April 3, 1964. Fauntroy, the first person to represent the District of Columbia in the U.S. House of Representatives in 100 years, was elected delegate to the House in 1971. He brought to his seat in the Congress a rich background as a civil rights activist and Christian minister.

Dr. Martin Luther King, Jr., appointed him director of the Washington Bureau of the Southern Christian Leadership Conference where he performed many valuable services for the movement in the 1960s. He was D.C. coordinator for the historic March on Washington for Jobs and Freedom in 1963. He was also coordinator of the Selma-to-Montgomery March in 1965, vice chairman of the White House Conference "To Fulfill These Rights" in 1966, and leader of a historic urban renewal project which is revitalizing housing, businesses and public facilities for the low- and moderate-income families of his own neighborhood. Fauntroy served as the first appointed vice chairman of the D.C. City Council from 1967 to 1968, and as national director of the Poor People's Campaign in 1969.

In recognition of his record of humanitarian community service, both Virginia Union in 1968, and Yale University in 1969, have conferred honorary D.D. degrees upon him. He was the chief architect of legislation in 1973 that permitted the District of Columbia to elect its own mayor and city council and engineered the passage by both the House and Senate of a Constitutional Amendment calling for full Congressional representation for District of Columbia citizens in the U.S. Congress. That resolution is now before state legislators in the nation's capital. The Georgetown University Law School awarded him an honorary LL.D. degree in 1979.

Since his election to Congress, Fauntroy has continued to build a record of achievement, having played key roles in the mobilization of black political power from the National Black Political Convention of 1972 to the presidential elections of 1972 and 1976. In the 95th Congress, Rep. Fauntroy was a member of the House Select Committee on Assassinations and chairman of its Subcommittee on the Assassination of Martin Luther King, Jr. He is now a member of the House Banking, Finance and Urban Affairs Committee and a member of the House District Committee where he serves as chairman of the Subcommittee on Government Affairs and Budget. He also heads the Congressional Black Caucus Braintrust on Voter Participation and Network Development. He is chairman of the board of directors of the Southern Christian Leadership Conference, vice president of the Martin Luther King, Jr. Center for Social Change, and a member of the board of trustees of Virginia Union University.

FERGUSON, LLOYD N., was born February 9, 1918, in Oakland, California. He is the son of Noel Swithin Ferguson and Gwendolyn Louise Johnson Ferguson. He married the former Charlotte Welch and they have three children, Lloyd, Jr., Stephen Bruce and Lisa Annette. He received a B.S. degree from the University of California, Berkeley, in 1940 and in 1943, he received a Ph.D. From 1941 to 1944, he was a research assistant on a National Defense Project at the University of California. From 1944 to 1945, he served as an assistant professor at A&T College in Greensboro, North Carolina. In 1950, he served as a chemist for the National Bureau of Standards in Washington, D.C. In 1951, he was a chemist for the Naval Ordnance Laboratory in White Oak, Maryland.

In 1958, he joined the faculty at Howard University, Washington, D.C., as head of the chemistry department. Through more than 50 years of teaching and research, Dr. Ferguson has influenced the thinking of a generation of chemists. He is the author of six chemistry textbooks and numerous articles, and has worked to increase the representation of minorities in science professions. The recipient of many national awards, Ferguson won the Outstanding Professor Award for the California State University System in 1981.

FIGURES, MICHAEL ANTHONY, was born October 13, 1947, to the Rev. and Mrs. Coleman Figures. He is married to Vivian Davis Figures and is the father of four sons, Derik, Akil, Shomari and Jelani. Figures graduated from Hillsdale High School in 1965; he received a B.A. degree in history from Stillman College, Tuscaloosa, Alabama, in 1969; exchange student University of Nebraska, Lincoln, 1966–1967; J.D. degree, 1972, University of Alabama School of Law, Tuscaloosa. In 1978, he was elected to the Alabama State Senate, District 33, and was a partner in the law firm of Figures, Jackson & Harris in Mobile, Alabama. Prior to taking office he was treasurer for the Democratic Party of Alabama; vice chairman of the Alabama Delegation of the Democratic National Convention in 1980; elected delegate pledged to Jesse Jackson, 1984–1988; state chairman of the Jesse Jackson for President Campaign, 1984–1988.

Figures is the recipient of numerous awards: Citizen of the Year, 1977, Omega Psi Phi Fraternity and Kappa Alpha Psi Fraternity; Outstanding Young Man of Mobile, 1978, Mobile Jaycees; Outstanding Legal Service Award, National Association of Landowners, 1979; Distinguished Alumni Award, Stillman College National Alumni Association, 1979; Outstanding Service Award, Alabama Law Institute, 1982; Southern Christian Leadership Legacy of the Dream Award, 1984; Outstanding Legislator, 1986, selected by the Alabama Senate; Trial Lawyer of the Year, 1987; Candace Award, 1988, National Coalition of Black Women. He has been active in community and public service: first vice president, Alabama New South Coalition; member, board of trustees, Stillman College; founder, vice-president and member of board of directors of Emergency Land Fund, Inc.; president, Alabama Lawyers Association, 1976; treasurer, Alabama Lawyers Association, 1977; member, Alabama Port Authority; member, Alabama Bar Association; executive secretary, Non-partisan Voters League, June. His professional presentations include a paper at the Southeastern Conference of the Judiciary in November of 1976 on the Quality of Justice for Black

People in the Southeast, and an address at the Alabama Judicial College on January 28, 1980. The subject of the presentation concerned partition sales in the state of Alabama and Alabama's new sale law.

FINLEY, MORRIS, was born June 11, 1939, in Atlanta, Georgia. He is divorced and the father of two children, Rhonda and Marguerite. Finley attended David T. Howard High School in Atlanta; Clark College, Atlanta, 1958–1959; Boston School of Lithography, 1960–1962; A.A. degree, University of Marietta, 1970–1972. He served in the United States Army. Finley was elected in 1975 to the city council of Atlanta. Prior to being appointed councilman he was executive president of the Diamond Printing Company where he was responsible for public relations. It is one of the largest black printing firms in the south. He served as director in the graphic art department for Southern Rural Action in Atlanta.

Finley was the recipient of numerous awards: Outstanding Men in the South; Outstanding Blacks in America; Outstanding Community Service, to Youth, Dekalb County in 1972; YMCA Public Service Award in 1973; Coach of the Year/YMCA, 1972; and Omega Psi Phi Fraternity Scroll of Honor/Government. He has been active in many civic, social, church, business and community organizations, some of which are: NAACP; National and Atlanta Business League; Atlanta Coalition of Current Community Affairs; Atlanta Urban League; National Association of Market Developers, American Academy of Political and Social Science.

FINNEY, JAMES NATHANIEL, was born June 10, 1939, in New York City. He is the son of Joseph Finney and Carrie McDowell. He is divorced and has one child from that marriage,

Karen. In 1963, he received a B.S. degree from Columbia University, New York. In 1966, he received an LL.M. degree from Columbia University. He was a staff attorney with Schiffer & Cohen in New York, from 1966 to 1967. From 1967 to 1973, he was a staff attorney for the NAACP Legal Defense Fund in New York. From 1973 to 1976, he was an assistant counsel for the Human Resources Administration in New York. From 1976 to 1980, he was the director and chief counsel for Harlem Legal Services in New York. Since 1980, he has served as an associate general counsel for the Equal Employment Opportunity Commission (EEOC), Washington, D.C.

FLEMING, CHARLES W. Judge Charles W. Fleming received his pre-law degree from Kent State University and his J.D. degree, in 1955, from Cleveland Marshall Law School. Prior to being elected to the bench, he served as assistant county prosecutor from 1961 until 1968, special assistant to the Attorney General of the State of Ohio from 1969 until 1975, professor at Case Western Reserve University from 1969 until 1973, and from 1968 until 1976 was engaged in the private practice of law. He was elected to his third six-year term in 1987.

During his tenure with the Cleveland Municipal Court, Fleming served as the presiding and administrative judge in 1989. He was recently re-elected to both positions by his colleagues. Fleming is a member of the Ohio State Bar Association, the Cleveland Bar Association, and is past chairman of the Judicial Council of the National Bar Association, and past president of the John Harlan Law Club (now the Norman S. Minor Bar Association). Judge Fleming is the president of the Association of Municipal and County Judges of Ohio, Inc., and he was recently elected to the Court of Appeals of the American Judges Association. He is also a member of many other civic and professional organizations.

FLEMMING, TIMOTHY, was born on December 31, 1950, to the late Mr. and Mrs. Ransom Flemming, Sr., of Macon, Georgia. He married Virginia Lee and they have three sons, Aric Bernard, Kenneth Lee, and Timothy, Jr. He received his elementary education at the B. S. Ingram and G. W. Carver Elementary Schools. He received his high school education at the Ballard-Hudson High School. He was awarded a diploma in theology from American Baptist Extension Seminary Center, where he studied for five years. He studied for two years at Mercer University, Macon, Georgia, and a short while at Mercer University in Decatur. He received his B.A. degree in philosophy of religion at Morehouse College in Atlanta, a Master of Divinity degree and an Honorary Doctorate of Ministry degree from National Theological Seminary.

On May 9, 1962, at age 11, Timothy preached his trial sermon at the Ross Street Baptist Church in Macon. By age 14, he became youth minister of five churches and brought many young people to Christ. At age 19, he was ordained as the assistant pastor of the greater Friendship Baptist Church where he was a member. Two months later he was called to pastor his first church, Forest Chapel Baptist Church in Pinehurst, Georgia. He had pastored five churches when he was invited to the Mount Carmel Baptist Church to preach on the first Sunday in March 1975. The congregation was immensely impressed with this dynamic young minister and he became their pastor. Under his leadership, Mount Carmel has grown tremendously. Early in 1980, the church purchased eight acres of land valued at over a quarter of a million dollars. This land had a five-year loan repayment plan; however, the church paid it off in exactly one year. Five additional acres have since been purchased.

As one of his achievements, Flemming was given two special awards for "Special Studies in Christian Education and Negro Works" at the Georgia Baptist Convention in 1968 and 1969. In 1979, he was invited to the White House and was honored by former President Jimmy Carter as Georgia's Outstanding Young Minister. Over the years, the Rev. Flemming has been viewed on many of the local television stations, such as Channel 46, Cable Channel 8, and has appeared as the special guest on the "Breakfast Club" with Bob Gass on Channel 36. He was the first black minister to appear on CBS Channel 5's television program "Moments of Reflection."

FLETCHER, ARTHUR A., was appointed chairman of the U.S. Commission on Civil Rights in February 1990. A Republican, he was appointed by President Bush to serve a term expiring in November 1995. Fletcher was born in Phoenix, Arizona, on December 22, 1924. He served in the United States Army from 1943–1945, and received his B.A. degree from Washburn University in Topeka, Kansas, in 1950. He and his wife Bernyce reside in reside in Washington, D.C. Fletcher is president of Arthur A. Fletcher and Associates, a management consulting firm with offices in Maryland. He served at the White House as deputy assistant to the president for Urban Affairs from 1976–1977; as president of Arthur A. Fletcher and Associates, Inc., 1973–1976; and as executive director of the United Negro College Fund, 1972–1973. He was an alternate delegate to the 26th session of the United Nations Assembly in 1971; and was an assistant secretary of labor for employment standards at the U.S. Department of Labor from 1969–1971.

for the pending *Brown vs. School Board of Topeka* desegregation suit, which was successfully fought up to the United States Supreme Court. In the early 1950s, he played professional football with the Los Angeles Rams and the (then) Baltimore Colts until an injury cut his career short.

FLOWERS, MARY EVELYN, was born July 31, 1951, in Inverness, Mississippi, the second oldest of seven children. She attributes her professional and political success to her very supportive family and an unshakeable

Fletcher was a special assistant to the governor of the state of Washington in 1968–1969; a member of the city council in Pasco, Washington; and an employee relations consultant at the Hanford Atomic Energy facility, 1967–1968. He was a public school teacher in Berkeley, California, 1961–1965; a reports control manager at Aerojet-General Corporation in Sacramento, 1957–1961; and an assistant director for the public information office of the Kansas State Highway Department in Topeka, 1955–1957. In 1954, while teaching in a rural elementary school in Kansas, Fletcher helped raise money

faith in God. She attended parochial school from 1957 to 1966, and upon graduation attended Simeon Vocational High School, graduated in 1970 and went on to Kennedy-King College and the University of Illinois at Chicago Campus. Flowers was elected to the Illinois General Assembly in November 1984. She represented the people of the 31st Representative District, which primarily comprised the Englewood, Auburn, and Foster

Park communities on Chicago's South Side. Prior to becoming a full-time legislator, she was a supervisor in the Physical Plant Management Department of the University of Illinois at Chicago; office supervisor, Department of Building Operations, University of Illinois Chicago Circle, 1982–1984; administrative clerk, associate vice chancellor, Health Sciences, Medical Center, 1979–1982; and administrative assistant, vice chancellor for Academic Affairs, University of Illinois Chicago Circle, 1977–1979.

Flowers' commitment to serve the people of her community is reflected in her previous professional and volunteer activities, which included community advocacy, youth motivation and political organization/participation. She has worked in public services for the past 13 years in both salaried and non-salaried capacities, in private industry as well as public institutions. These experiences included constituent research for political campaigns, credit investigation, medical insurance investigation, legal research, preparation of unemployment appeal cases, implementation of CETA programs, administration of a State Library Delivery System, financial aide counseling, adult education counseling and social work with the Correctional Center inmates.

These experiences, coupled with those as a black female in a predominately white, male world, have provided Flowers with insight and a sense of mission to address the needs of her community and society in general. Moreover, managerial and administrative experiences had prepared her with the organizational skills necessary to tackle the job at hand as a state legislator. Rep. Flowers' legislative focus for the 31st District intensified economic and business development, resulted in the improvement of housing conditions, improved public education, increased public safety, and expanded youth training and recreational programs.

FLOYD, DONALD J., was born on October 1, 1943, in Port Arthur, Texas. Married to the former Marie Comezux, he is the father of two children, Kristi and Karla. He attended Lincoln High School in Port Arthur and graduated in 1962. He received a B.A. degree upon graduation from Dillard University in New Orleans, Louisiana, in 1966. He attended Thurgood Marshall School of Law at Texas Southern University in Houston, Texas, where he received a J.D. degree upon graduation in 1972. On April 20, 1972, he passed the Texas bar examination and was licensed to practice law in the State of Texas. From April 1972 to August 1974, he worked as a trial attorney for the United States Department of Justice, Civil Rights Division, Housing Section in Washington, D.C.

In September 1974, he entered the private practice of law in Port Arthur. In September 1982, the City Council of the City of Port Arthur appointed him judge of the Municipal Court. He was the first black to occupy the position in Port Arthur. In December of 1983, the Jefferson County Commissioners' Court appointed him judge of the newly created County Court at Law #3. He was the first black to occupy the position in the history of Jefferson County. During the general election in November 1984, he was elected as judge of County Court at Law #3, becoming the first black to hold a countrywide elective office. On December 5, 1989, the Hon William P. Clements, Jr., Governor of the State of Texas, appointed him judge of the 172nd District Court, the position he presently holds.

Judge Floyd was the first black to be appointed to a statewide district judgeship by Gov. Clements during his term of office. He was also the first black to occupy the position of state district judge in the history of Jefferson County. He has received many honors and awards: a four-year United Negro College Fund scholarship to Dillard

University; Ford Foundation scholarship to Thurgood Marshall School of Law at Texas Southern University; *Who's Who Among Black Americans*, 1976–1977; Three Rivers Council Boy Scouts of America Award of Appreciation, 1977; U.S. Jaycees Outstanding Young Men of America Award, 1978; Port Arthur Alumni Chapter of Kappa Alpha Psi Fraternity Achievement Award, 1981, 1984, 1989; Golden Gate Civic and Social Club of Port Arthur 1983 "Man of the Year" Award; Royalist Civic and Social Club Outstanding Achievement Award, 1982.

Also, he received the Mary Alphin District of Federated Clubs Outstanding Community Service Award, 1983; Port Arthur Branch NAACP Freedom Award, 1983; Lincoln High School Class of 1962 Outstanding Achievement Award, 1983; Kiwanis Club of Port Arthur Outstanding Club Leadership Award, 1987–1988; National Women of Achievement, Inc., Beaumont Metroplex Chapter Certificate of Service Award, 1989. Judge Floyd has always been very active in many civic, social, church, business and community organizations. He was admitted to practice before all of the courts in Texas and the District of Columbia, and many other courts across the United States.

FORD, FRED, was born February 14, 1930, in Memphis, Tennessee. He attended Douglas Elementary School and Douglas High School. His first musical performance was at the age of 13 (in 1943) when he played clarinet at Douglas Elementary. Later he played with a teen group called the "Douglas Swingsters" under the direction of Mr. Sharp, principal and bandmaster of Douglas High School. In 1945, at the age of 15, Ford was given his first job playing music with Andrew Chaplin, Jr., at the Elks Club on Beale Street. He started playing saxophone quite by ac-

cident. His first love had been trumpet and clarinet. The late Onzie Horne, Sr., had a big band in 1946 and Ford played trumpet in the brass section. They had many trumpet players and an opening came in the saxophone section. He has been playing the instrument ever since.

From 1945 until 1952, he played with Onzie Horne, Sr., "Big Mama" Willie Mae Thornton (on the original recording of "Hound Dog"), Bill Harvey, Gatemouth Brown, B. B. King, George Coleman, Frank Strozier, Jamil Nassar, and Phineas Newborn, Jr. In 1952, he entered the Army and was sent to Korea where he played in the Army band. Early recording studio experience was with Bill Harvey at Peacock and Duke Records, owned by Don Robey of Houston. Upon returning to Memphis the band played at "Sunbeam" Mitchell's Domino Lounge, where the great jazz musicians came to play. Other studio work included: Chips Moman's American Studios, where Ford played behind such famous artists as Dionne Warwick, Burt Bacharach, Hal David, B. J. Thomas, Aretha Franklin, Wilson Pickett, and Joe Tex.

At MGM Studios, Ford was staff manager and worked with the Ovations, Solomon Burke, and D. Clark, arranging and scoring sound tracks and recordings. He worked at Sam Phillips' Sun Records, playing behind Jerry Lee Lewis and Charlie Rich. In 1975, he produced "Solo Piano" the come-back album for the great jazz pianist Phineas Newborn, Jr. The album was nominated for a 1976 Grammy award. He produced Cybill Shepherd's "Vanilla" album in 1978 (the album was re-released in early 1990). He co-produced the 1977 Beale Street Festival, in addition to performing. In 1979, with Phineas Newborn, he performed at the renowned Montreux Jazz Festival in France.

The Fred Ford/Honeymoon Garner Trio recorded "Bear Water: The Beale

Street Scene" in 1984. This album was followed by "Madame Honeybuns" in 1989. He participated on a monthly basis in Artists in Education programs in the Memphis public schools and at Memphis State University, 1984–1986. In 1988, he and Arkansas musician Bill Haymes (an Arkansas Arts Council Fellowship recipient) conducted a week-long music workshop for elementary students in West Memphis and Marion, Arkansas, sponsored by Crittenden Arts Council and funded by a grant from the Arkansas Arts Council. Ford and Haymes also performed at the Steudlein Learning Center, a countywide educational cooperative serving physically and mentally handicapped children and adults.

From 1985–1989 the Fred Ford/Honeymoon Garner Trio originated the Sunday night live broadcasts "Jazz from the Peabody" on FM 92, the Memphis State University radio station. He served as musical director for the 1986 "Blue Gardenia" tribute to Billie Holiday, sponsored by Crittenden Arts Council (West Memphis, Arkansas). He also performed in the 1988 Memphis tribute to the late Duke Ellington. He was narrator and musical director for "Beale Street's Blues," a documentary for television; performed four original compositions ("Beale Street After Sundown," "Living Legend," "Douglas Special," and "Moving On") in this celebration of Beale Street's influence on the world of popular music.

Ford interviewed Furry Lewis in the video "Slide Master Furry Lewis" on Mother Blues Video. He has hosted dignitaries from China, the Sudan, England and Switzerland, and participated in activities at the University of Mississippi during the visit of the vice president of the Chinese Writers' Association. In 1985, a painting of the Memphis musician was included in the New Orleans Music Hall of Fame and he was selected to appear on the Tennessee Homecoming 1986 poster. Additional

honors include: 1985 dinner and testimonial roast by United Music Heritage; 1986 "Good Neighbor" award from the Memphis chapter of the National Conference of Christians and Jews; 1987 and 1989 editions of *Who's Who in Black America*; and the 1989 edition of *International Who's Who in Music*, published by Cambridge University Press, Cambridge University.

Also, Ford was named "Tennessee Colonel" by Gov. Lamar Alexander; received proclamations from (then) President Reagan, Mayor Dick Hackett, Mayor Bill Morris, Congressman Harold Ford, Shelby County Commissioners, Memphis City Council, Tennessee State Legislature. In a 1985 *New York Times* article, he was dubbed "Memphis' best kept secret." He moderated two radio programs for K97's show "Concerns '86" discussing Memphis music. He was featured in *Black Music Heritage* catalogue by the Center for Southern Folklore. He has played for benefits for the Film, Tape and Music Commission, the NAACP, National Conference of Christians and Jews, Overton Park Shell Restoration Benefit, United Music Heritage, and United Way. In 1987, the trio opened for The Spinners at the grand opening celebration of the Peabody Orlando. Ford was featured in the 1988 opening of Lord & Taylor's Memphis store.

The Fred Ford/Honeymoon Garner Trio has been a mainstay at the annual Folk Life Festival sponsored by the Center for Southern Folklore, as well as the Memphis in May Beale Street Festival. During the 1989 Arts in the Park, the group performed on the Festival stage. Ford presented five workshops on jazz as an Artist-in-Action in the children's area of Arts in the Park. These workshops were funded in part by Arts in the Park and by the Memphis Arts Council's Innervisions program. Additionally, he served on the Festival's Performing Arts Advisory Committee. He appeared in the movie *On the Road* with Janet Leigh and Harry Guardino, as well as in the 1989 holiday commercial for Memphis Cablevision. Although he concentrated on playing the alto and baritone saxophones, Ford also plays the tenor saxophone and the saxello, an early (around 1926) forerunner of the soprano saxophone.

FORD, HAROLD, was born May 20, 1945, in Memphis, the eighth of 15 children of N. J. and Vera Ford. He is married to the former Dorothy Bowles of Memphis and they are the parents of three sons: Harold, Jr., Newton, and Sir Isaac. He received a B.S. degree in business administration from Tennessee State University, an A.S. degree in mortuary science from John Gupton College in Nashville, and an M.B.A. degree from Howard University in Washington, D.C. Congressman Ford represents Tennessee's 9th Congressional District. He has served this district, comprising solely the city of Memphis, since 1974, and is currently serving his eighth term in the Congress of the United States. He is the first and only black Tennessean ever elected to Congress. He serves as a ranking member of the powerful and prestigious House Committee on Ways and Means, which has jurisdiction over all tax and revenue-raising legislation, as well as the Social Security and Medicare programs.

Ford is the youngest member of Congress ever to be selected as a Ways and Means Subcommittee chairman. Since 1981, he has served as chairman of the House Ways and Means Subcommittee on Human Resources, formerly known as the Subcommittee on Public Assistance and Unemployment Compensation. This subcommittee has jurisdiction over approximately $40 billion in programs including Aid to Families with Dependent Children (AFDC), Title XX and Supplemental Security Income under the Social Security Act, Child Welfare and Foster Care, Low Income Energy Assistance, and Unemployment Compensation Insurance. Because of his leadership in crafting a comprehensive Welfare Reform bill in the 101st Congress, Ford was named Child Advocate of the Year for 1987 by the Child Welfare League of America. In early 1987, he was appointed to the Democratic Steering and Policy Committee by Speaker of the House Jim Wright. This Democratic Leadership group helped to define official Democratic policy within the House and chooses the leaders of House committees.

Ford also served as a ranking member of the Ways and Means Subcommittee on Oversight and the House Select Committee on Aging. Along with his committee responsibilities, he holds membership on the Congressional Arts Caucus, the Congressional Black Caucus, and the Congressional Caucus for Women's Issues. He was also re-elected to serve as a Democratic Zone Whip, represented the states of Tennessee, Louisiana and Mississippi during the 100th Congress, and is a member of the Democratic Study Group. Prior to his election to Congress, he served two terms in the Tennessee Legislature. He was elected to this state office at the age of 25, and represented the same geographic area of Memphis in which his great-grandfather served as a squire during the post–Reconstruction Era. Rep. Ford is active in social and community activities in Memphis and throughout the country. He is a member of the National Advisory Council of St. Jude's Children's Research Hospital, and the Metropolitan Memphis YMCA board. He is also affiliated with Alpha Phi Alpha Fraternity.

FOREMAN, GEORGE, was born January 22, 1948, in Marshall, Texas.

He dropped out of the seventh grade and joined the Job Corps. He was sent to the Grants Pass, Oregon, conservation camp. Persuaded to join the camp's recreational boxing program, he won the Corps' Diamond Belt Tournament. In 1967, he entered the Golden Gloves competition which he lost by a split decision. He won a position on the U.S. Olympic boxing team. In the 1968 Olympiad at Mexico City, he won the Heavyweight Gold Medal by a second-round knockout over Russia's Chepulis.

Foreman turned professional in July 1969, after winning 19 of 22 amateur bouts in two years. His first professional bout was on June 23, 1969, with Don Waldhelm, and he knocked Waldhelm out in the third round. He had won 37 heavyweight fights, 35 by knockouts, when he got a shot at the heavyweight title against Joe Frazier on January 22, 1973. He knocked out Frazier in the second round, a birthday gift to himself. He knocked Frazier down six times in two rounds and took the heavyweight championship. He had one other fight in 1973, on September 1, when he knocked out Jose Roman in the first round.

In 1974, Foreman had two fights, the first on March 6 with Ken Norton whom he knocked out in the second round. Then on October 30, 1974, Foreman, the World Heavyweight Champion, and Muhammad Ali, the people's champion, finally met for the world's heavyweight championship in Kinshasa, Zaire, Africa. Both Foreman and Ali each won $5 million dollars and training expenses for their respective efforts. Early Wednesday in Zaire, Tuesday night in the United States, Foreman was knocked out in the eighth round by Ali at 2:58 of Round 8. On June 15, 1976, he again knocked out Joe Frazier in the fifth round. On March 17, 1977, he lost a fight to Jimmy Young in the 12th round, only the second loss of his career. After the loss, he retired from the ring and became a lay minister

in the Church of the Lord Jesus Christ. He then lived a life of contentment as pastor of the church.

On March 9, 1987, Foreman decided to come out of retirement and in his first fight knocked out Steve Zouski in the fourth round. By 1990, he had run his record to 68-2 with 64 knockouts overall and 23-0 since ending a 10-year retirement from the ring in 1987. On April 19, 1991, Foreman at 42 years of age got the opportunity to fight Evander Holyfield for the heavyweight championship of the world. The fight, that grossed over $100 million, was the biggest grossing boxing event of all time. No other fight has come close to the $100 million mark. He was guaranteed $12.5 million for the fight but would likely surpass that when closed-circuit and pay-per-view receipts were counted. In a memorable fight, with Foreman momentarily young again but swinging leaden hands, Holyfield was unable to figure him out. A 42-year-old man can still fight; the young champ was hugging him at the last bell and not letting go. Final statistics credited Holyfield with 584 punches thrown and a 60.8 connection rate. Foreman threw 444 punches, landing 42.3 percent. The bout was the first heavyweight championship fight to go the distance since 1987. Holyfield won the fight — his first title defense — by unanimous decision.

———   ———

FOSTER, SHIRLEY M., is a graduate of the University of Hartford, West Hartford, Connecticut. She received a B.S. degree in special education in 1980 and an M.E. in administration and supervision in 1989. From 1987 to present, she has served as a special education teacher for Simpson-Waverly School, Hartford Board of Education, where she provides learning experiences and peer tutoring to enable youngsters to grow in self-esteem and academic understanding. Prior positions include:

special education teacher for Fox Middle School, Hartford Board of Education, Hartford; consultant, Title I/Chapter I for the Department of Education, State of Connecticut, Hartford; organizer/director for Connecticut Toy Resource Program, Hamden, Connecticut; consultant, Chapter I for Massachusetts, Ohio, Delaware, Wisconsin, New Hampshire, California, where she conducted numerous workshops to enable communities to establish networks of exchange regarding the interpretation/functioning of Chapter I programs; formed advisory councils; developed local/regional newsletters; benefits administrator for Cigna Corporation, Bloomfield, Connecticut, 1985–1987; and field service representative for Prudential Insurance Company, South Windsor, Connecticut, 1980–1982.

Foster is the recipient of many awards and citations: Outstanding Young Women in America, 1985; Scroll/Emeritus status bestowed by Chapter I ESEA; Hartford Chapter I Parents; Waterbury P.A.C.; School Readiness Program; selected to participate in Teacher Learning Cooperative Program, Johns Hopkins University and CCSU (in Baltimore, 1989). Her professional affiliations include: Bloomfield Town Council, Democratic Town Committee; Bloomfield Black Democratic Club; Concerned Black Parents for Quality Education, Bloomfield; IMPACT; Delta Sigma Theta Sorority and several of its committees; founder/board member for the National Coalition of Chapter I ESEA; and Black Caucus of American Federation of Teachers and the Hartford YWCA.

FRANKLIN, ARETHA, was born March 25, 1942, in Memphis, Tennessee, and is the mother of four sons, Clarence, Edward, Teddy and Kecalf. She was one of five children of the Rev. Clarence L. Franklin and Barbara Sig-gers Franklin. The Rev. Franklin, a well-known revivalist Baptist preacher, brought his family north when Aretha was two years old, and five years later they settled in Detroit, Michigan, where he took over the pastorate at the New Bethel Baptist Church. Among the house guests at the Franklin home during her childhood were Mahalia Jackson, Clara Ward, James Cleveland, Arthur Prysock, B. B. King, Dorothy Donegan, Dinah Washington, Lou Rawls, and Sam Cooke. By the time Franklin was eight or nine, she had taught herself to play the piano and sang gospel songs at local churches in a group made up of her older sister Erma and two other girls. Her mother died and she became deeply immersed in music.

Franklin was already a veteran member of her father's church choir and she cut her first record for Chess Records as her first solo at the age of 12. She attended Northern High School in Detroit and toured with her father's evangelist group as a featured singer when not in school. The tours gave her valuable performing experience that taught her a few painful lessons such as driving eight or ten hours and passing restaurants all along the road but having to go off the highway into some little city to find a place to eat because you're black. Having conquered the gospel circuit, in 1960 she decided to try her luck in the pop music field. She came to New York City, where she took dancing and vocal lessons and hired a manager.

In 1961, she signed a five-year contract with Columbia Records, but although she often seemed to be on the verge of achieving stardom during those five years, she never quite made it. Singing standard jazz tunes and novelties, she recorded nine long-playing albums that sold only moderately, although some of her songs were praised by the critics. Among her Columbia albums were "Electrifying Aretha Franklin," "Laughing on the Outside," "Runnin'

Out of Fools," and "Unforgettable," a tribute to Dinah Washington. In 1963, she appeared at the Newport Jazz Festival and the Lower Ohio Jazz Festival and later toured Bermuda, the Bahamas, and Puerto Rico. Most of the time, however, she made the rounds of the dingy jazz and rhythm and blues nightclubs along "the chitlin' circuit," where she was often so frightened by her surroundings that she sang to the floor.

In 1966, she signed with Atlantic Records, a small New York company that for the past 15 years had specialized in the rhythm and blues music. She recorded her first single for Atlantic in 1967, "I Never Loved a Man," which sold a million copies. She recorded four more golden singles that year, including "Respect" and "Baby, I Love You." Her first 1967 album entitled "I Never Loved a Man," passed the 1,000,000 mark, and her second, "Aretha Arrives," sold only somewhat less briskly. The major trade magazines of the music business, *Cashbox*, *Billboard*, and *Record World*, all named her top female vocalist of 1967. Franklin attributed her sudden stardom to Atlantic Records, because she wrote many of her own songs and blocked out her own arrangements. Except for a few cuts, she played her own piano accompaniment on all her recordings on "Aretha Arrives" that she made while recuperating from a broken elbow. At live performances she was accompanied by the Sweet Inspirations, consisting of Carolyn and two long-time friends from Detroit.

As a star who has become a standard bearer for the black movement of the 1960s, Franklin has helped to define a Negro sense of identity. Her Grammies and Golden Mike award-winning recording of "Respect," a song written by the late Otis Redding, has been called "the new Negro national anthem." She described herself as just mom and the lady next door. The real Aretha Franklin was just what you see on stage and off; she was domestic at home and theatrical on stage. She sang around the house in the shower, in the bathroom and of course with her records.

In 1967, she was awarded a special citation by the Southern Christian Leadership Conference for her support of various civil rights activities. On the other hand, she made it clear that she didn't address her music just to black people: "It's not cool to be Negro and Jewish or Italian or anything else. It's just cool to be alive, to be around. You don't have to be a Negro to have soul." In an age that believed in the basics, in getting down to the nitty gritty and being loose, Franklin embodies a whole new slant on life. Her success continued through 1968 with her album "Lady Soul" passing the 1,000,000 mark in September, and her single cut of "Chain of Fools" selling over 1,000,000 copies. She helped to open the 1968 Democratic Convention in Chicago with her soul version of "The Star Spangled Banner."

She has appeared on television with Jonathan Winters, Merv Griffin, Johnny Carson, Steve Allen, Mike Douglas, Joey Bishop, and Les Crane, and became the subject of a television documentary on ABC. Atlantic released two more albums, "Aretha Now" and "Aretha in Paris," and the latter was recorded live at a theatre in Paris. Singing in a style once considered suitable only for a limited Negro market in the deep South and the urban ghettoes of the North, the "queen of soul" to her fans reigns over the pop music field.

FRANKLIN, SHIRLEY CLARKE, was born May 10, 1945, in Philadelphia, Pennsylvania. She is the daughter of Eugene H. Clare and Ruth Lyons White and is the mother of three children, Kai Ayanna, Cabral Holsey, and Kali Jamilla. She received both her B.A. and M.A. in sociology from Howard University and the University of Pennsylvania, respectively. Prior to moving to Atlanta in 1972, she was a contract compliance officer with the U.S. Department of Labor and a member of the faculty of Talladega College in Alabama. In 1987, Mayor Maynard Jackson appointed her as the director and later as commissioner of the Department of Cultural Affairs. Under her leadership, the department developed innovative programs such as the first Atlanta Free Jazz Festival and the arts project at the Atlanta Hartsfield International Airport.

After successfully managing Andrew Young's campaign for mayor of Atlanta, Franklin was appointed the city's first female chief administrative officer in 1982. She held this important position during the eight years of Young's administration. Upon being elected as mayor of Atlanta for a third term, Jackson reorganized city government and appointed Franklin as his executive officer for operations, with responsibility over the operating departments and offices; i.e., Department of Fire, Department of Police, Office of Emergency Management Services, Office of Corrections, Department of Parks, Recreations and Cultural Affairs, Department of Public Works and Department of water and Polluion and Control.

Franklin has been lauded in *Ebony, Essence* and *Atlanta* magazines. She was inducted into the Academy of Women Achievers by the YWCA of Greater Atlanta and had received other civic recognition for the unique leadership role. In early 1991, Franklin, the chief executive officer for the city of Atlanta, was appointed senior vice president for external relations for the 1996 (XXV Olympiad), Atlanta Organizing Committee.

FUNDERBURG, I. OWEN, was born on August 21, 1924, in his hometown of Monticello, Georgia. He is married to the former Clara Comeaux of Chicago, and has one son. His education began in the public school system of Monticello where his father was a practicing medical doctor. He entered Morehouse College in 1940 only to have his education interrupted in 1943 by World War II. His three-year term in the U.S. Army ended in 1946 with his honorable discharge from military service. He then returned to Morehouse College to finish his work for a B.A. degree in business administration. After graduate studies at the University of Michigan, he entered the Graduate School of Banking at Rutgers University in New Jersey, where he was the banking school's first black graduate in 1959.

His banking career began in 1948 as a teller at the Mechanic and Farmers Bank in Durham, North Carolina. In 1951, at the age of 27, he became a bank officer. During his 18 years with the bank, he served as cashier, corporate secretary and a member of the board of directors. In 1966, his career broadened as he joined Gateway National Bank in St. Louis, Missouri. He served as

Gateway's chief executive officer and as a member of its board of directors and the executive committee. During his nine years with Gateway, he was honored numerous times. A significant appointment by the governor of Missouri was to the post of commissioner of the Bi-State Development Agency which was responsible for area economic development and operation of the metropolitan transit system.

In January 1975, Funderburg accepted the position of president and chief executive of Citizens Trust Bank. Along with filling those key posts, he also serves on the bank's holding company, Citizens Bancshares Corporation. Since 1975, Citizens Trust Bank has moved successfully through perilous times of deregulation, recession and recovery under the skilled leadership of its president and chief executive officer. When he assumed his position, Citizens Trust Bank, like the entire banking industry, was facing serious challenges in the marketplace. Many smaller banks and some larger institutions did not survive those years. But through the right combination of fiscally sound actions, the bank prospered, growing from $30 million in assets in 1975 to over $118 million in 1988.

Those actions included recapitalization, strengthening of the board of directors and management, development of staff skill levels bank-wide, improvement of operating policies and systems, and implementation of a formal program to present the bank in an accurate image of service to the community. Funderburg acknowledges that since its founding in 1921, Citizens Trust Bank has been both a symbol of hope and a provider of important day-to-day financial services for its customers. His goal was to be certain that the bank always understands and adapts to the needs of the market segment that it is serving. For example, the business of the bank was more heavily consumer oriented than many other financial institutions which serve mostly the larger industrial and business accounts. Because customers of Citizens tend to be individuals or smaller businesses, the bank must serve their special needs in such areas as mortgage, consumer and small business loans.

Funderburg came to Atlanta well prepared to be president and chief executive officer of Citizens Trust Bank. He was college-educated in business and banking matters, and he had nearly 30 years of front-line management experience with significant banks in two other cities. As evidence of his active commitment to keep Citizens Trust Bank in a leadership position in the Atlanta Community, he maintains a wide variety of significant relationships with a host of organizations and institutions. Among these board memberships are the following: the Atlanta Action Forum, the Georgia World Congress Center, Georgia State University Foundation, the Butler Street YMCA, Central Atlanta Progress Executive Committee, Atlanta University School of Business Administration Advisory Council, Metro-Atlanta Advisory

Board of the Salvation Army, Underground Atlanta Festival Development Company, Georgia Commission on the Holocaust, Auburn Area Revitalization Committee, Inc. (board chairman), the Georgia Tech National Advisory Board, the Atlanta Partnership of Business and Education, Inc., the Georgia Council on Economic Education, the Business Council of Georgia, the Atlanta Chamber of Commerce, and the Morris Brown College Advisory Board.

Funderburg also served for six years as a member of the board of trustees of the National Urban League, and was a past director of the National Urban Coalition and the Interracial Council for Business Opportunity. He is also a former board member of the St. Louis Chamber of Commerce and the internationally renowned RCA Corporation. His business affiliations include board membership with the North Carolina Mutual Life Insurance Company. Long active in the professional banking associations, he served two terms as president of the National Bankers Association. He has also been a member of the investment committee of Minbanc Capital Corporation, a capital assistance organization sponsored by the American Bankers Association to help minority banks strengthen their capital structure. Currently he serves on the board of the Georgia Bankers Association–Group 5.

FUTRELL, MARY HATWOOD, was born May 24, 1940, in Altavista, Virginia. She is the daughter of Josephine Austin and is married to Donald Futrell. She received a B.A. degree from Virginia State University and an M.A. degree from George Washington University. Also, she did graduate work at Maryland University and the University of Virginia Polytechnical Institute and State University. With her mother as her role model, she was inspired to stretch her

mind and appreciation for education and has a deep love for teaching and helping others, as well as sharing with the community as a whole.

Futrell has devoted her life to a career in education (her way of giving something back), first serving as head of the business education department at Alexandria's George Washington High School. From 1973 to 1975, she was elected to serve as president of the Education Association of Alexandria. She served as president of the National Education Association of Virginia from 1976 to 1978; in 1978, served as a member of the board of directors of the National Education Association; and in 1980, was elected secretary-treasurer, and that same year was again elected president of the National Education Association. She served as the NEA's president until 1989.

Futrell has served on numerous boards of civic and educational associations, which include: member of the Task Force on teaching Carnegie Forum on Education and the Economy, 1985; member of the National Commission on the Role and Future of State Colleges and Universities; member of the Select Commission on the Education of Black Youth; member of the United States National Commission for the United Nations Education, Scientific and Cultural Organization; and member of the Executive Commission of World Confederation of Organizations of the Teaching Profession. She has also received numerous honors and awards, including: honorary doctorates from over ten colleges and universities; being named to the Academy of Women Achievers, YWCA; recipient of the NAACP's President's Award; and the Anne and Leon Schull Award.

GALIBER, JOSEPH L., born October 26, 1924, in New York City, is the son of Joseph F. and Ethel Galiber. He married the former Emma E. Shade and they have a daughter, Ruby. He received a B.S. degree from New York City College in 1950. While in college he was co-captain of the basketball team which won both the Nit and the NCAA Championships in 1949–1950. He graduated from New York Law School and received his J.D. degree in 1962. He worked as a youth counsellor to the Borough Director of the Youth Council in the Bronx County District Attorney's Office, from 1950 to 1963. And also as a drug abuse counselor and recreation director for Riverside Hospital in New York, from 1953 to 1959. He served as executive director for JOIN from 1963 to 1965. Since 1965, he has been a private practicing attorney.

Galiber was elected to the New York State Senate in 1963, and began serving his first two-year term in January 1969. He has won re-election every two years since then. He has served longer than any other black legislator in the senate and assembly. As a member of the committee which initially proposed the decentralization of the New York City Board of Education, Galiber and then–Senator Basil Paterson voted against the legislation because they saw fatal weaknesses in the proposal. Time has proven his foresight to be accurate.

Senator Galiber continues to be concerned about the education of our children. The public education system is the basic training ground for the future, and our children must be properly trained in order to be independent and successful participants in the state's economy. To that end, as chairperson of the senate Minority Task Force on Affirmative Action, he has challenged the State Education Department and the NYC Board of Education to assure that all the students of this state have access to an education that prepares them for what is an increasingly competitive job market and teaches them to accept and respect, in the work place and in the community, those persons of different cultures and ethnicities. Galiber became nationally known in the 1980s for the boldness of his proposal to legalize all drugs and regulate their manufacture, distribution and sale. He is a veteran of World War II, is a life member of the NAACP, and is active in several professional and community organizations.

———

GAMMAGE, ANDRE, a graduate of Valparaiso University, Valparaiso, Indiana, received a B.S. in criminal justice in May 1985; was on the dean's list 1984–1985; was on the Academic All Conference team; and received a J.D. from Valparaiso University School of Law May 1988. His work experience, 1989 to date, includes: St. Joseph County Prosecutor's Office, South Bend, Indiana, as deputy prosecuting attorney analyzing and investigating reports for filing criminal charges; advocate the state's position at trial and in other criminal proceedings in St. Joseph County Superior Court. He has had experience in felony, misdemeanor, bond, child support, and sentencing hearings in addition to bench and jury trial background in the traffic and misdemeanor division.

Prior positions include: legal research/intake work where he conducted research to resolve trial issues and answer inquiries made by attorneys, handled petitions for post-conviction relief, and gathered case information from complainants for the filing of criminal charges; 1985, Michigan City Probation Department, Michigan City, Indiana, probation officer where he monitored job search and rehabilitation attendance of six felony probationers. He insured the submission of signed paperwork proving their participation in court-appointed programs.

In 1984, Gammage served an internship with Evans and Evans Attorneys at Law, Valparaiso, as a research assistant where he elicited information and compared statutes to gain

Social Security benefits for clients removed from the program under federal reorganization. His achievements include: co-founder/vice president of Leaders and Positive Role Models, participant in South Bend–Mishawaka Chamber of Commerce Leadership Program; YMCA Outstanding Achievement Award; and a member of the Indiana Bar Association.

GANTT, HARVEY BERNARD, was born January 14, 1943, in Charleston, South Carolina. He and his wife Cindy have three daughters, Sonja, Erica, and Angie, and one son, Adam. He received a B.A. degree in architecture from Clemson University, in 1965, and a master's from M.I.T., in 1970. From 1970 to 1972, he was a lecturer at the University of North Carolina Chapel Hill. From 1972 to 1973, he was elected to the Charlotte City Council. When he joined the City Council, only one black at a time sat on the council. In 1974, the black council member was Frederick Alexander, who was elected to the state senate the same year. In 1979, after five years on the council, Gantt made his first run for the mayor's job. He was elected mayor on his second try in 1983. The chief duties of Charlotte's part-time mayor are to preside over council meetings and to issue proclamations and commendations. He held this post until 1987.

In 1990, Gantt ran for the United States Senate against Sen. Jesse Helms. He was able to weather blistering television attacks on his support for the National Endowment for the Arts and abortion rights and opposition to the death penalty. His counterattack against the incumbent's record on education and the environment in fact propelled him into a significant polling lead. But in the final days of the campaign, Helms resorted to a tactic that had suited him in each of his three previous elections, racial divisiveness.

It was the element of his political career that has endeared him to mostly rural "Jessecrats." Helms explicitly polarized the state on racial lines. On November 6, 1990, the first black mayor of Charlotte lost in his bid to be the first black United States Senator from North Carolina.

GASKILL, ROBERT CLARENCE, was born on April 12, 1931, in Yonkers, New York. He received a B.A. degree from Howard University and an M.B.A. from George Washington University. Gaskill was commissioned a second lieutenant in the United States Army in 1952, after completing with distinction the Army Reserve Officers Training Course (ROTC) at Howard University. Initially, he served in various infantry positions. Following assignment to the Quartermaster Center, Fort Lee, Virginia, he held numerous key Army logistical positions. He served as deputy commanding general, 1st Support Brigade, United States Army in Europe. He served as the commanding general of Letterkenny Army Depot in Pennsylvania, and in staff positions with the Military Assistance Command, in Vietnam, and in the Office of the Deputy Chief of Staff for Logistics, Department of the Army, Washington, D.C.

Gaskill is a graduate of the United States Army Command and General Staff College, the Army Forces Staff College, the Army Logistics Management Center, the Army Institute for Military Assistance, and Navy Postgraduate School. From 1971 to 1972, he was a student at the Army War College and became a faculty member teaching in the areas of command management and executive development until 1974. In 1977, he was promoted to the two-star grade of major general. In October 1978, he was assigned as the deputy director of the Defense Logistics Agency. As the deputy director, his responsibilities encompass the Agency's worldwide activities which provide all the Armed Forces with a vast range of supplies and logistic support services. He has received numerous awards and decorations which include: the Distinguished Service Medal; the Legion of Merit; the Meritorious Service Medal (with oak leaf cluster); and the Honor Medal 1st class (Republic of Vietnam).

GASTON, ARTHUR G., SR., was born July 4, 1892, in Demoplis, Alabama. He graduated from Tuggles Institute in Birmingham, Alabama. Gaston eventually built a small conglomerate that included Booker T. Washington Insurance, Citizens Federal Savings and Loan, WENN-FM and WAGG-AM radio stations, New Grace Hill Cemetery and Zion Memorial Gardens. A. G. Gaston Corp. is the holding company for these companies, with a total of 270 employees. Gross income figures for A. G. Gaston Corp. subsidiaries' latest fiscal years include: Booker T. Washington Insurance — which was the holding company's flagship operation — $12.6 million; WENN-FM and WAGG-AM, $2.5 million; New Grace Hill Cemetery and Zion Memorial Gardens, $1 million; and A. G. Gaston Construction Co., $2.4 million. The holding company also included Vulcan Realty & Investment, which was a small part of the overall organization.

The Birmingham-based Booker T. Washington Insurance Co. was named "Insurance Company of the Year" in the June issue of *Black Enterprise* magazine in 1984. The company's selection was based on "how they handle their business and their overall involvement in community and civic activities," according to Paula Ward, public affairs administrator for the magazine. She said the founder of the company, A. G. Gaston, was specifically cited for "not just running a company in the city, but

for contributing to the community as well." "They were very excited and proud that they were selected. It's an honor that you don't seek, but when it comes, you're very glad to hear it," said Louis Willie, executive vice president of the company. Willie said the company has three reasons for its success. "We try to keep the company profitable, we offer good service to policy holders and we try to treat our employees right."

The genesis of A. G. Gaston Corp. can be traced to the 1920s when a young A. G. Gaston observed poor people asking steelworkers for money during shift changes at U.S. Steel's Birmingham plant. Gaston heard the people say they needed money to bury relatives, friends or other acquaintances in the community. And he saw that some steelworkers were contributing. From that scene Mr. Gaston saw opportunity: if steelworkers would give money to strangers for funerals, wouldn't they be interested in buying burial insurance for themselves? With virtually no capital, Gaston started the Booker T. Washington Insurance Co. to carry out his idea.

After a shaky beginning, the company made it.

Gaston started the insurance company in 1923, selling 25-cent burial insurance policies to area blacks. The company listed total assets of more than $23 million, making it the eighth largest black-owned insurance company in the country, according to *Black Enterprise*. The company no longer sells burial policies, concentrating on life insurance instead. It has $559 million in insurance policies in force. Gaston sold his interests in all his companies except Citizens Federal in 1987, and also retired from those businesses.

GASTON, MACK CHARLES, was born on July 17, 1940, in Dalton, Georgia. He married the former Lillian Bonds of Dalton, and they have a daughter, Sonja. He received a B.S. degree in electrical engineering from Tuskegee Institute in 1964, and an M.S. degree in business administration from Marymount College of Virginia, in 1984. On August 20, 1964, he enlisted in the United States Navy. From 1965 to 1967, he served on the USS *Buck* (DD-761). He attended Naval Destroyer School in Newport, Rhode Island, from March 1967 to September 1967. He served on the USS *O'Brien* (DD-725) from September 1967 to May 1969. Then until May 1971, he served on the staff of the commander of Destroyer Squadron 5. From May 1971 to December 1972, he was assigned to the Office of CNO (OP-098) (personal aide to the Director, Research, Development, Test and Evaluation).

Gaston had numerous assignments until December 1985, when he was assigned to the Surface Warfare Officers School Command (DUINS). In February 1986, he served as commander of USS *Josephus Daniels* (CG-27). In July 1988, he was assigned to the Office of CNO as director of Surface Warfare Manpower and Training Requirement (OP-39). In June 1990, he

served as the commander of field command of Defense Nuclear Agency. In 1990, he was selected rear admiral (lower half). He has received numerous medals and awards which include: the Meritorious Service Medal with one Gold Star; the Navy "E" Ribbon; the Vietnam Campaign Medal with Device; the Vietnam Service Medal with one bronze star; Navy Commendation Medal with Combat "V."

GATES, JACQUELYN, a native of Brooklyn, New York, Gates attended Brooklyn College–City University of New York, where she earned a B.A. degree in history. She continued her graduate education at the New School for Social Research, New York. She is a devoted Christian and a member of the First SDA Church of White Plains. She is married and the mother of three children, four-year-old Tiffany, Antoinette Burch, an education major at Central State University, and Anthony Burch, a biology major at Morehouse College. At age 38, Gates is the youngest national president in the history of the National Association of Negro Business and Professional Women's Clubs, Inc. (NANBPWC), and is focused on moving NANBPWC to action with new directions. Professionally, she is the director of Employment and Employee Relations at NYNEX.

Formerly manager of human resources for Time Inc. magazine company, she directed the corporation's college relations and affirmative action programs. As PepsiCo's manager of corporate relations in Purchase, New York, her career also included various personnel management positions at the Corporate Headquarters of Pepsi-Cola USA, Paramount Pictures Corporation, Revlon, Inc., and J.C. Penney Corporation. She was cited in the November 1989 issue of *Ebony Man* as a Woman of Distinction, and in the May 1990 issue of *Ebony* magazine as one of America's Most Influential Blacks. In 1986, she received the Industry Award from the National Council of Negro Women, the Young Achiever Award from the National Council of Women, and named one of America's Top 100 Black Business and Professional Women by *Dollars and Sense* magazine. In 1985, she received the Cecelia Cabiness Saunders Award, and was named among 100 Young Women of Promise by *Good Housekeeping* magazine.

In 1984, Gates was named an Outstanding Young Woman of America, and a 1984 Harlem YMCA Black Achiever in Industry. She is most proud of the Intern Programs that she initiated at three major corporations—Revlon, Inc., Paramount Pictures Corporation, and PepsiCo, Inc. She believes in exposing youth to successful role models and personally serves as a mentor to eight protégés who are making their mark in corporate America. She also developed the first "Return to Work" program for displaced homemakers at the corporate headquarters of J.C. Penney Company.

GIBSON, ALTHEA, was born on August 25, 1927, in Silver, South Carolina, the eldest of the five children of Daniel and Anna (Washington) Gibson. Brought up in the Harlem area of New York City, she played paddle tennis in a Police Athletic League. She later entered the city's Park Department competition and won the Manhattan girls' championship. In 1943, she won the New York State Black Girls' Singles Championship, and in 1945 and 1946 captured the National Black Girls' Championship. Dr. R. W. Johnson, a black physician and tennis fan, invited Gibson to stay with his family while she attended the Industrial High School at Williston, North Carolina.

Coached by another black physician, Dr. Hubert A. Eaton, she was the runner-up in 1947 to the winner of the National Black Women's Singles Contest, and in 1948 won the national championship which she successfully defended for nine years. In 1949, she entered Florida Agricultural and Mechanical University on an athletic scholarship and played on the tennis and basketball teams. She was the winner of the USLTA Eastern Indoor Championship. In 1950, she became the first black to appear on the Forest Hills, Long Island, courts.

In June 1951, Gibson became the first black American invited to compete in the All-England Championships at Wimbledon. She was eliminated in the quarter finals. In 1952, she was ranked ninth nationally, and in 1953 she was seventh. She graduated from Florida A&M with a B.S. degree in 1953 and was appointed to an athletic instructorship at Lincoln University, Jefferson City, Missouri. In 1954, she was ranked thirteenth by the American Tennis Association (ATA). In 1955, she was named one of four American tennis players to be sent on a six-week "good will" tour of Asia. In 1956, she won both the Indian National and Asiatic Women's Singles championships and was ranked second among American women tennis players.

In 1957, Gibson won the lawn tennis singles titles in the Surrey, Northern and Kentish tournaments, before proceeding to Wimbledon, where she was "seeded" first among the women players. Having eliminated various other opponents, she defeated Britain's 16-year-old Christine Truman in the semi-finals, then on July 6, 1957, she faced fellow American Darlene Hard in an all–American finals contest which was played in 100-degree heat. The match took 49 minutes, and Althea's victory by 6–3, 6–2, made her the first black American ever to win at Wimbledon, and the thirteenth straight American winner of the All-England Women's Singles Championship. She teamed with Darlene Hard to win the doubles title, and at the conclusion of the tournament she was presented to and congratulated by Queen Elizabeth II.

On her return to New York City on July 11, she was given an enthusiastic ticker-tape and official reception. On September 8, 1957, she won the United States Women's Singles title at Forest Hills. She also won the National Clay Courts Championship in 1957. In 1958, she returned to Wimbledon and won the women's singles and, teaming up with Maria Bueno of Brazil, won the women's doubles. Gibson went on to become a women's golf champion and a member of the New Jersey Boxing Commission. She was inducted into the International Tennis Hall of Fame in 1971.

GIBSON, KENNETH ALLEN, was born in Enterprise, Alabama, on May 15, 1932. He is the son of Willie Foy and Daisy Gibson and is married to the former Muriel Cook. They have one child. He has two other children from a previous marriage. When he was eight the family moved north to Newark, New Jersey. He was an honor student in Newark public schools. While attending Central High School, he added to his family's income by playing saxophone in a dance band and working part-time as a porter. After graduating from high school in 1950, he worked for two years and then spent two years in the United States Army.

When he returned from the Army, he enrolled in Newark College of Engineering. He continued his studies there into the 1960s while working for the New Jersey State Highway Department. In 1963, he received a degree in civil engineering and became an engineer with the Newark Housing Authority, in charge of the basic engineering in urban renewal projects. He became active in the Urban League, the NAACP, the YMCA, the YWCA, and CORE, and he headed Newark's Business and Industry Coordinating Council, a job-finding organization, and served as vice president of the United Community Corporation, an anti-poverty agency.

The Newark Junior Chamber of Commerce named him Man of the Year in 1964. The leaders of the black community in Newark asked him to run for mayor in 1966 and he agreed. Entering the mayoralty race six weeks before the election and with only $2,000 in funds, he ran, in his own words, not so much a campaign as "a civil rights demonstration." But he took enough of the votes to force a runoff election. On July 16, 1970, Gibson defeated incumbent Hugh J. Addonizio in an election in which the voting was along racial lines. In the predominantly black south and central wards, he received 93 and 95 percent of the vote, respectively. On May 14, 1974, he was re-elected, defeating a state senator.

GOODALL, HURLEY CHARLES. Goodall has led a life of firsts. He was the first black on the Muncie fire department, the first black elected to the Muncie school board and the first black elected to the legislature from Delaware County. He was born in Muncie on May 23, 1927, the son of Hurley C. and Dorene Mukes Goodall. He attended the public schools of Muncie, graduating from Central High School in 1945. He spent the next two years in the U.S. Army, rising to the rank of private 1st class. After discharge he continued his education at Indiana Business College, Purdue University, and Michigan State University. He married Fredine Wynn in 1948 and they have two children. He belongs to the African Methodist Episcopal Church.

Goodall was a factory worker until 1958, when he was accepted for the Muncie fire department. He retired in 1978. He spent the next two years as assistant to the Delaware County Engineer and, since 1980, has been director of a youth project. He has also served his city as a member of the Human Rights Commission from 1964 to 1970, and the school board from 1970 to 1978. He was school board president 1974 to 1975. A Democrat, he has been a precinct committeeman since 1966. In 1976 and 1980, he was a delegate to the Democratic National Convention.

As a legislator, Goodall is particularly interested in labor, welfare, and minority legislation. He has been a member of various unions and active in the Muncie chapter of the NAACP. His civic activities include service on boards of the Muncie Children's Museum, WIPB-TV (Muncie public television), and the Multi-Service Center of Muncie. He was elected to the Muncie Black Hall of Fame. He is the co-author of a *History of Negroes in Muncie, Indiana* (1976).

GOODE, W. WILSON, was born August 19, 1938, in a wooden shack on Jordan Mill Pond Road just outside Seaboard, North Carolina. His parents were Albert and Rozella Goode. His wife, Velma, is an administrator at the University of Pennsylvania Veterinary Medicine School. They have three children, two daughters and one son. He moved with his family to Philadelphia in 1955, where he attended John Bartram High School and graduated with honors in 1957. He received his bachelor's degree from Morgan State University, then served as a lieutenant in the U.S. Army. In 1968, he received a master's degree in governmental administration from the Wharton School of the University of Pennsylvania.

In 1969, Goode became executive director of the Philadelphia Council for Community Advancement, a nonprofit organization established to help neighborhood groups and promote housing construction. In 1972, he was named outstanding young leader of the year, by the Philadelphia Jaycees. In 1978, he was appointed a member and then chairman of the Pennsylvania Public Utility Commission. In the aftermath of the March 28, 1979 disaster at the Three Mile Island nuclear generating station near Harrisburg, Goode conducted an investigation into the incident and suspended a rate-hike recently granted to the Metropolitan Edison Company which owned the plant. It was Goode who was largely responsible for ensuring that the public was protected and at the same time provided with an uninterrupted flow of power.

In 1980, he was appointed as Philadelphia's first African American managing director. He held this position until December of 1982, when he resigned to seek the mayor's office. He assumed that position in January of 1984, after a distinguished record of community and governmental service. As mayor, he has presided over the rebirth of the central business district, with some $5 billion invested in the downtown development. He also developed the North Philadelphia Plan, a strategy for revitalizing the most depressed area of Philadelphia. He appointed women and minorities to key cabinet, commissioner, and board positions. He dramatically increased the number of contracts going to female-owned and minorities firms (increasing from less than $1 million per year to nearly $500 million over the six and a half years. He was awarded 14 honorary degrees from national universities, including from the University of Pennsylvania, Temple University, and honorary doctorates from Holy Cross, Wittenberg, Morgan State, and Lincoln University.

GORDEN, FRED AUGUSTUS, was born February 22, 1940, in Anniston, Alabama. He received a B.S. degree from the United States Military Academy, and an M.A. in foreign language and literature from Middlebury College. From August 1962 to October 1962, he was a student at the Field Artillery Officer Basic Course, United States Army Artillery and Missile School, Fort Sill, Oklahoma. From November 1962 to January 1963, he was a student in the Ranger Course at the United States Army Infantry School, Fort Benning, Georgia. From January 1963 to November 1965, he served as a forward observer, later liaison officer, later assistant executive officer, and later executive officer, of Battery B, 22d Artillery, 193rd Infantry Brigade, Fort Kobbe, Canal Zone, Panama. He was promoted to the rank of first lieutenant on December 6, 1963.

From November 1965 to March 1966, he served as assistant S-3, 193rd Infantry Brigade, Fort Kobbe. He was promoted to the rank of captain on November 9, 1965. From March 1966 to December 1966, he was a student in the Artillery Officer Advanced Course, United States Army Air Defense School, Fort Bliss, Texas. From December 1966 to January 1968, he first served as the assistant S-3 (operations), liaison officer; commander of Battery C; and then as assistant S-3 of 2d Howitzer battalion, 320th Artiller, 1st Brigade, 101st Airborne Division, United States Army, in Vietnam. From May 1968 to August 1969, he was a student at Middlebury College, Middlebury, Vermont. He was promoted to the grade of major on December 31, 1968.

From August 1969 to June 1972, he was appointed instructor of Spanish, then later assistant professor of Spanish, Department of Foreign Language, United States Military Academy, West Point, New York. From June 1972 to January 1973, he was a student in the Armed Forces Staff College, Norfolk, Virginia. From January 1973 to May 1975, he was an assignment officer. He was later personnel management officer, Field Artillery Branch, United States Army Military Personnel Center, Alexandria, Virginia. From May 1975 to July 1976, he was assigned as executive officer, 1st Battalion, 15th Field Artillery, 2nd Infantry Division, in Korea. On June 7, 1976, he was promoted to the grade of lieutenant colonel.

From July 1976 to March 1977, he served as special assistant to the commander; later S-3, Division Artillery, 25th Infantry Division, Schofield Barracks, Hawaii. From March 1977 to September 1978, he was the commander of the 1st Battalion, 8th Field Artillery, 25th Infantry Division, Schofield Barracks. From September 1978 to June 1979, he served as inspector general for the 25th Infantry Division, Schofield Barracks. From August 1979 to June 1980, he was a student in the National War College, Fort McNair, Washington, D.C. From June 1980 to August 1982, he served as the executive officer in the Office of the Chief of Legislative Liaison, United States Army, Washington. He was promoted to the grade of colonel on August 7, 1980.

From August 1982 to October 1984, Gorden was the commander of the Division Artillery, 7th Infantry Division, Fort Ord, California. From October 1984 to October 1986, he served as director of the Inter-American Region, Office of the Assistant Secretary of Defense (International Security Affairs), Washington. He was promoted to the one-star grade of brigadier general on October 1, 1985.

From October 1986 to August 1987, he served as assistant division commander for the 7th Infantry Division, Fort Ord. From August 1987 to January 1990, he served as the commandant of cadets, United States Military Academy, West Point. On July 1, 1989, he was promoted to the two-star grade of major general. In January 1990, he was assigned as the commanding general of the 25th Infantry Division (Light), at Schofield Barracks.

Gorden has received numerous awards and decorations which include: the Defense Distinguished Service Medal; the Legion of Merit; the Bronze Star Medal with "V" Device (with oak leaf cluster); the Meritorious Service Medal (with oak leaf cluster); the Air Medal; the Army Commendation Medal (with oak leaf cluster); the Parachutist Badge; and the Ranger Tab.

GORDON, LEVAN, was born in Philadelphia, Pennsylvania, and married Vivian J. Goode (Gordon). He is the father of one child, Sharilyn L. Pinkett. He received all elementary schooling in Philadelphia (Hawthorne

Elementary School, Bartlett Jr. High); attended West Philadelphia High; Pennsylvania State University and Lincoln University, B.A. degree, and received his LL.B degree from Howard University Law School. He served in the U.S. Army in 1953–1955, and the U.S. Naval Reserve in 1958–1961. He was admitted to the bar November 5, 1962, and appointed judge of the Municipal Court of Philadelphia, in 1974. He was elected judge of the Municipal Court of Philadelphia in 1975 and elected judge of the Court of Common Pleas of Philadelphia in 1979. He has served as an instructor, Temple University School of Criminal Justice, from 1980 to date.

Prior positions include: serving as an instructor at Georgetown University Intensive Session in Trial Advocacy Skills (NITA), 1984 to present; served as hearing examiner for Pennsylvania Labor Relations Board, 1971–1974; assistant city solicitor, counsel to the Philadelphia Human Relations Commission; executive director of Philadelphia Housing Information Service, a program designed to help low-income families obtain better housing, 1966–1968; former partner for the law firm of Schmidt, Williams, Gaskins & Gordon.

Gordon served as associate counsel to the Governor's Commission that investigated charges of Police Brutality in Chester, Pennsylvania, during 1964 civil rights demonstrations. He is the recipient of many awards: Community Service Award, Strawberry Mansion Civic Association Puerto Rican Community Service Award; Zeta Omicron Lambda Chapter, Alpha Phi Alpha "Man of the Year" Award, 1975; the Association of Business and Professional Women of Philadelphia and Vicinity "Man of the Year" Award, 1984; McMichael Home and School Association, Distinguished Service Award; the Methodist Men, Tindley Temple United Methodist Church, 1986 Award of Excellence; and Father of the Year, 1989, Tindley Temple United Methodist Church.

GORDY, BERRY, JR., was born November 28, 1929, in Detroit, Michigan. He is married to the former Grace Eaton. He attended Detroit public schools where he obtained his musical education. During the early 1950s he gave increasing attention to writing songs, went to New York to develop the necessary contacts, and produced a number of successful "rhythm 'n' blues" songs. His first music business experience was as the proprietor of a record shop in Detroit. His record shop went bankrupt in 1955, and he went to work first as a plasterer with his father and then as a chrome trimmer at the Ford Motor Company. He relieved the monotony of the Ford assembly line by making up songs in his head, and some of the compositions, when perfected, were recorded by local singers and groups he had met in the nightclubs he frequented. Dissatisfied with the way some of the songs were handled, he began producing his own recordings in a rented recording studio with hired musicians and singers.

His master recordings of Jackie Wilson singing songs by Gordy and his sister Gwen were sold to Decca Records and, when issued on Decca's Brunswick label, boosted Wilson to success. The first big Wilson hits were renditions of Gordy's "Reet Petite," "Lonely Teardrops," and "That's Why." A teenaged singer with whom Gordy was working, William "Smokey" Robinson, Jr. (now a vice president of Motown), suggested to him that he form his own company for manufacturing and marketing records. Following the suggestion, Gordy in 1959 borrowed $700 from his family and founded Motown in a bungalow on Detroit's Grand Boulevard. The company was composed of: Jobete, music publishers; Hitsville USA, a recording studio; the Motown Record Corporation, umbrella for the labels Motown, Gordy, Tamla, VIP, and Soul; a songwriting team headed by Brian and Eddie Holland and Lamont Dozier; International

Talent Management, Inc., which sought out and handled new young black performers; and the Motown Artist's development Department, a finishing school where the company's potential stars were trained in grooming, charm, deportment, and so on, until they emerged as polished pros.

The first Motown issue was "Bad Girl," recorded by Smokey Robinson and the Miracles in 1959. Motown's first gold record, issued nationally on the Tamla label, was "Shop Around," cut by Robinson and the Miracles in 1960. Susequent hits issued on Motown labels included the Marvelettes' "Please Mr. Postman" in 1961; Stevie Wonder's "Fingertips, Part 2" in 1963; Marvin Gaye's "How Sweet It Is to Be Loved by You" in 1964; Mary Wells' "My Guy" in 1964; Martha Reeves and the Vandellas' "Dancing in the Streets" in 1964; the Temptations' "My Girl" in 1965; The Four Tops' "Reach Out, I'll Be There" in 1966; and Tammi Terrell and Marvin Gaye's "Your Precious Love" in 1967. By far the most popular exponents of the Motown Sound in the 1960s were Diana Ross and the Supremes, the most successful of all female singing trios internationally. The Supremes had an incredible string of solid gold singles, beginning with "Where Did Our Love Go?" in 1964.

The Jackson Five turned out to be the most lucrative property in the Motown stable during the early 1970s. The Motown group that continued to win more Grammy awards than any other, however, was the durable Gladys Knight and the Pips, which began to record on the Soul label in 1967. In 1970, Gordy moved his company, Motown Industries, to Hollywood, California. Thereafter he added film directing and producing to his activities; the best-known of his films are: *The Wiz, Mahogany, Lady Sings the Blues,* and *The Bingo Long Traveling All-Stars* and *Motor Kings.*

GRAHAM, LOUIS, was born February 28, 1939, in Washington County, Georgia. He and his wife Leslie Graham, have two children, Kevin and Karen. As a child growing up in rural Washington County, he was introduced to hard work at an early age. Picking cotton, plowing with a mule, and many other farm chores. After moving to Atlanta, he joined the Atlanta Police Department in 1965. He was assigned to the uniform patrol until 1967. In 1967, he was assigned to the community relations division. In 1968, he was promoted to detective and assigned to homicide. In 1970, he served as a school detective. In 1971, he was promoted to sergeant, and assigned to uniformed patrol, district 71. In 1972, he was promoted to lieutenant and assigned to homicide, becoming the first black to command a Homicide Division on a major police department.

In 1975, ten years after starting his law enforcement career as a uniformed patrol officer for the Atlanta Police Bureau in 1965, he transferred to the Fulton County Police, a newly created police department. In July 1975, he was hired as a captain in charge of detectives. He organized the detective division and served six weeks as acting chief in 1979. In 1979, he was promoted to assistant chief. Graham helped transform the department from an under-equipped 100-member force, to a department of 240 officers with some of the most sophisticated communications and computer technology in the state. Graham would surface as a candidate nearly every time a local law enforcement command position opened.

In January 1991, he was promoted to chief of police for the Fulton County Police Department. He was the first black captain, assistant chief, and first black chief, in the history of Fulton County. His memberships include: International Association of Chiefs of Police, Georgia Association of Chiefs of Police, National Organization of Black Law Enforcement, and Georgia

Peace Officers Standards and Training Council, from 1977 to the present.

Graham was appointed by Governor George Busbee in 1977 to the Georgia Post Council and was reappointed by Gov. Busbee in 1980 to serve a four-year term. Governor Joe Frank Harris reappointed him to the Georgia Post Council to serve 4-year terms in 1984 and 1988 (expires in 1992); he is presently the longest-serving member to date on the council. He was appointed by Gov. Harris, 1987, to the Governor's Commission on Drug Awareness and Prevention and chaired the Criminal Justice Committee of the Drug Awareness Commission, and was appointed by Gov. Harris on January 3, 1990 to the board of directors of Drug Abuse Resistance Education.

GRANT, EDITH INGRAM, was born in Hancock County, Sparta, Georgia. After receiving her elementary and high school training in Hancock County, she entered Fort Valley State College where she received a B.S. degree in elementary education. Since graduating from Fort Valley State her exposure in society has been wide and varied. She taught in Griffin and Sparta, Georgia, as an elementary teacher. Her teaching career soon came to an end when, in 1968, she was elected as probate judge in Hancock County, being the first black in the United States to be elected to this position. Believing that all help comes from the Lord, Grant sees to it that God gets plenty of her time. She is a member of the Macedonia Baptist Church where she sings in the Inspiration choir, works in the Missionary Society, and serves as director of the Baptist Training Union. She is truly a civic-minded person.

Grant holds membership in several organizations, and many honors and awards have been bestowed upon her. They include: *Who's Who in America*, *Who's Who in American Law*, *The World Who's Who of Women*, May 1973, Cambridge, England; named Woman of the Year by the *Mirror* newspaper in Augusta, 1973; Fulton County's Outstanding Citizen's Award, 1978; Atlanta Branch NAACP—Outstanding, Courage in Southern Political Arena, 1979; PUSH's Pioneer Award, 1983; and the Service Award from the Probate Judges' Association of Georgia, 1988. It is interesting to note that she was recognized for her excellency by two governors, and they saw it almost imperative to have her an integral part of their team.

Grant was appointed a member of the State Democratic Executive Committee by Jimmy Carter (then governor of Georgia), and lieutenant colonel aide de camp, Governor's Staff in 1983, by Governor Joe Frank Harris. She has certainly had a busy, interesting, and rewarding life. She has also found the time to give her hand in holy matrimony to Roy L. Grant.

GRAVELY, SAMUEL LEE, was born June 4, 1922, in Richmond, Virginia. He is married to the former Alma Clark and they have three children, Robert, David, and Tracey. He is a graduate of Virginia Union University (A.B., 1948). He enlisted in the U.S. Naval Reserve (1942) and completed midshipman school at Columbia University (1944), becoming the first black man to be commissioned as an ensign in World War II. He was assigned to the submarine chaser PC-1264, on which he served successively as communications officer, electronics officer and personnel officer. Released from active duty in 1946, he completed college in 1948.

The Navy recalled him to active duty, in August 1949, and he saw both sea and shore duty during the Korean War. He transferred from the Navy Reserve to the regular Navy in 1955. In February 1961, as temporary skipper of the destroyer USS *Chandler*, he

became the first black man ever to command a Navy ship. Rising to lieutenant commander, he was given his own ship, the radar picket destroyer USS *Falgout*. Two other ship commands followed. He was promoted to captain in 1967, and to rear admiral and director of Naval Communications in 1971. In 1973, he was named commander of a flotilla of 30 ships.

Gravely distinguished himself as a naval communications expert, shop captain and eventually commander of the third fleet. He was the Navy's first black three-star naval officer, as well as the first black ever to attain the rank of admiral. He retired from the Navy in 1980 and since that time has served on several corporate boards and as consultant to defense contractors, while living in rural Haymarket, Virginia.

Gravely has been awarded the Legion of Merit, Bronze Star Medal, the Meritorious Service Medal, the Joint Services Commendation Medal, and the Navy Commendation Medal with bronze star and Combat "V." He is also authorized to wear the World War II Victory Medal; the Naval Reserve Medal (for 10 years' service in the U.S.

Naval Reserve); the American Campaign Medal; the Korean Presidential Unit Citation; the National Defense Medal with one bronze star; the China Service Medal (extended); the Korean Service Medal with two bronze stars; the United Nations Service Medal; the Armed Forces Expeditionary Medal; the Vietnam Service Medal with six bronze stars; the Vietnamese Campaign Medal; the Antarctica Service Medal; and the Venezuelan Order of Merit Second Class.

GRAVES, CURTIS M., was born in New Orleans, Louisiana, and is married to Joanne Gordon Graves. They have three children, Gretchen, Christopher and Gizelle. He earned a B.A. degree from Texas Southern University and was a Woodrow Wilson Fellow at Princeton University. He has co-authored two books called *Famous Black Americans*, written for elementary students. Graves is deputy director for civil affairs of the Defense and Intergovernmental Relations Division at the National Aeronautics and Space Administration in Washington, D.C. He is responsible for all communications and relationships with the Federal civil agencies and with state and local governments. He represents NASA on programmatic and policy issues to develop cooperative undertakings.

Before taking his present NASA position, Graves was deputy director for academic services in Public Affairs and chief of Community and Education Services. Before coming to NASA, he was managing associate and director of continuing education for the National Civil Service League in Washington for four years. He served for six years as a member of the Texas House of representatives, elected from a Houston district. He served on the following legislative committees: Elections, Higher Education, Juvenile Crime and Delinquency, School Districts and Military Affairs.

When elected in 1966, Graves was the first black elected to the Texas House of Representatives since 1891. He has received awards from the Council of Negro Women, Delta Sigma Theta Sorority, the National Association of College Women, Kappa Alpha Psi Fraternity, Texas Southern University, the National Congress on Aviation and Space Education, two honorary doctorate degrees, and the Frank G. Brewer Trophy in 1989.

GRAVES, EARL G., was born January 9, 1935, in Brooklyn, New York, the son of Earl G. and Winifred Graves. He married the former Barbara Kydd and they have three sons, Earl, Jr., John Clifford, and Michael Alan. While attending high school in Bedford-Stuyvesant in Brooklyn, he worked as many as three jobs at once. He paid his way through Morgan State College in Baltimore by selling both his energy and his know-how: teaching swimming and after-school programs, taking any odd job he could find, monitoring his dorm, running track for his meal ticket, and selling flowers on cam-

pus for local florists. He majored in economics, and by his junior year in 1956 he started his first business, cutting grass for local homeowners. He had a friend type up a flyer that promised experienced and knowledgeable lawn trimming at a reasonable price.

He graduated from Morgan State College in 1958 with a B.A. degree. Graves, who had been in the Reserve Officers Training Corps all the way through college, entered the Army two days after graduation. The Army was just what Graves needed. He learned how to organize people without any nonsense, and how to lead and discipline people with respect. He made first lieutenant, but it was clearly not a career. He left the Army and returned to New York, but joined the National Guard Reserves. He then married Barbara Kydd, then a school teacher and now general manager for Earl G. Graves, Ltd.

Graves went to work for the Justice Department as a narcotics agent. After a year, he went back to selling houses as he had before taking the Justice Department job. He sold a lot of houses, and by 1965 he had become manager of a Bedford-Stuyvesant real estate office, supervising six salesmen. In 1963, after an officer told him blacks should not be company commanders, he switched to the National Guard's Green Beret Reserves. There he commanded an elite unit of gung-ho types, men who hadn't joined just to avoid going to Vietnam. It was also in 1965 that Graves went to work for United States Senator Robert Kennedy. His job title was administrative assistant, responsible for making sure that events came off with military precision. In 1968, Kennedy was shot dead while campaigning for the Democratic presidential nomination. Graves was stunned by the trauma and lost his way for a while. Several large companies offered him jobs, but he turned them down.

A few months later an uncle of Graves' who operated a drugstore in Bedford-Stuyvesant was killed by a 14-year-old during a robbery. Graves moved his wife and three sons out of the city and started a management consulting firm, mainly as an excuse to give himself time to think about what he wanted to do, about what kind of business he could get into. One of his first clients sparked the idea for *Black Enterprise*. The Ford Foundation gave him a grant to study black-owned business in Caribbean countries. In 1969, he started piecing together a business plan for the magazine. He put together an editorial prospectus with the help of an experienced black reporter. He recruited a board of advisors of well-known black leaders from politics and business to give the magazine credibility.

Graves found a willing partner at Chase Manhattan Bank's Manhattan Capital Corp. They lent him $150,000 and bought 25 percent of the company for another $25,000. He sold 90 percent of the ads that brought the first year's revenues of $900,000, and his military

approach helped him keep expenses under that figure. The magazine was promoted as a how-to magazine for black entrepreneurs. The cover story in the first issue, entitled "How I Started in Business with $1,000," was about Charles Evers, who was mayor of Fayette, Mississippi, and the owner of a flourishing shopping center in that town. That first issue had 17 pages of ads among the total of 64. By 1972, people had begun to take the magazine seriously, and by 1975, Graves was being called on to make speeches.

Earl G. Graves Ltd. has come a long way, too. Officially there are six companies under the parent's banner: Earl G. Graves Publishing Co., Inc.; EGG Dallas Broadcasting, Inc.; Earl G. Graves Development Co., Inc.; Earl G. Graves Marketing and Research Co., Inc.; B.C.I. Marketing, Inc.; and the Minority Business Information Institute, Inc. "I believe that we can make a difference, are making a difference and have made a difference in terms of black people in this country having a piece of the economic action," Graves said. *Black Enterprise* became profitable after its 10th issue. In 1990, the magazine had a circulation of 230,000, had revenue of $15.1 million, compared with $900,000 after its first year.

Graves is in partnership with Earvin "Magic" Johnson in a Pepsi franchise, the largest minority-controlled Pepsi franchise in the nation. Also, he is grooming the next generation to take over. His son, Earl Graves, Jr., is vice president of advertising and marketing; Michael is involved in his father's Pepsi venture; and his third son, John, is an attorney in New York. Graves, who has become a respected authority on black businesses, is taking his knowledge into other arenas. He sits on the boards of many major corporations. Graves "found a vacuum in the black publishing field," the need for a black business publication. His military background has shaped the tone of the company and his approach to management, someone who does not consider his dreams to be out of reach.

GRAY, C. VERNON, was born July 30, 1939, in Sunderland, Maryland. He married the former Sandra Trice Gray and they have two children, Michael and Angela. He received a B.A. degree from Morgan State University, Baltimore, in 1961; an M.A. from Atlanta University, Atlanta, Georgia, in 1962; and a Ph.D. from the University of Massachusetts, Amherst, Massachusetts, in 1971. From 1962 to 1966, he served as an instructor at Philander Smith College in Little Rock, Arkansas. From 1970 to 1971, he was an assistant professor at Oakland University in Rochester, Michigan. Since 1972, Gray has has been a professor and chairman of the Department of Political Science at Morgan State University. He has also served as visiting professor at the University of Maryland, and Goucher College.

In 1988, he served on the U.S. State Department Foreign Review Panel. His public service record includes: first elected to Howard County Council in 1982, re-elected in 1986; chairman of the Howard County Council from 1985–1987; Chairman of the Howard County Zoning Board in 1990. He has also served on numerous state, local, and national committees and organizations, including the following boards: Maryland Children's Museum, Howard County Hospital Capital Fund, Inc.; United Way Community Partnerships; Maryland Museum of African Art; Howard County Red Cross; and National Association of Counties (NACO).

GRAY, ROBERT EARL, was born on October 18, 1941, in Algoma, West Virginia. He received a B.A. degree in computer science from Ohio State University. He enlisted in the United States Army in July 1959. From 1966 to March 1967, he was a student in the Signal Officer Basic Course, United States Army Signal School, Fort Monmouth, New Jersey. From March 1967 to October 1968, he served as a communications officer in the 56th Artillery Group, United States Army in Europe. He was promoted to the rank of first lieutenant on May 26, 1967, and was promoted to the rank of captain on May 26, 1968. From October 1968 to May 1969, he was the commander of Company C of the 97th Signal Battalion, 7th United States Army Communications Command, in Europe.

From May 1969 to June 1970, Gray served as the S-4 (logistics officer), and as commander of Company A, 501st Signal Battalion, 101st Airborne Division (Airmobile), United States Army in Vietnam. From July 1970 to June 1971, he was a student in the Signal Officer Advanced Course, United States Army Signal School, Fort Monmouth. From June 1973 to November 1974, he served as an automatic data processing officer, in the Computer Security Element of the Counterintelligence and Security Division, Defense Intelligence Agency, Washington, D.C. From November 1974 to July 1976, he was assigned as a communications-electronics staff officer in the Plans and Policy Branch of the Systems Management Division, Information Systems Directorate, Defense Intelligence Agency, Washington.

Gray was promoted to the grade of major on August 19, 1975. From July 1976 to June 1977, he was a student at the United States Army Command and General Staff College, Fort Leavenworth, Kansas. From June 1977 to August 1978, he served as the executive officer of the 50th Signal Battalion of the 35th Group, XVIII Airborne Corps, Fort Bragg, North Carolina. From August 1978 to April 1980, he served as the tactical plans officer, G-3 (operations), Contingency Plans Division, XVIII Airborne Corps, Fort Bragg. He was promoted to the grade of lieutenant colonel on August 13, 1979. From May 1980 to June 1983, he served as the commander of the 82nd Signal Battalion, 82nd Airborne Division, Fort Bragg. From June 1983 to June 1984, he was a student at the United States Army War College, Carlisle Barracks, Pennsylvania. From June 1984 to February 1986, he served as the chief of the Command, Control, and Communications Division, United States Army Combined Arms Combat Development Activity, Fort Leavenworth.

From February 1986 to June 1988, he was the commander of the 35th Signal Brigade, XVIII Airborne Corps, Fort Bragg. He was promoted to the grade of colonel on November 1, 1984. From July 1988 to October 1988, he served as special assistant to the commanding general, XVIII Airborne Corps, Fort Bragg. In October of 1988, he was promoted to the one-star grade of brigadier general, and was assigned as the deputy commanding general of the United States Army Signal Center

and Fort Gordon/assistant commandant of the United States Army Signal School, Fort Gordon, Georgia. In August of 1990, he was assigned as the deputy director for Plans, Programs and Systems, Office of the Director of Information Systems for Command, Control Cmmunication and Computers, in the Office of the Secretary of the Army, Washington. In August 1991, Brigadier General Robert Gray became the first African American commanding general for Fort Gordon and the U.S. Army Signal Center. He has received numerous awards and decorations which include: the Legion of Merit; the Bronze Star; the Air Medal; the Meritorious Service Medal (with two oak leaf clusters); the Army Commendation Medal (with oak leaf cluster); and the Master Parachutist Badge.

GRAY, WILLIAM H., was born August 20, 1941, in Baton Rouge, Louisiana, to Hazel Yates and the late Dr. William H. Gray, Jr. He is married to the former Andrea Dash and they have three sons, William H. IV, Justin Yates, and Andrew Dash. He was raised in

North Philadelphia and attended Simon Gratz High School. He received a B.A. degree from Franklin and Marshall College in 1963, a master's degree in divinity from Drew Theological Seminary in 1966, and a master's degree in theology from the Princeton Theological Seminary in 1970. He served six terms as the representative of Pennsylvania's 2nd Congressional District. Gray was majority whip of the House of Representatives, the number three leadership position in the House. In that position, he was responsible for helping to set legislative priorities and assembling legislative majorities to implement them.

Gray served for four years as chairman of the House Committee on the Budget, a position that brought him national attention for his fiscal expertise and legislative leadership. He was then elected chairman of the Democratic Caucus. He served on the Committee on Appropriations where he was the ranking member of the Subcommittee on Transportation and a member of the Subcommittee on Foreign Operations. He was also a member of the Committee on Fiscal Affairs and Health and the Subcommittee on Government Operations and Metropolitan Affairs. He was a former vice chairman of the Congressional Black Caucus and served as chairman of the Platform Drafting Committee for the 1988 Democratic National Convention.

Gray has been a leading spokesman on African policy. He authored the House version of the Anti-Apartheid Acts of 1985 and 1986 — legislation to limit American financial support for apartheid. He was one of the first congressmen to warn of famine conditions in Africa. He sponsored the emergency food aid bill for Ethiopia in 1984, and in 1980 he authored the bill that established the African Development Foundation which delivers U.S. aid to African villages — the only new agency created by a freshman and passed by Congress in this century.

In 1983, Gray authorized the first of a series of set-aside provisions to require participation by minority and women business owners, historically black colleges and minority private agencies in the U.S. Agency for International Development's development assistance programs. As a result, minorities and females received $300 million in AID contracts in the past three years, with $1 billion anticipated over the next ten years. He was also responsible for measures that have provided $10 million to minority business owners for bonding assistance in connection with transportation and highway projects. In 1989, the 101st Congress elected Gray majority whip which made him one of the most powerful and influential men in Congress. He performs the critical function of intelligence gathering (who will vote yes, who will vote no).

———

GREEN, DIANNA, a graduate of Golden Gate College, also holds an M.B.A. degree from Golden Gate University. She serves on the board of Point Park College, and numerous other civic organizations. She is vice president of the Administrative Services Group for Duquesne Light Company. She has responsibility for human resources, corporate affairs, general services and corporate security and reports directly to the Chairman and CEO of Duquesne Light. She joined Duquesne Light in May 1988 as general manager of human resources and was elected a vice president in September 1988.

Green was previously employed by Xerox Corporation in Fremont, California, as vice president of personnel for the Information Products Division. Before joining Xerox, she held positions in the personnel area for Ford Motor Company and served four years in the United States Air Force. She was selected by *Business Week* in 1987 as one of "Fifty Women to Watch" in corporate

America, and both *Dollars and Sense* and *Ebony* magazines named her as one of the nation's top 100 black business and professional women. She is also the recipient of the NAACP's outstanding service award.

GREEN, MELVIA B., was born November 13, 1953, in Miami, Florida, and is married. She graduated from Northwestern University, Evanston, Illinois, B.S., 1975 (dean's list all four years, academic scholarship, Alpha Lambda Delta–Collegiate, Women's Honor Society); University of Miami School of Law, Coral Gables, Florida, J.D., 1978 (academic scholarship, Dean's List senior year). She has served as one of Dade County Circuit Court judges from 1989 to date.

Prior positions include: Dade County Court judge, 1987–1989; senior litigation associate for Morgan, Lewis & Bockins, Philadelphia, Pennsylvania (Miami office), 1983–1987; Assistant United States Attorney, Department of Justice, Southern District of Florida, 1980–1983; staff attorney, Florida Power Corporation, St. Petersburg, Florida, 1978–1980.

Green is the recipient of the 1990 Outstanding Government Role Model presented by Transplant Foundation of South Florida; 1990 Outstanding Community Leader in the Judicial System, presented by Zeta Phi Beta Sorority, Inc., Beta Tau Zeta Chapter; and 1989 Achievement Award presented by Negro Business and Professional Women's Association. Professional affiliations include: American Judges Association; Dade County Bar Association; Florida Association of Women Lawyers, Florida Bar Association; the Miami Forum; National Bar Association; Negro Business and Professional Women's Association; and the Women Lawyers Association of the National Bar Association.

GREENE, BILL, was born in Kansas City, Missouri, November 15, 1931. He attended Kansas City schools, Lincoln Junior College (Kansas City), and the University of Michigan. Married to Yvonne LaFargue, they have two daughters, Alisa Rochelle and Jan Andrea. He is a United States Air Force veteran. The first black to serve as clerk to the assembly and consultant to former Speaker Jesse Unruh, and legislative assistant to Assemblyman Mervyn M. Dymally (former Lt. Governor). He was legislative advocate for the Building Service Employees International Union; field representative for the Los Angeles Democratic Central Committee; and regional director of the California Federation of Young Democrats. He is a former business representative of the Los Angeles City Employees, and former Freedom Rider and field representative for the Congress of Racial Equality.

Greene has served on numerous committees: Senate Industrial Relations, chairman; Senate Budget and Fiscal Review; Senate Elections and Reapportionment; Senate Governmental Organization; Senate Review and

Taxation; Budget and Fiscal Review Subcommittee #3 on Health, Human Services and Labor, chairman; Elections and Reapportionment Subcommittee on the Census, chairman; Governmental Organization Subcommittee on State Tidelands, chairman; Industrial Relations Subcommittee on Women in the Workforce; Elections and Reapportionment Subcommittee Women and the 1990 Reapportionment; Select Committee on Governmental Efficiency; Select Committee on Health Hazards of the Workplace; Select Committee on the Arts; Joint Committee on Legislative Budget; Joint Committee on Oversight Committee on GAIN Implementation; Joint Committee on 1992 California Quincentennial of the Voyages of Christopher Columbus.

Greene represents south-central and portions of the southeast sections of Los Angeles and Compton, and the contract cities of Bell, Cudahy, Huntington Park, and South Gate.

GREGORY, FREDERICK D., was born January 7, 1941, in Washington, D.C. His mother was Mrs. Nora D. Gregory, a resident of Washington. He married the former Barbara Archer of Washington. He graduated from Anacostia High School, Washington, in 1958; received a B.S. degree from the United States Air Force Academy in 1964, and a master's degree in information systems from George Washington University in 1977. After graduating from the United States Air Force Academy in 1964, he entered pilot training and attended helicopter training at Stead AFB, Nevada. He received his wings in 1965 and was assigned as an H-43 helicopter rescue pilot at Vance AFB, Oklahoma, from October 1965 until May 1966. In June 1966, he was assigned as an H-43 combat rescue pilot at Danang AB, Vietnam.

When he returned to the United States in July 1967, Gregory was assigned as a missile support helicopter pilot flying the UH-1F at Whiteman AFB, Missouri. In January 1968, he was retrained as a fixed-wing pilot flying the T-38 at Randolph AFB, Texas. He was then assigned to the F-4 Phantom Combat Crew Training Wing at Davis-Monthan AFB, Arizona. He attended the United States Naval Test Pilot School at Patuxent River Naval Air Station, Maryland, from September 1970 to June 1971. Following completion of this training, he was assigned to the 4950th Test Wing, Wright-Patterson AFB, Ohio, as an operational test pilot flying fighters and helicopters. In June 1974, he was detailed to the National Aeronautics and Space Administration (NASA), Langley Research Center, Hampton, Virginia. He served as a research test pilot at Langley until selected for the Astronaut Program in January 1978.

Gregory has logged more than 6,500 hours flying time in over 50 types of aircraft, including 550 combat missions in Vietnam. He holds an FAA commercial and instrument certificate for single- and multi-engine qualities and cockpit design. He was selected as an astronaut in January 1978. His technical assignments have included astronaut office representative at the Kennedy Space Center during initial Orbiter checkout and launch support for STS-1 and STS-2, flight data file manager, lead capsule communicator (CAPCOM), chief, operation safety, NASA Headquarters, Washington, chief, astronaut training, and a member of the Orbiter Configuration Control Board, and the Space Shuttle Program Control Board. He has flown on two shuttle missions, STS-51B and STS-33.

On his first mission, Gregory was pilot on STS-51B/Spacelab-3 which launched from Kennedy Space Center, Florida, on April 29, 1985. The crew on board the Orbiter *Challenger* included spacecraft commander, Robert Overmyer; mission specialists, Norman Thagard, William Thornton, and Don Lind; and payload specialists, Taylor Wang and Lodewijk Vandenberg. On this second flight of the European Space Agency (ESA) developed laboratory, the crew members conducted a broad range of scientific experiments ranging from space physics to the suitability of animal holding facilities. The crew also deployed the Northern Utah Satellite

(NUSAT). After seven days of around-the-clock scientific operations, *Challenger* and its laboratory cargo landed on the dry lakebed at Edwards AFB, California, on May 6, 1985.

Gregory was the spacecraft commander on STS-33 which launched, at night, from Kennedy Space Center, Florida, on November 22, 1989. On board the Orbiter *Discovery*, his crew included the pilot, John Blaha, and three mission specialists, Manley (Sonny) Carter, Story Musgrave, and Kathryn Thornton. The mission carried Department of Defense payloads and other secondary payloads. After 79 orbits of the earth, this five-day mission concluded on November 27, 1989, with a hard surface landing on Runway 4 at Edwards AFB. With the completion of his second mission, Gregory has logged over 288 hours in space. In March 1991, he was working on his third mission, the STS-44 which he commanded in the later part of the summer of 1991. The mission deployed a Department of Defense satellite and participated in other military activities. During this ten-day mission his crew conducted extensive studies evaluating medical countermeasures in long duration space flights.

GRIFFEY, DICK, was born November 16, 1943, in Nashville, Tennessee. For over two decades Griffey, chairman of the board of Sounds of Los Angeles Records (SOLAR), has accomplished great things in the entertainment world and returned profits from his business activities to the community. His dreams began when he was a promising young drummer and Tennessee State University student. Armed with a rich musical heritage developed and encouraged by his mother, he progressed from an ambitious young man with a dream to owner of the second largest African American–owned record company in the United States.

Despite the tremendous demands of his business, he maintained an unwavering record of community support and service rooted to his conviction that a strong African American community was essential to African American economic growth.

Griffey entered the entertainment business in the mid–60s when he discovered he possessed the entrepreneurial spirit, "he started thinking how entertainers come and go, but business people are always here." He first used his talents as the booking agent for a highly successful nightclub which he co-owned with former schoolmate and ex–New York Knickers player/coach Dick Barnett. He quickly branched out into concert promotion under the company name Dick Griffey Productions and earned the distinction as the most prominent African American promoter in town. At that time he was promoting domestic and international tours for some of the nation's biggest acts such as Stevie Wonder and The Jacksons.

Not content with these achievements, Griffey became talent coordinator for the nationally syndicated television dance program "Soul Train." Concerts were being routed to him. When you promote a concert you basically do the same things every time. He was always looking for new challenges. The "Soul Train" venture was so successful that in 1975 he and the show's producer, Don Cornelius, went on to form Soul Train Records. With only one small act, he carefully nurtured the label. After an amicable separation from Cornelius, he reorganized the company and founded the Solar label in 1977. Since that time he has directed Solar Records to both national and international prominence. Recording under the Solar and Constellation labels are numerous R&B and pop acts, including Shalamar, The Whispers, Lakeside, Midnight Star, Klymaxx, Carrie Lucas, The Deele and Babyface.

Griffey has always believed in giving new talent the opportunity to create and develop their crafts. He was the first to recognize songwriters/producers James "Jimmy Jam" Harris and Terry Lewis, Reggie and Vincent Calloway, Leon Sylvers and Antonio "L.A." Reid and Kenny "Babyface" Edmonds, to name a few. With the opening of a Solar branch in Lagos, Nigeria and distribution of Solar records in the United Kingdom, France, Germany, and Benelux, Griffey's acts have consistently reached and scored well on the music charts, selling millions of records throughout the world. From Dick Griffey Productions and the Solar and Constellation record labels, he expanded his business to include Griffco, a talent management company, which handles various entertainment and public figures including the Rev. Jesse Jackson; and Spectrum VII Music and Hip Trip Music, publishing companies that administer additional publishing catalogues including copyrighting, television licensing, royalties and print music.

The newest addition to his empire is Galaxy Studio. This facility includes a sound studio, rehearsal room and writers' room with state-of-the-art equipment. All of Griffey's corporate holdings occupy space in the four-year-old, $5 million, multi-story, Griffey-owned and operated Solar Tower located in Hollywood. A man of strong convictions, he has always felt the need to return some of his profits to the community, in particular, the African American community. "Music was the greatest natural resource in the African American community, and the industry generates more dollars by and for African Americans than any other single industry." Therefore it is important, "that African Americans who are successful in the music business return something to the community which helped them succeed." To that end, he has demonstrated his beliefs by giving of his time, his money and himself.

Griffey has reinvested in numerous organizations over the years. They include: the Black Music Association, PUSH Trade Association, Black Entertainment Lawyers Association, Hollywood Chamber of Commerce, City of Hop, Recording Industry Association of America, United Negro College Fund, American Cancer Fund and Tennessee State University. One of his charitable endeavors was the Save the Children, They Are the Future Telethon held in June 1989. Over a period of three years, Griffey and Assemblywoman Maxine Waters created the Coalition for a Free Africa in an effort to raise funds to aid the children in southern Africa.

On February 13, 1984, the United Nation's Special Committee Against Apartheid in New York, Griffey announced that "all of Solar Record royalties for publishing from South Africa would be donated to help improve the quality of life for the people there." While most people can only dream of major accomplishments, they are for Griffey already a reality. He is still a young man and with his drive and ability, a lifetime of accomplishments must lie ahead.

GRIMES, HUBERT L., was born in Bartow, Florida. He married the former Peggy Williams and they have two children, Ebun Iman and Jamal Kenneth. He received a B.S. degree from Kentucky State University in 1975, and a J.D. degree from the University of Georgia Law School in 1980. From 1980 to 1983, he was employed as a staff attorney/unit director of Central Florida Legal Services. In 1983, he was a founder and executive director of Central Florida Community Development Corp. In 1985, he became a partner in the law firm of Grimes & Polk, P.A. He also served as an adjunct instructor of criminal law at Bethune-Cookman College, and in 1987, he served as an adjunct instructor of business law at the University of Central Florida.

In 1988, when elected county judge, Grimes became the first black judge of Volusia County, Florida. He has received numerous awards, and served numerous organizations which include: president of the student government association at Kentucky State University in 1974; co-authored the Georgia Law Enforcement Training Manuals on Criminal Arrest and Searches and Seizures, in 1978; president of the University of Georgia Chapter of Black Law Students Association, from 1978 to 1980; served as a member of Volusia County Charter Review Commission, in 1986. He chaired the Beach Subcommittee which successfully created the merger of all county beaches under the authority of a Beach Trust Commission. Grimes is a member of the NAACP, and a member of Alpha Phi Alpha which named him brother of the Midwest United States in 1975.

GROFF, REGIS F., was born April 8, 1935, in Monmouth, Illinois. He married Ada Brooks and is the father of two children, Peter and Tracy. He graduated from Monmouth High School; received a B.S. degree in education (social science) from Western Illinois University, Macomb, Illinois, 1962; M.A. degree in secondary education (history); and an M.A. degree in secondary education (history) from the University of Denver, Denver, Colorado, 1972. He graduated from the John F. Kennedy School of Government, a program for senior executives in state and local government, Harvard University, in 1980. He served in the United States Air Force, 1953–1957, and received an honorable discharge with the rank of A/1c in 1957.

The former minority leader of the Colorado State Senate was first elected to the State Legislature in 1974 to fill the remaining years of the senate seat vacated by former Lt. Gov. George L. Brown. Groff was elected to his first full four-year term in 1976. Immediately following the 1976 election, he was elected by his colleagues to the leadership position of assistant minority leader. In 1978 he was elected as Senate minority leader, and he was re-elected to that post in 1980. Prior positions included: intergovernmental relations specialist, Denver Public Schools Administrative Offices, 1974–1984; taught history and government for 14 years before working in the Planning and Development Department; caseworker, Cook County Department of Public Aid, Chicago, Illinois, where he determined eligibility of aid for dependent children, disability assistance and blind assistance.

Groff has received numerous civic, international and social awards from a wide cross-section of the community. From 1974 to date, he has served on the following committees: Education; Finance; Judiciary; Health, Environment, Welfare, and Institutions; Transportation; Procedures; and Legislative Council.

GUITON, BONNIE, was born October 30, 1941, Springfield, Illinois. She is the daughter of Henry Frank Brazelton and Zole Elizabeth Newman Brazelton. She is divorced with one child, Nichele M. She received her B.A. degree in 1974 from Mills College, Oakland, California; an M.S. degree in 1975 from California State University; and an Ed.D degree in 1985 from the University of California, Berkeley. As president and CEO of the Earth Conservation Corps, a national, privately funded, nonprofit organization, Guiton's commitment was to linking vital conservation work such as reforestation, wetlands protection, disaster clean-up and other environmental rebuilding projects with the energy and idealism of young men and women throughout the country.

Prior to assuming this position with ECC, Guiton served two U.S. presidents in three separate appointments, most recently as special adviser to President Bush for Consumer Affairs and director of the United States Office of Consumer Affairs, where she forged new coalitions to address consumer concerns about the privacy and accuracy of personal computerized information. In addition, she launched the first National Symposium of Minority Consumer Issues, to address the unique problems and contributions of these consumers. She also served in the Department of Education as an assistant secretary for Adult and Vocational Education, where she successfully advocated incorporating basic skills into vocational-technical education.

Prior to that appointment, Guiton was vice chairman of the U.S. Postal Rate Commission. She came to Washington, D.C., from Oakland, California, where she had been a vice president with Kaiser Aluminum and Chemical Corporation, executive director of the Marcus A. Foster Education

Institute, and assistant dean of students at Mills College in California.

Guiton serves on the board of directors of the National Museum of Women in the Arts, and is a recipient of the YWCA's Tribute to Women in International Industry (TWIN) award, the National Coalition of 100 Black Women's Candace Award, the National Future Farmers of America's honorary American Farmer award, and numerous others. "Our goal," says Guiton, "is to preserve two of our greatest resources – the environment and our youth. Both are at risk."

GUMBEL, BRYANT CHARLES, was born on September 29, 1948, in New Orleans, Louisiana. He is the son of Richard Dunbar Gumbel and Rhea Alice (LeCesne) Gumbel. He is the second of four children; he has an older brother Greg, and two younger sisters, Rhonda and Renee. He married the former June Baranco, and they have two children, Jillian and Bradley. He graduated from the Roman Catholic elementary and high schools in Chicago. In 1970, he received a B.A. degree in Russian history from Bates College in Lewiston, Maine. He was one of only three blacks in a student body of 900. His first job after graduating from Bates was as a salesman for the Westvaco Corporation, a firm that manufactures paper bags and folding cartons. After about six months he quit.

In 1972, Gumbel took a job writing for a small monthly, *Black Sport*, and soon became editor-in-chief. In April of 1972, at the age of 23, Gumbel was hired by KNBC-TV in Los Angeles. An acquaintance at KNBC asked him to try out for the weekend sports anchor job. After eight months, he became the weeknight sportscaster on the 6:00 p.m. news, and in 1976, he was promoted to the post of KNBC's sports director. He held that position from 1976 to 1980. He commuted to

and from New York City on weekends to anchor major league sports, doing a wrap-up for his own affiliate, using NBC cameras.

In 1976, he won an Emmy award for producing an Olympics sports special. He won a second Emmy in 1977 and the Los Angeles Press Club Golden Mike Award in 1978 and 1979, and he was slated to co-anchor NBC's coverage of the 1980 Summer Olympics in Russia until the United States boycotted the Moscow games. In June 1980, he signed a three-year contract with the NBC network that included three sports features a week, for the "Today" morning show, a role that escalated in 1982 when he beat out various others for a co-host job. He became the first black to co-host "Today" in its 30-year history, the oldest morning program.

Gumbel first hosted "Today" alone with Jane Pauley and Chris Wallace. In 1986, he was voted the Best Morning TV News Interviewer by more than 1,000 journalists in the *Washington Journal Review* readers' poll. By 1991, Gumbel had become one of the most important figures in television broadcasting, and has taken an active role in revamping "Today."

HACKER, BENJAMIN T., was born September 19, 1935, in Washington, D.C., the son of Rev. C. Leroy Hacker and Alzeda C. Hacker. He married the former Jeanne House of Springfield, Ohio, and they have three children: Benjamin, Jr., Bruce and Anne. He attended high school in Daytona Beach, Florida, and Dayton, Ohio. After two years at the University of Dayton, he transferred to the University of Wittenberg in Springfield, Ohio, where he received a B.A. degree in 1957. In September 1958, he graduated from the United States Naval Aviation Officer Candidate School, Pensacola, Florida. Following completion of Aviation Officer

Candidate School in Pensacola, he was commissioned an ensign in September 1958. His operational assignments have included serving concurrently as commander Fleet Air Mediterranean; commander Maritime Surveillance and Reconnaissance Forces, United States Sixth Fleet; and commander Maritime Air Forces Mediterranean headquartered in Naples, Italy, from 1982–1984. In 1973, he reported to Patrol Squadron 24 in Jacksonville, Florida, where he served as executive officer and later as commanding officer. During this tour the squadron made highly successful deployments to Keflavik, Iceland, and was heavily tasked in major operational exercises in the Northern and Central Atlantic.

Hacker reported in 1970 to Patrol Squadron 47 based at Moffett Field, California, where the squadron completed numerous deployments in the P3c "Orion" aircraft to Adak, Alaska, and the Western Pacific. His first operational assignment was to Patrol Squadron 21 stationed in Brunswick, Maine, where he flew the P2V "Neptune" anti-submarine warfare aircraft. His shore assignments have included serving on the staff of the Chief of Naval Operations in 1984 as director, Total Force Training and Education Division (OP–11). In 1972, he established the NROTC unit at Florida A&M University in Tallahassee, where he served as its first commanding officer and professor of Naval Science. Additionally, he served as the commanding officer of the United States Naval Facility in Argentia, Newfoundland, and as personnel officer and instructor in the P–3A aircraft while attached to Patrol Squadron 31 at Naval Air Station, Moffett Field.

In 1975, Hacker was assigned to the Bureau of Naval Personnel as a division director and special assistant to the Chief of Naval Personnel, Washington, D.C. In 1980, he assumed duties as commander, United States Military Enlistment Processing Command headquartered in Fort Sheridan, Illinois. On March 1, 1981, he was promoted to the one-star rank of rear admiral. His last assignment was commander of the Naval Training Center/Commander Naval Base, San Diego, California.

HALL, ARSENIO, was born February 12, 1955, in Cleveland, Ohio, the only child of Fred and Annie Hall. During his teenage years, Hall played the drums in his high school marching band and orchestra and in his own group. Following his graduation from high school, he enrolled at Ohio University in Athens. In 1975 he transferred to Kent State University, where he became involved in theater arts and worked as a disc jockey at the campus radio station. He received a B.A. degree in general speech from Kent State in December 1977. After graduation, he went into advertising, but nursed an ambition to be a stand-up comic.

Hall moved to Chicago in 1979 and started performing in comedy clubs where he got his first big break on Christmas night in 1979, when he emceed a show featuring the singer Nancy Wilson. She was so impressed, she financed his move to Los Angeles where he soon appeared on the "Merv Griffin Show" and other programs. In 1983, ABC-TV selected him to co-host a summer replacement series, "The Half-Hour Comedy" Hour. More television engagements followed, such as: "Thicke of the Night," "Solid Gold," "Joan Rivers," and the "Tonight Show." His second big break came when "The Late Show," Fox Broadcasting's attempt to sell Joan Rivers to an audience five nights a week, crashed and burned in 1987. Hall, who had served as guest host, took over and ratings climbed, spurred by his brash, self-described bad-boy wit.

Despite his success, Fox wanted something new. When the show left the air in November 1987, Fox was deluged with letters from viewers demanding its return. The network offered Hall a $2 million contract to stay, but he rejected that deal to sign a two-year movie-television pact with Paramount worth almost $3 million. He made his film debut in *Amazon Women on the Moon*, in 1987. In June 1988, his first film, the comedy *Coming to America*, was released, in which Hall played second to Eddie Murphy.

Hall's good fortune continued with the announcement in August 1988, by Paramount Domestic Television, that he would host a new syndicated late-night talk show, beginning in January 1989. Premiering on 141 stations, the Arsenio Hall Show quickly became the late-night viewing choice for the hip young crowd. His new show started a revolution around the late-night dial. After years of failed attempts to take on seemingly invincible Johnny Carson, Hall's show was making inroads. He was drawing 50 percent of the late-night audience under the age of 35. Also in 1989, he appeared in Eddie Murphy's movie *Harlem Nights*.

In 1990, Hall was really on a roll. First Paramount executives raised the ante with a new contract worth guaranteed millions for Hall through 1995. He also had a four-movie deal, plus the opportunity to develop and produce movies and television shows. He took over the Gloria Swanson Building and turned it into Arsenio Hall Communications. That same year, he was named "Television Personality of the Year" by *TV Guide*, voted "Entertainer of the Year" in *US* magazine's readers' poll, and won the People's Choice Award for "Favorite Late Night Talk Show Host." He was also selected for Hollywood's most coveted honor, a star on the Walk of Fame. In 1991, Hall's show was airing on 175 stations, and in 20 percent of his markets it was aired on bigger stations. He decided in 1991 to put his power behind a late-night party of his own, creating "The Party Machine with Nia Peeples," which was a syndicated show that premiered on 150 television stations.

HALL, JAMES REGINALD, JR., was born July 15, 1936, in Anniston, Alabama. He married the former Helen A. Kerr, and they have three children, Sheila, James and Cheryl. Upon completion of work toward a B.A. degree in political science at Morehouse College, he enlisted in the Army. Following basic training at Fort Chaffee, Arkansas, and advanced individual training at Fort Carson, Colorado, Hall attended Officer Candidate School where he was commissioned a second lieutenant in 1958. He also holds an advanced degree in public administration from Shippensburg State College. His military schooling includes completion of the Armed Forces Staff College, and the United States Army War College.

Among his command and staff positions, he has served as commander of Company C, 2d Battalion (Airborne), 503d Infantry, 173d Airborne

Brigade, United States Army Okinawa, and Vietnam; 1st Battalion, 9th Infantry, 2d Infantry Division, Eighth Army, in Korea; 4th Regiment, United States Military Academy Corps of Cadets, West Point; 197th Infantry Brigade, Fort Benning, Georgia; assistant division commander, 4th Infantry Division (Mechanized), Fort Carson; commanding general, United States Army Military Personnel Center, Alexandria, Virginia; commanding general, 4th Infantry Division (Mechanized), Fort Carson; commanding general, Fourth Army, Fort Sheridan, Illinois. On January 22, 1982, Hall was promoted to brigadier general. On June 1, 1986, he was promoted to major general, and on May 31, 1989, he was promoted to lieutenant general.

HALL, ROBERT, is a native of Miami, Florida. His present career as Environmental Research Analyst comes after a colorful background as a media expert and educator. Hall earned his broadcast qualifications from the Columbia School of Broadcasting in Los Angeles, California. He went on from there to become the first black radio announcer on "Top 40 Radio" in Florida. Later, he joined the news staff of a Miami television station. During all of this, he still had time to take intensive study in religion and black history. This led to his desire to become an educator. After his brief stint in television, he became media-program director at Florida Memorial College in Miami and taught history classes in the adult education program of the Dade County school system in Miami while hosting a weekend radio-talk show on black history and affairs, on a white-oriented radio station, also in Miami.

The later part of the 1970s and the early 1980s put the spotlight on Hall, as he became a recognized, authoritative source in black history. National recognition came to him as the young man who created the first black, all-talk, news and information radio station in the United States—WMBM on Miami Beach. His programs on black history earned him many awards and strong public popularity. There are those today who credit Hall with saving many lives during the May 1980 disturbance in Miami. Because he understood the mood of the community, he stayed at WMBM radio station for three days and three nights talking people off the streets. His was a vibrant voice that pierced the airwaves and forced people to stop and listen. His was a no-nonsense approach that addressed the idea of "mental militancy—no compromise" as he reiterated so often on his mid-day talk show.

Currently, Hall is a recognized ambassador to America's only aboriginal nation, The Moors, in the Federal District of South Florida, and director of Historical Research at the Regis Historical Society of American Science.

HALSEY, H. RANDOLPH, was born November 5, 1932, in Marion, Virginia. He is married to Coralyne

Jessie Collier and is the father of three daughters, Robyn, Terri and Christy. He is a graduate of Lincoln University, B.S. degree in education, 1951–1955; attended Graduate School at the University of Missouri, Columbia, Missouri, 1957–1958; took postgraduate studies at Central Missouri State College, 1958–1959; received master's degree in education, M.Ed. in counseling and guidance, from Lincoln University, 1973; and attended the University of Missouri Postgraduate Studies (major in community development, and minor in Missouri Rural Development Leaders School). Halsey served in the U.S. Military as athletic and recreation director at Fort Campbell, Kentucky. He has served as assistant professor–local government state specialist for the University Extension, Lincoln University, in Jefferson City, Missouri, from 1986 to date.

Halsey's prior positions include: executive assistant to the president, Lincoln University; assistant professor, and instructor, Community Development State Specialist Cooperative Extension Service, Lincoln University; state coordinator of Model Cities Department of Community Affairs; state director of housing, Missouri Office of Urban Affairs; director, Housing and Relocation, Jefferson City Housing Authority and instructor of history and social studies, basketball and football coach for C. C. Hubbard High School in Sedalia, Missouri.

Halsey is the recipient of numerous awards and recognitions including: Outstanding Young Man of America, U.S. Junior Chamber of Commerce; Outstanding Personalities of the West and Midwest; 64th edition of *Who's Who in the Midwest*; commissioned as a member of Admiral Flagship Fleet; Meritorious Service Award, Lincoln University, selected as one of the Two Thousand Men of Achievement; Public School Award for Education Exemplary Programs, Kansas City, Kansas; Distinguished Alumni Award, Lincoln University; Citizen of the Year, Politics and Community Involvement, Omega Psi Phi Fraternity; First Black Official for the City of Jefferson, Missouri; Creative and Successful Personalities of the World; United States Department of Agriculture Service Award; State Campus-Based Extension Specialist of the Year; Community Service Award Man of the Year, Omega Psi Phi Fraternity; Optimist International Service Award; Delta Sigma Theta Sorority Invaluable Services Award.

Also, Halsey received awards from: Missouri Chapter of National Association Housing and Redevelopment; Officials Outstanding Service Award; Certificate of Appreciation, Student Affairs, Lincoln University; Outstanding Service Award, Missouri Association of Housing Development; Mayor Pro-Tem, Jefferson City, Missouri; Outstanding Achievers Award, Missouri Black Legislative Caucus; AKA Award to Citizens for 30 Years Service to Community; President Citation National Association for Equal Opportunities in Higher Education, Washington, D.C.; Jefferson City

Ambassador, Chamber of Commerce; Board of Directors 83–88 Award, Chamber of Commerce; Missouri Lottery Salute, "Real Winner"; Outstanding Achievement Award, Second Baptist Church, Jefferson City, Missouri; and Bootheel Service Award, Delmo Housing, Lilbourn, Missouri.

HARPER, RUTH B., is the widow of the late James Harper and the mother of one daughter, Catherine Brown. She is a graduate of the Berean Institute of Cosmetology and Business, the Flamingo Modeling and Charm School, and Philadelphia University. She also attended LaSalle University's Evening Division and the Moore College of Art. She served seven terms as the state representative from the 196th Legislative District representing Philadelphia. Harper was the House of Representatives' Democratic Majority Chairman to the Urban Affairs Committee. She represented the state as a board member on the Logan Assistance Corporation for the sinking homes of Logan. She was also a National Democratic Committeewoman, member of the Pennsylvania Legislative Black Caucus of State Legislators.

Harper was the founder and director of Ruth Harper's Modeling and Charm School in Philadelphia and was also the producer of the annual Miss Ebony Pennsylvania Scholarship Pageant. She served the community in a variety of ways as an active member of various community local and national organizations. The recipient of numerous awards and honors which included: AFL-CIO Woman of the Year Award; the Pennsylvania Association for Adult Education Award; the Philadelphia Women's Political Caucus Award; the Bright Hope Baptist Church Service Award; the Elks Pyramid Award; and the *Philadelphia Tribune* Charities Service Award.

Harper has been honored by the United Black Business Association

(UBBA); Theta Ne Sorority, with the Gamma Chapter Award; with the World Culture Center at Cheyney University; the Outstanding Service Award; the Mabel M. Keys Chapter 99 of the Elks, from which she received the OES-PHA Award; the Richard Allen for Mother Bethel Founders Award; the Philadelphia Council of the National Council of Negro Women Distinguished Service Award; the North Philadelphia "Action" Branch NAACP Freedom Fund Award; the Lambda Kappa Mu Kopelles Community Service Award; the Southwest Human Relations Council, Inc., Community Service Award; and the Margaret Carden Community Service Award.

HARRELL, ERNEST JAMES, was born on October 30, 1936, in Selma, Alabama. He received a B.S. degree in civil engineering–construction from

Tuskegee Institute, and an M.S. degree in engineering, from the University of Arizona. He attended military schools: the Engineer School, Officer Basic and Advanced Courses; the United States Army Command and General Staff College; and the United States Army War College. He joined the United States Army in 1960 and had numerous assignments. In 1960, he was a student in the Engineer Officer Orientation Course at Fort Belvoir, Virginia. In April 1963, he was appointed commander of Company B, 94th Engineer Battalion, of the United States Army in Europe. From June 1965 to December 1967, he was a civil engineer with the 539th Detachment 1st Special Forces Group (Airborne), 1st Special Forces, in Okinawa. From December 1967 to July 1970, he served as an instructor, later assistant professor of Military Science, at Arizona State University, Tempe, Arizona.

From July 1970 to May 1971, he served as executive officer, 809th Engineer Battalion (Construction), in Thailand. From June 1974 to June 1976, he was appointed inspector general, assigned to the Inspector General Office, Washington, D.C. From October 1977 to July 1979, he served as the commander of the 43rd Engineer Battalion (Combat, heavy), Fort Benning. From July 1979 to July 1982, he served as a personnel assignments officer in both the lieutenant colonels and colonels divisions. He was also promoted in September 1981, to lieutenant colonel, and in October 1982, to colonel, while serving at the United States Army Military Personnel Center, Alexandria, Virginia.

From June 1984 to July 1985, Harrell served as the commander of the 2nd Engineer Group, Eighth Army, in Korea. On March 1, 1988, he was promoted to brigadier general and assigned as the commanding general of the United States Army Engineer Division on the Ohio River, Cincinnati, Ohio. In July 1988, he was assigned as the commanding general of the United States Army Engineer Division, in Europe.

HARRIS, BARBARA ANN, born July 18, 1951, in Atlanta, Georgia, is the daughter of the Rev. and Mrs. Thomas Harris, Sr. She is a graduate of the University of Michigan Law School, 1976, and graduated cum laude with an A.B. degree from Harvard University, in 1973. She moved back to Atlanta and worked as a law clerk for Justice Charles L. Weltner from 1976 to 1977. She served as an assistant United States Attorney for the Northern District of Georgia, from 1977 to 1982.

Since May 1982, Harris has served as associate judge for the City of Atlanta Municipal Court. She presides over preliminary hearings for felonies and misdemeanors and conducts nonjury trials of offenses under the Atlanta City Code. She has been an active member of the Gate City Bar Association and a co-founder of the Georgia Association of Women Attorneys, having served both organizations in elected official positions. She was a 1984 alumna of Leadership Atlanta, and has served on the executive and program committees, as well as on the board of directors of the Atlanta Women's Network and the United Servicemen's Organization.

HARRIS, BARBARA CLEMENTINE, was born in Philadelphia, Pennsylvania, in 1930. Her mother, Beatrice Harris, was a church organist, and her father a steelworker. She was the second of three children, growing up with her brother and sister in the Germantown section of Philadelphia. After graduating from the local girls high school, she joined Joseph V. Baker Associates, a black-owned public relations firm specializing in relations between corporate clients and the African American community. At the beginning of her career she studied and graduated from the Charles Morris Price School of Advertising and Journalism in Philadelphia. In 1958, she became the president of Joseph V. Baker Associates, a position she held for ten years until she joined the Sun Oil Company's community relations department, of which she became manager in 1973.

Harris spent much of her time away from business in the 1960s in the civil rights cause, participating in NAACP picket lines and selective patronage projects, in church-sponsored voter-registration drives in Mississippi, and in such demonstrations as Dr. Martin Luther King, Jr.'s historic 1965 "freedom march" from Selma to Montgomery, Alabama. In the late 1960s she discovered the Church of the Advocate, an Episcopalian parish in North Philadelphia. She devoted herself zealously to the parish's work, which ranged from feeding the poor to hosting a Black Panthers conference that attracted thousands to Philadelphia.

Harris began her divinity studies at Villanova University, Metropolitan Collegiate Center in Philadelphia, Episcopal Divinity School in Cambridge, Sheffield, England, and graduated from the Pennsylvania Foundation for Pastoral Counseling. She received the diaconate in September 1979. In October 1980, she was ordained a priest by Bishop Lyman Ogilby of the Diocese of Pennsylvania. Having left her last position with the Sun Oil Company, the Rev. Harris devoted herself full-time to her priestly duties the earliest of which included assignment to St. Augustine in Norristown, Pennsylvania.

In February 1989, Harris of the Episcopal Diocese of Massachusetts, broke 20 centuries of Christian orthodoxy by getting the 60 votes needed from bishops around the country to win confirmation as the first female bishop of the Episcopal Church and the worldwide Anglican Church Community. A 2,000-year-old, deeply embedded, firmly held tradition was broken when the Rev. Harris was consecrated as a bishop in the Episcopal Church before more than 8,000 people at Boston's Hynes Convention Center. She became the first black woman bishop in the 450-year history of the Episcopal Church.

HARRIS, EARL LYNN, was born November 5, 1941, at Kerrville, Tennessee. His parents were Collins and Magnolia Hall Harris. His home until 1960 was the nearby town of Millington. He attended public schools at Millington and neighboring Woodstock, where he graduated from high school in 1959. He moved to East Chicago the following year. He attended Indiana University–Northwest in 1961–1962, and Purdue University, Calumet, in 1966–1967. His marriage to Donna Jean Lara took place in 1969; they have one child. Harris is a member of the Missionary Baptist Church. From 1963 to 1969, he served in the U.S. Navy Reserve.

Harris formerly worked for Inland Steel Company and as a laboratory tester at American Maize Products Company. He is now the owner-operator of his own businesses, Kentucky Liquors and Kentucky Snack Shop.

His first bid for public office was in 1980 when he sought the nomination for East Chicago city clerk in the Democratic primary. He has served on various boards, including the East Chicago Air Pollution Board. As a legislator, Harris has sponsored bills dealing with welfare and economic development. His civic activities include the East Chicago Black Coalition and the East Chicago Sunny Side Homeowners Association, which he organized. He belongs to the NAACP, and to associations of small businessmen. Harris has been a state representative since 1983.

HARRIS, EDWARD L., is married to Louise Harris and is the father of four children. His educational background consists of: Richwood High School, 1960; Grambling State University (four years); Fort Monmouth Signal School (six months); Ouachita Valley Technical Institution School of Nursing (13 months); LPN Ambulance Driver, First Aid Instructor and E.M.T. Monitor, at E. A. Conway Hospital (five years); and People's Law School (6 weeks). As chief administrator for the town of Richwood, Mayor Harris has served this municipality, with a citizenry of approximately 2,500, for six and a half years.

This job as a rule is most demanding; nonetheless, Harris confronts each day as a challenge only to be conquered. Such an attitude could not be so and jobs could not be accomplished, as he would often point out, without the strength provided by his family. The township of Richwood under the auspices of Harris has, among other notable achievements, installed a

sewerage system. In addition, a housing rehabilitation grant awarded by the Louisiana Community Development Black Grant Department is being implemented. This grant will financially enable the town to make needed renovations on homes; demolish condemned abandoned houses and in some instances where such activity would cost less — homes would, for the most part, be rebuilt. Both the named projects are considered milestones under Harris' administration.

HARRIS, PATRICIA ROBERTS, was born May 31, 1924, in Mattoon, Illinois, and is married to William Beasley Harris. She spent her early years in Mattoon and Chicago, and when she graduated from high school she had five offers of college scholarships from which to choose. Deciding upon Howard University in Washington, D.C., she received a B.A. degree summa cum laude in 1945. After graduation she went back to Illinois for two years of graduate work in industrial relations at the University of Chicago. She was employed in Chicago from 1946 to 1949, as program director of the YWCA.

Returning to Washington in 1949, she enrolled in American University for further graduate study and took a position, which she held until 1953, as assistant director of the American Council on Human Rights. From 1953 to 1959, she served as executive director of Delta Sigma Theta at its national headquarters in Washington. Meanwhile, in 1955, she married Washington attorney William Beasley Harris. She entered George Washington University Law School, where she was a research assistant in 1959–1960. She graduated from law school with the J.D. degree in 1960. She then served as a United States Assistant Attorney, 1960–1961, in the appeals and research section of the criminal division of the Department of

Justice, where she met Robert F. Kennedy, who became attorney general in 1961.

Harris accepted an appointment as associate dean of students and lecturer in law at Howard University. In July 1963, President John F. Kennedy appointed her co-chairman of the National Women's Committee for Civil Rights. In March 1964, President Lyndon B. Johnson named her to the newly created 13-member commission on the assignment of studying the question of what form of change would be best for Puerto Rico, statehood, independence, or improvement in commonwealth status. On May 19, 1965, President Johnson selected Harris as Ambassador to Luxembourg, an appointment that easily won Senate confirmation the following June. She became the first black woman to serve as a United States ambassador. In January 1977, President Jimmy carter selected her as Secretary of Housing and Urban Development (HUD). She served as secretary of Health, Education and Welfare (HEW), in 1979.

HARVEY, WILLIAM R., was born and reared in the small town of Brewton, Alabama. He was awarded an academic scholarship to Talladega College, where he was also a standout in basketball and tennis. After a tour in Europe with the Army, he soured on the idea of law school and turned to education as a career. He took a master's degree in history at Virginia State and went on to Harvard, where he earned a Ph.D. degree in college administration and served as assistant to the dean of governmental affairs. He then spent two years as administrative assistant to the president of Fisk University and four years at several administrative posts at Tuskegee Institute.

Harvey has been active as a panelist and consultant on educational issues and has published widely, but he insists that he is a "management and budgeting specialist." In 1978, he was appointed president of Hampton University. He issued his fund-raising edict within his first 18 months at Hampton. Besides the edict, Harvey implemented new budget controls and persuaded influential businessmen and social notables to serve on the school's board of trustees. Included were the chief executive officers of AT&T and Best Products, NAACP Executive Director Benjamin Hooks, HUD Secretary Samuel F. Pierce, and actress Elizabeth Taylor.

The owner of a Pepsi-Cola bottling franchise reflected on the sweet deal he got. With good management in place and profits predictable, the situation at the Houghton, Michigan, franchise is as different from what Harvey inherited at Hampton in 1978 as the taste of Pepsi is from Blue Nun. Far from being profitable when he took over, Hampton had earned an F in finance with a $486,000 deficit and five consecutive years of red ink. And far from being a caretaker, Harvey shook the administrative structure, reformed spending policies and put himself on a barnstorming tour in search of funds. Hampton has balanced its budget each year of his tenure. During the same period, its endowment has grown from $29.5 million to $65 million. Enrollment has climbed from 2,800 to more than 4,200, in 1986. At a time when most private schools had been happy to stay even.

Harvey's reputation has grown much like the limbs of the huge, old Emancipation Oak that is a landmark on the 204-acre campus. He has been featured in numerous publications; served as a consultant to Sen. Paul S. Trible, Jr., R-Va., former Gov. Charles S. Robb, and former President Reagan; and has been offered jobs in private business. He has published articles in such journals as Columbia University's *Teacher College Record, Phi Delta Kappan,* and *Harvard Graduate School* of Education Bulletin. He has received several presidential appointments to National Advisory Councils on Education. His achievements have been recognized in numerous publications. Dr. Harvey married the former Norma Baker, of Martinsville, Virginia, and they have three children, Kelly Renee, William Christopher, and Leslie Denise.

HATCHER, RICHARD GORDON, was born on July 10, 1933, in Michigan City, Indiana, 25 miles south of Gary, to Carleton and Caroline Hatcher. He married the former Ruthellyn Rose, August 3, 1976 in St. Louis, Missouri, and they have three children, Ragan, Rachelle, and Renee. He graduated from Michigan City High School in 1951 and enrolled at Indiana University on a track scholarship in 1951. He received a B.S. degree in economics and government in 1956 from Indiana University, and graduated from Valparaiso University Law School in 1959, earning honors in criminal law. From 1961 to 1963, he served as a deputy prosecuting attorney in Lake County, Indiana.

Hatcher was elected to the Gary City Council in 1963, and after serving four years he ran for mayor. He won the Democratic primary by a 3.082 plurality over the incumbent, and in the general election he defeated the Republican Radigan. It is believed that Hatcher's victory, preceding Carl Stokes' election in Cleveland by hours, made him the first black to be elected mayor of a major American city and signaled the beginning of a new era in American politics. In 1971, he ran for re-election, which he won easily over both his Democratic and Republican opponents. He was the mayor of Gary until 1988. In 1988, he retired to private life and his business, Hatcher and Associates, Inc.

Hatcher has served as legal advisor to the Gary Chapter of the NAACP; is a member of the Indiana State Executive Board of NAACP; executive committee member of the National Urban Coalition; member, board of directors, of the U.S. Conference of Mayors, and numerous others.

HAWKINS, ANDRÉ, was born in Jacksonville, Florida. He is married and the father of three children. He graduated from Andrew Jackson High, 1971; received a B.A. degree from the University of Southern California, Los Angeles, 1975; M.E. degree from Florida Atlantic University, Boca Raton, 1979; an educational specialist degree from Florida Atlantic University, 1985; and Doctor of Educational Leadership Program. Prior positions include: associate dean of instruction, Indian River Community College, Fort Pierce, 1986–1989; Florida director of instructional services, Indian River Community College, 1983–1986; interim assistant dean, Okeechobee Center, Indian River Community College, Okeechobee, 1982–1983; director of education, Okeechobee Training School Division of Indian River Community College, Fort Pierce, 1979; classroom teacher, Florida School for Boys, Okeechobee, 1976–1979; and occupational guidance and counseling coordinator, Florida School for Boys, Okeechobee, 1975–1976.

Hawkins received special projects and grants from the Adult Basic Education Grant; College Reach Out Grant; McKnight Articulation and Cooperation Grant; Single Parents and Displaced Homemakers Grant; Sex Bias and Stereotyping Grant. He was honored by Governor Bob Graham at Governor's Reception for Who's Who Among Florida Black Americans, 1986; listed in Who's Who Among Black Americans, listed in Who's Who in American Education. Service and membership in educational organizations included: Phi Alpha Theta International History Honor Society; president-elect of the Florida Association of Community

Colleges, 1989 to present; vice president of the Florida Association of Community Colleges, 1988–1989; second vice-president of the Florida Association of Community Colleges, 1987–1988; executive board of the Florida Association of Community Colleges; board of directors of the Florida Association of Community Colleges; president-elect Florida Association of Community Colleges, Indian River Community College Chapter; chairman-elect, Florida Association of Community Colleges Lifelong Learning Commission, 1986; chairman, Florida Association of Community Colleges Lifelong Learning Commission, 1987; representative, Indian River Community College, Florida Association of Community Colleges, Community College Week, 1985 to present.

Additionally, Hawkins has memberships in: Education Standing Committee of the Council on Instructional Affairs-State Board of Community Colleges, 1983–1986; Continuing Education Steering Committee of the Council on Instructional Affairs, State Board of Community Colleges, 1984–1986; St. Lucie County School Board Dropout Prevention Task Force, 1987–1986; St. Lucie County Program of Excellence Committee, 1987–1989; Florida Adult Education Association, 1983–1987; Florida Association of Community Education, 1983–1987; National Council on Community Services and Continuing Education, 1985–1987; Community Instructional Services Task Force of the Continuing Education Standing Committee of the Council of Instructional Affairs, State Board of Community Colleges, 1984–1986; Florida Adult Education State Plan Task Force, 1985; Correctional Education Task Force of the Continuing Education Standing Committee, State Board of Community Colleges, 1985–1986; and 310 Project Review Committee of the State Board of Education/Division of Adult and Community Education, 1985. He has memberships in: Southern Regional Council on Black American Affairs of the American Association of Community and Junior Colleges, 1983 to present; Association for Supervision and Curriculum Development, 1987 to present; NAACP of Black Americans in Vocational Education, 1990 to present.

Hawkins is also a member of the following: the Lucie County Chamber of Commerce, board of directors; Indian River Community Mental Health Center, treasurer; Martin Luther King Commemorative committee and board of directors; and the New York Mets Booster Club.

HAWKINS, AUGUSTUS F., was born August 31, 1907, in Shreveport, Louisiana. He is married to the former Elsie Taylor. A graduate of Jefferson

High School in Los Angeles, he received an economics degree from the University of California at Los Angeles and attended graduate class at the University of Southern California (U.S.C.). On his first professional venture into

politics, Hawkins was elected to the California State Assembly, a post he held for 28 continuous years. His election upset an incumbent who had held that post for 16 years. As a member of the California State Assembly, he compiled an impressive legislative record, which eventually led to his assuming the powerful position of chairman of the Rules Committee.

During his tenure Hawkins authored over 100 laws, including: slum clearance and low-cost housing; workman's compensation for domestics; disability insurance; the Fair Housing Act; old age pension; child care centers; the Fair Employment Practices Act of 1959; and the 1961 legislation establishing the construction of the Los Angeles Sports Arena, the Department of Employment Building at 15th and Broadway, and the Law and Medical Schools at U.C.L.A. As a result of his efforts, blacks were appointed, in some cases for the first time, to positions as: judges, state commissioners, a member of the State Highway Patrol, and supervisory positions in the U.S. Postal service.

Hawkins was elected in 1962 to the U.S. Congress with the strong support of the late President John F. Kennedy. The support of his constituents has remained steadfast. In 1986, he was re-elected by 85 percent of the vote — the highest in the California congressional delegation. Early in his congressional career, he introduced a bill which helped to change the dishonorable discharge status to "honorable" for the black soldiers involved in the so-called Brownsville Incident. This incident was the result of a group of townspeople framing 170 black soldiers of the 25th Infantry for a local crime. Although the white commanders of the fort proved that the accused were not guilty, they were drummed out of the Army, without honor, without fair trial and without a shred of evidence against them. Sixty-six years later, Hawkins was able to have the charges dropped and their names cleared.

In December of 1986, he released a "Report on Children in America: A Strategy for the 100th Congress," which detailed a social and economic agenda to improve the health and education of our nation's children. In the 100th Congress (1987–1988), he authored two landmark pieces of legislation which became law: The School Improvement Act, which reauthorizes virtually all major elementary and secondary education programs, and the Civil Rights Restoration Act, which strengthened four important civil rights laws which protect all Americans against discrimination based on race, sex, age or handicap by institutions that receive federal money.

In the 101st Congress, which marked the close of Hawkins' distinguished career on Capitol Hill, he introduced another series of legislative bills to promote the nation's economic and social agenda. His impressive legislative record was a tribute to his mastery of the art of political compromise. He continues to be an exemplary image of his own personal view of public service: "The leadership belongs not to the loudest, not to those who beat on the drums or blow the trumpets, but to those who day in and day out, in all seasons, work for the practical realization of a better world — those who have the stamina to persist and to remain honest and dedicated. To those belong the leadership."

HAYES, CHARLES A., was born in Cairo, Illinois, and educated in the public school system there. He is serving his fourth full term in the United States House of Representatives, having been elected in August of 1983 to fill the seat left vacant by the late Mayor Harold Washington. He represents the First Congressional District of Illinois, an area including most of South Central

Chicago. He is a member of the Education and Labor Committee and serves as chairman of the Subcommittee on Postal Personnel and Modernization of the Post Office and Civil Service Committee.

Hayes is the first elected representative of rank-and-file trade unionists to serve in Congress. He has been a leader in the successful fight for women in labor; for representation of blacks and women on all levels of union leadership; and for increased benefits and better conditions for all workers. He saw the need to address the disturbingly high incidence of dropouts among elementary and secondary school children and introduced H.R. 738, "The School Dropout Demonstration Assistance Act of 1987," which was passed by the House as part of H.R. 5, "The School Improvement Act of 1987" (P.L. 100–297). In an effort to improve the "quality" of the lives of all Americans, He introduced H.R. 1398, "The Quality of Life Action Act." When enacted, this measure will put teeth into the "Hawkins-Humphrey Full Employment and Balanced Growth Act of 1978." He also introduced H.R. 2870,

"The Economic Bill of Rights." The latter measure proposes to protect and improve the quality of life of all the people of the United States through various legislative and presidential actions.

Other measures Rep. Hayes has introduced include: a resolution commemorating "Soweto Remembrance Day"; H.R. 2788, legislation to revise P.O. 81–874, Impact Aid; and H.Con. Res. 1111, a concurrent resolution expressing the sense of the Congress that high unemployment rates in the United States are morally unacceptable.

HAYNES, LLOYD R., SR., was born in Dublin, Georgia, in 1916, on a 48 acre farm owned by a white family by the name of Bedenfield. His parents were Moses Haynes and Elizabeth McClendon Haynes. He doesn't remember having worn shoes on his feet until he reached the age of seven. His wearing apparel was simply one of his father's or older brother's cast-off shirts. He came from a very large family, three sisters and ten brothers. When he was young on the farm he recalls one day seeing a beautiful multicolored object in an old tree stump that served to help support his home above the ground. It was definitely not a plaything for a child. He soon learned from his father that it was a deadly cottonmouth water moccasin snake. Fortunately for him, the snake had pulled away and had resisted Haynes' efforts to pull it out of the stump.

Haynes' mother was his first teacher; she taught him his alphabet and how to read at an early age. Even before he had attended school, he knew his basic mathematics and how to read. To his mother learning was a must for all of her children. This simple but harsh life-style created in him a fighting spirit and a desire to be the best in everything he attempted to do in life. His family came to the north in search of a better life-style. His father found work in the steel industry but died when Lloyd was 9. Life did not improve for Lloyd. It only grew worse. During the Great Depression of the 30s, he began carrying newspapers and later mowing lawns for people to help augment his family's income.

Haynes' teachers began to notice something special in him. He seemed to have had a talent of superior being in his intellect above his peers. Therefore, he was advanced in his grade school classes far beyond the other students of his age group. One of his greatest pleasures in his early life was listening to his mother read to him about a very famous lawyer by the name of Clarence Darrow, who was constantly in the news, concerning a criminal case he was working on at that time. It was at this tender age around ten years old that he determined that he would become an attorney. His grades never faltered but continued to be excellent throughout all his high school years.

Upon graduation from high school,

he enrolled in a local college taking his pre-law course on a part-time basis. His first real job was in the local steel-making plant. The work was hard and very dirty and not to his liking. His dream of becoming a lawyer someday kept him always trying to advance himself along those lines. A strike for higher wages at the steel-making plant afforded him a chance to be a special policeman for keeping the peace at the steel mill. This part-time opportunity encouraged him to take a civil service policeman's examination. Then came World War II and he received a transfer to a defense plant making airplane parts. Immediately, the supervisor saw the leadership qualities and the potential in him and began schooling him to be a foreman at the plant.

About this time his work was interrupted by his appointment as a city rookie patrolman. Thus, knowing full well the war would soon be over and the defense job brought to an end, he accepted the policeman's position. The pay was very meager. This made him return to school. The thoughts of realizing his dream never left his mind of becoming a lawyer. His police work afforded him the time to attend night law classes at the local college. He acquired his B.A. degree and LL.B. law degree, and his J.D. degree. All of these accomplishments he received not through any scholarships of any kind, but by the sweat of his own brow and deliberate determination to succeed in reaching his goal while working two jobs at one time.

Haynes made it through all these steps upward to achieve his goal in life. His zeal in working hard at every endeavor helped him to advance in the police department to become the only black detective in the city. After serving 25 years on the police force and practicing civil law cases during the daytime as an attorney, he was appointed assistant prosecutor for the Mahoning County Court. It was not long after becoming a prosecutor for the county that notification was brought to his attention that he was being considered by the governor of the state of Ohio to become the city's first black judge. His hard work and persistence of prosecuting to the fullest many of the criminal cases and his success in winning them had not gone unnoticed by others.

Haynes became the first, and to this day the only, black judge to sit on the Youngstown Municipal Court bench as a judge in the history of that city. He was re-elected three times with an overwhelming vote city-wide. The mandatory law for the state of Ohio is that judges for the municipalities must retire from the bench upon reaching the age of 70. In 1989, after completing his third six-year term as a municipal judge, the Hon. Lloyd R. Haynes, Sr., retired and relinquished his robe to his successor, thus proving all of his endeavors helped him reach his lifetime achievements. Haynes was a charter member of the Kappa Alpha Psi fraternity in the city of Youngstown, and a member of the board of trustees of the Ohio Judicial College while he served on the bench. He was a member of the U.S. Supreme Court, U.S. District Court, and all courts and agencies in the state of Ohio. He has been married to the former Helena Harvey for 50 years. They have four children and six grandchildren.

HEARNS, THOMAS, was born October 18, 1958, in Grand Junction, Tennessee. He is the oldest of the three children of the first marriage of Lois Hearns. By a failed second marriage, Hearns had six additional children. Raised by their mother with the help of government welfare, Thomas and his siblings and half-siblings grew up in Grand Junction and Detroit, Michigan, where their mother moved when Thomas was five. At the age of eight, he became interested in boxing. He later began to fight in King Solomon's Gymnasium at first, and then at the Kronk Recreation Center. The Kronk became his second home and Emanuel Steward, Hearns' manager, then his coach at the Kronk, served as a surrogate father. Hearns dropped out of school in the twelfth grade to become a full-time member of the Kronk amateur team, which Steward drove to tournaments throughout the Midwest in his car.

As an amateur, Hearns had difficulty getting leverage into his punches. He lost two of his first six fights, but he suffered only eight more defeats in 163 subsequent matches. His hopes for an Olympic try in 1976 were dashed when early that year he lost by decision to Howard Davis in the finals of the Amateur Athletic Union's 132-pound competition. After winning both the 1977 National A.A.U. title and 1977 Golden Gloves championship, he turned pro in November 1977. He began his professional career with 17 consecutive victories by knockouts, and while working his way up the weight divisions to the W.B.A. welterweight championship he won all of his 28 fights, 26 by knockout and 22 before the end of the fourth round.

In the World Boxing Association championship fight with incumbent Jose ("Pipino") Cuevas, who had defended his title 11 times, 10 by knockouts, and never been decked, until he was knocked out by Hearns who hit him with a short overhand right at two minutes and thirty seconds into the second round. Cuevas lost his title to Hearns in Detroit on August 2, 1980. Hearns successfully defended his W.B.A. title against Luis Primera in December 1980; against Randy Shields in April 1981; and against Pablo Baez in June 1981. In Las Vegas on September 16, 1981, Hearns lost his fight and his W.B.A. Championship Belt to Sugar Ray Leonard, the W.B.C. welterweight champion. After the Leonard fight, he moved up to the super-welterweight division (147–154 pounds), and confronted

Wilfred Benitez, the W.B.C. champion, in the Superdome in New Orleans on December 4, 1982.

Like Hearns, Benitez had suffered his sole professional loss at the hands of Sugar Ray Leonard. Hearns won the fight by a majority decision. Hearns, whose popular nickname was "Hit Man," was a knockout artist who was as crafty as he was rangy — six feet one and a half inches tall, possessing a 78-inch reach, quick hands, and a whip-like, paralyzing right. In 1986, he lost to Iran Barkley, but in 1988, he claimed the W.B.C super-middleweight crown with his win over Kinchen. Then with his 45th victory in 47 fights, the "Hit Man" won the W.B.C. middleweight championship and became the only man to win four different titles in four different weight classes. On June 3, 1991, at age 33, Hearns won a unanimous 12-round decision over Virgil Hill and took the W.B.A. light-heavyweight championship at Caesars Palace.

HEATH, COMER, III, was born February 22, 1935, in Eastman, Georgia. He attended Highland Park Junior College, A.A. degree, 1956; Wayne State University, M.A. degree, 1962; University of Michigan, Ed.D. degree, 1971; and Wayne State University. He served his country as a personnel specialist in the United States Army, Bordeaux, France. From 1984 to the present, he has been a Highland Park city councilman. Prior to this position he was a teacher and developmental career guidance consultant, Detroit Public Schools and Wayne State University, 1961–1968; school community coordinator, 1968–1974; administrative assistant, counselor, instructor, Wayne State University, 1969–1972; assistant professor guidance/counseling, Wayne State University, European Program, Berlin, Germany, and Karamursal, Turkey, 1972; instructor, Highland Park Community College,

1974–1976; vice president of college services, Highland Park Community College, 1977; president, Highland Park Community College, 1978–1981; and dean of Liberal Arts and Sciences, 1981–1986.

Heath was the first alumnus to become president of Highland Park Community College. He has received many honorary proclamations, awards and certificates. He was listed in *Who's Who in America*; was chosen Distinguished Alumnus by the Highland Park Community College Alumni Association; awarded Certificate of Appreciation for outstanding service to the community as a School Community Coordinator, a citizen, an educator and civic leader by the City of Highland Park; awarded Resolution by County of Wayne, Michigan — in recognition of his many attributes and contributions to humanity; and was awarded State of Michigan, Michigan Legislature, Senate Concurrent Resolution No. 924, of Tribute, Praise and Recognition as President of Highland Park Community College Academician and Civic Activist.

Heath is also a member of the Highland Park Caucus Club, the Association of Black School Administrators, the Michigan Community College Association, the NAACP, Kappa Alpha Psi, and Phi Delta Kappa fraternities.

HEIGHT, DOROTHY IRENE, was born on March 24, 1912, in Richmond, Virginia, to James Edward Height and Fannie (Burroughs) Height. When she was four the family moved to Rankin, Pennsylvania, where she attended integrated schools. In school she was an outstanding student, earning high grades in her classes and winning spelling bees, debates, essay and oratorical contests. At Rankin High School she excelled as a center on the girls basketball team and co-authored the high school song. She graduated from high school with a $1,000 college scholarship, her prize for winning a national oratorical contest sponsored by the Elks.

Height's first choice among colleges was Barnard, in New York City, but when she applied there she was informed that the school already had two black students and that she would have to wait a term or more. At the suggestion of a half-brother, she turned to New York University, where she was readily accepted because of her superior scholastic record. As a student at NYU she helped organize the all-black Rameses Club. She earned her B.S. degree in three years, her master's degree in one year, and later she did further postgraduate work at the New York School of Social Work.

Height's first job was a caseworker for the New York Welfare Department, where she worked for two years. In 1937, she was one of ten young church people representing the United States in an international church youth conference in Oxford, England. In 1944, she moved into the Harlem apartment that remained her New York home throughout her rise in the executive ranks of the YWCA. Among the YWCA positions in which she served over the years were the directorship of the Emma Ransom House in New York City and the executive directorship of the Phyllis Wheatley YWCA in Washington, D.C. At the same time she was devoting much of her energy to the National Council of Negro Women, an "umbrella" organization serving as a coordinating point, clearing house, and public voice of conscience for groups ranging from sororities and women's auxiliaries to professional associations.

The NCNW had observer status at the United Nations, and it is represented on the Council for United Civil Rights Leadership. In 1957, she became the fourth president of the NCNW. She led the NCNW for 34 years. It's a reign longer than any major civil rights leader, including the NCNW's venerated founder, the late Mary McCleod Bethune. The NCNW serves as an umbrella organization; a clearinghouse for 30 national women's groups. It also has 100,000 dues-paying members and claims an outreach of four million women. Its focus over the years has been on programs dealing with issues such as teen pregnancy, child care and black women's history. The idea for an annual event to celebrate the black family came to Height in 1986 after seeing a television documentary "The Vanishing Black Family." Since 1986, four million people have participated in the annual event, with the concept of the extended family joining together for a picnic. The "picnic" has been expanded to include entertainment, workshops and health checks.

———————

HENDERSON, ERMA, was born August 20, 1917, in Pensacola, Florida. She is the mother of two children. She was educated in Detroit's public schools. She attended Detroit Institute of Technology, graduated from Wayne County Community College and received a master's degree in social work from Wayne State University. She served as executive director of the Equal Justice Council, Inc., before being appointed to the Detroit City Council to fill a vacancy. In November 1973, she was elected to a four-year term on the Detroit City Council. In 1977, she was elected president of the Detroit City Council, and was re-elected in 1981, 1985, and 1989 to four-year terms.

Henderson has served in numerous civic and professional organizations, which include: (former) board member of the United Community service; member of the National Council of Negro Women; member of the National Association of Black Social Workers; advisory board member for the Black United Fund; founder-director of the National Women's Conference of Concerns; (former) national chairwoman for the Women in Municipal Government of the National League of Cities. She holds a lifetime membership in the NAACP.

Henderson has received a long list of awards and honors which include: Woman of the Year in 1972 and 1978; Citizen of the Year recognition in 1975 and 1978; the Sojourner Truth Award in 1977; "Michiganian of the Year" in 1978; in 1979, Michigan Gov. William G. Milliken issued an Executive Declaration, "Erma Henderson Day in Michigan"; in 1984, she was named honorary mayor and given the key to the city of Selma, Alabama.

HENDERSON, HENRY F., JR., is a graduate of State University of New York Agricultural and Technical Institute, Alfred, New York; Henderson attended William Paterson College, Seton Hall University, New York University. He founded H. F. Henderson Industries in 1954 and guided the company through the growth period to make it currently one of the top 100 minority companies in the U.S. specializing in the design and manufacture of control panels, automatic weighing systems including mixing and conveying scales, etc. The company is considered one of the top suppliers of complex material handling and scale systems. Under his direction, the company diversified into military electrical systems and hardware. The two divisions, commercial and government, were considered models of success.

From 1953-1967, Henderson was an applications engineer where he was responsible for electrical proposals and technical support throughout the U.S. for the Howe Richardson marketing group. In 1952, he founded System Control Services Corp., where they concentrated on industrial electrical contracting and specializing in electrical installations in hazardous areas. Although activity with System Control Services Corp. ended for all intents and purposes in 1970 due to activity with Henderson Industries, Henderson still held an electrical contractors license for the state of New Jersey. In 1950-1953, he worked with Howe Richardson Scale Company, in Clifton, New Jersey, as part of the engineering team that pioneered complex control systems for material control by weight. Research and development included digital weight systems, electro-mechanical servo units, motion detection equipment, load sensors, high speed printers and recording equipment.

Henderson is an accomplished instrument-rated multi-engine pilot and has traveled extensively in the Far East including China, Europe, Russia, Australia and South America. He traveled with DOCA (Defense Orientation Civilians Association) to numerous military installations throughout the U.S. including Cuba and Central America.

HENDERSON, RICKEY, was born December 25, 1958, in Chicago,

Illinois. His father, a truckdriver, abandoned the family early in 1959, leaving his wife Bobbie Henderson, a nurse, to care for the couple's eight children. She took the children to live with her mother in Pine Bluff, Arkansas. When Henderson was seven, his mother moved the family again, this time to Oakland, California. He began playing baseball at the age of eight, and later at Oakland Technical High School, he was an outstanding baseball player. He also enjoyed playing basketball and football. His first love was football and he was a high school All-American in that sport. He rushed for 1,100 yards during his senior year at Oakland Tech and received scholarship offers from two dozen colleges and universities.

After being selected by the Oakland A's in the fourth round of the June 1976 free-agent draft, he signed with the A's and was sent to their rookie league farm team at Boise, Idaho. There, the former first baseman was converted to an outfielder. After an impressive minor-league career, he joined the Oakland A's on June 23, 1979. He immediately entered the A's starting lineup. By the end of the season, he had compiled an average of .274 in 351 at-bats. He led the Oakland A's (Athletics), with 33 stolen bases, on each of which he employed his patented head-first slide. In 1980, his first full major league season, he batted .303; he was second in the league in walks (117), third in on-base percentage (.422), and fourth in runs. His most notable achievement was becoming only the third player in major-league history to steal at least 100 bases in a season. In 1981, he won his first Gold Glove Award for defensive excellence.

In 1982, during spring training, he promised to steal a base a game, a pace that would easily allow him to break Lou Brock's single-season stolen-base record of 118. He stole 51 bases in his first 51 games. On August 2, in his 105th game, he stole his 100, becoming the first man ever to reach triple figures in steals in two different seasons. On August 26, he tied Brock's record, and the following day he shattered it with four stolen bases. In 1983, he stole 108 bases to win his fourth straight stolen-base title.

On December 8, 1984, the Athletics traded Henderson to the New York Yankees. On June 20, 1989, the Yankees traded him back to the Oakland A's. In 1990, he won the American League Most Valuable Player Award. In April 1991, he tied Brock's all-time stolen base record of 938 stolen bases. For the record, Brock was caught stealing 307 times, Henderson was caught only 214 times. It took Brock 19 seasons to set the record, and took Henderson only 12 seasons to break it. Brock's best season was 118 stolen bases, while Henderson's best season was 130 bases stolen. In May 1991, he went on to become baseball's all-time king of stolen bases, having broken Brock's record, and went on in 1991 to add up numbers that will last for a long time to come.

HICKS, JUANITA, was born to Estelle Hicks-Powell, a registered nurse, and Joseph Hicks, a retired U.S. Army Master Sergeant. She was the oldest of five girls. After attending Spencer High School in Columbus, Georgia, she studied history at Bennett College in Greensboro, North Carolina. She furthered her education by obtaining an M.S. degree in urban administration from Georgia State University. She was elected clerk of Fulton County Superior Court in Atlanta, Georgia on August 9, 1988. She has several philosophies which she lives by, one of which was "It Can Be Done." She believes that anything and everything you set out to accomplish, you will achieve. It was this positive thinking which motivated her to run for this office the second time after being defeated in 1984.

During both campaigns she worked very hard to make the public aware of her outstanding qualifications, her many years of experience in public service with Fulton County, her preeminent educational background in public administration, her dedicated commitment to community service, her steadfast belief and commitment to her religious upbringing, and her continued willingness and desire to serve the public as the clerk of superior court. Hicks convinced over 25,000 voters county-wide when she was elected to office. She set a goal and she accomplished that goal.

When Hicks took office on January 1, 1989, she told over 100 employees that she made two campaign promises to the voters of Fulton County. Those two promises were that she would run a very professional office and that "if you call or come to our offices [she had offices at the North and South Annex Buildings], you would be treated like we were glad you called or came in." She insists that her employees be courteous, helpful, and very pleasant to clients. The theme for the year 1990 was "Doing Our Best." So if you had a need to call the clerk's office or a need to come into either of these offices, you could expect the best service anywhere in Fulton County.

Before being elected clerk of the court, she had over 15 years of experience with Fulton County. From 1973 until 1976, she worked as a program analyst. She began working as the insurance manager in 1976, coordinating property and casualty insurance programs for Fulton County. In 1980, she left the finance department to become the chief of the Delinquent Tax Office. She supervised a staff of professional, technical, and clerical workers in collecting delinquent tax accounts for Fulton County and the city of Atlanta.

Hicks is very active in numerous civic organizations and served as a board member/officer with a number of non-profit organizations. She is a member of Cascade United Methodist Church. If you ever have the opportunity to visit there, you can hear her beautiful voice among the many beautiful voices of the Chancel Choir. Some of her professional memberships include: board of directors, YWCA of Atlanta; board of directors, Friends of Zoo Atlanta; Leadership Atlanta; National Women's Political Caucus; League of Women Voters; Business and Professional Women, Atlanta Urban Chapter; American Business Women's Association, ISIS Chapter; Friends of the Library; Black/Jewish Coalition; Bennett College Alumni Association; Georgia State University Alumni Association; Phi Alpha Alpha (Public Administration Honor Society), University of Georgia; Ponderosa Neighborhood Association and Kiwanis International, Government Walk Chapter.

HICKS, MARYELLEN WHITLOCK, was born March 10, 1949, in Odessa, Texas, the daughter of Albert G. Whitlock and Kathleen Durham.

She has one child, Kathleen. In 1970, she received a B.A. degree from Texas Woman's University. She then went on to Texas Woman's University Graduate School, Texas Tech School of Law, where she received a J.D. degree in 1974. She also attended Harvard University School of Law in 1987, Golden Gate Law School, University of Colorado School of Law in 1977. She was the first black to graduate from Texas Tech School of Law. From 1974 to 1975, she was an attorney with Bonner & Mitchell. From 1975 to 1977, she was a partner in Bonner & Hicks, Attorneys at Law. In 1977, she was appointed a Municipal Court Judge for the City of Fort Worth, Texas, becoming the third black female judge in the state of Texas, and the first in the city of Fort Worth.

In 1978, Hicks was appointed chief judge of the Municipal Court, becoming the first black and first female to hold this position. In 1983, she made history again when she was appointed a district court judge. She was the first black female to serve as judge of Probate Court of the 231st Judicial District Court of Tarrant County, Fort Worth, Texas. Hicks is a member of Delta Sigma Theta Sorority, National Women of Achievement, Eastern Star, Board of Regents for Oakridge School, Golden Heritage member of the NAACP and holds a lifetime membership in the NAACP, Sojourner Truth Cultural Arts Center vice president, and board of directors for Fort Worth Girls Club. In 1989, Hicks was the first African American to receive the Alumna Award from the Texas Woman's University.

HIGGINBOTHAM, A. LEON, JR., was born February 25, 1928, in Trenton, New Jersey. He married the former Evelyn Brooks, and they have three children, Stephen, Karen, and Kenneth. He attended Antioch College, where he received a B.A. degree in 1949. He received an LL.B. degree from Yale Law School in 1952. From 1954 to 1962, he was a partner in the law firm of Norris, Green, Harris, and Higginbotham. From 1962 to 1964, he served as a commissioner with the Federal Trade Commission.

In 1964, Higginbotham was appointed a United States District Court Judge in Philadelphia, where he served until 1977 when (then) President Jimmy Carter elevated him to the Federal Appeals Court there. He has lectured at Harvard Law School, and has authored more than 100 published articles and *In the Matter of Color: Race and the American Legal Press*, Oxford University Press, 1978. He has received over 40 honorary degrees.

HIGHTOWER, MICHAEL, was born and raised in College Park, Georgia. He and his wife, the former Sandra Deshields, and their daughter, Evie, reside in East Point and are members of the Friendship Baptist Church in College Park. He was educated in the public schools in College Park and received his high school diploma from College Park High School in 1975. In May 1979, he received his B.A. degree in music education from Clark College in Atlanta. He regularly appeared on the dean's list and honor roll. Some of his affiliations while attending that institution included the Clark College board of trustees, president and vice president of Alpha Phi Alpha Fraternity, Inc., and president of the college band.

Hightower was the first black and youngest member elected to the College Park City Council. He was elected to represent the Second Ward in September 1979, and was re-elected in 1981, and again in October 1985, without opposition. He was elected to serve as mayor pro-tem (vice mayor) in 1985. In September 1986, he continued his service in public office and was elected to the Fulton County Board

of Commissioners. Fulton County is the largest county in the state of Georgia and encompasses ten cities, including Atlanta, and a population of more than 700,000 citizens.

Hightower is also employed at Georgia State University in Atlanta. He has been employed there since June 1979, initially working in the capacity of CETA program coordinator. At present, he is an administrative services unit head and also responsible for affirmative action adherence and compliance. He has experience in various aspects of human resource administration and personnel management. Included in his years of experience at Georgia State University and in the public sector, are personnel administration, employee relations manager, EEO office, and staff/employee trainer, governmental and community relations responsibilities. He is involved in a host of civic and professional organizations.

Presently, Hightower is a member of the National Association of Counties (1987 to present) where he also

serves as a member of the organization's board of directors, vice chairman of the Transportation Committee (1987 to present), past chairman of the Community and Economic Development Committee (1988–1989); the National Democratic County Official (1987 to present); American Cancer Society board of directors (1983 to present); member of the Association of County Commissioners of Georgia and serves on the board of managers for the organization (1987 to present); Atlanta and South Fulton Chambers of Commerce (1979 to present); Fulton County Building Authority (1987 to present); Atlanta-Fulton County Water Resources Board (1987 to present); Grady Memorial Hospital Oversight Committee (1987 to present); Alpha Phi Alpha Fraternity (1976 to present); and the board of directors for the Southwest YMCA (1987 to present).

In addition, Hightower has served as a member of the National League of Cities (1979–1986); Clark College Board of Trustees (1978–1981); Georgia Municipal Association (1979–1986); Georgia Gov. George Busbee's Policy Committee for the Community Development Black Grant Program (1981–1983); board of directors, Jesse Draper Boys Club (1983–1987); Fulton County Private Industry Council (1982–1983); vice chairman of the Fulton County CETA Youth and Advisory Council (1980–1982); and the Airport International Jaycees (1982–1986). He has been the recipient of numerous awards. In 1990, he was named vice chairman of the Transportation Steering Committee of the National Association of Counties by NACo president S. Michael Stewart.

HILL, JESSIE, JR., married the former Azira Gonzalez, and they have two children, Nancy and Azira. He received a B.S. degree from the University of Maryland in 1947, a B.A. degree from Lincoln University, and an M.B.A.

degree from the University of Michigan. He joined the Atlanta Life Insurance Company in 1949, as an actuarial assistant. In the 1950s, he was the driving force behind the successful voter registration drive. In the 1960s, Hill's involvement allowed Atlanta Life to become a communications center and home for the student sit-in movement. His personal investment and leadership enabled the *Atlanta Inquirer* to begin as a public forum for the movement.

In the 1970s, Hill chaired Maynard Jackson's historic and successful campaign for mayor of Atlanta. He was a close friend of former President Jimmy Carter, and the city's most influential black businessman. He was a frequent visitor to the White House and would hold private meetings with President Carter to talk about things he felt needed to be done. He worked on Andrew Young's campaigns for Congress and mayor. In 1977, he was elected president of the Atlanta Chamber of Commerce, the first black to head a chamber in a major American city. He was the first black appointed to the State Board of Regents and served as chair of the Atlanta Crime Commission and National Alliance of Business.

Hill rose to become actuary and vice president of Atlanta Life and in 1973 was elected president and CEO. He is the company's third president, succeeding Norris B. Herndon. Under Hill's direction, the new corporate headquarters was built at 100 Auburn Avenue, a testament to the success of the company's quest for economic dignity. In September 1980, Hill chose the week of the company's 75th anniversary, which included the opening of its Auburn Avenue headquarters and a visit by former President Jimmy Carter, to disclose ambitious expansion plans. Atlanta Life, founded by a former slave, was set for substantial expansion in the insurance field and a restructuring that will make it "a holding company owning businesses

that are not insurance-related," Hill said in an interview.

In December 1990, Hill led the acquisition of the Chicago Metropolitan Life Assurance Company, the sixth-largest black-controlled life insurance company. He became chairman of the Illinois company. He stated, "We will operate Chicago Met as a separate subsidiary indefinitely." Atlanta Life, under Hill's direction, rose to become the nation's largest minority insurance firm from the standpoint of net worth, with over $30 million in capital and surplus. It was second largest measured by assets. Hill has served in several volunteer capacities. He was on the presidential advisory group on wage guidelines and the board of the Communications Satellite Corp., and was chairman of the advisory board of the Minority Business Resource center of the Department of Transportation.

HILL, ROBERT L., a native of Spartanburg, South Carolina, spent most of his young adult years in New Haven, Connecticut, where he received

his formal education, married, started a family, and began his professional experiences. He resides with his wife, the former Marcia Norcott, in Silver Spring, Maryland. They have two daughters, Robin and Lisa. He graduated from Southern Connecticut State University in 1960, and soon after began a career in public education. He served four years in the U.S. Air Force during the Korean War.

Shortly after President Lyndon Johnson announced this country's war on poverty in 1965, Hill joined this effort as a key staff member of Community Progress, Incorporated, of New Haven and soon moved on to become executive director of the New Haven Opportunities Industrialization Center. In 1969, he was appointed national coordinator for the National Urban Fellows program established by the Ford Foundation to increase the number of minorities in management positions in all levels of government. Hill was appointed vice president of consumer and community affairs for the American Gas Association in April of 1985. In this position, he serves as the natural gas industry's guide and technical assistance officer for programs and matters affecting individual consumer concerns and ongoing community relations.

Prior to this position, Hill spent the bulk of his career with the public sector, serving as director of human resources and public safety for the National League of Cities. In the '70s, he received numerous awards and built a national reputation as director of veterans' affairs for the League of Cities and U.S. Conference of Mayors by establishing a prototype network of multi-service centers in 27 cities to assist returning Vietnam-era veterans with problems of readjustment to civilian life. He served these municipal associations for a 12-year period — spanning four presidential administrations in the process.

Hill is a member of the board of

directors and corporate roundtables of several organizations, including the National Forum for Black Public Administrators, American Association of Blacks in Energy, National Black Caucus of State Legislators, and National Association of Black County Officials. He serves on the energy committees of the National Conference of Black Mayors and the NAACP. He is an active supporter of other prominent groups such as the National Urban League, Ibero-American Chamber of Commerce, National Association of Latin Elected Officials, and the Indochina Resource Action Center.

HILLIARD, EARL F. was born April 9, 1942, in Birmingham, Alabama. He is married to Mary Franklin and they have two children, Alesia Lyneete and Earl, Jr. He attended Morehouse College and received a B.A. degree in 1964; J.D. degree from Howard University in 1967; and an M.B.A. degree in 1970. He is a life member of the NAACP; National Bar Association; Morehouse Alumni Association;

Alpha Phi Alpha Fraternity. Hilliard has been a member of the Alabama State Senate since 1980 and was a member of the Alabama House of Representatives, 1974–1980.

HILLS, CARLA ANDERSON, was born on January 3, 1934, in Los Angeles, California, the younger of the two children of Carl and Edith (Hume) Anderson. Her father, who died in 1965, was originally a rural Missourian. He moved to Los Angeles and started a multimillion-dollar building supplies business. He also became president of the Hollywood Chamber of Commerce. Carla Hills' brother Stephen runs the family business, Modern Materials, Inc. On September 27, 1958, she married Roderick Maltman Hills. They have four children, Laura Hume, Roderick Maltman, Jr., Megan Elizabeth, and Allison Macbeth.

Hills was educated in the exclusive Marlborough School for Girls, and after graduating from high school in 1951, she went to England to study at St. Hilda's College, Oxford University. She graduated from Stanford in 1955, with a B.A. degree cum laude. In 1958, she graduated from Yale with an LL.B. degree. In 1959, she was admitted to the California bar. She worked for the next two years as an assistant United States attorney. In 1962, she and her husband joined with other lawyers in establishing the Los Angeles law firm of Munger, Tolles, Hills, & Rickershauser.

In 1974, Attorney General William B. Saxbe, who was impressed by Hills' credentials, invited her to head the Justice Department's Civil Division as an assistant attorney general. On February 18, 1974, she was nominated and on March 7, 1974, she was confirmed by the United States Senate. That April she took office becoming the highest ranking woman in the Justice Department. She was also the first female assistant attorney general since

the early 1920s. As an assistant attorney general, Hills was in charge of some 250 Justice Department lawyers in Washington, D.C., as well as some 95 United States Attorneys across the country. On February 13, 1975, President Ford nominated her to be the Secretary of Housing and Urban Development. She was confirmed by the Senate on March 5, 1975, and sworn in as Secretary of Housing and Urban Development on March 10, 1975, becoming the first woman cabinet member in 20 years, and the first black.

Some of Hills' achievements are as follows: In 1963, she was president of the Los Angeles chapter of the Federal Bar Association; in 1965, she was president of the National Association of Women Lawyers; in 1970, she became a member of the standing committee on discipline of the United States District Court for California's central district; in 1969 to 1971, she served on a corrections task force under the California Council on Criminal Justice; from 1972 to 1974, she was on the Council of the Administrative Conference of the United States. She has been described as self-confident and hard-working. She has had to contend with her share of male chauvinist remarks, but she has a reputation for maintaining her poise in most situations.

HINES, GREGORY OLIVER, was born February 14, 1946, in New York, New York, the son of Maurice Hines, Sr. and Alma Iola (Lawless) Hines. He has a daughter, Daria, by his first wife, Patricia Panella, and a son, Zachary, by his second wife, Pamela Koslow. He has a brother, Maurice, who is two years older. Growing up in Harlem and Brooklyn, the boys were steered toward a tapdancing career by their mother. In addition to enrolling both boys in dancing school, Mrs. Hines regularly took them to the Apollo Theatre.

The Hines brothers began performing together locally when Gregory was five. They were held over "for a total of two weeks" at the Apollo when he was six. By the time he was seven, they were enrolled in professional children's school and were touring during summer vacations. In 1954, Maurice and Gregory were cast, respectively, as the newspaper boy and the shoeshine boy in the short-lived Broadway musical comedy "The Girl in Pink Tights." Their father learned to play the drums and, in 1963, joined the act, which accordingly underwent a name change from the Hines Brothers to Hines, Hines and Dad. With Gregory functioning as comedian, Maurice as straight man, and the elder Hines as percussionist, the trio went on television programs, including Johnny Carson's "Tonight Show."

In 1973, the Hines act disbanded and Gregory moved to the beachfront town of Venice, California. In Venice he organized a jazz-rock group, Severance, for which he wrote songs, sang, and played guitar. In addition, he worked as a waiter, busboy, and Karate instructor (he is a black belt). He was "the brightest star" in the all-black galaxy of the Broadway musical revue "Eubie!" (1978–1979). In 1981, he appeared on the screen as a Roman-era slave in Mel Brooks' *History of the World, Part I*. He received a Tony nomination for best actor in the musical "Sophisticated Ladies."

In late 1984, Hines won the role of "Sandman" Williams in the hit movie *The Cotton Club*. A review of Hines' great performances includes: appearances with The Hines Kids, 1945–1955; Hines Brothers, 1955–1963; Hines, Hines and Dad, 1963–1973; in "Severence," "Eubie," "Comin Uptown," "Sophisticated Ladies," and *Wolfen, History of the World, Part I, The Deal of the Century, Taps, The Cotton Club, White Nights, Running Scared*, and in April 1991, he appeared in the movie *A Rage in Harlem*.

HOLDEN, MELVIN LEE, is married to the former Lois Stevenson and the father of five children, Melvin II, Angela, Monique, Myron and Brian Michael. A graduate of Scotlandville High, he received B.A. degree in journalism from Louisiana State University; M.A. degree in journalism from Southern University; and J.D. degree from Southern University School of Law. Holden has served in numerous outstanding positions which include: news director WXOK Radio; reporter WWL Radio in New Orleans; reporter WBRZ-TV; public relations specialist for the Census Bureau; public information officer for the Baton Rouge City Police; law clerk for the Louisiana Department of Labor Worker's Compensation Division; and councilman District #2, 1984–1988. He is presently a public relations specialist and attorney-at-law and state representative for District #63.

Holden was selected as outstanding legislator by the Louisiana Association of Educators and the American Federation of State, County and Municipal

Employees Environmental Groups. He is the recipient of many honors: Lawmaker Award presented by the Brown Pelican Awards; Best Bets Award, Environmental Award presented to ten legislators in the United States by the Center for Policy Alternatives, Washington, D.C.; Southern University Law Center Hall of Fame Inductee; selected as one of the Outstanding Young Men of America; won an award for the Best Editorial on Radio and Television in Louisiana, 1975–1976; won award for the Best Spot News in Louisiana; won the award for the Best Story in the City of New Orleans in Radio, 1977–1978.

Holden has received numerous community awards and appeared on NBC "Nightly News," ABC "Nightline," CNN, and CBS. His professional affiliations include: legislative committee member of Natural Resource Committee Ways and Means, Municipal, Parochial and Cultural Affairs; vice chairman House Subcommittee on Environment; member House Oversight Committee for Natural Resources; chairman Joint Legislative Capital Outlay Committee; Special Budget Task Force Committee; Alternative Environmental Quality and Natural Resources Committee of the Southern Legislative Conference; member of the Xi Nu Lambda Chapter of Alpha Phi Alpha; member of the Louisiana Bar Association, the American Bar Association, and the National Bar Association; and a member of the Greater Baton Rouge Airport Commission.

HOLLOWAY, ERNEST L., is a graduate of Boley High School. His higher education was received from the Oklahoma university system and included a B.S. degree from Langston University, 1952; an M.S. degree from Oklahoma State University, 1955; and a doctorate degree from the University of Oklahoma 1970.

He has done additional study at the University of California, Berkeley, and at Ohio State University. His concern for young people is evidenced by the fact that, throughout his working career, he has been associated with helping to shape the lives of young men and women.

He served as a science teacher, coach and principal at Boley High School during the years, 1952–1962. In 1963, he accepted employment at Langston University. During his tenure at Langston University, he had served as assistant professor of biology, assistant registrar, registrar, dean for student affairs and professor of education, vice president for administration, acting president, and interim president. He was elected president of Langston University on October 10, 1979.

Holloway has made program appearances for "Candid Campus," KETA-TV; Student Services Management and Staff Improvement Conference, speaker; First Annual Logan County Branch NAACP of Guthrie

Membership Banquet, banquet speaker; dedication of the Henry Ponder Fine Arts/Humanities Center, Benedict College, gave dedication address. He has also served as consultant for many education and civic groups. He is the recipient of numerous awards and honors, and his professional organizational affiliations were numerous as well.

HOLLOWAY, HERMAN M., SR., was born February 4, 1922, in Wilmington, Delaware. He is married to the former Ethel Johnson of Wilmington, they are the parents of three daughters and two sons. Educated in both parochial and public schools of Wilmington, he graduated from Howard High School and later attended Hampton University, Hampton, Virginia. In June of 1969, he was awarded an honorary LL.B degree by Delaware State College. In 1972, he was awarded an honorary associate's degree of applied science by the Georgetown Branch of Delaware Technical and Community College.

Holloway began a new phase in the political history of the First State when on November 31, 1964, he became the first Afro-American ever to be elected to the Delaware State Senate. Representing the Second Senatorial District in Wilmington, he was the holder of the highest elective office attained by a member of his race in Delaware. His prior legislative experience consisted of one year in the Delaware House of Representatives. He was elected on November 23, 1963, to serve out the unexpired term of the late Rep. Paul F. Livington.

In 1988, Holloway became the most tenured legislator in the present Delaware General Assembly. He has 25 years' continuous service, more than any minority legislator elected at the state or congressional levels of government throughout the nation. For 20 consecutive years, Holloway has served as a member of the Joint Finance Committee and 16 years as chairperson on the Senate Committee on Health and Social Services and Aging. He served as a member of the Senate Committees on Labor, Revenue and Taxation and the Committee on Corrections. He was a member of Delaware's Interstate Cooperative Commission and a member of the Human Resource Task Force, Eastern Region of the National Legislator Conference.

Holloway has been the recipient of numerous commendations and awards from various professional, civic and social groups, including fraternities, business and industry, labor, religious and educational organizations. He was identified by the local press in 1974 as having sponsored and passed more socially progressive legislation than any legislator in Delaware history, such as Delaware's Public Accommodations law, Open Housing legislation, mandating education and training for all handicapped children within the state's public education system, Adult Protective Services and various programs and benefits for the state's aging population, effective Child Support Collection legislation, child protective laws, consumer protection legislation and numerous enactments to provide opportunity and benefits for women, the disadvantaged and the poor.

Holloway's legislative interest and participation removed him from and above the narrow confines of special interest or group problems. He says, "This is as it should be. As a State Senator, regardless of my elective district, I am a representative of all the people, special considerations and interest notwithstanding." He is the recipient of numerous recognitions, commendations and awards: the New Castle County Vocational and Technical School District, special recognition for Sen. Holloway for his outstanding contributions, support and enrichment of the community, 1990; National Sorority of Phi Delta Kappa, Inc., Eastern Region Citation, "For Outstanding Community Service"; Delaware Technical and Community College, Wilmington Campus, established an annual Herman M. Holloway, Sr. Scholarship in recognition of his firm support for Del-Tech, 1990; "The Keeper of the Flame Freedom Award" presented by he Council of the City of Wilmington, and the 1989 Civil Rights Commemorative Commission; selected by the Afro-American Historical Society of Delaware to become a member of the Delaware Afro-American Hall of Fame, 1989.

A park located at 7th and Lombard streets in Wilmington dedicated the Herman M. Holloway, Sr. Park by the mayor and council of Wilmington, 1989; the Delaware State Bar Association, "Distinguished Legislative Service Award, 1988; Delaware State Education Association, "Outstanding Achievements in Human and Civil Rights Award," 1985; Delaware King Memorial Foundation, "Recognition of Senator Holloway's Tireless Efforts to Upgrade the Quality of Life of all Delaware Citizens," 1983; Delaware Heart Association Award for dedica-

tion to "The Improvement of Health Care," in the state of Delaware, 1977; Alpha Phi Alpha fraternity, "Outstanding Citizen and Public Service Award," 1972; Distinguished Alumni Award, Howard High School, 1969; Psi Iota Chapter, Omega Psi Phi fraternity, "Outstanding Citizen Award," 1967; Monday Club, Inc. "Man of the Year Award," 1966; founding member of the National Black Legislators Caucus.

Churchman and fraternalist, he is a member of My Joy United Methodist Church, and past Worshipful Master of Union Lodge #21, Prince Hall Masonic Order. Holloway has served as a member of the Board of Managers of the Walnut Street YMCA and the Monday Club, Inc. He was the founder and president of the Citizens Political Issues League.

HOLMES, ARTHUR, JR., was born May 12, 1931, in Decatur, Alabama. He married the former Alice Louise Basnight, and they have four children, Deborah Lynn, Sharon, Lorene Key, and Arthur Orin. He received a B.S. degree from Hampton Institute in 1952, and an M.B.A. degree from Kent State University in 1967. From 1970 to 1971, he served in the United States Army in Vietnam as commander of the 62nd Maintenance Battalion. From 1972 to 1974, he was assigned to the Joint Chiefs of Staff as a staff officer. From 1974 to 1975, he served as chief of the Ordnance Branch, Military Personnel Center. From 1975 to 1977, he was assigned as commander of 1st Infantry Division Support Command. From 1977 to 1979, he served as executive officer to the secretary of the Army.

HOLMES, DAVID S., JR., was born August 11, 1914, at Covington, Kentucky. He is married to Avis E. Greene and they have one daughter, Patricia Ann. He attended Virginia

State University and received a B.S. degree; graduate study, University of Michigan. He is employed as a UAW-AFL-CIO aide; is a member of Allen Temple A.M.E. Church, Detroit; Masons; Alpha Phi Alpha Fraternity; 13th District Business and Professional Men and Women's Club; Trade Union Leadership Council; and a delegate, 1974 Democratic Charter Conference.

Holmes was elected to the House of Representatives to fill a vacancy in 1959 and served until March 1974; elected to the Michigan State Senate, March 1974, to fill a vacancy in the 4th Senatorial District. Legislative Committees he has served on include: minority vice chairman of Appropriations; Appropriations Subcommittees on General Government, Capital Outlay, Regulatory, Budget and Oversight; and chairman of Senate Democratic Caucus. His national affiliations include: treasurer, National Black Caucus of State Legislators; National Conference of State Legislatures; and Conference of Insurance Legislators. In 1986, Sen. Holmes received an honorary doctorate degree from his alma mater, Virginia State University.

HOLMES, LARRY, was born on November 3, 1949, in Cuthert, Georgia. He is the son of John and Flossie Holmes, seventh of 12 children. The family moved north in 1954 to Easton, Pennsylvania. At the age of 13, he dropped out of school in the seventh grade and held a succession of jobs, in a car wash, a paint factory, a rug mill, and an artillery shell factory. His second home during adolescence was the St. Francis Youth Center in Easton, where he learned to box and where he was entrusted with locking up at night. On Saturday nights he, his brother Lee, and some friends did exhibition boxing in bars in and around Easton.

In 1970, he began to fight as an amateur, and over the next three years he had 22 fights, winning 19, including the New Jersey A.A.U. championship and the Eastern Olympic championship. He turned professional in March 1973. During his early years as a pro, he served as sparring partner for Joe Frazier, Jimmy Young, Ernie Shavers, and Muhammad Ali. By June 9, 1978, with a five-year career record of 28-0, he fought Ken Norton, the World Boxing Council champion for that title belt. During the fight Norton appeared in control after the 12th round as he was jabbing well, and scoring with hooks and effective body punches. But in the 13th round, Holmes had Norton reeling in the final minutes from eight punches to the head, and Norton almost went down at the bell from four slashing rights. Norton staggered to his corner. He came back in the 14th round, but in the 15th, which was three minutes of nonstop punching that had a crowd of about 5,600 cheering wildly, Holmes won the fight by again having Norton reeling from punches to the head as the round came to an end.

Holmes, at 28 years of age had done the unexpected that night. First, he upset Ken Norton for the World Boxing Council heavyweight championship. Then, he jumped into the Caesars Palace swimming pool with his championship belt. In his first title defense, he knocked out Alfredo Evangelista in the seventh round on November 10, 1978. On October 2, 1980, he stopped Muhammad Ali in the 11th round after Ali wasn't able to answer the bell for the 11th round. Until September 22, 1985, he ruled the heavyweight division, achieving most of his goals. His record as a professional remained unblemished for a record of 48-0, until he was stunned and stripped of his title by Michael Spinks, a lighter fighter who was not expected to succeed as a heavyweight. Seven months later in a rematch he lost to Spinks a second time; he did not fight again for 21 months.

Then on January 22, 1988, Holmes

tried to recapture his glories, and redeem failures, by stepping into the ring with 21-year-old Mike Tyson. Tyson had become the youngest heavyweight champion in history, with a record of 32-0, with 28 knockouts. Holmes was 38 years of age, the same age Ali was when he fought Holmes; Tyson was 14 when he watched Holmes defeat Ali. Tyson successfully defended his title against Holmes at the Atlantic City Convention Center with a convincing fourth-round knockout of the former champion.

Holmes' record now stood at 48-3. Holmes, a man of quiet determination, has always formulated his goals and driven himself to achieve them. He had seven years as one of history's most successful, artful and dignified heavyweight champions. He amassed enough wealth to transform his tiny hometown of Easton, Pennsylvania, into his personal financial kingdom.

HOLMES, ROBERT A., was born July 3, 1943, and is the father of one son, Robert, Jr. He is a graduate of Shepherd College and received his Ph.D. degree in public law and government from Columbia University at the age of 25. He was a former administrator and faculty member of the City University of New York (Bernard Baruch College, Hunter College, and Herbert Lehman College), Columbia University, and Southern University. He was a professor of political science at Clark Atlanta University and acting director of the Southern Center for Studies in Public Policy. During 1986–1987, he served as a United Negro College Fund Distinguished Scholar. He is to date in his 8th term as a state representative in the Georgia General Assembly where he is a member of the Budget Subcommittee, Appropriations Committee, Ways and Means, and serves as chairman of the Governmental Affairs Committee.

Holmes was a real estate broker with the Unique Realty and Property Management, Inc., of Atlanta. He has authored or co-authored 12 books/monographs and has published more than 30 articles and reviews in journals throughout the world. He serves on the editorial boards of the *Journal of Social and Behavioral Sciences* and *Phylon*. He is active in numerous professional associations and has served as a chairperson panelist, local arrangements chairperson, and paper presenter at more than 50 conferences.

Holmes is a past president of the National Conference of Black Political Scientist and the Association of Social and Behavioral Scientists. He served as a consultant to many government agencies and businesses and has presented lectures on more than 25 college campuses. He is a member of the board of directors of ten local and national organizations and has been the recipient of numerous honors and awards for his civic activities including: Atlanta Jaycees Outstanding

Young Man of the Year Award, Ten Outstanding Young People of Atlanta, Metro Atlanta YMCA Layman of the Year, Southwest Atlanta District YMCA Volunteer of the Year Award (three times), American Association of Adult Educators' Legislator of the Year Award, Atlanta NAACP Lobbying Network Hall of Fame and the Georgia Municipal Association Legislative Services Award.

HOLYFIELD, EVANDER, was born October 19, 1962, in Atmore, Alabama, the son of Annie Holyfield. He and his wife Paulette have three children, Evander, Jr., Ashley, and Ewin. He grew up in an Atlanta housing project called Bowen Homes, the youngest of eight children (four girls and four boys). They were raised by Annie Holyfield, a single mother who was divorced at a young age. All the children chipped in and helped Annie, who had worked as a head cook at the Old Grady Hotel until a 1972 heart attack disabled her. But it was Evander, whom she nicknamed "Chubby," who really toiled. She never took his boxing too seriously even though he was eight when he first put on boxing gloves at Grant Park's Warren Memorial Boy's Club, where he and his brothers spent nearly every afternoon. He talked about dropping out of Fulton High School to focus more time on boxing, but his mother put her foot down.

Only when Holyfield became a member of the United States Olympic boxing team did she realize he was for real. But before he made the Olympic team, he worked a number of odd jobs such as selling Coca-Cola at the Atlanta Braves games, life guard at the city park, and pumped gas at the Peachtree-Dekalb Airport. He won the Olympic bronze medal in 1984, after a controversial disqualification in the semifinals. He had cruised through Taju Akay of Ghana, Ismail Salman of Iraq, and Syivaus Okello of Kenya. But

after virtually knocking out Kevin Barry of New Zealand with seconds left in the second round, referee Gligorije Novicic said Holyfield hit after the break and disqualified him.

Six years later on October 26, 1990, in front of a celebrity crowd of 16,350 at the Mirage Hotel, Holyfield, an 8-to-5 favorite, knocked out Buster Douglas with a savage right hand only 70 seconds into the third round. He came to the fight weighing 208 pounds; it was his 25th victory in as many pro fights and was his 21st win by knockout. He became the undisputed heavyweight champion of the world. His purse was $7,484,750.

Holyfield's personal timeline record: 1971, has first bout at age 9; 1973, suffers first loss to Cecil Collins at age 11; June 28, 1983, wins National Sports Festival by defeating Ricky Womack; April 22, 1984, wins 57th National Golden Gloves tournament; July 8, 1984, disqualified during Olympic semifinals; November 15, 1984, wins in fight with Lionel Byarm; January 20, 1985, wins in fight with Eric Winbush; March 13, 1985, knocks out Freddie Brown in first round; April 20, 1985, knocks out Mark Rivera in the second round; May 17, 1985, marries wife Paulette; July 20, 1985, wins in fight with Tyrone Booze; August 29, 1985, knocks out Rick Meyers in the first round; October 30, 1985, knocks out Jeff Meachum in the fifth round; December 21, 1985, knocks out Anthony Davis in the fifth round; March 1, 1986, knocks out Chisanda Mutti in the second round; April 6, 1986, knocks out Jesse Shelby in the third round; May 28, 1986, knocks out Terry Mims in the fifth round; July 12, 1986, wins first pro title (WBA cruiserweight) by defeating Dwight Muhammad Qawi in 15 rounds; July 16, 1988, wins his first heavyweight fight, a fifth round knockout of James "Quick" Tillis; December 9, 1988, knocks out Pinklon Thomas in the seventh round; March 11, 1989, knocks out Adilson

Rodrigues in the second round; November 4, 1989, knocks out Alex Stewart in the eighth round; June 1, 1990, knocks out Seamus McDonagh in the fourth round; October 26, 1990, knocks out James "Buster" Douglas in the third round, to take the undisputed World Heavyweight Title. On April 19, 1991, Holyfield made his first title defense against George Foreman. He won the fight in 12 rounds; it was the first heavyweight championship fight to go the distance since 1987.

———

HOMER, RONALD, was born and raised in Brooklyn, New York. He is married to Cheryl Bell Homer and they reside with their two sons in Lexington, Massachusetts. He received a

B.A. degree from the University of Notre Dame in 1968 and an M.B.A. degree from the University of Rochester in 1971. He began his banking career as a management trainee at Marine Midland in 1971 and a year later became the bank's youngest com-

mercial loan officer. In 1976, he was made responsible for Marine Midland's corporate banking activities in New England. In 1979, he joined Freedom National Bank of New York as its senior vice president and senior loan officer, and then was promoted to executive vice president and chief operating officer in 1981. During this period Freedom was the largest and most profitable black-owned bank in the United States with assets in excess of $100 million and net income over $1 million.

In 1983, Homer left Freedom to become president and CEO of the Boston Bank of Commerce, a fledgling and troubled bank. Since 1984, Boston Bank of Commerce has grown at an average annual rate of 35 percent and has had net income averaging a 1 percent return on assets and a 19.5 percent return on equity. In addition to his banking career, he is active in real estate development, serving as treasurer and managing partner of Columbia Plaza Associates, a 50 percent joint venture with Metropolitan Structures in a $300 million office tower development in downtown Boston and a $200 million mixed use development in a revitalized area of Roxbury.

Homer is a director of the New England Telephone Company and the New England Student Loan Marketing Corporation and is treasurer of the Massachusetts Industrial Finance Agency. He is a past president of the National Bankers Association and currently serves as a member of the American Bankers Association task force on government regulation and community involvement.

Homer also serves as a member and director of numerous civic and cultural organizations in Boston, including the Chamber of Commerce, the Coordinating Committee, the Boston Symphony, the Greater Boston Convention and Visitors Bureau and the YMCA. He was a co-chair and a senior advisor to the "Dukakis for President" campaign and he is a trustee of the Democratic National Committee. He is vice chairman of the board of trustees of Cambridge College and a member of the Board of Overseers of the New England Medical Center and the Trustees Council of the University of Rochester. He has received an honorary doctorate of humane letters from the University of Massachusetts.

HONOR, EDWARD, was born March 17, 1933, in Melville, Louisiana. He married the former Phyllis Whitehurst. He received a B.A. degree in education from Southern University in Baton Rouge, Louisiana, in 1954. From 1969 to 1970, he commanded the 36th Transportation Battalion, AUS Support Command Cam Ranh Bay. From 1970 to 1971, he was chief of Passenger Services Division, CONARC Military Traffic Management and Terminal Services; from 1972 to 1973, chief of the Transportation Service Branch, Office DCOS for Logistics; from 1973 to 1975, AUS Europe, commander of 37th Transportation Group; from 1976 to 1978, Military Traffic Management Command, commander of Terminal Group, Europe; from 1978 to 1979, USA Material Development and Readiness Command, director of Plans Doctrine and Systems. In 1979, he was assigned to the Joint Chiefs of Staff at the Pentagon, deputy director for Plans and Research.

HOOKS, BENJAMIN LAWSON, was born January 31, 1925, in Memphis, Tennessee, the fifth of seven children of Robert B. Hooks, Sr., and Bessie (White) Hooks. He married Frances Dancy, and they have one child, Patricia. He attended Porter Elementary School and Booker T. Washington High School in Memphis. After graduating from high school in 1941, he enrolled at LeMoyne College in Memphis. After two years at Le

Moyne College, Hooks was drafted for World War II service in the United States Army, where he once found himself in the ironic position of guarding Italian prisoners of war who were allowed to eat in "for white only" restaurants in Georgia that were off limits to him. At the end of the war he was discharged from the Army in the rank of staff sergeant.

Because no law school in Tennessee would admit blacks at that time, he matriculated at De Paul University in Chicago, where he took his J.D. degree in 1948. In 1961, he became assistant public defender of Shelby County, the Memphis jurisdiction. In 1965, Gov. Frank G. Clement appointed him to fill out a vacancy in the Shelby County Criminal Court, thus making him the first black criminal court judge in Tennessee history, and the following year Hooks won election to a full term in the judgeship. An ordained Baptist minister, he became in 1964 the pastor of the Greater New Mount Moriah Baptist Church in Detroit, where he flew to conduct services twice a month.

On December 31, 1968, he resigned his seat on the criminal court bench in order to devote more attention to his ministries and to assume the presidency of Mahalia Jackson Chicken Systems Inc., a fast-food chain. In 1972, President Richard Nixon nominated Hooks to succeed Robert T. Bartley, who was retiring from the seven-member Federal Communications Commission, which licenses radio and television stations and regulates those stations as well as telephone, telegraph, and satellite communication. On July 6, 1972, he was confirmed by the Senate. As the first black member of the FCC, Hooks was especially concerned with the influence of minorities in radio and television, because, as he observed, "until we become part of the image-making process we are foredoomed to failure."

On November 6, 1976, the board

of directors of the National Association for the Advancement of Colored People elected Hooks executive director of that civil rights organization, effective with the retirement of Roy Wilkins nine months later. He stressed the plight of blacks and other minorities in American society, describing "affirmative action" (which takes past inequities as well as present ability into account in such matters as hiring and education) as the "only workable, humane means" of redressing "handicaps growing out of centuries of black exclusion." On the other hand, he acknowledged that, the degree of opportunity aside, the problem transcends race it is employment, education, and a decent welfare system.

In 1990, Hooks as executive director of the NAACP, had over 2,200 chapters with 500,000 members. He stated, "Our agenda is designed to do what it always was designed to do, bring Blacks to first-class citizenship. It is designed to solve problems rather than appeal to certain sectors. We believe that we Blacks have been here too long, fought, died, suffered, got beaten, and made too many contributions in blood and sweat and toil for us to jump ship now. Our primary concern remains the protection and enhancement of civil rights, sheltering the homeless, defending the powerless, finding jobs for the jobless, caring for the helpless, fighting the scourge of crack and other drugs, and making our communities safe. Any discussion of saving Black youths in America today must deal with the stratification of the Black community which is based upon socio-economic background. There are now one million Black youngsters in post-secondary education, a number undreamed of in earlier times. For those young people, we must make sure that all civil rights laws are strongly enforced, the right to access to open housing, to jobs, to upward mobility."

HORN, WILLIAM FRED, was born in Bessemer, Alabama, but has lived most of his life in Birmingham. He is an active member of St. Paul Lutheran Church, is married to Mildred D. Horn. They are the parents of four children. He was educated in city schools, graduated from Parker High School and Miles College, as well as the University of Montevallo where he received a master's degree in administration. He serves in the Alabama State Legislature, representing the 18th Senatorial District in Jefferson County and chairs the Finance and Taxation Committee.

Horn was first elected to the State Legislature in 1978. During the one and one-half terms he served in the House of Representatives, he chaired two major committees, Constitutions and Elections and the Jefferson County Legislative Delegation. Then, in 1984, after a special election, he moved to the Senate and is now serving his first full term. Quietly but effectively, he has represented the interests of his electoral constituents and has championed the cause of public education in Alabama.

Among important legislation sponsored by Horn is the significant legislative act which allows Boards of Registrars to register non-registered voters without restrictions as to time or place. As chairman of the Senate Finance and Taxation Committee, he has worked to ensure passage of the largest budget ever and was responsible for securing equitable funding of approximately $9 million for black institutions in Alabama. Without his leadership, these black institutions most likely would not have received these funds. Also, as a state legislator, his successful intervention in negotiations with U.S. Steel resulted in the corporation's relocation to Jefferson County.

Presently, Sen. Horn is employed by the Birmingham City School System as director of middle school athletics. He has enjoyed an illustrious career as an educator, counselor and high school coach and was the first to integrate high school athletics He has been named "Coach of the Year." His more recent awards and honors include: University of Montevallo "Outstanding Area Public Official of the Year"; Delta Sigma Theta Sorority, Birmingham Alumnae Chapter "Dedicated Service and Outstanding Leadership Award"; Alabama Democratic Conference "Lyndon Baines Johnson Political Freedom Award"; Birmingham Press Club "Razzberry Award"; Hi-Y "Service Award"; Omega Psi Phi Fraternity "Outstanding Governmental service Award"; Titusville Community "Recreational Leadership Award"; "Eighteen Senatorial District Core Group Leadership Award"; and an induction into the Zeta Phi Beta Sorority Black Hall of Fame.

HOUSTON, WHITNEY, was born August 9, 1963, in Newark, New Jersey, to John Houston and Emily (Drinkard) "Cissy" Houston. She has two older brothers, Gary Garland and Michael. She graduated from Mount St. Dominic Academy in Caldwell, New Jersey. When she sang her first solo at the New Hope Baptist Church in Newark at the age of 12, she knew she was going to be a singer. With a childhood filled with music and musicians – first cousin Dionne Warwick, family friend Aretha Franklin, and mother, a veteran gospel and R&B singer – she lived in a musical dream world.

While in high school, she often sang with her mother in clubs and recording studios as a backup singer, and for such singers as Lou Rawls and Chaka Khan. After one performance at Carnegie Hall, a photographer suggested that she try modeling, and check out "Click," a new modeling agency. So she launched a career as a fashion model, appearing in the pages of *Vogue* and on the cover of *Seventeen* and *Cosmopolitan* magazines. Luther Vandross offered to produce her as a solo artist when she was 15, but her parents insisted that she finish high school first. When she graduated from high school, she signed with Tara Productions, a talent management company. She later signed with Arista Records.

In February 1985, her album "Whitney Houston" was released. The album was commercially successful, especially in the adolescent market, and its success mounted with the measured release of singles from it, videos to match the singles, television appearances, and a national tour by Houston beginning in June 1985 and culminating in sold-out performances at Carnegie Hall in November 1985. In addition to a Grammy, she won two national music awards early in 1986. The "Whitney Houston" album hit the top of the pop charts that spring and remained there on and off into the summer. Her once-planned release of her second album for the spring of 1986 was postponed for at least six months because of the unexpected resurgence of her first, which had been on the charts longer than any other LP in the top ten.

In 1988, she won the People's Choice Award. In 1989, Houston performed a benefit concert for Grambling State University, in addition to making a sizable personal contribution to the university. That same year, the National Center for Birth Defects in Boston named a wing in her honor in recognition of the fund-raising she has done for the center. In 1990, she received an award from the United Negro College Fund. She was one of the first black artists to agree to perform at the salute to South African freedom fighter Nelson Mandela. Her biggest soft spot is for children, and in 1990, she formed the "Whitney Houston Foundation for Children" to tackle illiteracy. She has used her fame to help others as she urges youth to say "NO" to drugs. By the end of 1991, Houston, one of the top female singers in the world, had raised a lot of money for numerous charities.

HUDSON, LIZANN R., was born in Mobile, Alabama. She is the mother of two adult children. She is presently pursuing her education in the field of physiology at Capital University and is also employed as a deputy bailiff in the referees department of Cleveland Municipal Court. While she was growing up, her family continued to travel in Alabama and other parts of the South. Because of family closeness and her excitement of seeing relatives during the summer and holidays, she was unaware that racism was present. As she grew older, not only did she become aware of racism in the South, but she realized that racism was alive and well in America.

After the riots in Cleveland, Hudson began working for the Hough Center (a center of EEO, equal opportunity program), as a youth counselor. It was during this time that she met the Rev. Jesse Jackson, who was recruiting people for the Breadbasket Program. Once the program started, she worked with the Rev. James Orange, who was essential in her meeting Dr. Martin Luther King, Jr., when he came to Cleveland in 1962. Through research of Dr. King's life and writings, he continues to be her spiritual mentor.

For many years Hudson had kept secret her inner frustrations of not getting the opportunity to fully express her natural talents. After an early marriage that ended in divorce and through many broken dreams, she continued to raise her children and pursue her education, while writing short skits and stories and performing for churches and organizations. Finally in 1989, while working on a class project which became the beginning of the future of "Okoa Watoto Wetu Inc," translated, "Save Our Children Inc.," she reached what she called "The Peak of the Jeremiah State."

Hudson plans to first finalize the organization in Cleveland and seeks to help others form similar culture centers in othe major cities. Okoa Watoto Wetu Inc., will not serve as a fine arts cultural center; it will have educational, vocational, drug prevention and drug crisis programs. The center will emphasize the cultural spirituality of the African American people as well as networking with other organizations. Hudson is a writer and singer who uses her talents to spread a message of love and hope. Her favorite quote is her own, "Our children need so much and we must be there for them." We are a race of people who must heal ourselves and begin to love ourselves with an unselfish fervor. "You cannot destroy a man's life for what he believes in, only share your beliefs with him . . ."

HUDSON, SAMUEL W., III, was born November 6, 1940, in Houston, Texas. He married the former Henrie Suldon, and they have eight children, Sam, Cynric, Lelalois, Samzie, Stacy,

Tracy, William, and Frenchelle. He received a B.S. degree from Texas Southern University, in 1963, and a J.D. degree from Thurgood Marshall School of Law, in 1967. From 1967 to 1968, he worked as a staff attorney for the Legal Foundation of Houston. From 1968 to 1970, he was a member of the legal staff of Collin Radio Company. In 1972, he became a staff attorney for the Federal Aviation Administration. In 1973, he was elected a State Representative for District 100, in Dallas. He is a member of the NAACP, and numerous political and bar associations.

HUGHES, CATHERINE LIGGINS, was born April 22, 1947, in Omaha, Nebraska. She is the daughter of William A. Woods and Helen E. Jones-Woods. She has one son, Alfred Charles Liggins, III. She credits her parents and the demanding Midwest

environment for honing her independence and confidence. "In Omaha, Nebraska, you work or you perish," she says, "because the elements will literally consume you." If the elements taught her how to survive, it was her mother who taught her how to live. The family lived in a low-income apartment complex in Omaha, a home where racial pride was the norm. "We were taught to achieve because we were black," she remembers. "My mother always told us, 'If you fail, you let your people down.' So she shackled my brothers, my sister, and me with the burden of all black people."

The roots of political activism were nurtured early. Against her mother's wishes, 15-year-old Hughes traveled halfway across the country to take part in the March on Washington in 1963. At 17, she became president of the Omaha NAACP Youth Council. Soon after, she mobilized the blacks in her neighborhood and the white students at her school to protest the segregation of a local pool. During her last year in high school, she became pregnant. When she refused to get an abortion, her mother, in Hughes' words, "invited me to become mistress of my own home." She moved out, found an apartment and, within a few months, married the father of her child.

For the next year she juggled motherhood, marriage, a job, and political activism, but still finished high school and entered Creighton University. Her marriage ended, but she continued taking classes at Creighton and became involved with a troubled black radio station in Omaha, both as a volunteer staffer and as a small investor. It was her first exposure to the inner workings of radio. She also stayed politically active, working as Midwest regional director of a Ford Foundation-funded organization that monitored non-profit groups for adherence to affirmative-action and equal-opportunity laws.

Then, in 1971, she was offered a chance to join the staff of Howard University's new School of Communications, headed by veteran black journalist and broadcaster Tony Brown. After a year as a lecturer,

Hughes was appointed sales manager of WHUR-FM, the campus radio station. Soon she was general manager. With graduates of the Howard University Law School, in Washington, D.C., she organized a protest over the 85 percent bar exam failure rate of the school's students. Her most lasting contribution as general manager had more to do with programming than with protest. She had attended a six-week program at the University of Chicago on psychographic programming. She left Howard in 1978 to become vice president and general manager of WYCB-AM, a gospel music station.

Opportunity presented itself in 1980 when WOL-AM went on the market. For 14 years WOL had been the voice and sound of D.C.'s black working class, pumping out a constant stream of soul and rhythm and blues. With her second husband, Dewey Hughes, an Emmy Award–winning producer at WRC-TV, Hughes formed Almic Broadcasting, named for her son Alfred, and Dewey's son Michael. Almic's purchase of WOL was partly financed by Syndicated Communications, a venture-capital group that aids minorities in the purchase of broadcast stations. Among the original investors in WOL were Samuel Jackson, a former HUD undersecretary, and Lebaron Taylor, vice president of CBS Records.

By the time Hughes purchased WMMJ in 1987, again with the assistance of Syndicated Communications, she had dispelled any doubts about her business acumen. WOL has not just survived, it has thrived under her management. Using a small northwest apartment building she owned as collateral, Hughes and her investors bought WOL for $950,000. By itself WOL is hardly a media heavyweight, but the purchase in 1987 of WMMJ-FM for $7.5 million has made Almic Broadcasting a media operation to be reckoned with. Hughes was also in the final stages of purchasing WINN-AM and FM in Baltimore, the next step in her plan to develop a network of radio stations geared to black communities. She has broken into television, too, hosting an interview show every Saturday evening at 7 p.m. on Channel 50.

HUGHES, HOLLIS E., JR., was born March 14, 1943, in South Bend, Indiana. He is married to Lavera Ruth Knight. From 1958 to 1961, he attended South Bend Central High School, graduating in 1961. He enrolled at Ball State University in 1961, and graduated in 1965 with a B.S. degree in education. In 1972, he received an M.A. degree in sociology from Ball State University. From August 1965 to September 1969, he worked for the South Bend Community School Corporation as a secondary level social studies teacher and coach. From 1969 to 1970, he worked for the city of South Bend Model Cities Program as assistant director for citizen participation, and in 1970, as deputy director.

In December 1973, Hughes received a mayoral appointment as director of the city's new Bureau of Housing. He was appointed executive director of the South Bend Model Cities Program and served from 1972 to 1974. From 1974 to 1978, he worked for Housing Allowance Office, Inc., as chief, division of client services. From 1978 to 1986, he was appointed executive director/secretary-treasurer of Housing Allowance Office, Inc., and St. Joseph County Housing Authority. From 1986 to the present, he has served as president of Housing Systems, Inc.

Hughes has a long list of community affiliations which includes: member, United Way Planning and Allocation Division, and chairman of the Health Services Allocation Panel; member, board of trustees, Memorial Hospital, South Bend; member and president, board of trustees, South Bend Community School Corporation; and member and president, board of directors, South Bend Public Library.

HUGHES, TERESA P., was born in New York City. She is married to Frank E. Staggers, M.D., and they have two children, Vincent and Deirdre. She earned a B.A. degree in physiology and public health and completed her graduate work in sociology at Hunter College. She received her M.A. degree in education administration at New York University, and a Ph.D. degree in education administration at Claremont Graduate School. Hughes, a Democrat, was elected to the Assembly in a special election in 1975. She represents the 47th Assembly District which includes south central Los Angeles, and the cities of Bell, Cudahy, and Huntington Park. She is a former legislative and education consultant to the State Commission on teacher credentialing, and professor of education at California State University, Los Angeles.

Hughes' professional experience as a former social worker, teacher, school administrator and professor is evidenced by the variety of her legislative efforts. She is the successful author of legislation mandating affirmative action reporting for California's universities, authorizing $800 million in bond money to construct school classrooms; the Hughes Earthquake Safety Act of 1987 that allocates state funds for the reconstruction of nonconforming school buildings; creation of a State School of the Arts; and the Hughes-Hart Education Reform Act of 1983 that funded education proposals to upgrade California's scholastic programs. In the field of health, she led the fight to provide research grants for lupus disease and high blood pressure; to protect physicians from civil and criminal liabilities for informing the spouse of a patient of a positive test result for the AIDS antibodies; the financing of Displaced Homemaker Centers; and to provide for adequate compensation for development disabilities work-activity programs.

Hughes, in the area of public safety, authored laws establishing a gang and drug prevention program in public schools; increasing the prison terms for gang-related drive-by shootings; instituting a training program for prosecutors on gang-related crimes; and developing a pilot program for burglary prevention. During her terms as an elected official she was responsible for laws to provide $100 million to construct or rehabilitate low- and moderate-income housing; establish anti-redlining home loan laws; provide adequate notices before a person loses their home due to foreclosure; and institute a replacement housing program for Redevelopment Agencies established before 1975. In addition, Hughes carried and supported legislation protecting consumers' interests, and creating the California Museum of Afro-American History and Culture and locating it in Los Angeles, a major center of commerce and the home of her constituents. She continues to serve on the board of directors of the Afro-American Museum and is on the Foundation Board of the Museum of Science and Industry.

Dr. Hughes is the founder of Aware Women, an active member of the California State Employees Association, the California Teachers Association, the Coalition of Labor Union Women, the Democratic Women's Caucus, and Delta Sigma Theta, Inc., a public service sorority. She is on the board of directors for the local coalition of One Hundred Black Women, the Black Agenda, and on the corporate board of Blue Shield. She serves as a member of Los Angeles Mayor Bradley's Education Committee, the board of trustees of the Los Angeles County High School for the Arts, and the education council of the Music Center of Los Angeles County. In November 1988, the Los Angeles Unified School District, by unanimous approval, honored Hughes by dedicating and renaming an elementary school in the city of Cudahy, Los Angeles County, the "Dr. Teresa Hughes Elementary School."

As a credit to her legislative leadership role, Hughes has been the chairwoman of the Assembly Committees on Human Services, Housing and Community Development, Education Subcommittee on Postsecondary Education, California Legislative Black Caucus, California Woman Legislators Caucus, and presently chairs the Assembly Committee on Education. She serves on the Assembly Committees on Public Employees and Retirement, Housing and Community Development, and local government. She also represents the Assembly on the State Allocation Board.

HUNTER, TEOLA P., a graduate of Cass Technical High School in Detroit, Hunter received her B.S. degree from the University of Detroit, and a master's degree in education from Wayne State University. A mother and businesswoman who is highly respected and very involved in community leadership, she resides in Detroit. She was a school teacher in the Detroit school system for 14 years, has served on several boards of directors, and is a member of Mayflower Congregational United Church of Christ. She is the founder, owner and operator of the Buttons and Bows Nurseries and Preparatory Schools.

After her election to the House of Representatives in 1980, she organized the Fifth District Task Force to enable her constituents to discuss issues of concern with her on a one-to-one basis. This group met monthly and attempted to assist those in the community in need. She assisted the Task Force in securing a grant to participate in celebrating Michigan's Sesquicentennial. She has been a member of the Michigan House of Representatives since January 1981, representing the 5th District.

As chairperson of the House Social Services and Youth Committee, Hunter also serves on the following House committees: Urban Affairs (majority vice chair); Public Health;

Legislative Council; House Oversight; and Oversight Committee on Family and Children Services (chair). The speaker of the House appointed her to a special committee to study the status of the Medicaid system in the state of Michigan. She has served as the chair of the Public Health Subcommittee on AIDS, and introduced legislation on confidentiality in AIDS testing. Through her determination and efforts in protecting the rights of persons with AIDS, the legislation was signed into law by the governor in 1988. She also founded Resource Endowment Aiding Children Together (REACT) with Love. This non-profit foundation was established to help children and families with AIDS.

In November and December of 1982, Hunter toured the Soviet Union along with nine other persons from diverse backgrounds as a concerned citizen of peace. In July 1985, she traveled to Nairobi, Kenya, to attend the Decade of Women World Conference. And in 1986, she was a representative to the NOBEL (National Organization of Black Elected Legislators) Women's Conference in Bermuda. In January 1990, Hunter was one of several legislators invited to visit Israel by the Jewish Community Council to get a more complete perspective on Middle East developments.

Rep. Hunter has received many honors and awards, including Pathfinders Award, Black Students of Oakland University; Citizen of the Year Award, presented by the Detroit Medical Society; Outstanding Citizen Award, presented by Gentlemen of Wall Street; recognition from Blue Cross/Blue Shield of Michigan as Black Legislator in honor of Black History Month; Award of Merit for Outstanding Achievement/Leadership Development and Community Relations, by the Core City Neighborhoods Inc., Detroit; Outstanding Contribution to the City of Detroit and State of Michigan, The Detroit Squaws; Woman of

the Year Award, National Association of Black Women Entrepreneurs, 1987; Michigan Legislator of the Year Award, presented by Michigan Association of Children's Alliances; Susan B. Anthony Award, presented by the Michigan Women's Political Caucus; Distinguished Citizen of the Year Award, presented by the National Association of Social Workers, Metro Detroit Chapter, 1990; and the Public Citizen of the Year Award, by the Michigan Chapter, National Association of Social Workers, 1990.

HURLEY, SAMUEL W., JR, a native Chicagoan and a product of the city's public school system (John Marshall High School), Hurley graduated from the Illinois Institute of Technology with a B.S. degree in civil engineering in 1958, and received his master's degree in public works from the University of Pittsburgh in 1973. He has served as commissioner of Chicago's Department of Water from 1987 to date. Prior positions include commissioner of the Chicago Department of Sewers, 1986–1987; deputy commissioner, Chicago Department of Public Works, 1983–1986; engineer of construction in the Bureau of Construction, Department of Public Works, Chicago, 1981–1983; chief records and estimates engineer, Department of Public Works, Chicago, 1975–1981; supervised engineer/civil engineer, Project Administration Section, Department of Public Works, Chicago (2 1/2 years as supervisor), 1969–1975.

Hurley has been a participant in the Youth Motivation Program, Chicago Association of Commerce and Industry; a board member of South East Community Organization; a Block Club president; a member of SOS (Save Our School) steering committee for Caldwell-McDowell Elementary, and a life member of Kappa Alpha Psi fraternity. He is also a

member of the Water Utility Council of the American Waterworks Association and serves on the board of directors of the Association of Metropolitan Water Agencies. He is a member of the National Society of Professional Engineers, and former vice president of the Chicago Chapter of the American Public Works Association.

INGRAM, ROBERT B., was educated and has served as adjunct professor in the School of Public Affairs at Florida International University, the School of Psychiatric Medicine at the University of Miami and the School of Graduate Management of Nova University. He has been a professor of psychology at Florida Memorial College. He is married to the former Delores Newsome and has two daughters and five granddaughters. Ingram is the mayor of Opa-Locka, Florida. He brings a tremendous advantage to the political table because he comes with the patient understanding of a preacher, the political knowledge of a professor and the assurance of an administrator with experiences valuable for guiding the rebirth of a com-

munity. He is seen as the perennial "point-man."

Ingram was the first black police officer to be assigned to an all-white section of downtown Miami; the first black police officer to be assigned to the prestigious motorcycle unit and then later to the imposing Internal Security unit; the first black police officer to achieve the position of chief prior to retiring from the Miami Police Department; and the first black city manager of South Miami, Florida. He has a tradition of breaking down color barriers, and as impressive as his list of accomplishments has been, his present role as mayor of the seventh largest city in Dade County is the one that is especially close to his heart. "Because there were so many good people in Opa-Locka, with the ability, willingness and desire to stand up for what they know to be right, they had made great strides in bettering their community."

Ingram believes that "Every boy and girl, man and woman deserve[s] a neighborhood where opportunity to succeed [is] assured." Hence there are extended families and church outreach programs to take care of their people. While the problem appeared overwhelming, Ingram believed "When our local ministers come together, and they will, when we galvanize our families and we will, and when we get other community-based groups working to develop the qualities of character that was good enough for their parents and mine, we will solve the most immediate problems impacting on our life and our liberty and it won't be a long time coming." His method: "God's Servant in the Service of God's People." His motto: "Keep on struggling."

INNIS, ROY, was born June 6, 1934, in St. Croix, Virgin Islands. His father, a policeman, died when Roy was a child. Innis, with his mother, moved to New York's Harlem ghetto in early adolescence. When he was 16, he dropped out of Stuyvesant High School in Manhattan to join the United States Army. Following his discharge, he finished high school and then studied chemistry at the City College of New York. He left college before graduation and found jobs as a chemical technician for the Vicks Chemical Company and as a research assistant in the cardiovascular research laboratory at Montefiore Hospital in New York City.

In 1963, he joined the Congress of Racial Equality, Harlem chapter. In 1968, he succeeded Floyd McKissick as national director of CORE. Under Innis' direction, CORE was concentrating its energies on winning political, social, and economic autonomy for black communities throughout the United States. Among other innovations in CORE, brought about largely by Innis, was an affirmation of the right to self-defense against white racist violence. In 1989, he served as National Chairman of CORE, and opened a branch office in Washington, D.C., to provide job training, substance abuse counseling, and legal assistance for minorities and immigrants.

JACKSON, JANET, was born May 16, 1966, in Gary, Indiana, the daughter of Joseph and Katherine Jackson. She is the youngest of nine children in the famous Jackson family. Each child—Janet, Rebbie (Maureen), Jackie, Tito, Jermaine, LaToya, Marlon, Michael and Randy—has been involved in the music industry. From the cradle, the Jackson children were imbued with music by both parents. Katherine Jackson taught them folk songs, and Joe Jackson, who with his brothers had formed the Falcons, a short-lived Chicago rhythm and blues combo, played the guitar. The children sang together spontaneously, especially after the family television set broke down, and eventually they did so to guitar accompaniment after Tito taught himself to play on his father's instrument.

Janet acted in the following television shows: "Good Times" (1977-1979), "A New Kind of Family" (1979-1980), "Diff'rent Strokes" (1981-1982), and "Fame" (1984-1985). In 1982, she released her first album, "Janet Jackson," followed by "Dream Street" in 1984, "Control" in 1986, and "Rhythm Nation 1814" in 1989. Her "Rhythm Nation" album made recording industry history by notching the most top ten hits from one album and went on to dominate the music awards. Janet took home eight prizes at the first Billboard Music Awards on the strength of "Rhythm Nation": number one rhythm and blues artist, rhythm and blues album, rhythm and blues singles artist, Hot 100 singles artist, top dance album, top dance singles artist, best pop album, and best rhythm and blues album. The awards, given by *Billboard* magazine, are based on record sales, and "Rhythm Nation" sold more than 7 million copies. Her "Rhythm Nation" world tour lasted most of 1990; with a nine-piece band and six dancers, she performed on a five-story, $2 million aluminum stage.

JACKSON, JANET E., a graduate of Wittenberg University in Springfield, Ohio, with a B.A. degree, 1975; received a J.D. degree from the National Law Center, George Washington University, Washington, D.C., 1978. Jackson has served as a judge for Franklin County Municipal Court since January 1987. Prior positions include: chief of Worker's Compensation Section, Ohio Attorney General's Office, Columbus, chief of Civil Rights Section, Sindell, Sindell & Rubenstein; other positions with the Ohio Attorney General's Office, including assistant attorney general in the Civil Rights Section, assistant chief of the Civil Rights Section and chief of the Crime Victims Compensation Section. Jackson was admitted to the Ohio bar in 1978, to the United States District Court Southern District of Ohio in 1979, and to the United States District Court Northern District of Ohio in 1983.

Jackson has received many awards: Franklin County Democratic Women's Outstanding Accomplishments Award, 1988; Omega Psi Phi Citizenship Award, 1987; Distinguished Barrister Award, presented by the National Conference of Black Lawyers, Columbus chapter, 1988; Warren Jennings Award, presented by the Franklin County Mental Health Board to an individual who did the most to improve services to the black community, 1989; Sharon Wilkin award from the Metropolitan Women's Center; Political Leadership Award presented by the 29th District Citizens Caucus, 1987; Community Service Award presented by the Metropolitan Democratic Women's Club, 1989; and the Martin Luther King, Jr. Humanitarian Award from the Love Academy, 1987. Her professional affiliations include: Ohio

Bar Association; Columbus Bar Association; National Conference of Black Lawyers; and the Women Lawyers of Franklin County, Inc.

JACKSON, JESSE LOUIS, was born October 8, 1941, in Greenville, South Carolina. He is the son of Charles Henry and Helen J. He married the former Jacqueline Lavinia Brown, and they have five children: Jesse Louis, Jonathan Luther, Yusef DuBois, Jacqueline Lavinia, and Sanita. In 1964, he received a B.A. degree in sociology and economics from North Carolina A&T State University. In 1966, he was founder (with others) of Operation Breadbasket, a joint project of the Southern Christian Leadership Conference, in Chicago, Illinois. In 1967, he was named national director of Operation Breadbasket joint project for the SCLC. In 1968, he was ordained a Baptist minister.

Jackson, who developed much of his leadership style while serving as a lieutenant to the late Dr. Martin Luther King, Jr., would later call King "my father figure, my brother figure and my teacher." He helped expand King's economic efforts to other cities and was at the Memphis Hotel when King was assassinated. He left the SCLC in 1971 and founded his own organization, Operation PUSH (People United to Save Humanity). He is an activist for social change, with a message for the American people and for black people in particular. "For black folks," he said, "the crisis is doubly serious. The doors of opportunity that have been knocked open by the civil rights movement can't be taken advantage of because many of our young men are too drunk to stagger through them. Many of our young girls become pregnant prematurely. The crime rate where we [blacks] live is so high our businesses can't flourish. Our women cannot walk the streets in safety and our homes have so many bars they look like prisons. Dope is flowing through our schools and our young people are influenced by the movies that glorify hustling and nonwork. What I've seen in the schools is a breakdown in moral authority, discipline and development. Youth are looking for something, even if it's something wrong. It is up to adults to show them what is worth emulating."

On November 3, 1983, Jackson stood on the stage of the Washington, D.C., Convention Center and announced that he was a candidate for the presidency of the United States of America. He gained enough delegates and support to go into the Democratic National Convention as a strong voice in the construction of the 1984 Democratic platform. In 1987, he was on the road with a new campaign for the Democratic nomination for president of the United States. This time he had a vision of a Rainbow Coalition. His candidacy, at first dismissed by the presumed experts as an exercise in minority politics, flourished into the spring, outlasting all but one of his rivals.

At the 1988 Democratic National Convention in Atlanta, Jackson was once again a force to reckon with. There were some 962 black delegates, 23 percent of the total. He did not win the nomination, but his campaign had broken through the psychological barrier that prevented blacks from reasonably seeking offices beyond traditionally black districts. On the stage at the convention, he gave a 49-minute, nationally televised speech and received a 15-minute ovation at its conclusion, In 1989, responding to the white media on the new mainstream "black politicians," he said, "The items I have struggled for are in the mainstream of this country's interest. You cannot name one that I am not in the center of that stream." He volleyed reporters' questions about policies that many say mark him as a liberal. Affirmative action? "That's the law of the land," he replied. "You can't get any more mainstream than that."

In 1990, Jackson made his first run for an office other than president, and won the Democratic nomination for one of two "shadow senator" seats from the District of Columbia. In September 1990, he traveled to Baghdad, Iraq, and Kuwait City, Kuwait. Jackson met Iraqi President Saddam Hussein and left Kuwait with 500 freed hostages.

JACKSON, MAYNARD, was born March 23, 1938, in Dallas, Texas, to Dr. Maynard Holbrook Jackson, who served as pastor of Friendship Baptist Church, and professor Irene Dobbs Jackson, whose father, John Wesley Dobbs, was a legend in Atlanta long before Maynard was born. One of six children, Maynard distinguished himself academically early on. As a Ford Foundation Early Admission Scholar, he graduated from Morehouse College at age 18 with a B.A. degree in political science and history. He later earned the J.D. degree (cum laude) from the School of Law at North Carolina Central University. After law school he settled in Atlanta, where he practiced law with the National Labor Relations Board, offered free legal services to low-income Atlantans through

the Emory Community Legal Service Center and helped establish the private law firm of Jackson, Patterson, Parks and Franklin.

In June 1968, Jackson announced his decision to run for public office. He quit his job, borrowed enough money to pay the qualifying fee and, on the last possible day, started what was described as a quixotic race for the U.S. Senate seat held by Herman Talmadge, until then the unchallenged symbol of the Old South. Predictable, Talmadge won. But the young unknown confounded the experts when he carried Atlanta by a majority of 6,000 votes. A year later, at the age of 31, he was elected vice mayor of Atlanta with a healthy majority of all votes cast. In 1973, at the age of 35, he ran for mayor, and the voters responded favorably to the theme that Atlanta needed "leaders, not politicians" by electing him. In 1977, he was re-elected to a second term with strong bi-racial support.

Jackson served as mayor for two terms (1974–1982), the maximum number of consecutive terms allowed by the city charter. For those eight years, he presided over a period of economic development, fiscal stability, job creation, neighborhood revitalization, improved delivery of city services, effective public safety and construction of the new Atlanta airport. Characterizing his policies as the "politics of inclusion," he also opened the doors of the city government to all; for the first time, minorities and women truly had the opportunity to compete for jobs and contracts on an equal basis. When he first became mayor, less than one-half of one percent of those contracts went to minority and female-owned businesses, and after he became mayor employment of minority and female managers gained national and local acclaim. Accurately reflecting the accomplishments of these years, Rand-McNally, in the prestigious *Almanac of Places Rated*, named Atlanta as the best major city in which to live and work in the United States as of December 1981.

In 1982, Jackson returned to the private practice of law as managing partner of the Atlanta office of Chapman and Cutler, one of the nation's leading firms in corporate, municipal and state finance. He has served as president of the National Conference of Democratic Mayors; is a member of the executive committees of the Democratic National Committee and the Democratic Party of Georgia; president of the National Black Caucus of Local Electre Officials; chairman of the U.S. Local Government Energy Policy Advisory Committee; founding chairman of the Committee of the Arts, U.S. Conference of Mayors; founding chairman of the Atlanta Authority of city of Atlanta; and member of the President's National Commission on Neighborhoods. A trustee of Morehouse College, Jackson has received numerous honorary degrees, citations, and awards for civic, humanitarian, academic and business achievements.

Jackson is married to Valerie

Richardson and is the father of four daughters and one son. He was inaugurated as Atlanta's 56th mayor January 2, 1990. Three months earlier, he had won the mayoral race garnering over 80 percent of the vote and carrying every precinct in the city. His victory on October 3 marked the third time that Atlanta voters have chosen Maynard Jackson to fill the top elected post in the city.

JACKSON, MICHAEL JOSEPH, was born on August 29, 1958, the fifth of nine children of Joseph and Katherine Jackson. The oldest Jackson sibling is (Rebbie) Maureen (Jackson) Brown, who lives with her husband in Kentucky. Michael's older brothers are Jackie, Tito, Jermaine, and Marlon, the four who, with him, formed the original Jackson Five. The Jackson children were taught music by both parents; Katherine taught them folk songs, and Joe, who with his brothers had formed the Falcons, played guitar. Tito taught himself to play his father's guitar, and the Jackson boys would play at talent contests and pass-the-hat gigs in and around Gary. They moved on to paid engagements in such venues as the Apollo Theatre in New York's Harlem and the Uptown in Philadelphia. Joe Jackson was their manager and drove them around in a borrowed Volkswagen van.

It was at the Apollo that they were "discovered," not by Motown singer Diana Ross, as apocrypha has it, but by Motown singer Gladys Knight and pianist Billy Taylor. Knight and Taylor were the first to alert Berry Gordy, Motown's founder and president, to the Jacksons' potential. Ross served to reinforce decisively their recommendation of the Jacksons to Gordy. The Jacksons proved to be more than just pre-teenybopper heartthrobs. Black and white audiences from all age groups went for them, and the group earned four number one hits in 1970. In

1971, Michael established a solo career with the ballad "Got to Be There," followed the next year with another ballad, "I'll Be There." As the 1970s elapsed, Jackson's voice began to change and the hits came fewer and farther between.

In 1978, Michael played the role of Scarecrow in the Motown/Universal film *The Wiz*. It was on the set of *The Wiz* that he met Quincy Jones, the film's musical director, and the two began sharing musical ideas. Jones produced Michael's Epic debut solo album, the disco-oriented "Off the Wall" (1979), which exploded with huge success in the record industry at a time when that industry was in a severe depression. The new Michael Jackson was more like the horned god Pan than the eternal boy Peter Pan, and he beckoned his audience into a sweaty dance that was equal parts gyration and copulation. He trumpeted the new style from the album's first cut, opening with the steamy "Don't Stop 'Til You Get Enough." "Off the Wall" sold 8 million copies, making it at that time the largest selling album by any black artist, and placed three singles in the Top 10 simultaneously.

In 1982, his "Thriller" album so dominated the record-buying public that it effectively eclipsed "Off the Wall." "Thriller" became the largest selling album ever recorded. Since its release in 1982, "Thriller" has sold over 35 million copies worldwide. Jackson wrote four songs on the album, including the hits "Beat It" and "Billie Jean." In 1984, on tour with his brothers, the Michael Jackson "Victory Tour" attracted the largest concert crowds and sold the most tickets in the history of show business. Also in 1984, Jackson and his brothers signed a three-year contract to make commercials for Pepsi for an estimated $10 million. In 1987, Jackson came out with his "Bad" album. The album sold over 18 million copies and had an unprecedented five number one singles. Jackson received an honorary doctorate from Nashville's Fisk University at the United Negro College Fund's 44th Anniversary dinner in Manhattan.

JACKSON, SHIRLEY A., a native of Washington, D.C., received an S.B. degree in physics from Massachusetts Institute of Technology (MIT), Cambridge, Massachusetts, in 1968. In 1973, she was the first black woman to earn a Ph.D. from MIT, in theoretical particles. After earning her doctorate, she was a research associate (1974–1974, 1975–1976) at the Fermi National Accelerator Laboratory in Batavia, Illinois, and a visiting scientist (1974–1975) at the European Center for Nuclear Research (CERN), where she worked on theories of strongly interacting elementary particles. Since 1976, Jackson has been at AT&T Bell Laboratories, Murray Hill, New Jersey, where she has done research on various subjects including charge density waves in layered compounds, polaronic aspects of electrons on the surface of liquid helium films, and most recently, optical and electronic properties of semiconductor strained layer superlattices.

In 1986, she was elected a Fellow of the American Physical Society for her research accomplishments. In 1985, New Jersey governor Thomas Kean appointed Jackson to the New Jersey Commission on Science and Technology. She was reappointed and confirmed for a five-year term in 1989. She has also served on committees of the National Academy of Sciences, the American Association for the Advancement of Science and the National Science Foundation promoting science and research and women's roles in these fields.

Jackson is a trustee of MIT, Rutgers University, Lincoln University (Pennsylvania) and the Barnes Foundation. She is also a director of Public Service Enterprise Group (Newark, New Jersey), New Jersey Resources Corporation (Wall, New Jersey), and Core States/New Jersey National Bank (West Trenton, New Jersey). She has received ten scholarships, fellowships and grants; has studied in Colorado, Sicily and France; has taught at MIT, and has lectured at several institutes. She has received numerous awards, is a member of the American Physical Society and its governing board, and the Council of the American Physical Society, a past president of the National Society of Black Physicists, and a member of a half-dozen other professional societies, including the American Institute of Physics, on whose governing board she also sits.

During her student years at MIT, she did volunteer work at Boston City Hospital and tutoring at the Roxbury (Boston) YMCA. She has been a vice president of the MIT Alumni Association, and is on three MIT visiting committees. She is married and has a son.

JACKSON, VINCENT EDWARD (BO), was born on November 30, 1962, in Bessemer, Alabama, the son of Florence Jackson and A. D. Adams. He and his wife Linda have three children, Garrett "Spud," Nicholas and Morgan. He ran track as a third-grader. He graduated from McAdory High School in McCalla, Alabama, 15 miles west of Birmingham. While in high school, Jackson set a national high school record by hitting 20 home runs as a senior, despite missing seven games because he was competing in track meets. He was a two-time state decathlon champion and set state records in the 60- and 100- yard dashes, the 60- and 120-yard hurdles, the long jump and the high jump.

The New York Yankees drafted him during his senior year of high school. They offered him $250,000 in 1982 to bypass college. But he enrolled at Auburn University in Auburn, Alabama, where he won the Heisman trophy in

1985 as a running back. He was the first choice in the 1986 National Football League draft, but he turned down a multimillion dollar offer from the Tampa Bay Buccaneers to play baseball. The Kansas City Royals also selected him in its 1986 college draft. Jackson signed a three-year contract with the Royals totaling $1.06 million. His first year with Kansas City he played in 25 games and had 17 hits, 9 home runs and a batting average of .207.

In 1987, Jackson signed a five-year contract with the Los Angeles Raiders for $1.2 million a year, and he renegotiated his contract with the Royals. He became pro sports' first outfielder/running back. When he went to the Raiders, his first year he set a new team record with a 91-yard touchdown run and a 221-yard rushing performance on "Monday Night Football." In 1987, he hit 22 home runs as an outfielder with the Kansas City Royals, and scored six touchdowns as a Los Angeles Raiders running back. He became one of five pro athletes to have hit a home run and scored a touchdown in the same season.

On May 23, 1989, Jackson ripped a 461-foot homer to center field off Nolan Ryan, the longest measured home run in the history of Arlington Stadium, in a game between the Royals and Texas Rangers. That same year at the 60th All-Star Game, played before 64,036 at Anaheim Stadium, consecutive home runs by Jackson and Boston Red Sox third baseman Wade Boggs against National League starter Rick Reuschel erased a 2–0 deficit and set the AL on a tear of five consecutive runs. Bo homered; Bo stole a base; Bo caught a ball that could have ended the game before it began. Bo beat out what might have been a routine double-play ball to most mortals. Bo stole the show. Bo was named the game's Most Valuable Player.

In 1990, Jackson was selected to the AFC Pro Bowl Squad, becoming the first pro athlete chosen for all-star games in two sports. His 88-yard run that put the ball on the 1-yard line led to a touchdown to make the score 24–7 in a game between the Raiders and Cincinnati to clinch the AFC playoff game. The marketing of America's newest sports hero was moving into a new dimension. Jackson and his agent, Richard Woods of Mobile, Alabama, agreed in 1985 to be selective with the endorsement process. Even before his Most Valuable Player performance in the All-Star Game, Jackson had signed several endorsement deals, including a four-year arrangement with Nike, Inc., in Beaverton, Oregon, that doubled sales of cross trainer shoes and apparel; and deals with Salem Screen Printers of Salem, New Hampshire, for T-shirts, baseball and football pennants; Costacos Brothers Sports of Seattle, Washington, for "Black/Blue" poster (Raider/ Royals); Franklin Sports Inc., of Stoughton, Massachusetts, for batting gloves; Donruss, Fleer, Topps for baseball cards; Tiger Electronics for hand-held baseball and football computer games; and Sports Impressions for porcelain figurine in Royals uniform.

Beyond all that, Jackson still found time to donate his services to charity. He served as a spokesman for the Marillac Foundation of Kansas City, which works with children who have learning disabilities. He served as spokesman for the President's Fitness Council; for the American Library Association "The Read Poster" which shows Jackson reading his favorite book, *The Old Man and the Sea*; and for Hughston Sports Medicine, which produced a medical poster for high school students dealing with sports injuries. At Methodist Hospital Systems, he made an anti-drug television commercial. By 1991, he had become a legend, if not for baseball and football, for his commercials. Every kid in the country knows who Bo is.

On January 13, 1991, in an AFC semifinal game against Cincinnati,

Jackson's 77 yards on 6 carries ran his career per-carry average against Cincinnati to a stunning 13.1 before he took his last hit of his first playoff game, injuring his left hip, on a play where he had broken loose for 34 yards. As the 1991 baseball season spring training got under way, the Kansas City Royals physicians were not pleased with Jackson's recuperation, and the Royals released him. In April 1991, he found a home in Chicago with the White Sox. He signed with the Chicago White Sox on April 3, 1991, his salary dependent on how much he is able to play. The White Sox have options for 1992 and 1993. The contract does not prohibit Jackson from fulfilling the final year of his $7.4 million contract with the NFL's Los Angeles Raiders if his health permits.

JACOB, JOHN EDWARD, was born on December 16, 1934, in Trout, Louisiana, one of five sons of Emory and Claudia (Sadler) Jacob. The family moved to Houston, Texas. Jacob enrolled at Howard University in Washington, D.C., on an E. E. Worthing scholarship, and graduated with a B.A. degree in economics in 1957. After spending two years on active duty in the United States Army, and obtaining the rank of 2nd lieutenant, he returned to Washington. He at first found a job with the United States Postal Service as a clerk. In 1960, he began work at the Batimore Department of Public Welfare as a public assistance caseworker.

In 1965, he left a supervisor position with the Public Welfare Department, after graduating from Howard University with a master's degree in social work. He then joined the Washington Urban League as director of education and youth incentives. After the riots of 1967, in the black ghetto of northwest Washington, when on one day 34 persons were arrested for arson, vandalism, or looting, the Washington Urban League created Project Alert, in which ghetto youth leaders were hired to lessen neighborhood tensions by putting residents with problems in touch with the League and other agencies.

In 1968, Jacob was appointed acting executive director of the Washington Urban League. In 1970, he served briefly as director of community organizing and training for the National Urban League's Eastern region, and from 1970 to 1975, he was director of the San Diego Urban League. Meanwhile, Vernon E. Jordan, Jr., had become president of the National Urban League, succeeding Whitney M. Young, Jr., who died in a drowning accident in 1971. In 1975, he returned to Washington as president of the Washington Urban League. In 1982, he became the third president of the National Urban League. In a period of political and financial retrenchment for black civil rights organizations, he guided the interracial league in new service initiatives. He applied league resources to self-help solutions to the black community's internal problems, such as out-of-wedlock teenage pregnancy, poor single-mother households, black-on-black crime, and voter education and participation.

Jacob said, "This is a time of hopelessness and despair for millions of Black youths. We cannot, however, succumb to the lost-generation notion that young blacks are both hopeless and expendable, these are our children and their survival is our future. We must do what we can to protect them against the constant onslaught of outside forces that prey upon them. We advocate increased mobilization of the Black community, through our churches, schools and civic organizations, to uphold values, high expectations and motivation. One of our numerous programs, 'Crime Is Not a Part of Our Black Heritage,' is one of many efforts to motivate community institutions to create a sense of culture, an appreciation of history, and a rededication to the values that have meant Black survival. Our National Education Initiative seeks to increase the achievement levels of Black students in public schools. What has distinguished us organizationally is that in addition to our civil rights portfolio, we have always been a direct service organization."

JACOBS, TRACIE B., is a graduate of the University of Colorado, where she received her B.A. degree in psychology and an M.P.A. degree in public administration. She has served as minority affairs coordinator for Indiana Vocational Technical College to date. She served as the manager of the Equal Employment Opportunity Program for approximately 1,200 employees, which included the following programs: High School Stay-in-School Program, Federal Women's Program, Complaint Processing, Worker-Trainee Program, and Management Training. She coordinated committees composed of staff and management to develop and maintain programs.

Jacobs' prior positions include: director of personnel for the Holiday Inn–Downtown; marketing/public relations manager for Bethel Business Machines; director of development for the YWCA of St. Joseph County; manager, project business for the Junior Achievement of Michigan; co-host, Minority Forum television program for WSBT-TV; producer, script editor and host, radio program "Especially for You" for WHME-FM, WAUS-FM and WAMJ-FM; president/speaker, for Especially for You Consulting Co. (motivational seminars, counseling, and newsletter); instructor, for Lake Michigan College; associate director, coop and placement for Andrews University, and an Equal Employment Opportunity manager/personnel manager, for the Bureau of Reclamation. Jacobs was a candidate for City Council at Large in 1987, and has served on the mayor's Minority Affairs Council as chair, employment committee from 1984 to date.

---

†JAMES, DANIEL, JR., was born on February 11, 1920, in Pensacola, Florida, the youngest of 17 children of Daniel James, Sr., and Lillie Anna (Brown) James who ran an elementary school for black children in her home. He married the former Dorothy Watkins of Tuskegee, Alabama. They have three children, Danice, Claude and Daniel, III. He graduated from Washington High School in June 1937. From September 1937 to March 1942, he attended Tuskegee Institute, where he received a B.S. degree in physical education and completed civilian pilot training under the government-sponsored Civilian Pilot Training Program. He remained at Tuskegee as a civilian instructor pilot in the Army Air Corps Aviation Cadet Program until January 1943, when he entered the program as a cadet and received his commission as a second lieutenant in July

1943. He next completed fighter pilot combat training at Selfridge Field, Michigan, and was assigned to various units in the United States for the next six years.

In September 1949, James went to the Philippines as flight leader for the 12th Fighter-Bomber Squadron, 18th Fighter Wing, at Clark Field. In July 1950, he left for Korea, where he flew 101 combat missions in F–15 and F–80 aircraft. He returned to the United States and in July 1951 went to Otis Air Force Base, Massachusetts, as an all-weather jet fighter pilot with the 58th Fighter-Interceptor Squadron (FIS) and later became operations officer. In April 1953, he became commander of the 437th FIS, and in August 1955, he assumed command of the 60th FIS. While stationed at Otis, he received the Massachusetts Junior Chamber of Commerce 1954 award of "Young Man of the Year" for his outstanding community relations efforts.

James graduated from the Air Command and Staff College in June 1957. He became Deputy Assistant Secretary of Defense (Public Affairs) in March 1970, and during his tenure at the Pentagon, he was promoted from the one-star rank of brigadier general to the three-star rank of lieutenant general. He assumed duty as vice commander of the Military Airlift Command, with headquarters at Scott Air Force Base, Illinois, on September 1, 1975, and he was promoted to "Four Stars" that day. James was the first black American to be promoted to a Four-Star General in the history of the United States Military Service.

James was assigned as commander in chief NORAD/ADCOM, the North American Air Defense Command. He had operational command of all United States and Canadian strategic aerospace defense forces. He was responsible for the surveillance and air defense of North American aerospace and for providing warning and assessment of hostile attack on the continent by bombers or missiles.

On February 1, 1978, Gen. Daniel "Chappie" James, Jr., ended a long military career at "the top of the heap" after beginning as a young black lieutenant who risked court martial to fight racial segregation. The Air Force arranged full military honors for James' retirement ceremony marking the close of his nearly 35 years of service which spanned three wars. At a farewell Pentagon news conference, he reflected with obvious satisfaction that he had made it to the top of the heap, and a dream fulfilled.

General James was widely known for his speeches on Americanism and patriotism for which he was editorialized in numerous national and international pulications. Excerpts from some of the speeches have been read into the *Congressional Record*. He was awarded the George Washington Freedom Foundation Medal in 1967 and again in 1968. He received the Arnold Air Society Eugene M. Zuckert award in 1970 for outstanding contributions to Air Force professionalism. His citation read "fighter pilot with a magnificent record, public speaker, and eloquent spokesman for the American Dream we so rarely achieve." The F–3C Phantom warplane flown by James sits outside the Aerospace Science and Health Education Center named in his honor at Tuskegee University. He died on February 25, 1978.

JAMES, HAROLD, was born in Philadelphia, Pennsylvania. In 1964, after receiving an honorable discharge from the United States Army, he became a member of the Philadelphia Police Department in 1965, where he served with honor until his retirement in 1987. During the 1970s, he decided to continue his education in the areas of law enforcement and sociology. He earned a certificate in police science, an associate's degree in criminal justice, and a B.A. degree in sociology from Temple University. He also attended the Philadelphia School of Law.

During his tenure with the police department, James received many honors including several Police Merit commendations, Police Officer of the Year Award from the National Black Police Association, the American Police Hall of Fame Community Service Award, the Guardian Civic League Al Deal Courage Award and Civic Achievement Award, and the Philadelphia Human Relations Commission Outstanding Service Award. After being wounded during off-duty police action, James received the Chapel of Four Chaplains Award for Heroism and the Police Valor Award, the Philadelphia Police Department's highest honor. In 1980, he was also named one of the Outstanding People of the Year by *Philadelphia* magazine.

James has held many elected offices in the law enforcement profession over the years, including national chairman of the National Black Police Association, president of the Guardian Civic League, state and national delegate for the Fraternal Order of Police, founder and chairman of the Black Coalition of Service Organizations, and historian for the Eastern Region of the National Black Police Association. In addition, James coordinated the successful campaign of John Green, the first African American sheriff of Philadelphia County. In January of 1989, he was elected as a state representative for the 186th Legislative District. He is a member of numerous civic organizations, including the NAACP and the Philadelphia Urban League.

JAMES, SHARPE, was born February 20, 1936, in Jacksonville, Florida. He spent his life in Newark. He is married to Mary and the father of three sons, John, Elliott and Kevin. He graduated from Miller Street Elementary School, Malcolm X. Shabazz (formerly South Side) High School and with honors from Montclair State Col-

lege. James received a master's degree from Springfield College, where he received the 1961 Department of Physiology Award, and completed advanced studies at Washington State, Columbia, and Rutgers universities. In 1988, he was awarded an honorary LL.B. degree from Montclair State College.

James was an Essex County College professor for 18 years. He was the first black department chairman and athletic director within the state college system. He also served as vice-president and president of the Garden State Athletic Conference (GSAC). He served with the U.S. Army in Europe, and was a Newark public school teacher for seven years, coaching city, county and state championship track and cross-country teams.

James was elected mayor of Newark on May 13, 1986, and was sworn into office on July 1 of that year. He had lived up to his campaign slogan, "It's time for a Sharpe change." During his four-year term, he inspired the creation of public/private partnerships, which spur growth in the city of Newark. Bond rates and housing stock figures had risen, along with increases in city revenue created by the heightened collection of taxes, water bills, and fines for parking and traffic violations. Many affordable housing complexes had been built and many businesses had relocated or expanded within Newark. Cultural revitalization was also underway. James had rallied for a $200 million, 2,500-seat New Jersey Performing Arts Center and Cultural District. The plan uses the arts center as the centerpiece for renewed night life in the community, where one could relax in a major hotel, go shopping nearby and be surrounded by a wealth of art and culture.

James was first elected to public office as South Ward Councilman in 1970 and easily won re-election on the first ballot in 1974 and 1978, when he became the first public official in the

city's history to run unopposed. He again made history in 1982 when he won the post of councilman at large, becoming the first person to serve Newark as both ward councilman and councilman at large. He continued to set records by being the first incumbent to run unopposed in the May 1990 mayoral election. James was the 35th mayor of New Jersey's largest city, and the first councilman to be elected mayor. He gained nationwide attention by defeating the city's first black mayor, Kenneth A. Gibson, who was seeking an unprecedented fifth term in office.

James was co-chairman of the Essex County's Committee to Elect Ted Kennedy for President in 1980, and served as a delegate whip at the Democratic Convention. In 1988, he served as state chairman of the "Jesse Jackson for President" campaign. He served on the board of directors for the National League of Cities, the Advisory Board of the U.S. Conference of Mayors, and served as chairman of the Newark Collaboration Group. He was appointed as a member of the State Council on Affordable Housing by Gov. Jim Florio, and was a member of

the board of governors of the New Jersey Historical Society. In addition to his other accolades, James was named one of the nation's Ten Best Dressed Men of 1987 by the Fashion Foundation of America. He was also Newark's senior tennis champion and a former New Jersey State Tennis Association champion.

JASMIN, ERNEST A., was Kentucky's first black chief prosecutor and was one of the first blacks elected to countywide office in Jefferson County, Kentucky. In November 1987, he was elected commonwealth's attorney by an overwhelming 70 percent of the vote. He has brought a wealth of experience to his current position. He served as an assistant commonwealth's attorney for 11 years. During that time, he became known as the "Preacher for the Prosecution" because of his powerful style of arguing in front of a jury. He has successfully handled some of Jefferson County's most pressure-packed and highly publicized criminal cases. He also served as trial commissioner in the Louisville Police Court and as an assistant city law director.

Narcotics cases make up a third of the caseload for prosecutors in the commonwealth's attorney's office. Since taking office, Jasmin has established a Narcotics Unit with four prosecutors assigned to the unit, working drug cases only. In an effort to improve the quality of prosecuting attorneys in the office, he established prosecuting training seminars. These seminars are held monthly, training young prosecutors in a number of areas relating to criminal law. Recognizing the need to educate young people about the dangers of drugs and alcohol, he has sponsored several programs in the local school system to discourage youth from getting involved in drug abuse.

Jasmin is also involved in criminal law at the national level. He has served as director-at-large for the National Association of Government Attorneys in Capital Litigation (NAGACL) and is a member of the National Black Prosecutors' Association, National District Attorneys Association and the Kentucky Academy of Justice. He is also a member of the Louisville and Kentucky Bar Associations. In addition to his

legal background, Jasmin has had an impressive military career. He is a lieutenant colonel Army Reserve, retired with 28 years of military experience. During the last four years, he served as the chief legal advisor in Kentucky's 100th Division. He is a 33rd degree Mason, and holds memberships in Shriners, Elks, Order of the Eastern Star, Saber and Blade, Phi Alpha Delta and Kappa Alpha Psi. He is a member of the NAACP and a number of local Democratic clubs.

JASPER, MABEL M., received her B. S. degree from Kent State University and her J.D. degree from Cleveland Marshall Law School. After graduating from law school, she went into private law practice, which included general

counsel for a local savings and loan association. She later served as an assistant attorney general and as a trial attorney for the Bureau of Worker's Compensation for three years. She was then appointed a general trial referee for Cuyahoga County Court of Common Pleas Domestic Relations Division for four years, after which she was elected judge to the Cleveland Municipal Court. She is a member of many civic and professional organizations which include the Ohio State Bar Association, Bar Association of Greater Cleveland, Norman S. Minor Bar Association (past president, 1985), and Harambee board of directors.

JEMISON, MAE C., was born October 17, 1956, in Decatur, Alabama, to Charlie and Dorothy Jemison. She considers Chicago, Illinois to be her hometown. In 1973, she graduated from Morgan Park High School, Chicago; received a B.S. degree in chemical engineering from Stanford University in 1977 (also fulfilled the requirements for a B.A. in African and Afro-American studies); and an M.D. degree from Cornell University in 1981. Her background was in both engineering and medical research. She worked in the areas of computer programming, printed wiring board materials, nuclear magnetic resonance spectroscopy, computer magnetic disc production and evaluation of trophic factors for rat epididymides.

Jemison completed her internship at Los Angeles County/USC Medical Center in July 1982, and worked as a general practitioner with INA/Ross Loos Medical Group in Los Angeles until December 1982. From January 1983 through June 1985, she was the Area Peace Corps Medical Officer for Sierra Leone and Liberia in West Africa. Her task of managing the health care delivery system for U.S. Peace Corps and U.S. Embassy personnel included provision of medical care, supervision of the pharmacy and laboratory, medical administrative issues, and supervision of medical staff. She developed curriculum for and taught volunteer personal health training, wrote manuals for self care, developed and implemented guidelines for public health/safety issues for volunteer job placement and training sites.

Jemison developed and participated in research projects on hepatitis B vaccine, schistosomiasis and rabies in conjunction with the National Institute of Health and the Center for Disease Control. On her return to the United States, she joined CIGNA Health Plans of California in October 1985, and was working as a general practitioner and attending graduate engineering classes in Los Angeles when selected to the astronaut program. She was selected as an astronaut candidate by NASA in June 1987, and completed a one-year training and evaluation program in August 1988, which qualified her for assignment as a mission specialist on space shuttle flight crews.

Jemison's technical assignments include astronaut office representative to the Kennedy Space Center, Cape Canaveral, Florida, which involves participation in the processing of the space shuttle for launch, especially its payloads and thermal protection system (tiles); launch countdown; and work in the Shuttle Avionics Integration Laboratory (SAIL) performing verification of shuttle computer software. She is assigned as a mission specialist on STS–47, Spacelab–J. This cooperative mission between the United States and Japan, to conduct experiments in life sciences and materials processing, is scheduled for launch in August 1992.

Some of Jemison's special honors include: National Achievement Scholarship (1973–1977); Stanford representative to Carifesta '76 in Jamaica; American Medical Student Association (AMSA) study group to Cuba; received grant from International Travelers Institute for health studies in rural Kenya (1979); organized New York citywide health and law fair for National Student Medical Association (1979); and worked in a refugee camp in Thailand (1980). She is the recipient of several awards: CIBA Award for Student Involvement (1979), Essence Award (1988), and Gamma Sigma Gamma Woman of the Year (1989). She is a member of American Medical Association and American Chemical Society;

honorary member, Alpha Kappa Alpha Sorority; member, NAACP; board member, World Sickle Cell Foundation; and honorary board member, Center for the Prevention of Childhood Malnutrition.

JENKINS, FERGUSON, was born December 13, 1943, in Chatham, Ontario. Jenkins, 6'5", 205 lbs., with a 20-victory season in 1972, the sixth consecutive year he reached this number, didn't want to be starting pitcher when he joined the Chicago Cubs. He had been a relief man for Philadelphia in the NL. His shift from a fireman's job to starter paid off artistically and financially. He won the coveted Cy Young Award, 1971, then signed a two-year contract for a salary estimated at $125,000, taking him through the 1973 season. Jenkins frankly said that Joe Becker, former Cub pitching coach now retired, was a vital factor in his transformation. He told Jenkins he was going to help him make millions of dollars and listed four things he had to do: (1) work hard, (2) concentrate, (3) make batters hit his pitch, and (4) be ready to go out and pitch every fourth day. Becker got him to reduce his big windup, and study movies of his own pitching, enabling him to correct mistakes. The result proved highly successful for both Jenkins and the team.

As Jenkins went into the 1973 campaign, he had 135 NL victories against 93 defeats. Despite the fact he pitches home games in relatively small Wrigley Field, he had 3.03 ERA for 2,031 innings pitched in the majors. He worked in 304 games, struck out 1,650 men, and walked the amazingly low total of 432 batters. He rarely needed the help of a relief man and usually pitched complete games. A factor, besides mound skill, was the power at the plate; for this reason he wasn't pulled out for a pinch hitter as often as other pitchers when the club was trailing. At the end of the 1972 season he had 13 home runs to his credit. Six of them came in the banner 1971 season. He was one of a limited number of Canadians in the majors.

In earlier days, he was a stand-out hockey and basketball player. He turned down several offers from pro hockey teams to follow baseball as a career. He started with the Miami, Florida, State League in 1962, winning seven of nine decisions. He later played with Buffalo, Chattanooga, and Arkansas clubs before joining the Phillies in 1965. He had two wins, one loss in his first part-season in the NL. The following spring the Cubs got him in trade April 21, 1966; that year he had six wins, eight losses. Then began the skein of 20-victory seasons: 20-13, 20-15, 21-15, 22-16. In 1971, when he captured the Cy Young Award, he reached 24 wins against 13 losses and led the league in innings pitched, with 325. With a bit of luck, Jenkins might have had a better won-lost record. In 1968, he tied the major league record for being starting pitcher in five 1-0 losses; he also was starting pitcher in nine games when Cubs were shut out. He led the NL in complete games in 1967 with 20; in 1970 with 23; in 1971 with 30. He was a member of the NL's All-Star squads in 1967, 1971, and 1972.

JETSON, RAYMOND A., was born to the late Rep. Louis Jetson and Mary Jetson. He is married to the former Tammy Williams. He attended school in East Baton Rouge Parish, and was an honor graduate of Capitol Senior High School. Further educational training was secured at Grambling State University, Southern University, and Arizona State University. His major areas of study were political science and advertising.

Jetson was elected to the House of Representatives for District 61. In his first term, his main areas of interest were economic development and criminal justice. He handled the so-called "Boot-Camp" bill which allowed first-time offenders to be sent to a Marine Corps–style boot camp as a deterrent and far less expensive alternative to incarceration. He also sponsored a bill to expand enterprise zones in Louisiana which gave businesses incentives to locate and hire workers in underdeveloped areas. He sponsored a welfare reform bill with incentives for work training and benefits for all participants as well as the business that trained them.

Jetson serves on the following committees in the legislature: Health and Welfare, Transportation, Highways and Public Works, Labor, and Industrial Relations, where he served as vice-chairman, and Joint Committee on Budget Oversight. He was voted one of the six most valuable members of the legislature, and selected one of the "New Breed" of leaders by both the Baton Rouge Chamber of Commerce and the *Baton Rouge Business Report* magazine. He received the "Outstanding Legislator" award from the Louisiana Association of Educators and the Louisiana Federation of Teachers. His extensive community involvement has included positions as president of the Gus Young Civic Association, sergeant at arms of the Louisiana Black Caucus, chairman of the East Baton Rouge Legislative Delegation, member of the Governors Commission on Black-on-Black Crime, member of Kappa Alpha Psi Fraternity, advisory committee member for the Casey Family (a child placement agency for foster families), member of the Region II Council (representing early intervention for school-age children).

JIMISON, Z. MAE, born June 29, 1943, in Indianapolis, Indiana, is married to Robert Jimison and is the mother of two sons, Robert, Jr., and Willard. A graduate of Shortridge High School in Indianapolis, she earned a certificate of proficiency in secretarial

science from Indiana Central Business College in 1962, completing a two-year curriculum in one year. She received a B.A. degree in pre-law, with minors in Latin, Afro-American Studies, English and United States History, from Indiana State University in Terre Haute, in 1973; and an M.S. degree in United States History, with thesis on the Constitutional Rights of Prisoners, from Indiana State University, in 1976. (She also did graduate study in England, France and Scotland in 1973 on comparative judicial systems.) She received her J.D. degree from Ohio State University, College of Law, in Columbus, in 1977.

Jimison was admitted to the State Bar of Indiana and to the United States District Court for the Southern District of Indiana in 1979, and admitted to the bar of the United States Tax Court in 1980. She has served as the associate presiding judge of the Marion Superior Court, Criminal Division, since January 1, 1990. Her duties include convening a monthly meeting for all criminal court judges, addressing all issues that pertain to the criminal bench in Marion County, and reporting monthly to the full General term.

Jimison worked part time in a restaurant while in high school. After business college, she worked as secretary to the registrar of the United States Army Finance School for three years. While a full-time undergraduate student at Indiana State University, she made the dean's list every semester while working full time as secretary of the art department. During the same period of time, she was a student leader and a feature writer for the school newspaper. As a graduate student she worked as assistant dormitory director and as a graduate assistant in the history department. When she began her private law practice in 1979, she also taught law-related courses at Clark College. As a practicing attorney she represented many small businesses and cooperatives, engaged in collections, family law, probate, tort claims, disability, personal injury, juvenile and criminal law.

Jimison worked part time as a public defender in the Marion Superior Court, Criminal Division II, representing indigent defendants charged with felonies. As an advocate, she has been sole or principal counsel in the trial of at least 59 felony cases before juries, and several civil cases. She has won 92 percent of her trials before juries and 97 percent of her court trials. As the Master Commissioner (part-time) in the Marion Superior Court, Criminal Division II, she presided over jury and court trials, guilty pleas and sentencing hearings, mental hearings, initial hearings and review of bond hearings.

On April 7, 1988, Jimison was appointed judge pro-tempore of the Marion Superior Court, Criminal Division VI, by the Indiana Supreme Court. On August 3, 1988, the governor appointed her presiding judge of the court, and in this capacity, she presides over felony cases, administers a staff of 18 people, prepares, justifies and disburses various budgets. She is the recipient of numerous awards and is associated with a number of professional affiliations.

JOHNSON, EARVIN, JR., was born on August 14, 1959, in Lansing, Michigan. He is the sixth of 10 children of Earvin Johnson, Sr., and Christine Johnson. He graduated from Everett High School in Lansing where he led his high school basketball team to the Michigan Class A championship his senior year. He entered Michigan State University, Lansing, as a communications major. The presence of Johnson revitalized basketball at Michigan State, where the 9,886-seat Jenison Field House began selling out in advance for the first time in its history and the Spartans were transformed from losers into National Collegiate Athletic Association regional finalists.

On March 26, 1979, the Michigan Spartans beat Indiana State, led by Larry Bird, to win the NCAA championship. After the 75–64 victory over Indiana State, Johnson was named the championship tournament's Most Valuable Player (MVP). He was also voted the Most Valuable Player in the Big Ten. He left Michigan State after his sophomore year, in 1979, and joined the Los Angeles Lakers. On February 3, 1980, Johnson became the first rookie to start in the NBA All-Star game since Elvin Hayes of San Diego in 1969. Johnson, with 127 steals, led the NBA in steals average for the 1980 1981 season.

In 1982, under new Laker coach Pat Riley, Johnson (nicknamed "Magic") lifted his season average to more than 18 points a game and finished the season second in assists in the NBA. The Lakers won the NBA's Western Conference, swept the conference playoffs and went on to win the NBA championship with a victory over the Philadelphia 76ers on June 8, 1982. He led the Lakers to their 10th straight division title and their three NBA championships, 1982, 1987, and 1988. In 1990, he was named the NBA's Most Valuable Player for the second straight year and, having previously won the award after the 1986–1987 and 1988–1989 seasons, became the sixth player in NBA history to win the award three times. He added the only basketball award to elude him to his collection by garnering enough votes to be named Most Valuable Player in the 1990 NBA All-Star game.

In 1990, Johnson teamed up with *Black Enterprise* publisher Earl G. Graves to buy a $60 million Pepsi franchise in the nation's capital. The franchise will be located on 400 acres in Washington, D.C. Johnson has received numerous awards and honors which include: an honorary doctorate of humanities degree from Rust College, and the 16th annual Whitney M. Young, Jr., Award.

On November 7, 1991, Johnson revealed that he had tested positive for the Human Immunodeficiency Virus and was retiring from professional basketball. Johnson's stature brought increased attention to the AIDS crisis, leading many to hope that his illness could destigmatize the disease. In announcing his retirement, Johnson vowed to become a spokesman in the fight against AIDS, particularly among young people.

JOHNSON, EDDIE BERNICE, was born in Waco, Texas, and is the mother of Dawrence Kirk and grandmother of Dawrence Kirk, II. She received a diploma in professional nursing from Holy Cross Central School of Nursing, St. Mary's College of the University of Notre Dame, South Bend, Indiana, in 1955; a B.S. in nursing from Texas Christian University in 1967; and an M.P.A. degree in public administration from Southern Methodist University in 1976. She won a landslide victory to the Texas House of Representatives in 1972, becoming the first

black woman elected to public office in Dallas, the first woman elected to the House since 1935, and, with her second term, became the first woman in the history of the state to chair a major House Committee. In her third term as State Representative, she resigned her seat when President Jimmy Carter appointed her as regional director of the Department of Health, Education and Welfare (currently, the U.S. Department of Health and Human Services, and the Department of Education).

Following the Carter administration, Johnson again took an active role in community and civic activities. She has received honorary doctoral degrees from three Texas colleges for her service and contributions in the field of education and the community. She rekindled her political career in 1986 after nine years away from elective office and won a decisive victory for the senate seat in District 23. Currently, Johnson is completing her first four-year term in the Texas Senate, where she is the first woman and the first black to represent the Dallas area since Reconstruction. She is a member of the Finance, Health and Human Services and Education committees. She was also the chair of the subcommittee on Health and Human Services of the Finance Committee. In addition, she served on the Southern Legislative Conference Committee and was a representative to the National Conference for State Legislators.

During the 1987–1988 interim of the regular legislative session, Johnson served on the following interim committees: Council on Disabilities, Texas Literacy Council, Task Force on Affordable Housing, Alcohol and Substance Abuse Services Oversight Committee, Select Committee on Education, Texas Department of Health, Minority Health Ad-Hoc Committee, Texas Committee for Health Care Reimbursement Alternatives, Intermediate Care Facilities Committee on the Mentally Retarded, Hospital Data Advisory Committee, and most recently, the Attorney General's Task Force on Non-profit/Charitable Trusts.

During the 1989–1990 term, she was appointed to serve on the following interim committees: Joint House/Senate interim study on Drug-Related Crime; Special Advisory Committee on Bishop College—to study educational utilization alternatives of the former Bishop College Campus; Joint House/Senate Interim Special Advisory Committee on the creation and expansion of Small, Socially and Economically Disadvantaged Businesses; Senate interim study on child care to be conducted by the Senate Standing Committee on Redistricting. In addition, she was appointed to the Health and Human Services Coordinating Council statutorily created in 1983. She is the recipient of numerous awards and citations.

JOHNSON, ERIC G. Johnson and his wife Pamela have four children, Lacretia, Erin, Cara and John. He was elected president of Johnson Products Company, Inc., a Chicago-based man-

ufacturer and marketer of personal care products on December 14, 1988. On October 2, 1989, upon the resignation of his father, George E. Johnson, he was elected chief executive officer of Johnson Products. Since 1972, he has held various other posts, including chief operating officer; executive vice president, sales and marketing; senior vice president, corporate sales; president of the private label division; director of franchising; and director of the company's sales division.

Johnson has served on many civic, charity and educational organizations which include: board member of the American Health and Beauty Aids Institute; member of corporate board of Babson College; member of the executive board of the Boy Scouts of America, Calumet City Council; member of the board of directors of the Dr. Martin Luther King, Jr., Center.

JOHNSON, GLORIA TAP-SCOTT, a native of Washington, D.C., and married 40 years to Dr. David F. Johnson, she is the mother of two children, Toni and David, and has one grandson, David. She attended

Dunbar High School and Howard University where she received both her B.A. and M.A. degrees (1950). Prior to 1954, she taught for a brief period at Howard University and served as an economist with the U.S. Department of Labor and Old Wage Stabilization Board. She has been with the International Union of Electronic, Electrical, Salaried, Machine and Furniture Workers AFL–CIO since 1954, and is currently the director of the Department of Social Action, responsible in particular for education and women's activities.

Johnson is also chair of the IUE Women's Council and in this position she is a member of the IUE Executive Board. She was one of the recipients of the PUSH Award for Outstanding Women in the Labor Movement in 1975; delegate to the 1975 Houston, Texas, meeting of the Decade of Women; appointed by Gov. Mandel as a member of the Maryland Commission on the Status of Women; appointed by President Carter to serve on the National Advisory Council on Vocational Education, 1980–1981; recipient of the 1981 Economic Equity Award from Women's Equity Action League (WEAL) for outstanding achievement in the labor movement and the 1985 recipient of an award from Southern Christian Leadership Conference for her work for human rights.

Johnson's related affairs and international work include: 1977, 1 of 118 U.S. union women selected by the German Marshall Fund to participate in a three-week study of child care systems in Israel, France and Sweden; 1979, one of six U.S. union women selected by the American Institute for Free Labor Development to attend and participate in the women's conference in Central and South America; 1984, one of five U.S. representatives selected to attend the women's conference in West Berlin; 1985, selected by the AFL–CIO to serve as delegate to the annual meeting of the International Confederation of Free Trade Unions held in Madrid, Spain; 1985, one of ten trade unionists selected by the African American Labor Center to visit and study in four African nations, including a stop-over in Nairobi for the 10th Anniversary of the Decade for Women. She spoke at various meetings and conducted workshops at others on subjects such as "Comparable Worth, the Economics of Discrimination," "The Role of Women in the Modern World," etc.

Johnson has been affiliated with numerous professional organizations which include: Washington Union Women, Equal Rights Ratification Council, Labor Committee for ERA, Clearinghouse on Women's Issues, National Executive Board, Coalition of Labor Union Women, the Advisory Board of the Institute for Education and Research on Women and Work, Cornell University School of Labor and Industrial Relations, National Commission on Working Women Wider Opportunities for Women, the Board of Overseers, Wellesley College Center for Research on Women, NAACP, National Urban League, National Executive Board, A. Philip Randolph Institute, Delta Sigma Theta Sorority, member of Democratic National Committee, Advisory Council on Technical and Career Education, Prince George's Community College, Advisory Council of the Women's Institute, American University, AFL–CIO Standing Committee on Education, a founding member of the Coalition of Labor Union Women, for which she has served as treasurer since its founding in 1974, and also chairs the AFL–CIO Committee on Salaried and Professional Women.

JOHNSON, JOHN HAROLD, was born on January 19, 1918, in Arkansas City, Arkansas. He and his wife Eunice were married in 1941, and they have two children, John Harold, Jr., and Linda. He was the only child of

Leroy Johnson and Gertrude (Jenkins) Johnson. His father was killed in a sawmill accident when John was six years old. Johnson attended a segregated elementary school in Arkansas City, which had no black high school. Rather than drop out of school after receiving his elementary school diploma, he repeated the eighth grade. In 1933, his mother took him to the world's fair in Chicago and they decided to stay. He graduated from DuSable High School on Chicago's south side. He was an honor student, a member of the debating team, president of the student council, and president of his class. He was also managing editor of the school paper and business manager of the yearbook.

On the basis of his record at DuSable High School, Johnson was invited to speak in 1936 at a banquet given annually by the Urban League in Chicago to honor outstanding black high school seniors. Harry Pace, then president of the Supreme Liberty Life Insurance Company, was the featured speaker on the same program. Impressed with Johnson, Pace took him into his company as an office boy and made it possible for him to study part time on a scholarship at the University of Chicago. After two years, when he became an assistant to Pace, he quit classes at the University of Chicago. From 1938 to 1940, he took night courses at Northwestern University's School of Commerce in Chicago and then devoted himself full time to his work at Supreme Life.

One of Johnson's chief responsibilities as assistant to Pace was to help publish the company house organ, which contained some general black news and information in addition to company reports and insurance business information. Pace selected the general items from a monthly digest of articles about blacks in the national press, prepared for him by Johnson. It occurred to Johnson that such a culling service deserved a wider market, and

thus was born the idea of the *Negro Digest*. Using his mother's furniture as collateral, he borrowed $500 from a loan company and with the money he mailed out to Supreme Life customers 20,000 letters offering charter subscriptions to the *Negro Digest* at $2 each. Three thousand people responded, and the *Negro Digest*, with a first-issue run of 5,000 copies, was launched in November 1942. The *Negro Digest* was similar to the *Reader's Digest* in format.

Inspired by the success of the *Negro Digest*, which had a circulation jump to 150,000, Johnson began to plan for a picture magazine, patterned after *Life*, that would cover black news and personalities in a more entertaining way than the *Digest*. The first issue of *Ebony* went on the newsstands in November 1945 and immediately sold out its press run of 25,000 copies. At first manufacturers of consumer goods were reluctant to buy space in a magazine aimed exclusively at the black market, but in 1946 Zenith Radio Corporation, Chesterfield Cigarettes, and International Cellucotton signed advertising contracts with Johnson. Others followed, and *Ebony* became the first black publication to carry, in addition to ads for hair straighteners and other ethnic products popular at that time, a significant amount of advertising of general consumer merchandise.

Johnson went on to expand his empire which, by 1991, was worth $245 million. It included: *Jet*, *Ebony*, and *Ebony Man* (EM) magazines; a cosmetics company, Fashion Fair; Supreme Liberty Life Insurance Company; WJPC radio in Chicago; and he was president of WLOU radio station in Chicago. His daughter Linda Johnson-Rice serves as president and chief operating officer of Johnson Publishing Company, Inc., in Chicago. Johnson, Sr., now serves as publisher, chairman and CEO.

Johnson has received numerous awards and honors which include:

accompanying United States vice president to Russia and Poland in 1959; was appointed Special U.S. Ambassador to Independence Ceremonies of the Ivory Coast, by the president of the United States, in 1961; Special United States Ambassador to Independence Ceremonies of Kenya in 1963; received the National Press Foundation Award; *Black Enterprise* No. 1 Black Business Award; Salute to Greatness Award, Martin Luther King, Jr., Center for Nonviolent Social Change; Harold H. Hines, Jr., Benefactors' Award; and the NAACP 1966 Joel E. Springarn Medal, the highest honor bestowed by the nation's oldest black organization.

JOHNSON, JULIUS FRANK, was born on February 8, 1940, at Fort Leavenworth, Kansas. He received a B.S. degree in social science from Lincoln University and an M.D. degree in

counseling psychology. He received a ROTC commission to 2nd lieutenant in February 1964. From February 1964 to April 1964, he was a student in the United States Army Infantry Center and School, Fort Benning, Georgia. From June 1964 to July 1965, he served as a Rifle Platoon leader, later Reconnaissance Platoon Leader, and later assistant S-3, Operation Officer, in Headquarters, 3rd Battalion, 32nd Infantry, Eighth Army, in Korea. From July 1965 to January 1967, he was assigned as a platoon leader, later commander, of Company E (Honor Guard), 1st Battalion, 3rd Infantry (Old Guard), Fort Myer, Virginia. He was promoted to the rank of 1st lieutenant on August 1, 1965, and was promoted to the rank of captain on November 1, 1966.

From January 1967 to March 1976, Johnson was a student in the Special Forces Officer Qualification Course, at the United States Army Special Warfare School, Fort Bragg, North Carolina. From July 1967 to June 1968, he served as adjutant and later as commander of Company A, and later as the S-4 Logistics Officer, of the 1st Battalion, 327th Infantry, 101st Airborne Division, United States Army in Vietnam. From June 1968 to July 1969, he was a platoon advisor, 2nd Student Battalion, the Student Brigade, later student at the United States Army Infantry Center and School, at Fort Benning. From July 1969 to July 1972, he served as assistant professor of Military Science, Lincoln University, Jefferson City, Missouri.

From July 1972 to February 1973, he was the commander of the Mobile Security Training Team, later the S-3 (Operations) Officer, in the Field Training Command, at the United States Military Advisory Group, Military Assistance Command, in Vietnam. From April 1973 to June 1974, he was assigned as the operations officer, Department of Non-Resident Instruction, later student at the United States Army Command and General Staff College, Fort Leavenworth. From July 1974 to May 1976, he served as first operations officer, G-2 (Intelligence) Staff, United States Army Element, I Corps

Group, Eighth Army in Korea, later as the S-3 (Operations) officer, of the 3rd Brigade, 2nd Infantry Division, United States Army, in Korea.

From June 1976 to April 1981, he was first assigned as personnel management officer, Officer Personnel Management Division, United States Army Military Personnel Center, Alexandria, Virginia, later personnel staff officer, Officer Division, Office of the Deputy Chief of Staff for Personnel, United States Army, Washington, D.C. He was promoted to the grade of major on June 9, 1976, and was promoted to the grade of lieutenant colonel on July 14, 1979. From June 1981 to June 1983, he was the commander of the 2nd Battalion, 36th Infantry, 3rd Armored Division, United States Army, in Europe. From June 1983 to June 1984, he was a student at the United States Army War College, Carlisle Barracks, Pennsylvania. From June 1984 to March 1985, he was assigned as director of operations (J-3), Armed Forces Inaugural Committee, at Fort Lesley J. McNair, Washington.

Johnson was promoted to the grade of colonel on November 1, 1984. From February 1988 to July 1989, he served as director of the Joint Staff, Armed Forces Inaugural Committee, in Washington. From July 1989 to June 1990, he was assigned as the assistant division commander, of the 1st Armored Division, United States Army in Europe, and the Seventh Army. He was promoted to the one-star grade of brigadier general on September 1, 1989. In June of 1990, he was assigned as commanding general of the First Reserve Officer Training Corps Region, Fort Bragg.

General Johnson has received numerous awards and decorations which include: the Silver Star; the Bronze Star medal (with two oak leaf clusters); the Defense Meritorious Service Medal; the Defense Superior Service Medal; the Meritorious Service Medal; the Air Medal; the Army Com-

mendation Medal (with oak leaf cluster); the Combat Infantryman Badge; the Parachutist Badge; and the Air Assault Badge.

JOHNSON, LEROY R., was born July 28, 1928, in Atlanta, Georgia. He married the former Cleopatra Whittington, and they have one son, Michael V. Johnson. He graduated from Booker T. Washington High School in 1945. He received a B.A. degree in sociology from Morehouse College in 1949 and an M.A. degree in political science from Atlanta University in 1951. He enrolled at North Carolina School of Law (Durham, North Carolina) where he earned an LL.B. in 1957. He served as a teacher of social science in the Atlanta Public School System from 1950 to 1954.

After receiving his law degree in 1957, Johnson was employed as a member of the district attorney's staff from 1957 to 1962. He was the first black in the southeastern United States to be employed as an assistant district attorney. He was employed by the Fifth Judicial District, Fulton County, Atlanta. In 1962, he became the first black to win a seat in the Georgia Senate. Since his election to the Georgia Senate occurred before passage of the Voting Rights Act in 1965, his legal and political career spans almost all of the Civil Rights Era. Johnson was a contemporary of Dr. Martin Luther King, Jr. During his tenure, he rose to the chairmanship of the Fulton County Senate delegation, the first black person ever to head a legislative delegation in the state.

In 1969, Johnson was named by the lieutenant governor as chairman of the Scientific Research Committee, the first black senator to be named chairman of a standing committee in the Georgia Legislature. He reached the peak of his legislative influence when he was appointed chairman of the powerful Senate Judiciary Committee in 1970, a position he held until he left the Senate in 1974.

JOHNSON, LINDA DIANNE, was born February 5, 1954, in Richland, Mississippi. She is divorced and the mother of one son, J. Carson, III. She is a 1971 graduate of Florence High School, Florence, Mississippi; a 1974 graduate of Jackson State University, Jackson, Mississippi, with a B.S. degree in biology pre-med; and a 1978 graduate of Indiana University School of Optometry, Bloomington, Indiana, with a doctor's degree in optometry. In 1978, she became the department head of optometry at Jackson Hinds Comprehensive Health Center.

Johnson is the recipient of numerous awards and recognition, including: Mississippi's first black female optometrist, 1978; Outstanding Young Women in America, 1978 and 1980; Outstanding Professional Achievement Award, Jackson State University National Alumni Association, 1980; nominated for *Who's Who Among Black Americans*, 1980–1981; Who's Who in Mississippi—This Century, 1980; Distinguished Service Award, Jackson State University, Hinds Alumni Chapter, June 1982; nominated for the *World Who's Who of Women*, 1989; Certificate of Appreciation as Public Relations co-chairman of the Mississippi Optometric Association, June 1990; and Volunteer of the Month, Central Mississippi Chapter of the American Red Cross, July 1990.

Johnson has been active in many professional and social organizations: National Optometric Association, member and secretary of the board of directors; Mississippi Optometric Association, member, Legislative Committee, and chairman of the Public Relations Committee; Southern Council of Optometrists; Jackson Hinds Chapter of the Jackson State National Alumni Association; and the American Red Cross, Central Mississippi Chapter, board of directors and chairman of the Community Volunteers Service Committee and served on the Executive Committee.

JOHNSON, MARLENE E., a native of Milwaukee, she is a graduate of North Division High School and has attended M.A.T.C. She holds a B.S. degree from the University of Wisconsin-Milwaukee. She was elected to the Common Council in April 1980. Alderwoman Johnson serves on the Judiciary and Legislative Committee, the Zoning and Development Committee, and is a member of the Community Development Policy Committee. She is also president of the M.A.T.C. board, vice-president of the M.E.C.C.A. board, a commissioner on the Redevelopment Authority, the Pabst Theater board, and board member of the Private Industry Council.

Johnson is also a member of the Milwaukee Urban League, a lifetime member of the NAACP, member of OIC-G.M., the Democratic Party of

Wisconsin, the Black Women's Network, the National League of Cities, and the National Association of Housing and Redevelopment Officials.

JOHNSON, MARY J., was born on June 17, 1917, in Newcomb, Tennessee, 1 of 12 children. She married

Robert Johnson, and they have four children. She attended school in Newcomb and Jelico, Tennessee, and worked at odd jobs to obtain extra money for herself and family. After graduating from high school, she was provided an opportunity to work in Detroit, Michigan. She lived and worked on the east side of Detroit. One of the first organized groups she joined was the Democratic Club in Detroit. In 1945, she and her husband moved to Ecorse, Michigan, where she immediately became involved with the Democratic Club in Ecorse.

In 1979, Johnson was elected to the Ecorse City Council, and mayor pro tem. She is a leader in the political arena and in many civic organizations as well. She is an active member in the Women's Conference of Concern, Silver Star Temple, Eastern Star, and River Rouge-Ecorse NAACP, and founder and organizer of Women Equally Involved Organization.

JOHNSON, WENDELL NORMAN, was born in Boston, Massachusetts. He married the former Helen L. Underwood of Boston. They have three children, Laura, Lois, and W. Norman, Jr. He graduated from the

New England College of Pharmacy and holds an M.A. degree in international communications from American University. He was commissioned an ensign in May 1957, and began his Navy career as a first lieutenant on board the auxiliary ship USS *Lookout*. A graduate of the United States Naval Postgraduate School Engineering Curriculum and the Armed Forces Staff College, he also attended the National War College where he was recognized for outstanding scholarship by the college commandant and the Chief of Naval Operations.

Subsequent sea duty assignments included fire control and gunnery officer on board the aircraft carrier USS *Coral Sea*, and weapons officer on the destroyer USS *Ingraham*. While serving as the executive officer on the destroyer USS *Jonas Ingram*. Johnson served as commander of the Charleston

Naval Base, in February 1987, and in August 1987, he assumed command of Mine Warfare Command, in an additional duty capacity.

Johnson was promoted to the one-star rank of rear admiral in 1983. He retired from the Navy on April 14, 1989. His outstanding civic contributions were recognized by his mayoral appointment as a community relations commissioner serving Duval County and the city of Jacksonville, Florida.

JOHNSON-BROWN,   HAZEL W., was born October 10, 1927, in West Chester, Pennsylvania. She is the daughter of Clarence L. and Garnett Johnson, and is married to David B. Brown. She earned a diploma in nursing from Harlem Hospital in New York City, a B.S. degree in nursing from Villanova University, a master's degree in nursing education from Teacher's College, Columbia University, and a Ph.D. in educational administration from Catholic University. In addition,

she holds honorary doctorates from Morgan State University, Villanova University, and the University of Maryland.

From 1950 to 1953, she worked as a beginning level staff nurse in the emergency ward of Harlem Hospital. Her responsibilities included evening and night duty, and initial admission work-up for all patients except obstetrics. From 1953 to 1955, she was a staff nurse in the medical cardiovascular ward of the Veterans Administration Hospital, Philadelphia, Pennsylvania. There she became head nurse on the ward within three months of employment. Entering the Army Nurse Corps in 1955, she served for the next 12 years in a variety of positions at Walter Reed Army Medical Center, the 8169 Hospital in Japan, Madigan General Hospital, Letterman General Hospital, 45th Surgical Hospital at Ft. Sam Houston, and Valley Forge General Hospital. From 1967 to 1973, she was assigned to the staff of the United States Army Medical Research and Development Command as a project director in the Army Medical Department field hospital system.

Upon completion of her doctoral studies, she was appointed director of the Walter Reed Army Institute of Nursing. In 1978, she was transferred to Korea to assume the positions of assistant for nursing, Office of the Surgeon, 8th Army Command; chief, Department of Nursing, United States Army Hospital/121 Evacuation Hospital, in Seoul, South Korea, and chief consultant for nursing matters to the Senior Medical Officer, 8th Army Command. In 1979, she was selected to the position of chief, Army Nurse Corps and was promoted to the rank of brigadier general. General Johnson-Brown became the 116th chief of the Army Nurse Corps, the first chief holding an earned doctorate, the fourth chief to hold the rank brigadier general, and the first black woman general in the history of the United States Military Services.

Among Johnson-Brown's significant recognitions are: Army Nurse of the Year Awards from Letterman General Hospital and the Daughters of the American Revolution, the Army Commendation Medal with Oak Leaf Cluster, the Meritorious Service Medal, and the Legion of Merit. Upon retirement from active duty in 1983, she served as assistant professor in the Graduate Nursing Administration program at Georgetown University and director of Governmental Affairs for the Washington Office of the American Nurses' Association. During the period 1983 to the present, she has endeavored to translate her leadership skill and concern for young people, especially black youth, to work in her civilian position. As director, Division of Governmental Affairs, she worked diligently to increase the minority participation in professional positions with her office and the professional organization. That work continues in her teaching opportunities in her present organization, George Mason University. Within the university, she serves as chair of the Minority Affairs Committee, consultant to the George Mason University Alumni Association, and member of the Cultural Diversity Committee of the School of Nursing. Also, serving as a mentor to three black nursing students provides additional indication of her interest in furthering the careers of young black men and women.

In addition to these activities, Dr. Johnson-Brown maintains her membership in the Black Women United for Action of Northern Virginia, and has recently been appointed a member of the Board of Military Affairs for the Commonwealth of Virginia by the Hon. Douglas Wilder, governor of Virginia. In 1984, she was 1 of 13 women to receive the Outstanding Women of Color Award and 1 of 12 women to receive the National Coalition of 100 Black Women's Candace Award. In August 1989, she was named director, Center for Health Policy, a new center within the School of Nursing. She teaches health care public policy and health care administration.

JONES, CLARA STANTON, was born May 14, 1913, in St. Louis, Missouri. She was educated in the St. Louis public schools and went on to earn an A.B. degree from Spelman College, Atlanta, Georgia, in 1934, and an A.B. degree in library science from the University of Michigan in 1938.

In 1938 she began her distinguished library career as a reference librarian at Dillard University in Baton Rouge, Louisiana. She moved in 1940 to a post as associate librarian at Southern University, also in Baton Rouge. Her next move was to the Detroit Public Library, where she became a junior librarian in 1944 and soon advanced to senior librarian. In 1949 she became first assistant librarian, and in 1950 she became division chief, a position she was to hold for 13 years before becoming department chief in 1963. In 1968 she was made library neighborhood consultant.

In 1970 Jones became director of the Detroit Public Library. She was the first African American and the second woman to serve as director of a major city library system. During her tenure she was also elected the first black president of the American Library Association, in 1976. Jones retired in 1978.

During her long career Jones was a centenary guest of The (British) Library Association (1977), a workshop lecturer on information and referral service in public libraries for the Library Association of Australia, Melbourne (1977), a guest of the West German Federal Republic during a month-long comprehensive library tour (1972), a reference librarian for the ALA's "Library 21" model library at the Seattle World's Fair (1962) and a co-director and lecturer of the Institute on Public Library Service to the Black Urban Poor at Wayne State University, Detroit (1969). She was a Regents lecturer at the University of California at Berkeley's Graduate School of Library and Information Science during the spring quarters of 1979 and 1980, and has been a guest lecturer on urban public library service and African American literature at various universities and state library associations.

Jones has received honorary doctoral degrees from Shaw College, Detroit; Ball State University, Muncie, Indiana; North Carolina Central University, Durham; Grand Valley State College, Allendale, Michigan; St. John's University, Jamaica, New York; Pratt Institute, Brooklyn, New York; Northern Michigan University, Marquette; Wayne State University, Detroit; and Spelman College. Her awards include the Golden State Achievement Award for Service to the Community from Golden State Mutual Life Insurance Company (1970); the Award for Distinguished Service to Librarianship from the Black Caucus of the American Library Association (1970); the Distinguished Alumnus Award, for outstanding service to the library profession, from the University of Michigan School of Library Science (1971); the Athena Award, for humanitarian service, from the University of Michigan Alumnae (1975); and an Award for Distinguished Service to the Community from Wayne County Community College, Detroit (1978). She is listed in *Who's Who in America*, *Who's Who in American Women* and *Who's Who Among Black Americans*.

Jones is a member of the American Library Association, the Michigan Library Association, the Special Library Association, the American Civil Liberties Union, the Women's International League for Peace and Freedom, the NAACP, the Association for the Study of Afro-American Life and History, the National Commission on Libraries and Information Science (1978–82), the board of directors of City National Bank in Detroit and Amnesty International.

Her community service activities include serving on the boards of trustees of New Detroit, Inc. (1971–78), the Historical Society of Michigan (1971–73) and the Metropolitan Fund (1972–73); the advisory boards of United Foundation (1974–76) and Western Michigan University School of Library Science (1973–75); and the board of advisors of Wayne State University Press (1971–78).

Jones has published many works dealing with library science and various special issues in librarianship, including the textbook *Public Library Information and Referral Service* (Gaylord, 1978), a collection of lectures from the ALA President's Program entitled *The Information Society: Issues and Answers* (Oryx, 1978), and numerous lectures and addresses.

Jones and her husband, retired social worker Albert D. Jones, have three children — Stanton, Vinetta and Kenneth — along with seven grandchildren and one great-grandchild.

JONES, HERBERT C., was born August 1, 1936, in Demopolis, Alabama, to Thomas Allen Jones and Bettie Young Jones. He is married to Bessie C. Jones, M.D., M.P.H. (public health physician, Dekalb County, Georgia). They have four children, Sandra Jo, Nancy G., Herbert Chapman, and Lis C. He is a graduate of U.S. Jones High School, Demopolis, Alabama; Talladega College, Talladega, Alabama; Indiana University, Bloomington, Indiana (A.B. degree), and Indiana University School of Medicine, Indianapolis (M.D. degree). He received postgraduate education at Rotating Internship, Brooke General Hospital, San Antonio, Texas, and did residency in general otolaryngology, University of Illinois Medical Center, Chicago.

Jones served in the United States Air Force Medical Corps in 1960–1965, including service during his senior year of medical school and internship. He is licensed with the states of Georgia, Indiana, and Illinois, and certified by the American Board of Otolaryngology and the American College of Surgeons. He has been in solo practice since 1968–1989 in otolaryngology, head and neck surgery, Atlanta, Georgia.

Jones' professional honors include: Alpha Omega Alpha Honor Medical Society (1961); cited as Father of the Year in Medicine, by Concerned Black Clergy of Atlanta, 1988; and cited as an Outstanding Physician, *Black Enterprise* magazine, October 1988. His academic appointments include: Clinical Associate Professor (Dept. of Surgery), Morehouse School of Medicine (1985 to date); and instructor in otolaryngology, Emory University School of Medicine (1970–1980).

JONES, LEONADE DIANE, was born November 27, 1947, in Bethesda, Maryland, to Leon Adger and Landonia Madden Jones. She received a B.A. degree from Simmons College, Boston, Massachusetts, in 1969; and an M.B.A. in 1973 from Stanford Law School and Graduate School of Business, Stanford, California. She has been the treasurer for the Washington Post Company, Washington, D.C., since 1987. Prior to taking this position she was: financial analyst, Capital Research Company, Los Angeles, California, 1973–1975; assistant secretary and assistant treasurer, The Washington Post Company, Washington, 1975–1979; director of financial services, Post-Newsweek Stations, Inc., Washington, 1979–1984; vice president, business affairs, Post-Newsweek Stations, Inc., Washington, 1984–1986; assistant treasurer, The Washington Post Company, Washington, 1986–1987.

Jones has been active in many civic, social, church, business and community organizations, some of which are as follows: member of California Bar, 1973–; member of District of Columbia Bar, 1979; American Women in Radio and Television, 1979–1984; American Bar Association, 1973–; president (1984–1985) and member of board of directors (1982–1989) Washington, DC–Baltimore, MD Chapter of Stanford Business School Alumni Association; treasurer and member of board of directors, Big Sisters of Washington Metropolitan Area, 1984–1985; board of directors, Stanford Business School Alumni Association, 1985–1988; board of directors, D.C. Contemporary Dance Theatre, 1987–1988; advisory council, Charlin Jazz Society, 1988–; advisory board, WHMM-TV, 1989–; assistant chairperson of budget and audit, the Edges Group, Inc., Metropolitan Washington, DC Chapter, 1989– .

JONES, MARY E., was born on May 3, 1943, in Ft. Meade, Florida. She is the daughter of Albert and Gladys L. Tucker. She married Tommy Jones and they have four children. She graduated from Union Academy High in 1958, and then attended Gibbs Junior College, in St. Petersburg, Florida, for one year. In 1962, she became the first secretary for Anna Woodbury Junior High. In 1963, she transferred and became the first secretary of Gibbons Street Elementary School and Union Academy High, both of Bartow, Florida. In 1975, she was employed as the first black banker of Polk County Citrus & Chemical Bank of Bartow. She served as a bank teller, teller supervisor, customer counselor and new accounts.

In 1986, Jones was elected the first black city commissioner for the city of Ft. Meade, Florida. In 1988, she was appointed the first black officer for the Citrus & Chemical Bank. In 1989, she

was elected the first black mayor of the city of Ft. Meade. In 1990, she became the first black to seek the office of County Commissioner for Polk County, including the first commissioner of Ft. Meade to serve on the board of directors for the Florida League of Cities. She has been active in many civic, social, church, business, and community organizations, and is the recipient of numerous awards and citations.

JONES, QUINCY DELIGHT, JR., was born on March 14, 1933, in Chicago, Illinois. He is the son of Sarah and Quincy Delight Jones, Sr. He has six children from his three marriages. He obtained his musical education in the public schools of Chicago and Seattle. He attended Seattle University and the Berklee School of Music in Boston, Massachusetts. His parents divorced soon after his younger brother, Lloyd, was born and both boys were raised by their father and stepmother. The stepmother, who already had three children of her own, subsequently had three more, bringing the total number of children to eight. In 1943, the family moved to the Seattle suburb of Bremerton, Washington. It was in Seattle that he met pianist-singer Ray Charles. When Jones was 15 he approached Lionel Hampton, who was passing through Seattle with his orchestra, and showed him a suite he had written called "The Four Winds."

Hampton invited Jones to join his band, but Jones had to finish high school. After graduating from high school, he went on scholarship to the Berklee College of Music in Boston, and while studying in Boston he worked nights playing local night clubs. From Boston he went to New York City to do some recording arrangements for bassist Oscar Pettiford and then went on the road with Lionel Hampton. After the 1957 tour he remained in Europe. In 1960 and 1961, he toured Europe and the United States with a big band he had formed, and was now directing. After he scored his first United States film, *The Pawnbroker*, in 1965, critics hailed the music, and movie score offers poured in.

Encouraged by his success, he decided to move wholly into film work and settled in Los Angeles, California, in 1968. He wrote music for such films as *In Cold Blood* (1967), *For the Love of Ivy* (1968), *Cactus Flower* (1969), *Come Back, Charleston Blue* (1972), *The Getaway* (1972), *Thriller* (1982), *Roots* (1977), *ET* (1982), and *The Color Purple* (1985), to name a few. He has recorded numerous albums and records which include: "You've Got It Bad, Girl," "Body Heat," "Mellow Madness," "We Are the World," and "Back on the Block." By the 1990s, Jones had become the undisputed king of the music industry. His "Back on the Block" LP went double-platinum. In 1990, he teamed up with Time/Warner which partly financed the Quincy Jones Entertainment Company's production of two television series: NBC-TV's "Fresh Prince of Bel Air" and the syndicated "Jesse Jackson Show."

JONES, ROXANNE H., is the mother of two daughters and the grandmother of four children. Long-time community activist Jones made her mark on Pennsylvania history in 1984 when she became the first black woman elected to the state senate. She was overwhelmingly re-elected in 1988 by the 3rd senatorial district voters. She had been a leader in the struggle to improve the lives of people in need since 1950. In 1966, she began working with the Philadelphia Opportunities Industrial Center and soon after became active in the Philadelphia Welfare Rights Organization, rising from chairperson of the Southwark Chapter to citywide chair in 1968. Under her leadership, the organization's membership rose from 600 to 3,000 and her efforts resulted in an increase in cash assistance grants for welfare recipients and lead-based paint eradication.

Jones' lobbying successes led her to form Philadelphia Citizens in Action (PCIA), a grassroots lobbying group. The PCIA scored a number of victories in the areas of job training, welfare reform and lead-based paint eradication. Upon assuming her senate seat in 1985, she made job training for welfare recipients her number one priority. She put her skills as an organizer and coalition builder to work generating support for her job training legislative package. After holding public hearings and bringing in experts from across the nation her efforts paid off when Act 61 of 1987 was enacted into law. She co-wrote and co-sponsored that legislation which created state-of-the-art job training programs to help break the cycle of dependency for welfare recipients. Her efforts helped obtain $15 million in state and federal funding targeted for these job training programs.

Jones next focused her attention on combatting drug abuse. She had been the state's leading advocate for expanding special residential treatment programs where addicted mothers can receive treatment with their children. Again, she introduced legislation and held public hearings on the issue. In 1988, her efforts led to state funding directly aimed at residential treatment centers for addicted mothers and their children — a first in Pennsylvania. Funding for such centers was doubled by the administration in 1989. She then turned her attention to the problem of affordable housing for low- and moderate-income persons. Since 1987, Jones has served as the Democratic chair of the Senate Urban Affairs and Housing Committee; she has also served on the Public Health and Welfare, Community and Economic Development, Aging and Youth, and the Senate Democratic Policy committees, and was an active member of the Pennsylvania Legislative Black Caucus.

Jones served as a member of the Pennsylvania Long Term Care Council and the Pennsylvania Minority Business Development Authority; she also served on the board of the Allegheny West Foundation in Philadelphia. Her efforts to raise the living standards of poor people had been recognized by a variety of organizations across the state and nation. She has been honored by many groups including: the NAACP, the National Council of Negro Women, Inc.; the National Association of Black Social Workers; Delta Sigma Theta Sorority, Inc.; the Pennsylvania AFLCIO, the Woodstock Civic Association; AFSCME; Martin Luther King, Jr., Association, and numerous church groups. Sen. Jones is an active member of the United House of Prayer for All People, where she works with many youth groups.

JONES, RUFUS E., was born August 21, 1940, in Memphis, Tennessee, to S. L. and Ida Jones. He is married to Marvis LaVern Kneeland Jones and they have four children, Gladys, Rufus, Jr., Ida, and Dorothy. He attended Weaver Elementary, in Shelby County, 1945–1953; Booker T. Washington High School, Memphis, 1953–1957; and Michigan State University, East Lansing, 1957–1961, receiving a B.A. degree in business administration. From 1981 to date, he has been the state representative, Tennessee General Assembly. Jones has been president of GRID, Inc., Jones Big Star Supermarket, #102, Memphis, since 1968.

Prior to becoming state representative, he was with Brittenum and Associates (mutual funds and insurance), 1967–1968; Tennessee Department of Revenue, Memphis Office, Sales Tax Auditor, 1965–1967; and S. L. Jones Supermarket, Memphis, 1953–1968. He is affiliated with numerous organizations: member of the board of directors of PUSH, Memphis NAACP, Memphis Urban League, Memphis Chamber of Commerce, Memphis and Shelby County Board of Adjustment, the Goodwill Boys Club, New Memphis Development Corporation, Southern Education Foundation, Tennessee Task Force on the Supply of Minority Teachers, Mid South Fair Executive Committee, and charter member of the Tennessee Retail Grocers Association.

Jones is also a member of the Memphis Museum, Inc., board of direc-

tors, Memphis, Arkansas; Mississippi Council of Government; Shelby County Democratic Club, former president of Black Merchants Association; chairman, Martin Luther King State Holiday Committee; 1986 delegate to White House Conference on Small Business; chairman of State Committee on International Trade; participant in 1986 SEC forum on Capitol Formation; 1988 recipient of the Government Service Special Award from the National Conference of Christians and Jews; chairman of Tennessee Black Caucus of State Legislators; member of National Black Caucus of State Legislators; National Conference of State Legislators; vice-chairman of House Government Operations Committee; serves on the Finance, Ways and Means Committee; and Calendar and Rules Committee. He was involved with the Business Tax Study: SJR 174, and AIDS Testing for Food Handlers: SJR 233 House member of the 92nd, 93rd, 94th, 95th and 96th General Assemblies.

JONES, STEPHANIE TUBBS, is married to Mervyn L. Jones and the mother of one son, Mervyn L. Jones, II. She was a product of the Cleveland public schools, graduating from Collinwood High School. She attended Case Western Reserve University where she received a B.A. degree in 1971, and the LL.B. degree in 1974. In 1974, she was awarded the Martin Luther King, Jr., Award by her law school graduating class. She has been admitted to practice in the state of Ohio before the Sixth Circuit Court of Appeals, the Federal District Court, and the United States Supreme Court.

Jones' past employers include the Equal Employment Opportunity Commission, the Cuyahoga County Prosecutor's Office, and the Northeast Ohio Regional Sewer District. On November of 1981, she was elected to the Cleveland Municipal Court for a six-year term. In April 1983, she was appointed by Governor Dick Celeste to the Court of Common Pleas of Cuyahoga County. She became the first woman to serve on the Common Pleas Court in the state of Ohio. In November 1984, she was elected to the Common Pleas Court, and in November 1988, she was re-elected to a full six-year term on the Common Pleas Court. The Ohio

Supreme Court had appointed Jones to sit by assignment on the Eleventh District Courts of Appeals (Portage and Geauga counties), the Court of Claims of the state of Ohio, and the Franklin County Common Pleas Court.

In 1982, she was selected as an outstanding young woman of America. In 1984, she was awarded the Young Alumnus Award by Case Western Reserve University for her achievements in the field of law. She has been featured in *Ebony* magazine on two occasions: in the February 1983 issue in an article entitled, "Black Women on the Bench: Wielding the Gavel of Change," and in the August 1984 issue in an article entitled, "New Faces for an Old Struggle." In 1986, she received an award from the Urban League of Greater Cleveland for outstanding volunteer services in law and justice. In 1987, she was named Woman of the Year by the Cleveland Chapter of the Negro Business and Professional Women's Clubs, Inc. In 1988, she received the Value Alumnus Award from the 1988 graduating class of Collinwood High School in recognition of her continued support, service and dedication to her alma mater.

In the same year, Jones received a centennial citation from her undergraduate college, Flora Stone Mather College of Case Western Reserve University, during its One Hundredth Anniversary Celebration, for her achievements in the field of law. Jones has served as a member of the board of trustees of Bethany Baptist Church, the Federation for Community Planning, the Cleveland Public Library, the Urban Library Council, and the Community Re-entry Program. She is a member of various legal organizations, the Greater Cleveland Alumnae Chapter of Delta Sigma Theta Sorority, Inc., the NAACP, the National Council of Negro Women, and many other civic organizations. She has also served as a judicial instructor for the Ohio Judicial

College, and as a faculty advisor for the National Judicial College in Reno, Nevada.

JORDAN, BARBARA CHAR-LINE, was born on February 21, 1936, in Houston, Texas, the youngest of three daughters of Benjamin M. and Arlyne Jordan. She graduated from Phyllis Wheatley High School in 1952, and enrolled at Texas Southern University, an all-black college in Houston. In 1956, she obtained her B.A. degree, magna cum laude. She earned an LL.B. degree at Boston University in 1959 and later that same year, she was admitted to the bar in both Massachusetts and Texas. She opened a private law practice in Houston and worked as an administrative assistant to a county judge in Harris County, Texas. During the 1960 presidential campaign, she worked for the Democratic nominee John F. Kennedy.

In 1962, Jordan ran for public office, in a losing bid for a seat in the Texas House of Representatives. In 1966, she won a seat in the Texas Senate, and in doing so became the first black female to win election to the senate in Texas. In 1968, she ran unopposed and was re-elected. In 1971, she announced she would run for the United States Congress from a new Congressional District (18th). On November 7, 1972, she won election to Congress, with 85 percent of the vote. She took office on January 3, 1973, and right from the start she consistently backed legislation to raise the standard of living of impoverished Americans. She voted for increased aid to elementary and secondary schools, the continuation of the guaranteed student loan plan, and the extension of the national school lunch program.

In 1976, Jordan stole the Democratic National Convention show as a keynote speaker. With her stunning speech that night, she burst upon the national scene as a certified folk her-oine. A comet in the political sky, they called her, but she moved quickly to squelch a movement to place her name in nomination for vice president. Thousands of telegrams urging presidential nominee-apparent Jimmy Carter to add her to his list of potential running mates arrived at the Georgian's headquarters and were being "sorted" by aides. Carter already had narrowed his field to two or three senators before Jordan's spectacular performance brought her prolonged standing ovations of delegates and won her new admirers all over the country.

In 1977, Jordan, the first black congresswoman elected from the Deep South, announced that she would not seek a fourth term in Congress in 1978, saying she was acting "for reasons predicated totally on her internal compass." She stated her single, greatest accomplishment was representing hundreds, thousands of heretofore nameless, faceless, voiceless people.

JORDAN, KENNETH U., was born in South Pittsburg, Tennessee. He received a B.S. degree in public administration from the University of Tennessee, Knoxville, in 1966; a J.D. degree from Vanderbilt University School of Law, Nashville, Tennessee, in 1974. He was commissioned a 2nd lieutenant in the United States Air Force, through the R.O.T.C. program, while at the University of Tennessee. From 1966 to 1968, he served as a squadron section commander, Minot Air Force Base, in North Dakota. From 1968 to 1969, he was the executive support officer, Udron Royal Thai Air Force Base, in Thailand. From 1969 to 1970, he was the commander of Headquarters Squadron, McDill Air Force Base, Florida. He joined the Tennessee Air National Guard in 1976.

Jordan left active duty in 1970 and accepted a position as an employee relations specialist, General Foods Corporation, White Plains, New York.

From 1974 to 1975, he was an associate director of Fair Employment Practices Clinic and clinical instructor, Vanderbilt Law School, Nashville. From 1975 to 1977, he was the assistant dean for administration, at Vanderbilt Law School. From 1977 to 1981, he was the director of the Opportunity Development Center at Vanderbilt University.

From 1981 to 1983, he served as executive assistant to the president, later as interim vice president for development and public relations, later vice president for administration and general counsel, at Meharry Medical College, Nashville. From 1983 to 1984, he was a student at the Air Command and Staff College, at the Air University, on Maxwell Air Force Base, Montgomery, Alabama. From January 1985 to October 1985, he served as an attorney-advisor, director, Equal Employment Opportunity Staff, Department of Justice, Washington, D.C. From October 1985 to January 1987, he served first as executive assistant to the Assistant Attorney General for Administration, then as chief of staff,

Justice Management Division, Department of Justice, Washington. He also served on the board of directors for the Department of Justice Federal Credit Union.

From January 1987 to August 1988, he served as an executive assistant to the governor (cabinet-level appointment), in the state capitol, Nashville. He also served as chairman of the Governor's Task Force on Housing. In September of 1988, he was promoted to the one-star rank of brigadier general, becoming the first black to serve as the assistant adjutant general for the Tennessee Air National Guard.

Jordan has served on numerous boards, both civic and community, which include: member, Tennessee Task Force on the Supply of Minority Teachers (governor's representative); member, Statewide Area Health Education Centers (AHEC) Advisory Committee, Meharry Medical College; member, Boy Scouts' Inner-City Task Force Finance Committee; chairman, Project Blueprint Committee, United Way of Middle Tennessee; member, National Committee for Employer Support of the Guard and Reserve (Tennessee Committee), and United States Department of Defense (term expires January 1994).

JORDAN, MICHAEL, was born February 17, 1963, in Brooklyn, New York. He is the son of James Jordan and Deloris Peoples Jordan. He married the former Juanita Vanoy, and they have a son, Jeffrey Michael. He grew up in Wilmington, North Carolina, with his two brothers and two sisters. He attended North Carolina University but left school in 1985 to play basketball as a pro for the Chicago Bulls. He was an instant success as a pro. In his first season 1984–1985, he led the NBA in points with 2,313, and was named Rookie of the Year, a starting All-Star, and winner of the Seagram Award for best player in the NBA.

Jordan averaged 28.2 points per game, 5.9 assists, and 2.4 steals and led the Bulls in rebounds. In the slam-dunk championship at the NBA All-Star weekend in Seattle in February 1987, he out-dunked Jerome Kersey 146–140 to claim the top prize of $12,500. He then shared the prize money with his teammates, giving 11 of them $1,000 each. At Chicago Stadium on April 16, 1987, he scored 61 points and became the second player in NBA history, after Wilt Chamberlain, to surpass the 3,000 mark in a season. In 1988, Jordan was named the National Basketball Association's Most Valuable Player, upstaging previous winners Larry Bird of the Boston Celtics and Magic Johnson of the Los Angeles Lakers. Jordan guided the Bulls to a 50–32 regular season record, their best in 14 years.

For the second straight season, Jordan posted more than 200 steals and 100 blocked shots and remained the only player in NBA history to achieve the feat. His phenomenal record-breaking performances have lifted basketball to new heights of excitement and intensity. In January 1991, he scored 40 points, including the 15,000th of his career, as the Chicago Bulls defeated the Philadelphia 76ers 107–99. His career scoring average of 32.6 is the highest for any player in NBA/ABA history. With ProServ, the sports management firm that represents Jordan, signed deals to promote Nike sports apparel and "Air Jordan" basketball shoes is one of the most lucrative ever signed by an NBA player.

In addition, Jordan has endorsement contracts with McDonald's, the Wilson sporting goods company (for an autographed basketball), Coca-Cola, Chevrolet automobiles, Johnson Products, Excelsior International ("Time Jordan" watches), and Guy LaRoche watches. Jordan has been called one of the most recognized sports figures in the world.

The year 1991 could be called the year of Michael Jordan; he led his team, the Chicago Bulls, into the NBA championship by first knocking off the defending champions, the Detroit Pistons. Before game two with the Pistons, he was presented the league's Most Valuable Player award in a ceremony; after that he had the upper hand emotionally. He guided the Bulls to their first-ever championship in 25 years, as the Chicago Bulls took four of five games with the L.A. Lakers. Jordan was voted unanimously as MVP of the series. He finally won a championship ring and joined an elite club.

JORDAN, VERNON EULION, JR., was born August 15, 1935, in Atlanta, Georgia, the second of three sons of Vernon and Mary Belle (Giggs) Jordan. He and his wife Shirley have one child, Vickee. In 1953, he enrolled at DePauw University in Greencastle, Indiana, and was the only black student in his class. He majored in political science and minored in history and speech. During his first year at DePauw he won the Margaret Noble Lee Extemporaneous Speaking Contest. The next year as a sophomore he took first prize in the Indiana Interstate Oratorical Contest, only the second time that the prize was won by a DePauw student. After graduating in 1957, with a B.A. degree, he enrolled at Howard University. He graduated from Howard University's Law School in 1960 with a J.D. degree.

Soon after graduation he became a clerk in the office of Atlanta civil rights attorney Donald Hollowell. In 1961, Hollowell won a landmark civil rights decision when the Federal District Court ordered the University of Georgia to admit two qualified blacks, in the first desegregation at any level in the state's school system. Using his body as a shield, Jordan personally forced a path through an angry white mob so that Charlayne Hunter, a black coed, could enter the university grounds. In 1962, he took on the additional job of field secretary for the Georgia branch of the NAACP, becoming responsible for organizing, for speech making, and for servicing local branches, many of which, at the time, were engaged in marches, demonstrations, and other direct action techniques.

In late 1962, he led a boycott against stores in Atlanta that refused to hire blacks. The NAACP won, essentially, all the concessions it had sought. With another civil rights lawyer, Wiley A. Barnton, in 1964, Jordan set up a law partnership in Arkansas, taking over at the same time Barnton's duties as director of the Voter Education Project of the Southern Regional Council. He succeeded the late Whitney M. Young, Jr., as executive director of the National Urban League. Although only in his mid-thirties, he had played a crucial role in all the stages of the contemporary civil rights movement. At the National Urban League's Annual Conference, July 28, 1971, in Detroit, Jordan pledged that the agency would continue to be: "A forceful advocate for the cause of black people and other minorities; a result-oriented, issue-oriented organization dedicated to serving the people; a bridge between the races, forging unity and harmony in a land torn by strife and division."

When Jordan took over the leadership of the Urban League, he made the league more of an activist organization than it had been under Young, and broadened its sources of funds. He offered corporations careful plans for regular contributions to the league, and he tapped sources in the South for the first time. His success in establishing ties with big business was best demonstrated by his election to the board of directors of one corporation after another: Bankers Trust Co., Xerox, Celanese Corp., J. C. Penney, and American Express, as well as the Rockefeller Foundation, the John Hay Whitney Foundation, the New World Foundation, and the Urban Institute.

He was also on the board of directors at Massachusetts Institute of Technology and several other educational institutions. He served as executive director of the United Negro College Fund, and was elected to the Ryder System board of directors.

In 1977, at the National Urban League's Annual Conference in Washington, D.C., he became the first black leader to voice the disenchantment that many blacks were beginning to feel toward the Jimmy Carter Administration. When he attacked President Carter at the NUL's 69th Annual Conference at the Conrad Hilton Hotel, he did not specify what individuals were playing political games. "The black strategy should be to hang loose and make the candidates come to us," he said to the 4,000 delegates and observers squeezed into the Hilton's International Ballroom. "No one can win without the black vote," he said. He did not hesitate to enumerate the advancements made by blacks in high positions, including corporate jobs and other employment "never before open to us."

Jordan noted that blacks are in schools and colleges that never allowed them through their doors. "Yes, there has been progress, for some of us," he declared. "But the myth of black progress is a dangerous illusion used as an excuse to halt further efforts to extend real progress to all of our people. It purports to show that blacks have made progress and those who have not have only themselves to blame. It sanctions the vile myth that the poor are really an underclass, incapable of being helped, unwilling to rise out of their poverty. Let us acknowledge the great progress some of us have made but at the same time, let us recognize the true plight in which the vast majority of black people find themselves," he said. "While blacks in public life and private industry are holding job titles and receiving paychecks unheard of for black people a decade ago," he said, "the black unemployment rate was higher than it was when the Brown decision was handed down (in 1954), and higher than it was when we marched on Washington for jobs and freedom."

Jordan warned Carter that the black vote that swung the South behind him and provided the margin of victory in several northern states was not the same. He described the Carter Administration as cautious on black issues and the Congress as hostile. To make the speech required a measure of courage, for Jordan was risking a rupture of relations with the White House and loss of federal funding for various league projects. The responses from black leaders around the country overwhelmingly supported his criticism. He said, "If the speech hadn't been on the mark, it wouldn't have been the event that it was."

In 1980, he was shot by someone with a deer-hunter's rifle, which placed a wound the size of a fist an inch from his spine. The FBI had been investigating a number of brutal killings of blacks but said there was no link to the unsolved Jordan attempt. Lying on the asphalt that cool May morning in 1980, in Fort Wayne, Indiana, his blood gushing from the gunshot wound, he thought, oddly enough, of the daily letters his mother wrote him in college. "Son," she wrote, "if you trust Him, He will take care of you." After two weeks in Fort Wayne, he was transferred to New York.

Jordan became a partner in the Washington-based law firm of Akin, Gump, Strauss, Hauer and Feld, and was elected a director of the Revlon board. In 1989, he gave the elements of leadership. He said, "I believe leadership is instinctive, intuitive and self-motivated. From first grade on, I wanted to be a leader. I always wanted to be in charge and out front. I wanted to be class president, head of the school patrol, and the winner of all the essay, oratorical and declamation contests. I don't think that's a bad thing. Ego

doesn't have to be the prime motivating factor, but you show me a leader without ego, and I'll show you a nonleader. The ability to articulate needs, aspirations, hopes, dreams and fears is a key to leadership."

JOYNER, DELOREZ FLORENCE GRIFFITH, was born December 21, 1959, in the Mojave Desert, California. She is the daughter of Robert and Florence Griffith. She married Al Joyner and they have one child, Mary Ruth Griffith Joyner. She was the seventh of 11 children, and her mother nicknamed her "Dee Dee" to avoid confusion over their names. She grew up in the Jordan Downs housing project in the Watts section of Los Angeles. She began to run track at the age of seven. In elementary and junior high school she competed in the 50- and 70-meter dashes with the Sugar Ray Robinson Youth Foundation, a program for underprivileged youngsters.

At the age of 14, Joyner won the annual Jesse Owens National Youth Games and was awarded an all-expenses paid trip to a meet in San Francisco. She won the Jesse Owens Games again the next year, and was congratulated personally by Jesse Owens. In 1978, she graduated from Jordan High School in Los Angeles, where she set school records in sprinting and the long jump. In 1979, she enrolled at California State University at Northridge as a business major, but the lack of funds forced her to drop out after her freshman year and accept a job as a bank teller. Bob Kersee, the assistant track coach at Northridge, sought her out and helped her apply for financial aid. In 1980, Kersee accepted an assistant coaching position at UCLA, and Joyner followed him there.

The move proved beneficial to Joyner's track career, as she competed against the top American runners. In 1982, she became NCAA champion in the 200 with a time of 22.39 seconds.

After winning the 400 in the NCAA chanpionships in 1983 and placing second in the NCAA 200 that year, she continued to train with Kersee and his World Class Track Club. In 1984, at the Olympics in Los Angeles, she won the silver medal in the 200 with a time of 22.04 seconds, behind Valerie Brisco's 21.81 seconds. After the 1984 Olympics she became a customer service representative for the Union Bank company in Los Angeles and worked at night braiding women's hair.

By 1986, she was in semiretirement, but in 1987 she asked Kersee to help her train for the 1988 Olympic trials. She received moral support in her efforts from her husband-to-be, Al Joyner, the triple jumper who won the 1984 Olympic gold medal and the brother of her World Class Track Club teammate Jackie Joyner-Kersee. Al Joyner and Florence Griffith Joyner were married in October 1987, in Las Vegas. In September 1988, at the Summer Olympics in Seoul, South Korea, she set an Olympic record in the trials with a 10.62 in the 100 meter. She then set another Olympic record on September 25, erasing the world record of 10.76 set by Evelyn Ashford in 1984. Joyner blew away the mark by the largest margin since 1968 when automatic timing was introduced. At the Seoul Olympics, she won the 100 in 10.54, set a world record of 21.34 in the 200 meters, and won another gold in the 4x400 relay and a silver in the 4x400 relay

In a Tass poll that encompassed 31 countries, Joyner, affectionately nicknamed Flo Jo, was voted World Athlete of the Year for 1988. In March 1988, she won the 1988 Sullivan Award as the top American amateur athlete. In February 1989, she received the United States Olympic Committee Award, the Golden Camera Award in Berlin, and the Harvard Foundation Award for outstanding contributions to society. On February 25, 1989, she retired from competition. She had earned the un-

official title of the world's fastest woman, who brought unprecedented glamour to women's track with her fingernails at lengths of anywhere up to six inches, with artistic designs painted on them. She also wore sheer, one-legged running suits that garnered considerable attention, with her bikini briefs, and her flowing, immaculately coiffed hair shoulder length. She became an inspiration to all children to find the winner within themselves.

JOYNER, GORDON L., is a native of Fort Valley and Atlanta, Georgia. He graduated from Morehouse College summa cum laude and Phi Beta Kappa with majors in business administration and political science. He received the J.D. degree from Harvard Law School. He is a member of the bar in Georgia and Washington, D.C., and has practiced before the United States Supreme Court. Joyner is married to Gail Tusan Joyner, an attorney and judge, and they practice law together in the law offices of Joyner and Joyner. They have two children, Ashley and Shannon.

Joyner practiced law in Atlanta with the corporate law firm of Kilpatrick and Cody for several years before temporarily relocating to Washington, D.C., to serve as assistant director in the Governmental Relations Office of the American Bar Association. While in Washington, he was appointed director of the U.S. Department of Housing and Urban Development's Office of Fair Housing Enforcement. In that position, he worked in coordinating the federal government's nationwide program under the Civil Rights Act of 1968 to combat housing discrimination.

Joyner returned to Atlanta to serve as government executive-in-residence and visiting professor in political science and urban studies at Morehouse College, and to re-enter private law practice. At Morehouse, he developed and taught a course on Federal Civil Rights Laws and Enforcement. Among his civic and community activities in Atlanta, he has served as a member of the boards of directors of the Butler Street YMCA and the Metropolitan YMCA. He served as a member of Mayor Andrew Young's Task Force on Public Education, and is a founding member of the Robert H. Brisbane Institute of Law, Government, and Public Affairs at Morehouse College. He has served as an officer of the Gate City Bar Association and the Georgia Bar Association's section on Individual Rights.

Joyner is a member of the board of trustees and is former president of the Usher Board at Friendship Baptist Church. In 1985, he was sworn in by Mayor Young as a judge on the Atlanta Municipal Court, and he was installed as chairman and chief registrar of the Fulton County Board of Elections and Voter Registration. That same year, the Atlanta NAACP presented him with its "Thurgood Marshall Award" for his achievements as a Civil Rights lawyer, and he was honored as one of "The Ten Outstanding Young People of Atlanta." In 1987, Governor Joe Frank Harris appointed him as a member of the Fulton County Board of Commissioners. He was elected to that position in January 1990.

Joyner has been a speaker at conferences, bar conventions, seminars, and universities throughout the country including the Atlanta University Center, the Harvard Kennedy School of Government, Talladega College, Yale Law School, the University of Florida, Alabama State University, and Georgetown Law School. *Ebony* magazine honored him by selecting him as one of its "Leaders of the Future," and he and his family were the subject of a feature article in *Ebony*. Joyner has traveled throughout America. His priorities in public service has been ethics, accountability, and efficiency in government.

JOYNER-KERSEE, JACQUELINE, was born March 3, 1962, in East St. Louis, Illinois. She was named for Jacqueline Kennedy, who was the First Lady, at the insistence of her grandmother, who predicted that someday this girl would be the first lady of something. Her parents, Alfred and Mary Joyner, were 17 and 19 years old respectively when she was born and had been married for three years. Their youth made family life an economic struggle, especially in East St. Louis, a depressed industrial town so crime-ridden that by the time she was 11 she had seen a murder in front of her house. At the age of 9 years she enrolled in a special community track program where she was the fourth or fifth fastest in her group. But by age 13 she came into her own and out-performed all the other runners.

Joyner-Kersee first took up a multi-event sport, the five-event pentathlon, when a coach at the Mayor Brown Center informed her that the quickest way to the Olympics was to master a variety of specialties. Blossoming quickly, she won the first of four consecutive National Junior Pentathlon championships when she was 14, and while attending Lincoln High School, she became known as perhaps the finest athlete in the state of Illinois. She set a state high school record of 20 feet, 7½ inches, in the long jump in her junior year, played volleyball, and contributed to the Lincoln basketball team. After graduation in 1980 in the top 10 percent of her class, she was recruited for both basketball and the pentathlon by the University of California at Los Angeles. Opting for the basketball scholarship, she went on to star as a forward for the U.C.L.A. Bruins.

A few months later her mother died from meningitis. Her Aunt Oella Gaines took care of her two younger sisters. She returned to UCLA filled with grief. The first person to offer comfort was an assistant track coach, an intimidating man named Bob Kersee. She was concentrating on basketball and long jumping at the time, maintaining a B average and allowing her multievent skills to languish. Taken aback by this, she has said that Kersee saw a talent walking around that everyone was blind to. No one was listening to her mild request to do more. He went to the athletic director of UCLA and threatened to quit unless he was allowed to coach Jackie Joyner. His ultimatum was met.

He then went to her, tallied up her personal best performances in heptathlon events, and showed her that even without special training she was only 400 points behind America's then-reigning heptathlete, Jane Frederick. Her sprinting ability in particular made her almost invincible in a heptathlon 200-meter dash and she lamented that although her raw speed was the best everyone could beat her in the hurdles. She agreed to take up the heptathlon, although she rankled for some time at having to train for the 800 meters and the throws, feeling that she would

spread herself too thin and compromise her long jumping and basketball training. But Kersee, who has been described as demanding and strong willed on the track, persisted. By 1982, he could see that she would be the world record holder. In 1983, Joyner-Kersee and her brother Al, who had excelled in the triple jump as a student at Arkansas State University, were selected to represent the United States at the track and field world championships held in Helsinki, Finland. Along with her brother, she qualified for the United States team selected for the 1984 Los Angeles Olympics.

Joyner-Kersee arrived in Los Angeles favored to win a gold medal, but with a heavily taped leg because of a new hamstring injury sustained a few weeks before. Although Al Joyner, Jr., was not expected to win a medal, he has recalled that both he and his sister were determined to show that there were better things to come out of East St. Louis than just crime. In 1984, she was the Olympic silver medalist in the heptathlon, a two-day, seven-event competition that included running, long jumping and javelin throwing.

Two years later she had a pretty full calendar. She married her coach on January 11, 1986. She then became the first woman to break 7,000 points at the Goodwill games in Moscow. She caught her breath and one week later scored 7,158 at the U.S. Sports Festival. That world record stood as long as she needed to get really serious about the 1988 Olympics.

Joyner-Kersee scored 7,215 at the Olympic Trials and admitted she was holding herself back for the Summer Games. She went on to win two gold medals in the heptathlon and the long jump during the 1988 Summer Olympics in Seoul. She established her own community foundation; her place in athletics was secure and she was a world champion. In 1988, she won the McDonald's Amateur Athlete of the Year by the Women's Sports Foundation for the second year in a row. At the Goodwill games in 1990, she had to settle for just winning the heptathlon rather than approaching her world record of 7,291 points. A time of 24.26 in the 200 meters, her slowest since 1984, when she competed with a sore leg, left her far off record pace, and she finished with 6,783 points, 547 ahead of her closest challenger, Larisa Nikitina of the Soviet Union. She was named 1988 Woman of the Year by the *Sporting News*.

Joyner-Kersee parlayed her heptathlon world championship into commercial success. The record holder for the long jump inked a contract with McDonald's, 7-Up and Primatene Mist. By any standard, her athletic achievements were remarkable, without the fact that she has asthma. This condition didn't develop until 1982; she said that it never affected her during competition because her husband Bob was always waiting at the finish line with water or medication to help clear out her system. In 1986, she won the best amateur athlete Sullivan Award. Only six other blacks have won this award since 1954.

KAUFMAN, MONICA, married to Clarence P. Lott, III, is the mother and stepmother of two children, Claire Patrice and Nicole. The University of Louisville graduate was a reporter with *The Louisville Times* for four years. In 1969, she participated in the summer program for minority groups later called The Michelle Clark Fellowship, at the Graduate School of Journalism, Columbia University, New York. She worked in public relations for Brown-Forman Distillers before joining WHAS-TV in Louisville as a reporter and anchor for two years. She was WSB-TV's 5, 6, and 11 p.m. "Action News" anchor. She joined the Channel 2 staff in August 1975.

Kaufman has received numerous awards which reflect her outstanding abilities. The following is a partial list of her most recent achievements. She has received 10 Emmy awards in 1978, 1982 and 1984 for Outstanding News Talent; in 1981 for Outstanding Achievement in Educational Programming for "The Making of 'Nightline' "; and in 1987 for TV Excellence/Entertainment Program (series) — "Monica Kaufman Closeups." In 1988, she won two more Emmys for Best Entertainment Series and Best Magazine Program, "Monica Kaufman Closeups." In 1989, she received three Emmys — Best Documentary, "Behind Closed Doors"; Best Entertainment Program (series), "Monica Kaufman Closeups VI." "The Making of Nightline" won two national awards in 1982 — the award for local TV productions at the Chicago International Film Festival in 1983, and an Iris Award, presented by the National Association of Television Program Executives.

In 1985, Kaufman was named to the Metropolitan Atlanta YWCA Academy of Women Achievers. In 1986, *Glamour* magazine selected her as one of the All-Time Ten Top Working Women in the United States. That year she was awarded an honorary Doctorate of Humane Letters from Atlanta University. She was the 1988 recipient of the University of Louisville Alumni Association Order of Merit Award. In January 1989, she received the Distinguished Service to Broadcasting Award, presented by DiGamma Kappa honorary society at the University of Georgia. Previous recipients of this award include Barbara Walters, Ed Bradley, and John Chancellor.

Kaufman's recent work has been honored nationally. The series "When Love Hurts" won Honorable Mention at the AWRT National Awards. This series and the hour-long documentary "Behind Closed Doors" was awarded an American Bar Association Certificate of Merit in the 1989 ABA Gavel Awards competition. "Behind Closed Doors" also won the Documentary Public Affairs Award, presented by the Associated Press, in April 1989. Kaufman is a member of various professional organizations, including: the Society of Professional Journalists, Sigma Delta Chi; the National Association of Black Journalists; and the Atlanta Junior League.

KEARSE, AMALYA LYLE, was born June 11, 1937, in Vauxhall, New Jersey. In 1959, she received a B.A. degree from Wellesley College, and received her J.D. degree from the University of Michigan Law School at Ann Arbor, in 1962. From 1962 to 1969, she worked as a lecturer for New York University Law School. She was a partner in a Wall Street law firm before President Jimmy Carter appointed her to the 2nd Circuit of the United States Court of Appeals in New York, in 1979.

Kearse was the first black woman on the United States Court of Appeals in New York. She has served as a member of the President's Commission for Selection of Judges, the board of directors of NAACP LD&E Fund and

the board of directors of the National Urban League.

KEITH, DAMON J., was born July 4, 1922, in Detroit, Michigan. He married the former Rachel Boone, and they have three children, Cecile, Debbie, and Gilda. In 1943, he received a B.S. degree from West Virginia State College; he received an LL.B. degree from Howard University Law School in 1949. He received an LL.M. degree from Wayne State University. He has received numerous honorary degrees.

From 1952 to 1956, he worked in the Detroit office of Friends of the Court. From 1958 to 1963, he was a member of the Wayne County Board of Supervisors. From 1964 to 1967, he was in private law practice and the senior partner of Keith, Conyers, Andrews, Brown and Wahls in Detroit. In 1967, he was appointed to the federal court by President Lyndon Johnson, during the civil rights movement and Vietnam. On October 12, 1967, he assumed office as United States District Court Judge. He was later named chief judge and remained on the United States District Court, for the Eastern District of Michigan until 1977. In 1977, he was appointed to the United States Court of appeals for the 6th Circuit in Detroit by President Jimmy Carter.

Keith made history in 1971 when he ruled against then–President Richard Nixon. It was revealed that President Nixon had sanctioned wiretaps on the home of a political activist suspected of bombing the Ann Arbor, Michigan, branch of the CIA in 1968. The go-ahead for the wiretaps, Keith ruled, was in violation of the Fourth Amendment, which requires wiretaps to be approved by the court. In his ruling, he wrote: "We are a country of laws and not of men, the president is, of course, still subject to the constitutional limitations imposed upon him by the Fourth Amendment. The Fourth Amendment protection is derived from the Court's declaration that the Fourth Amendment protects a defendant from the evil of the uninvited ear." Attorney General John Mitchell appealed the ruling to the United States Supreme Court, for the Nixon Administration. But the Supreme Court upheld Keith's ruling by a unanimous decision.

Some of Keith's other public offices have included appointment to the Committee of Manpower Development and Vocational Training and Coordinating, and as chairman of the Subcommittee of Administration and Organization of the Citizens Advisory Committee on Equal Educational Opportunities for the Detroit Board of Education. United States Supreme Court Chief Justice William Rehnquist named Keith to serve as chairman of the Bicentennial of the Constitution for the duration of its activities, which continued through the celebration of the 200th anniversary of the adoption of the Bill of Rights, in 1991. He has served as vice president of the United Negro College Fund in Detroit, and the first vice president emeritus in the Detroit Chapter of the NAACP. He has also served as a member of numerous civic organizations and bar associations.

KELLY, JOHN PAUL, JR., was born March 8, 1941, in New Orleans, Louisiana, the son of John Paul Kelly, Sr., and Dorothy M. Jones Kelly. He married the former Lethia A. Robinson. He received his B.S. degree from Manhattan College, Riverdale, New York, in 1963; and an M.A. degree from the City University of New York, in 1965. He worked various jobs while in college, such as a self-employed barber, for a taxi service and at a record shop. From September 1963 to October 1965, he worked in the New York City school system as a teacher. In October 1965, he left the school system to join the United States Air Force. He served

as a captain and assistant professor at Chapman College, on Vandenberg Air Force Base Division, Orange, California (1966–1967); then as an instructor at Allen Hancock Junior College, Vandenberg Air Force Base Division, Santa Maria, California. He left the Air Force in March 1970, and that April he accepted a job as a trainee with Surface Transportation Department, Corporate Banking Group, Citibank N.A., in New York.

In January 1971, Kelly moved up to assistant cashier in the Correspondent Banking Division at Citibank. By June 1973, he had been appointed assistant vice president of Information Systems and Electronics Division, Corporate Banking Group, Citibank N.A., in New York. In December 1973, he had moved over to the World Corporation Group, a division of Citibank, as its assistant vice president. He left New York in November 1974 to accept a job as president of the Midwest National Bank, in Indianapolis, Indiana. In August 1982, he was named the new president and chief executive officer of the Midwest National Corporation in Indianapolis. He also chaired a $750,000 capital building fund campaign for the Alpha Home, the oldest black nursing home in Indianapolis.

Kelly also served on the board of the Indianapolis Airport Authority, and the board of Citizens Gas and Coke Utility, Indianapolis. He is a member of the board of the Indianapolis Chamber of Commerce, and a member of the Governor's Fiscal Policy Task Force. In 1983, while still president and CEO at Midwest National, he started and successfully operated three distinct and separate businesses: Jackson Controls, Castine Financial, Inc., and Unibind of Washington, D.C. He has served as a board member of the American Society of Association Executives, the Minority Business Enterprise Legal Defense and Education Fund, and the National Center for Missing and Exploited Children.

KILPATRICK, CAROLYN CHEEKS, was born June 25, 1945. She is a native of Detroit and has two children, a son Kwame and daughter Ayanna. She spent her undergraduate years attending Ferris State University and Western Michigan University, and earned her J.S. degree in education administration from the University of Michigan in 1977. She taught in the Detroit public schools eight years prior to serving in the Michigan legislature. Her church, The Shrines of the Black Madonna of the Pan African Orthodox Christian Church, was the inspiration behind her political career.

As a politically aware member, Kilpatrick was coordinator of political action for the Shrine. In that role she served as community organizer for the then–Senator Coleman A. Young in his first mayoral election in 1973. She was first elected to the Michigan House of Representatives in 1978 and re-elected five times. She was a delegate to the Democratic conventions in 1980, 1984 and 1988. She was a Majority Whip of the House of Representatives and served on the powerful House Appropriations Budget. She chairs the Corrections Budget.

Kilpatrick is the first black woman in the history of Michigan statehood to serve on the House Appropriations Committee. She was a member of the Detroit Substance Abuse Advisory Council, and served as chairperson of the Michigan Legislative Black Caucus for the legislative session in 1983–1984.

Rep. Kilpatrick was affiliated with the National Organization of 100 Black Women, National Black Caucus of State Legislators and the National Order of Women Legislators. She was a member of the highly acclaimed television documentary "Your Children, Our Children" Resource Committee. She owns an American Speedy Printing Center in downtown Lansing, Michigan. She was selected in 1984 to participate in the first of its kind Michigan African Trade Mission and visited several African countries. In 1985, she returned to Nairobi, Kenya, to participate in the United Nations International Women's Conference. In 1986, she led an 11-member delegation for the Michigan Department of Agriculture to Nairobi to participate in Kenya's International Agriculture Show.

Kilpatrick was chairperson of the National Black Caucus of State Legislators' International Affairs Committee, and on the board of trustees of Henry Ford Hospital. She has been awarded the Anthony Wayne Award for leadership from Wayne State University, the Distinguished Legislator Award from the University of Michigan, the Woman of the Year Award from the Gentlemen of Wall Street, Inc., and the Burton-Abercrombie Award from the 13th Democratic Congressional District. She is listed in *Who's Who in Black America, Who's Who in American Politics* and the Detroit Historical Museum's exhibit, "Black Women in Michigan 1785–1985."

KING, BARBARA LEWIS, was born August 26, 1930, in Houston, Texas. She has a son, Michael Lewis. She received her bachelor's degree from Texas Southern University in 1955, and her master's degree from Atlanta University in 1957. She also received honorary doctorate degrees from the University of Metaphysics, the Christian Church of Universal Philosophy, and Bethune-Cookman College.

From the age of 13, King knew she wanted to become a minister. She says, "Believe an idea strongly, with faith, and the idea will manifest into reality." Following her own advice, she started with a handful of people in her living room in 1971, and went on to build one of Atlanta's most influential and fastest growing churches, with a congregation of over 5,500. She is the founder and minister of Hillside International Truth Center in Atlanta, Georgia. She is also founder and president of the Barbara King School of Ecumenical Ministry in Atlanta.

Despite the time demands that being a leader of her stature requires, she remains committed to other religious organizations. She was third vice president and board member of the International New Thought Alliance, member of the board of trustees of the Christian Council of Metropolitan Atlanta, and international president of the International Congress of Women in Ministry. She has been active in community organizations: as a member of the state Committee on the Life and History of Black Georgians, the Women's Chamber of Commerce of Atlanta, Zeta Phi Beta Sorority, Inc., and the National Council of Negro Women. She also served as chaplain of Black Women Entrepreneurs.

Dr. King is hostess of her own television program, "A New Thought, A New Life," which airs in the metropolitan Atlanta area on Channel 69 on Sunday evenings. She has delivered extensive sermons and speeches throughout the United States, and was invited to speak in Johannesburg, South Africa, in November 1990.

KING, CORETTA SCOTT, was born April 27, 1927, in Heiberger, Alabama, one of three children of Obie and Bernice Scott. She married the late Dr. Martin Luther King, Jr., and they had four children, Yolanda Denise, born in 1955; Martin Luther 3rd, born 1957; Dexter Scott, born 1961; and Bernice Albertine, born in 1963. Her first years of schooling were spent in a one-room schoolhouse in Heiberger. She obtained her secondary education in nearby Marion, Alabama, at the Lincoln School, a private missionary institution. There she had her first contact with college graduates, her teachers both black and white.

At Lincoln School she studied piano and voice, and sang as leading soloist in many school musical productions. After graduating first in a class of 17, Scott matriculated in 1945 at Antioch College in Yellow Springs, Ohio, where her sister had pioneered two years previously. She was granted a scholarship by the college's Race Relations Committee. Majoring in education and music, Scott took part in the college's trailblazing work-study program. By the time she graduated in June 1951, she had decided not to become a teacher but to continue her music studies.

That fall Scott entered the New England Conservatory of Music in Boston with a fellowship from the Jessie Smith Noyes Fund. Since the fellowship barely covered tuition, to eke out a living she worked part time as a mail order clerk and cleaned for a Beacon Hill family who provided her with breakfast and a place to sleep. Much of the time she subsisted on a diet of Graham crackers, peanut butter, and fruit. After the first year her financial condition improved when she began receiving aid from the state of

Alabama which was provided for black students not allowed into the state's white institutions. At the Conservatory, she studied voice and sang with the Conservatory Chorus and the Old South Choir.

While studying in Boston, Scott was introduced to a brilliant young Atlanta minister named Martin Luther King, Jr., who was doing graduate work in philosophy at Boston University. Scott decided to give up her career for marriage. The couple were wed on June 18, 1953, in a ceremony presided over by the Rev. Martin Luther King, Sr., and held in the garden of the Scott's home in Heiberger. After Martin Luther King, Jr., completed his program for the Ph.D. degree and his wife graduated from the New England Conservatory, the couple moved back to the South, where in September 1954, Dr. King became pastor of the Drexel Avenue Baptist Church in Montgomery, Alabama. In 1957, he became head of the Southern Christian Leadership Conference.

In 1960, the Kings moved to Atlanta where Dr. King shared the pastorate of the Ebenezer Baptist Church with his father. Meanwhile, Coretta King devoted herself to housekeeping and raising their growing family. In 1962, she taught voice in the music department of Morris Brown College in Atlanta. Long active in the peace movement, she was a Women's Strike for Peace delegate at the 17-nation Disarmament Conference held in Geneva, Switzerland, in 1962. In December 1964, when Dr. King was presented with the Nobel Peace Prize in Oslo, she was at his side. Her faith was put to its supreme test by her husband's assassination in Memphis, Tennessee, on April 4, 1968. At a peace rally in New York City in April 1968, she composed a speech from notes Dr. King had left. Soon, however, she began to speak in her own words.

When, on Solidarity Day, June 19, 1968, she fulfilled her husband's last appointment by speaking before the Poor People's Campaign at the Lincoln Memorial in Washington, she called upon American women "to unite and form a solid block of women power to fight the three great evils of racism, poverty, and war." Early in January 1969, King announced plans for the creation of a Martin Luther King, Jr., Memorial in Atlanta. For two decades after Dr. King was slain, she worked diligently to raise more than $10 million to build the King Center. And she was adamant that "nonviolent social change" be a part of its official name. She is the founding president and chief executive officer.

In undertaking the task of making the dream come true, King enlisted the support of business leaders, politicians, entertainers, educators, heads of local and national organizations along with the countless blacks who supported the civil rights crusade of her husband, the Nobel Peace Prize winner. And after 15 years of protest and marches, in 1986, she saw another dream fulfilled when January 15, Dr. King's birthday, was designated a national holiday. Dr. Martin Luther King, Jr., was the first black American to be so honored.

KING, DON, was born December 6, 1932, in Cleveland, Ohio, the fifth child of seven children of Clarence and Hattie King. His father was a steelworker at Jones and Laughlin Plant who died on Pearl Harbor Day in an explosion. King was once married and is the father of three children, Debbie, Carl and Eric. At the age of 39, he decided to become a boxing promoter, scorning a tradition in which that role was reserved for white men. He fitted the guidelines in neither color nor manner. This 200-pound plus, 6'4" black hyperbolist from the entrails of a Cleveland ghetto was meddling with their sport. "There ain't no others like me," booms King, who bills himself as the "World's Greatest Promoter," and with good reason, since he is indisputably the most powerful promoter in boxing.

King's flamboyant public image is marked by his wild hairdo, flashy jewelry and evangelical monologues embellished with quotations from Shakespeare and other literary immortals. Money is what makes a man step into the ring, and it is a criterion that permeates the sport. With a master's degree in gambling and a doctorate with honors in hustling, this context fits perfectly. King spent a good portion of his adolescence running a numbers operation in Cleveland.

His first job was a chicken runner for Hymie's Chicken Shack. He served four years in Marion Correctional Institution for stomping a fellow numbers runner to death. He spent those lonely years behind bars reading and pondering Shakespeare. Somehow this prepared him to move, once released, unswervingly to the top of the world of pugilism. In 1974, he had become the world's foremost prizefight promoter, while professional boxing was enjoying a period of heightened interest due to the sorcery of Muhammad Ali. It was on Ali's wings that King rode to prominence. The opportunity arose when the aspiring promoter persuaded the champ to put on a charity boxing exhibition in 1972. The exhibition was a success.

Then the inexperienced promoter took an uncharacteristic route, bewitching the heavyweight king's advisers: manager Herbert Muhammad, and Charles Lomax, the lawyer who has since become King's counsel and perhaps his most trusted ally. The events that established his supremacy was the "Rumble in the Jungle," Ali's stunning 1974 upset of George Foreman "Thrilla in Manila," the Larry Holmes, Gerry Cooney "The Pride and the Glory" and the doubleheader "The Crown Affair." King's stable has included Greg Page, Michael Dokes, Victor Galindez, Sugar Ray Leonard, Roberto Duran, Wilfredo Gomez, Leon Spinks, and Aaron Pryor. His power structure has expanded to the third world where he has raised many millions for prize fighters. He has served as president and owner of Don King Sports Entertainment Network; owner of King Training Camp, and president, chairman and CEO of Don King Productions. He is the recipient of numerous awards and honors, along with giving support to a number of professional organizations.

KING, REATHA CLARK, was born April 11, 1938, in Pavo, Georgia. She married N. Judge King, Jr., and they have two children, N. Judge, III, and Scott Clark. She received a B.S. degree from Clark College, Atlanta, Georgia, in 1968; an M.S. degree in 1960, and Ph.D. degree in 1963, from the University of Chicago; and an M.B.A. degree from Columbia University in 1977. From 1963 to 1968, she served as a research chemist at the Natural Bureau of Standards in Washington, D.C. From 1970 to 1974, she served as an associate dean for natural sciences and math at New York City College, New York, and associate dean for academic affairs from 1974 to 1977. In 1977, King was named president of Metropolitan State University in St. Paul, Minnesota.

King has been a pioneer in thermochemistry research and in university administration. She has received numerous honors and awards which include: Educational Leadership Award from the YWCA of St. Paul, in 1984; Exceptional Black Scientist Award from the CIBA-GEIGY Corporation, in 1984; the Drum Major for Justice Award from the SCLC in Atlanta, in 1986. She also holds membership, and serves in numerous organizations, boards and associations which include: the NAACP; the Urban League; chairelect of the board of the American Association of Higher Education, in 1987; corporate director of Norwest

Corporation (bank holding company), in 1986; board member of St. Paul Foundation, St. Paul, and Carnegie Foundation for the Advancement of Teaching, in Princeton, New Jersey.

KING, ROBERT LEWIS, SR., was born June 15, 1940, in Washington, D.C. He graduated from Bell Vocational High School in 1958, in Washington. He also attended Federal City College and Southeastern University. From October 1983 to October 1987, he served as a Housing Management Specialist for the Department of Housing and Community Development, Washington. He was responsible for developing election procedures and assisted the properties in holding elections for residents/officials. He served as the primary troubleshooter to solve resident complaints by coordinating agency resources. He was also responsible for bringing together the residents of the Property Management Administration's properties. King was responsible for identifying and developing employment and training opportunities for the residents of D.C. public housing.

As the deputy director for the Department of Housing and Community Development Summer Youth Program, he was responsible for placing and supervising the field staff in addition to 500 youth involved in meaningful work experiences. From October 1986 to August 1987, he served as an appointed member of the "Housing Reorganization Task Force" as established by mayoral order, to separate the Property Management Administration of the D.C. Department of Housing and Community Development into a separate housing agency to operate public housing. From October 1987 to February 1988, he was assigned to the Office of General Assistant to the Mayor, where he advised the general assistant on matters involving how programs affect the community, and

helped design community outreach programs.

In March 1988, he was assigned as a special assistant in the Department of Consumer Regulatory Affairs where he served as special assistant to the program manager, for Pharmaceutical and Medical Devices Control Division, and performs, plans, develops, and coordinates projects and programs under the direction of the program manager. He has served as president of the Fort Lincoln Civic Association; president of Change Inc.; parliamentarian of the Advisory Neighborhood Commission 5A; member of the Citywide Housing Coalition; member of Justice within the Media, and coordinator, Children's Hospital Advisory Council.

KNIGHT, GLADYS M., was born May 28, 1944, in Atlanta, Georgia. She is the mother of three children, Shanga, Kenya and Jimmy. She made her first public appearance at the age of four as a gospel singer. Both parents sang with Over Jordan, a gospel group. At the age of seven she won first place in a "Ted Mack Amateur Hour" television show, in 1952, and won a $2,000 grand prize for her rendition of Nat King Cole's "Too Young," and two other songs. In 1953, she became one of the original members of the Pips and signed with Motown in 1965. Under the guidance of Motown's "Hits Ville Staff" she became known worldwide with such hits as "I Heard It Through the Grapevine," "Friendship Train," and "If I Were Your Woman." The Pips members were Knight and her brother Bubba, and their cousins William Guest and Edward Patten.

Knight's version of Marvin Hamlisch's nostalgic "The Way We Were" sounds like a mature woman singing from the struggle and strife she has seen. In 1991, the group celebrated its 36th year in show business. Knight starred in a movie entitled *Pipe Dreams*, which co-starred and was coproduced by her then husband Barry Hankerson, Jr., and in 1985, she costarred with Flip Wilson in a weekly television show, the CBS sitcom "Charlie & Co." A true artist of true talent, Knight has traveled the roads of pain and glory.

LABELLE, PATTI, was born October 4, 1944, in Philadelphia, Pennsylvania; Patti LaBelle is the stage name of Patricia Louise Holte. She married Armstead Edwards and they have three sons, Stanley Stocker-Edwards, Dodd Stocker-Edwards, and Zuri Edwards. The couple adopted Dodd and Stanley. It was in the Beulah Baptist Church in Philadelphia, that her stunning vocal powers were first displayed. As a teenager, she performed in city parks with the Ordettes, a group that also included Cindy Birdsong. In 1961, the Ordettes' manager brought Patti and Cindy together with Nona Hendryx and Sarah Dash in a new singing sensation group called Patti LaBelle and the Bluebells. The group made the top 40 with "Down the Aisle" in 1963, and their version of "You'll Never Walk Alone" in 1964.

In 1970, Patti, Sarah and Nona changed their image and their name to just LaBelle. Their song "Lady Marmalade" went to the top of the charts, in 1970. LaBelle was the first rock group to perform at the Metropolitan Opera House. Since 1977, LaBelle has been a solo artist, with such hits as: "New Attitude," "On My Own," "If Only You Knew," and "Winner in You." She had two Top Ten singles on the hit soundtrack of the movie *Beverly Hills Cop*. She had the only female part in the movie *A Soldier's Story*, and in the early eighties critics raved about her costarring role in the Broadway gospelmusical revival "Your Arm's Too Short to Box with God."

LaBelle has worked with several major charities such as: the United Negro College Fund, Black Health Research Foundation, Save the Children, and Big Sisters of America.

LAFONTANT-MANKARIOUS, JEWEL, was born in Chicago, Illinois, and is married to Naguib S. Mankarious, an international business consultant. She is the mother of John W. Rogers, Jr. She received a B.A. degree in political science from Oberlin College

and a J.D. degree from the University of Chicago in 1946. She became the first female deputy solicitor general of the United States in 1973. As deputy solicitor general, she successfully argued United States government cases before the United States Supreme Court. Lafontant-Mankarious, known nationally for her contributions to civil and human rights, has served as a United States Representative to the United Nations, a commissioner of the Martin Luther King, Jr., federal holiday commission, is a member of the National Advisory Board of the Salvation Army, and is a director of Project Hope.

Lafontant-Mankarious' worldwide travels, which include visits to Europe, Africa, Asia, the Middle East, and the Caribbean, have greatly enhanced her insight and understanding of international affairs. In 1983, she became a partner of Vedder, Price, Kaufman and Kammholz and practices in the corporate and labor areas of the firm's Chicago office. In 1989, President George Bush appointed her as Ambassador-at-Large and U. S. Coordinator for Refugee Affairs. As United States Coordinator for Refugee Affairs, she is responsible to the president for the development of overall United States refugee assistance, admission and resettlement policy and for government-wide coordination of United States refugee programs. Under the direction of the secretary of state, she negotiates on behalf of the United States with foreign governments and international organizations in discussions on refugee matters.

Lafontant-Mankarious also served as director of more than a dozen of America's most important business corporations and has received numerous civic and professional awards including the service award of the United States Department of Justice Drug Enforcement Administration, the National Bar Association's C. Francis Stradford Award for contributions to the legal profession, and the B'nai B'rith International Abraham Lincoln Marovitz Award for outstanding achievement in the legal profession. She is a Fellow of the International Academy of Trial Lawyers.

LANE, BENSONETTA TIPTON, was born in Washington, D.C., and grew up in Bridgeport, Connecticut, where she was an honors-curriculum high school graduate. She went on to earn a bachelor's degree in political science at New York University. Graduation, however, was somewhat in question the year she cut several weeks of classes and headed South to help with voter education in Huntsville, Alabama, and Albany, Georgia. She met a veteran activist in Albany who became a source of personal inspiration and a significant influence on her eventual career choice, the legendary civil rights attorney C. B. King. Encouraged by her mother, she reluctantly returned to New York University and graduated in 1972.

Lane enrolled at the University of Massachusetts in Amherst, where she received a master's in education, in 1973. As part of the program, she taught adult education at a prison in Cranston, Rhode Island, where she gained special insight into the lives of prisoners. In an interview she stated, "I became and remain very concerned about these people, many of whom are very intelligent and all of whom, of course, are human beings. Too often they are in jail because of poor lawyers who didn't try hard enough or have no understanding of the sociology of being black in America."

By late 1973, she had chosen her profession and entered the University of Virginia Law School. When she approached a dean about arranging an internship at the Southern Poverty Law Center, however, his reaction convinced her that she was not at the best school for learning law the way she planned to

practice it. "For a while, I actually feared that becoming a lawyer might separate me from the values and beliefs that I hold so dearly as a black woman," she said. Nonetheless, she graduated in 1976, with a J.D. degree and her value system intact. Soon after graduation she moved to Atlanta to become a partner in the experimental "Law Project," a private, pro bono firm. There she gained experience in civil rights, prison litigation and employment discrimination.

Over the years, Lane has built a successful law practice and enviable professional reputation around her commitment to helping brothers and sisters of various colors. From prison litigation to employment discrimination, she has made a difference for thousands of everyday folks who took on the system. High on her long list of professional accomplishments was the 1982 Central State Hospital case, in which she represented 2,300 workers in a class-action, racial-discrimination suit. The court found in favor of her clients and issued relief to the tune of $3 million, at that time the largest radial

discrimination award in Georgia's history.

If African American history boasts countless leaders who have periodically and persistently reminded the race's more privileged members of their responsibility to less-advantaged brothers and sisters: "Don't forget where you came from," they admonish the black professional. "Reach back and help someone." If such leaders could mass produce black role models to specification, they might well select Lane, attorney at law, as one prototype. From 1983 to 1984, she served on the board of directors, Georgia Office of Air Employment Practices. Since 1985, she has served as an arbitrator for the Fulton County, Georgia, Superior Court. Also since February 1986, she has served as Judge Pro Hac Vice, Municipal Court for the City of Atlanta. In 1983, she was named "Lawyer of the Year" by the National Conference of Black Lawyers.

LANGFORD, ARTHUR, JR., was born October 4, 1949. He is a native Atlantan and is married to Susan Elaine Pease. They have one daughter, Shara Elizabeth. He received his high school

education from Luther Judson Price High School. A political science major, he graduated from Morris Brown College in 1971. He also attended Interdenominational Theological seminary, and in 1989 he earned a certificate in the field of gerontology from Georgia State University for Continuing Education. In 1972, at the age of 23 years, he was the youngest person ever elected to the Atlanta City Council. He distinguished himself while serving two four-year terms in that body. The founder and president since 1972 of the United Youth-Adult Conference, he has directed and led that organization in projects such as: job training and placement for youths; youth anti-drug abuse programs; shelter for the homeless; and organized searches for missing children in metro Atlanta and persons throughout the state of Georgia.

An ordained minister, Langford was commissioned to pastor the Rush Memorial Congregational Church, Atlanta, in 1981, where he served until 1989. An associate minister of the historical West Hunter Street Baptist Church, he was elected to the Georgia Senate in 1984 to serve the constituents of the 35th senatorial district. He served as chairman of the Senate Consumer Affairs Committee. During the interims of legislative sessions, he has been named by the lieutenant governor to represent the legislature by serving on standing committees of the nationally known Southern Legislative Conference. Previously, Sen. Langford served on the Retirement and Offender Rehabilitation Committees, and headed the Tuition Payment Alternatives Study Panel and Joint Adoption Study Committee.

As a legislator, Langford served as an advocate for children and youth issues, assisted in obtaining funding for business development projects and community enhancements, voted for more aid to senior citizens, played a major role in creating the new Atlanta Airport, and worked toward promot-ing progressive change that ultimately benefited all Georgians. After serving one term in the senate, he was elected to chair the Fulton County Senate Delegation, a nine-member panel of senators focused on legislation affecting Atlanta and Fulton County. During his second term, he became the senate's second black to chair a committee when Lt. Gov. Zell Miller named him head of the Consumer Affairs Committee. In addition, he served on the following committees: secretary, Children and Youth, Economic Development and Tourism, Human Resources; and vice chairman, MARTOC. Subcommittees he served on include: Regulated Beverages, Small Business, AIDS, and chairman, Aging.

Langford's long-standing community services have been recognized by numerous organizations in Atlanta, including the 1985 Intown Extra Community Service Award for public service. He was the author of the stage production, "Life of a King," a heartwarming drama based on the life of Martin Luther King, Jr. In addition to writing the play, he has given highly acclaimed performances in the lead role as "Dr. King" in city auditoriums, churches, public schools and universities across the United States. It has been performed on numerous occasions since it was written in 1969.

LAWSON, LAWYER, is married to Mary Bates Lawson and the father of four children, Mary, Kenneth, George and Robert. He attended Ohio College of Applied Sciences and received an associate degree, and had also pursued a degree in electrical engineering at the University of Cincinnati. He worked for Dover Elevator Company in the capacity of Regional Safety Coordinator. Lawson has served as mayor of Woodlawn, Ohio, for several years. He has been involved in local government since 1977, when he was elected to serve on the city council. As mayor he is involved in many community service organizations and has received many honors and awards, some of which include: 2nd vice president of the National Conference of Black Mayors; president, since 1983 of Woodlawn Scholarship Fund, Inc., which he created; vice president of the Hamilton County Municipal League since 1984; served as vice mayor of Woodlawn in 1979; served as president of the Ohio Chapter of Black Mayors, of which he has been a member since 1985; and was president of the Community Housing Resource Board, of which he had been a member since 1985.

Lawson has also been a member, board of trustees, National Conference of Black Mayors, since 1985; member, board of trustees, American Red Cross, from 1983 to 1987; member, board of trustees of the Hamilton County Development Company from 1983 to 1989; member of the Kiwanis Club from 1979 to 1987; served as council person, Village of Woodlawn, 1977 to 1980; member of National League of Cities since 1981; member of Ohio Municipal League since 1980, and named in *Who's Who Among Black Americans* in 1985.

†LEE, BERNARD SCOTT, was born October 2, 1935, in Norfolk, Virginia. He graduated from Howard University Divinity School, M.Div. degree, 1985. During the civil rights movement, he was one of the leaders of the movement that traveled and worked closely with Dr. Martin Luther King, Jr. Lee was a founding member in 1960 of the Student Nonviolent Coordinating Committee, and was expelled from Alabama State College in Montgomery for his role in sit-ins. Later, he helped organize the Freedom Rides, and the frustrating civil rights efforts in Albany, Georgia. he served as vice president of the Southern Christian Leadership Conference (SCLC), in Atlanta, and took part in the Selma March.

In 1976, Rev. Lee went to Washington with President Jimmy Carter as special assistant to the administrator of the Environmental Protection Agency. In 1980, he was Carter's deputy campaign manager in Mississippi. He was assistant pastor at Gethsemane Baptist Church in Washington in the 1970s and chaplain at Lorton Penitentiary in Virginia in the late 1980s. On February 10, 1991, the Rev. Lee died at home of heart failure. He was survived by two sons, Khalil and Kincherlow, and five daughters, Denita, Chiquita, Toinette, Bertha Lee, and Bernadette Scott.

LEE, GEORGE L., was born July 27, 1906, in Jamestown, New York, a short distance from the spot where a marker was later placed to honor his great-great-grandmother Catherine Harris, who had helped fugitive slaves escape to freedom in Canada. In 1914, Lee moved with his mother and older brother to Spokane, Washington. The family later moved to Wenatchee and Seattle; Lee graduated from Garfield High School in Seattle in 1925. He became interested in art during his senior year but received no formal training beyond high school. He earned money by picking fruit, shining shoes and working as a bellboy and waiter on boats to Alaska and California.

In 1927, Lee went to Chicago, where he still resides. Always fascinated by the action of sports drawings, he made contact with the boxing journal *BANG* while working as a messenger for the Pure Oil Company, just outside the Loop. His first drawings appeared on the cover of *BANG* in 1929. Soon Lee met Eddie Geiger, sports editor of the *Chicago Evening American*, who was impressed with Lee's drawings. Lee began drawing freelance for the *American*, his first piece appearing on the front page of the sports section on August 24, 1930. The president of Pure Oil congratulated Lee and arranged for him to make drawings of company executives which would appear in the company's monthly magazine.

In March 1933, Eddie Geiger arranged to have Lee's work syndicated, but the deal collapsed when it was revealed that Lee was black. Fate stepped in when Lucius Harper, editor of the black sports weekly the *Chicago Defender*, created with Lee a series called "Sporting Around." Then, in 1934, the Pittsburgh Courier asked Lee to design and illustrate a history feature called "Your History," which would be written by noted black historian J. A. Rogers. Also in 1934, Lee created ten posters advertising the first professional fight of Joe Louis. Lee and Louis each received $50 for their work. That was as close as Lee ever got to the great Joe Louis.

Lee married a beginning schoolteacher, Jennie Hicks, in 1936. The couple had one son. Mrs. Lee taught school for 38 years. Meanwhile Lee joined the Postal Service in 1937, continuing his freelance drawing in his spare time. In 1945, he created "Interesting People," a series of drawings and short biographies of significant black Americans, for the black press. A newsprint short-age in 1948 forced the cancellation of the series. During the 1950s Lee drew all of the publicity materials for the International Boxing Club, which organized major fights at Chicago Stadium until it was disbanded in 1959.

After retiring from the Postal Service in 1969, Lee revived "Interesting People" in 1970. This time the series continued for 16 years, until Lee retired from active drawing in 1986 at age 80. Since then he has published four books of his drawings: *Interesting People* (1989), *Interesting Athletes* (1990), *Inspiring African Americans* (1991) and *Worldwide Interesting People* (1992; all McFarland).

LEE, SPIKE, was born March 20, 1957, Shelton Jackson Lee, in Atlanta, Georgia, the oldest of the five children of Bill and Jacquelyn (Shelton) Lee. He has three brothers and one sister. His mother, who died in 1977, nicknamed him "Spike." His father and grandfather both obtained degrees from Morehouse College in Atlanta, and his mother and grandmother attended Spelman College. Following Lee's birth, the family moved to Chicago, where they lived briefly before moving, in 1959, to New York City, and settling in the predominantly black Fort Greene section of Brooklyn. He graduated from John Dewey High School in Brooklyn, and enrolled in Morehouse College in 1975. Majoring in mass communications, he immersed himself in such extracurricular activities as writing for the school newspaper, working as a disc jockey for a local jazz radio station, and in his senior year, directing Morehouse's lavish coronation pageant on homecoming weekend.

It was at Morehouse that Lee first took an interest in making films, and bought his first super-8 camera. After graduating from Morehouse in 1979, he obtained a summer internship at the Columbia Pictures studio in Burbank,

California. He returned to New York that fall to begin work toward a master's degree in filmmaking. His first attempt at independent filmmaking was to be a film entitled *Messenger*, a drama about a New York City bike messenger. It was in preproduction for eight weeks in the summer of 1984 before a dispute between Lee and the Screen Actors Guild killed the project because the union felt that his script was "too commercial" to qualify for a waiver that would allow nonunion actors to appear in it. Such waivers are often granted to low-budget, independent films, and he believed that the Screen Actors Guild's refusal to award him one was "a definite case of racism."

Lee's efforts failed, and he lost some $40,000. In the summer of 1985, Lee was ready for his next film, but he had to come up with a script that could be done for as little money as possible, yet be commercial, have very few characters, and needed next to no location work, sets, or costumes. Shot in 12 days in the summer, that same year, was *She's Gotta Have It*. He had scraped together $175,000 to make this film, about a young, attractive, and independent-minded black woman who simultaneously juggles three lovers with widely divergent personalities. *She's Gotta Have It* was a success, becoming the first movie by an independent black filmmaker to receive major international distribution since Melvin Van Peebles' *Sweet Sweetback's Baadasss Song* in 1971. *She's Gotta Have It* ultimately grossed over $7 million, including $1.8 million in its first three weeks.

Lee went on to make other movies now that the door had been knocked down by his determination. His films include *School Daze* (1988), *Do the Right Thing* (1989), and *Mo' Better Blues* (1990). His latest film is *Jungle Fever*. His latest television commercials include: Levi's 501 jeans, Nike, The Gap, Barney's of New York, and Scholastic Inc. His collection of merchandise

consists of Spike Garb–Brooklyn Dodgers baseball caps, T-shirts and jackets blazoned with the title of his 1989 hit movie *Do the Right Thing*, and a bicycle cap worn by him in his movie *She's Gotta Have It*.

Lee has founded a minority student scholarship fund at New York University's film school, and he has a "40-Acres and A Mule" film-training program at Long Island University. In addition, he actively supports a number of charities, including the United Negro College Fund. He directed a commercial for the Rev. Jesse Jackson's 1988 campaign.

LEIGH, FREDRIC HOMER, was born on March 29, 1940, in Ohio. He received a B.A. degree in history from Central State University and received an M.S. degree in public relations from Syracuse University. Leigh entered the United States Army in 1963, with an ROTC commission of 2nd lieutenant. From September 1963 to November 1963, he was a student in Infantry Officer Basic Course, United States Army Infantry Center and School, Fort Benning, Georgia. From December 1963 to February 1964, he was a student in the Ranger Course at the United States Army Infantry Center and School. From February 1964 to May 1964, he was a Platoon Leader, Company B, 1st Battalion, 2nd Infantry Brigade, Fort Devens, Massachusetts. From May 1964 to September 1964, he served as a member of the Infantry Committee, First Army Demonstration and Instruction Team, Camp Drum, New York.

Leigh was promoted to the rank of 1st lieutenant on February 4, 1965. In March of 1965, he was assigned as an assistant operations officer, in the 2nd Brigade, 5th Infantry Division (Mechanized), Fort Devens. He was promoted to the rank of captain, on August 25, 1966. In July 1966, he was the commander of Company B, 2nd Infantry Brigade, 1st Infantry Division, United

United States Army in Vietnam. From September 1966 to November 1968, he served as an assistant professor of military science, at Tuskegee Institute, Tuskegee, Alabama. From December 1968 to December 1969, he served first as an assistant S-3 (Operations), then as assistant G-3, plans officer, at Headquarters and Headquarters Company, 101st Airborne Division (Air Assault), United States Army in Vietnam.

From January 1970 to September 1970, Leigh was a student in the Infantry Officer Advanced Course, United States Army Infantry Center and School, Fort Benning. He was promoted to the grade of major on January 20, 1970. From August 1972 to June 1973, he was a student in the United States Army Command and General Staff College, Fort Leavenworth, Kansas. From June 1973 to January 1976, he served as a plans, program, and budget officer, Command Information Division, Office of the Chief of Information, United States Army, Washington, D.C. From January 1976 to May 1978, he served first as executive officer of the 2nd Battalion, 503rd Infantry, and second as executive officer of the 101st Airborne Division (Air Assault), Fort Campbell, Kentucky. He was promoted to the grade of lieutenant colonel on August 4, 1977.

From July 1978 to July 1979, he was the commander of the 1st Battalion, 38th Infantry, 2nd Infantry Division, United States Army in Korea. From August 1979 to August 1981, he served as a military assistant in the office of the Assistant Secretary of the Army (Manpower and Reserve Affairs), United States Army, Washington. From August 1981 to June 1982, he was a student at the National war College, Fort McNair, Washington. From June 1982 to June 1983, he served as the senior military assistant, Office of the Secretary of the Army, United States Army, Washington. From June 1983 to June 1985, he served as the deputy director of the Army Staff,

Office of the Chief of Staff, United States Army, Washington. He was promoted to the grade of colonel on September 1, 1983. From July 1985 to May 1987, he was the Chief of Staff, 19th Support Command, Eighth Army, in Korea.

From August 1987 to August 1989, Leigh served as the commander of the 1st Brigade, 101st Airborne Division (Air Assault), Fort Campbell. From August 1989 to March 1990, he served as the director of the senior leadership research, United States Army War College, Carlisle Barracks, Pennsylvania. In March 1990, he was assigned as the assistant division commander, 7th Infantry Division (Light), Fort Ord, California. He was promoted to the one-star grade of brigadier general on August 1, 1990.

Leigh has received numerous awards and decorations which include: the Legion of Merit (with two oak leaf clusters); the Bronze Star Medal (with four oak leaf clusters); the Bronze Star Medal with "V" Device; the Meritorious Service Medal (with two oak leaf clusters); the Air Medal; the Army Commendation Medal (with oak leaf cluster); the Combat Infantryman Badge; the Parachutist Badge; Air Assault Badge; and Range Tab.

LENHARDT, ALFONSO EMANUAL, was born on October 29, 1943, in New York, New York. He received a B.S. degree in criminal justice from the University of Nebraska, Omaha, and a master's degree of law administration from Central Michigan University. He enlisted in the United States Army in November 1965. In October 1966, he entered the Tactical Officer, Infantry Officer Candidate School, 60th Company, 6th Student Battalion, Student Brigade, at the United States Army Infantry School, Fort Benning, Georgia. From October 1967 to September 1968, he was a platoon leader in Company C,

4th Battalion, 12th Infantry, 199th Infantry Brigade, United States Army in Vietnam. From October 1968 to June 1969, he served as the commander of Company A, 10th Battalion, 4th Advanced Individual Training Brigade (Military Police), United States Army Training Center, Fort Gordon, Georgia.

Lenhardt was promoted to the rank of captain on October 19, 1968. From June 1969 to December 1969, he served as the chief of the Military Police Subjects Committee, 4th Advanced Individual Training Center, Fort Gordon. From December 1969 to August 1970, he served as an assistant S-2 (Intelligence)/S-3 (Operations) officer, 4th Advanced Individual Training Brigade (Military Police), Fort Gordon. From August 1970 to May 1971, he was a student at the Military Police Officer Advanced Course, Fort Gordon. From May 1972 to August 1972, he served as an action officer in the Special Activity Division, Operations Directorate, United States Army Criminal Investigation Command, Washington, D.C. From August 1972 to February 1973, he served as chief of the Operations Center, United States Army Criminal Investigation Command, Washington.

From February 1973 to June 1973, Lenhardt served as chief of the Region Coordination Division, United States Army Criminal Investigation Command, Washington. From June 1973 to September 1973, he was a student at the Federal Bureau of Investigation National Academy, Quantico, Virginia. From September 1973 to August 1975, he was the commander of Fort Eustis Field Office, 1st Regional United States Army Criminal Investigations Division Command, Fort Eustis, Virginia. From August 1975 to June 1976, he was a student at the United States Army Command and General Staff College, Fort Leavenworth, Kansas. He was promoted to the grade of major on June 5, 1976.

From June 1976 to December 1976, he was a student at Wichita State University, Wichita, Kansas. From December 1976 to June 1977, he served as operations officer in the Provost Marshal Office, Fort Dix, New Jersey. From June 1977 to June 1978, he served as the executive officer, 759th Military Police Battalion, Fort Dix. From June 1978 to June 1980, he served as company tactical officer of staff and faculty, United States Army Military Academy, West Point, New York. From June 1980 to June 1981, he served as chief of the policy branch, Office of the Provost Marshal, United States Army in Europe and the Seventh Army. He was promoted to the grade of lieutenant colonel on July 13, 1980.

From June 1981 to May 1983, Lenhardt served as the commander of battalion commander, 385th Military Battalion, VII Corps, United States Army in Europe. From May 1983 to June 1984, he was a student at the National War College, Fort Lesley J. McNair, Washington. From June 1984 to March 1985, he was the deputy director of research and assistant to Director of Strategic Defense Initiative Organization, Office of the Secretary of Defense, Washington. He was promoted to the grade of colonel on November 1, 1984. From March 1985 to June 1986, he served as the executive officer and assistant to the Director of Strategic Defense Initiative Organization, Office of the Secretary of Defense, Washington. From June 1986 to June 1988, he was the commander of the 18th Military Police Brigade, V Corps, United States Army in Europe.

From July 1988 to August 1989, Lenhardt served as the deputy provost marshal, Office of the Provost Marshal, United States Army in Europe and Seventh Army. In September 1989, he was promoted to the one-star grade of brigadier general and assigned as the deputy commanding general, of East, United States Army Recruiting Command, Fort Sheridan, Illinois. General

Lenhardt has received numerous awards and decorations which include: the Defense Superior Service Medal; the Bronze Star Medal; the Purple Heart; the Meritorious Service Medal (with two oak leaf clusters); the Air Medals; the Joint Service Commendation Medal; the Army Commendation Medal (with two oak leaf clusters); the Army Achievement Medal; the Humanitarian Service Medal; the Combat Infantryman Badge; the Parachutist Badge.

LEONARD-DENT, MARVA J., was born in South Bend to Henry and VerNeal Leonard. She is married to Dorian N. Dent, a native of Washington, D.C., and they have one daughter, Dionne JeNae. After graduating from South Bend's own LaSalle High School, she completed her undergraduate work at and earned her B.A. degree from Howard University, Washington, D.C., on December 21, 1979. She graduated from Indiana University School of Law, Bloomington, Indiana, earning her J.D. degree on May 7, 1983, and was honored with the special distinction and honor of being elected Student Commencement Speaker, and was appointed by the dean to the Faculty Hiring Committee. Leonard-Dent sat for and passed the Indiana Bar while finishing her third year of law school and was admitted to practice before the Indiana Supreme Court, June 1983. She is in-house corporation counsel for the South Bend Community School Corporation, South Bend's third largest public employer. She has held this position since July 1989. As the corporation staff attorney, she serves as general legal counsel to the board of school trustees, the superintendent and other school administration officials on all legal issues pertaining to the operation of public schools, including governance, pupils, finance, property, employees and liability; drafts legal documents, including pleadings, con-

tracts, leases, policies, and resolutions; monitors state and federal legislation activity for interpretation of impact on school district; coordinates the legal services of all outside law firms; and prepared and presents in-service programs and newsletters as a preventative/risk maintenance program.

Prior to being appointed to her present position and for only a short period of time, Leonard-Dent was asked to take a leave of absence from her position as an assistant city attorney by South Bend Mayor Joseph Kernan to serve as the executive director of the South Bend Human Rights Commission. Honored and flattered by the mayor's faith and confidence in her, she served as interim executive director for approximately six months. During this interim period, she was instrumental in improving the public image and work product of the commission and in the selection and appointment of the current director, Cynthia Love-Bush.

From 1983–1989, Leonard-Dent held the position of assistant city attorney in the City Attorney's Office, South Bend. In this position she served as the city's representative before various governmental, civic and community entities, including serving as the Human Rights Commission Attorney from 1983 through 1985. She was the first attorney to organize and conduct training sessions for commissioners in the area of discrimination. She was a proficient communicator, both orally and in writing; she was responsible for legal advice and resolving citizen complaints and inquiries on illegal acts.

Leonard-Dent is active and affiliated with numerous professional and civil organizations. She holds membership and leadership positions in the following, among others: Indiana State Bar Association, National Bar Association, American Bar Association, National School Board Association's Council of School Attorneys, Indiana

School Board Association, American Trial Lawyers Association, International Association of Human Rights Agencies, National Association of Trial Advocacy, St. Joseph County Bar Association, Delta Sigma Theta National Sorority, Inc., NAACP, St. Joseph County Commission on the Status of Women, Boys' and Girls' Clubs of America board of directors, Community Action Center board of directors, Forums for Youth Self-Sufficiency Committee, and the St. Joseph County Head Start Policy Council.

LEWIS, BRENDA J. EARLY, born January 29, 1955, in Montgomery, Alabama, is the daughter of James L. and Ida M. Early. She is the divorced mother of three children, Roger, Justin and Aiyana. She received her elementary education at St. Jude Educational Institute, graduating in 1972. She attended college at Alabama State University, where she majored in sociology. While at Alabama State University she was the editor-in-chief of the *Hornet Tribune*, a member of the university's tennis team and a member of Delta Sigma Theta sorority. She completed her studies at Alabama State and received a B.S. degree in 1976.

In 1977, Lewis received her Peace Officers Standards and Training at the Montgomery Police Academy. In August 1978, she graduated from Auburn University at Montgomery, receiving a master's degree in criminal justice. In 1987, she was appointed by Governor Guy Hunt of Alabama as constable of Precinct 4-C in Montgomery County, to fill a vacancy in that office for the unexpired term of one year. In 1988, she was elected to that position for a four-year term, which expires in 1992. She also held a position on the board of directors for the Alabama Prison Project, and the school board for St. John the Baptist Catholic School.

LEWIS, DELANO E., was born on November 12, 1938, in Arkansas City, Kansas. He and his wife Gayle reside in Potomac, Maryland, and have four sons, Delano, Jr., Geoffrey, Brian and Phillip. They are also the grandparents of three grandsons. He received a B.A. degree in political science and history from the University of Kansas in 1960, and was awarded a J.D. degree in 1963 from Washburn School of Law. He is a member of the Kansas and District of Columbia Bar Associations. He is president and chief executive officer of C&P Telephone Company, a Bell Atlantic subsidiary. He is responsible for C&P telecommunication services ranging from basic residential service to complex business systems and broadcast circuits. His scope of administration includes all of Washington, D.C., as well as operations responsibilities in the Washington metropolitan area.

In 1963, Lewis was appointed as an attorney for the U.S. Department of Justice. In 1965, he joined the Office of Analysis and Advice to the U.S. Equal Employment Opportunity Commission.

From 1966 through 1969, he served in the U.S. Peace Corps in Africa, holding positions of associated director in Nigeria and country director in Uganda. From 1969 to 1971, he was a legislative assistant to the administrative assistant to Congressman Walter E. Fauntroy of the District of Columbia. In 1973, he joined C&P as public affairs manager. Three years later, he was promoted to assistant vice president, Revenue Requirements and Public Affairs. Subsequently, he held the positions of assistant vice president, Public Affairs and Administration and assistant vice president, External Affairs, until his promotion in January 1983 to vice president. On July 1, 1988, he was elected president of C&P Telephone Company.

He is active in many civic and public service activities in the nation's capital. Lewis is the past president of several groups, such as the Cultural Alliance of Washington, Friendship House, and the United Planning Organization, and has served on the boards of trustees of Catholic University, Mount Vernon College, Group Hospitalization, the United Negro College Fund, the Capital Children's Museum, and the greater Washington Research Center. He is an honorary board member of Mainstream, a national board member of AFRICARE, and an emeritus member of the Washington Performing Arts Society. He is also on the boards of the Eugene and Agnes Meyer Foundation, the Psychiatric Institute of Washington, GEICO, and the Lincoln Theatre. He was a co-founder and chairman of the board of City National Bank.

In 1978, Lewis was named "Washingtonian of the Year" by *Washingtonian* magazine, and was awarded Catholic University's President's Medal. Also in 1978, he was appointed by District of Columbia Mayor Marion Barry, Jr., to serve as chairman of his transition committee. In 1987, Lewis was invested in the Sovereign Military Order of Malta, Federal Association,

U.S.A. In 1988, he was awarded a Doctorate of Humane Letters from Marymount University for dedicated community service. During 1988, he served as president of the Greater Washington Board of Trade, using the office to promote regional solutions to metropolitan area problems. He is also a member of the Council Against Drug Abuse, a consortium of local business leaders and medical professionals.

LEWIS, JAMES B., was born November 30, 1947, in Roswell, New Mexico. He is married to the former Armandie Johnson of Artesia, New Mexico, and is the father of four children, Terri, James, Jr., Shedra and LaRon. He received a B.S. degree in education from Bishop College, Dallas, Texas; B.S. degree in business administration from National College of Business, Albuquerque, New Mexico; and an M.A. degree in public administration from the University of New Mexico. Benefits from the G.I. Bill made it possible for him to engage in academic pursuits and consequently earn his degrees. In the November 1986 general election, he was elected state treasurer with 210,351 votes, more than any other opposed candidate, including the governor of the state of New Mexico. Prior to becoming state treasurer, he was elected Bernalillo County Treasurer in 1982, where he received more votes than any candidate on the county Democratic ticket. He was re-elected in 1984, and again he received the greatest number of votes on the Democratic ticket.

Prior to Lewis' commitment to public service, he served in the following positions: military policeman/drug education specialist in the United States Army; personnel counselor for Public Service Careers; director of administration for Public Service Careers for Bernalillo County (State Personnel); consumer advocate for Consumer Affairs

Division; investigator with White Collar Crime Section; and director of the purchasing Division of the District Attorney's Office (Second Judicial District). He has devoted much of his adult life to the belief that government should be conducted professionally and that those in public life are accountable to the people. His career accomplishments clearly evidence his professionalism in government. His driving administrative philosophy was that any public office must be conducted in an efficient, proficient and productive manner.

In adhering to this philosophy, Lewis has taken major steps toward automating and streamlining the state government general investment ledger system as well as all of the collateral, depository and custodial operations within the State Treasurer's Office. Also, in keeping with this philosophy, he has implemented a comprehensive intra- inter-agency communications system to assure maximum cooperation among all state agencies, between public entities and financial institutions, as well as many divisions within the State Treasurer's Office. During the first year following his appointment as state treasurer by Gov. Anaya, he successfully reorganized the office through his uniquely designed comprehensive administration plan to facilitate the management of human and fiscal resources. This reorganization has resulted in maximum productivity of all personnel given the current budgetary constraints.

Lewis advocates an open-door policy to familiarize New Mexico's taxpayers with all of the functions and corresponding fiscal responsibilities inherent in the duties of the state treasurer. Furthermore, he was most receptive to any ideas from anyone who will offer suggestions for improving the operations of the office. Lewis has been active in many civic, social, church, business and community organizations, some of which are: vice president, National Association of State Treasurers; president-elect, Western State Treasurers; National Association of State Treasurers; president-elect, American Society for Public Administration, New Mexico Chapter; past president, Treasurer's Affiliate New Mexico Association of Counties (two terms); and past treasurer, American Society for Public Administration New Mexico Chapter.

LEWIS, JOHN, was born February 21, 1940, in Troy, Alabama, to the son of a sharecropper. He grew up on his family's farm and attended segregated public schools in Pike County, Alabama. He received a B.A. degree in religion and philosophy from Fisk University, and was a graduate of the American Baptist Theological Seminary in Nashville, Tennessee. Elected to Congress in 1986, he represents Georgia's Fifth Congressional District. He was re-elected by an overwhelming majority to a second term in Congress in November 1988. He has displayed a sense of ethics and morality that had won him the admiration of many of his House colleagues.

At an early age, Lewis developed an unwavering commitment to the Civil Rights Movement. For more than three decades, he has been in the vanguard of progressive social movements and human rights struggles in the United States. During the height of the Civil Rights Movement from 1963 to 1966, he was chairman of the Student Nonviolent Coordinating Committee (SNCC) which was largely responsible for the sit-ins and other activities of students in the struggle for civil rights. As a student in Nashville, he joined other students to organize sit-in demonstrations at segregated lunch counters in the city. As a result of his activity as a sit-in demonstrator, he joined others to form SNCC.

In 1961, Lewis volunteered to participate in the Freedom Rides to challenge segregation at interstate bus terminals. He risked his life with other Freedom Riders and was beaten severely by mobs for participating in the rides. Despite his youth, he became a recognized leader in the civil rights movement. By 1963, he was recognized as one of the "Big Six" leaders of the movement (the other leaders were Whitney Young, A. Philip Randolph, Martin Luther King, Jr., James Farmer, and Roy Wilkins). He was one of the planners and a keynote speaker at the "March on Washington" in August 1963. In 1964, he coordinated SNCC efforts to organize voter registration drives and community action programs during the Mississippi Freedom Summer.

The following year, Lewis led demonstrators in one of the most dramatic nonviolent protests of the movement. He and fellow activist Hosea Williams led 525 marchers across the Edmund Pettus Bridge in Selma, Alabama, on March 7, 1965. Alabama state troopers attacked the marchers with billy clubs and tear gas in a confrontation that became known as "Bloody Sunday." That fateful march and a subsequent march between Selma and Montgomery led to passage of the Voting Rights Act of 1965. Despite 40 arrests, physical attacks and serious injuries, he remained a devoted advocate of the philosophy of nonviolence.

After leaving SNCC in 1966, Lewis remained active in the Civil Rights Movement through his work as a field foundation director and his participation in the Southern Regional Council's voter registration programs. He went on to become the director of the Voter Education Project (VEP). Under his leadership, the VEP transformed national politics by adding nearly 4 million minorities to the voter rolls. In 1977, he was appointed by President Jimmy Carter to direct more than 250,000 Volunteers for Action, the federal volunteer agency. In 1980, he left

Action and became community affairs director of the National Consumer Co-op bank in Atlanta.

Lewis' first taste of electoral success came in 1981 when he was elected to the Atlanta City Council. While serving on the council, he was an advocate for ethics and neighborhood preservation. He resigned from the council in June 1986 to run for Congress. In Congress, he was a member of the Public Works and Transportation Committee, the Interior and Insular Affairs Committee, and the Select Committee on Aging. He also served as an at-large majority whip in the 101st Congress. He was a member of the Congressional Coalition on Soviet Jewry and the Democratic Congressional Campaign Committee.

Since joining the Congress, Lewis has drawn much praise from political observers who had predicted a bright future for him in national politics. *The National Journal*, in a recent issue, named him as 1 of 11 "rising stars in Congress." The journal stated, "Few House members, let alone those with little seniority or clout, have had such momentous experiences before coming to Washington that other members of Congress want to hear about them. John R. Lewis, D-Ga., had that cachet, and he had made it a plus in his House service. In so doing, he also had begun to show the reasons for his earlier success."

LIPMAN, WYNONA M., was born in Georgia and achieved her higher education at Talladega College and Atlanta University. She earned a Rockefeller Grant to study at Columbia University where she received a Ph.D., and was named a Fulbright Scholar to study at the Sorbonne in Paris. She holds honorary doctorates in humane letters and law from Kean and Bloomfield colleges, respectively, and was an associate professor at Essex County College. She is the mother of

two children, Karyne, and William John, who died at the age of 24 and was commemorated in a scholarship at the Newark Community School of the Arts.

Lipman was the only woman in the all-male Senate from 1978 to 1984, and is currently the only black female member of the New Jersey Senate. She was a former Essex County Freeholder director and has served on many national and state committees. She chaired the Senate State Government Committee; served on the Senate Revenue, Finance and Appropriations Committee; was chair of the Commission on Sex Discrimination in the Statutes; served on the board of overseers of the Governor's School, and was on the New Jersey International Trade Commission. She also was a former director of the Interracial Council of Business Opportunity; a member of State Legislators; life member of the National Council of Negro Women; life member of the Newark branch of the NAACP; and was a coordinator of the New Jersey Legislative Black Caucus.

Lipman has been the recipient of numerous awards and citations. She was given a Human Rights Award from the State Division of Human Rights, and a Distinguished Service Award in State Government by the NAACP. In 1983, awards for her included a "Senator of the Year" award by the New Jersey Division of the National Association of Industrial and Office Parks and an award from the American Association of Affirmative Action. She appeared in the 1983 edition of *Who's Who Among American Women*; was recognized as one of New Jersey's most powerful women by the *New Jersey Monthly*; and was the Iron Bound Manufacturer's "Woman of the Year" in 1984.

Among the numerous awards made to Lipman in 1985–1986 are advocacy awards from the Essex-Newark Legal Services and from the Office of Minority Business Enterprise, a Service Award for Educational leadership from Essex County College; a Citation from the New Jersey Commission on Sex Discrimination in the Statutes; and the New Jersey Minority brain trust has honored her by establishing the "Wynona M. Lipman Scholarship" at the Seton Hall Graduate School of Business.

LOMAX, MICHAEL L., was born October 2, 1947, in Los Angeles, California. He is married to Cheryl and the father of one daughter, Deignan. A graduate of Morehouse College, B.A. degree (magna cum laude), English and Spanish, 1968; M.A degree (high honors), Columbia University, in English literature; Ph.D. degree, Emory University, in American and Afro-American literature. His employment background is impressive; he holds four important positions at this time: 1989 to date, serves as president and chief executive officer of Amistad Corporation, an Atlanta-based firm spe-

cializing in the acquisition and operation of funeral homes which traditionally had served the African American community; from 1979 to date, holds the position as Fulton County Commissioner; from 1981 to date, holds the position as chairman for the Board of Commissioners, Fulton County; and from 1989 to date, is visiting associate professor for Emory University.

Some of Lomax's prior positions include: associate professor of English, Spelman College; director of cultural and international affairs for the city of Atlanta; special assistant to mayor of Atlanta; assistant director, for Atlanta University Center, Summer Institute in Afro-American Studies; assistant professor of English, Morehouse; tutor in English, Yale University Harvard-Yale-Columbia Intensive Summer Studies Program; and inter-reporter for *The Washington Post*.

Lomax is the recipient of many scholarships, honors and awards: Morehouse College, Charles E. Merrill Early Admission Scholarship; Phi Beta Kappa; Columbia University Graduate Fellowship; UNCF, IBM Faculty fellow; UNCF, Lily Faculty Doctoral Fellowship; Emory, NEH Doctoral Fellowship; Southern Fellowship Fund Doctoral Fellowship; Five Outstanding Young Men of Atlanta; SCLU of Georgia, Freedom of Speech Award; Bronze Jubilee Award for Outstanding Service to the Arts; Rockefeller Fellow of the Aspen Institute for Humanistic studies; *US* magazine, 35 Most Promising Young Adults Under 35; Leadership Atlanta; Leadership Georgia; participant, Aspen Institute Tradition and Change Seminar U.S.A.; Past Present and Future and participant, United States/United Kingdom Successor Generation (Oxford, U.K., 1985).

Lomax is the publisher of *Countee Cullen: A Key to the Puzzle*, and *Fantasies of Affirmation: The 1920s Novel of Negro Life*. His professional affiliations include: chairman, Fulton County

Development Authority; Fulton County Board of Health; Delta of Georgia Chapter, United Chapters of Phi Beta Kappa; chairman and founder, National Black Arts Festival; board of trustees, Atlanta-Fulton County Public Library; board of Atlanta Regional Commission; chairman, Environmental Committee; member, Executive Committee; member, Transportation Committee; board of directors, Atlanta Convention and Visitors Bureau, the Atlanta Botanical Garden, Inc.; board of trustees, Atlanta Historical Society, the Studio Museum in Harlem, School of Advanced International Studies, Johns Hopkins University; Kappa Boule, Sigma Pi Phi Fraternity, Emory University Museum Visiting Committee; vice chairman, Democratic Leadership Council, Democratic Leadership Council; Schomburg Commission for the Preservation of Black Culture and Commission of the National Museum of African Art, Smithsonian Institution.

LOVELACE, GLORIA E., is the mother of one son, Jabrie. She holds a B.S. degree from Virginia State University, Petersburg, Virginia, and an M.S. degree from the University of Illinois, Champaign-Urbana, Illinois. She is the former owner and operator of Preston Highlands Day School, Dallas, Texas. She is director, Human Resources Eastern Business Market Group, US Sprint, located in Reston, Virginia. As director, her responsibilities are to oversee an annual budget of $1,804,000 and approximately 2,000 personnel spanning the East Coast from Maine to Florida, and west to Louisiana and Tennessee. She also directs a staff of 18 while ensuring the short- and long-term growth of the company through effective acquisition, maintenance and development of human resources. Effective policy implementation and interpretation to provide a productive, positive, fair work environment was a major focus. Additionally, training, compensation, benefits, and employee relations programs are provided to employees.

Under Lovelace's direction, all Human Resources issues impacting the region receive priority attention. Guidance was supplied to management on concerns surrounding the company's most important asset, people. Prior to joining US Sprint, she served as director, personnel for the National Captioning Institute, a nonprofit corporation specializing in captioning television programming and video tapes for the hearing impaired, non–English-speaking, the elderly, and children. Located in Falls Church, Virginia, she was responsible for developing and implementing a full range of personnel programs and policies, and providing advice and counsel to senior management and staff there, and in New York and California.

Before that, Lovelace was owner of General Business Services, a Washington, D.C.–based full-service business counseling company, where she developed comprehensive programs custom tailored for each business to develop their profits; to organize, simplify and improve their record keeping; establish financial goals; and develop tax planning and tax saving methods. She also served as senior vice president of human resources of Old Stone Bank, Providence, Rhode Island, a $6 billion thrift holding company. Her responsibilities included staffing and development, compensation, salary and benefit administration, personnel policy development and administration, personnel management information systems, employee relations, charitable foundation, and EEO and affirmative action.

Lovelace supervised the personnel component of a $135 million savings and loan acquisition which represented a 7 percent increase in the employee population, and was successful in retaining and placing 100 percent of the acquired employees within the parent. While with Xerox Corporation, Office Products Division, Dallas, she served as manager of human resources and manager compensation, affirmative action, safety/security and health services. In Chicago, she served as Midwest Region personnel manager, where the region ranked first in human resource management. She has also held positions at Xerox as personnel relations manager for the Information Systems Group, Rochester, New York, and in administration/control in the mid–Atlantic Region in Rosslyn, Virginia.

Prior to joining Xerox, Lovelace was employed as marketing systems coordinator, Scovill Manufacturing Company, Waterbury, Connecticut, and assistant director, Pearl Street Neighborhood House, Waterbury. She has taught school in Connecticut, West Berlin, Germany, and Washington, D.C. She belongs to numerous civic organizations, and other professional organizations. She has been a frequent speaker at schools, organizations, and conferences. She has had a collection of poems published, and a thesis entitled "Responses of Educable Mentally Handicapped Children and Normal Children to a Unique Plaything."

LOWERY, JOSEPH E., was born October 6, 1924, in Huntsville, Alabama. He married the former Evelyn Gibson and they have three children, Yvonne, Karen, and Cheryl. He was educated at Clark College; Knoxville College; Alabama Agricultural and Mechanical College; Paine College and Paint Theological Seminary; Wayne State University; Garrett Theological Seminary; and the Chicago Ecumenical Institute. Before entering the ministry of the United Methodist Church, he was editor of the small black Birmingham, Alabama, newspaper the *Informer* (now the *Mirror*). After his ordination, he was pastor of the Warren Street United Methodist Church in Mobile, Alabama, for nine years beginning in 1952. From Mobile he went to Nashville, Tennessee, as administrative assistant to the United Methodist bishop there. After three years in Nashville, he became pastor of St. Paul's United Methodist Church in Birmingham.

In 1968, Lowery assumed the position as pastor of the Central United Methodist Church in Atlanta. In 1967, he was a co-founder and vice president of SCLC under Dr. Martin Luther King, Jr., and a member of the National Board of Directors of SCLC. In 1977, he was elected national president of SCLC. In 1986, he assumed the position as pastor of Cascade United Methodist Church, in Atlanta. As president of SCLC, he has taken a new course, adapting its strategy and tactics to changing time. "Now the struggle is on the cash register side of the lunch counter. All black people have won the right to check into the Hilton and Hyatt Regency hotels, but few blacks have the means of checking out. That's why we're going to have to wrestle with real, basic systemic changes."

In 1990, speaking on young

blacks, the Rev. Lowery stated, "We at SCLC are trying to get them before their heads hit that ceiling and to have their heads screwed on right so they will be able to join in an organized effort to remove that ceiling. Toward that end, we are challenging Afro Americans to embrace Liberation Lifestyles, a program that would make us free at last, not in death but in this life. Liberation Lifestyles grew out of my fear that we are falling victim to the assault from without by our fault from within. Liberation Lifestyles compels us to seize the initiative, to reclaim the values of the past which helped us through the stormy and turbulent waters of racism, and would now do it again."

The Rev. Lowery is the recipient of numerous honors and awards which include: awards from the National Conference of Black Mayors, Medal of Honor Moscow Theological Seminary, twice named Citizen of the Year, OEO Award Atlanta Urban League, honoree 1985 Religion Award for accomplishments as pastor of Central United Methodist Church, and for leadership as National President of the Southern Christian Leadership Conference.

LOWRY, JAMES H., was born on May 28, 1939, and grew up on Chicago's south side. After graduating from Francis Parker High School, he earned a B.A. degree in political science from Grinnell College (Iowa) in 1961. The following year, he received a Grinnell Travel Fellowship and became a volunteer instructor of business and political leaders in Dar-es-Salaam, Tanzania. He then served in the U.S. Peace Corps for five years, as director of program training in Arecibo, Puerto Rico, and as associate director of economic and community development projects in Lima, Peru. As a John Hay Whitney Fellow, he attended the University of Pittsburgh, where he received an M.A. degree in

international economics in 1965. He was then appointed special assistant to the president at Bedford-Stuyvesant Restoration Corporation of New York City by the late Senator Robert Kennedy.

Lowry spent the next eight years as a management consultant and director of the Chicago public sector practice at McKinsey & Company, Inc. While associated with McKinsey, he attended the Harvard Graduate School of Business Administration and was elected president of his Program for Management Development class in 1973. In 1975, he founded James H. Lowry and Associates, headquartered in Chicago. Today the firm employs a staff of 25 people. Lowry, president and chief executive officer of the firm, is a recognized authority on small business development, management, human resource development, and education.

Lowry has twice been named one of the country's Outstanding Young Men, and is listed in *Who's Who in the Midwest* and *Men of Achievement*. He is a member of the Harvard University Visiting Committee and is a trustee of both Northwestern Memorial Hospital and Grinnell College. He is the immediate past president of the Chicago Public Library board of directors and is on the board of the Academy, the Goodman Theater, Partners in International Education and Training, Independence Bank and Johnson Products, Inc. He is a principal of Chicago United and a member of various professional and civic organizations, including the Institute of Management Consultants, the Economic Club of Chicago, the University Club, the Chicago Council on Foreign Relations, the Japan-American Society, and the advisory committee of Kellogg School of Management (Northwestern University).

LYGHT, JOHN RICHARD, was born October 1, 1927, in the township of Lutsen, Cook County, Minnesota, and has lived in Cook County most of his life. He married the former Anne Matage of Thunder Bay, Ontario, Canada. They have three children and six grandchildren. He was appointed sheriff in 1972. In 1974, he was elected to the office, winning 93 percent of the vote. In 1978, he was re-elected with 97.4 percent of the vote. He is the first black sheriff of Grand Marais, Cook County.

Lyght easily has the most popular black family in Cook County because his family members are the only blacks among the county's 4,200 residents. Most of the residents are of Scandinavian descent. He did not have a murder there his first eight years in office. "We keep a pretty tight ship," he says. While his three children have grown, married and left the area, Lyght and his wife Anne plan to stay. "The way I feel now, I'm in great shape and I'll keep on serving until they vote me out. And with 97 percent of the vote last time, I don't think they'll do that too soon." He served in the United States Air Force, and received an honorable discharge from Colonel B. O. Davis of Lockborne Air Base, Columbus, Ohio.

McCALL, JAMES FRANKLIN, was born on June 25, 1934, Philadel-

phia, Pennsylvania. He received a B.S. degree in economics from the University of Pennsylvania, and an M.B.A in comptrollership from Syracuse University. He entered the United States Army in March of 1958, and became a platoon leader, Company A, 12th Battalion, 4th Training Regiment, United States Army Training Center, Fort Knox, Kentucky. From December 1958

to August 1959, he was the commander of Company A, 12th Battalion, 4th Training Regiment, United States Army Training Center. From August 1959 to March 1960, he was an instructor in the 12th Battalion, 4th Training Regiment. On September 4, 1959, he was promoted to the rank of first lieutenant. From March 1960 to June 1961, he was a platoon leader, Combat Support Company, 1st Battle Group, 7th Cavalry, United States Army in Europe.

From June 1962 to January 1963, he served as assistant S-2, 1st Battle Group, 3rd Infantry, Fort Myer, Virginia. He was promoted to the rank of captain on September 4, 1962. From January 1963 to June 1963, he was the commander of Company C, 1st Battle Group, 3rd Infantry, Fort Myer. From August 1963 to July 1964, he was a student, Infantry Officer Advanced Course, later Ranger Course, United States Infantry School, Fort Benning, Georgia. From July 1964 to October 1965, he served as the S-2, 2d Battalion, 6th Infantry, Berlin Brigade, United States Army in Europe. From November 1965 to April 1966, he served as secretary of the General Staff, Headquarters, Berlin Brigade, United States Army in Europe.

From June 1966 to November 1966, McCall was the commander of Company M, 4th Battalion, 2d Basic Training Brigade, Fort Dix, New Jersey. He was promoted to the rank of major on November 23, 1966. From April 1967 to May 1968, he served as an advisor on Advisory Team 96, United States Military Assistance Command, in Vietnam. From May 1968 to May 1969, he was a student at the United States Command and General Staff College, Fort Leavenworth, Kansas. From August 1970 to July 1973, he served as a military assistant in the Office of the Assistant Secretary of the Army (Financial Management), Washington, D.C. He was promoted to the rank of lieutenant colonel on November 9, 1971.

From August 1973 to August 1974, he was the commander of the 1st Battalion, 31st Infantry, 2d Infantry Division, in Korea. From September 1974 to August 1975, he served as a staff officer with the Army Materiel Acquisition Review Committee–Armament, United States Materiel Command, Alexandria, Virginia. From August 1975 to June 1976, he was a student at Industrial College of the Armed Forces, Fort Lesley J. McNair, Washington. On February 1, 1976, he was promoted to the rank of colonel. From June 1976 to June 1977, he served as executive in the Office of the Director of the Army Budget, Office, Comptroller of the Army, Washington. From July 1977 to April 1979, he was the commander of the 4th Training Brigade, United States Army Armor School, Fort Knox, Kentucky.

From June 1979 to July 1980, McCall served as the chief of the Procurement Programs and Budget Division, Materiel Plans and Programs Directorate, Office of the Deputy Chief of Staff for Research, Development, and Acquisition, United States Army, Washington. He was promoted to the one-star rank of brigadier general on March 1, 1980. From July 1980 to June 1984, he served as the Comptroller of the United States Army Materiel Development and Readiness Command, Alexandria. He was promoted to the two-star rank of major general on September 1, 1983. From June 1984 to July 1988, he served as the director of the Army Budget, Office of the Comptroller, United States Army, Washington.

On July 1, 1988, he was promoted to the three-star rank of lieutenant general. In July 1988, he was assigned as Comptroller of the Army, Office of the Secretary of the Army, Washington. Gen. McCall has received numerous awards, decorations and badges which include: the Parachutist Badge; the Distinguished Service Medal; Legion of Merit (with oak leaf cluster); the Meritorious Service Medal; the Air Medals; Army Commendation Medal (with oak leaf cluster); and the Combat Infantryman Badge.

McCLURE, FREDERICK D., was born in San Augustine, Texas, but presently lives in Falls Church, Virginia, with his wife, the former Harriet Jackson of Pleasanton, Texas, and their two children, Lauren and Frederick, Jr. He received his B.S. degree in agricultural economics from Texas A&M University in 1976, graduating summa cum laude. While at Texas A&M, he served as student body president, was elected to Phi Kappa Phi, was a member of the Singing Cadets, and received the Brown-Rudder Outstanding Student Award. After graduating, he served as a member of the Target 2000 Committee and as vice president of the Texas A&M University Association of Former Students. He is president of the National Capital A&M Club in Washington, D.C.

McClure received his J.D. degree in 1981 from the Baylor University

School of Law, where he was elected president of the Student Bar Association and was a member of the National Order of Barristers. He was also a director of the National Fraternity of Alpha Zeta. Prior to entering law school, he served as agricultural assistant and state office director for Senator Tower. In 1976, former President Gerald R. Ford appointed him as a White House intern. He was appointed by President Bush in January 1989, and served as government affairs staff vice president of Texas Air Corporation. He joined Texas Air in November 1986 after serving as special assistant to President Reagan for Legislative Affairs.

McClure had also served as Associate Deputy Attorney General of the United States and as legislative director to former U.S. Senator John Tower of Texas. Before joining Sen. Tower's staff, he was a trial attorney

with the Houston firm of Reynolds, Allen and Cook. A former national secretary and Texas state president of the Future Farmers of America, he was appointed by former Texas Governor Dolph Briscoe to the State Advisory Council for Technical-Vocational Education and has served as a member of the Real Estate Research Advisory Committee for the state of Texas since his appointment by Texas Governor William P. Clements in 1979. He is a member of the American Council on Germany, and the Alpha Gamma Rho Fraternity.

McCOLLUM, ALICE O., a graduate of Hillside High School (valedictorian) in Durham, North Carolina, she received a B.A. degree in mathematics from the University of North Carolina at Greensboro; a J.D. degree from the University of Cincinnati, College of Law, Cincinnati, Ohio, and attended the National Judicial College, University of Nedada, Reno, where she took courses in general jurisdiction and search and seizure. She was admitted to the Ohio state bar in 1972, the Michigan state bar in 1974, and accompanying federal bars. She has served since 1979 as judge, Dayton Municipal Court; presiding judge, 1984–1986; administrative judge, 1983–1984. She is also an adjunct professor for the University of Dayton, College of Law.

McCollum's prior positions include: 1976 to 1979, assistant director of clinical legal studies, and assistant professor of law, University of Dayton School of Law; hearing examiner for the Ohio Civil Rights Commission, 1978–1979, and from 1974–1975, served as codirector of the Legal Aid Society of Dayton. She was appointed the first woman on the Dayton Municipal Court by Governor James A. Rhodes, in February 1979, and was the first woman elected to the Dayton Municipal Court, in November, 1979.

McCollum is the recipient of the

Outstanding Black Woman Award of 1979 from Sinclair Community College, Student Government; Woman of the Year, 1980, from Iota Beta Lambda Sorority; Woman of the Year, 1983, from Metropolitan Civic Women; Salute to Career Women Special Achievement Award, in 1983, from the YWCA; Unique Woman of the Year, 1985, from Unique Study Club; and recipient of the Supreme Court of Ohio Superior Judicial Award and Excellent Judicial Award from 1979 to the present. She was a contributing author to A. J. Giannini and R. L. Gilliland, *The Neurologic, Neurogenic, and Neuropsychiatric Disorders Handbook* (1982).

McCOY, GLADYS, was born in Atlanta, Georgia. She married William McCoy and is the mother of seven children, Krista, William, Paul, Mary, Cecila, Peter and Martha. She attended Talladega College in Alabama and earned a bachelor's degree in sociology with a minor in economics. In 1965, she enrolled at Portland State University and received a master's degree in social work. In 1970, she received her ACSW (Academy of Certified Social Workers) certificate in mental health. McCoy serves over Multnomah County, Portland, Oregon, in the role of county chair, a position to which she was elected in 1986. As county chair, she not only administers the government as the County Executive, she also sits as chair of the five-member Board of County Commissioners.

In 1975, she accepted a three-year appointment from the governor as State of Oregon Ombudsman. In 1978, she was elected to a four-year term as Multnomah County Commissioner, the first black to serve in this capacity. She won re-election to this post in 1982. She directed social services for Project Head State in the Vancouver school system in 1967. This position gave her an opportunity to demonstrate how effectively and efficiently her management style complemented the work place. She developed, implemented and coordinated parent services and training as well as coordinated social services for children. The excellent results she achieved in that position prompted friends and associates to encourage her to enter her first race for public office.

In 1970, she was elected to the Portland School Board where she served two four-year terms. During this period, 1970–1974, she also taught undergraduate sociology and social work courses at Clark College in Vancouver; Pacific University, Forest Grove, Oregon; Portland Community College, and a term at International College of Cayman Isle, British West Indies.

She continues to be active on boards and councils on a local, state and national level. She consistently participated in all levels of continuing education. As an example, she established a model for the provision of human and justice services within Columbia Villa, a housing project in North Portland. Social service agencies had been brought directly into the neighborhood which has resulted in increased job referrals, reduced vulnerability of at-risk youth, and the provision of recreational and educational opportunities for residents. The Villa project has revitalized living conditions, enhanced the potential of citizens, and substantially reduced the presence of drug and gang-related crime within Columbia Villa.

McCoy has been the recipient of numerous honors, prizes and awards, including the Oregon Mother of the Year, the Oregon Assembly for Black Affairs Political Development Award, and the Central City Concern Community Award, to name a few. To McCoy, her accomplishments have been no more than an ordinary way of life.

McCOY, WILLIAM, married to Gladys McCoy, is the father of seven children, Krista, William, Paul, Mary, Cecilia, Peter and Martha. He is a graduate of the University of Portland with a B.A. degree in business administration and political science; University of Oregon, graduate work in public administration; University of Southern California, graduate work in gerontology, and the University of Portland, honorary doctorate.

McCoy serves as a state senator for the Democratic 8th District. His Democratic Party experience includes: a lifelong Democrat; National Democratic Committee person, 1976–1980; chairperson of the Multnomah County Democratic Central Committee, 1968–1972; precinct conditioners, 1948–1984. He supported health care programs and practices which are affordable and could meet the wide variety of individual needs; and senior citizens' issues of concern. The fact that jobs are the #1 concern of most Oregonians, is why he has devoted so much time and energy to keeping and bringing new business and industry to District 8. McCoy is recognized as one of Oregon's leading environment legislators, and strongly encourages alternative resources development and conservation by governments and individuals.

McCULLOUGH, GEORGE W., JR., was born May 18, 1950, is married and the father of two children. He is a graduate of Indiana University at South Bend, Indiana, B.S. degree in secondary education, sociology-political science, and M.S. degree in counseling and guidance. He has served as guidance counselor and head football coach for Washington High School in South Bend from 1980. Prior positions include: consultant, A.C.T.I.O.N., Inc., programming and planning department; career counselor/teacher, Upward Bound Program, Center for Educational Opportunity, University of Notre Dame; teacher in the social science department, Washington High School, South Bend, and assistant varsity football defensive coordinator; teacher, Upward Bound Program, Department of Urban Studies, University of Notre Dame; coordinator, C.E.T.A. Summer Youth Employment Program, Department of Human Resources and Economic Development; teacher/coach, social science department, Riley High School, South Bend.

McCullough has also been coordinator of school service programs and counselor, Outreach, Youth Services Bureau, Department of Public Safety, South Bend; and playground director and program supervisor of structural recreational activities, South Bend Recreation Department.

He is the recipient of many honors and awards, which include the following: Outstanding Citizens Award, presented by the mayor of South Bend; Outstanding Service to the Community Award, South Bend's Solidarity Committee; chosen by Washington High School student body as one of the Outstanding Teachers on the staff, and chosen by the I.U. Foundation as one of the Most Outstanding Students at Indiana University. His professional community activities and affiliations are numerous.

McHENRY, DONALD F., was born October 13, 1936, in St. Louis, Missouri, and grew up in an impoverished black neighborhood in East St. Louis, Illinois. He is the son of Limas and Dora Lee (Brooks) McHenry. At Lincoln Senior High School in East St. Louis, he was president of the civics club and a member of the honor society, the student council, the Latin club, the library guild, the staff of the newspaper, and the choir. After graduating, he entered Illinois State University, where he took part in debate, became involved in civil rights,

and organized a chapter of the NAACP. He received a B.S. degree in 1957 and an M.S. degree in 1959. He then moved to Washington, D.C., where he served until 1962 as an instructor of English at Howard University and undertook graduate studies in international relations at Georgetown University.

In 1963, he joined the Department of State and served from 1963 to 1966 as a foreign affairs officer in the Dependent Areas Section of the Office of United Nations Political Affairs; and from 1965 to 1968 he was the officer in charge of that section. In 1966, he was a consultant to the United States Congressional delegation to the Inter-Parliamentary Union. After a stint as assistant to the secretary of state in 1968–1969, he became special assistant to the counselor of the Department of State. In 1971, he took a leave of absence from the state department, and in 1973 he resigned.

From 1971 to 1973, McHenry was a guest scholar at the Brookings Institution, an international affairs fellow to the Council on Foreign Relations, and a lecturer at American University in 1975. In early 1977, at the request of Andrew Young, the new ambassador to the United Nations, President Carter named McHenry Deputy Representative in the United Nations Security Council. On August 31, 1979, President Carter announced that McHenry would replace Young as the American Permanent Representative to the United Nations and Representative in the Security Council.

McHenry's reputation as an experienced diplomat, highly regarded at the state department, made him an obvious possibility as a successor to Young, who resigned August 15, 1979. McHenry had performed many of the duties of the chief delegate during Young's frequent trips abroad on diplomatic missions or in the United States on behalf of the Democratic Party. The divorced father of three was little known by the public until he was thrust into his new United Nations post.

---

†McKISSICK, FLOYD BIXLER, SR., was born on March 9, 1922, in Asheville, North Carolina. He married the former Evelyn Williams, and they had four children, Joycelyn, Andree, Floyd, Jr., and Charmaine. He attended Morehouse College in 1949, the University of North Carolina in 1951, before receiving an A.B. degree from North Carolina Central University in 1951. He received a law degree from North Carolina Central in 1952. He was admitted to the North Carolina bar in 1952, then the United States Supreme Court bar in 1955. After serving as an Army sergeant during World War II, he sued to gain admission to the University of North Carolina at Chapel Hill Law School in 1951. A federal appeals court ordered him admitted. He was represented in the case by Thurgood Marshall, the former Supreme Court Justice.

From 1960 to 1968, he served as counsel to the Congress of Racial Equality (CORE). From 1957 to 1966, he was in private law practice as a partner in McKissick & Bertry, Attorneys. During the 1963 March on Washington, D.C., McKissick, then a vice-president of CORE, shared the podium with Martin Luther King, Jr., and others during a historic rally at the Lincoln Memorial. He represented CORE that day because its president, James Farmer, was in jail for civil disobedience.

From 1968 to 1974, he served as president of Floyd B. McKissick Enterprises Inc., and from 1974 to 1980, he served as president of the Soul City Co. It was around 1979 that he was ordained a gospel minister, and also switched to the Republican Party. He capped his legal career in 1990 when he was appointed a North Carolina district judge by Governor Jim Martin.

Judge McKissick had been unable to hold court for several months because of illness. He died of cancer on April 28, 1991, and he was buried at his Soul City project in Warren County, North Carolina. He served numerous organizations, which include: CORE; co-chairman of the National Conference of Black Lawyers; United States Commission on Civil Rights Advisory Committee; founder of the National Association of Black Manufacturers; co-founder of the North Carolina Center for the Study of Black History; and a life member, NAACP. He received numerous awards and honors which include the Man of the Year Award in Durham and the Ike Smalls Civil Rights award, NAACP.

---

†McNAIR, RONALD, was born October 12, 1950, in Lake City, South Carolina. He married Cheryl Moore of Jamaica, New York, and they had two children, Reginald and Joy. His mother taught elementary school and his father worked as an auto body repairman. Growing up in a small southern town in the waning days of Jim Crow segregation, he learned early how to maneuver around racial discrimination. "It means trying a little harder, fighting a little harder to get what you perhaps deserve," he once told an interviewer. "It means building up a tolerance and not being discouraged by some of the obstacles that get put in front of you." McNair graduated from Carver High School in 1967; received a B.S. degree in physics (magna cum laude) from North Carolina A&T University in 1971; and earned his Ph.D. degree in physics from the Massachusetts Institute of Technology in 1976. He did research in laser physics while at MIT and at the École d'été Théorique de Physique at Les Houches, France. In 1976, he joined the Hughes Research Laboratories in Malibu, California, and was a scientist there when chosen by NASA. He was one of the 35 astronauts selected by NASA in January 1978.

use the manned maneuvering unit. He had been the second black American astronaut in space.

In August 1979, McNair completed a training and evaluation course that qualified him as a shuttle mission specialist. He worked at the Shuttle Avionics Integration Laboratory and was assigned to STS-11 (later Mission 41-B) in February 1983. He also served as a capcom for flights 41-G and 51-A in October and November 1984. He was the author or co-author of several technical papers. He also held a black belt in karate along with 30 trophies he had won in competitions and was probably the first person to have played a saxophone in orbit.

He was one of the seven space travelers killed in the explosion of the shuttle *Challenger* on January 28, 1986. During the planned six-day flight, mission specialist McNair was to have operated the Spartan scientific package during observations of Halley's Comet. McNair was also mission specialist aboard Mission 41-B in February 1984. During that eight-day flight he took part in the deployment of two communications satellites, and also operated the *Challenger*'s remote manipulator arm during the first space walks to

McPHAIL, IRVING PRESSLEY, a native of New York City, is the father of one daughter, Kamilah Carole. He received his B.A. degree in sociology at Cornell University in 1970, an M.A.T. degree in reading/language arts at the University of Pennsylvania in 1976. He was awarded academic scholarships at Cornell and Harvard and was a National Fellowships Fund Fellow at the University of Pennsylvania. He was named the seventh president of LeMoyne-Owen College in May 1987 and assumed his position on July 6, 1987. He came to LeMoyne-Owen College from Delaware State College in Dover, Delaware, where he was vice president and dean of Academic Affairs and professor of education.

McPhail had previously been a faculty member and or academic administrator at Morgan State University, the University of Maryland at College Park, and the University of Pennsylvania. He had also served as a research scientist and as chief operating officer of the Baltimore city public schools. He was an American Council on Education Fellow in Academic Administration at the Johns Hopkins University in 1978–1979. He completed the Harvard University Institute for Educational Management (IEM) in summer 1988.

McPhail is the recipient of numerous honors and awards, and has earned a national reputation for his research in test-wiseness, effective urban schools, sociolinguistics and reading, and his test-wiseness curriculum. He has published more than 25 referred journal articles, book chapters and monographs on issues in testing and literacy development of black children, youth and adults. He was selected by the United States Jaycees as one of America's Ten Outstanding Young Men for 1982 for his contributions to equal educational opportunity.

Active in his profession, McPhail was co-founder and past president of the National Association of Black Reading and Language Educators, a member of the Affirmative Action Advisory Group of the International Reading Association, and a member of the Advisory Committee on Testing of the NAACP; president of Kamilah Educational Enterprises, a national consulting and publishing firm dedicated to the improvement of black education. He served on the advisory board of Memphis Partners, Inc., and on the board of directors of the American Cancer Society, Memphis/Shelby County Unit; National Association for Equal Opportunity in Higher Education (NAFEO), Methodist Hospitals Foundation, Amistad Research Center, and Free the Children Corporation.

McPhail also served on the Executive Committees of the Harvard/Radcliffe Alumni(ae) Against Apartheid, Council for Higher Education of the United Church of Christ, and Council of Fellows of the American Council on Education. He was co-

chairman of the Education Committee of the Free the Children Corporation, a member of the Memphis Rotary Club, and a member of the Alpha Delta Lambda Chapter of Alpha Phi Alpha Fraternity, Inc. He is listed in *Who's Who Among Black Americans* and *Men of Achievement.*

MAIR, JOY, was born in Jamaica and immigrated to the United States at the age of 11. She graduated from grade and high school in St. Louis, Missouri. She earned undergraduate and master's degrees in business from the Wharton School of Finance and Commerce, University of Pennsylvania. Mair is currently vice president at the Chase Manhattan Bank in New York City. She was previously vice president at Bankers Trust Company. Her entire 10-year career has been in banking.

MALLORY, WILLIAM L., was born in Cincinnati, Ohio. A former high school drop-out, he received his diploma, graduated with honors, and became the recipient of the honorary doctorate of law degree from Central State University in Wilberforce, Ohio. He was elected to the majority floor leader position in 1974. As representative for the people of the 23rd House District of Cincinnati, he held the leadership position of the Speaker of the Ohio House of Representatives. A member of the National Conference of State Legislatures, he has also served on a national level as vice-chairman of the State Federal Assembly, and chairman of the National Housing Task Force of NCSL.

In his years of service, Mallory has sponsored and co-sponsored over 600 pieces of legislation. One of five has been enacted into law. His major areas of concentration are senior citizens, education, the homeless, jobs for Ohioans, drug prevention, mental health, utilities, finance, and transportation. The Ohio Commission on Aging, renamed Department of Aging in 1986, was established through legislation principally sponsored by him.

Mallory also sponsored legislation that would provide free college tuition to low- and moderate-income students if they study math or science, maintain a 2.5 grade point average, and agree to stay in Ohio to work for four years after graduation. Substitute House Bill

780 was unanimously approved by the House of Representatives. As majority leader, Mallory was also a member of important committees of the House. Committee work was important to the functioning of the legislature. He is often called upon to speak to groups on behalf of the House Leadership.

MANLEY, AUDREY FORBES, was born March 25, 1934, in Jacksonville, Mississippi. She is married to Albert Manley, former president emeri-

tus of Spelman College. She received a B.A. degree from Spelman College in Atlanta, in 1955; an M.D. degree from Meharry Medical College in Nashville, Tennessee, in 1959; and an M.P.H. degree from Johns Hopkins University, School of Hygiene and Public Health, Baltimore, Maryland, in 1987. She took residency in the pediatrics department at Cook County Children's Hospital and received additional training in neonatology at the Abraham Lincoln School of Medicine, University of Illinois. She was appointed deputy assistant secretary, Department of Health and Human Services, on May 5, 1989, by HHS Secretary Louis W. Sullivan, M.D.

As deputy assistant secretary for Health, Manley is the principal advisor and assistant to James O. Mason, M.D., Dr. P.H., the assistant secretary for Health, and shares with him the responsibility of directing the U.S. Public Health Service. The Public Health Service includes the Alcohol, Drug Abuse and Mental Health Administration (ADAMHA); the Centers for Disease Control (CDC); the Food and Drug Administration (FDA); the Health Resources and Services Ad-

ministration (HRSA); the Indian Health Service (IHS); the National Institutes of Health (NIH); and the Agency for Toxic Substances and Disease Registry (ATSDR).

Before assuming her present duties, Manley was director of the National Health Service Corps, HRSA component that delivers primary care to medically under-served communities throughout the country. Prior to that, she was HRSA's chief medical officer and deputy associate administrator for planning, evaluation and legislation. She joined the public health service in 1976. In 1962, she was the first African American woman to be named chief resident of Cook County's 500-bed Children's Hospital and, in 1988, was the first to achieve the rank of assistant surgeon general in the U.S. Public Health Service. She is the first woman to be named to the post she now holds. She had held adjunct or associate positions at the University of California at San Francisco, Howard University in Washington, D.C., and the Uniformed Services University of Health Services in Bethesda, Maryland.

Dr. Manley is a member of numerous professional and community organizations, including the American Academy of Pediatrics, the American Public Health Association, and the Institute of Medicine of the National Academy of Sciences. She was licensed with the state medical board of Georgia (written), 1959; state medical board of Illinois (oral and practical), 1961; state medical board of California (oral), 1969; and medical board of the District of Columbia (reciprocity), 1977. She is the recipient of numerous awards and honors, and professional affiliations.

MARBURY, CARL HARRIS, was born March 24, 1935, in Leeds, Alabama. He graduated magna cum laude with a B.S. degree from Alabama Agricultural and Mechanical University; obtained M.A. and B.D. degrees from Oberlin College; an M.Div. degree from Vanderbilt; and received a Ph.D. degree from Harvard University. Prior to coming to Alabama A&M University, he was assistant director for instructional programs for the Alabama Commission on Higher Education.

Additionally, he previously served as vice president/dean of college, Stillman College, Tuscaloosa, Alabama; vice president for academic affairs and coordinator of joint Garrett-Northwestern graduate programs, Garrett-Evangelical Theological Seminary and Northwestern University, Evanston, Illinois; academic dean and professor of Garrett-Evangelical Theological Seminary, Evanston; associate professor of New Testament Interpretation, Garrett-Evangelical Theological Seminary; director, The Center for Research, Information and Technical Assistance (CRITA), Institute for Services to Education, Washington, D.C.; director, Institutional Research, AAMU; professor and dean, School of Library Media, AAMU: lecturer in philosophy (part-time), University of Alabama at Birmingham; associate professor of philosophy, AAMU; teaching fellow in Greek, theology and biblical studies, Oberlin College; traveling research fellow to Europe (France, Germany, Switzerland, Great Britain), and the Middle East (Lebanon, Jordan, Israel, Greece); teaching fellow at Harvard; instructor of Classical Greek Studies, Language and Literature, Concord Academy; and faculty researcher for Meiron Archaeological Project: Meiron, Israel, Garrett-Evangelical, Northwestern and Duke University.

Marbury has written numerous publications, monographs and study reports on a variety of educational issues and subjects. He is proficient in the scholarly reading and use of Greek, Hebrew, Latin, Aramaic, Ethiopic, Syriac, German and French. His

studies and research seminars have taken him to France, Germany, Great Britain, Norway, Switzerland, Greece, Lebanon, Syria, Jordan and Israel. Moreover, he serves as a consultant in higher education to numerous institutions, educational agencies and foundations, and is a sought-after speaker for churches, conferences, workshops, etc.

Marbury's achievements have been recognized through meritorious awards and citations from numerous professional and civic organizations. He has been selected to appear in: *Outstanding Young Men of America; Who's Who in the South and Southwest; Personalities of the South; Outstanding Educators of America; Alabama's Distinguished;* and *Who's Who in Religion.* Moreover, he was given a Service/Dedication Award in 1988 by the Nu Epsilon Chapter of Omega Psi Phi; the Meritorious Service Award by the Alabama Cooperative Service Employees Organization in 1989; and a Dedication, Commitment, Outstanding Service Award by the Pasadena Chapter of the Alabama A&M University National Alumni Normalite Association in 1989.

Extremely active in civic and professional organizations, Marbury has held membership and or leadership roles in numerous organizations and many boards, including Alabama Humanities Foundation, Alabama League for the Advancement of Education, Montgomery Council for the Aging, Alabama Historical Records Advisory Council, Montgomery National Issues Forum, Alabama Initiative for Recruitment and Retention (Black Students in Higher Education), Alabama Black Historical Association, UNICEF of the United Nations, National Alumni Normalite Association, Association for Educational and Professional Opportunities Foundation (AEPO), Kappa Alpha Psi Fraternity, National Education Association, Society for the Study of Religion, Society of Biblical Literature, American Association for Higher Education, The Society for Religion in Higher Education, Ecumenical Center for Stewardship Studies of the National Council of the Churches in the USA, NAACP and life member of Tuscaloosa Chapter, Mayor's Advisory Committee on the Handicapped and the Elderly (Tuscaloosa), and Kiwanis Club of Tuscaloosa.

Dr. Marbury is an academician, a patron of the arts and a staunch supporter of charitable organizations. At AAMU, he launched a strategic plan designed to move the institution toward university greatness in the year 2000.

MARSHALL, THURGOOD, was born July 2, 1908, in Baltimore, Maryland, the son of William C. and Norma A. Marshall. In 1929, he married Vivian Burey, who died in February 1955. On December 17, 1955, he married Cecila A. Suyat. They had two children, Thurgood, Jr., and John William, and made their home in Virginia. He attended public schools in Baltimore, graduating with honors from Lincoln University in 1930, where he had first gone with the intention of becoming a dentist. His aims changed to law and he graduated, in 1933, at the head of his class, from Howard University Law School in Washington. He has received numerous honorary LL.B. degrees.

Upon graduation, Marshall entered the private practice of law in Baltimore and, in 1934, became counsel for the Baltimore branch of the NAACP. In 1936, he joined the organization's national legal staff and, in 1938, was appointed chief legal officer. He served, from 1940 until his appointment to the federal bench, as director-counsel of the NAACP Legal Defense and Educational Fund. President Kennedy nominated him for appointment to the Second Circuit Court of Appeals on September 23, 1961. He was given a recess appointment in October 1961, and his nomination was confirmed by the Senate on September 11, 1962. President Johnson nominated him for appointment as Solicitor General of the United States on July 13, 1965. He took the oath of office on August 24, 1965.

Marshall was nominated by President Johnson as Associate Justice of the Supreme Court of the United States on June 13, 1976, confirmed by the Senate on August 30, 1967, and took the constitutional oath on September 1, 1967. He took the judicial oath and was seated on October 2, 1967, as successor to Justice Tom Clark. He was the first Negro to become a justice of the Supreme Court. In 1951, he visited Japan and Korea to make an investigation of court-martial cases involving Negro soldiers. He served as a consultant at the Constitutional Conference on Kenya in London in 1961, and as President Kennedy's personal representative to the independence ceremonies of Sierra Leone in 1961.

Just prior to becoming Solicitor General, he was chief of the United States Delegation to the Third United Nations Congress on the Prevention of Crime and the Treatment of Offenders which convened in Stockholm in August 1965. He was former President Truman's personal representative to the laying of the cornerstone ceremony at the Center for the Advancement of Peach (Harry S Truman Centre) in Jerusalem on July 11, 1966. He attended, as special ambassador and head of the United States delegation, the funeral of the late Prime Minister Sangster of Jamaica on April 17, 1967.

Marshall was the recipient of scores of national and local medals, awards and citations for his work in the field of civil rights. He was a member of the board of directors of the John F. Kennedy Library; the American Bar Association; New York City County Lawyers Association; the Research Institute; the Alpha Phi Alpha Fraternity and the College of Electors, Hall of Fame, New York University. At the height of the celebration of the 1987 Bicentennial of the United States Constitution, he caused an uproar by pointedly reminding everyone that the nation's Founding Fathers had held "a woefully incomplete conception of the people," and that their vision as reflected in the Constitution had only been enlarged through unrelenting social struggle, including a bloody civil war.

In 1988, in his first televised interview after 20 years on the Supreme Court bench, Marshall candidly suggested to journalist Carl Rowan that in terms of concern for racial justice, Ronald Reagan should be ranked at "the bottom"—a condemnation of a sitting president by a sitting justice that was probably unprecedented. Still more recently, he criticized his colleagues arguing that the Court's recent decisions eroding antidiscrimination laws, narrowing reproductive rights, and enlarging the powers of the police "put at risk not only the civil rights of minorities but the civil rights of all citizens." On September 8, 1989, in a speech to the federal judges who sit in New York, Connecticut and Vermont, he bitterly accused the Supreme Court majority of engaging in "a deliberate retrenching of the civil rights agenda.... We could sweep it under the rug and hide it, but I'm not going to do it."

It seems as though Justice Marshall, at age 81, was intent upon ensuring that the twilight of his grand career will be just as memorable, productive, and controversial as the earlier phases that already assure him a large place in American history. On June 27, 1991, Justice Marshall announced he was retiring from the Supreme Court.

MARTIN, CHARLES E., SR., a graduate of Ball State University, received a B.S. degree in political science in 1967; completed 30 hours toward a master's degree in counseling and guidance from Indiana University, South Bend, Indiana; was certified as YMCA senior director, George William College, 1977; received International Quest Program certification, 1989; and is certified in various other areas of youth services. He serves as director of Urban Youth Service in South Bend.

Martin is the recipient of many awards: presented the Key to the City of South Bend, by Mayor Peter Nemeth; Sagamore of the Wabash Award; Outstanding Service to Youth Award, U.S. Senator Richard Lugar; Distinguished Alumni Award, Ball State University; Outstanding Leadership Award, John Adams High School Cultural Awareness Society; Community Service Award, Urban League of St. Joseph County; Lewis Hine Award, National Child Labor Committee in New York, in recognition as one of the top 110 youth workers in the nation; two-time recipient, Prince Hall Lodge Freedom Award; Martin Luther King, Jr., Community Service Award, LaSalle High School Black Culture Society; Exemplar Award, Community Education Roundtable of South Bend, the highest award presented in recognition of outstanding service in promoting educational achievement and meeting the needs of youth; *Outstanding Young Men of America; Who's Who in the Mideast; Who's Who*

Among Black Americans; and *Who's Who in America.*

Martin's professional affiliations include: board of directors and member of Scholarship Committee, Hoosier Fund for Excellence; member, Kiwanis Club of South Bend; Steering Committee, Forums for Youth Self-Sufficiency; member, Indians Black Expo Scholarship Committee; member, South Bend Community School Corporation's Youth-at-Risk Committee; member, Martin Luther King, Jr., Foundation of St. Joseph County; chairman, Outreach Committee, Healthy Babies Project; chairman, Martin Luther King, Jr., Scholarship Committee; founder and president, Black Community Scholarship Fund, Inc.; advisor, Leaders and Positive Role Models, Inc. (LPM); member, Admissions Advisory Council, Ball State University; member, Kappa Alpha Psi National Fraternity; member, South Bend Community School Corporation Parent Communication Network (PCN); board of directors, South Bend School Boosters; and sponsor/advisor, Ladies of Distinction (LOD).

MATTHEWS, VIRGINIA L., was born in Jonesville, Virginia, to the late John and Ella Goode Lee. After high school graduation she attended West Virginia State College at Institute, West Virginia. She started teaching school in Virginia and North Carolina, and attended summer school in Petersburg, Virginia, and Bluefield State at Bluefield, West Virginia. After teaching several years, health problems caused a change in life. Not wishing to remain idle, she started catering, and relocated to Cape May, New Jersey, for a short time. She came to Washington, D.C., December 31, 1941, continuing her career catering for some of the very influential and political people, learning the ins and outs of politics.

Matthews became involved with the Edgewood Civic Association as membership chairman and with the Federation of Civic Associations as chairman of the patrons and sponsors for a number of years. While serving in the capacity as membership chairman for the Edgewood Civic Association, the membership was tripled. The Recreation Department tried to eliminate Edgewood and Langley playgrounds and she went before both Houses of Congress, and both playgrounds were made available to the children. While still doing catering, she was associated with the late Supreme Court Justice John Harlan. Through this exposure she became acquainted with some of the outstanding political figures. As a result, she was invited to the Supreme Court along with her protégée. Through this experience she became interested in politics.

In 1975, when the District asked for volunteers to collect registered voters she did so, collecting several hundred names. With this background in community involvement she decided to cast her hat in the ring to become an Advisory Neighborhood Commissioner. She gathered enough signatures on her petition to enable her to get her name on the ballot to become an ANC commissioner. Her campaign was a success and in 1976, she was sworn in, along with many others, as the first ANC commissioners in the District of Columbia.

Since 1976, Matthews has served her constituents and has been re-elected each time. As a commissioner, she has served the commission as financial secretary, treasurer, and in her present position as financial secretary. Through her diligence, a shopping center at 4th and Rhode Island Avenue was made a reality.

MATTHEWS, WESTINA L., was educated at the University of Dayton in 1970 and received her B.S. degree in education. While teaching elementary school for six years in Yellow Springs, Ohio, she earned an M.S. degree in education from Dayton in 1974. She proceeded to earn a Ph.D. degree in education from the University of Chicago in 1980, and then served as a postdoctoral fellow at both Northwestern University and the University of Wisconsin at Madison. In 1982, she joined the Chicago Community Trust, where she became senior program officer. She served on the boards of the Ms. Foundation and the Middle States Association of Colleges and Schools.

On July 1, 1990, Matthews was appointed to a year term by Mayor David N. Dinkins as a member of the Board of Education for the city of New York. She was the 1989–1990 chair based in the Greater New York City area. In addition, she served as secretary of the New York Regional Association of Grantmakers from 1988–1989, and has been a member of the Governor's Advisory Committee on Black Affairs since 1987. She was vice president of corporate staff and manager of corporate contributions and community affairs at Merrill Lynch & Co., Inc. She also served as secretary of the Merrill Lynch & Co. Foundation, Inc., where she was the architect of the Scholarship Builder Program. The Merrill Lynch Foundation, in conjunction with the National Urban League and 10 of its affiliates, adopted 250 first graders—the Class of 2000—from 10 inner-city schools in Atlanta, Boston, Chicago, Detroit, Houston, Los Angeles, Miami, New York, Philadelphia and Washington, D.C. In the year 2000, each student who graduates from high school will be eligible to receive up to a four-year scholarship for either college or vocational study.

Matthews was the director of the First-Day-Back-to-School N.Y.C. 1990 program, a city-wide initiative between the private and public sector to support education in New York City. Chaired by Joyce B. Dinkins, the program included a multi-media public service campaign that targeted all city school-aged children (both public and nonpublic). Matthews is a member of the Association of Black Foundation Executives, the Women and Foundations/Corporate Philanthropy, the Coalition of 100 Black Women and the NAACP (life member), and was listed in the 1990/91 edition of *Who's Who Among Black Americans*. In 1989, she was selected as a Harlem YMCA Black Achiever in Industry awardee and as a National Council of Negro Women Salute to Women in Industry honoree.

In addition, Dr. Matthews was included among the "100 of the best and brightest black women in corporate America" in the January 1990 *Ebony*, and received the 1990 Corporate Special Recognition Award from the NAACP. She was selected also to receive a 1990 Special Achievement Award from the University of Dayton National Alumni Association, and the Bronx Community College Foundation's 1990 Hall of Fame for Great American Distinguished Business Achievement Award.

METCALFE, LETHA MAE (HOWARD), was born January 24, 1929, in Alexandria, Louisiana, one of 11 children. She married Uel Othello Metcalfe in 1949 and they had 10 children, six boys and four girls. A graduate from Peabody High School in Alexandria in 1947 with honors, she ranked third in her class and received a gold cup. She couldn't afford college so she moved to Flint, Michigan, with one of her older sisters and got a job working in a cafeteria. Later, she enrolled in Hurley School of Nursing. In addition, she had training in cooking and catering. She was a teacher's aid and a Sunday school teacher. While raising the children, she worked one shift and her husband worked another shift so they would not need to hire a babysitter. She also worked in two schools as a para-

professional in Girl Scouting, Cub Scouts and Boy Scouts.

In 1974, Metcalfe received the Naskapi District Award of Merit for Outstanding Service to Scouting in the Naskapi District. She entered Mott Jr. College to major in criminal justice and child development in 1975. She had only been enrolled for a few months when her husband of 26 years died, and as a result she dropped out of college. She moved to Baldwin, Michigan, in 1977 with her six children and remarried. She worked as a program assistant for the 4-H Program in Lake County to recruit and orientate adults and children. The program was very successful until she had both arms broken in a car accident.

Metcalfe strived for her children to get an education or training in a special field. Some have graduated from college; others have pursued doctorate degrees. With the help of the Lord her children attended college and all worked their way through school. She served as a trustee for Webber Township and also on the planning board. She also served as a member of the Goodwill Baptist Church, as the president of Peacock Post Auxiliary, and notary for the state of Michigan.

---

†METCALFE, RALPH HAROLD, was born May 30, 1910, in Atlanta, Georgia. He was the son of Clarence and Marie (Attaway) Metcalfe. He married the former Madalynne Fay Young, and they had one son, Ralph, Jr. He grew up in Chicago and attended Doolittle Elementary, Wendell Phillips Junior High, and Tilden Tech High School. He enrolled at Marquette University and received a B.P. Degree in 1936; in 1939, he received a master's degree in physical education from the University of Southern California. While at Marquette he was captain of the school's track team in 1934.

Metcalfe was a member of the United States Track Team in 1932 and finished undefeated in the 100 meters. He bested Eddie Tolan at 100 and 200 meters at the 1932 U.S. Olympic trials and was favored at the Los Angeles games. The Olympic 100-meter finish ended in a near dead heat. Seven judges spent several hours studying film to determine that Tolan had won by 2 inches. Metcalfe captured the bronze medal in the 200-meter dash, after which it was discovered that his lane measured 2 meters too long. He declined to protest because Americans Metcalfe, Tolan, and Simpson swept the event.

In 1936, at the Olympic Games in Berlin, Jesse Owens broke the tape in 10.3 seconds, 1 yard ahead of Metcalfe (10.4 seconds). Metcalfe won a silver medal, a repeat performance of four years earlier. He won a gold medal in the 400-meter relay, teaming with Foy Draper, Frank Wykoff, and the legendary Jesse Owens to win by 15 yards. This United States team ran the event in 39.8 seconds, a world's record that lasted 20 years.

Metcalfe served as track coach and political science and physical education instructor at Xavier University in New Orleans, Louisiana, from 1936 to 1942. He served as a first lieutenant during World War II, and was decorated with the Legion of Merit while serving in the United States Army from 1943 to 1945. He served as director of the department of civil rights, Chicago Commission on Human Relations from 1945 to 1949. From 1949 to 1952, he was a commissioner with the Illinois Athletic Commission. He then served as an alderman from the South Side wards on the Chicago City Council from 1955 to 1970.

Metcalfe was elected in 1970 as a member of the United States House of Representatives from Illinois, 1st District, Chicago. He was the founder of the Ralph H. Metcalfe Foundation in Chicago, and was active in numerous athletic, youth and civic groups. He was a director of the Illinois Federal Savings & Loan Association and the North Bank of Chicago. He died October 10, 1978.

MILLER, STANLEY A., was born January 13, 1947, in New York, New York. He graduated from Borough of Manhattan Community College, August 1966, with an A.A.S. degree; John Jay College of Criminal Justice, June 1968, B.S.; New York University, Graduate School of Social Work, June 1970, M.S.W.; and the University of Wisconsin, School of Law, May 1974, receiving a J.D. degree. On August 1, 1988 he was appointed Municipal Court judge for the city of Milwaukee, where he tries cases involving violations of the Municipal Code, including housing code violations, traffic matters, and disorderly conduct.

Prior to this position, he served as an Assistant Family Court Commissioner; Principal Assistant Corporation Counsel; Legal Counsel for Milwaukee County Institutions and Departments;

executive director, Clinical Services, Inc.; director of Frederick Douglass Center; and was a partner in Miller Law Offices.

MILLER, YVONNE BOND, was born in Edenton, North Carolina, the oldest of 13 children of John and Percy Bond. She grew up on Howard Street in Norfolk, lived in Moton Park, Huntersville and Lindenwood. She attended S. C. Armstrong Elementary School and Booker T. Washington High School; two years at the Norfolk Division of Virginia State College and received a B.S. degree; Teachers College, Columbia University, New York City, M.A. degree; Ph.D. from the University of Pittsburgh, and further study at Queens College City College of New York.

Miller ran unopposed and was elected to the Virginia House of Delegates, 89th District, on November 8, 1983 and was sworn in on January 11, 1984. She became the first black woman in the Virginia legislature. She

was unopposed and re-elected on November 5, 1985 and was sworn in for a second term on January 8, 1986. On November 3, 1987, she was elected over two opponents to the Virginia Senate, 5th District, sworn in on January 13, 1988. She became the first black woman in the Virginia Senate, serving numerous committee assignments.

Prior to this position Miller had worked as a grocery store cashier, librarian's helper, first grade teacher, Head Start teacher and college teacher; and began service with the Norfolk public schools 1956–1968. She was an assistant professor, associate professor, and professor at Norfolk State University beginning in 1968. Also, she was the former department head of Early Childhood/Elementary Education at Norfolk State, 1980–1987. She was on leave as professor of education during the General Assembly Session.

Miller has worked as consultant for churches, parent organizations, and other community groups. She served as choir member, Sunday School teacher, youth leader and usher, at C. H. Mason Memorial Church of God in Christ; member of Zeta Phi Beta Sorority, Inc., past Basileus of Beta Theta Zeta Chapter of Zeta Phi Beta Sorority, Inc.; former commissioner, Eastern Virginia Medical Authority; former advisory board member of Virginia Division of Children; elected to the board of directors of the National Alliance of Black School Educators; and former member, board of directors of the Virginia Association for Early Childhood Education.

MILLIGAN, HUGH D., was born December 8, 1931, in Washington, D.C. He married the former Phyllis Louise Bivins, and they have two children, Sean Michael and Sharon

Leslie. He graduated from Overbrook High School in Philadelphia, Pennsylvania. In 1958, he joined the Federal Aviation Administration (FAA), as an air traffic controller trainee. He received his training at the Federal Aviation Administration Academy. He served as a controller in the Pittsburgh Air Route Traffic Control Center and in the Control Tower at the NAFEC–Atlantic City Airport.

From 1974 to 1976, Milligan served successively as an associate project manager, project manager, program manager, and from 1976 to 1978 he served as a technical analyst at NAFEC, which is the FAA's national test center. In recognition of his work at the center, he has received several awards. In 1978, he was appointed manager of the NAFEC–Atlantic City Airport, he was the first black airport manager appointed at any of the three airports owned and operated by the FAA. The NAFEC–Atlantic City Airport is located within the 5,000-acre FAA experimental center, approximately 10 miles northwest of Atlantic City, New Jersey. It is owned and operated by the FAA along with Washington National and Dulles International.

MILLIONES, JAKE, was born in Marietta, Georgia. He attended Lincoln University in 1958–1961, graduated from the University of Pittsburgh, 1961–1966, with a B.S. degree in psychology; from Langley Porter Neuropsychiatric Clinic, San Francisco, California, 1971–1972, clinical psychology; 1968–1973, University of Pittsburgh, Ph.D. degree in clinical psychology. From 1980 he has been assistant professor of psychiatry and psychology at the University of Pittsburgh Western Psychiatric Institute and Clinic Adolescent/Young Adult Module, Pittsburgh.

In 1977–1980, Milliones was a research assistant professor of psychology at the University of Pittsburgh as well as assistant professor of psychology; also, associate director of Right Start, an Early Intervention program from 1973–1977. He has received numerous awards: Florence Reizenstein Award, 1987; Lucy Stone Community Service Award, 1987; Distinguished Black Alumnus Award, University of Pittsburgh, 1987; Very Important Person Award, Pittsburgh City Council of PTA, 1987; Community Service Award, Bon Ami Temple Elks, 1986; Community Service Award, National Association of Black Accountants (NABA), 1982; First Decade Award, Department of Black Community Research & Development, University of Pittsburgh, 1980, and Distinguished Service Award, Black Graduate Student Organization, University of Pittsburgh, 1980. He has a number of publications.

Milliones' professional affiliations have included: board of directors, Boys Club of Western Pennsylvania; board director, Hill Community Development Corporation; board of directors,

Hill District Project Area Committee; trustee, The Carnegie; board director, Pittsburgh Peach Institute; consultant, Spectrum Drug Treatment Program; board director, American Civil Liberties Union; board member, Pittsburgh Board of Public Education (president, 1983–1988); board of directors, Community Action Pittsburgh, Inc.; board of directors, Allegheny Children's Youth Service; board director, Pittsburgh Psychoanalytic Center; consultant, Pennsylvania Department of Education; consultant, Alpha House, a therapeutic community for the treatment of drug addiction; course instructor in group dynamics, Western Pennsylvania State Correctional Institution; consultant, House of the Crossroads, a therapeutic community for drug addicts; member of Synanon's Square Club (nonaddicts), San Francisco; board of directors, Program to Aid Citizens Enterprises (PACE), and observer, Phoenix House, a therapeutic community, New York City.

MITCHELL, PARREN J., is a graduate of Morgan State University in Baltimore, Maryland. In 1950, he filed suit to compel the University of Maryland to enroll him as its first black graduate student. There, he completed his master's degree in sociology and was admitted to the school's honor society. After taking his master's degree, he returned to teach at his alma mater, Morgan State University. As executive director of Baltimore's anti-poverty program in the late 1960s, he lobbied Washington for his agency's programs. Also, during the 1960s he served as executive secretary for the Maryland Human Relations Commission, and played the pivotal role in the enactment and implementation of Maryland's statewide Public Accommodations Law.

In 1970, Mitchell was elected Maryland's first black congressman, for the seventh district. In 1976, he attached to President Carter's $4 billion Public Works bill an amendment that compelled state, county and municipal governments seeking federal grants to set aside 10 percent of the money to retain minority firms as contractors, subcontractors, or suppliers. His single amendment resulted in more than $625 million (15 percent) going to legitimate minority firms. He also introduced the legislation which, in 1978, became Public Law 95-507, that requires proposals from contractors to spell out their goals for awarding contracts to minority subcontractors. This law potentially provided access to billions of dollars for minority businesses.

During his 20 years in Congress, Mitchell has served with distinction as a member of the House Budget Committee; vice chairman of the Joint Committee on Defense Production; and chairman of the Congressional Black Caucus. To date he has served as Whip-at-Large; a senior member of the House Banking, Finance and Urban Affairs Committee, chairman of its Subcommittee on Domestic Monetary Policy; a member of the Small Business Committee, chairman of its Task Force on Minority Enterprise; chairman of the Subcommittee on Housing, Minority Enterprise and Economic Development of the

Congressional Black Caucus; a member of the Joint Economic Committee; and the Presidential Commission on the National Agenda for the Eighties.

Mitchell holds a total of five honorary degrees, i.e., two Doctor of Humane Letters; two Doctor of Law; and one Doctor of Social Sciences. More than 150 awards have been presented to him from organizations such as: national and local consumer groups; civil rights groups, business and economic groups; fraternities; sororities; religious groups, and educational organizations. He has also received awards from such diverse groups as: the National Alliance of Black Educators; the Southern Christian Leadership Conference; the Morehouse Alumni; the Joint Center for Political Studies; the Greater New Haven (Connecticut) Business and Professional Association; the Minority Contractors of Dayton, Ohio; the Alaska Black Caucus; and the Consumer Federation of America.

MONROE, JAMES W., was born on March 12, 1942, in North Carolina. He received a B.S. degree in electrical engineering from West Virginia State College in 1963, and an M.A. degree in political science from the University of Cincinnati in 1973. From October 1963 to December 1963, he was a student in the Ordnance Officer Basic Course, United States Army Ordnance Center and School, Aberdeen Proving Ground, Maryland. From February 1964 to April 1964, he was a student in the Armor Officer Basic Course, United States Army Armor School, Fort Knox, Kentucky. From August 1964 to February 1966, he served as platoon leader, Armored Cavalry, B Troop, later platoon leader, Troop A, 2nd Squadron, 9th Cavalry, 24th Infantry Division, United States Army in Europe.

Monroe was promoted to the rank of first lieutenant on April 5, 1965.

From February 1966 to June 1967, he was commander of the 621st General Supply Company, United States Army in Europe.

He was promoted to the rank of captain on September 20, 1966. From June 1967 to June 1968, he was a student in the Defense Language Institute, East Coast Branch, United States Naval Station, Anacostia, Washington, D.C. From June 1968 to June 1969, he was assigned as ordnance advisor, United States Military Training Mission, Saudi Arabia. From July 1969 to June 1970, he was a student in the Ordnance Officer Advanced Course, United States Army Ordnance Center and School, Aberdeen Proving Ground, Maryland.

From June 1970 to June 1972, he served as assistant professor of military science, First United States Army, at Fort Meade, Maryland, with duty at the University of Cincinnati, Cincinnati, Ohio. From August 1973 to July 1976, he was assigned as strategic intelligence officer, Office of the Assistant Chief of Staff for Intelligence, United States Army, Washington. From August 1976 to June 1977, he was a student in the United States Army Command and General Staff College, Fort Leavenworth, Kansas. From June 1977 to July 1978, he was the commander of the 61st Maintenance Company, Eighth Army, in Korea. From July 1978 to October 1979, he was assigned as executive officer, 709th Maintenance Battalion, 9th Infantry Division, Fort Lewis, Washington.

From November 1979 to June 1982, Monroe served as deputy commander, later commander, Division Materiel and Management Center, and executive officer of Division Support Command, 9th Infantry Division, Fort Lewis. He was promoted to the grade of lieutenant colonel on November 7, 1979. From June 1982 to March 1985, he was the commander of the 71st Maintenance Battalion, VII Corps, United States Army in Europe. From

June 1985 to June 1986, he was a student in the Industrial College of the Armed Forces, Fort Lesley J. McNair, Washington. He was promoted to the grade of colonel on February 1, 1986. From June 1986 to June 1987, he served as a member of the faculty of the Senior Service College, National Defense University, Fort McNair. From July 1987 to July 1989, he was the commander of the Division Support Command, 24th Infantry Division (Mechanized), Fort Stewart, Georgia.

From July 1989 to July 1990, Monroe was assigned assistant chief of staff, G-4 (Logistics), Third United States Army, Fort McPherson, Georgia. In July 1990, he was promoted to the one-star grade of brigadier general and assigned as deputy commanding general for Procurement and Readiness, United States Army Tank-Automotive Command, Warren, Michigan. Monroe has received numerous awards and decorations which include: the Legion of Merit; the Defense Meritorious Service Medal; Meritorious Service Medal (with three oak leaf clusters); and the Army Commendation Medal.

MOON, ARCHIE, was born in Atlanta, Georgia, and grew up in East Point, Georgia. She is the daughter of Arthur and Brozell Fears Dixon, and is the mother of three children. She attended East Point Elementary and attended South Fulton High School in East Point, where she dropped out in the 11th grade and became a teenage wife and mother. She continued her education and received her high school diploma. She then enrolled in Grady Hospital's School of Nursing in Atlanta. After graduating she became a Licensed Practical Nurse, first working at Grady Memorial Hospital, a public hospital, then at Egleston Pediatric Hospital, and from there she went to Dekalb General Hospital.

In 1964, Moon was employed by the United States Postal Service as a clerk assigned to the Federal Annex in Atlanta. During this time she enrolled in Atlanta Area Tech in a typing/secretarial course. In 1968, when the position became available as an assistant training instructor for the LSM machine, which required typing skills, she applied for the position and was accepted. In 1974, she was promoted to supervisor in mail processing at the main post office in Atlanta. It was also during this time she accepted additional responsibility as the coordinator for women programs and instructing classes in equal opportunity for employment with the postal service in Atlanta metropolitan areas. At night on her own time she did volunteer work at the Atlanta Job Corps for women, instructing them on "How to Pass the Postal Exam," and nine young women graduated.

In 1977, Moon was transferred to the Briarcliff Postal Unit in the Atlanta Division, where she began her training to become a station manager and was subsequently transferred to several stations where she continued her training. In early 1978, she was appointed as a station manager and she worked a number of assignments in the Atlanta area. She was promoted to an area manager becoming the first female area manager in the state of Georgia. As an area manager, she manages the operation of 12 carriers stations and detached delivery and collection units within her jurisdiction. From 1989 to 1990, she was placed on temporary assignment as the postmaster of Stone Mountain, Georgia, where she became the first and highest ranking female to serve in that position.

In 1990, Moon returned to her position as area manager in the Atlanta Postal Division, In 1991, as area manager she had the responsibility of the day-to-day management and operation of 12 of the largest post offices in Atlanta. These units deliver mail to over 200,000 Atlanta residents on a daily basis. When asked what's the most significant gains minorities have made during her tenure with the postal service, she stated, "The ability to move from the entry level craft positions to technical and managerial positions. The postal service has out paced the private sector in terms of its equal opportunity and upward mobility of all its employees who have worked hard, came to work on time and applied themselves through further education and training." Her advice offered to high school students is: "Regardless of the field a student is contemplating entering, he/she must first obtain as much education as possible to ensure success in that particular field of employment." She said, "Young people fail to take advantage of opportunities, set goals for themselves, then work hard to fulfill them. . . . They should begin early in life, setting goals for themselves."

MOON, WARREN, was born November 18, 1956, in Los Angeles, California. He and his wife Felicia Moon have three children, Blair, Chelsea and Josh. He attended Hamilton High School and earned the city MVP title his senior year. Remaining in Los Angeles after high school graduation, he played college football for one year at West L.A. College. He is a member of their Hall of Fame and a scholarship is named in his honor. Desiring to gain greater laurels, Moon continued his academic and athletic career at the University of Washington. Along with a B.A. degree in communications, he racked up other achievements and honors while a Washington Husky. During his senior year, he was elected Pacific Athletic Conference 8 Player of the Year.

When Moon was growing up, there were few black quarterbacks he could dream of becoming. He says, "James Harris, former quarterback for the L.A. Rams, was a role model even though he didn't get the kind of exposure he deserved." In a sense Moon didn't get what he deserved his senior year at the University of Washington. In 1978, he took the Washington Huskies to the Rose Bowl and was selected the game's Most Valuable Player. But when the National Football League's draft time rolled around he found the

NFL teams unwilling to pay a black quarterback more than his white counterparts. So he signed with the Canadian Football League. It was his standout play with the Edmonton Eskimos that made the NFL scouts take notice. He led the Eskimos to the league title five consecutive seasons.

In 1983, the CFL presented the Schenley Award (CFL version of the League's MVP) to Moon for breaking all previous records for a single season. He came to the Houston Oilers as a free agent in 1984, from the CFL, expected to rally a team that had lost its drill bit. He has successfully and skillfully led the Oilers through their rebuilding process. At the same time, he has continued to build his own arsenal of strength and character. He took the Oilers to the Central Division playoffs in both 1987 and 1988. The 1988 NFL season proved to be the best yet for the All-Pro Houston Oilers quarterback. An untimely shoulder injury forced him to miss five games early in the season, but he charged back for a finish. That finish included being elected, for the first time, to the Pro Bowl in Hawaii where he was starting quarterback for the AFC team.

In 1990, Moon threw five touchdowns in the Oilers' win over the Cincinnati Bengals, to become the first quarterback in history to throw for 20,000 yards in both the National Football League and the Canadian Football League. On December 16, 1990, in a game with the Kansas City Chiefs, he threw for 527 yards, a passing total "the second-highest in NFL history." It was said, "he shot for the moon and almost made it." Only Norm Van Brocklin ever passed for more yards in a game, "554" on September 28, 1951. In January 1991, after six spectacular seasons in the CFL and another six good years in the NFL, Moon still wasn't getting much notice. So he did something about it. He went on the field, masterfully guided the run-and-shoot and had his best year ever. For doing so, he was voted Offensive Player of the Year by the Associated Press on January 9, 1991. In 15 games, he led the league with 362 completions in 584 attempts for 4,689 yards and 33 touchdowns.

Moon has been very active in community affairs, by donating his time, talent, and money to Ronald McDonald House, Olympiads, Special Olympics, the March of Dimes, Muscular Dystrophy Association, Sickle Cell Foundation, United Negro College Fund, Urban League, and the American Heart Association. He has served on the board for the United Negro College Fund, Houston Visitors & Convention Bureau, and the Houston Sports Association advisory Board. In April 1989, he founded the Crescent Moon Foundation, demonstrating once again his commitment to his community. "The Foundation will allow me the opportunity to conceive and develop my own fundraising ideas," Moon says. "We will be able to see first hand where the money goes and how it is used to benefit those in need. Before any of us can be truly successful, we must first give back to our community." He was awarded the "Superstar of the Year" award from the National Urban Coalition, and was elected 1989 "NFL Man of the Year" from Travelers.

MOORE, FARNEY, married to the former Sudie Monk of Greenville, is the father of six children, Matthew, Susan, Daphne, Aissa, Sharon and Brent. He is a graduate of Washington High School (presently the P. S. Jones School) in Washington, he was awarded a B.S. degree in education at Elizabeth City State University. He studied administration and supervision at Columbia University, New York City, and religious doctrine under the auspices of Shaw University, Raleigh, North Carolina. He earned his M.A. degree in administration and supervision from East Carolina University. He was a three-time recipient of the National Science Foundation Fellowships from Saint Augustine College, Raleigh.

Moore served as assistant minister at Cornerstone Missionary Baptist Church, Greenville, for eight years, and as youth pastor at Macedonia Missionary Baptist Church, Farmville, for seven years. He was regarded as an organizer, Christian leader, and loyal supporter. He was a founding member of the Washington, North Carolina, City Unit (North Carolina Teacher Association), and served as its first president. He later served the Pitt County unit of the North Carolina Association of Educators-National Education Association as president after serving as vice president of membership and vice-president of orientation.

Moore represented Pitt County educators as a delegate to the National Educational Association's Annual Convention at Atlantic City, New Jersey, and Miami, Florida. He has also served as principal of Nichols Schools; vice-principal of North Pitt High School; was a member of the Phi Beta Sigma

Fraternity; as vice-president of the Greenville Division of the NAACP; and board chaplain and presidential advisor of the Southern Christian Leadership Conference, Pitt County Chapter. He was the author of the published work *The Washington March of Martin Luther King*, and of a second book *Of One Blood: The American from Africa*. He has held numerous positions in a number of professional organizations, and is the recipient of many honors and awards.

MOORE, GWEN, was born October 28 in Michigan. She is married to Ronald Dobson and is the mother of a son Ronald Dobson II. She received her B.A. degree from California State University at Los Angeles and her teaching credential from UCLA. Her professional career has led her from a position as a deputy probation officer with the Los Angeles County to director of public affairs and director of personnel with a community action agency in Los Angeles. She also taught at Compton Community College where her educational commitment led her to her first elected public office in 1975 as a member of the Los Angeles Community College District Board of Trustees. She was elected assemblywoman for the Democratic-49 District, where she has represented since 1978 the ethnically and economically diverse communities of Crenshaw, Ladera Heights, Baldwin Hills, Culver City, Playa del Rey, Marina del Rey, portions of Venice, Westchester and Cheviot Hills. She was elected by overwhelming margins.

Moore serves as a majority whip of the California State Assembly. She is chair of the prestigious Assembly Committee on Utilities and Commerce which also has jurisdiction over the California cable television industry. Her work on this committee gained her national acclaim and much of her legislation has become models for other states. She also served on the Committee on Finance and Insurance; Health; Local Government; Governmental Efficiency; and Consumer Protection. She is a member of the subcommittees on Health and Workers Insurance and Savings and Loan, Law and Regulation. She chairs the Select Committee on Regional Government, and was a member of the Select Committee on State Public Procurement Practices. She co-chaired the Task Force on Televising the Legislature. Moore also serves as a legislative member of the Commission on California State Government Organization and Economy, the "Little Hoover" Commission.

Moore is affiliated with several legislative associations. She was finance director of California Elected Women's Association for Education and Research; active with the National Conference of State Legislatures; served as a member of the executive committee and as western region director of the N.C.S.L. Woman's Caucus; handles the western region chair responsibilities for the National Black Caucus of State Legislators; and served as Secretary of the National Organization of Black Elected Legislative Women (NOBEL/Women).

Respected in many arenas, Moore's honors include awards from U.S. Department of Commerce, Minority Enterprise Development Appreciation Award; NAACP Legal Defense Fund, Black Woman of Achievement; California Association of Nutritional Directors; California Independent Gas Producers Association; National Dental Association; Association of Municipal Court Clerks Legislator of the Year; California Trucking Association, Truck Safety Legislation Award; Black American Political Association of California (1988 Willie L. Brown, Jr. Award); and Joint Conference, Inc. (1987 Economic Parity Award).

Known in the legislature as an authority on utility and telecommunications issues, she has authored legislation which opened the utility rate setting process to more public scrutiny. As a business advocate, she has encouraged the multimillion dollar utility industry to aggressively proceed with outreach programs to women and minority-owned businesses for business contract purposes. She has received national acclaim for her legislation regarding privacy rights of subscribers to the cable television network. The Moore Universal Telephone Service Act, which ensures availability of telephone service to all Californians, has become a model for legislation across the country. Through legislation and her membership on the Little Hoover Commission, she has become the primary force in the enhancement of California's telecommunications network.

Close to home, Moore has been instrumental in the development of the Kenneth Hahn State Recreational Area by legislating millions of dollars for acquisition and development of land for the park. She has spearheaded legislation dealing with child nutrition, family leave, truck and bus safety, and consumer protection in the areas of utility concerns, medical practice, telecommunications and insurance. She has signed into law landmark legislation which disallows businesses tax deductions on memberships in private clubs that discriminate on the basis of race, religion, or sex.

MOORE, GWENDOLYNNE S.

The mother of three children, she is a 1969 graduate of North Division High School in Milwaukee. From there, she went on to earn a B.A. degree in political science from Marquette University. In 1983, she earned her certification in Credit Union Management from Milwaukee Area Technical College. Besides a strong educational background, she has been active in numerous community service organizations. She has specialized in economic development and community reinvestment.

Moore was elected to the Wisconsin State Assembly in 1988. Drawing on her long history of service to the Milwaukee community, she campaigned on the theme of economic development and fighting for her district's share of state resources. As a VISTA volunteer, she spearheaded the start-up of the Cream City Community Development Credit Union. In 1986–1987, she was president of that organization's board of directors. She was also employed by the City of Milwaukee as a neighborhood development specialist from 1985 to 1988. This solid background in business and development gives her a unique perspective in dealing with the problems that confront her district.

Moore is not new to state government. She worked for the state of Wisconsin as a program and planning analyst for both the Department of Employment Relations and the Department of Health and Social Services. These experiences gave her extensive knowledge of legislative research, analysis, bill drafting and the entire legislative process. She has served on the following legislative committees: Housing, Securities and Corporate Policy (vice-chair), Health, Children and Human Services, Financial Institutions and Insurance and the Small Business and Employment Training.

In addition to these committee assignments, Moore has also been appointed by the governor to his Task Force on Housing Policy, and was a board member of the Wisconsin Housing and Economic Development Authority. She was also assigned to three legislative council committees: Fair Housing, Homelessness, and Privacy and Information Technology. She was pursuing an active agenda of advocacy for her constituents. The people of the 7th Assembly District have a strong, thoughtful representative standing up for them in Madison.

MOORE, MELBA, was born October 27, 1945, in New York City. She is the daughter of singer Melba ("Bonnie") Smith and jazz saxophonist Teddy Hill. She was raised in Harlem during her early years, and after her mother married pianist Clem Moorman, the family moved to Newark, New Jersey. Between 1968 to 1970, she graduated from Newark Arts High School and Montclair State College in Upper Montclair, New Jersey. Since then she has risen through the ranks of the cast of "Hair" to become the first black female lead in that hippie rock musical, and in 1970 she reached stardom with her Tony Award–winning portrayal of Lutiebelle, the drawling back-country Georgia girl in the musical "Purlie."

In 1972, she and singer-actor Clifton Davis teamed up on "The Melba Moore–Clifton Davis Show," a weekly music-variety hour production. Moore, a very proud black woman who has resisted pressure from producers who complained that her hairline didn't "look right," insisted on playing the television series (with Davis), with her hair in its natural, nappy state. She stated "I'm a nigger, and I'm proud of being a nigger. I don't want to be made into something else," and elsewhere she has been quoted as saying: "What's happened to me is important . . . in terms of black kids who might want to emulate me. That's why it's important for me to stay in contact with black folks, and one of the reasons I don't get my hair straightened. I have subtle ways of saying I am black."

Moore's accomplishments in the entertainment industry don't stand alone, but are instead accompanied by a sturdy foundation she has continued to build within the community. Creation of the Melba Moore Foundation for Children, her leadership role in the National Council of Negro Women, and volunteer efforts at Harlem Hospital, to name a few, help to convey her sensitivity, intelligence and compassion for mankind. She has donated partial proceeds from the singles' sales to the NAACP, National Association for Sickle Cell Disease and the United Negro College Fund. by 1990, she had seven impressive albums:

"I'm in Love," "Never Say Never," "A Lot of Love," "Read My Lips," "What a Woman Needs," "The Other Side of the Rainbow" and her new album, "Soul Exposed."

On the "Soul Exposed" album, she rounded up other vocalists and musicians to produce and perform the remake of James Weldon Johnson's "Lift Every Voice and Sing" (the black national anthem). Joining her on the production's vocals were Stevie Wonder, Bobby Brown, Anita Baker, Freddie Jackson, BeDe and CeCe Winans, Take-6, Jeffrey Osborne, Gerald Albright, the Rev. Jesse Jackson, Howard Hewett, The Clark Sisters, Dionne Warwick, Terri Lyne Carrington, Karen Clark, and Stephanie Mills. She was quoted as saying, "I've been singing this song a long time because it makes me happy to sing about freedom and victory. But I decided I didn't want to sing it by myself anymore so I invited some of my dear friends to help. Together we'll make freedom ring."

MORIAL, ERNEST N., was born October 9, 1929, in New Orleans, Louisiana. He is married to Sybil Haydel and is the father of five children, Julie, Marc, Jacques, Cheri and Monique. He attended parochial and public schools in New Orleans; received a B.S. degree in business administration from Xavier University, 1951; J.D. degree, 1954, first black graduate from Louisiana State University Law School and the University of Nevada; and a graduate of National College of Juvenile Justice. He served in the U.S. Army Intelligence Corps, 1954–1956. In 1978, he was the first black mayor in the history of New Orleans to be elected.

Morial's prior positions include: councilman at large, New Orleans, 1969, ran and lost runoff election (5,100 votes); was the first black elected to the Fourth Circuit Court of Appeals, 1974–1977; was the first black to serve in

Juvenile Court, 1970-1973; Louisiana House of Representatives, 1967-1970, the first black in the legislature since Reconstruction; U.S. Attorney, 1965-1967, he was the first black to serve in Louisiana; and practiced law in association with civil rights leader A. P. Tureaud, in 1945-1965. He used his legal training to advance the cause of equal justice under the law.

Together with A. P. Tureaud, he brought and won suits to eliminate segregation in the city of New Orleans and the state of Louisiana. When Louisiana law prohibited teachers from holding memberships in organizations such as the NAACP, he successfully challenged the law under the First Amendment, his wife Sybil being the sole plaintiff. He filed suit to end race discrimination in many of the city and state educational institutions, including Delgado Trade School, Louisiana State University in New Orleans, University of Southwestern Louisiana, Southeastern Louisiana University, New Orleans, public schools, and New Orleans Recreation Department Facilities. All were "off limits" to black citizens. He filed suit to end segregation practices in the city's taxicabs. He sued to desegregate the New Orleans Municipal Auditorium and the New Orleans International Airport.

Morial served as president of the New Orleans branch of the NAACP from 1962-1965. He was named by President Kennedy to be a founding member of the Lawyer's Committee for Civil Rights Under Law. When offered the position of First Black Delegate to the Democratic National Convention in 1968, he asserted his interest in additional black memberships in the delegation, but would not serve as a "token" representative of his race, which constituted a quarter of the state's total population. As a result, the size and vote of the Louisiana delegation was increased to reflect the black population of Louisiana.

While in the Louisiana Legislature,

he continued his leadership by authoring legislation such as welfare reform, civil service employment, consumer credit protection, housing reform and voter registration. He successfully advocated lowering the voting age to 18. As a judge of the Juvenile Court, he worked for the needs of the city's disadvantaged youth, and dispensed justice with compassion and understanding. His professional community and civic affiliations were numerous.

He is the recipient of many awards: 100 Most Influential Black Americans, *Ebony* magazine; *Who's Who in American Politics; Who's Who in the South and Southwest; Who's Who in America; Outstanding Young Men of America*; A Knight of Mark Twain, recognized for his contributions to modern municipal government; Distinguished Alumni Award, Xavier University; A. P. Tureaud Medal, Louisiana Conference of the NAACP: Silver Torch of Liberty Award, Anti-Defamation League B'nai B'rith; Outstanding Political Leader of 1978, Voter Education Project; *Personalities of the South*, 1978-1979 edition; Social Justice Award, NAACP, Shreveport Chapter; C. Alvin Bertel Memorial Award for 1979, presented by the New Orleans Traffic and Transportation Bureau; and American Society of Mechanical Engineers Silver Medallion on their 100th Anniversary — to selected mayors of American cities for outstanding support of engineering projects.

MORROW, CHARLES, III, was born July 21, 1956, in Chicago, Illinois. He attended school in Chicago: Martha Ruggles Elementary; DeLaSalle High School, and Illinois Institute of Technology. He has served since 1977 at the People's Gas, Light & Coke Co., in Chicago, as a customer service representative for six years and phone representative for three years. Prior positions include: Metropolitan Sanitary

mond W. Ewell; 17th Ward Young Democrats; member of Illinois Black Elected Officials, member of National Conference of Black Legislators, member of Illinois Legislature Black Caucus; member of National State Conference of Legislators; East Auburn Block Club; 500 Black Men; member of West Chatham Improvement Association; Boy Scouts of America; NAACP, Operation PUSH, Urban League; member, Pilgrim Baptist Church and sponsor, Soul Children of Chicago.

MORSE, MILDRED S., is a graduate of the University of Arkansas, B.A. degree, and Howard University School of Law, J.D. degree. Morse has lectured, taught courses, and conducted numerous seminars on major civil rights and the administrative law process. She is president of Morse Enterprises, Inc. (MEI), a communications consulting firm responding to: (1) the challenge of reaching and serving multi-cultural groups; and (2) the need to develop and nurture strong minority group linkages to information and resources through various communications media. The firm provides a wide range of services for telecommunications, communications, media-related

Sanitary District for Chicago, 1975–1976; a drivers education instructor who maintained and cleaned the vehicles, 1971–1974; student driver instructor classroom teacher.

He is the recipient of an Outstanding Young Men in America Award, 1987; *Who's Who Among Black Americans*, 1988; IVI-IPO Ethel Parker Best Legislator, 1988; received Distinguished Service Certificate, AMVETS, 1988; *Personalities of America*, 1989; and the Friends of Labor Award-AFL/CIO, 1990. He has served on the following House committees: Housing (vice chairman), Urban Redevelopment, Mental Health, Consumer Protection Public Utilities and Energy Environment & Natural Resources.

Morrow's political activities have included: 17th Regular Democratic Organization, volunteer; volunteer for Alderman Alan Streeter; volunteer for Committeeman William Shannon, volunteer for campaign of Mayor Harold Washington; volunteer for campaign for Congress of Eugene Barnes; volunteer, campaign for Rep. Lewis A. Caldwell; aide to Rep. Ray-

companies and individuals. Services include: Outreach and Networking; Representation; Brokerage and Consultation, including general consulting services to ventures, businesses, and industries outside of the communications field.

From 1980–1989, Morse served as assistant to the president and director, Human Resources Development of the Corporation for Public Broadcasting (CPE), the primary organization charged with the national growth and development of public radio and television in the United States. As a member of the corporation's senior management team and director of three major national programs, her responsibilities included the administration of programs in a broad range of fields: training and professional development; work force diversity; and program and institutional diversity. These included the development of minority radio and television programs, enhancement of station management capabilities, and the expansion of multicultural audiences.

Morse's expertise in broadcasting has been enhanced through participation in such practitioner experiences as: Master Seminars in Television Production, Sundance Institute (Utah, 1988, 1990); International Public Television Producer's Conferences (Columbia, S.C., 1984; Marseille, France, 1985; Philadelphia, PA, 1988; and Edmonton, Canada, 1990); as well as broadcast seminars in development, fund raising, marketing, promotion, strategic planning, and financial management. Prior to joining CPB, between 1968–1977 and in 1980, she administered and or directed major civil rights compliance and enforcement programs in cabinet-level departments of the federal government. At the executive level of government, she served as deputy director, Phase II of the President's Civil Rights Task Force from 1977–1979.

Morse has been recognized through numerous awards, certificates of merit,

and special achievement for her work. She is listed in *The World's Who's Who of Women, Outstanding Women of America,* and *Who's Who Among Black Americans.* She is active in church, civic, public service, and professional organizations. She is a public speaker on numerous topics: the Ohio State University: keynote speaker topic "Women in Communications in the 1990s"; American University School of Law: topics, equal employment opportunity law requirements for broadcasters, employment in the broadcast field, outreach to special radio and television audiences, and marketing/promotion of broadcast programs to target audiences; Howard University School of Law: guest lecturer during a course on Civil Rights Law and the Constitution; University of Maryland: guest lecturer during a course on Civil Rights Law Enforcement; and the department of HEW and HUD, instructor for classes in the investigation and enforcement of civil rights laws.

Morse's professional organizational affiliations have included: Americans for Indian Opportunity; American Indians in Media Association board of directors; American Women in Radio and Television; Broadcast Education Association; Council on Education in the Electronic Media; National Bar Association; National Black Media Coalition; Capital City Links; Delta Sigma Theta Sorority; NAACP and Sigma Pi Phi Fraternity Archousa.

MORTON, MARGARET E., a native of Pocahontas, Virginia, she was raised in Bluefield, West Virginia. She attended public schools in Bluefield and graduated from Genoa High School in 1941. Presently she is living in Bridgeport, Connecticut, with her husband of 49 years, James F. Morton. They are both licensed funeral directors and owners of a family mortuary which is operated by one of their three sons, Robert Morton. They are also parents of one daughter. She represents the 23rd District, City of Bridgeport. She is an active member of Walters Memorial A.M.E. Zion Church, an executive board member of Hall Neighborhood House, and a member and former executive board member of the NAACP. She also continues to fulfill her commitment to numerous community and church organizations.

When the General Assembly convened in 1973, Morton became the first black woman to serve in the Connecticut House of Representatives. She continued in that chamber for four consecutive terms, serving on numerous committees with distinction and eventually serving as assistant majority leader. In 1980, following a tremendous party fight, she sought and won the Senatorial seat for the 23rd District in spite of not receiving the party endorsement.

Morton has served five terms in the Senate and was re-elected for a sixth term in November of 1990. In 1985–1986, she served as ranking member of both the public Health Committee and the General Law Committee. She has also served as chairman of the Legislative and Executive Nominations Committee, member of the Human Services Committee, member of the Judiciary Committee, and member of the black and Hispanic Caucus since its inception in 1980. She was named deputy president pro-tempore of the Senate in February of 1990. With this appointment, she became the highest ranking black woman to serve in Senate history. In this leadership position, Morton will focus on the development of a long-range plan to address the problems of the cities.

MURPHY, EDDIE, was born April 3, 1961, in Brooklyn, New York, the son of Charles and Lillian Murphy. The Murphys were divorced when Ed-die was three, and Charles Murphy died about five years later. When Eddie was nine, his mother married Vernon Lynch. Eddie attended Roosevelt Junior-Senior High School, which is the alma mater of basketball star Julius Erving. While there, he dabbled in karate, baseball, and astronomy, and worked for a time as a shoe store clerk. Developing his comedy skills (while other kids in Roosevelt whiled away afternoons in the park emulating "Dr. J" Julius Erving), he spent hours in his basement, impersonating such characters as Bugs Bunny, Tom and Jerry, and film comics like Laurel and Hardy, and Richard Pryor. He would also rehearse his impressions of Jackie Wilson, Al Green, Elvis Presley, Bill Cosby and the Beatles.

Murphy took his first step toward superstardom on July 9, 1976, when he hosted a talent show at the Roosevelt Youth Center. After that he was confident and determined, and began calling local talent agents who found work for him in such Long Island night spots as Richard M. Nixon's White House Inn in Massapequa, the Blue Dolphin in Uniondale, and the East Side Comedy Club in Huntington. By the time he was 17 his weekly income was from $20 to $300. He was voted the "most popular" boy in his graduating class of 1979. He attended Nassau Community College for a short time.

Murphy left school when he learned that the producers of NBC-TV's "Saturday Night Live" were looking for a black cast member for the late-night show's 1980–1981 season. After weathering six auditions, he was hired as a featured player, or an extra. His chance to shine came about halfway through the season when the producers suddenly discovered that they had about four minutes of air time remaining and no skits or other material to fill it with. In desperation, they pushed Murphy before the camera and told him to do his stand-up comedy routine. Shortly after that, he was named a regular member of the "Saturday Night Live" repertory company. Murphy grabbed the spotlight on "Saturday Night Live" and held it. He created a variety of characters, such as Mr. Robinson, a ghetto interpretation of "Mister Rogers," Little Richard, and Buckwheat.

It was on the basis of some videotapes of "Saturday Night Live" that director Walter Hill chose Murphy for the role of the urbane, fast-talking convict Reggie Hammond in the film 48 Hours, a 1982 Paramount film. In June 1983, his second movie was released, Trading Places, a comedy. But 1984 proved to be the year that put Murphy at the top in Hollywood. In a role originally slated for Sylvester Stallone, his popularity soared through the roof when he portrayed streetwise Detroit cop Axel Foley in the mega-smash Beverly Hills Cop. The movie became the ninth most successful movie in film history.

In addition to the box-office success, Murphy received a Golden Globe nomination as Best Actor, was named Star of the Year at the 1985 ShoWest Convention of motion picture exhibitors, and was selected co-winner of the Favorite All-Around Male Entertainer Award at the People's Choice Awards. Next, he teamed up with R&B artist Rick James to produce his third album, which featured his singing, rather than his comic talent. He next starred in The Golden Child. In 1987, His Beverly Hills Cop, II was the No. 1 hit of the year and grossed $155 million. His next release was Raw, a concert film which grossed more than $37 million.

In 1988, Murphy starred as Prince Akeem in Coming to America, cast as an African prince who travels to New York in search of an American bride. His friend Arsenio Hall played the prince's companion. In 1989, he released Harlem Nights, a 1930s gangster drama, co-starring Richard Pryor, and Arsenio Hall. In 1990, he starred in the sequel to 48 Hours entitled Another 48 Hours. Murphy once again played the role of "Reggie Hammond." His mother and step-father run Panda Merchandising, which handles the rights for Eddie Murphy products, with his older brother Charles and half-brother Vernon, Jr.

NEWMAN, CONSTANCE BERRY, was born July 8, 1935. She is a graduate of Bates College, Lewiston, Maine, A.B. degree, 1956; and B.S.L. degree from University of Minnesota Law School, 1959. She has served as director, U.S. Office of Personnel Management, a presidential appointment, U.S. Senate confirmation, since 1989. Her prior positions included: co-director of Outreach, Presidential Personnel, Presidential Transition Team (primary recruiter for black Americans in the Bush Administration), 1988–1989; deputy director, National Voter Coalitions, Bush-Quayle '88, advisor to the chairman of the Republican Convention, 1988; consultant, 1984–1988, for Ministry of Interior, Government of Lesotho (CHF), Coopers & Lybrand, U.S. Department of Labor, and Equal Employment Opportunity Commission; 1984–1985, consultant, African Development Foundation Securities Dealer, First Investors Corporation; 1982–1984, president, Institute for American Business; 1977–1982, president, the Newman and Hermanson Company; 1976–1977, assistant secretary, Department of Housing and Urban Development (presidential appointment, Senate confirmation); director, VISTA (presidential appointment), 1971–1973; special assistant to the Secretary and the Deputy Under Secretary, U.S. Department of Health, Education and Welfare, 1969–1971; chief, Midwest Section, Migrant Division, Office of Economic Opportunity, 1967–1969; research analyst, National Advisory Commission on Civil Disorders Commission on Political Activity of Government Personnel 1967;

personnel management assistant and officer, Department of Interior, 1961–1967, and instructor, Air Force/University of Maryland pre-college course, Laon, France, 1958–1961.

Newman was the recipient of the Secretary of Defense Medal for Outstanding Public Service (December 1985); Doctor of Laws, Amherst College, 1980; Secretary's Award for Excellence, Department of Housing and Urban Development, 1977; Doctor of Laws, Bates College, 1972; Outstanding Young Women of America, 1969 and Bates Keys, 1956. She has been listed in *Who's Who in American Women*, *Who's Who in American Politics*, the *World Who's Who of Women*, *Who's Who Among Black Americans*, *Who's Who in Government* and *Directory of International Biography*. She is the author and member of numerous publications and professional organizations.

NICKLEBERRY, HENRY H., was born in 1927, in Wichita Falls, Texas. He married the former Alice F. Bland and they have two children. He has five children from a previous marriage. He is a graduate of the University of Wisconsin School of Labor, Cornell University School of Law and Michigan State University. He serves as the 41st mayor of Saginaw, Texas.

Nickleberry started working at Grey Iron on his 18th birthday in 1945. He accepted hot, hard, and fast, repetitious work, because he wanted to save money for college. A strike started less than two weeks after he took the job, and his leadership role was linked to property his father owned. His father had a garage across the street from the Grey Iron, and that became the strike headquarters. They fed the families of the strikers. After the strike ended, he was elected to serve on the UAW local 668 shop committee. His 1948 appointment as the UAW's first black international representative was tied to a union goal of integrating the top hierarchy. Nickleberry's work during the next 34 years focused on training for union leaders, contract negotiations and equal job opportunities for minorities and women. In 1982, he was appointed to serve as an administrative

assistant to UAW Vice President Marc
Stepp. He retired in 1986 and won a
council seat in November 1987. He said
he followed city council politics during
his work career, but that he could not
seek a seat on the panel until after he
retired. He noted that his role in the
labor movement would have been jeop-
ardized if he had spent all his time performing in government activities. His
labor background helped him work to
involve municipal employees in an effort to improve city services. He believed
that he could bring together the forces
of city government and city employees,
and they could become more responsive
to the needs of the public.

Nickleberry served on the Sagi-
naw Downtown Development Author-
ity; Saginaw County Tuberculosis
Association; Saginaw Housing Appeals
Commission; Saginaw Vocational
Educational Advisory Committee;
Saginaw Community Action Commit-
tee; St. Mary's Medical Center Ad-
visory Board and Catholic Bishops
Committee for Community Affairs.

NORTON, ELEANOR HOLMES,
was born June 13, 1937, in Washington,
D.C. She married Edward Norton, and
they have two children, Katherine and
John. She graduated from Dunbar
High School, in Washington, and
enrolled in Antioch College in Yellow
Springs, Ohio, in 1955. She received a
B.A. degree from Antioch College in
1960. She then enrolled at Yale University, where she received her M.A.
degree in 1963, and her J.D. degree in
1964. In late 1964, she moved to
Philadelphia where she spent a year
clerking for a federal judge. There she
met Edward Norton, then a naval
officer stationed in the city. They were
married on October 9, 1965. Later that
year, the Nortons moved to New York
City, where she took a job as the assistant legal director of the American
Civil Liberties Union.

In October 1968, Norton argued
and won her first case before the United
States Supreme Court. In April 1970,
Mayor John V. Lindsay appointed her
chairman of the New York City Commission on Human Rights. She helped
push through the New York state
legislature the nation's strictest law
prohibiting discriminatory real estate
practices. Horrified by the imbalance
between minority students and minority teachers in New York City's schools,
she convened public hearings on the
Board of Education's employment
practices in January 1971. Citing a 1969
Board of Education survey which
showed that minority groups comprised 55 percent of the students, 9 percent of the teachers, and 4 percent of
the principals, she ordered Human
Rights Commission investigators to
look into and outline constructive proposals for "immediate change and improvement in the way blacks and Puerto
Ricans were treated by the educational
system."

Turning her attention to municipal government, Norton conducted a
census of city employees to check for
racial or sexual discrimination, set
up affirmative action programs, and
broadened maternity leave policies. In
a memorandum to Mayor Lindsay
made public on January 25, 1973, she
complained that because only 3 of the
14 members of the Human Rights Commission were attorneys qualified to
conduct hearings, vital work of the
commission was being unnecessarily
delayed. She recommended that the
mayor hire two professional hearings
officers to replace the 14 unpaid commissioners and raise the commission to
the status of a full-fledged city department. Impressed by her ability and her
aggressiveness, Mayor Abraham D.
Beame asked her in 1974 to stay on for
a second term.

Norton's reappointment was supported by 100 Black Men, the NAACP,
the National Urban League, and
leading city politicians, and both of
New York City's black newspapers. In

1977, President Jimmy Carter appointed her chairperson of the United States Equal Employment Opportunity Commission. She served in that position until 1980, the end of President Carter's term in office. She accepted a job at Georgetown University as a law professor. In 1990, she declared her candidacy for D.C.'s nonvoting Congressional seat. She won that seat easily on November 6, 1990, in her first bid for public office.

OBI, JAMES E., was born and raised in Lagos, Nigeria. He and his wife Rose and their four children reside in Stamford, Connecticut. He operated a successful business in Nigeria until his departure for the U.S. in December 1966. In July 1966, he joined the Equitable Life Assurance Society for the U.S. as a sales representative, and was appointed a district sales manager in 1968. He won the National Builders Trophy as the leading manager in the company in each of the three subsequent years. In March 1972, he was appointed an agency manager in New York City with the responsibility of building and developing his own agency organization. In 1982, the agency was number one in the U.S., and was awarded the Gold President's Trophy. He has earned three additional President's Trophies.

Obi has also won the Presidential Citation Award several times. In 1985, he was admitted to the Order of Excalibur. His agency force presently consists of more than 250 sales people in addition to a team of several managers and clerical staff. He is well-known and respected in the insurance industry. He is a member of the Million Dollar Round Table and the General Agency's and Managers Conference. He has been awarded the National Management Award six times, and the Master Agency Award twice. His accomplishments have been published in several U.S. publications. A book was written on his management style entitled *Theories of Management and the Executive in the Developing World*. A videotape entitled "The Jim Obi Story" is in circulation throughout the United States, and is used in the company and industry for motivational purposes.

Obi is a director of the TLC Group, L.P.– Beatrice Goods International, and board chairman of International News Link Corporation. He is a member of the Business Advisory Committee of the Business Council of the United Nations; the Jackie Robinson Scholarship Foundation; and the Glaucoma Foundation. He is president of the Nigerian-American Alliance.

OWENS, DARRYL T., a native Louisvillian, is married to Faye McBride Owens, and is the father of two daughters. He is a graduate of Central High School, and a trustee and lifetime member of Green Street Baptist Church. He received his college education at Central State University, and his legal training at Howard University Law School. He has practiced civil and criminal law in Louisville. From 1975 to 1983, he was a board member of the Kentucky Worker's Compensation Board. From 1970 to 1975, he served as a trial commissioner with the Juvenile Division of the Jefferson County court system. In 1966 and 1967, he was appointed as assistant attorney general for the Commonwealth of Kentucky. From 1965 to 1966, he was an assistant prosecutor for the Louisville Police Court.

Owens was elected County Commissioner in Jefferson County in 1983. He was elected with a solid majority of the countywide vote. He has sponsored legislation such as collective bargaining for public employees, a landlord tenant ordinance, and a minority vendors contract.

Owens has served as a member of the Kentucky State Democratic Central Executive Committee. During the 1984

Democratic National Convention, he served on the staff of Governor Martha Layne Collins, the convention chair. He previously has served as: field representative for U.S. Senator Wendell Ford; campaign chair for the re-election of state Senator Georgia Davis Powers; state campaign co-chair for the re-election of U.S. Senator Wendell Ford; and Jefferson County co-chair for the re-election of U.S. Senator Walter "Dee" Huddleston, to name a few. Owens is the recipient of numerous awards and citations from organizations in Louisville, Jefferson County and the Commonwealth of Kentucky.

Owens has served the Louisville community as a civic leader in a broad range of organizations: Louisville Bar Association; Kentucky Bar Association; National Association for the Advancement of Colored People; National Bar Association; Louisville Urban League; Kappa Alpha Psi Fraternity; Psi Boule Sigma Pi Phi Fraternity; Rohm & Haas Citizens Advisory Board; Juvenile Justice Commission; Kentuckiana Regional Planning and Development Agency Board; president of the Louisville Legal Aid Society; executive committee member of the Southern Association of Workmen's Compensation Administrators; board of directors of the Kentucky Health System Agency West; board of directors, Mammoth Life and Accident Insurance Company; Kentucky Attorney General's Consumer Protection Council; board of directors of the Kentucky Youth Council, and the Kentucky Commission on Women.

---

†OWENS, JAMES CLEVELAND "JESSE", was born September 12, 1913, in Danville, Alabama. He was the seventh child of a poverty-stricken sharecropper. When he was six years old, he was already working in the cotton fields. His family called him "J.C.," which was later changed to "Jesse" by his classmates and teachers. After graduating from East Technical High School, he enrolled at Ohio State University. He did not receive a scholarship and was forced to wait on tables and run elevators to pay his tuition. On May 25, 1935, a little more than a year before the Olympics, the Ohio State sophomore achieved international fame in "the greatest day in track history" and "the most astounding single day ever experienced by any athlete in any sport." He set new national AAU track records at the Big Ten Track and Field Championships at Ann Arbor, Michigan.

As a member of the United States contingent at the 1936 Olympic Games in Berlin, he tied the world record for the 100-meter dash in 10.3 seconds. He set an Olympic broad jump record by leaping 26 feet 5 5/16 inches. He set an Olympic and world record of 39.8 seconds in the 400-meter relay. He won four gold medals in the 1936 Olympic Games and was given a "hero's welcome" on his return.

During the following three years Owens led a swing orchestra, appeared as a detective in a Hollywood film, ran and won a sprint against a race horse in Havana, served as a WPA official with the Cleveland Park Department, established his own dry-cleaning business, and became a salesman for a distilling corporation. And, during this time, received an A.B. degree from Ohio State University.

From 1940 to 1942, Owens was employed in the Office of Civilian Defense in Philadelphia as national director of physical education for Negroes, and from 1942 to 1946, he worked for the Ford Motor Company as director of Negro personnel. He went on military leave in 1944. In 1946, he became the director of sports and sales for the Leo Rose Sporting Goods Company in Detroit. In 1950, he joined the board of directors of the South Side Boys Club in Chicago.

In 1952, he was appointed secretary of the Illinois Athletic Commission; he held this post until the fall of 1955 when he resigned to undertake a three-weeks "good will" tour of India for the State Department. In 1976, President Gerald Ford, presented Owens with the Medal of Freedom. Jesse Owens died in 1980.

OWENS, MAJOR, was born June 28, 1936, in Memphis, Tennessee, one of eight children of furniture factory worker Ezekiel Owens and homemaker Edna Davis Owens. He and his wife Maria have five children: Christopher, Millard, Geoffrey, Carlos and Cecilia.

Despite a constant struggle with poverty, Owens' parents instilled in him the belief that he could always overcome life's challenges, and that education would be an important tool for achieving success. Owens earned a Ford Foundation Scholarship to Morehouse College in Atlanta, Georgia, when he was only 16 and in his second year in high school. At Morehouse, Owens majored in mathematics and minored in education and library science. After graduating from Morehouse in 1956, Owens received his Master of Library Science degree from Atlanta University in 1957.

Owens moved to New York City during the mid–1950s and settled in Brooklyn. During this period, he held a number of specialized and supervisory positions in the Brooklyn Public Library. He also became involved in community activism, civil and housing rights demonstrations and neighborhood community renewal. From 1964 to 1966 he chaired the Brooklyn Congress of Racial Equality (CORE). During the '60s he was also appointed New York's commissioner of community development. His six years of service with the multi-million dollar community action agency won him the trust and praise of thousands of New Yorkers.

Owens' civil rights and grassroots organizing work became the foundation for his entry into electoral politics.

In 1974, Owens became the first New York state senator elected from Brooklyn's 17th Senatorial District. As the chairman of the Senate Day Care Task Force and as a member of the Senate Finance and Social Services Committees, he consistently fought attempts to slash social spending, particularly during a state fiscal crisis.

Owens remained a New York State Senator until 1982, when he was first elected to the U.S. House of Representatives. He has been returned to the Congress every election year since; in 1990, he was overwhelmingly re-elected for a fifth term by 95 percent of the vote. He is a senior member of the House Education and Labor Committee and chairs its Subcommittee on Select Education.

His numerous memberships include 100 Black Men, Beta Phi Mu, CORE and the NAACP.

PAIGE, EMMETT, JR., was born February 20, 1931, in Jacksonville, Florida, son of Emmett and Elizabeth Core Paige. He married the former Gloria McClary and they have three children, Michael, Sandra and Anthony. He dropped out of high school at age 16, not to hang out in the streets, but to fulfill his lifelong dreams of a military career. After leaving Stanton High School, he enlisted as a private in the United States Army. He began his Army career in August 1947. He held a host of important assignments in the United States and abroad, including Japan, Germany, Korea, the Philippines, and Vietnam. Earlier in his 39-year military career, Paige was with the 25th Infantry Division in Nara, Japan, as a Morse code radio operator. A very short while after enlisting, he had earned his GED high school diploma and later received a B.A. in general arts from the University of Maryland. Later, he received a master's degree in public administration from Penn State University.

He entered Officer Candidate School at Fort Monmouth, New Jersey, graduating in July 1952. When asked why he chose the army, he said, "The Army and Air Force were all one and the same back then, and they sent me down to MacDill Airbase in Tampa. I took a battery of tests and the Sergeant said, 'Well, you qualified for the ground forces or the Air Corps,' and I said, 'Where does the Air Corps give basic training?' He said, 'Sheppard Field in Texas.' When I found out the temperature there was 110 degrees, I told him I'd go with the ground forces — they trained at Fort Dix in New Jersey." Asked if race made a difference in his career, he said, "Officer Candidate School comes to mind. I've never forgotten who I am, having been born and raised in the South. When I went to Officer Candidate School in Fort Gordon, Georgia, I was the first and only black in the leadership course you had to finish to get into OCS. The commandant of the school, a West Pointer, said at the end of the course, 'Student Paige, I guess you think that we've been very unfair and given you a harder time than necessary,' and I said, with a smile on my face, 'As a matter of fact, sir, I do.' Then he said, 'You're right. You have set the standard for the Negroes who are going to have to be just as good as your white contemporaries, you're going to have to be twice as good. I'm not saying that that's fair or that's right, but those are the facts.'

"As he went on talking, I could see he was about to come to tears. Inside, the tears were there, but I didn't let them come out because I was pissed that I had to go through this. But I knew he was right. I had seen it as an enlisted man, black lieutenants sitting at a separate table in the officers' mess, in a black field artillery battalion where the bulk of the officer corps was white. And then, at OCS in Fort Monmouth, N.J. it was the same thing. But I was determined not to let the bastards kick me out. So yes, race has made a difference, but if anything I think it's made me a better person."

After OCS, tours followed at Fort Bliss, Texas (1952–1953), Karlsruhe, Germany (1954–1956), and still later at Fort Devens, Massachusetts, and Fort Carson, Colorado. Paige was in Korea (1959–1960), and in the Philippines with the Defense Communications Agency at Clark Air Force Base (1962–1965). In 1969, he commanded the 361st Signal Battalion in Vietnam as a lieutenant colonel with the famed 1st Signal Brigade, returning to the Defense Communications Agency in Arlington, Virginia, in 1970. University and War College training followed. In April 1976, he made history when he was promoted to brigadier general, the first black to reach general officer rank in the United States Army Signal Corps.

Gen. Paige's second star came in 1979 and the third in 1984 when he came to historic Fort Huachuca (black "Buffalo Soldiers" were stationed there in 1913) to command the ISC and direct about 40,000 civilian and military personnel. In November of 1986, he was honored for his outstanding accomplishments with the Information Systems Command when he received the Distinguished Service Medal from the Army's Chief of Staff at a special ceremony in the Pentagon. Included among his other decorations are three Legion of Merits, the Bronze Star and Meritorious Service Medals, and the Joint Service Commendation Medal. He retired from the Army in 1987.

---

†PAIGE, LEROY ROBERT (SATCHEL), was born July 7, 1906, in Mobile, Alabama. As a boy, he earned money toting suitcases at the Mobile train depot, where he rigged a pole and some rope to carry three or four bags at once. That ingenious arrangement prompted friends to call him Satchel. He would toss stones at cans, which

helped him later with accurate control. He won a job with a local semi-pro team in 1923. Two years later he advanced to the Chattanooga Black Lookouts of the Negro Southern League and later pitched for the Birmingham Black Barons, New Orleans Pelicans, Baltimore Black Sox, and Chicago American Giants.

Between league games and in the off-season, Paige barnstormed, often opposing the best white major league players. When the money was right, he journeyed to Mexico, Venezuela, and the Dominican Republic. He drew huge crowds everywhere and was able to earn an annual income near $40,000, higher than most major leaguers. He reportedly won 31 games, lost 4 in 1933; had 21 consecutive victories, and 62 straight scoreless innings. In 1934, when the major league season ended, Bill Veeck saw Paige pitch a 1-0 victory over major league pitcher Dizzy Dean in an exhibition game. In the fall of 1946, Veeck saw Paige beat another major pitcher, Bob Feller, in exhibition games, shutting out Feller's team.

Jackie Robinson broke the color line with the Brooklyn Dodgers, in 1947, becoming the first black player in the majors. Bill Veeck signed Paige to a Cleveland Indians contract on July 7, 1948, making him the first black pitcher in the American League. He was 42 when he made his debut. He won six important victories for the Cleveland Indians, losing one. Without those six victories, the Indians could not have won the pennant that year, 1948. Paige not only helped the Indians win the pennant, but more than earned his salary in his first three starts when more than 200,000 fans jammed stands to see this legendary black man pitch in the big league.

Paige worked in 31 games in 1949 but was released after the season when Veeck sold the Indians, only to be signed by Veeck again in 1951 for the St. Louis Browns. In 1954, Paige was released again and resumed barnstorming. He played another year for the Monarchs and three for Veeck's International League, Miami Marlins. He continued to pitch into the 1960s and finished his career with a farewell, three-inning stint as a starter for Charley Finley's A's on September 25, 1965.

For more than four decades in the Negro Leagues and the Majors, Paige used his pitching prowess and flashy, outspoken style to fashion a legendary career. In his younger days, he threw a fast ball described as "just a blur, or noise in the catcher's glove." In retirement, he embellished his legend through frequent interviews and public appearances. He became known for his rules for longevity, including the classic maxim "Don't look back. Something might be gaining on you." He died in Kansas City, Missouri, June 8, 1982.

PARAMORE, GWEN, a graduate of Howard University, Paramore received a B.A. degree in French, and a master's degree in French education. She received a scholarship from the University of Massachusetts and two grants to study overseas. She has served as assistant principal for J. Hayden Johnson Jr. High School from 1990 to date. Prior positions include: assistant principal Anita J. Turner Elementary School, 1985–1990; principal of four summer schools, 1986–1990.

She is founder of Afro-American Chiefs which builds self-esteem and pride in black male children. The criteria for becoming a member is that the child must have excelled in at least one subject. The children are rewarded, motivated and taken on all kinds of trips. They are also members of the Entrepreneurs Club and the Junior Citizen's Club. Further, she wrote a program called "Coup-Cultural Operation Upward Push," reaching children through extracurricular clubs/activities. Several clubs involved are: It's Academic, the Astronaut Club, Photography, Future Nurses, Future Teachers, Afro-American Dance — you name it! These programs were used to enhance learning and to improve attendance so that students can enjoy their educational road to success.

Paramore served as chairperson for ANC 8E07 Commission, 1990. She is the recipient of the Golden Poet Award from the World of Famous Poets organization. She has been professionally involved in numerous community and civil organizations.

PARKS, ROSA LOUISE, was born February 4, 1913, in Tuskegee, Alabama. Rosa Louise McCauley is the daughter of James and Leona (Edwards) McCauley. At the age of two she moved to her grandparents' farm in Pine Level, Alabama, with her mother and younger brother Sylvester. At the age of 11 she enrolled in the Montgomery Industrial School for Girls, a private school founded by liberal-minded women from the northern United States. The school's philosophy of self-worth was consistent with Leona McCauley's advice to "Take advantage of the opportunities, no matter how few they were." In 1932, she married Raymond Parks, a barber who was active in black voter registration and other civil rights causes.

After attending Alabama State College (now Alabama State University) in Montgomery for a time, Parks worked for the Montgomery Voters League, the NAACP Youth Council, and other civic and religious organizations. In 1943, she was elected secretary of the Montgomery branch of the NAACP. It was a rather simple problem which arose that first week of December 1955, and with patience it might have been worked out and forgotten. But nothing was simple in the South during this period. Parks, a respected black woman, had been hauled off a city bus and arrested when she refused to give up her seat to a white man.

The Montgomery Improvement Association filed a federal suit challenging the constitutionality of the segregation law of February 1, 1956, and the boycott continued until December 20, 1956, when a Supreme Court order declaring Montgomery's segregated seating laws unconstitutional was served on city officials. The next day blacks returned to the integrated buses, but not without violent incidents.

In 1957, Parks moved to Detroit, Michigan, where she worked for nonviolent social change with Dr. Martin Luther King, Jr., and the Southern Christian Leadership Conference (SCLC). She earned her living primarily as a seamstress until 1965, when she went to work for Congressman John Conyers, Jr., Democrat from Michigan. She was his receptionist, secretary, and administrative assistant for over 25 years. In 1987, she founded the Rosa Parks Institute to provide leadership and career training to black youths.

PATIN, JUDE WILMOT PAUL, was born on January 25, 1940, in Baton Rouge, Louisiana. He received a B.S. degree in architectural engineering from Southern University, in 1962, and an M.S. degree in industrial engineering from Arizona State University, in 1971. He received a ROTC commission to second lieutenant in 1962, and from September 1962 to November 1962, he was a student in the Field Artillery Officer Basic Course, United States Army Field Artillery School, Fort Sill, Oklahoma. From December 1962 to October 1963, he was a reconnaissance survey officer, Service Battery, 1st Missile Battalion, 42nd Artillery, with the United States Army in Europe. From October 1963 to January 1964, he was a survey officer, 3rd Missile Battalion, 32nd Artillery, 214th Artillery Group, Fort Sill. On March 4, 1964, he was promoted to the rank of 1st lieutenant.

From January 1964 to February 1965, he was the commander of Headquarters Battery, 3rd Missile Battalion, 32nd Artillery, 214th Artillery Group, Fort Sill. From March 1965 to June 1966, he served as an architectural engineer in the Installation Section, 593rd Engineer Company, Fort Sill. He was promoted to the rank of captain on April 16, 1966. From July 1966 to May 1967, he first served as commander of the 697th Engineer Company (Pipeline), and later commander of the 561st Engineer Company (Construction), of the 44th Engineer Group (Construction), United States Army in Thailand. From June 1967 to March 1968, he was a student in the Army Engineer Officer Advanced Course, United States Army Engineer School, Fort Belvoir, Virginia. From March 1968 to December 1968, he was the chief of the structures and utilities section, General Engineering Branch, Department of Engineering and Military Science, United States Army Engineer School, Fort Belvoir.

From January 1969 to March 1969, he served as assistant division engineer, 65th Engineer Battalion, 25th Infantry Division, United States Army, in Vietnam. From April 1969 to December 1969, he was the operations officer, Operations Division, United States Army Engineer Construction Agency Vietnam. He was promoted to the rank of major on July 11, 1969. From January 1970 to June 1971, he was a student at Arizona State University, Tempe, Arizona. From June 1971 to June 1974, he served first as the technical operations officer, later chief of plans and program branch, Management Analysis Office, United States Army Logistics Doctrine, Systems and Readiness Agency; then as the program analysis officer of the Administration and Management Office, United States Army Logistics Evaluation Agency, Deputy Chief of Staff for Logistics, United States Army, New Cumberland, Pennsylvania.

From June 1974 to May 1976, he served first as the S-3 (Operations Officer), and later as executive officer, 84th Engineer Battalion, 25th Infantry Division, Schofield Barracks, Hawaii. From June 1976 to June 1977, he was a student at the United States Army Command and General Staff College, Fort Leavenworth, Kansas. From June 1977 to May 1980, he served as an advisor to the 1138th Engineer Battalion (Combat) (Reserve Component), United States Army Readiness Region V, Fort Sheridan, Illinois. He was promoted to the grade of lieutenant colonel on December 9, 1978. From May 1980 to May 1983, he was the commander of 293rd Engineer Battalion, 18th Engineer Brigade, United States Army in Europe. From May 1983 to April 1985, he was a student, later director, of Insurgency Operations, United States Army War College, Carlisle Barracks. He was promoted to the grade of colonel on October 1, 1984. From May 1985 to July 1987, he was the commander of the 1st Training Support Brigade, later commander of the 136th Engineer Brigade, United States Army Training and Engineer Center, Fort Leonard Wood, Missouri.

From August 1987 to September 1989, Patin served as the assistant chief of staff for engineering and housing, 21st Support Command, United States Army in Europe and the Seventh. He was promoted to the one-star grade of brigadier general on November 1, 1989. In October 1989, he was appointed commanding general of the United States Army Engineer Division, North Central, Chicago, Illinois. General Patin has received numerous awards and decorations, including: the Legion of Merit; the Bronze Star Medal; Meritorious Service Medal (with two oak leaf clusters); the Air Medal; Army Commendation Medal (with oak leaf cluster); and the Parachutist Badge.

PATRICK, JENNIE R., was born January 1, 1949, in Gadsden, Alabama. She is the daughter of James Patrick and Elizabeth Patrick. She attended Tuskegee Institute from 1967 to 1970, and later received a B.S. degree from the University of California, Berkeley, in 1973. She received a Ph.D. degree from the Massachusetts Institute of Technology (MIT), in 1979. She became the first black woman in the United States to earn a doctoral degree in chemical engineering. From 1972 to 1973, she was employed as an assistant engineer for the Dow Chemical.

From 1973 to 1974, Patrick served as an assistant engineer for the Stauffer Chemical Company. She also served as a research associate for MIT, from 1973 to 1979; as a research engineer with first Chevron, from 1974 to 1983; Arthur D. Little Inc., and General Electric Company. In 1983, she was employed as a senior research engineer at the Phillip Morris Research Center in Richmond, Virginia.

Dr. Patrick is committed to the education of minority youth and travels the country encouraging high school and college students to pursue scientific and technical careers. Her numerous awards and honors include the NOBCChE Outstanding Woman in Science & Engineering Award in 1980.

PAYTON, WALTER JERRY, was born on July 25, 1954, in Columbia, Mississippi. He is the son of Peter and Alyne Payton. He and his wife Connie have two children, Jarrett and Brittney. He attended Columbia High School, where he was a drummer in the school band. After school he played and sang in jazz-rock combos. While he set local schoolboy records in the long jump in track, he avoided football as long as his brother was starring at halfback for the school team. When his brother Eddie Payton graduated from Columbia High School, Walter, at the urging of the football coach, tried out for the team in his junior year. The first time he carried the football, he ran more than 60 yards for a touchdown.

After graduating from high school, Payton enrolled at Jackson State University. At Jackson State he registered the most points in National Collegiate Athletic Association history, with 464. Academically, he earned his B.A. degree in special education in three and a half years. In the 1975 professional draft of college players he was the first-round choice of the Chicago Bears. In his first year, while limited in his rushing opportunities, he averaged 3.5 yards per rush, and as a kickoff returner he led the league with 444 yards in 14 returns. In 1977, along with his fellow running back and friend Ron Harper, he paced the Bears to their first winning season (9-5) in 10 years and their first playoffs in 14. Payton led the National Football League in yards rushing with 1,852, and he did so in 339 attempts, for an average of 5.5 yards per rush. He set a new NFL single-game record for most yards in a game against Minnesota on November 20, 1977, with 275, two more than O. J. Simpson's previous mark.

Payton was voted the Most Valuable Player in the 1977 Pro Bowl, and he was the league's consensus MVP, the youngest player ever to achieve that distinction. He was also named UPI's Athlete of the Year. In 1980, he won an unprecedented fifth consecutive National Football Conference rushing title with 1,460 yards. In 1983, he had a combined total of more than 2,000 yards for the second time in his professional career. On October 7, 1984, he surpassed Jim Brown's career rushing record of 12,312 (which had stood for 19 years), and his running and blocking made the Bears the best team on the ground in the 1984 season.

Payton, whose nickname is "Sweetness," went on to become the NFL's all-time leading ground-gainer. He rushed for 16,726 yards during his

NFL career. He retired at the end of the 1988 football season. With the help of a lawyer, an accountant, and a secretary, he runs Walter Payton Enterprises, which encompasses a number of investments and businesses, including Mississippi and Tennessee timberland, real estate, and restaurants in Chicago and Jackson, Mississippi. He has done commercial endorsements for cars, shoes, and the Hilton hotel chain, but he has turned down most commercial offers. Most of his television spots have been public service ads for such causes as the Peace Corps and United Way. He is involved in many charities, especially benefits for deaf and retarded children.

———

PEAY, FRANCIS, a native of Pittsburgh, Pennsylvania, he is married to Patricia and the father of twin daughters, Aryca and Aisha. He earned All-American honors as an offensive tackle at Missouri. After graduating in 1966, he played two years with the New York Giants (1966–1967), five seasons with the Green Bay Packers (1968–1972), and two campaigns with the Kansas City Chiefs (1973–1975) in the NFL. He entered his fifth season as head coach at Northwestern determined to get the Wildcats back on the right path to success after a disappointing season. He was a first year assistant under head coach Dennis Green in 1981 when the Wildcats endured a winless season, and he had watched the program slowly improve. He took over as interim head in 1986 and Northwestern responded with a 4-7 record, its finest mark in 13 years.

With single season record holders in both rushing and receiving in 1990, Peay certainly had reason to believe that last year's 0-11 season was merely a stumble and not a complete fall from levels his first three Northwestern teams had reached. Under his guidance, the squad had earned its share of

individual honors. Running back Bob Christian broke Mike Adamle's 1970 school rushing mark with 1,291 yards in 1989. Wide receiver Richard Buchanan established a single season receiving mark with 94 grabs and also set Northwestern standards with 1,115 receiving yards and nine touchdown catches. Buchanan garnered first-team All-Big Ten honors from the Associated Press and second-team accolades from United Press International. Christian claimed second-team conference honors from AP. Buchanan captured third-team All America honors from AP, and both he and Christian earned honorable mention All-America recognition from the *Sporting News*. Punter/ linebacker Ed Sutter was selected the 1988 AP Big Ten Freshman of the Year while Sutter and running back Byron Sanders were named honorable mention All-America by UPI. Mike Baum, who finished his Northwestern career in '88, made history when he became the first offensive lineman in Division I to be named to the GTE/CoSIDA Academic All-America first team three times. During Peay's four-year tenure, six players had been selected Academic All-America All Big Ten.

Peay got his first test of collegiate head coaching experience with the Wildcats in 1986 when he was named interim coach and led Northwestern to a 4-7 mark. His efforts were recognized by *Sports Illustrated*, which termed his performance "brilliant" while honoring him with Coach of the Year recognition, and by the *Chicago Tribune*, which credited him with the "Best Coaching Job" of 1986. His achievements are even more remarkable considering the circumstances surrounding his move into the head coaching role. He was named interim head coach in March of 1986, after Dennis Green resigned one week before the start of spring practice, and was named coach for the season in early June. He was a natural choice to conduct spring drills, having come to Northwestern with

Green in 1980, and having been instrumental in building the improving Wildcats defense.

Since 1984, Peay had been NU's defensive coordinator. The initiative and leadership he demonstrated during the spring proved him to be the best candidate for the unusual interim coaching position. Circumstances may have brought him to the head coaching ranks earlier than expected, but hard work and dedication made him the man to answer opportunity's call. Following a nine-year career in the National Football League, he began coaching as the defensive coordinator at University Senior High School in St. Louis, Missouri. After a year on the prep level, he was hired as junior varsity and offensive line coach at Notre Dame by Dan Devine, who had coached Peay both at Missouri and the Green Bay Packers.

Peay coached at Notre Dame in 1976 and 1977, helping the Fighting Irish to a pair of bowl game wins and the 1977 national championship. In 1978, he moved to the University of California as outside linebacker coach and worked three seasons with the Golden Bears. He tutored future pros Ron Rivera (Chicago Bears) and Rich Dixon (Atlanta Falcons) and helped California gain its first bowl bid in 20 years during his second year. In his final two seasons at Cal, the Golden Bears beat arch-rival Stanford, and he was the first man asked to come to Evanston as an assistant when Stanford offensive coordinator Dennis Green was hired as Northwestern's head coach.

PENN, ROBERT W., was born in Athens, Alabama. He is married and the father of one child. He is a graduate of Tuskegee Institute, Tuskegee, Alabama, with a B.A. degree, 1950. He also attended A&T College in North Carolina, and graduated from Case Western Reserve University in 1953, with a J.D. degree. He served five years in the United States Army and was honorably discharged with the rank of first sergeant. He practiced law in private practice from 1953 to 1984, and serves as a judge in the municipal court from 1984 to date.

Penn's prior positions include: president of Civil Service Commission of the city of Toledo from 1971 to 1984 where he enforced the Civil Service Provisions of the Charter of the city of Toledo, including classifications of all positions in the classified service for appointment and employment based on merit, efficiency, moral character and industry. He heard and decided all cases which were appealed from persons employed in the classified Civil Service ranks of Toledo who were suspended, reduced in rank or dismissed.

Penn served on the administrative board of zoning appeal of the city of Toledo from 1962 to 1978, and served as its president for approximately five years. His duties were to hear all appeals from persons who requested waivers of any zoning ordinance for the city of Toledo. A former member of the executive committee of the Toledo Bar Association, where he served for approximately eight years with the responsibility of giving advice and counsel and directing the affairs of the Toledo Bar Association.

Penn was a former member of Gov. Gilligan's Judicial Election Committee, where he screened and recommended candidates for appointments as judges in all county and city courts for Central and Northern District for the state of Ohio. He served on numerous boards: former president of the Toledo Opera Association and board member for a number of years; formerly a board member of the Lyric Opera Association; member of the board of trustees of Toledo Hospital; former member of the board of directors of Toledo Trust Company; and former member of the board of directors of Sea Gate Community Development Corporation — decisions regarding providing consulting services and making investments for projects designed to primarily promote community welfare and consulting assistance to local governmental agencies making applications for UDAC.

Penn also served on the Metropolitan board of trustees of YMCA; Indiana board of trustees of YMCA and former chairman of the board; Volunteers of America; Epilepsy Foundation board member; former member of Charter Revision Committee for the city of Toledo; former member of mayor's "Blue Ribbon" Committee to report on the propriety of recommending an increase in the tax levy for Toledo; former vice chairman of the board of trustees of Maumee Valley Hospital, served on that board for approximately 12 years; former board member of NAACP; former member of Advisory Group of Northwestern Ohio Regional Medical Program; former member of Task Force Committee on special programs of youths in Dorr Detroit area; former member of United Federate executive board; former member of the trustees of Community Planning Council of Northwest Ohio; former member of the trustees of Hospital Planning Association; former member of board of Community Relations; former member of Child and Family Services of Greater Toledo, and former member of board of trustees of Links Neighborhood Center.

PEREZ, ANNA, was born June 13, 1951, in New York City, and serves as press secretary to Barbara Bush, wife of President George Bush. She attended Hunter College where she majored in journalism and minored in political science. She is married to Theophilus Sims and resides with their two children in the Washington, D.C. area. Beginning in 1972, she worked five years as a flight attendant followed by two

years as a small business marketing specialist in Oakland, California.

From 1979 to 1981, Perez co-owned the *Tacoma Facts*, a weekly newspaper in Tacoma, Washington. From 1981 to 1985, she served as assistant press secretary to U.S. Congressman John Miller (R-WA). In August of 1988, she served as regional press secretary for Bush '88 at the Republican National Convention in New Orleans, Louisiana.

PERRY, CARRIE SAXON, was born in Hartford, Connecticut. After high school she enrolled at Howard University in Washington, D.C., in 1949, staying for two years. She served as executive director of Amistad House Inc.; as administrator of Community Renewal Team of Greater Hartford Inc.; as administrator of Ambulatory Health Care Planning Inc.; as administrator of Hartford Community Trainers; and as administrator of the Connecticut Welfare Department. She spent seven years in the Connecticut General Assembly as a State Representative. She was assistant majority leader, chaired the Bonding Subcommittee and was a hard-working member on the Education, Finance and Housing committees.

In November 1988, she became the first black female to be elected mayor of a major northeastern city. The Democratic candidate defeated her white male Republican opponent by a vote of 10,304 to 7,613. Perry doesn't dwell on the fact that she is a black woman, but she does emphasize how important it is for blacks and women to have a voice in all levels of government. She was selected the first woman treasurer of the National Conference of Black Mayors, Inc. She is a lifetime member of the NAACP; president of the Hartford Chapter of 100 Black Women; and executive board member Greater Hartford Black Democrats, and numerous other organizations.

PETERSEN, FRANK E., JR., was born in Topeka, Kansas. He enlisted in the Navy in 1950. While attending the Naval Aviation Cadet Program, he was determined to become the first black Marine pilot. His determination paid off. He completed Naval Flight Training at Pensacola, Florida, and received his wings on October 22, 1952. He flew 64 combat missions in the F-4U Corsair in Korea, earning the Distinguished Flying Cross, America's highest aviation medal, and six air medals. He was the first black in the Naval services to command a tactical air squadron.

In 1968, Petersen commanded the Marine Fighter Attack Squadron 314 in Vietnam. Under his command, this squadron received the Hanson Award for Aviation as the best fighter squadron in the Marine Corps. In 1979, while serving as the chief of staff of the 9th Marine Amphibious Brigade on Okinawa, Japan, President Jimmy Carter nominated him for advancement to the grade of brigadier general. With the Senate confirmation, Petersen, the Marine Corps' first black aviator, became the first black Marine to attain Flag rank.

PHILLIPS, JOHN F., was born on September 3, 1942, in Neches, Texas, and graduated from Climons High School there in 1959. He received a B.S. degree in biology and chemistry with honors from Jarvis Christian College in 1963, and an M.S. degree in logistics management from the Air Force Institute of Technology in 1975. He also pursued additional studies at North Texas State University and Texas Southern University. He is an honor graduate of the Institute of Aerospace Safety Engineering (graduate and undergraduate school), University of Southern California. He completed Squadron Officer School in 1971, Industrial College of the Armed Forces in 1976, and the National War College in 1983. He was commissioned a second lieutenant through Officer Training School, Lackland Air Force Base, Texas, in December 1963 and earned his navigator wings at James Connally Air Force Base, Texas.

After completing KC-135 combat crew training at Castle Air Force Base, California, in February 1967, Phillips was assigned to Travis Air Force Base, California, where he flew as an instructor navigator. During this time he flew regular combat missions in Vietnam, accumulating more than 300 combat flying hours. He entered pilot training at Williams Air Force Base, Arizona, and graduated with top honors in July 1970. He then was assigned to the 1st German Air Force Squadron, Sheppard Air Force Base, Texas, as a T-37 instructor pilot and was awarded German pilot's wings. From December 1973 to August 1975, he served as an inspector and flight examiner with the Air Training Command inspector general's staff, Randolph Air Force Base, Texas.

Phillips then attended the Air Force Institute of Technology, Wright-Patterson Air Force Base. Upon graduation in September 1976, he became system manager for the F-100 and J-85 engines at Kelly Air Force Base, Texas. In December 1978, he was assigned as a logistics systems analyst at Doshan Tappeh Air Base, Iran, until the fall of the shah of Iran. Phillips remained in Iran under the Khomeini regime until his expulsion in February 1979. He transferred to Wright-Patterson and served as deputy program manager for logistics, KC-10 Joint Program Office.

In January 1982, Phillips was appointed system program director for the TR-1 and later became director of all airlift and trainer systems. He attended the National War College from August 1982 to September 1983, and distinguished himself in both academics and athletics. He then was assigned to the Weapons System Program Division, Directorate of Logistics Plans and

Programs, at the headquarters of the United States Air Force, Washington, D.C. He first served as deputy division chief, then as chief, and later as deputy director of logistics plans and programs.

From July 1985 to July 1986, Phillips was military assistant to the assistant secretary of the Air Force for Research Development and Logistics. After this assignment he served as vice commander of the Logistics Management Systems Center at Wright-Patterson. He assumed his current position in October 1988, and he was promoted to brigadier general on October 1, 1988. He is a senior pilot with more than 3,000 flying hours. His military awards and decorations include: the Legion of Merit; the Meritorious Service Medal (with two oak leaf clusters); the Air Medal; the Air Force Commendation Medal (with oak leaf cluster); the Combat Readiness Medal; and the Republic of Vietnam Gallantry Cross with Palm.

PHILLIPS, WILBUR L., is married to Barbara C. Phillips and is the father of one daughter, Lynda. A graduate of Central Park Elementary School, Omaha, Nebraska; North High (Secondary) School, Omaha; J.D. and LL.B. degrees from Drake University, Des Moines, Iowa. He served as Revenue Agent, Employee Plans, I.R.S. and Revenue Agents E.P. Examiners, I.R.S. Since 1970 he has served as a part-time instructor in the Black Studies Department, University of Nebraska of these courses: Law in the Black Community, Introduction to Black Studies, Black Culture, Minority Economic Development and the International Relations of the Black Community. He was in general practice with specialties in commercial/corporate enterprises doing business in West African imports, exports, joint ventures, economic development and other forms of in vestments; also, consultin on the draft-

ing and management of pension, profit sharing and other retirement plans.

Prior positions include: tax law specialist for the Internal Revenue Service; planning director, Technical Assistance Agency, state of Nebraska; director and consultant, Entrepreneurial and Management; part-time hearing examiner for the State Labor Department; director of consulting unit conducting feasibility studies and making reports on the feasibility of Black Community Radio Station Management; staff attorney, Legal Aid Society, Omaha; field legal representative for the Veteran's Administration and staff attorney for a Real Estate Acquisition Branch, Omaha district.

Phillips was admitted to practice before the Iowa Supreme Court in 1956; Federal District Court for the Southern District of Iowa, 1956; admitted to practice before the Nebraska Supreme Court, 1957, and Federal District Court for the District of Nebraska, in 1957. His professional affiliations include: member, Omaha-Council Bluffs Bicentennial Commission, 1975–1976; president, chairman of the board of directors and legal counsel, Great Plains Black Museum from 1974–1976 and from 1988 to date;

Administrative Appeals Board, city of Omaha, 1970–1973, chairperson 1972–1973; legal counsel: Citizens Coordinating Committee for Civil Liberties (4CL, social activist organization), 1965–1967; president, Negro Historical Society of Nebraska, 1963–1973; president, North Branch, Omaha, NAACP, 1964–1965; board member, Omaha Urban League, 1957–1959; Second District representative, Nebraska Young Democrats, 1960–1961; board chairman, Calvin Memorial Presbyterian Church, 1958; and president of the Omaha De Porres Club, a social activist organization, 1950–1958.

PIERCE, LAWRENCE W., was born in Philadelphia, Pennsylvania, and married the former Cynthia Straker, a law professor at St. John's University School; they have three sons, Warren, Michael and Mark. After three years in the U.S. Army, where he served as a sergeant in the infantry in

Italy during World War II, he completed his undergraduate education at St. Joseph's College in Philadelphia. He was inducted into Alpha Sigma Nu National Jesuit Honor Society and graduated with honors in the class of 1948. He attended Fordham University School of Law, where he was a dean's list student, and an associate editor of the *Fordham Law Review*; he graduated in the class of 1951. He was admitted to the New York State Bar that year and for the next 20 years he was a civil law practitioner, a prosecutor, a deputy police commissioner, a state commissioner, and a university professor. For 10 years he was an active member and later president of the Catholic Interracial Movement founded by Father John La Farge.

Pierce has served as a board member and officer of the Sons of the Revolution at Fraunces Tavern in Manhattan, and was a member of the Black Revolutionary War Patriots Foundation. In the early 1960s he was a founder of the civic organization known as 100 Black Men. In 1971, he was appointed by President Nixon as a United States District Judge for the Southern District of New York. From 1979–1981, he was a member of the United States Foreign Intelligence Surveillance Court by appointment of Chief Justice Warren Burger. In 1981, he was appointed by President Reagan as a judge of the United States Court of Appeals for the Second Circuit, which covers New York, Connecticut and Vermont. On January 1, 1990, he assumed the status of a senior circuit judge of that court. Earlier, he had served as chairman of the Second Circuit Bicentennial Committee and chairman of the Circuit's Historical Events Committee.

For over 25 years he has been a member of the United States delegations studying criminal justice systems in England, Sweden, Japan and South Africa. He has served on the secretary of the Army's Special Civilian Committee to study and report on Army confinement facilities in the United States, Europe and the Far East; and headed a delegation of judges and lawyers which studied the legal and judicial systems in the People's Republic of China. He has served on the board of trustees of St. Joseph's University; vice-president of the board of managers of Lincoln Hall for Boys in the Archdiocese of New York; served on the board of trustees of the Practicing Law Institute; and as a member of the board of directors of CARE, USA and the Havens Fund Society; and completed service to the American Bar Association's Alternate Observer to the United States Mission to the United Nations.

POITIER, SIDNEY, was born February 20, 1924, in Miami, Florida, to Reginald and Evelyn (Otten) Poitier, the youngest of eight children. He is married to Joanna Shimkus and is the father of six children, Beverly, Pamela, Sherri, Gina, Anika and Sydney. He was educated by private tutors in his childhood, in the Bahama Islands on his parents' tomato farm. He is a graduate of Western Senior High School and Governor's High School in Nassau. During the Depression he was forced to leave school and go to work because the demand for tomatoes had decreased and his father, who had become a victim of rheumatism and arthritis, was unable to work. As a teenager living in Miami, he really became conscious of the "barbed wire" that surrounded the white world.

Poitier's life was full of frustration and confusion, and he experienced tremendous loneliness as a result of realizing for the first time that he could not trust adults. Wanting to go to New York, but not having the funds, he rode the rails and reached Harlem with $1.50 in his pocket. He worked as a dishwasher and slept on a roof across from the Capitol Theatre. After the attack on Pearl Harbor, he enlisted in the United States Army. He was trained to be a physiotherapist, served with the 1267th Medical Detachment, and was discharged in 1945. Back in New York, he held a series of menial jobs and found none of them satisfying.

Reading a story in the *Amsterdam News* that the American Negro Theatre was looking for actors, Poitier decided to apply. His audition was unfavorable, and director Fredrick O'Neal made it clear that he lacked the required talents. He was determined so he bought a radio and spent as much as six months listening to cultivated voices and improving his enunciation of words. He returned to the theatre and O'Neal gave him acting lessons in exchange for doing backstage chores. As a member of the group, he alternated with Harry Belafonte in the leading role of "Days of Our Youth" and portrayed a butler in "Strivers Road" and Boris Kolyenkov in "You Can't Take It with You," "Rain," "Freight," "The Fisherman," "Hidden Horizon," and "Riders to the Sea."

In 1946, Poitier was hired by James Light at $75 a week to play Polydorus in an all Negro production of "Lysistrata." In 1949, he made his first film appearance in an Army Signal Corps documentary called *From Whom Cometh My Help*. He made his Hollywood film debut in *No Way Out*. Other motion pictures in which he has appeared include: *Cry, the Beloved Country; Red Ball Express; Go, Man, Go; Goodbye; My Lady; Edge of the City; Band of Angels* and *Blackboard Jungle* in 1955, a movie dealing with juvenile delinquency in the New York schools. He played the part of a gifted student whose truculence creates havoc in every classroom.

Poitier's acting career continued with *Something of Value, The Mark of the Hawk,* and *The Defiant Ones* which received the Silver Bear Award at the Berlin Film Festival of 1958. The film won the New York Film Critics award and was named to six of the ten-best lists. In the film adaptation of the George Gershwin-DuBose Heyward opera "Porgy and Bess," in 1959, he took the stellar role of Porgy which was sung by Robert McFarren. On Broadway, he starred in Lorraine Hansberry's drama "A Raisin in the Sun." It depicts the problems of a black family in Chicago who were trying to cross the boundary line that separated lower-class status from the middle class. As the highstrung son William Lee Younger, he had to decide whether he would compromise himself to pander to his family's material needs or whether he would stand firm for freedom and dignity.

Poitier was written up in the *New York Times* in 1959 as a remarkable actor with enormous power that was always under control. He was as eloquent when he had nothing to say as when he had a pungent line to speak. When acting, Poitier said that what he wanted was the kind of role that makes him feel worthwhile. He said that he would work anywhere — movies, theater, TV — provided the material had texture, quality, and something good to say about life. Such work as *A Warm December; Little Nikita; Hard Knox; In the Heat of the Night; To Sir, with Love* and *Guess Who's Coming to Dinner* had good texture and quality as well.

From the beginning of his screen career Poitier has displayed an exceptional talent that promised to place him in the front rank of black actors in the world today. In spite of the limited casting opportunities that the Hollywood film industry offered the serious black actor, he has established his reputation on the strength of his acting alone. He was the first black to be nominated as the best actor by the Academy of Motion Picture Arts and Sciences, for his performance in *The Defiant Ones*. At the age of 37 he was presented an Oscar in 1963 for his performance in *Lilies of the Field* and became the first black actor to ever cop the coveted statuette, along with the first black to record footprints in concrete at Grauman's Chinese Theater in 1967.

In 1972, Poitier made his debut as a director-actor with Harry Belafonte in *Buck and the Preacher* and later was producer-director-actor in the comedy series, *Uptown Saturday Night, Let's Do It Again* and *A Piece of the Action* with Belafonte, Bill Cosby and James Earl Jones. He joined with stars Paul Newman, Steve McQueen, Dustin Hoffman and Barbara Streisand to form First Artists Productions, Inc., an independent film production company. Poitier's autobiography *This Life* was published in 1980 and has the unique distinction of being a true autobiography written by the star himself.

As a director he created a box-office hit in 1980, *Stir Crazy* starring Richard Pryor and Gene Wilder, followed in 1982 by Wilder in *Hanky Panky*, and rock music film *Fast Forward* in 1985. *Shoot to Kill* turned out to be a good vehicle for Poitier's return as an actor after ten years. The story was a simple one. As an FBI special agent, he was assigned to track down a cold blooded killer who had to prove himself as a black man, a lawman and a human being. He is undoubtedly the most successful black actor in history.

PORTER, JOHN W., was born in Fort Wayne, Indiana, August 13, 1931. Porter's professional career has demonstrated an outstanding dedication and commitment to teaching and education. He earned a B.A. degree in political science from Albion College in 1953, an M.A. degree in counseling and guidance from Michigan State University in 1957, and a Ph.D. degree in higher education administration, also from Michigan State, in 1962. He taught in the Albion and Lansing school systems for five years before joining the Michigan Department of Public Instruction as a research consultant in 1958. At the age of 26, he was the youngest person and the only black professional employed in the Michigan Department of Education.

In 1960, Porter was appointed director of the Guaranteed Student Loan Program for College Students, a program he designed following on-site visits to similar programs in New York and Massachusetts. Once the Guaranteed Student Loan Program was operational, he established the Michigan State Scholarship Program, which began in 1964. Today, the scholarship program awards approximately $70 million annually to deserving college students.

In 1965, Dr. Porter was appointed director of education, and from 1966 to 1969 he served as the associate superintendent of the Bureau of Higher Education of the Michigan Department of Education. He was unanimously elected state superintendent of public instruction by the Michigan State Board of Education in October 1969. At age 38, he was the youngest chief state school officer in the nation and the first black state school superintendent in the United States. During his ten-year term as head of the Department of Education, he implemented numerous education programs and was recognized for his outstanding contributions to higher education. Among his accomplishments were the "Six Step Accountability Model," which he designed, and the concept of the "Educational Health Check-Up."

Porter is recognized as a leading supporter of vocational rehabilitation and disability determination and has served as a national spokesperson for retraining school staffs. During his 37 years of public service, he has received many honors. In 1979, he went to Eastern Michigan University as the 17th president of the institution. he introduced the "Decade of Advancement," which was designed to revitalize the troubled university. His plan – and much hard work – produced unbelievable success. In January 1989, he joined the National Board for Professional Teaching Standards as vice president, and at that time also became chief executive officer of the Urban Education Alliance. Inc. He has made a commitment to raise $1 million to endow a Distinguished Chair in Urban Education.

In May 1989, Dr. Porter agreed to serve as the Interim General Superintendent for the Detroit Public Schools. His term began on July 1, 1989. He has published many books and articles relating to education and has served on several state and national commissions and advisory boards, including the National Commission on Manpower Policy and the National Advisory Council on Social Cooperative Education, the Governor's Blue Ribbon Commission on Welfare Reform, and the Michigan Martin Luther King, Jr. Holiday Commission. He is a member of the boards of directors of the Michigan Bell Telephone Company, the Economic Club of Detroit, past chairman of the board of trustees of the College Board, and is a member of the National Urban League.

POSEY, EDWARD W., was born May 29, 1927, in Youngstown, Ohio. He is married to the former Fanny Berryman of Warren, Ohio, and the father of three children, Bruce, Ada and Michael. He is a graduate of Meharry Medical College in Nashville, Tennessee, with an M.D. degree in 1952. His internship (rotating) was served at Brooklyn-Cumberland Medical Center, 1952–1953. He served with the U.S. Marine Corps as battalion surgeon and as Naval medical officer from 1953–1955.

Dr. Posey has served as chief, Mental Health Clinic from 1979 to date. Prior positions include: General Surgery Residency, Crile V.A. Hospital, Cleveland; Family Physician Practice, Minneapolis, Minnesota; psychiatry residency, V.A. Hospital, Minneapolis, and the University of Minnesota; director, Day Hospital, Psychiatry Service, Minneapolis V.A. Medical Center; instructor for the University of Minnesota Department of Psychiatry; and assistant professor, Department of Psychiatry, University of Minnesota Medical School, since 1968. He was certified in psychiatry by the American Board of Psychiatry and Neurology as a Diplomat in 1968. His professional affiliations include: member, for the National Medical Association, Minnesota Psychiatric Association, Fellow of American Psychiatric Association and examiner for the American Board of Psychiatry and Neurology.

POWELL, COLIN L., was born April 5, 1937, in New York, New York. He married the former Vivian Johnson, and they have three children, Michael,

Linda, and Annemarie. In about 1940 the family, which Powell recalls as having been "strong and close," moved to the South Bronx, where he graduated from Morris High School in 1954. At the City College of New York, he majored in geology and got his first taste of military life as a cadet in the Reserve Officers Training Corps (ROTC). He has explained that he enrolled in ROTC because, as an ambitious young black man in the 1950s, he had learned to take advantage of what few attractive opportunities existed and he found his temperament well suited to military discipline. Former classmates remember that he displayed rare leadership ability on campus, motivating many other students to succeed.

Powell was appointed commander of the Pershing Rifles, the ROTC precision drill team, and graduated at the top of the college's ROTC class of 1958 with the rank of cadet colonel, the highest rank in the corps. On graduation, he was commissioned a second lieutenant in the United States Army. As one of the more than 16,000 American military advisers sent to

South Vietnam by President John F. Kennedy, Powell was assigned from 1962 to 1963 to a South Vietnamese infantry battalion patrolling the border with Laos. While marching through a rice paddy one day in 1963, he stepped into a Punji-stick trap, impaling his foot on one of the sharpened stakes concealed just below the water's surface. After that injury, he was given a Purple Heart, and in that same year he was awarded the Bronze Star.

In 1968, Powell returned for a second Vietnam tour of duty with the United States Army infantry as a battalion executive officer and division operations officer. He was injured a second time in a helicopter crush landing. In 1971, he earned an M.B.A. degree from George Washington University. in 1972, he was selected to be a White House Fellow and served his fellowship year as special assistant to the Deputy Director of the Office of the President. In 1973, he assumed command of the 1st Battalion, 32d Infantry in Korea. Upon completion of the National War College in 1976, he assumed command of the 2d Brigade, 101st Airborne Division (Air Assault), Fort Campbell, Kentucky.

In 1977, Powell went to Washington to serve in the immediate office of the Secretary of Defense. Over the next three years, he served as senior military assistant to the Deputy Secretary of Defense. For a brief period in 1979, he served as executive assistant to the Secretary of Energy. In 1981, he became the assistant division commander for Operations and Training, 4th Infantry Division (Mechanized), Fort Carson, Colorado. In 1983, he returned to Washington to serve as senior military assistant to Secretary of Defense Caspar W. Weinberger. In July 1986, he assumed command of the V U.S. Corps in Frankfurt, Federal Republic of Germany.

In January 1987, Powell returned to the White House to serve as deputy assistant to National Security Adviser Frank Carlucci. When Carlucci took over as Secretary of Defense, in 1989, Powell became assistant to then–President Reagan on National Affairs (Military Matters). In April 1989, he took over as commander-in-chief of Forces Command, Fort McPherson, Georgia. In September 1989, he returned to Washington as President Bush's choice for Chairman of the Joint Chiefs, a selection that leap-frogged him over many senior officers. In October 1989, he was confirmed as chairman.

General Powell played a key role in the decision to invade Panama and argued for the massive Gulf deployment. Military experts say he represents a new breed of post–Vietnam soldier/politicians, and Powell has been called the most politically astute U.S. general since Eisenhower. At age 52, in April of 1989, he was promoted to his first four-star position as head of Forces Command. And in August of the same year nomination for the top post in the armed forces, becoming the first black to become the chairman of the Joint Chiefs of Staff. Since taking over this post, he has been more willing to use military force than any of his predecessors since the 1960s. Other Joint Chiefs chairmen, fearing another Vietnam-type disaster, have been reluctant to commit U.S. troops. But Gen. Powell tells the president: "If you want to use force, we can do it."

The 1990s are the best of times for General Colin Luther Powell: the president of the United States follows his advice, the Congress hangs on his every word, and the nation is reassured by his confidence. In political circles, he is even touted as a potential running mate for President Bush in 1992, perhaps even a candidate for president someday.

Gen. Powell was selected as the recipient of the NAACP's 1991 Spingarn Award, the highest honor bestowed by the nation's oldest and largest civil rights organization. The announcement of his selection was made by Dr. Benjamin L. Hooks, the NAACP Executive Director/CEO. Instituted in 1914 by the late Joel E. Spingarn, the NAACP chairman, the medal is presented annually to the man or woman of African descent and American citizenship who has made the highest achievement during the preceding year or years in any honorable field of human endeavor. "General Powell in every way, reflects the high standards of achievement and integrity that have always been applied in selecting the Spingarn medalist. His service to the nation has been truly outstanding. He is living proof of the heights to which African Americans can rise, if given the opportunity," Dr. Hooks said.

---

†POWELL, ROMAE TURNER, was born August 3, 1926, in Atlanta, Georgia, the daughter of Paul D. Turner, a dry cleaner, and Mary Hubert Turner, a school teacher. She graduated from Booker T. Washington High School and received a bachelor's degree from Spelman College. She received her law degree from Howard University in 1950 and practiced law in Atlanta. She was active in the civil rights movement in the late 1950s and early 1960s and was one of the six attorneys in Atlanta who represented citizens in desegregation of city buses, hotels and motels, and the preservation of the Atlanta Branch of the NAACP.

In March 1968, the then-judge of the Fulton County Juvenile Court appointed Powell to serve as referee (assistant to judge) of the court. This was the first time a woman and a black person had held such a position in the state of Georgia. During the time she served as referee of the court, 1968 to 1973, she developed the Girls' Citizenship Training Program and a tutorial program for the court. In January 1973, the judges of Superior Court of Fulton County appointed her as judge of the

Fulton County Juvenile Court. On January 17, 1973, she was sworn in by the Hon. Clarence Shaw as judge of the court. She then became the first full-time black judge of a court of record in the state of Georgia.

Through her work and dedication, the Child Treatment Center of Fulton County Juvenile Court began a nutrition program for the children detained, which was designed to provide good nutrition as an element of delinquency prevention and behavior control. A drug addiction program has also been developed at the court through her initiative. The Child Treatment Center received an award in 1983 from the National Council of Juvenile and Family Court judges as having the most outstanding detention program in the country.

From 1980 to 1990, Judge Powell served on the board of directors of Fledgling Foundation and SEARCH, Inc.; as president of the National Council of Juvenile and Family Court Judges, and National Council of Juvenile Court Judges Fund, Inc.; as a member of the Atlanta University Council Justice Advisory Committee and on the Constitution Revision Committee for the state of Georgia. She has received many honors and awards, and has presented papers and lectures in numerous states. She received certification of specialized study at Emory University in Atlanta, and the University of Nevada in Reno. She became a familiar and welcome face to members of the Georgia General Assembly while pursuing legislative goals as an advocate for children and the needs of the Juvenile Courts of Georgia.

Judge Powell was a firm believer in the role of family in the development of children. As evidence of the important example she set for others, the Atlanta public school system published a biography of her in 1989 and shared with all of us her valuable contributions to humankind through her civil rights and legal activities. She was hospitalized in May 1990, and on July 20, 1990 died at her home.

POWELL, WILLIAM E., was born April 12, 1936, in Indianapolis, Indiana. He married Loretta Braxton Mitchell of Norfolk, Virginia, and they have two sons, William Clinton Powell, III, and David Anthony Powell. He received a B.S. (Naval Science) degree from the United States Naval Academy in 1959, and an M.B.A degree from George Washington University in 1969. His first duty after Supply Corps School in Athens, Georgia, was as the supply officer aboard the USS *Nicholas* (DDE-449). In 1962, he was assigned as the planning officer at the Naval Air Station, Point Mugu, California.

This assignment was followed by two years at the Naval Supply Depot, Subic Bay, Philippines, where he obtained experience in inventory management and assisted in special support projects in Vietnam. From July 1966 until 1968, Powell served as ship design and fleet support coordinator for the Naval Supply Systems Command in Washington, D.C. In May 1969, he was assigned as the financial management and planning officer on the Staff Commander Cruiser Destroyer Force Atlantic. Reporting to USS *Intrepid* (CV-11) in August 1971, he assumed duties as the supply officer and participated in deployments to northern Europe and Mediterranean areas. In April 1974, he reported to the Aviation Supply Office and was initially assigned as industrial support officer and later as stock control branch head for power plants.

Powell attended the Industrial College of the Armed Forces in 1977, and upon completion in 1978, he reported to the Naval Supply Center, Oakland, California, as director of the planning department. In July 1980, he returned to Washington, D.C., and served as the assistant for supply policy to the Director Aviation Programs Division, Office of the Chief of Naval Operations. From 1982 through 1984, he served as commanding officer, Naval Supply Depot, Subic Bay. He was then assigned to Naval Supply Systems Command as director of supply corps personnel until May 24, 1985, when he assumed command of the Naval Supply Center, Norfolk, Virginia.

A chronological list of one-star, Rear Admiral Powell's dates of rank are as follows: June 27, 1955, entered the U.S. Naval Academy as a midshipman; June 3, 1959, graduated from the Naval Academy as an ensign; December 3, 1960, promoted to lieutenant (junior grade); June 1, 1963, promoted to lieutenant; May 1, 1968, promoted to lieutenant commander; November 1, 1971, promoted to commander; July 1, 1979, promoted to captain; October 17, 1985, promoted to rear admiral; November 1, 1988, retired.

PRATHER, THOMAS LEVI, JR., was born on June 25, 1940, in Washington, D.C. He received a B.S.

degree in music from Morgan State University; an M.S. degree in contracting and procurement management from Florida Institute of Technology; and a ROTC commission of second lieutenant on July 19, 1962. From July 1962 to October 1962, he was a student in the Army Ordnance Officer Basic Course, United States Army Ordnance School, Aberdeen Proving Ground, Maryland. From October 1962 to May 1964, he was assigned as a platoon leader in the Service, Supply and Recovery Platoon, 546th Ordnance Company, later ordnance supply officer of the 84th Ordnance Battalion, United States Army, in Europe. He was promoted to first lieutenant on January 19, 1964.

From May 1964 to August 1965, Prather was assigned as the ordnance supply officer, 66th Ordnance Battalion, in Europe. From August 1965 to October 1965, he was a student in the Armor Officer Basic Course, United States Army Armor School, Fort Knox, Kentucky. From October 1965 to April 1966, he served as the executive officer, Headquarters Company, 1st Battalion, 66th Armor, 2nd Armored Division, Fort Hood, Texas. He was promoted to the rank of captain on April 1, 1966. From April 1966 to May 1967, he served as the commander/battalion maintenance officer/S-4 (Logistics), Headquarters Company, 1st Battalion, 66th Armor, 2nd Armored Division, Fort Hood.

From June 1967 to September 1968, he was the assistant brigade supply officer, later supply officer, 9th Support Battalion, 198th Infantry Brigade, United States Army, in Vietnam. From September 1968 to September 1969, he was a student in the Ordnance Officer Advanced Course, United States Ordnance School, Aberdeen Proving Ground, Maryland. He was promoted to the grade of major on May 23, 1969. From September 1969 to July 1970, he was assigned as chief of the Consolidated Equipment Mainte-

nance Division, Mobility Training Department, School Brigade, United States Army Ordnance School, Aberdeen Proving Ground, Maryland. From July 1970 to June 1971, he was a student at the United States Army Command and General Staff College, Fort Leavenworth, Kansas.

From June 1971 to August 1973, Prather served as a personnel management officer, Assignment Section, Ordnance Branch, Officer Personnel Management Directorate, United States Army Military Personnel Center, Alexandria, Virginia. From September 1973 to September 1974, he was a student at the Florida Institute of Technology, Melbourne, Florida. From September 1974 to June 1975, he served as a project officer, Industrial Planning Branch, Industrial Management Division, United States Army Materiel Command, Alexandria. From June 1975 to June 1977, he was assigned as a military assistant, Office of the Assistant Secretary of the Army (Installations and Logistics), Washington, D.C. From June 1977 to January 1979, he was the commander of the Division Materiel Management Center, 8th Infantry Division, United States Army, in Europe. He was promoted to the grade of lieutenant colonel on July 11, 1977.

From August 1981 to June 1982, he was a student at the United States Army War College, Carlisle Barracks, Pennsylvania. From July 1982 to December 1984, he was assigned as director of the Materiel Management Directorate, United States Army Communications-Electronics Command, Fort Monmouth, New Jersey. He was promoted to the grade of colonel on August 1, 1983. From December 1984 to July 1987, he was the commander of Tobyhanna Army Depot, Depot Systems Command, United States Army Materiel Command, Tobyhanna, Pennsylvania. From July 1987 to July 1989, he served as the deputy commander of 2nd Support

Command, VII Corps, United States Army Europe and Seventh Army.

From July 1989 to August 1990, Gen. Prather was assigned as the deputy commanding general, United States Army Armament, Munitions and Chemical Command, Rock Island, Illinois. He was promoted to the one-star grade of brigadier general on September 2, 1989. In August of 1990, he was assigned as the commanding general, Army Troop Support Command, St. Louis, Missouri. He has received numerous awards and decorations which include: the Legion of Merit; the Bronze Star; the Meritorious Service Medal (with three oak leaf clusters); and the Army Commendation Medal (with two oak leaf clusters).

PRATT, MARVIN, was born on May 26, 1944, and has been a resident of the 1st District for 28 years. He and his wife Dianne have two children, Michael and Andrea. They are members of St. Boniface Church. He graduated from North Division High School, received his B.A. degree in political science from Marquette University in 1972 and has graduate credits in urban affairs from the University of Wisconsin-Milwaukee. A former president of AFSCME Local 40, District Council 48, Alderman Pratt is a former chairman of the Wisconsin State Board of Veterans Reserves, 84th Division. He is also a member of the North Side Democratic Unit, LaVarnway Boys and Girls Club Advisory Board and an alumnus of Future Milwaukee. He won a special election in the spring of 1987 to serve as alderman of the 1st District. He was re-elected unopposed in April 1988 to a four-year term.

Alderman Pratt presently serves as chairman of the Economic Development Committee, is vice chairman of the Zoning & Development Committee, a member of the Finance & Personnel Committee, and is a member of the Milwaukee Metropolitan Sewage Commission, the Labor Policy Committee, Urban Committee, Equal Opportunities Enterprise Committee, and the MECCA Board. Prior to his election, he was director of consumer relations with HealthReach, a health maintenance organization, has had 15 years' experience as a property appraiser, was a graduate intern in the mayor's office, and a library assistant with the Milwaukee Public Library System.

PRICE, ALBERT, was born April 6, 1930, in Port Arthur, Texas. He is married to the former Elizabeth Tanner and they are the parents of three children, Terri, Anita and Albert, Jr. He is a graduate of Herbert High School, Beaumont, Texas, 1946, valedictorian; received a B.A. degree in sociology from Morehouse College in Atlanta, Georgia, in 1950; and did graduate study in sociology at Atlanta University, 1950–1951. He has served as state legislator for the state of Texas, District 22 in Beaumont, from 1977 to date. He had retired in 1990 as a captain for American Airlines in New York.

Price enlisted in the United States Air Force in 1951; graduated from Air Force Officer Candidate School in 1953; graduated from Air Force Pilot Training School in 1953; pilot (Air Rescue Service) in Greenland, 1955–1955; graduated from Air Force Navigation and Radar Observer's School in 1955; pilot (B-47), Strategic Air Command, Portsmouth, New Hampshire, 1955–1958; graduated from Air Force Instructor's Program, Maxwell AFB, Alabama, in 1958; Afrotic Instructor at Tennessee A&I University, Nashville, Tennessee, in 1958–1962; pilot (B-47), Strategic Air Command, Plattsburg AFB, New York, 1962–1963; and received honorable discharge in 1963.

Price's prior positions include: director of Beaumont Community Program; assistant personnel officer, Veterans Administration Hospital in Houston, Texas, and assistant training officer for NASA, Manned Spacecraft Center in Clear Lake, Texas. His professional affiliations include a long list of activities: Allied Pilot's Association; member, Plymouth United Church of Christ of Beaumont; member of board of trustees of Plymouth United Church of Christ of Beaumont; past moderator of the South Central Conference of the United Church of Christ, Austin, Texas; member of the board of directors of the American Conference of the World Council of Churches, New York City; delegate to the 5th Assembly of the World Council of Churches, Nairobi, Kenya; member of the Central Committee of the World Council of Churches, Geneva, Switzerland; board of directors, United Black Christians; the Young Men's Christian Association; Omega Psi Phi Fraternity; board of directors of People Organized with Economic Resources, Inc.; board of directors, Plymouth Village Trust; YMCA Luncheon Club and Leadership Beaumont, Beaumont Chamber of Commerce.

PRICE, MARY LEONTYNE, was born on February 10, 1927, in Laurel, Mississippi, to James Anthony and Kate (Baker) Price. She married William Warfield, August 31, 1952, and they divorced in 1973. She graduated from Oak Park High School in 1944. She received a B.A. degree from the College of Education and Industrial Arts (now Central State College) in Wilberforce, Ohio, in 1948. She was awarded a four-year scholarship at Juilliard School of Music. Former concert singer Florence Page Kimball was her vocal coach at Juilliard, and has been her teacher, adviser, and friend ever since.

After Price's appearance as Mistress Ford in the student production of Verdi's "Falstaff," composer Virgil Thomson selected her to sing the role of Saint Cecilia in a revival of his "Four Saints in Three Acts," which was presented on Broadway for two weeks in April 1952. After she made her nationally televised American opera debut on NBC in 1955, she became a pacesetter as the first black to appear in opera on television. She then made a grand opera stage debut two years later in San Francisco. In 1961, she made her first appearance at the prestigious Metropolitan when she appeared as Leonora in "Il Trovatore." From 1961 to 1969, she made 118 performances at the Metropolitan.

The National Academy of Recording Arts and Sciences has honored her with 15 Grammy awards. On October 8, 1978, Price performed at the White House. In 1989, at the age of 62, she performed at the Fox Theatre in Atlanta, with her awesome powerful voice which allowed her to fill the cavernous theatre even though the stage was set with soft, sound-absorbing curtains instead of the sound shell ordinarily used for a solo recital program. In 1989, after more than 35 years, she was still going strong.

Price is the recipient of 20 Grammy awards, which include a Lifetime

Achievement Award; the Presidential Medal of Freedom, America's highest civilian award, from President Lyndon B. Johnson; the Kennedy Center Honor; and three Emmy awards for prime-time television appearances; the Spingarn Medal, NAACP; and numerous other awards and honors.

PRIDE, CHARLEY FRANK, was born March 18, 1938, in Sledge, Mississippi, in a small cotton town near Memphis. His father was a sharecropper of 40 acres on a 124-acre farm, with the help of eight sons and three daughters. He started working in the fields at the age of five, chopping and picking cotton. Listening to the Grand Ole Opry from Nashville on Saturday nights, he learned all the lyrics and sang along with his favorite stars, Hank Williams, Ernest Tubb, Roy Acuff and Eddie Arnold. Eager to escape picking cotton, he pursued playing professional baseball. He had begun playing at the age of 14, dreaming of breaking Babe Ruth's records and setting some new ones of his own. His ambition was to join the Brooklyn Dodgers in 1947 and then turn to singing as a career. A graduate of Sledge Junior High School, he left home for Memphis in 1955 at the age of 17 to join the Negro American League.

Pride played for Detroit, Birmingham Black Barons and the Memphis Red Sox, hitting .367. He had a good earned run average. Two years in the U.S. Army suspended his career from 1956–1958. He returned to the Red Sox and played with the team until 1959, when he quit because the managers would not give him the pay raise he thought he deserved. Ambitious to play in the major leagues, he went to the California training camp of the Los Angeles Angels in 1961 as a pitcher and outfielder, lasting two and a half weeks with the team.

Living in Helena and working the swingshift in the smelting factory, Pride found that his sleep was being interrupted by a country music group practicing next to his apartment. After introducing himself to the group, they invited him to appear with them as guitar player and singer on occasional club engagements around Helena. He was also playing baseball with the semipro Amvets and had the chance to sing over the public address system before the games. A newspaper featured a story on the singing baseball player which made him a local celebrity. He continued working at Anaconda and performing in night clubs on weekends. In 1963, Red Sovine, one of the top country and western singers stopped while on tour at the Great Falls club where he was singing. Impressed with his talent, Sovine urged him to visit Nashville and offered to help him get an audition there.

Giving baseball one more chance, he went to Tampa, Florida, and presented himself to Casey Stengel who said that later in the day he was running a tryout camp. On his way back to Montana, he stopped in Nashville and met Jack D. Johnson who was delighted with his singing, but surprised that a black man sounded so much like a white country singer. Two days after he arrived in Montana he received a management contract from Johnson, who is still his manager. After hearing two test recordings, country guitarist Chet Atkins, head of RCA Victor in Nashville, signed him to a long-term contract under which he cut his first record, "Snakes Crawl at Night."

Still worried about the reception of a black country singer by white listeners, the company released it, as well as Pride's two succeeding records, without any of the usual publicity or photographs. All three recordings proved quite successful on the country music charts, particularly his second release, "Just Between You and Me," which won a Grammy nomination for the singer in 1966 as the Best Country and Western Male Vocal Performance.

He had attracted a large following of country music fans who were not yet aware that he was black. At his first big public performance, before a crowd of 10,000 in Detroit in 1966, his appearance evoked a din of applause that lessened noticeably when he stepped out on stage. However, when the first shock over the discovery of his color subsided, his singing was enthusiastically cheered and color lines were forgotten.

Pride, who never believed that being black would be a hindrance to him explained, "I didn't have any doubts. I always had felt people were just people." His fans numbered in the thousands and he had won Most Promising Male Artist award from several of the country music publications. At the Country Music Convention in Nashville in October 1966, he sang before his peers and they met him with a standing ovation and an encore. At the Grand Ole Opry in Nashville in 1967, he was introduced by one of the idols of his youth, Ernest Tubb, and he enjoyed a singularly successful debut as the Opry's first black singing star. His first recorded album, "Country Charley Pride," was proving to be a best seller and although his later recording "The Best of Charley Pride" won him his first Gold Album, "Country Charley Pride" eventually achieved a sale of over a million copies.

Pride's career grew and he made road tours and appeared on television: "The Lawrence Welk Show," "Hee Haw," "The Tom Jones Show," "Flip Wilson" and "The Johnny Cash Show." In 1970, his "Kiss an Angel Good Morning" became a million record seller and won him his first Gold Single award. In October 1971, at the nationally televised fifth annual presentation of awards by the Country Music Association at the Grand Ole Opry in Nashville, he became the only double winner at the ceremonies being named Entertainer of the Year and Male Vocalist of the Year. Shortly thereafter he was honored by receiving the Entertainer of the Year Award by the Music Operators of America.

After being nominated for Grammy awards for three consecutive years, Pride won two 1971 Grammys when his album "Did You Think to Pray" was named Best Sacred Performance and his single record "Let Me Live" was named Best Gospel Performance. His 1972 album, "Charley Pride Sings Heart Songs," earned him another Grammy, this time for Best Country Performance for a male singer. Among his other awards has been Cashbox's Top Male Vocalist on the country music list and Billboard's Top Country Artist on albums. According to *Time* magazine, 1974, he had sold more records for RCA than any singer since Elvis Presley, earning over $20,000,000 with 21 records.

In the *Time* article Pride was called the "Marian Anderson of country music," because of his breaking of racial barriers and the "black superstar of white soul." From the beginning of his career white people had asked him, "How come he sounds like us and looks like them?" and black people had told him "You know you look like us, but you sound like them." He explained that all he was trying to do was just be a total individual who fit into what society had become over the years. It goes beyond music, it took being what he called American and eliminating as best you can what he called "skin hang-ups." He was pleased to be the first black star in the country music field and hoped his success would lead to other blacks becoming performers of that typically American music.

PROCOPE, ERNESTA GERTRUDE, born and raised in Brooklyn, New York, is the daughter of Clarence and Elvira Forster, West Indian immigrants. She is married to John L. Procope, attended Brooklyn College and has received numerous honorary degrees. She originally aspired to being a concert pianist, but in her early twenties she realized this was not a guaranteed way to pay the rent. Her career in insurance began as a result of her first marriage to Albin Bowman, a real estate broker. As it happened, her husband needed someone to handle the insurance coverage for the property he was buying and selling. Ernesta Procope became that person.

A year after Bowman's death in 1952, Procope started E. G. Bowman Co., Inc., an agency specializing in personal lines. A year after that, she married John Procope. Although the business grew steadily over the next decade and a half, it was the racial troubles of the mid–1960s that really pushed the company into the brokerage big leagues. Riots and the threat of riots were frightening insurers away from many of the accounts E. G. Bowman was servicing. During the late 1960s, she asked Governor Nelson Rockefeller for help, the same day fire insurers cancelled 88 of her policies.

Rockefeller introduced her to his secretary of state, and several months later, the New York Property Insurance Underwriting Association (FAIR Plan) was born. Procope was a tremendous help and played a leading role in getting the FAIR Plan off the ground. She worked to get the brokers and the companies lined up, working for her community and for her people who lacked insurance. She marched uninvited into the downtown Manhattan offices of several insurance executives and demanded that they take a look at the areas of Brooklyn they were effectively redlining through their underwriting policies. She ended up taking the executives on a bus tour of Crown Heights, Park Slope and Bedford-Stuyvesant.

As a result, availability began to pick up again in many areas. E. G. Bowman is the New York area's leading broker for independent churches, in-

suring a total of 420 churches. The next push, the one that set Bowman squarely on the path to Wall Street came from Procope's husband John, who had maintained close links to his wife's business while building a successful business career of his own. (He is now E. G. Bowman's board chairman, in charge of sales and marketing.) John Procope's suggestion was that Bowman take the almost unheard of step (for a black-owned brokerage house) of approaching Fortune 500 companies as potential clients.

The company moved to Wall Street in 1979, which was part of an effort to integrate into the economic mainstream. When Procope opened the office, she became the first black in history to do so. By 1989, the commercial brokerage house of E. G. Bowman earned $21 million in premiums, and in 1990, had 45 Fortune 500 companies, including Pepsico, General Motors, Avon Products, Mobil Oil, Monsanto, and Philip Morris, among its nearly 400 commercial clients. Procope serves on the boards of several corporations, including: The Chubb Corporation, Columbia Gas System, Inc., the New York Zoological Society, the Salvation Army of Greater New York, and Avon Products, Inc., and is a trustee of numerous others.

RANDOLPH, BERNARD P., was born July 10, 1933, in New Orleans to Philip J. Randolph (deceased) and Claudia Randolph. He was married in 1956 to Lucille Robinson Randolph and they have six children, Michelle, Julie, Michael, John, Liane and Mark. He received a B.S. degree in chemistry from Xavier University of Louisiana, New Orleans. He also earned bachelor (magna cum laude) and M.S. degrees in electrical engineering from the University of North Dakota, Grand Forks, through the Air Force Institute of Technology program in 1964 and 1965, respectively. He completed Squadron

Officer School in 1959; Air Command and Staff College as a distinguished graduate, concurrently earning a master's degree in business administration from Auburn University, Auburn, Alabama, in 1969; and was a distinguished graduate of the Air War College in 1974, all at Maxwell Air Force Base, Alabama.

Randolph's first assignment after completing aviation cadet training at Ellington Air Force Base, Texas, and Mather Air Force Base, California, was with the Strategic Air Command at Lincoln Air Force Base, Nebraska, from June 1956 to June 1962. He instructed and evaluated KC-97 and B-47 flight crews. While there, he was a member of a select crew. He attended the University of North Dakota until July 1965 and was then assigned to Los Angeles Air Force Station as chief, on-orbit operations, Space Systems Division. He was next assigned as assistant deputy program director for launch and orbital operations and was responsible for all payload operations.

From August 1968 to October 1969, Randolph attended Air Command and Staff College and Auburn University. He was then assigned to the Republic of Vietnam as an airlift operations officer at Chu Lai and airlift coordinator at Tan Son Nhut Air Base. He was responsible for the total operation of about 50 C-7 and C-123 airlift sorties daily from Chu Lai and later coordinated the operations of all airlift control elements throughout the Republic of Vietnam.

Upon his return to the United States in November 1970, Gen. Randolph was assigned to Headquarters Air Force Systems Command, Andrews Air Force Base, Maryland, as chief of command plans in test evaluation, and then as the executive officer to the deputy chief of staff for operations. He attended the Air War College from August 1973 to June 1974. In 1987, he was promoted to the four-star grade of general, and assigned as the commander of the Air Force Systems Command (AFSC), headquartered at Andrews Air Force Base near Washington, D.C.

RANGEL, CHARLES B., was born June 11, 1930, in Harlem. He is married to Alma and they have two children. He was a high school dropout before enlisting in the United States Army in 1948. He was awarded a Bronze Star during the Korean War after being wounded while bringing some 40 men out from behind Chinese lines. He is a graduate of New York University and St. John's University School of Law. He has served as Congressman for ten terms as the representative of New York's 6th Congressional District which covers the neighborhood of East and Central Harlem, the Upper West Side, Roosevelt Island, and Washington Heights/Inwood.

In Congress, Rep. Rangel has attained the following positions and responsibilities: senior member, Committee on Ways and Means; chairman,

Subcommittee on Select Revenue Measures, Committee on Ways and Means; chairman, Select Committee on Narcotics Abuse and Control and deputy whip for the House Democratic Leadership. During his legislative career, Rangel has served as chairman, Congressional Black Caucus, is a member, Judiciary Committee, and member of the New York State Assembly. He is the recipient of seven honorary doctorate degrees from: Atlanta University, Wagner College, St. John's University, Columbia University, Mt. Sinai School of Medicine, New York University, and Howard University.

RATTLEY, JESSIE MENIFIELD, was born May 4, 1929, in Birmingham, Alabama. She is the daughter of the late Mr. and Mrs. Alonzo Menifield. She married the late Robert L. Rattley, who was a civil service supervisor at Fort Eustis. They were the parents of two daughters, Florence and Robin. She earned a B.S. degree from Hampton Institute in 1951. After graduation, she established the business department at Huntington High School in Newport News, the first black high school in Newport News to offer business training to its students.

On June 9, 1952, Rattley founded

the Peninsula Business College which provided an opportunity for youths and adults to be trained for careers in business. In 1960, she purchased the present site of the school, 2901 Jefferson Avenue. Later, the three adjacent houses to the school were added as dormitories for students. They are named for the three persons closest to her: namely, Robert Hall, Florence Hall and Robin Hall.

In 1970, she was the first black and first woman elected to the Newport News City Council. She was top vote-getter in the 1974 Councilman Election, being re-elected to another four-year term. On May 1, 1978, she was again top vote-getter, being re-elected for a third term. On May 4, 1982, she was re-elected to a 4th four-year term with the highest vote ever recorded for any candidate for council in the history of Newport News. In July 1976, she was elected vice-mayor of the city; she became the first black and first woman ever elected mayor of Newport News, in 1986. She served as mayor from July 1986 until June 1990.

Rattley has been very active in the National League of Cities and has served on various committees and task forces. She served as vice chairman of the Municipal Government and Administration Committee. She was appointed vice-chairman of the Effective Government Policy Committee by Mayor Tom Bradley, former president of the National League of Cities, and was later appointed chairperson of the Effective Government Committee. She was the first black elected to the Virginia Municipal League Executive Committee in 1974; elected second vice president in 1976; first vice president in 1977; and elected president of the League in 1978. In April 1987, Rattley visited Bologna, Italy, as part of the National League of Cities delegation to participate in a program sponsored by the Bridge Association. She was part of the delegation that visited Germany in 1989. She was the first black female to serve as president of the National League of Cities.

In 1990, Rattley was a Fellow at the Institute of Politics, John F. Kennedy School of Government, Harvard University, Cambridge, Massachusetts. Her study group was entitled "Local Government Stands Alone." In 1991, she served as the senior lecturer at Hampton University teaching political science and urban affairs. When she retired from electoral politics in June of 1990, she didn't know if she would do anything more rewarding than local government. She has found teaching at Hampton University and sharing her experiences with students very gratifying.

—————————

†RAWLS, CHARLES ALLEN, was born January 25, 1905, in Haywood County, Tennessee, one of 11 children born to Ned and Tex Anna Love Rawls. Al, as he was affectionately called, married Maude Ellis Crofton and they have two children, William Donald, Sr., and Charles Cynthia Rawls Bond. At the age of 24, Rawls graduated with honors from Gupton Jones College of Mortuary Science in Nashville, Tennessee. On March 4, 1934, he organized and established the Rawls Funeral Home. In 1935, he began writing burial insurance when he founded the Rawls Mutual Benefit Burial Association. By 1940, total membership had reached a peak of 50,000 members in Tennessee.

In 1940, Rawls built and established the Service Sundry Drug Store, employing the first black pharmacist in Haywood County. Next, he began operating the GEM Theatre, the first black movie house. In 1950, during the 11 o'clock services at First Baptist Church, the Sons and Daughters of the Golden Circle was organized. By June 1958, the Golden Circle Life Insurance Company was formed and operated in Brownsville, Memphis, Nashville and Knoxville. Today, the Golden Circle

Life Insurance Company ranks among the top 100 black-owned companies in the nation.

The last accomplishments of Al Rawls occurred in 1986. He was appointed to the board of directors of the Brownsville Bank and was designated a Paul Harris Fellow of Rotary International. He died February 7, 1987, in Haywood County. Rawls was a man of many dreams and these dreams touched the lives of numerous people, his friends, family, associates and the community at large.

—————————

RAWLS, LOUIS ALLEN, was born on December 1, 1936, in Chicago, Illinois. He is the son of Virgil and Evelyn Rawls. He attended Forrestville Elementary and Dunbar High, on the Chicago south side. At the age of seven he joined the junior choir at the Greater Mount Olive Baptist Church. At 14 he joined a gospel quintet, the Chosen Gospel Singers, which competed with other local groups at Friday night gatherings. In his mid-teens, he lied about his age and joined the National Guard to supplement his income. He was later drafted into the United States Army, where he served for two years with the 82nd Airborne Division, based at Fort Bragg, North Carolina.

After his discharge from the Army, Rawls toured churches and gospel programs across the United States with the Pilgrim Travelers, a gospel group whose other members included Sam Cooke, Eddie Cunningham, and Cliff White. Driving from St. Louis to Memphis one rainy night in 1958, the quartet collided with an 18-wheeler truck. Cunningham was killed, Cooke suffered minor eye injuries, White broke his collarbone, and Rawls received a brain concussion.

Rawls made the transition from gospel halls to nightclubs by concentrating on such songs as "Every Day I Have the Blues." In 1959, he performed in a Dick Clark show at the Hollywood

Bowl and had non-singing roles in episodes of the ABC network television series "Bourbon Street Beat," "77 Sunset Strip" and Steve Allen's late-night show on ABC. In 1961, Capitol Records signed him; his first album for Capitol was "Stormy Monday" in 1962. In 1966, his first live album "World of Trouble" was released. In 1967, he made his first appearance at Carnegie Hall. In 1970, he was nominated for a Grammy for his single "Your Good Thing Is About to Come to an End."

In 1971, he signed with MGM Records and under the MGM label released his first single "A Natural Man," which won him his second Grammy in 1972. In 1975, he signed with Philadelphia International records, a CBS subsidiary, thus placing himself under the guidance of two masters, Kenny Gamble and Leon Huff. In 1976, he released "You'll Never Find Another Love Like Mine," which turned out to be his first gold single and won an American Music Award. It was also nominated for a Grammy, along with the song "Groovy People." In 1977, his album "All Things in Time" reached third place on the soul charts and became his first platinum LP and won his third Grammy.

Rawls launched "The Lou Rawls Parade of Stars," his annual telethon for the United Negro College Fund. The telethon served to give "Public awareness of the College Fund and its needs." In 1982, he moved from Philadelphia International to Epic Records, a CBS subsidiary. It was under the Epic label that he released the album "When the Night Comes," among the tracks of which was "Wind Beneath My Wings." The Lou Rawls sound was born of the blues, of gospel halls, of those that have been kicked and kicked again, of anguish, of servility, of protest, of losers, loners and lovers.

Rawls has won five Gold albums, one Platinum album, and Grammy awards in 1967, 1971, 1977, and 1978. In 1983, he went on a Christmas tour of military bases in Korea, Japan and the Philippines. In 1987, he was honored in Chicago where a street was named after him, a salute to him for his legendary music career as well as for his longtime humanitarian efforts. At the time his latest hit album was "At Last." By 1991, his twelve annual "Parade of the Stars" telethons had raised more than $100 million for the United Negro College Fund. Citing the UNCF's motto "A mind is a terrible thing to waste," Rawls encouraged black youth to attend college. "Educating the youth of our nation is priority one," he said.

REASON, JOSEPH PAUL, was born March 22, 1941, in Washington, D.C. He married the former Dianne Lillian Fowler of Washington, D.C., and they have two children, Rebecca L. and Joseph P. Reason, Jr. He graduated from the United States Naval Academy in 1965 with a B.S. degree (Naval Science). Prior to being trained in nuclear propulsion engineering, he served as operations officer on USS *J. D. Blackwood* (DE 219). Upon completion of training, he was assigned duties in USS *Truxton* (DLGN 35) and participated in her first deployment to Southeast Asia in 1968. In 1970, he earned an M.S. degree in the management of computer systems from the U.S. Naval Postgraduate School, Monterey, California. Joining USS *Enterprise* (CVN 65) as electrical officer in 1971, he deployed twice to the Southeast Asia and Indian Ocean areas.

After service as combat systems officer, again in USS *Truxton* (CGN 35), Reason commenced a tour as surface nuclear assignment officer at the Bureau of Naval Personnel. In late 1976, he was assigned as naval aide to the president of the United States. He served as aide to President Carter until mid-1979. Subsequent duties included executive officer, *Mississippi* (CGN

1973, promoted to lieutenant commander; September 1, 1978, promoted to commander; October 1, 1983, promoted to the rank of captain; October 1, 1987, promoted to rear admiral (Lower Half); April 21, 1989, promoted to the rank of rear admiral; January 1991, promoted to the rank of vice admiral.

---

40); commanding officer, USS *Coontz* (DDG 40); and commanding officer, USS *Bainbridge* (CGN 25). Prior to assuming his duties as commander Naval Surface Force, U.S. Atlantic Fleet, he commanded Cruiser-Destroyer Group One. He led Battle Group ROMEO through operations in the Northern and Western Pacific and Indian Ocean regions and the Persian Gulf.

As commander Naval Base Seattle, from 1986 through 1988, Reason was responsible for all naval activities in Washington, Oregon, and Alaska. His awards include the Legion of Merit, Navy Commendation Medal, and the Republic of Vietnam Honor Medal. He also wears the Navy Unit Commendation, Navy Meritorious Unit Commendation, and numerous other medals. A list of the three-star Vice Admiral's dates of rank and promotions, are as follows: June 28, 1961, entered the Naval Academy, a midshipman; June 9, 1965, graduated from the Naval Academy, an ensign; December 9, 1966, promoted to lieutenant (junior grade); July 1, 1968, promoted to lieutenant; July 1,

REESE, MAMIE BYNES, was born September 3, 1913, in Gibson, Georgia. She is the widow of Dr. William J. Reese, an Albany, Georgia, osteopathic physician. In 1933, she received a B.S. degree from Spelman College in Atlanta and an M.S. Degree from Drake University in 1948. She also studied at Ohio State University, University of Southern California, Simmons College, and Boston University. She taught high school in Waycross and in Des Moines, Iowa, where she earned her master's degree. After 25 years in teaching and as an associate professor and dean of women at Albany State College, she was appointed to the State Board of Pardons and Paroles by former Georgia Governor Jimmy Carter.

In 1976, Reese was elected by her colleagues as chairwoman of the State Board of Pardons and Paroles. She became the first black paroles chief and reached the highest position ever attained by a black in Georgia state government. She was no stranger to public life when she began her board tenure. In 1963, then–Governor Carl Sanders appointed her to the Governor's Commission on the Status of Women, and Governor Lester Maddox chose her as a delegate to the 1968 Democratic National Convention in Chicago where she served on the credentials committee. Reese is a member and past president of the National Association of Colored Women's Club, Inc. She also serves as a member of the Albany Urban League and the NAACP.

RICE, CONDOLEEZZA, grew up in Birmingham, Alabama, where both her parents were teachers. She received a B.A. degree from the University of Denver, Phi Beta Kappa and cum laude. She then obtained her M.A. degree from the University of Notre Dame, and her Ph.D. from the University's School of International Studies, specializing in Soviet and East European Politics and foreign and defense policy and international security policy. She first accepted a job as associate professor of political science at Stanford University, where she was a member of the Center for International Security and Arms Control. In 1986, she was the recipient of a one-year fellowship, acting as special assistant to the director of the Joint Chiefs of Staff assigned to Strategic Nuclear Policy.

In 1989, when President George Bush needed an articulate adviser on Soviet Affairs, he selected Dr. Rice. She was one of the few people to personally advise the president on Soviet policy. She also joined the National Security Council at the personal request of NSC Adviser Brent Scowcroft, where she was the highest-ranking black woman on the Council. In 1990, she was President Bush's chief adviser during his global summit with Soviet President Mikhail Gorbachev, in Washington, D.C. She was there during the brainstorming sessions of the American advisers when the United States approach on some of the most delicate and important foreign policy questions of the last two years were discussed.

In 1991, Rice left her White House post to return to her professorship at Stanford University. She is the author of *The Soviet Union and the Czechoslovak Army*, and with Alexander Dallin, *The Gorbachev Era*, as well as numerous articles on Soviet and East European military policy. In 1984, Rice was awarded the Water J. Gores Award for excellence in teaching at Stanford. She has been a Hoover Institution National Fellow and a Council on Foreign Relations Fellow. She has also served as a consultant to ABC News on Soviet affairs.

RICE, NORMAN, B., was born in 1943, in Denver, Colorado. He is married to Dr. Constance Rice and they have one son, Mian. He moved to Seattle in 1968 to attend the University of Washington, earning a B.A. degree in communications, and a master's degree in public administration. He was elected mayor in November 1989, with broad support from 57 percent of Seattle's voters. His term expires at the end of 1993. As mayor, Rice wants to build on all of Seattle's strength, beauty and diversity, in order to meet the challenges of the 1990s. Among his top priorities are: strengthening Seattle's public school system and ensuring a quality integrated education for all students; improving public safety by creating partnerships between police and community residents; preserving the quality of life in Seattle's neighborhoods and

restructuring the city government to be more responsive and accessible to citizens; meeting critical human service needs, including housing, health care and job training; providing regional leadership and working with other jurisdictions to address the serious concerns of transportation, growth, and environment protection.

Prior to his election as mayor, Rice served on the Seattle City Council for 11 years. He was president of the council for two years and chaired major committees including, Finance, Public Safety, and Energy. He also chaired the Metro Council's Personnel and Finance Committee for ten years, where he gained a reputation as a leader on transportation, solid waste, and environmental issues confronting the region. Among his many accomplishments on the City Council were: adding more than 100 Seattle police officers; chairman of the Public Safety Committee; securing funding for prevention and school safety officers to work with school children and officials; sponsored the creation of neighborhood "Anti-Crime Teams."

Rice also developed the Survival Services Fund to assist hungry, ill, and homeless people; and offset sharp federal budget cuts in the early 1980s; created a "pay as you go" system for maintaining Seattle's infrastructure; won federal funding to put rail in the Metro tunnel; to make future development of a regional rail transportation system more feasible and less expensive; secured a cap for the I-90 project in Southeast Seattle, to minimize the dislocations and noise in the local residential neighborhoods; provided critical block grant funding to maintain the Spice Senior Meals Program; funding for weatherization and energy assistance programs for low-income families and seniors.

In addition to his work as an elected official, Rice has been a leader in countless Seattle community groups and civic efforts. He had broad experience in both the private and public sectors, having worked as a reporter for KIXI-RADIO, writer/editor for KOMO-TV, assistant director of the Urban League, director of Government Services for the Puget Sound Council of Governments, and manager of Corporate Contributions and Social Policy for Rainier National Bank. His civic involvement includes serving as chair of the 1-2-3 Bond Committee, president of the Mount Baker Community Club, and on the board of directors of Planned Parenthood. Rice has been actively involved with the Governor's Urban League, NAACP, Washington Wildlife and Recreation Coalition, and the Municipal League.

RICHARDSON, EARL STANFORD, a native of Maryland and a graduate of the Maryland education system, he earned a B.A. degree in social science from the University of Maryland Eastern Shore (formerly Maryland State College), in 1965. His immediate family includes his wife, the former Sheila Bunting of Oklahoma City, and a son Eric Anthony. In August of 1972, Richardson merited a one-year fellowship from the Ford Foundation to pursue an M.S. degree which he received in May 1973. In December 1975, through the support of a second Ford fellowship, he completed his doctorate degree at the University of Pennsylvania.

After having served eight months as interim president, on November 1, 1984, Richardson became the 11th president of Morgan State University. Upon accepting the appointment, he asserted that, as a leader, he would seek primarily to build on Morgan's traditional foundation of excellence and achievement — the very lodestars that guided his academic undergraduate and graduate careers. Thereupon, he began the difficult tasks of fashioning strategies for strengthening academic programs, improving the fiscal

management of the university, stabilizing student enrollment, accelerating fund raising efforts, and renovating the physical plant.

In addition to his theoretical academic training in administrative leadership, Dr. Richardson brought to the Morgan State University presidency a widely ranging practical experience derived from his successful fulfillment over the last 19 years, of several administrative positions. He served as assistant to the president, University of Maryland College Park; and executive assistant to the chancellor, director of Career Planning and Placement, and acting director of Admissions and Registration at the University of Maryland Eastern Shore. He complements his administrative knowledge with teaching experiences at the undergraduate and graduate levels.

As a solution-oriented research fellow of the Ford and Kellogg Foundations, Dr. Richardson investigated critical problems in higher education relevant to "Health, Education and Welfare Guidelines: Implications for Maryland Black Higher Education"; "The Plight of the University of Maryland Eastern Shore: to Exist, to Merge, or to Close"; "Enhancing Interinstitutional Cooperation Between Black Institutions and Predominantly White Institutions"; and "Some Economic, Educational, and Racial Implications of a Proposed Merger of the University of Maryland Eastern Shore and Salisbury State College." In addition to his research interests, he is an active member of the leading professional associations in his field and a supporter of various organizations devoted to social welfare.

---

†RICHARDSON, HARRY VAN BUREN, was born June 27, 1901, in Jacksonville, Florida, the son of Martin Richardson and Bertha Witsell Richardson. He graduated from Western Reserve University and Harvard Divinity School, and he received a Ph.D. degree from Drew University. He was the chaplain of Tuskegee Institute in Alabama from 1932 to 1948. He led efforts to develop a statewide interracial ministers' alliance that was a catalyst for ecumenical, interracial services at Alabama Polytechnic Institute, now Auburn University.

In 1948, Richardson moved to Atlanta to become president of a small, predominantly black Methodist school, Gammon Theological Seminary. Atlanta then had two other primarily black seminaries, the Morehouse School of Religion, a Baptist school, and the Turner Theological Seminary, an AME school affiliated with Morris Brown College. In 1955, he began seeking funds for the interdenominational training of ministers. In 1956, he met with Dean Rusk, then the director of the General Education Board, a Rockefeller foundation. Dr. Richardson and Rusk discussed the proposed educational center and the funding it would require. A $15,000 study grant was provided, followed by approval of a $2.25 million grant. An Atlanta organizational committee within a year raised $250,000. The ITC opened in 1959 as part of the Atlanta University Complex.

Dr. Richardson was the founder and first president of the Interdenominational Theological Center at Atlanta University. His leadership spurred the development of ITC into what is now one of the nation's prominent theological schools. He was a nationally known and respected churchman.

RICHARDSON, LUNS C., a Hartsville, South Carolina, native, he graduated from Butler High School in 1945 as class valedictorian. He received an A.B. degree magna cum laude from Benedict College, and an M.A. degree in higher education administration at Teachers College, Columbia University. He has pursued additional studies at South Carolina State College, Rutgers University, and the University of Tennessee at Knoxville. He held several significant positions in secondary, vocational, and higher education before being elected as Morris College President in 1974. He served as dean of men, chaplain and teacher at Denmark Technical College (then known as South Carolina Area Trade School) for 15 years; principal of St. Helena High School, Frogmore, South Carolina, for two years; and principal of Wilson High School, Florence, South Carolina, for one year. He also served at Benedict College for six years, the last 16 months as acting president. His last position before assuming the presidency of Morris College was that of vice president of Voorhees College at Denmark, South Carolina. He has also served as pastor at the Thankful Baptist Church, Bamberg, South Carolina, for 31 years.

Under Richardson's leadership, numerous developments have taken place at Morris College: the liquidation of a half-million dollar indebtedness, the construction of several new buildings, an increase in library holdings from 21,000 to over 175,000 volumes, faculty upgrading to 50 percent earned doctorates, and curriculum expansion including at least two new majors along with an Army ROTC unit. He also led Morris College to its initial accreditations by the Southern Association of Colleges and Schools in 1978, and to membership in the United Negro College Fund in 1982. He served on the Sumter board of C&S Bank, the South Carolina Higher Education Tuition Grants Commission, and the board of directors of the United Negro College Fund. He had also served several terms on the Sumter County Development Board, the Sumter Chamber of Commerce Board, the South Carolina Chamber of Commerce Board, the Sumter-Clarendon United Way Board, Wateree Community Actions, Incorporated, and the South Carolina Committee for the Humanities. He served as a member of the South Carolina Desegregation Task Force, charged with completing the desegregation of the state's publicly supported colleges and universities.

Dr. Richardson has received well over one hundred honors and awards locally, statewide, regionally, and nationally — from Greek-letter organizations, churches, conventions, schools, colleges, civic organizations, states and cities. Morris College, Benedict College, and Coker College have conferred honorary doctorate degrees on him. Benedict College and Teachers College, Columbia University have both named him an outstanding alumnus. He is in constant demand as a preacher, speaker and lecturer. On March 8, 1990, at the annual spring meeting, he was elected to a two-year term as secretary of the member, of the United Negro College Fund.

RICHIE, LIONEL, was born June 20, 1949, in Tuskegee, Alabama, and married Brenda, a school sweetheart. His father, a retired Army captain, worked as a systems analyst, and his mother an elementary school principal. He grew up in the home of his grandmother, Adlaide Foster, on the campus of Tuskegee Institute, where his late grandfather had been a colleague of the founder, Booker T. Washington, and where Mrs. Foster was an instructor in classical piano. He received all of his elementary and half of his secondary schooling in Tuskegee. After completing high school in Joliet, Illinois, he enrolled in Tuskegee Institute in 1968, with the intention of becoming an Episcopal priest. He taught himself to play the piano by imitating his grandmother's playing. His Uncle Bertram, a big-band hornman, gave him his first saxophone.

It was many years, however, before Richie aspired to become a performer (before that, he was strictly a music lover, and listener). As a listener he was influenced from his earliest years by the ballets and symphonies he attended at Tuskegee as well as his grandmother's playing "Bach and Beethoven all day." A lot of it rubbed off, and the country flavor came from living in Alabama. His influence came from a classical background when he wrote "Three Times a Lady," and his R&B background came from the neighborhood, gospel, the Motown sound of the Temptations and the Supremes; in his late adolescence, from the recordings of such white rock 'n' roll artists as James Taylor and the groups Crosby, Stills and Nash, and Cream.

Most of his heroes when he was growing up were ministers. After about a semester at Tuskegee, Richie realized that being a minister in a church was not his thing. He finally majored in economics and minored in accounting with the idea of later going into law. He had taken his tenor saxophone along to Tuskegee with the intention of learning how to play it. Asked to play with the Commodores by Thomas McClary, the guitar player, in a school talent show, he said sure. Two years later the Commodores, originally the Mystics, comprised of McClary on guitar, William King on trumpet, Walter Orange drummer, Ronald LaPread on bass, Milan Williams on piano, and Richie. The Commodores' rise in the music business, on the other hand, was very carefully planned in accordance with a strategy laid down in a 251-page thesis that William King wrote at Tuskegee. They took not only the music approach, but a business approach from day one.

While studying at Tuskegee, the Commodores worked as entertainers weekends and summers. Benny Ashburn, a black New York City marketing consultant with no previous music business experience, became their manager and obtained bookings for them at Small's Paradise in Harlem and the Cheetah, then a popular rock 'n' roll club in midtown Manhattan. At the Cheetah they met Suzanne DePasse, a booking agent who later became a vice-president of Motown Records. Through DePasse, they auditioned as opening act for the Jackson Five's 1971 European tour, and with their tightly choreographed performance overcame the fierce competition in the auditions.

After their return from Europe, the Commodores signed a contract with Berry Gordy, the founder and president of Motown Records. They groomed themselves for two years with a compatible Motown producer/arranger in the person of James Anthony Carmichael, who has produced the Commodores' recordings ever since and who produced Richie's solo albums and singles as well. The title of the group's first album was "Machine Gun," the title cut along with "Bump" which became so popular that it gave its name to a dance, "I Feel Satisfied," "Slippery When Wet," "Fancy Dancer" co-written by LaPread and Richie, "Brickhouse" written by all of the Commodores.

By 1976, the group was one of the most successful party bands in pop music, with three gold albums behind them and their first platinum LP (1 million copies sold) in the works. Richie said that the Commodores wanted to write a musical résumé to show people that there was more to the Commodores than just, "Baby, baby, baby." Meanwhile, he was developing his skill at songwriting, taking lessons from the team of Holland, Dozier and Holland, and others at Motown. He started following producer and songwriter Norman Whitfield around, asking him to teach him how to write songs. He sat in on some Stevie Wonder sessions, and the transition in the Commodores' style and the ascendancy of Richie as the group's increasingly sophisticated ballad composer and lead singer began unobtrusively,

with Richie's slow-tempo romantic song "This Is Your Life" on the Commodores' 1975 album "Caught in the Act."

The fusion of country, soul and middle-of-the-road in his ballads was carried forward in "Zoom," "Sweet Love," and the gold single "Just to Be Close to You," in which Richie's voice was described as "oozing with country melancholy, projected lyrics as sentimental and courtly as roses on the first date." The trend continued with the Southern-flavored "Easy," a gold single that became an MOR standard and helped give the Commodores their first platinum LP and culminated in the triple-platinum "Three Times a Lady," a tribute to his wife, mother and grandmother, and in 1978 it jumped from the top of the soul charts to the top of the country and pop categories in the United States and number one in five countries.

The Commodores were ranked the number one R&B group in 1978 by the publications *Rolling Stone*, *Billboard* and *Cashbox*, and finished third in the pop category in *Billboard*'s chart. They contracted to do commercials for the Schlitz Brewing Company. Richie's progress toward slow stardom was accelerated by his gold, number one song "Sail On" and "Still," included in the Commodores 1979 triple-platinum album "Midnight Magic." The 1980 LP "Heroes" included allusions to James Cleveland's "Jesus Is Love," Deodato, James Conley's "Got to Be Together" and Otis Redding's "An Old Fashioned Love" as well as echoes of Bob Dylan, the group America, and the Isley Brothers.

Richie's solo career was launched with "Lady," written and produced for country-pop crossover king Kenny Rogers. It remained six weeks in the number-one spot nationally, and the lachrymose "Lady" was the biggest single of Rogers' career. Four more songs by Richie were included on Rogers' platinum album "Share Your

Love," in 1981, produced by Richie. While producing "Share Your Love," Richie was working with the Commodores on their LP album "In the Pocket," which included his country love plaint "Oh No," and "Lady, You Bring Me Up." The latter co-written by Harold Hudson with Richie coproducing and lead singing. In 1981, he wrote and sang with Diana Ross "Endless Love," the title song of the motion picture.

Richie's decision to leave the Commodores to concentrate on his solo career was a difficult one for him to make, because the Commodores were in his words "not a group but a family." This came after the family father image, manager Benny Ashburn, died of a heart attack in September 1982, and the success of Richie's first solo album "Truly," which headed straight to the top of the charts and won him his first Grammy after 11 nominations for Best Male Vocalist. Two other singles from the album made the top five, "You Are," co-written with his wife Brenda, and "My Love" on which Kenny Rogers sang harmony. The next step in his journey was "Can't Slow Down," and "All Night Long," released as a single. By the time the LP was issued, it had taken only six weeks to become the number-three song in the U.S. Other tracks included "Penny Lover," written with Brenda Richie. With the exception of "Can't Slow Down," "All Night Long" and "Running with the Night," the themes were romantic.

Richie is the recipient of numerous outstanding awards in the music industry. Among the more recent influences on Richie's music was the "We Are the World Experience" in which 45 top pop performers lent their voices to the Richie/Jackson composition. He has become increasingly dedicated to a variety of social causes.

RICHIE, SHARON IVEY, was born December 14, 1949, in Philadel-phia, Pennsylvania. She is the daughter of William Joseph Richie, Sr., and Helen L. Ogleby Richie. She received a B.S. degree in nursing from Wagner College, Staten Island, New York, and an M.S. in nursing (psychiatric, clinical nurse specialist), from the University of Texas, San Antonio. From November 1971 to July 1972, she was a staff nurse in the Orthopedic Ward, and later in Medical Intensive Care Unit, Walter Reed Army Medical Center, Washington, D.C. From December 1972 to July 1974, she was the assistant head nurse, Behavior Modification Ward, Walter Reed Army Medical Center. From August 1974 to August 1975, she was the assistant head nurse, Psychiatric Ward, Brooke Army Medical Center, Fort Sam Houston, Texas.

From August 1976 to September 1977, she was assigned as hospital psychiatric nurse consultant and head nurse, 2nd General Hospital, Landstuhl, Germany. From October 1977 to June 1979, she served as a psychiatric clinical nurse specialist, Alcoholism Treatment Facility, Stuttgart, Germany. From January 1980 to August 1982, she served as a nursing consultant and clinical liaison officer, United States Surgeon General Drug and Alcohol Abuse, the Pentagon, Washington. From September 1982 to September 1983, she served as a White House Fellow, Office of Intergovernmental Affairs, the White House, Washington.

From October 1983 to February 1984, Richie was the assistant chief nurse for evenings/nights, Letterman Army Medical Center, Presidio of San Francisco, California. From January 1984 to May 1986, she was profis chief nurse, 8th Evacuation Hospital, Fort Ord, California. From February 1984 to August 1985, she served as chief of ambulatory nursing service, Letterman Army Medical Center, Presidio of San Francisco. From August 1985 to May 1986, she served as director of quality assurance, Department of Nursing, Letterman Army Medical Center. From May 1986 to June 1987, she served as both chief and assistant chief of the Department of Nursing, Kimbrough Army Community Hospital, Fort Meade, Maryland.

From June 1988 to May 1990, she served as chief of Clinical Nursing Service, Walter Reed Army Medical Center, Washington. In May 1990, she was assigned as chief of the Department of Nursing, Letterman Army Medical Center, Presidio of San Francisco. She has written numerous publications which include: in 1989, "Combat Nurses: You Won't Be Alone," for the *Military Review*, Vol. LXIX (1), January, pp. 65-73; in 1984, "Combat Medical Support: Federal Roles and Responsibilities — Highlights of the 91st Meeting of the Association of Military Surgeons," *LAMC Network*, December, pp. 9-20; in 1983, "Drug Abuse in the Military: An Adolescent Misbehavior Problem," *Journal of Drug Education*, Vol. 13(1), pp. 83-93, John Beary, John Mazzuchi, and Sharon Richie. She has been a member of the White House Fellows Association and Foundation (secretary 1986–1988, and second vice president May 1989–December 1990).

RICKMAN, RAY, is the well-known co-owner of Cornerstone Books, located in Providence, Rhode Island. Rickman lectures widely on the subject of collecting black literature. He is currently serving his second term as a state representative in Rhode Island, the first African American elected from his district, which includes the prestigious Brown University. He is a commissioner on the Historic District Commission of Providence, which governs the preservation of all buildings within historic boundaries. He is a board member of the Rhode Island Historical Society. He was the first black elected to the post.

Rickman is actively involved in promoting African American literature in Rhode Island, and to that end he has mounted a lecture series which brought such authors as James Baldwin, Jamaica Kincaid, and Maya Angelou to Providence. He also co-coordinated New England's first Black Memorabilia Faire in Boston, which assembled 15 dealers of black collectibles and drew 500 people in December of 1989. In addition to this, he is host of a widely watched public television show entitled "Shades," which is devoted to exploring the Black American experience. This show has a viewership in Rhode Island, Massachusetts and Connecticut.

Rep. Rickman has written about African American culture for the *Providence Journal*, *The Detroit Free Press*, *The Maine Times*, *The Detroit News*, *The National leader*, *Chicago Leader* and *American Visions*. He also runs a bed and breakfast out of his 1850s home, which serves the Brown University and Rhode Island School of Design community.

ROBERTS, TOM, was born in Dayton, Ohio. He and his wife Regina

have two children, Edward and Erienne. He attended Sinclair Community College and graduated from the University of Dayton with a B.A. in communication arts. He was appointed to represent the 37th House District on January 8, 1986, and has been elected and re-elected since that time, most recently in 1990, and is serving his third term. He is a full-time legislator and serves not only his district well, but has become one of the most outstanding legislators in the state of Ohio.

Roberts' work includes: serving as vice chairman of the Aging and Housing Committee; chairman of the Select Committee for the Homeless, and Affordable Housing; served on the Judiciary and Criminal Justice Committee and the Select Committee on Child Abuse and Juvenile Justice. He also served on such committees as: Agriculture and Natural Resources, Children and Youth, Energy and Environment, Enterprise Zone Oversight and Policy Advisory Group (PAG) for the Department of Youth Services.

Roberts has devoted a great deal of his time to the needs of Ohio's Youth. He has served on the Advisory Committee of the Dayton Job Corps; and as a past president of the Mental Health Association in Montgomery County.

ROBINSON, FRANK, was born August 31, 1935, in Beaufort, Texas, the son of Frank and Ruth (Shaw) Robinson. He attended McClymonds High School where he played baseball, football, and basketball. He was signed by Cincinnati scout Bobby Mattick when he graduated from high school, in 1953, and was assigned to the Reds Class C Pioneer League team in Ogden, Utah. On the diamond he began at third base but was soon switched to the outfield, at his request. He was called up by Cincinnati in 1956, and in his first season hit 38 home runs, batting .290. He was also named Rookie of the Year by the National Baseball League. In

1960, his slugging average or extra-base-hit percentage was .595, the highest in the league.

During his career Robinson played on four pennant winners in Baltimore from 1966 through 1971 and later served as a coach and minor league manager for the Orioles. He managed the Cleveland Indians from 1975 to 1977, and the San Francisco Giants from 1981 to 1984. He compiled a 186-189 record in Cleveland and a 264-277 mark in San Francisco.

Robinson, who batted .294 in 21 major league seasons, was elected to the Baseball Hall Fame in 1982, the only man to win the Most Valuable Player Award in both leagues, and Manager of the Year awards. A righthanded-hitting outfielder, who belted 586 career homers, he is fourth on the career list behind Hank Aaron, Babe Ruth, and Willie Mays. In 1988, he was named the new manager of the Baltimore Orioles, and as the 1991 season began, it found Frank Robinson still on the diamond with the Orioles.

ROBINSON, HENRY, was born in Port Royal, South Carolina. He is a member of the Union Baptist Church in Port Royal and is married to the former Jannie Middleton. He is the father of four children and the grandfather of six grandsons. He attended the Robert Smalls High School, graduating in 1956. After graduating, he worked in a local drug store for six years. In 1961, he was employed on Parris Island, South Carolina, by the John Demosthenes Company as a tailor and is currently still with the company.

Robinson served on the board of directors for the Municipal Association of South Carolina for the years 1980–1984. In 1969, he ran for a Port Royal Council seat and was elected for a four-year term. He was re-elected for another four-year term in 1972. In 1971, he was elected mayor pro-tem and served until he was elected mayor of Port Royal in 1976. Robinson is the first black ever to run for a public office and the first black to be elected to public office in the town of Port Royal.

ROBINSON, ROSCOE, JR., was born on October 28, 1928, in St. Louis, Missouri, where he received his elementary and secondary education. After graduation from Charles Sumner High School, he was appointed to the United States Military Academy at West Point, New York. He graduated in 1951 with a B.S. degree in military engineering and was commissioned a second lieutenant. After graduation, he attended the Associate Infantry Officer Course and the Basic Airborne Course at Fort Benning, Georgia. He then joined the 11th Airborne Division at Fort Campbell, Kentucky, where he served as a platoon leader in the 188th Airborne Infantry Regiment until he went to Korea in October 1952.

In Korea, Robinson served in the 31st Infantry Regiment, 7th Infantry Division as a rifle company commander and battalion S-2. He was awarded the Bronze Star for his service in Korea. Upon returning to the United States, he served in a variety of school and airborne unit assignments highlighted by a tour with the United States Military Mission to Liberia in the late 1950s, and the receipt of a master's degree in international affairs from the University of Pittsburgh in the early 1960s. As a lieutenant colonel he served in Vietnam, first on the staff of the 1st Air Cavalry Division, then as the first black to command the 2nd Battalion, 7th Cavalry. For his Vietnam service, he was decorated with the Silver Star for valor.

Upon completion of the National War College in 1969, Robinson served in Hawaii until his promotion to colonel when he assumed command of the 2nd Brigade, 82nd Airborne Division in 1972. Among other assignments, he served as commanding general, United States Army Garrison, Okinawa; commanding general, 82nd Airborne Division; and commanding general, United States Army, Japan/1X Corps. In August 1982, he became the first black to become a four-star general in the Army and the second black in the armed forces, after Gen. Daniel "Chappie" James. Robinson also served as the United States representative to the North Atlantic Treaty Organization (NATO) Military Committee.

ROBINSON, SAUNDRA A., after graduating from Michigan State University, she spent two years in the United States Peace Corps teaching in the British West Indies. She then spent several years in various capacities, including directing the National Alliance of Businessmen's Program with Xerox Corporation, She attended Atlanta University, where she worked on her master's degree in political science. This led to work in city government where she conceived, designed and created Atlanta's Neighborhood Planning Process and its Neighborhood Planning Unit System. This system is still utilized today to allow individual citizens direct access to the city's planning process.

While working as a city planner, Robinson attended Georgia State University on a part-time basis to study a pre-med curriculum and ultimately attended medical school. She became the first black to attend the University of North Carolina Medical School from outside the state of North Carolina. She was divorced while in medical school, but she still successfully raised two daughters, Zahra and Asha, and a son, Khalid, while pursuing her career and personal commitments. After receiving her degree in adolescent psychiatry, she returned to Atlanta.

Dr. Robinson is committed full time to the mental health of the black community, and in addition to her practice which addresses adolescent mental health as well as the health of the family system, she serves as president and co-founder of the Rebecca Lee Society of Women in Medicine. Named after the first black woman physician in America, the society in its first two years has over 75 paid members, representing almost 70 percent of all the black female physicians in the Atlanta area.

Dr. Robinson has received numerous special awards and recognition from the Atlanta Medical Association for her efforts in mental health. She is active in numerous professional, civic and social organizations, including: the Alpha Kappa Alpha sorority; serves as consultant to numerous youth organizations; and is presently developing a new concept in parenting entitled "Parenting Without Violence." This latest project is her contribution to the epidemic of violence in which we find ourselves; it is her belief that if she can help one family at a time learn to love and live together without violence, in a society that is inherently violent, then perhaps one less cycle of violence will exist in our community.

RODGERS, JOHNATHAN AR-LIN, was born January 18, 1946, in San Antonio, Texas. He married Royal Kennedy, and they have two children, Jamie and David. In 1967, he received a B.A. degree in journalism from the University of California at Berkeley, and a master's in communications from Stanford University, in 1972. From 1968 to 1973, he was an associate editor for *Newsweek* magazine. He joined CBS in 1976 as assistant news director at WBBM-TV, and from 1978 to 1983, he worked at KCBS-TV, formerly KNXT, the CBS-owned station in Los Angeles, where he was executive producer, news director and station manager. In 1983, he moved to CBS News in New York as executive producer of "Nightwatch." He was later named executive producer of the CBS

"Evening News." In 1985, he became executive producer of the CBS "Morning News."

In March 1986, he was named general manager of WBBM-TV, the CBS-owned station in Chicago. He was named to that position on the heels of a boycott of the station by Operation PUSH, and a protest by area blacks because of the removal of a black news anchorman. He was the first black to be named manager at a network station and reached an agreement with PUSH to beef up hiring and promotion of blacks and women. In 1989, he was named president of the CBS Television Stations Division, making him the highest ranking black at a major network. As president he oversees stations owned by CBS in New York, Philadelphia, Miami, Los Angeles, and Chicago. The five television station general managers report directly to Rodgers, whose main job is to boost profits and revenues.

†ROGERS, CHARLES CALVIN, was born on September 6, 1929, in Claremont, West Virginia, the son of Clyde Rogers, Sr., and Helen Rogers. He married the former Margarete Schaefer and they have two children, Jackie Linda and Barbara. He received a B.S. degree in mathematics from West Virginia State College, and an M.S. in vocational education from Shippensburg State College. He also received an M.S. degree in theology from the University of Munich, West Germany.

Rogers served in the United States Army for over 33 years, and was promoted from second lieutenant in 1951 to the two-star grade of major general in 1975. From June 1966 to November 1967, he was the commanding officer of the 1st Battalion, 2nd Brigade, Fort Lewis, Washington. From November 1967 to February 1968, he was the commander of the 1st Infantry Division in Vietnam. He also served as operations chief J-3, United States Military Assist

Command in Vietnam. From 1969 to 1970, he was a staff officer in the United States Army's Readiness Division, Washington, D.C.

From 1971 to 1972, he served as the deputy commander of V Corps Artillery, in Europe. From 1972 to 1973, he was the commander of the 42nd Field Artillery Group in Europe. From 1973 to 1975, he served as the commanding general of the VII Corps Artillery in Europe. Rogers has been honored as the recipient of the Congressional Medal of Honor; the Distinguished Service Medal; the Legion of Merit (with oak leaf cluster); the Distinguished Flying Cross; the Bronze Star Medal; the Air Medal; the Joint Service Commendation Medal; the Purple Heart; and the Grand Service award (with star) from the German Army.

ROGERS, EARLINE SMITH, a native of Gary, Indiana, she was born December 20, 1934. Her parents were Earl and Robbie Hicks Smith. She was married to Louis C. Rogers, Jr., and they have two children. She belongs to St. Timothy Community Church. She attended the Gary public schools, graduating in 1952 from Roosevelt High where she was senior class president. She worked as a clerk-typist and enrolled in night classes at Indiana University-Northwest. After two years she transferred to Indiana University, Bloomington, where she majored in education and received her B.S. degree in 1957, and earned her M.S. in 1971. A teacher for 25 years, Rogers initiated Gary's first elementary school reading laboratory and did consulting work for an international reading laboratory company.

Rogers' political career was born out of another avid interest — teacher unionism. She has been active for years in local, state and national teacher organizations. She was elected in 1980 to the Gary Common Council and served as the council's first female presi-

dent until 1983, when she gave up the post after being elected to the General Assembly. In 1981, she was appointed to the Little Calumet River Basin Development Commission. Since 1984, she has been vice-chairman of the Indiana democratic national committee. She was a delegate to the 1984 Democratic National Convention.

ROSENTHAL, ROBERT E., was born April 9, 1945, in Phillips, Mississippi. He is married to Robertta Perry and is the father of two boys, Mike and Robert. He is a graduate of Jackson State University, B.S. degree in science education and chemistry; did graduate work in counseling and business at JSU, and studied at the University of Florida. He has completed many management and personnel management courses with the Air Force, Army and Office of Personnel Management. He is president of Mid-South Management and public relations director for the Black Music Association and the Young Black Programmers Coalition. He has developed a book that takes on the monumental task of capitalizing the black record industry for the common man. The book is entitled *Who's Who in Black Music*. The information in this book effectively gives the holder as nearly a complete communications network as has ever been put on paper. It was compiled by Rosenthal and Dr. Portia Maultsby. This reference took nearly four years to put together.

Contained in *Who's Who* is a comprehensive listing of black music organizations ranging from the Black Music Association, National Association of Black Promoters; a record label guide that includes both independent and major labels; booking agents, trade publications and black newspapers; broadcasting organizations such as cable, TV, radio and video companies; music licensing companies, record pools, record stores, billboard and Black Radio Exclusive stores and radio stations and more. Also included was a statistical breakdown on black listening habits as well as black populations by state and city. A biographical breakdown on the important movers and shakers within the industry was also given. A constant update of this book was issued, also, *Who's Who in Europe, Who's Who in Japan* as well as *Who's Who in Pop Music* scheduled for the future. Within the pages of this book one could successfully chart a full career.

Rosenthal's professional experiences include: working as a United States Postmaster for the U.S. Postal Service; in investment for Kimbrough Investments in Jackson, Mississippi; marketing manager for Philadelphia International Records (Lou Rawls and the O'Jays); national public relations manager for the Black Music Association and the Young Black Programmers Coalition; and as a staff manager for the Mississippi River Commission and the Lower Mississippi Valley Division of the U.S. Army Corps of Engineers. He has written over 180 publications and edited two books, and is listed in *Who's Who in Black Music* and *Programming Radio*.

Rosenthal has been appointed to the White House Area Council; Congressional Black Caucus-Minority Economic Development Brain Trust; Minority Colleges and University Clusters, and the Media Coordinator for Black Radio for Jesse Jackson. His professional affiliations include: Congressional Black Caucus Brain Trust; National Association of U.S. Postmasters; National Business League; Black Music Association; American Management Association; Young Black Programmers Coalition; American Marketing and Financial Services; National Counsel of Affirmative Action; Blacks in Government; Black Concert Promoters Association; and the National Academy of Films.

ROSS, CARSON, was born December 15, 1946, in Warren, Arkansas. He is married to Eloise Ross and they have three daughters, Shelly, Carla and Diana, and one granddaughter, Brittanie. The Ross family lives in Blue Springs, Missouri, which is a suburb of Kansas City. Ross was elected to the Blue Springs Board of Aldermen in 1981 and served until 1988, when he was elected to the Missouri House of Representatives. While serving as alderman, Ross served as Ward 2 alderman for 6 years (3 terms), Ward 3 alderman for 2 years (1 term); mayor pro tem 1983; vice president and president, Westgate Division of the Missouri Municipal League; Missouri Municipal League board of directors, 2 terms; National League of Cities: Transportation and Communication Policy Committee, Small Cities Advisory Board and Steering Committee, Human Development Committee; and was appointed in 1986 by Missouri Governor John Ashcroft to a 3-year term on the Missouri Air Conservation Commission.

Ross' other public and community services include: member, Comprehensive Mental Health board of directors; member, Blue Springs Board of Zoning Adjustments; chairman, Blue Springs First Personnel Board; chairman, R-4

R-4 School District Citizen's advisory board; president, St. Mary's Hospital of Blue Springs board of associates; member, Private Industry Council; vice president, United Services of Greater Kansas City; chairman, 1985 Major Gifts Division of the Heart of America United Way; director, National Alliance of Business Ex-Offender Program; member, the Parks Homeowners Association board of directors.

During Ross' first term in the Missouri House of Representatives, he was recognized with the Conscientious Legislators Award and Freshman of the Year Award on local issues. He serves on the Public Health and Safety, Motor Vehicle and Traffic Regulation, and Local Government committees. He was re-elected to a second term August 7. In addition to serving in the Missouri House, Ross has been employed by Hallmark cards for 25 years. He has a BSBA degree from Rockhurst College; is a Vietnam veteran, U.S. Army; member of the Church of Christ; recipient of the Southern Christian Leadership Conference (SCLC) Black Achievers in Industry Award in 1985. Ross serves a legislative district that is over 90 percent white and he was the only black state elected Republican in Missouri when the legislature convened in January 1991.

---

†ROSS, LESTER KEITH, was born May 8, 1946, to James and Barbara Ross in Terre Haute, Indiana. He married the former Joan Barnes, and they have a son Wesley Owens. After graduating from high school, he served in the military obtaining the rank of staff sergeant with the United States Marines. Following an honorable discharge from the Marines, he earned a B.A. degree in business management from Orange Coast College, and a B.S. degree in administrative services from Pepperdine University in Los Angeles, California.

Ross joined the Xerox Corporation in 1970 in manufacturing operations in Irvine, California, where he held a number of positions from production supervisor, production manager, operations manager to personnel manager. He joined Xerox Business Services in 1983 as the Southeast region production manager. In 1986, he became a sales manager in the Atlanta Center.

In this capacity, Ross received many awards, including: a Par Club winner twice, and a President's Club winner in 1989. He landed a lucrative contract for copying service at General Motors' Saturn Plant in Spring Hill, Tennessee. In early 1991, he was named center manager of Xerox Business services in Houston, texas. He was killed in a March 3, 1991 plane crash in Colorado Springs.

RUSSELL, HERMAN JEROME, was born December 30, 1930, in Atlanta, Georgia. He and his wife Otelia have three children, Donata, Michael, and

Jerome. He grew up in the southeast side of the city of Atlanta, in a neighborhood called Summerhill. He began as a plasterer with his father and bought his first property as a high school sophomore. He founded H. J. Russell & Company in 1953, as a subcontractor. Under his direction the company has evolved into a large diversified holding company providing management services and computer data processing to his nine affiliated companies. His business ranks third among minority Construction/Industrial/Service 100.

Russell's affiliated companies operate in the areas of apartment and property management/leasing, food and beverage concessions, beverage distribution, construction and construction management, real estate investment and development, and communications. H. J. Russell Construction Company, founded in 1962, has been a major joint venture partner on such projects as Atlanta Life Insurance Company, Five Marta Subway Stations, Hartsfield International Airport, Atlanta University's Woodruff Library, Benjamin E. Mays High School, Coca Cola Company Office Tower, and the Atlanta Dome Stadium.

Russell is the chairman of the board of Citizens Trust Bank and a member of the board of directors of Prime Cable, First Atlanta Corporation, Central Atlanta Progress, Business Council of Georgia, Morris Brown College, Tuskegee Institute, Georgia Institute of Technology, and other businesses and educational institutions. He was the first black invited to be a member of the Atlanta Chamber of Commerce and became its second black president in 1981. Sales growth of H. J. Russell in 1987 was $34.8 million; and in 1989, $130.9 million. The company's employee growth in 1987 was 345; and in 1989, 538.

In 1990, Russell was honored at the 4th Annual Black Business Day Luncheon, hosted by the Black Business Association of Los Angeles. He received the Black Business Days award in recognition of his exemplary business and community leadership. The California Legislature Assembly Resolution was presented to him by California State Representative Willie Brown. He also received the County of Los Angeles Recognition Award.

RUSSELL, WILLIAM FELTON, was born February 12, 1934, in Monroe, Louisiana. He and his wife Shirley have five children, Xavier, James, Alex, Vicki and Toby. He grew up in the Deep South where insults seemed to be absolute facts of existence which could not be overcome. School was held in a converted barn. His family moved to Oakland where his father found a job in a war plant. Later his family moved into the projects, and after his parents separated and his mother died, he learned to lean on his brother Charlie. He attended Hoover Junior High School in Oakland, an awkward, gangling boy with growing pains. As a sophomore he failed to make the high school basketball team. Even as a senior in his best game he only scored 14 points.

Hal De Julio, alumnus of the University of San Francisco, an avowed basketball fan and unofficial scout, saw something no one else had ever seen in Russell and referred him to USF for a basketball scholarship. Before he came along there was no systematic shot blocking in basketball, and the sight of a skyscraping, six-foot-nine center excelling at swift defense instead of perfunctory scoring was so odd that one college coach, when Russell was a sophomore, blindly criticized his style as "fundamentally unsound." Russell made fantastic progress during his freshman year and taught himself the fundamentals of playing defense. He became the leader of the team in his junior and senior years, 1954–1955 and

1955–1956, guided USF to two national championships and a streak of 60 consecutive wins to establish a national collegiate record.

Upon graduation, Russell opted to try for the 1956 Olympic team rather than turn professional. He led the United States basketball team to a rousing 89-55 victory over the USSR in the final and brought home a gold medal. When he returned he was drafted by the St. Louis Hawks, but Arnold "Red" Auerbach, Celtics coach and general manager, wanted him so badly that he convinced Walter Brown to trade two established pros for the young Olympic star. When Russell joined the Celtics in 1956, they became champions overnight and they remained such until he left them in 1969. He was a player/coach for the Boston Celtics and they won back to back championships in 1968–1969.

During those years Russell was named to the East All-Star team 11 times and won the Most Valuable Player award five times. He served as the first black to be head coach in pro basketball in 1973–1977, for the Sacramento Kings. He also served as a Network NBA Color Analyst for 13 years including serving at ABC, CBS and WTBS; and was a TV sportscaster for ABC in 1969. He has been a member of the National Basketball Association for over 17 years; the author of *Second Wind, Memoirs of an Opinionated Man* in 1979; the recipient of the Podoloff Cup as MVP in 1957–1965; MVP U.S. Basketball Writers 1960–1965; and Memorial Basketball Hall of Fame. He has been described as a man with God-given ability who made the most of the skills he had.

SAFFOLD, SHIRLEY STRICKLAND, is married to Dr. Oscar E. Saffold and they have a daughter, Sydney Strickland. She received her B.A. degree from Central State University, and her law degree from Cleve-

land-Marshall College of Law. After she was admitted to the Ohio State Bar, she engaged in the practice of law with the Legal Aid Society of Cleveland Defender's Office.

In 1987, Saffold was elected judge to the Cleveland Municipal Court. She is a member of the National Bar Association, Greater Cleveland Bar Association, Ohio Bar Association, Cuyahoga County Bar Association, Norman S. Minor Bar Association, and many other civic and professional organizations.

SANDERSON, WALTER H., JR., was born in Fulton, Missouri. He has been involved in the metal trades since he was a young apprentice. At the age of 15 he was running a lathe. He enrolled at Lincoln University of Missouri, in Jefferson City, Missouri, where he received a B.S. degree in 1941. From 1941 to 1942, he taught in the mechanical arts department at Lincoln University. From 1943 to 1945, he worked with the United States Cartridge Company as supervisor of the tool and die unit. From 1945 to 1948, he served in the United States Army, at Aberdeen Proving Grounds, in Maryland. From 1948 to 1952, after leaving the armed services, he accepted a position as superintendent at a roofing manufacturer, later plant superintendent for manufacturing radio and television parts, at Smith Manufacturing Company in Chicago, Illinois, where he was employed for 14 years.

In 1965, Sanderson established his own business at which time he began producing parts for Western Electric, IBM, Xerox, Honeywell and others. In 1968, Sanderson Industries began producing parts for Ford Motor Company and later for GM, Chrysler and International Harvester. In 1985, he made the decision to relocate his company from Chicago to Atlanta, Georgia. His company has expanded 300 percent since its relocation, with Ford being his primary customer.

Sanderson is a member of numerous business and trade organizations, which include: serving as a past president of the Chicago South Chamber of Commerce; as past director of the Chicago Assembly; as past director of Chicago Economic Development Corporation; past director of the National Association of Black Manufacturers; and a member of the American Society of Tool and Manufacturing Engineers. He has served as a member of various charitable and civic organizations, which include: as past vice president of the Corporate Board of the Chicago Boys' Club; and as past chairman of the Chicago Board of the YMCA.

SCHMOKE, KURT L., was born December 1, 1949, in Baltimore. He is married to Patricia, an ophthalmologist, and they have two children, Gregory and Katherine. He attended Balti-more city's public schools, graduating with honors from Baltimore City College High School in 1967, having won the top scholar-athlete award in Baltimore for that year. In 1971, he received his B.A. degree in history from Yale University. He studied at Oxford University, England, as a Rhodes Scholar, and in 1976, earned his J.D. degree from Harvard University Law School. After graduating from Harvard, he began his law practice with the Baltimore firm of Piper & Marbury.

In 1977, he was appointed by President Carter as a member of the White House Domestic Policy staff. In 1978, he returned to Baltimore as an assistant United States Attorney, where he prosecuted narcotics and white collar crime. He later returned to private practice. In November 1982, he was elected state's attorney for Baltimore, which was the chief prosecuting office of the city. As state's attorney, he created a full time narcotics unit to prosecute all drug cases, and underscored the criminal nature of domestic violence and child abuse by setting up separate units to handle those cases. Also while state's attorney, he hired a community liaison officer to make sure that his office was being responsive to neighborhood questions and concerns.

Schmoke was elected mayor of Baltimore on November 3, 1987. In his inaugural address, the mayor set the tone and future direction for his administration when he said that he wanted Baltimore to become known as "The City That Reads." Since then, the Mayor, in partnership with Baltimore's public and private sectors, has established a cabinet-level city agency, as well as a private foundation, to coordinate and expand literacy programs throughout the city. He has also overseen the passage of the largest increase ever in the city's education budget; and together with Baltimore businesses and community-based organizations, has developed programs to guarantee job opportunities to qualifying high school graduates and created a foundation to provide financial assistance to students going to college.

In addition to his emphasis on improving the city's schools, Schmoke has also begun major initiatives in housing, economic development and public safety. In December 1988, he announced the formation of the Baltimore Community Development Financing Corporation, which will pool private and public resources and expertise to renovate abandoned buildings and reinvigorate Baltimore's neighborhoods. He has also initiated several major new development projects in Baltimore's downtown and harbor areas. Since becoming mayor, he has traveled abroad to encourage international business and investment, to showcase Baltimore as an international city and to exchange ideas on matters of shared concern including housing and economic development.

In addition to being a former prosecutor, Schmoke has worked throughout his career to develop more effective criminal justice policies. He served on the Governor's Commission on Prison Overcrowding, the Maryland Criminal Justice Coordinating Council and the Task Force to Reform the Insanity Defense. He has also taken a national leadership position in the movement to reform drug policy in the United States. In recognition of his commitment to excellence in education and his service to the community, Mayor Schmoke has received honorary degrees from several colleges and universities.

SCOTT, DONALD LAVERNE, was born on February 8, 1938, in Hunnewell, Missouri. He received a B.S. degree in art from Lincoln University and an M.S. degree in human relations from Troy State University. He received a ROTC commission to second lieutenant in 1960, and from September 1960 to November 1960, he was a student in the Infantry Officer Orientation Course, United States Army Infantry School, Fort Benning, Georgia. From November 1960 to December 1961, he was assigned as a platoon leader, Company E, 2nd Battalion, 2nd Training Regiment, United States Army Training Center, Fort Leonard Wood, Missouri. He was promoted to the rank of first lieutenant on March 24, 1962. From December 1961 to July 1961, he was the commander of Company E, 2nd Battalion, 2nd Training Regiment, Fort Leonard Wood. From July 1961 to November 1962, he was a student in the Intelligence Research Course, United States Army Intelligence School, Fort Holabird, Baltimore.

From November 1962 to December 1964, he was assigned as intelligence research officer, Region I, 113th Intelligence Corps Group, Chicago, Illinois. He was promoted to the rank of captain on July 9, 1964. From December

1964 to December 1965, he was a student in Vietnamese language, Defense Language Institute, West Coast Branch, Presidio of Monterey, California. From December 1965 to September 1967, he served as an intelligence research officer, later chief of Counterintelligence Section, 441st Military Intelligence Detachment, 1st Special Forces Group (Airborne), 1st Special Forces, United States Army Okinawa. From September 1967 to May 1968, he served as a staff officer with the 97th Civil Affairs Group, 1st Special Forces, United States Army in Okinawa.

From May 1968 to June 1969, Scott was a student in the Infantry Officer Advanced Course, United States Army Infantry School, Fort Benning. From June 1969 to November 1969, he served as psychological operations officer, Office of the Assistant Chief of Staff, G-5, 4th Infantry Division, United States Army Vietnam. From November 1969 to March 1970, he served as executive officer, 1st Battalion, 35th Infantry, 4th Infantry Division in Vietnam. From March 1970 to June 1970, he served as the S-3, 1st Battalion, 14th Infantry Division, in Vietnam. From June 1970 to May 1972, he was an assistant professor of military science, Tuskegee Institute, Tuskegee, Alabama.

From August 1972 to February 1973, he was the senior advisor, Office of Territorial Forces, United States Military Assistance Command in Vietnam. From February 1973 to July 1974, he served as the project officer for the Threats Branch, War Games Division, Combat Operations Analysis Directorate, and later project officer (Combat Developments), Program Management Integration Office, United States Army Combined Arms Development Activity, Fort Leavenworth, Kansas. From August 1974 to June 1975, he was a student in the United States Army Command and General Staff College, Fort Leavenworth. From June 1975 to May 1977, he served as

chief of the Training Division, United States Army Garrison, Fort Lewis, Washington.

Scott was promoted to the grade of lieutenant colonel on September 9, 1976. From May 1977 to October 1978, he served as the executive officer for the 1st Infantry Brigade, 9th Infantry Division, Fort Lewis. From October 1978 to June 1980, he was the commander of the 3rd Battalion, 47th Infantry, 9th Infantry Division, Fort Lewis. From June 1980 to June 1981, he served as professor of military science at Tuskegee Institute, Tuskegee. From June 1981 to May 1982, he was a student in the Air War College, Maxwell Air Force Base, Alabama. From May 1982 to May 1983, he served as the deputy inspector general, Office of the Inspector General, United States Army in Europe and the Seventh Army.

Scott was promoted to the grade of colonel on October 1, 1982. From March 1985 to October 1986, he was the inspector general, VII Corps, United States Army in Europe. From October 1986 to August 1988, he served as the assistant division commander, 1st Cavalry Division, Fort Hood, Texas. On March 1, 1988, he was promoted to the one-star grade of brigadier general. In September 1988, he was appointed chief of staff of the 2nd Army, Fort Gillem, Georgia. Gen. Scott has received numerous awards and decorations, including: the Legion of merit; the Bronze Star Medal (with five oak leaf clusters); the Meritorious Service Medal; the Air Medal; the Army Commendation Medal; the Combat Infantryman Badge; the Parachutist Badge.

SCOTT, GLORIA DEAN RANDLE, was born April 14, 1938, in Houston, Texas. She is married to Will Braxton Scott. She attended Indiana University in Bloomington, Indiana, where she received a B.A. degree in

zoology, minor in botany and French; an M.A. degree in zoology, minor in botany; and a Ph.D. degree in higher education, minors in zoology and botany. She has served as president of Bennett College in Greensboro, North Carolina, from 1987 to date.

Scott's prior positions include: vice president of Clark College; assistant to the president for Educational Planning/Evaluation for Texas Southern University; director of Educational Research/Planning for North Carolina A&T State University, along with serving as director of Institutional Research/Planning, and special assistant to the president as well; and served as dean of students and deputy director of Upward Bound for Knoxville College. She is the recipient of three honorary degrees: Doctor of Laws, Indiana University, Doctor of Humane Letters, Fairleigh Dickinson University, and Doctor of Human Letters, from Westfield State College.

Dr. Scott was included in the Exhibit: "I Dream a World: Seventy-Five Black Women Who Changed the Face of America," 1989. She has served as secretary, for Africa University, 1989–1991; member of board, National Association of Independent Colleges of the United Methodist Church, 1988–1991; member of the board for the National Association of Independent Colleges and Universities, 1988–1992; co-chair for the Minority Task Force; member of the North Carolina Governor's Internship Council, 1988–1991; the First Home Federal; Greensboro Area Chamber of Commerce; Lowes Corporation, 1990; and the White House Initiative on Historically Black Colleges and Universities for 1990.

---

†SCOTT, WENDELL OLIVER, SR., was born August 21, 1921, in Danville, Virginia; he is married to Mary and they have seven children, Willie Ann, Wendell, Jr., Franklin, Deborah, Cheryl, Sybil and Michael. He broke stockcar racing's color barrier in 1949, when he began his racing career in Danville. On March 4, 1952, he started his first NASCAR Tour, and on December 1, 1963, in Jacksonville, Florida, he won the NASCAR, becoming the first black American to do so. In 1965, he was the recipient of the state of Florida's Citation for Outstanding Achievements. He competed in more than 506 Grand National races, and won a career record of 128 races. He started 147 NASCAR events in the top ten positions.

Scott's NASCAR point standing is as follows: in 1966, he was sixth, and tenth, in 1968 and 1969 he held the ninth position. In 1977, his career was highlighted in Warner Bros. Pictures' *Greased Lightning*, starring Richard Pryor as Wendell Scott, Pam Grier as Mary Scott, with Beau Bridges, Cleavon Little, Vincent Gardenia, Julian Bond, and Maynard Jackson. Also in 1977, he was the subject of the novel *Greased Lightning*. He was inducted into the National Black Athletic Hall of Fame in New York, and was named a lifetime member of Hollywood Screen Actors Guild.

Some of Scott's other honors and awards received were: in 1959, he won Virginia State Championship and the Southside Speedway Championship. In 1970, he was named Honorary Lieutenant-Colonel-Aide-de-Camp honor via the Governor of Alabama State Militia. In 1971, he received the 1st Curtis Turner Memorial Achievement Award; in 1974, he received a Special Olympics Service Award; in 1975, he was the recipient of the Schaefer Brewing Company Achievement award; in 1978, he was the recipient of the Tobaccoland 100 Award for the Finest NASCAR Driver via Major Henry Marsh, III.

Scott was the recipient of many awards and honors during the 1980s. In 1990, he was the recipient of the Early Dirt Racers Driver of the Year Award and honored with Wendell Scott Day, in his hometown of Danville. In June of 1990, Scott was diagnosed as having spinal cancer, and died Sunday, December 23, 1990, at Memorial Hospital in Danville. He had been hospitalized since July 28, 1990.

SEARS-COLLINS, LEAH J., was born June 13, 1955, in Heidelberg, Federal Republic of Germany, the daughter of Thomas E. Sears and Omnye Jean Rountree Sears. She is married to Love Sears-Collins, III, and they have two children, Addison and Brennan. She is a graduate of Cornell University, Ithaca, New York, with a B.S. degree with honors in 1976; Emory University School of Law, Atlanta, Georgia, with a J.D. degree in 1980, top 15 percent of class, 1978–1980; the National Judicial College, Reno, Nevada, received master of judicial studies degree program 1987–1989. She has served as judge for the Superior Court of Fulton County, Atlanta, Georgia, presiding over civil, domestic, felony and misdemeanor criminal cases from 1989 to date.

Sears-Collins' prior positions included: judge, for the City Court of Atlanta, a Georgia state traffic court that disposes of over 300,000 misdemeanors a year; attorney, Alston & Bird, Atlanta; judge pro hac vice, City Court of Atlanta; summer associate, Sirote, Permutt, Friend, Friedman, Held & Apolinsky, Birmingham, Alabama; reporter, *Columbus Ledge* newspaper, Columbus. She is the recipient of many honors: Leadership Atlanta, 1988–1989; Outstanding Young Women of America; NAACP (Atlanta Chapter) Award for Community Service; Certificate of Appreciation from Fulton County; Distinguished Leadership Award for Outstanding Service in the Judiciary, 1988, and chosen as honoree for *Dollars and Sense* magazine's "Salute to African-American Business and Professional Women," 1990.

Sears-Collins' professional affiliations include: board member, AMC Cancer Research Center; founding president and current committee member of Georgia Association of Black Women Attorneys; executive council member of Younger Lawyers Section (YLS), state bar of Georgia; board member, Georgia Association for Women Lawyers; board member, Women Judges Fund for Justice (an affiliate of the National Association of Women judges); board member, Atlanta Chapter of the American Red Cross; board member, Affordable Houses, Inc.; nominee to board, Georgia Chapter of the National Council of Christians and Jews; member, state bar of Georgia Committee to Advise Office of General Counsel; advisory member, state bar of Georgia Public Relations Committee; member, state bar of Georgia Commission on Children and the Courts; member, Kiwanis Club of Central Atlanta; National Association of Alcoholism and

Drug Abuse Counselors; American Business Women's Association; American Adjudicature Society; National Association of Women Judges; Joint Center for Political Studies; the High Museum of Art Members' Guild; Women's Forum of Georgia, Inc. (an affiliation of the International Women's Forum); the National Association of Women Judges' Committee on Judicial Selection and Resolutions; and the National Task Force on Gender Bias in the Court.

SHACKELFORD, LOTTIE H., was born April 30, 1941, in Little Rock, Arkansas, to Curtis Holt and Bernice Linzy Holt. She is the mother of three children, Russell, Karen and Karla. She received her B.A. degree in business administration from Philander Smith College; Broadway School of Real Estate, and received her diploma in 1973; JFK School of Government, Harvard University, Fellow, 1983. She has been a member of the Little Rock city Board of Directors since 1978, and was elected mayor in 1987.

Shackelford also has a long history of public service: vice chairman of the Arkansas Director State Committee, Urban League of Greater Little Rock, education director, 1973–1978; Arkansas Regional Minority Council, executive director, 1982. She has received many awards and honors, including: Outstanding Citizen, Philander Smith Alumni Award, 1982; Outstanding Community Service HOPE NLR, 1977; Trailblazer Award, Delta Sigma Theta Sorority, 1977; Outstanding Citizen, Business & Professional Women, 1984; honorary Doctorate of Humane Letters, Philander Smith College, 1988; and an honorary Doctorate of Humane Letters, Shorter College, 1987.

SHAKOOR, ADAM A. He is married to Nikki H. Shakoor, M.P.A.,

and they have seven children. He holds a J.D. degree from Wayne State University Law School, a master's degree in educational sociology, and a B.S. degree both from Wayne State University. In November 1977, while performing hajj, a pilgrimage to Mecca, he was awarded a certificate in Islamic Education from King Abdul Aziz University in Saudi Arabia. In 1969, he received a certificate in Local Union Administration from Wayne State University and the University of Michigan School of Labor. He has also participated in numerous judicial training and management seminars sponsored by the Michigan Judicial Institute, the Institute for Court Management of the National Center for State Courts, and the National Institute for Justice.

Shakoor served from 1986–1988 on the Video Tape Record Advisory Committee by appointment of Chief Justice Dorothy Comstock Riley. He has also served on the board for the State Judicial Council which administers all of the state reorganized courts in Michigan. He was cited for distinguished service by that body in 1989. After a distinguished judicial career, Judge Shakoor retired as a judge and was appointed by Mayor Coleman A. Young to the position of deputy mayor and chief administrative officer for the city of Detroit. He brought a wealth of experience to his present position.

Prior to his appointment, Shakoor served for two terms, by election of his fellow judges, as chief judge of the 36th District Court. This court is the largest court of its kind in America that is housed under one roof, and annually processes some 500,000 cases. He was appointed a Common Pleas Court Judge for Wayne County in February 1981, by former Governor William G. Milliken. His appointment marked the first time a Muslim had served as a judge in the history of the United States or Canada. At the time of his appointment to the court, he was engaged in the private practice of law and in that capacity distinguished himself as an outstanding trial attorney and civil rights advocate.

Shakoor has served since 1971 as an instructor in the Interdisciplinary, Criminal Justice and Business Law Divisions of Wayne County Community College. He also taught at Atlanta University in their Criminal Justice Institute. In his teaching capacity, he has taught criminal justice personnel from all over the nation. He has also been involved in numerous community and legal activities during the past 20 years and has received over 50 proclamations, awards and honors from state and local branches of government, as well as several community organizations. He has been listed in the Marquis Publications of *Who's Who in the World*, 8th edition, 1986, and *Who's Who Among Black Americans*, and *Who's Who in Law Enforcement*.

Deputy Mayor Shakoor also belongs to numerous civic and community organizations: American Bar Association; American Federation of Teachers/AFL-CIO; American Trial Lawyers Association; Association of Black Judges of Michigan, chairman, 1985–1986; Detroit Bar Association; Delta Theta Phi Law Fraternity, International; Kappa Alpha Psi Fraternity, Inc.; Michigan Bar Association; Operation Get Down, chairman of the board, 1987–1989; Optimist Club of Renaissance Detroit, president, 1982–1983; Trade Union Leadership Council; Wolverine Bar Association; and 13th Congressional District Democratic Party Organization.

SHANNON, JOHN W., was born September 13, 1933, in Louisville, Kentucky. He is married to Jean and they are the parents of a son John, Jr. He attended public school in Louisville, Kentucky, and in 1955, graduated from Central State University in Wilberforce, Ohio, with a B.S. degree. He received his M.S. degree in 1975 from Shippensburg State College, Shippensburg, Pennsylvania, pursued additional postgraduate studies at Catholic University, and was a graduate of the United States Army War College. Upon graduation from college, he was commissioned into the Regular Army as a second lieutenant, infantry. He served on active duty for over 23 years from 1955 to 1978. During that time, he served in various capacities as a commander and staff officer. His active duty service included two tours in the Republic of Vietnam as an advisor and as an infantry battalion commander. He retired in the grade of colonel.

Shannon's experience in the areas of military force development, force structure, personnel policy and administration, and congressional affairs activities includes working as a congressional liaison officer in the Office of the Secretary of the Army and serving as special assistant for Manpower, Reserve Affairs and Logistics to the Assistant Secretary of Defense for Legislative Affairs. He was sworn in as the Under Secretary of the Army August 14, 1989. Prior to this appointment, Shannon had served as Assistant

Medal, Vietnamese Cross of Gallantry (with palm), four Vietnam battle campaigns, Roy Wilkins Meritorious Service Award, and the Korean Gugseon Medal.

Secretary of the Army (installations and logistics) since December 7, 1984. In this position, he was the principal advisor and assistant to the Secretary of the Army for Department of the Army policy and activities in the areas of logistics installation operations and construction, environmental preservation and restoration, and safety. He also directed commercial activities and accompanying contract administration throughout the Department of the Army and managed the Army's Chemical Stockpile Disposal Program. Additionally, from June 1981 to December 1984, he served as the Deputy Under Secretary of the Army.

Among Col. Shannon's numerous awards are the Combat Infantry Badge, Parachutist Wings, and the Ranger Tab. He was also a recipient of the Department of the Army Distinguished Civilian Service Award, Legion of Merit, Secretary of Defense Award for Outstanding Public Service, Defense Meritorious Civilian Service Award, Defense Superior Service Award, Bronze Star, Meritorious Service Award, Defense Superior Service Award, Bronze Star, Meritorious Service Medal (with oak leaf cluster), Air

SHAW, LEANDER J., JR., was born September 6, 1930, in Salem, Virginia, the son of Leander J. Shaw, retired dean of the Florida A&M University Graduate School, Tallahassee, Florida and Margaret Shaw, retired teacher Lylburn Downing High School, Lexington, Virginia. He is married to Vidya and they have five children. He attended public schools in Virginia and received his B.A. degree in 1952 from West Virginia State College in Institute, West Virginia. After serving in the Korean conflict as an artillery officer, he entered law school and earned his J.D. degree in 1957 from Howard University in Washington, D.C. In 1986, he was awarded an honorary doctor of laws degree from West Virginia State College and an honorary doctor of public affairs degree from Florida International University in 1990. He served in the Korean Conflict in 1952–1954 as an Army Artillery and Ammunition officer.

Shaw came to Tallahassee in 1957 as an assistant professor of law at Florida A&M University and was admitted to the Florida Bar in 1960. Gov. Graham appointed him to the position of justice of the Supreme Court in January of 1983. He continued to serve in that capacity until July 1, 1990, at which time he became Chief Justice. He is a member of the American Bar, National Bar, Florida Bar, Florida Government Bar, and Tallahassee Bar Associations and was admitted to practice in all Florida courts, the United States Southern District Court of Florida, the United States Circuit Court of Appeals for the Eleventh Circuit, and the United States Supreme Court.

Shaw has an active background in

community, civic, and church activities where he received numerous awards for his outstanding service: Jacksonville Bar Association Award for Community Service; Nathan W. Collins Meritorious Service Award; plaque from Dayspring Baptist Church for Outstanding Community Service; National Bar Association Award; Outstanding Service in Government and Community Affairs Award, Jacksonville, Florida; O.I.C. Torch Bearer Award; Northwest Division chairman, March of Dimes; appointed to the mayor's Police Advisory Committee; appointed to Jacksonville JetPort Authority; board chairman, Jacksonville Opportunities Industrialization Center, Inc., and member, Advisory Committee, Jacksonville Community Council, Inc. (Offender Research Project).

SHEFFEY, FRED C., JR., was born on August 27, 1928, in McKeesport, Pennsylvania. He is married to the former Jane Hughes of Providence, Kentucky, and they have three children, Alan, Steven, and Patricia. He graduated from the ROTC program at Central State College, Wilberforce, Ohio, in June 1950, as a distinguished military graduate. At this time, he was commissioned as a second lieutenant of infantry and awarded a B.S. degree in economics. In October 1950, he joined the 25th Infantry Division fighting in Korea as an infantry platoon leader. He was wounded and medically evacuated to the United States in April 1951, several weeks after promotion to first lieutenant. After hospitalization, he was assigned as a weapon instructor with the 5th Infantry Division Faculty at Indiantown Gap Military Reservation in Pennsylvania. He was detailed to the Quartermaster Corps in 1953, and attended the Quartermaster Officer Basic and Advanced Courses at Fort Lee, Virginia.

During the period August 1953 to June 1962, in addition to attending these schools, Sheffey had a series of logistical assignments in inventory management, supply, and maintenance at the Nahbollenback Depot in Europe and at the Columbus General Depot in Columbus, Ohio. He was promoted to the rank of captain on July 9, 1954, and was promoted to the rank of major on November 28, 1961. While at Columbus General Depot, he engaged in business studies at Ohio State University and received an M.B.A. degree in June 1962. From June 1962 to December 1964, he served on the staff of the United States Army Communications Zone, in Europe. Following this assignment he attended the Command and General Staff College, graduating in May 1965. He was then assigned to the 4th Infantry Division at Fort Lewis, Washington, where he served as division supply officer and later as executive officer of the 4th Division Supply and Transport Battalion.

On January 11, 1966, he was promoted to the grade of lieutenant colonel and assigned as commander of the

266th QM Battalion, Fort Lewis. He deployed with this unit to the Republic of South Vietnam in June 1966. On his return to the United States, he was assigned to the Office of the Deputy Chief of Staff for Logistics, Department of the Army, as chief of the Base Operations Branch in financial management. He graduated from the National War College in June 1969 and continued studies in international affairs at George Washington University. For the latter, he was awarded an M.S. degree in September 1969. He was promoted to the grade of colonel on November 20, 1970, and in May 1971 took command of the 54th General Support Group in the Republic of South Vietnam.

In July 1972, he was again assigned to the Office of the Deputy Chief of Staff for Logistics, Department of the Army, where he served as the director of financial resources in the Pentagon until his promotion to the grade of brigadier general on July 1, 1973. On July 2, 1973, he became director of Operation and Maintenance Resources (Provisional) and served in this capacity until May 20, 1974, when he was assigned as the deputy director of Supply and Maintenance. He joined the United States Army Materiel Development and Readiness Command, Alexandria, Virginia, in August 1975 as the director of Materiel Management. In March 1976, he was nominated by the president for promotion to the two-star rank of major general and was promoted on August 2, 1976.

On September 29, 1977, Gen. Sheffey assumed command of the United States Army Quartermaster Center and Fort Lee, Virginia. In this capacity he also served as commandant of the United States Army Quartermaster School. His medals and awards include: the Legion of Merit (with two oak leaf clusters); the bronze Star Medal; the Meritorious Service Medal; the Army Commendation Medal (with two oak leaf clusters); the Purple Heart; and the Combat Infantryman Badge.

SHORT, ALONZO E., JR., was born January 27, 1939, in Greenville, North Carolina. He married the former Rosalin Reid of Orange, New Jersey, and they have a son Stanley, and a daughter Daniele. He holds a B.D. degree in business management from the New York Institute of Technology, Long Island, New York. His military education includes the United States Army Signal School Officer Basic and Advanced Courses, the Military Advisor and Technical Assistance School, the Armed Forces Staff College, the Communications/Electronics Systems Engineer Course and the Army War College. Since entering the Army in June of 1962, he has held a variety of assignments with progressively increasing responsibility throughout his career.

Short was a platoon leader and staff officer at Fort Riley, Kansas. From 1965 to 1967, he had assignments as a staff officer, company commander, and executive officer of a signal battalion in Europe. In 1967, he was assigned as a staff planning and engineering officer in the Republic of Vietnam, which was followed by an assignment to Okinawa first as battalion S-3, then executive officer and, finally, battalion commander in the Strategic Communications Command, Okinawa Signal Group. He also served a second tour in Vietnam in 1972–1973 as an advisor. In 1975, he was assigned as a staff officer in the Defense Communications Agency. Following that assignment, he was a battalion commander in the 101st Airborne (Air Assault) Division at Fort Campbell, Kentucky.

In 1979, Short began a tour as a staff planner with the Army Communications Command at Fort Huachuca. He then served as commander of the 3rd Signal Brigade at Fort Hood, Texas.

He was then assigned as the deputy commander of the Army Electronics Research and Development Command at (ERADCOM), Adelphi, Maryland, from July to October 1984. He was promoted to brigadier general on June 1, 1986, assuming command as deputy commanding general/deputy program manager, Army Information Systems, United States Army Information Systems Engineering Command, Fort Belvoir, Virginia. On September 7, 1988, Short was promoted to the two-star rank of major general, concurrent with becoming deputy commanding general, Information Systems Engineering Command (ISEC), becoming deputy commanding general, Information Systems Command, then commanding general, and was promoted to his three-star rank of lieutenant general before he retired in 1990.

SIMPSON, DONNIE, was born January 30, 1954, in Detroit, Michigan, son of Calvin and Dorothy Simpson. He is married to Pamela and they have two children, Donnie, Jr., and Dawn. He attended the University of Detroit, obtaining a B.A. degree in communication. Hailing from Detroit, Michigan, he started his first job at the age of 15 at WJLB Radio. Despite his youth, audiences were mesmerized by his deep voice and his eclectic tastes in music and he soon became Detroit's highest rated evening deejay. When one thinks of Washington's top-rated WKYS Radio, the first name that comes to mind is Donnie Simpson.

In 1992, radio and television personality Donnie Simpson entered his 23rd year in broadcasting and his 15th year at WKYS Radio. As if those are not remarkable accomplishments in and of themselves, Simpson's career and popularity have been as distinguished and extraordinary as it has been rewarding. Word of Simpson soon spread to Washington, where NBC, hoping to beef up its fledgling

ratings at WKYS Radio, hired him for the afternoon drive time shift. Two years later he was named program director and it was not long before his "special" brand of music — a format of soul, dance, jazz and rock music — caught on in Washington. It broke barriers by educating listeners to the universality of music — transcending race, color, income levels and geographical locale.

People who once listened to soul and rock exclusively began expanding their repertoire to include jazz and reggae. Under Donnie's direction, WKYS became the most "listened to" radio station in Washington — going from 16th place in the ratings to number one. For the last seven years, Simpson has been the leading radio personality in the Washington, D.C. metropolitan area for the 12-49 age group, and when you translate ratings into revenue, you know that his "special" brand of music has become a hot commodity. Endowed with a good sense of humor, sensitivity, and enthusiasm for his work and listening audience, he realizes that he alone often times has a tremendous influence on the masses, so he doesn't restrict his presence to the studio or office.

On any given day, Simpson can be found giving something back to the community, helping to raise funds for a variety of causes, from the United Negro College Fund to AIDS research. He also spends a good deal of time with children, urging them to "Just Say No to Drugs" or helping inspire them to pursue their dreams. In recent years, he has branched out to include television and film on his list of accomplishments. He appeared for a while as a weekend sports anchor on WRC-TV, NBC's Washington station. More significantly, he is the host of "Video Soul," a daily music video show that is seen nationally by over 25 million viewers on Black Entertainment Television.

Through "Video Soul" Simpson has become so popular that he regularly receives an avalanche of mail from viewers from around the country — including Alaska, Hawaii and the Virgin Islands! His natural, personable style before the cameras has now led him to film. He had a small part in 1985's *Krush Groove*, and appeared in 1987's *Disorderlies*, the Fat Boy's long-awaited musical comedy. Clearly, Simpson has a lot to celebrate in his 15th year in Washington. Every indication is that despite his accomplishments — a natural and personable style, strong excellence — this is still just the beginning.

SMITH, ADA L., was born in Amherst County, Virginia, the only child of the late Lillian and Thomas Smith. She was educated in the New York City public school system and graduated from the Baruch College of CUNY. She was the first female and the only black president of the Baruch College Alumni Association, and has served as trustee of the College Fund and is a life director. A leading community activist, she brings to the Senate more than 20 years of neighborhood commitment and public service. Profound interest in improving the quality of life

for her neighborhoods has resulted in an impressive history of community involvement.

A former member of Community Board 1 and chairperson of its Social Services Committee, Smith is also former chairperson of the New York Community Services Coalition, former chairperson of the Brooklyn Coalition of Area Policy boards; and is former treasurer of the Brooklyn Coalition of Area Policy boards; former treasurer of the Brooklyn Plaza Medical Center, the Friends of Lindsay Park Anti-Crime Committee, and 67 Manhattan Avenue Block Associations. She is a former member of the board of managers of the Eastern District YMCA, a former officer of the Williamsburg Tenants Association, a former member of the Community Action Board, and former executive member of the Center for Community Organizations, a former member of Woodhull Hospital Advisory board, and former member of Area Policy Board 4.

Sen. Smith is a past chairperson of Area Policy Board 1, a former board member and president of the Lindsay Park Housing Corporation, and a former president of the Williamsburg/Greenpoint Coalition of Community Organizations. Her efforts and accomplishments have resulted in numerous awards, including the Roberto Clemente Community Service Award; YMCA Woman of the Year Award; Pulaski Community Service Award; Baruch College Model Citizen Award; Williamsburg/Greenpoint COCO Community Service Award; and Baruch College Alumni Association Distinguished Service Award.

Prior to Sen. Smith's election to the state senate, she served as the deputy city clerk of New York City. She has also been extremely active in the mental health arena, initially appointed to the Board of Visitors of the Brooklyn Development Center for the Mentally Retarded and the Developmentally Disabled in 1981 and re-appointed in

1985. The full-time legislator has been assigned to the following committees: Mental Health (Ranking); Health; Social Services; Alcoholism; Substance Abuse; Child Care; Elections; Veterans; Task Force on Moderate Income Housing; Education Task Force of the Black and Puerto Rican; Legislative Caucus (chairperson) Task Force on Puerto Rican/Hispanic Affairs. She has recently been elected 1st vice chair of the African-American Clergy and Elected Officials and 2nd vice chair of the NYS Women's Legislative Caucus.

SMITH, CALVERT H., was born in Council Bluffs, Iowa, and reared in Chicago. He is married to he former Carrie Flowers of Goldsboro, North Carolina, and they are the parents of three children, Melanie, Calvert H., III, and Natobia. He attended the public schools of Chicago, and graduated third in his class from George Washington Carver High School in 1954. In 1955, he was awarded an athletic scholarship to Winston-Salem State University in Winston-Salem, North Carolina. In 1959, he graduated cum laude from Winston-Salem and received a B.S. degree in education; in February 1964, he received his M.E. degree in guidance from De Paul University; and in June 1969, he received a Ph.D. degree in management from Northwestern University.

Smith began his career in education by serving as a teacher and coach in North Carolina from September 1959 through June 1960. From 1960 through 1963, he worked as a teacher in the Chicago Public Schools and as assistant principal of the Central YMCA High School in Chicago. In 1966, he was promoted to principal of Central where he served successfully for two years. In September of 1968, he began his career in higher education by accepting a joint appointment with Northeastern Illinois University in Chicago and Northwestern University in Evanston, Illinois.

From 1971 through 1975, Smith served as chairman of the Department of Urban Affairs, professor of educational administration and assistant dean of the College of Education at the University of Cincinnati. In January 1975, he accepted a position with the General Electric Company as manager of organizational development and personnel relations. in July 1977, he joined the staff of the University of Cincinnati as vice provost for Continuing Education and professor of Educational Administration. In August 1984, he accepted the presidency of Morris Brown College. During his tenure as president, Morris Brown has experienced phenomenal growth. Enrollment at the 109-year old historically black college has doubled, moving from 900 students in 1984 to 1,800 students in 1989. The dramatic increase in enrollment has been accompanied by an increase in the average SAT score of the student body by 30 points.

Early in his tenure as president, Smith initiated a strategic planning process which revised the mission of the college, revamped the curriculum and produced a long-range plan of action for the institution to guide it into the 21st century. In addition to the dramatic increase in enrollment, under his leadership the financial health of the college had improved significantly. The endowment had doubled and the institution had finished the fiscal year in the black for four consecutive years. The quality of the faculty had improved with 65 percent of that group being hired in the last four years, the Nursing Program received state approval and national accreditation by the National League for Nursing, with 90 of its graduates passing state board examinations in the various states in which they were taken, and in December 1989, the Southern Association of Colleges and Schools reaffirmed the accreditation of the institution for the next ten years.

Under Smith's leadership, Morris Brown College has ranked 16th from the top among the 41 United Negro College Fund Colleges in endowment, ninth in total enrollment and 11th in terms of overall strength. For 22 years, he has served as educational consultant to state legislatures, school districts, universities and community groups throughout the country. In the midst of performing his responsibilities, he has found time to publish two books and to author numerous articles. Among his awards, he was selected as the Outstanding Black Educator in the state of Illinois (1969): selected as one of the 29 in a nationwide search for participation in the Rockefeller Internship Program (1972); and Who's Who Among Black Americans (1974).

Smith was active in church activities where he has served in several capacities including Sunday school teacher, advanced Bible class teacher and Director of the Board of Christian Education. Included among his community activities were membership on the board of directors of the Alliance Theater, membership on the boards of the Butler Street YMCA, the Citizens Trust Bank and the Martin Luther King, Jr. Center of Nonviolent Social Change, and the Collection of Life and Heritage, and membership in the Atlanta Ballet Society and the Atlanta Chamber of Commerce.

SMITH, CHARLES Z., was born February 23, 1927, in Lakeland, Florida. He is married to Eleanor Jane Martinez and they have four children. He received his B.S. degree from Temple University, Philadelphia, Pennsylvania (1952), and a J.D. degree from the University of Washington School of Law, Seattle (1955). He is a graduate of the National Judicial College, University of Nevada, Reno (1968), and from the Naval Justice School, Newport, Rhode Island (1973). He retired November 1, 1986 from the United States Marine Corps Reserve with the rank of lieutenant colonel. He serves as a justice of the Washington State Supreme Court, having been appointed to that position by Gov. Booth Gardner on July 13, 1988 to fill an unexpired term. He took his oath of office on July 18, 1988 and was elected unopposed on November 8, 1988, for the remainder of that term.

Since January 1983, Smith had been professor of law emeritus at the University of Washington School of Law. He retired from full-time teaching there, having been a professor of law since 1973. He was associate dean of the School of Law from January 1973 to July 1, 1978. He was director of University District Defender Services, a law school clinical program, from July 1978 to September 1, 1982, and was also director of the Law School Clinical Program. Previous professional positions include: principal in the law firm of Theodore M. Rosenblume, Charles Z. Smith and Associates, P.S., as a news commentator for KOMO Radio and KOMO Television (ABD Affiliate), Seattle. On January 8, 1973, he completed service as a judge of the Superior Court of Washington for King County, having been appointed to that position by Gov. Daniel J. Evans in November 1966. He was elected unopposed to a full term in November 1968.

Smith was a general trial judge and also served as a Juvenile Court judge on rotation assignment. He served as chairperson of the Juvenile Court Committee of the Washington State Superior Court Judges Association. He served as judge of the Municipal Court of Seattle, Criminal Department, under appointment by Mayor J. D. Braman to fill an unexpired term, beginning January 14, 1965. He was elected unopposed to a full term on that court, but resigned to accept appointment to the Superior Court.

Upon his graduation from law school in 1955, Smith served as law clerk for Justice Matthew W. Hill of the Washington State Supreme Court for one year. He served as a deputy prosecuting attorney for King County under Charles O. Carroll from June 1956 to April 1960. When he left the prosecuting attorney's office, he was assistant chief of the Criminal Division. He was in private practice of law in Seattle for approximately one year, 1960–1961. In March of 1961, he joined the United States Department of Justice at the request of the attorney general Robert Kennedy where he served until his resignation as a Special Assistant in September 1964.

Smith's professional awards are numerous: the 1966 Distinguished Service Award (Alcoholism), Washington State Department of Health; the 1974 Brotherhood Award, Washington Region, National Conference of Christians and Jews; the 1974 Professional Service Award, Washington Corrections Association; 1974 honorary membership, Washington Registry of Interpreters for the Deaf; the 1977 Martin Luther King, Jr. Award for Law and Justice, Seattle Benefit Guild; 1978 Community Service Award, Japanese American Citizen League, Seattle Benefit Guild; 1978 Community Service Award, Japanese-American Citizen League, Seattle Chapter; was Christian honoree for the Seattle Chapter, Jewish National Fund in 1980; 1980 Humanitarian Award, Seattle Chapter, American Association for the United National; the 1982 "Friend of the Community" Award from the Pacific Northeast Asian Pacific American Community; the 1983 "President's Award" of the Black Law Enforcement Association of Washington.

In addition, Smith received 1985 honorary membership, board of directors, Washington Association for the Deaf; 1988 Outstanding Lawyer Award, Seattle–King County Bar Association; 1988 Public Service Award, Community Relations Service, United States Department of Justice; Honorary Life member, board of directors, American Cancer Society, Washington Division (1988); and 1989 Distinguished Service Award, Zeta Phi Lambda Chapter, Alpha Phi Alpha Fraternity; the 1989 National Volunteer Leadership Award, American Cancer Society; the 1990 Edwin T. Pratt Award, Metropolitan Seattle Urban League; and the 1990 Hall of Fame, Polk County (Florida) School Board. Judge Smith was awarded honorary J.D. degrees by Eastern College, Saint Davids, Pennsylvania, in May 1978 and by Linfield College, McMinnville, Oregon, in May 1990.

SMITH, JOSHUA ISAAC, was born April 8, 1941, Garrard County, Kentucky. He married the former Jacqueline Jones and they have a son Joshua, II. He received a B.S. degree in biology/chemistry, in 1963. He went on to study at the University of Akron School of Law, University of Delaware, Central M.I. University. From 1969 to 1970, he worked as manager of the Data Book Division, Plenum Publishing Corp. From 1970 to 1976, he was the executive director of American Source of Information Science. From 1976 to 1978, he was the vice president of Herner & Company.

In 1978, Smith founded the Maxima Corporation, an information technology firm with revenues over $62 million. President George Bush named Smith to head a 14-person commission to study and advise him on ways to improve business development. The commission was comprised of the Small Business Administration, the Under Secretary of Defense, secretaries of Commerce and Transportation, along with representatives of trade associations, major domestic corporations and educational institutions. Smith also served as senior adviser to GOP Chairman Lee Atwater.

SMITH, ROLAND B., JR., is married to Valerie Smith and they are the parents of two children, Rovelle and Roland, III. He is a graduate of Bowie State University in Bowie, Maryland, with a B.A. degree in anthropology-sociology, 1969; received an M.P.A. degree from Indiana University, South Bend, Indiana, School of Public and Environmental Affairs, 1976, and Ed.D. degree from Harvard University, Graduate School of Education,

Cambridge, Massachusetts. A native of Washington, D.C., Smith first moved to South Bend in 1969. After working three years for the city of South Bend, he joined the University of Notre Dame in 1973. He served first as assistant director of Upward Bound, was named director of the program in 1976, and was also appointed to the faculty in the Institute for Urban Studies.

In 1980, Smith formed the Center for Educational Opportunity and became the director of the Center, which housed Upward Bound, Educational Talent Search, Project MASS COMM, Linkup, and other collaborative projects. He was named executive assistant to the president of Notre Dame University in 1988, while continuing as director of the center. He has received many honors and awards, including: the Distinguished Alumni Award from the School of Public and Environmental Affairs of Indiana University, South Bend, and the Distinguished Service Award from the United Negro College Fund.

Also, Smith has been named in *Who's Who Among Black Americans* and *Outstanding Young Men of America*. While at Harvard he was elected to the Harvard Educational Review. He has served as president of the Indiana Chapter of the Mid-American Association of Educational Opportunity Program Personnel. He continued to be active on many community boards and committees and was to date a member of the Minority Affairs Council of South Bend, the Private Industry Council of St. Joseph County, and the Community Education Round Table, to name just a few. He also served as Polemarch of the South Bend Alumni Chapter of Kappa Alpha Psi Fraternity.

SMITH, SAM, is a graduate of Seattle University with a B.S. degree, and a graduate of the University of

Washington with a degree in economics and government and practical politics. He is married to Marion King Smith and they have five sons and a daughter, and five grandchildren. He is in his sixth term as a member of the Council. He has also completed four terms as president of the Seattle City Council. He is currently chair of the Utilities Committee, vice chair of the Finance and Personnel Committee, and also a member of the Metro Rules Committee, as well as the Metro Finance Committee.

Prior to being elected to the Seattle City Council, Smith served five terms in the Washington State Legislature. He is a former member of the Board of Managers of the American Baptist Churches USA; life member of the NAACP; member of the Seattle Urban League; former president of the Brotherhood of the Mt. Zion Baptist Church for 26 years; church school-teacher for 34 years and area director of the National Black Caucus of Local Elected Officials. He organized and guided the Northwest Conference of Black Public Officials in Washington, Oregon, Idaho, Colorado and Alaska. He also founded the Prisoners Assist-

ance Coalition of Washington. He was honored by the Samoan National Chief's Council in 1989 for his many contributions to the Samoan Community, including the passage of the Samoan Flag Day.

Smith was awarded the 1987 NBL (National Business League) Booker T. Washington Award, and the 1986 NCCJ (National Conference of Christians and Jews) Recognition Award. He was selected "Most Outstanding Public Official for 1985" by the Municipal of Seattle and King County. He was honored by the Alpha Phi Alpha Fraternity for his achievements in the community and by the Mt. Zion Brotherhood for 26 years of excellent service as president. He received the Distinguished Alumnus Award from Seattle University in 1976; the Distinguished Service Award from the Central Area Jaycees; the Exemplary Leadership Award from the Mount Zion Baptist Church; the Community Service Award for outstanding service to his community; the Seattle Urban League Annual Award in 1968; the Legislator of the Year Award in the State House of Representatives in 1967. He is a 33° Mason and was awarded the Prince Hall Scottish Rite Gold Medal Achievement Award, "Most Outstanding Mason in 1983" by the Most Worshipful Prince Hall Grand Lodge of Washington Jurisdiction and the Medal of Honor from the Daughters of the American Revolution. He was presented the Meritorious and Distinguished Service Award by the Veterans of Foreign Wars; inducted in the Prince Hall Scottish Rite Hall of Fame in Philadelphia (1983); was awarded by the Central Area Public Development Authority for "Keeping Their Dream Alive" and was one of the three recipients of "Leading the Way for All of Us" (1989).

SMITH, VIRGIL C., JR., represents Michigan's Second Senatorial

District, comprising Highland Park, Hamtramck, and a Northeast portion of Detroit. Born on the 4th of July, the 43-year-old Smith is a graduate of Pershing High School in Detroit. He earned a B.A. degree in political science, and a J.D. degree from Wayne State University. Following law school, he became a legal advisor to community groups for Wayne County Legal Services rendering services for the Equal Justice Council, the Art Center Citizens Council, and for the Forest Park Development Project.

Sen. Smith has also acted as supervising attorney for Wayne County Legal Services and was a senior assistant corporation counsel for the city of Detroit Law Department. He served 12 years in the House of Representatives until his election to the Second Senatorial District in March of 1988. He previously served as chairman of Economic Development and Energy, Taxation, Judiciary, Elections, and the Special Committee on Court Reorganization. Sen. Smith presently serves on the Finance Committee, Local Government and Veterans Committee, Law Revision Commission, and the 21st-Century Commission on the Courts.

SMITHERMAN, CAROLE CATLIN, was born in Birmingham, Alabama, where she gained her education in public schools. She is married to Rodger Smitherman, an attorney in private practice, and they have three children, Rodger, II, Tonya Renee, and Mary Elaine. She graduated with honors from Spelman College, Atlanta, Georgia; earned a J.D. degree from Miles Law School where she graduated number one in her class and was the only female in that class. She has furthered her legal education by studying at Northwestern University School of Law, Chicago, Illinois. She was licensed to practice law in April 1982. For eight years she worked as an attorney in the Jefferson County District Attorney's Office, rising from an initial appointment as a law clerk to executive director of the first Victim-Witness Program in Alabama, and ultimately receiving an appointment as the first black female deputy district attorney in Alabama. She presently serves as the first female Municipal Court judge for the city of Birmingham.

Smitherman is a constitutional law and labor law professor at Miles Law School, and an active member of the local and national bar associations. As a member of the Birmingham Bar Association, she has served in the following capacities: chairperson of the Law Day (1985); co-chaired Continuing Legal Education Committee (1986); Entertainment Committee (1987); Criminal Court Procedures Committee (1989). In 1989, she was appointed by Chief Justice Hornsby to serve as a commissioner for the Commission on the Future of the Alabama Juvenile Justice System. She was appointed by 1989 State Bar President, Alva Caine, to serve on the State Bar Task Force on Legal Education. She was a charter member for the Magic City Bar Association and has been a Continuing Legal Education instructor for the Alabama Lawyers Association.

Smitherman is a member of the Alabama Municipal Judges Association where she serves as the 1989–1990 secretary/treasurer. She was vice-chairman of the Police Athletic Team board of directors and a member of the Service Guild Early Intervention Program Advisory Board. She is also the High School Mock Trial coach for the 4th Avenue YMCA Youth and Government Program where her team placed second in the 1989 state competition. She also serves as assistant Sunday school teacher and youth director of Westminster Presbyterian Church, of which she is an active member; and past president of Women's Work. Her community service work includes speaking to numerous civil and church groups which deserve recognition for outstanding service.

SPEARMAN, LEONARD H. O., JR., is native of Tallahassee, Florida, residing in the Washington, D.C. area with his wife and three daughters. He is a graduate of the University of Florida where he received a B.A. degree in 1975. He also has a J.D. degree from Texas Southern University's Thurgood Marshall School of Law. He was appointed executive secretariat and secretary to the Federal Housing Finance Board (FHFB) in April 1990. The newly created FHFB was established to supervise the Federal Home Loan Banks by the Financial Institutions Recovery, Reform, Enforcement Act of 1989.

Spearman previously served as the first executive director of the Commission on Minority Business Development. Before that, he was appointed deputy associate director, Presidential Personnel for the White House and the Office of the President-Elect. He has more than 14 years of experience in business and government, having served as the special assistant to the director, Community Relations Service, U.S. Department of Justice, and as special assistant for the associate administrator for Minority Small Business and Capitol Ownership Development, U.S. Small Business Administration.

Earlier, Spearman was director of the EEO Office of the governor of the state of Texas, and served as a legal assistant with the law firm of Burney, Caggins, and Hartsfield. He was also with AT&T in Florida and Texas in Marketing Management. He has spoken before several esteemed groups such as the National Newspaper Publishers Association, Paul Quinn College, National Urban Bankers Association, and the National Business League, discussing issues such as politics, government and business. He was appointed by President Reagan to the National Advisory Council for Career Education, under the Secretary of Education, Terrell H. Bell, in 1981. Spearman serves as a director in the Texas Lyceum Association, and is a trustee for the Black Texas Cultural Museum.

STAMPER, RUSSELL W., SR. He and his wife Virginia have three children, Russell II, Rashan and Cancade. They live in Milwaukee, Wisconsin, where he has worked as a teacher, as a director of a youth apprenticeship program, and as an attorney for ten years. Governor Anthony S. Earl of Wisconsin appointed Stamper a judge to the Milwaukee County Circuit Court, Branch 9, on March 30, 1983.

Stamper's reputation as an accomplished attorney, possessing an effective combination of toughness and sensitivity, convinced the Judicial Selection Committee to unanimously recommend the governor to appoint him judge. His noteworthy performance on the bench has won him respect and support from judges and attorneys throughout Milwaukee County and the state of Wisconsin. He won election to a full six-year term in April of 1984, and was re-elected to a second six-year term in April of 1990.

STANFORD, JOHN HENRY, was born on September 14, 1938, in Darby, Pennsylvania. He received a B.A. degree in political science from Pennsylvania State University, and an M.S. degree in personnel management/administration from Central Michigan

University. He received an ROTC commission to second lieutenant on June 10, 1961. From August 1961 to January 1962, he was a student at the Infantry Officer Basic Course and the Ranger Course, United States Army Infantry School, Fort Benning, Georgia. From January 1962 to May 1962, he was platoon leader of Company D, 2nd Air Reconnaissance Battalion, 36th Infantry, 3rd Armored Division, United States Army in Europe. He was promoted to the rank of first lieutenant on December 10, 1962.

In June of 1963, he was appointed commander of the 40th Transportation Company, 15th Quartermaster Battalion, 6th Quartermaster Group, United States Army in Europe. From June 1963 to November 1964, he was a student in the Officer Fixed Wing Aviator Course, United States Army Aviation School, Fort Rucker, Alabama. He was promoted to the rank of captain on January 6, 1965. From August 1965 to October 1965, he was assistant S-1, Headquarters, Troop brigade, Fort Rucker. From January 1966 to April 1966, he served as a fixed wing Army aviator, 55th Aviation Company, Eighth Army in Korea. From August 1966 to July 1967, he was a fixed wing aviator, 73rd Aviation Company (Aerial Surveillance), 222d Aviation Battalion, U.S. Army in Vietnam.

From July 1967 to February 1968, he was a student in the Aricraft Maintenance Officer Course, United States Army Transportation School, Fort Eustis, Virginia. From February 1968 to June 1968, he was assigned as chief of the electrical section, United States Army Transportation School, Fort Eustis. He was promoted to the rank of major on June 10, 1968. From June 1968 to February 1969, he was a student in the Transportation Officer Advanced Course, United States Army Transportation School, Fort Eustis. From February 1969 to September 1969, he was a platoon commander, 73rd Aviation Company, 210th Aviation Battalion (Combat), United States Army in Vietnam.

From September 1969 to May 1970, he was the commander of the 56th Transportation Company, 765th Transportation Battalion, 34th General Support Group, United States Army in Vietnam. From May 1970 to July 1971, he served as a personnel staff officer, Directorate of Personnel and Community Activities, United States Army Transportation Center, Fort Eustis, Virginia. From July 1971 to June 1972, he was a student at the United States Army Command and General Staff College, Fort Leavenworth, Kansas. From June 1972 to November 1972, he was a personnel management officer, Office of Personnel Operations, Washington, D.C. From November 1972 to September 1975, he served as an aviation assignments officer and later personnel management officer, Transportation Branch, Personnel Directorate, United States Army Military Personnel Center, Alexandria, Virginia.

Stanford was promoted to the rank of lieutenant colonel on June 1, 1975. From June 1975 to May 1977, he was the commander of the 34th Support Battalion, 6th Cavalry Brigade (Air Combat), III Corps, Fort Hood, Texas. From June 1977 to May 1979, he served as a military assistant to the Under Secretary of the Army, Office of the Secretary of the Army, Washington. From June 1979 to June 1980, he was a student at the Industrial College of Armed Forces, Fort Lesley J. McNair, Washington. He was promoted to the rank of colonel on August 1, 1979. From July 1980 to June 1981, he was the commander of Division Support Command, 2nd Infantry Division, United States Army in Korea. From June 1981 to June 1984, he was first executive assistant to the Special Assistant to the Secretary of Defense, later he served as executive secretary for the Department of Defense, Office of the Secretary of Defense, Washington.

From June 1984 to September 1986,

Stanford was the commander of the Military Traffic Management Command, Western Area, Oakland Army Base, Oakland, California. He was promoted to the one-star rank of brigadier general on September 1, 1984. From September 1986 to June 1987, he was deputy commander for research and development, United States Army Aviation Systems Command, St. Louis, Missouri. From June 1987 to August 1989, he was the commanding general of the Military Traffic Management Command, Washington. He was promoted to the two-star rank of major general on May 1, 1988. In September of 1989, he was appointed director of plans, J-5, United States Transportation Command, Scott Air Force Base, Illinois.

Gen. Stanford ended a 30-year military career August 1, 1991, to become the Fulton County, Georgia, County Manager. He has received numerous awards and decorations which include: the Master Army Aviator Badge; the Distinguished Service Medal; and the Ranger Tab.

STEPHENS, ROBERT LOUIS, JR., was born on September 21, 1940, in Welch, West Virginia. He received a B.S. degree in education from West Virginia State College, and an M.S. degree in vocational education guidance from Alfred University. He received a ROTC commission and entered the Army as a student in the Infantry Officer Basic Course, United States Army Infantry School, Fort Benning, Georgia. From November 1962 to April 1964, he served as a platoon leader for Company C, later as S-4 (Logistics), 1st Airborne Battle Group, 327th Infantry, 101st Airborne Division, Fort Campbell, Kentucky. From June 1964 to December 1964, he was a student at the Defense Language Institute, Presidio of Monterey, California.

From January 1965 to April 1965, he was a student in the Special Forces Officer Course, United States Army Special Warfare School, Fort Bragg, North Carolina. From April 1965 to June 1967, he served as executive officer, later commander, of Company B, 8th Special Forces Group (Airborne), 1st Special Forces, Fort Gulick, Panama. He was promoted to the rank of captain on April 11, 1966. From June 1967 to July 1968, he was assistant G-5 (Civil Affairs/Civic Action), later commander, Company B, 1st Battalion, 7th Cavalry Division (Airmobile), United States Army in Vietnam. From July 1968 to July 1969, he served as senior platoon advisor; later he was a student in the Infantry Officer Advanced Course, United States Army Infantry School, Fort Benning, Georgia. On June 27, 1969, he was promoted to the grade of major.

From July 1969 to May 1971, Stephens served as the assistant professor of military science a Alfred University, New York. From August 1971 to June 1972, he was a student at the United States Army Command and Staff College, Fort Leavenworth, Kansas. From June 1972 to March 1973, he was assigned as the S-3 (Operations) advisor, Delta Region Assistance Command, United States Military Assistance Command, in Vietnam. From March 1973 to June 1976, he served as the division race relations officer, later headquarters commandant, later executive officer, 3rd Battalion, 187th Infantry, later adjutant, 3rd Brigade, later assistant G-1 (Personnel), 101st Airborne Division (Airmobile), Fort Campbell, Kentucky.

From June 1976 to April 1978, Stephens served as a personnel staff officer, Alcohol and Drug Policy Branch, Leadership Division, Office, Deputy Chief of Staff for Personnel, United States Army, Washington, D.C. From April 1978 to April 1979, he served as military secretary J-3 (Operations), Organization of the Joint Chiefs of Staff, Washington. He was promoted to the grade of lieutenant colonel on September 12, 1978. From May 1979 to June 1981, he was the commander of the 2nd Battalion, 39th Infantry, 9th Infantry Division, Fort Lewis, Washington. From June 1981 to

June 1982, he served as the personnel staff officer, Leadership Division, Office, Deputy Chief of Staff for Personnel, United States Army, Washington. From June 1982 to June 1983, he was a student at the National War College, Fort McNair, Washington. From June 1983 to April 1985, he was assigned as inspector general, Military District of Washington, Fort McNair, Washington.

Stephens was promoted to the grade of colonel on October 1, 1983. From April 1985 to June 1987, he was the commander of Task Force Bayonet, later designated 193rd Infantry Brigade, United States Army South, Panama. From June 1987 to September 1988, he was appointed deputy director for readiness, mobilization and exercises, Office of the Deputy Chief of Staff for Operations and Plans, United States Army, Washington. From September 1988 to February 1990, he was assigned as the assistant division commander, 9th Infantry Division (Motorized), Fort Lewis. He was promoted to the one-star grade of brigadier general on July 1, 1989. In February 1990, he was appointed chief of Joint United States Military Assistance Group, in Thailand.

Gen. Stephens has received numerous awards and decorations, including: the Legion of Merit; the Bronze Star Medal with "V" Device (with two oak leaf clusters); the Purple Heart; the Meritorious Service Medal (with five oak leaf clusters); the Air Medal with "V" Device (with three oak leaf clusters); the Joint Service Commendation Medal (with oak leaf cluster); the Combat Infantryman Badge; the Air Assault Badge; the Master Parachutist Badge.

STEPP, MARC, was born in Versailles, Kentucky. He is married to the former Eleanor F. Hardy. A graduate of Lincoln High School, Evansville, Indiana, he completed Wolverine Trade School, automobile collision repair course in Detroit, Michigan, in 1949, received a B.B.A. degree in business administration from the University of Detroit in 1963, and received certificates from Wayne State University School of Law (Common Pleas Court in Service Training), in 1972. In 1986, he was awarded an honorary Doctor of Humane Letters degree, and Alumnus of the Year, from the University of Detroit. He served in the United States Army from 1943 to 1946. From 1989 to date, Stepp has served as executive director, Institute for Urban & Community Affairs, at the University of Detroit.

Stepp's prior positions included: vice president, International Union, UAW; assistant director, UAW Region 1B; clerk of the court (chief administrator) Common Pleas Court of Detroit at Wayne County; international representative, UAW Region 1B; assistant director for the Community and Membership Relations Division for the Community Health Association, and arc welder, machine operator for Chrysler Corporation, Highland Park Plant. His involvement with the union included: hired by Chrysler in 1942; joined the local Union 490, UAW in 1942; appointed to Veterans Committee (1950 strike) and deputy chief steward in 1950; appointed to the Fair Employment Practices Committee (FEPC) in 1952; appointed to Education Committee in 1953; elected chief steward in 1955.

Additionally, he was elected to Shop Bargaining Committee in 1956; elected chairman of the Shop Bargaining Committee in 1959; elected vice president of Local 490, UAW in 1960; and elected as negotiator, National Negotiating Committee (UAW Chrysler Corp.) in 1961. He was appointed to CHA, membership and community relations staff in 1961 for the union; appointed to International Union, UAW- Region 1B staff and elected vice-president of the International Union,

UAW in 1974. Stepp's professional affiliations are numerous.

STOKES, CARL, was born June 21, 1927, in Cleveland, Ohio. He and his wife Shirley have three children, Carl, Jr., Cordi, and Cordell. He was a high school dropout, quitting East Technical High School in 1944. He went to work in a foundry until shortly after his 18th birthday when he signed up for the Army. In 1946, he was discharged as a corporal and returned to Cleveland. Obtaining his high school diploma in 1947, he enrolled at West Virginia State College and Cleveland College of Western Reserve University, where he majored in psychology. He left college to take a job with the enforcement division of the Ohio State Department of Liquor Control. After three years he returned to school, this time to the University of Minnesota from which he received a B.S. degree in 1954. Two years later, he earned his LL.B. degree from Cleveland-Marshall Law School, and in 1957 was admitted to the Ohio bar and began to practice in Cleveland.

During the late 1950s he began taking a more prominent part in civic and civil rights activities, becoming a member of the executive committee of the Cleveland branch of the NAACP in 1958, and the Community Council of Mt. Pleasant, the residential section of Cleveland where he lives, in 1959. He spent several years as probation officer for the Cleveland Municipal Court and as assistant city prosecutor. In 1962, he resigned his job as prosecutor and opened a law firm with his brother Louis. That same year he was elected to the Ohio state legislature as a Democrat.

Stokes won the mayoralty election in Cleveland in 1967 with a coalition of black and white votes, becoming the first black to be elected mayor of a major American city. In November 1983, he was elected to the Cleveland Municipal Court, and within a short time the 12 other judges of the court elected him as the administrative and presiding judge of the court.

STOKES, LOUIS, was born February 25, 1925, in Cleveland, Ohio. He is married to Jeanette (Jay) Stokes and they are the parents of four children, Shelly, Angela, Louis C. and Lorene, and have three grandchildren. He attended Cleveland public schools (Giddings and Central High School) and received a J.D. degree from Western Reserve University, Cleveland Marshall Law School (the Cleveland State University). He served in the U.S. Army, 1943–1946, and received an honorable discharge. On November 6, 1986, he was elected congressman of the 21st Congressional District of Ohio on his first try for public office. By virtue of his election, he became the first black member of Congress from the state of Ohio. He is currently serving his 11th term in Congress.

In his second term of office, Stokes was appointed the first black member ever to sit on the Appropriations Committee of the House. On February 8, 1972, he was elected as chairman of the Congressional Black Caucus. He served two consecutive terms in this office. In addition to his seat on the powerful Appropriations Committee, on February 5, 1975, he was elected by the Democratic Caucus to serve on the newly formed Budget Committee of the House. He was re-elected to the Budget Committee twice, serving a total of six years. He was also chairman of the Congressional Black Caucus Health Brain Trust.

On September 21, 1976, Stokes was appointed by Speaker Carl Albert to serve on the select committee to conduct an investigation and study of the circumstances surrounding the death of President John F. Kennedy and the death of Dr. Martin Luther King, Jr. On March 8, 1977, Speaker Thomas P.

"Tip" O'Neill appointed Rep. Stokes chairman of this committee. On December 31, 1978, he completed these historic investigations and filed with the House of Representatives 27 volumes of hearings, a final report and Recommendations for Administrative and Legislative Reform. In February 1980, he was appointed by Speaker O'Neill to the House Committee on Standards of Official Conduct (Ethics Committee). In the 97th and 98th Congresses, he was elected chairman of this committee.

In January 1981, Stokes became Senior Democratic Representative from Ohio and he served as the dean of the 11-member Ohio Democratic Congressional Delegation. In February 1983, he was appointed by Speaker O'Neill to the House Permanent Select Committee on Intelligence. The committee had legislative authorization and oversight jurisdiction over the intelligence agencies and intelligence-related activities of federal agencies. In the 99th Congress, he was elected chairman of the Subcommittee on Program and Budget Authorization for the Intelligence Committee. In January 1987, the 100th Congress, Speaker Jim Wright appointed him chairman of the

Intelligence Committee. He also appointed him to serve on the House Select Committee to Investigate Covert Arms Transactions with Iran. His tenure on the Intelligence Committee terminated with the 100th Congress. In the 101st Congress, Stokes was appointed to serve on the Ethics Task Force and the Pepper Commission on Comprehensive Health Care.

His prior position was practicing law for 14 years in Cleveland and was chief trial counsel for the law firm of Stokes, Character, Terry, Perry Whitehead, Young and Davidson. Since being in Congress, he has been named by *Ebony* magazine as one of the 100 most Influential Black Americans each year since 1971. In 1979, he was nominated by *Ebony* in three categories for the Second Annual American Black Achievement Awards. His nomination was based upon the fact he was the first black to head a major congressional investigation and to preside over nationally televised hearings which revealed new facts on the assassination of Dr. Martin Luther King, Jr., and President Kennedy.

At the Congressional Black Caucus Weekend Awards Program, Stokes was awarded the William L. Dawson Award by his colleagues in the Congressional Black Caucus. This coveted and prestigious award was made to him in recognition of his "unique leadership in the development of legislation." He is the recipient of 18 honorary degrees from: Wilberforce University, Shaw University, Ohio College of Podiatric Medicine, Livingstone College, Oberlin College, Morehouse College, Meharry Medical College, Atlanta University, Howard University, Morehouse School of Medicine, Central State University, Xavier University of Louisiana, Tuskegee Institute, Defense Intelligence College, Bethune-Cookman College, University of Arkansas at Pine Bluff, Southeastern University and Cleveland State University.

Rep. Stokes has been honored in: *Who's Who in the Midwest, Who's Who in Health Care* and *Who's Who Among Black Americans, Community Leaders and Noteworthy Americans.*

STONE, JIM, a graduate of the University of Notre Dame, he received his B.A. degree in communications in 1981. He played professional football for: Chicago Blitz (USFL), 1983–1985; Tampa Bay Buccaneers (NFL), 1982–1983; and the Seattle Seahawks (NFL), 1981–1982. From 1986 to date, he has served as a life, health and investment agent for CM Financial Group. His prior positions included: life and health agent for American United Life, South Bend, Indiana; salesman for Rainbow Water Purification, South Bend; and accounting clerk, Pacific Northwest Bell, Seattle, Washington.

Stone is the recipient of the Howard Hodgen Award; Outstanding Young Men of America, 1987, and Junior Achievement Consultant of the Year, 1987 and 1988. He has served as professional designation of Life Underwriter Training Council Fellow, 1989; has given 10 to 15 professional speeches each year to various organizations centered on youth, goal setting, self-esteem, and insurance-related topics; conducted seminars on Goal Setting and Financial Planning for College Seniors; and consulted with undergraduate student athletes on academics, choosing an agent, and preparing for life after athletics.

Stone has served as Toastmasters International, for six years competent Toastmaster designation, 1986, distinguished Toastmaster designation, 1990. His professional affiliations include: Toastmaster, former president; Junior Achievement, consultant since 1985; Special Olympics volunteer, 1985 to present; Life Underwriters Board Public Service chairman; Notre Dame Alumni Association; Chamber of Commerce Leadership Program; Leadership Forum Planning Committee; Notre Dame Monogram Club, board member; Par Putters Golf Club, former president; chairman annual Special Olympics golf fundraiser; charter member of Leaders and Positive Role Models, and director of Bishop's Annual Appeal.

STRAND, ELOISE BROWN, was born June 5, 1929, in Stamford, Connecticut, and received her primary and secondary education in Bedford, Virginia, and Philadelphia. She enrolled in Virginia State College in 1946 and graduated with a B.S. degree in home economics in 1950. After college she taught in the Bedford public school system from 1950 to 1955. In 1955 she began post-graduate training at the University of Pennsylvania, receiving a certificate in occupational therapy in 1956. In 1956 she was commissioned in the U.S. Army; for the next six years, she was a student and staff therapist at Valley Forge and Walter Reed Army hospitals. In 1963 she became the supervisor of a general clinic, and the following year she began working as the occupational therapy clinical affiliation coordinator at Letterman General Hospital in San Francisco.

She enrolled in New York University in 1965, and, after receiving an M.A. degree in occupational therapy in 1966, served as educational coordinator for the occupational therapy section and occupational therapy clinical affiliation coordinator at Walter Reed Army Medical Center until 1969. In 1969 she became chief of the occupational therapy section at the 97th General Hospital in Frankfurt, Germany, moving later to the same position at Letterman Army Medical Center.

In 1972 she began working toward her second master's degree at the U.S. Army Academy of Health and Baylor University. She received a master's degree in health care administration in 1973. After serving as a health care administrative resident from 1973 to 1974, Strand became chief of the occupational therapy section at Walter Reed Army Medical Center and served in this capacity until 1978, meanwhile becoming chief of the occupational therapy section in the Office of the Surgeon General (1976–1982).

In 1978, Strand was made chief of the Army Medical Specialist Corps;

she was the first black to hold such a position. A full colonel, Strand held the second highest rank of all women in the Army Medical Corps. In 1982 she became special assistant to the U.S. Army surgeon general; in the same year she became recruitment coordinator for the occupational therapy department of Howard University's College of Allied Health Sciences. Since 1988 she has served as the international liaison of the national office of the American Occupational Therapy Association.

Strand has been featured in *Jet* and *Ebony* magazines. Her military honors include the "A" Professional Designator, the surgeon general's award for professional excellence; the Army Commendation Medal, with oak leaf cluster; the Meritorious Service Medal; the Legion of Merit; and U.S. Army service awards. She is also included in the Roster of Fellows of the American Occupational Therapy Association.

She is a longtime volunteer and coordinator of the Montgomery County (Maryland) Hospice Society and has served as a volunteer and coordinator of the Vietnam War Memorial in Washington, D.C.

STRAYHORN, EARL E., was born April 24, 1918, in Columbus, Mississippi. He married Lydia E. Jackson and the couple have two children, Donald and Earlene. He graduated from Edmund Burke Elementary High School in Chicago; received an A.B. degree from the University of Illinois, Urbana, 1941; and earned a J.D. degree from DePaul University College of Law, 1948. He is currently sitting on the Criminal Court of Cook County. He enlisted in the armed forces as a private, October 15, 1941; took basic training at Fort Custer, Michigan. In November 1941, he was assigned to Tuskegee Air Force Base where he assisted in the establishment of the

Military Police Section as sergeant-in-charge. Admitted to the Artillery School Officer Candidate School in April 1942, and was awarded a commission as a second lieutenant of artillery in June 1942. He was assigned to 184th Field Artillery Regiment, Fort Custer and saw foreign service with the 600th Field Artillery Battalion of the 92nd Division Artillery in Italy where he served as executive officer of a 155mm howitzer battery. He separated from service as a first lieutenant.

Strayhorn served as a member of the 184th Field Artillery Battalion, Illinois Army National Guard, from January 1948, and served successively as battery commander B Battery, battalion intelligence officer as a captain, and thence in the rank lieutenant colonel as commander, 2nd Battalion, 178th Infantry, Illinois National Guard. He was called from retirement April 1968, by Gov. Otto Kerner to assume command of 1st Battalion, 178th Infantry, with rank of lieutenant colonel, and commander, 2nd Battalion, 178th Infantry, Illinois National Guard.

Strayhorn was a senior founding partner in 1952 in the firm of Rogers, Strayhorn & Harth, attorneys, 109 North Dearborn, Chicago. He was a trial lawyer for the firm in criminal and civil cases, handling all criminal, probate and personal injury and appellate cases for the firm. He was a partner in association with R. Eugene Pincham and Charles B. Evins from January 1966 to his election to the Circuit Court of Cook County, November 7, 1970. From May 1959 to October 1963, he served as a member of the Civil Service Commission of the city of Chicago responsible for the administration and supervision of 45,000 city Civil Service employees, acting as presiding officer at all Trial Board hearings. From 1948-1952, he served as assistant state's attorney of Cook County where, for the last two years of that period, he was assigned to the Criminal Trial Division in trial of major cases.

Strayhorn served as hearing officer, Fair Employment Practices Commission from 1969-1970. Prior to that time he was a member of the 20th Ward Regular Democratic Organization; member, bar of United States Supreme Court; United States Court of Military Appeals; 6th Circuit Court of Appeals; 7th Circuit Court of Appeals; and U.S. District Court, North District of Illinois. He was secretary, Sanitary District Employees' Annuity & Benefit Fund, 1964-1970. He was appointed in October 1963 by Gov. Otto Kerner to vacancy as trustee, Metropolitan Sanitary District of Greater Chicago, and elected for a full six-year term, November 1964. He served as chairman, Judiciary Committee; chairman, Civil Service, Pension & Personnel Relations Committee; vice-chairman, Engineering & Finance Committees; and vice-president of Metropolitan Sanitary District from December 1966 to December 6, 1970.

Strayhorn was elected judge, Circuit Court of Cook County November 1970; and retained for 6-year term November 5, 1974, 1980, and 1986. He is a member of the Illinois Judges Association; member, Committee on Criminal Law; vice-chairman, Court Services Committee; and Illinois Judicial Council member, Judiciary Committee. He has been a former member of the Chicago Bar Association; American Bar Association/third vice-president and member of board of managers, Association of Defense Lawyers; American Judicature Society; National Association of Defense Lawyers in Criminal Cases; and Cook County Bar Association.

STRINGER, C. VIVIAN, a native of Edenborn, Pennsylvania, is married to William D. Stringer and they are the parents of three children, David, Janine and Justin. The Division I coaches summarized Stringer's abilities and accomplishments in one gesture — their selection of her as the 1988 Converse Coach of the Year. After her seventh year as head coach of the University of Iowa women's basketball program, she was the winningest coach in school history and the only coach to lead the Hawkeyes to 20-victory seasons and into postseason competition.

The Hawkeyes' dynamic head coach boasts a remarkable career record of 415-94 (.815), a mark that includes a current Iowa record of 164-43 (.792) and a 105-21 (.833) ledge against Big Ten Conference opponents. Her 415 wins were the fifth highest total in the profession and her .815 win percentage was the nation's best for coaches with better than 300 victories. She was the only coach to ever lead two schools to a number two or better ranking on the Associated Press poll. At the heart of the Iowa success story are the recruitment of only the very best athletes in the nation. The 1989–1990 roster included ten players who received All-American honors as high school seniors. Of those, two had played on national or international teams sponsored by the Amateur Basketball Association of the United States.

Stringer's presence in the Hawkeye state has resulted in unprecedented success in two other significant areas. Iowa was firmly established as one of the nation's top three schools in average attendance. In 1984, the Hawkeyes shattered the national attendance record as 22,157 fans filled Carver-Hawkeye Arena. In 1988, Iowa was the site of the first pregame sellout in women's basketball history when all 15,365 tickets were sold over 30 hours prior to the team's annual showdown against Ohio State. Each of the past four seasons, Iowa has ranked among the top three women's basketball programs for average attendance; 1989–1990 marked the fifth season in Iowa history that the Hawkeyes were ranked among the nation's top 20 from start to finish.

In 1988, Iowa's eight-week stint at number one on the nation's polls made Stringer the only coach in Division 1 history to lead two schools to a number two or better ranking. Among the most respected women's basketball coaches in the nation, she has received numerous awards but none more prestigious than the 1988 Converse Coach of the Year honor and the 1982 NCAA Division I Coach of the Year award. She was also named the 1988 and 1985 NCAA District V Coach of the year.

In 1989, Stringer was chosen to coach the United States entry to the World Championship Zone Qualification Tournament in Sao Paulo, Brazil, and in 1985, she coached the United States entry to the World University Games in Kobe, Japan. In 1979, she coached in Mexico and in 1981 she toured China as head coach of the United States Select Team. She also coached in the 1982 National Sports Festival in Indianapolis, Indiana. Also an active administrator, Stringer was instrumental in the development of the National Women's Basketball Coaches Association. She is also a voting board member of the Amateur Basketball Association of the United States of America, and the Nike Shoe Company Coaches Advisory Board. In 1987, Stringer began a three-year appointment as the Big Ten Conference's representative to the NCAA Division I Mideast Basketball Committee.

SULLIVAN, LOUIS W., was born November 3, 1933, in Atlanta, Georgia. He is married to Ginger and they have three children, Paul, Shanta and Halsted. He received his B.S. degree, magna cum laude, from Morehouse College in 1954, and earned his M.D., cum laude, from Boston University in 1958. His internship, 1958–1959, and medical residency, 1959–1960, were at New York Hospital, Cornell Medical Center. After a pathology fellowship at Massachusetts General Hospital, 1960–1961, he became a fellow in hematology at the Thorndike Memorial Research Laboratories of Harvard Medical School at Boston City Hospital.

Sullivan was an instructor in medicine at Harvard Medical School, 1963–1964, and an assistant professor of medicine at New Jersey College of Medicine, 1964–1966. In 1966, he became co-director of hematology at Boston University Medical Center. From 1966 to 1975, he was successively, assistant professor of medicine, associate professor of medicine and professor of medicine at Boston University School of Medicine. During 1972–1975, he also was co-project director and project director of the Boston Sickle Cell Center and director of Hematology at Boston City Hospital.

Sullivan returned to Morehouse College, his alma mater, in 1975 as professor of biology and medicine. He was a member of the American Medical Association, National Medical Association, Atlanta Medical Association, Medical Association of Atlanta, Medical Association of Georgia, and the Georgia State Medical Association. He has been certified in internal medicine and in hematology. His research interests were in hematology. He was the founding president of the Association of Minority Health Professions Schools. He was a former member of the Joint Committee on Health Policy of the Association of American Universities and the National Association of Land Grant Colleges and Universities.

Professional honors received by Dr. Sullivan included election to Alpha Omega Alpha Honor Medical Society in 1957, election to the American Society of Clinical Investigation in 1970, to Phi Beta Kappa in 1974, to the Institute of Medicine (National Academy of Sciences) in 1975, to fellowship and mastership in the American College of Physicians in 1980 and 1990, respectively. From 1985 to 1987, he was vice chairman of the Commission on Health and Human Services of the Southern

Regional Education Board. He also was the recipient of 17 honorary degrees. He served as associate editor of *Nutrition Reports International*, 1969–1973, was on the editorial board of the *American Journal of Hematology*, 1975–1977, and the editorial board of the *Journal of Medical Education*, 1977–1978.

Sullivan has served as consultant and advisor to numerous organizations and agencies, including several in HHS' Public Health Service, and for the Veterans Administration. Prior to becoming secretary, he was a member of the National Cancer Advisory Board of the National Cancer Institute, National Institutes of Health. He was a member of the boards of the Friends of the National Library of Medicine, the Boy Scouts of America, the Woodruff Arts Center, the Southern Center for International Studies, and an honorary member of the Board of Medical Education for South African Blacks, Inc. He has been a member of the Atlanta Rotary Club since 1977.

Other honors received by Dr. Sullivan include: Boston University Alumni Award for Distinguished Public Service in 1985; honoree of the Year of the State Committee on the Life and Health of Black Georgians in 1963, the Drum Major Award of the Southern Christian Leadership Conference in 1982, establishment of an endowed annual lectureship at the Morehouse School of Medicine in his honor in 1980, the Outstanding Alumnus award from New York Hospital-Cornell Medical Center in 1984, honoree of the National Association of Minority Medical Educators for Outstanding Contributions to the Education of Minorities in Medicine in 1984, the first Martin Luther King, Jr. Visiting Professorship at the University of Michigan in 1986, the Atlanta Urban League Award for Outstanding Community Leadership in 1989, and the Equitable Black Achievement Award in Education in 1989.

Dr. Sullivan was a member of

then–Vice President George Bush's official 12-member delegation to seven African countries in mid–November 1982. Dr. Sullivan was sworn in as Secretary of Health and Human Services on March 10, 1989, by U.S. Circuit Judge A. Leon Higginbotham, Jr. He was nominated by President Bush on January 20, 1989, and confirmed by the Senate on March 1, 1989. As head of the Department of Health and Human Services, he is responsible for the major health, welfare, food and drug safety, medical research and income security programs serving the American people.

SUMMERS, JOSEPH W., was born March 8, 1930, the son of Joe and Willie Mae Johnson Summers. He was married in 1948 to Joyce Benson and they have two children. He is a native not only of Indianapolis but of the district he represents. He has resided for 30 years in a house he built himself under a "Self-Help Program" sponsored by Flanner House Settlement. He attended Indianapolis public schools, graduating from Crispus Attucks High School. He took extension courses at Indiana University and graduated from the Indiana College of Mortuary Science, Indianapolis. In 1962 he opened the Summers Funeral Chapel, a business he still operates today. He belongs to the African Methodist Episcopal Church.

Summers has been active in politics for many years beginning in 1952 as a precinct committeeman. He has also been a ward chairman, member of the Indianapolis Board of Public Safety from 1965 to 1968, and Marion County chief deputy coroner from 1967 to 1978. Professionally, he is active in all levels of the funeral directors association and in the Better Business Bureau. He has been prominent for many years in the local and national NAACP, serving as national convention chairman in 1973. He is on the board of the Alpha Home, the Sickle Cell Center, and the Indianapo-lis-Scarborough Peace Games. As a lawmaker, Summers' special interests include education, the needs of the elderly, and welfare.

SUMMERS, WILLIAM E., III. He is married to the former Feryn Stigall, an artist and retired teacher from Somerset, Kentucky. They have three children, William IV, Seretha and Sherryl. Described by many as influen-tial, dynamic, energetic and dedicated, Summers has been a leader in the broadcast industry for 39 years. Al-though his professional career began at the *Louisville Defender* newspaper in 1941, his first broadcasting opportu-nity was during the late 1940s when he coordinated a talent program for WGRC radio. He experienced his first real break in broadcasting in 1951 when he was hired as a part-time sports an-nouncer for WLOU radio. After mov-ing into a full-time slot, he quickly ad-vanced to the position of assistant manager of Rounsaville Radio, a chain of seven black-formatted stations. He was promoted to vice-president and general manager in 1967 and became the first black in the U.S. to manage a radio station.

After forming Summers Broad-casting Company in 1971, Summers purchased WLOU and became the first black radio station owner in the state. Summers Broadcasting undertook another venture in 1973 with the pur-chase of WNUU-FM which was sold in 1976. He remained president and general manager of WLOU until 1982, when it was sold to Johnson Publishing Company of Chicago. He continued to work as the station's management con-sultant until 1988. Concurrent with his professional career, he pursued a voca-tional career as a minister, evangelist, and pastor.

In 1947, shortly after completing his time in the U.S. Army, he began to study and prepare to become a deacon in the African Methodist Episcopal Church. Following his first assignment as a pastor in Taylorsville, Kentucky, he left to become an evangelist. Once he returned to the pastorate in 1965, he accepted an assignment in George-town, Kentucky. In 1968, he was trans-ferred to St. Paul A.M.E. in Louisville and remained there until his retirement in 1988. He is presently serving as ad-ministrative assistant to the Bishop of the 13th Episcopal District of the A.M.E. Church and preaches on a reg-ular basis.

Summers has been involved with countless civic, educational, profes-sional and religious activities. His civic involvements include: Clothe-a-Child/ Food for the Elderly Consortium, Inc., president emeritus; Saints Mary and Elizabeth Hospital, board of directors; TARC, vice-chairman; NAACP, life, senate and thousandaire member; Mar-tin Luther King, Jr. Professional and Businessman's Group, inaugural presi-dent; West Louisville Development Commission, founding member; Ser-toma International, governor of Ken-tucky district; WKPC-TV, chairman of the board of directors; National Council of Community Mental Health Centers, member and president; Boy Scouts, volunteer, vice president and executive board member; Metro YMCA, board of directors, Southfield Committee; and past chairman of the Top of the South Cluster; Minority Venture Capital Corporation, chair-man; United Negro College Fund, ad-visory board; and the Kentucky Derby Festival, first and only black to serve as president-elect and board chair-man.

Summers' activities in the educa-tion area include: serving as a member of Jefferson County Board of Educa-tion, President's Society of Bellarine College, President's Council on Youth Opportunity, Kentucky Literacy Com-mission, and Jefferson County Public Schools Foundation. His broadcast affiliations date back to the late 1940s when he became a member of the National Disc Jockey Association. In the early 1950s he became involved with and later became president of the Association of Radio and Television Announcers. In 1977, he was their Man of the Year. While involved with the Kentucky Broadcasters Association (KBA), he became the first black in America to become the president of a Broadcasting Association, and as a member he worked to sensitize the organization to the needs of its black constituents. In 1980, he received the KBA Golden Mike Award. As a direct result of his work with the KBA, he became involved with the National Association of Broadcasters in the mid–1970s.

In addition to these organizations, Summers was a member of the board of directors of the Association of Public Broadcasters, Sales and Marketing Fraternity, and helped to form the Louisville Association of Public Broadcasters, Sales and Marketing Executives Louisville Area Radio Stations, Pi Sigma Epsilon Fraternity, and helped to form the Louisville Association of Black Communicators. His honors and awards are numerous and include among others: Louisville Urban League Distinguished Service Award; Black Achiever of the Year; Louisville Board of Education Pioneer Award; NAACP Educational Award; *Who's Who in the South*; *Ebony* magazine's Famous Blacks; National Association of Social Workers Private Citizen Award; and *Who's Who in America*.

Summers' religious involvements include the NAACP Ministerial Coalition, Kentucky Council of Churches, Kentucky Chapter of National Conference of Christians and Jews, Greater Louisville A.M.E. Ministerial Alliance; Interdenominational Ministerial Alliance; director of Camp Primm-Simmons and the Metro Louisville Chapter of the Inter-Religious Commission on Civil Rights.

SUTTON, PERCY E., was born November 24, 1920, in San Antonio, Texas. He married the former Leatrice O'Farrell in 1943. They were divorced in 1950 but later remarried. They have a son Pierre Monte, and Sutton has a daughter Cheryl Lynn, by his second wife. At age 13, he had a traumatic experience while passing out some NAACP pamphlets. A white policeman stopped him and asked, "Nigger, what are you doing out of your neighborhood?" and then proceeded to "beat hell out of him." Then, as throughout his life, he was guided by his father's admonition, "Suffer the hurts, but don't show the anger, because if you do it will block you from being able to do anything effectively to remove the hurt."

After graduating from Phyllis Wheatley High School and working for a year on the family cattle farm outside San Antonio, near Prairie View, Sutton attended Prairie View Agricultural and Mechanical College, Tuskegee (Alabama) Institute, and Hampton (Virginia) Institute, without taking a degree. While studying he earned his living at various jobs, including working as a stunt pilot at county fairs. When World War II broke out, he tried to enlist in the United States Army Air Corps. After being rejected by Southern white recruiting officers, he moved to New York City, where his enlistment was accepted. During the war he won combat stars as an intelligence officer with the 332nd Fighter Group's black 99th Fighter Squadron in the Italian and Mediterranean theatres of operation.

After his discharge from the Air Corps with the rank of captain, Sutton returned to New York City to pursue a law degree. He enrolled at Columbia University School of Law and worked in his spare time as a dishwasher, waiter, and bellhop, a clerk in the general post office, and a subway conductor while studying part-time at the Brooklyn School of Law. In 1950, he received an LLB degree from Brooklyn School of Law. During the Korean conflict, he again served in the military as an Air Force intelligence officer and trial judge advocate.

In 1953, Sutton, along with his brother Oliver, and George Covington, set up a law partnership on 125th Street, in the heart of Harlem. The socially conscious law firm handled many cases free of charge. Its clients ranged from an unknown Malcolm Little (who would later become world famous as Malcolm X) to the Baptist Ministers Conference of Greater New York. The dividing line between Sutton's legal practice and his involvement in public service and civil rights activity often disappeared. He was a consultant to the Student Nonviolent Coordinating Committee, and served in a succession of positions with the New York branch of the NAACP, including the presidency (1961–1962).

In 1964, Sutton was elected to the New York State Assembly. He took his seat in the lower house of the Albany Legislature on January 1, 1965. He and Clarence B. Jones, a lawyer and stockbroker, were cofounders of the Inner City Broadcasting Corporation, which purchased radio station WLIB-AM on July 14, 1971, for an estimated $1,900,000, making it the first black-owned New York City station, In 1991, Sutton served as chairman of Inner City Broadcasting Corp.

TAYLOR, KRISTIN CLARK, is married with two children. Taylor joined President Bush's White House staff in 1987 as assistant press secretary to the vice president. In August 1988, she was appointed special assistant to the vice president for Press Relations. She joined the White House from Gannett Co., Inc., the media conglomerate that publishes and owns, among many other newspapers, *USA Today*. She worked as a corporate writer and public affairs officer in the company's corporate communications division. While with Gannett, she also served briefly as a business correspondent for Gannett News Service. Taylor joined the Gannett Co. in 1982 as a founding member of *USA Today*'s editorial board, where she was an editor and writer.

TEER, BARBARA ANN, is a native of the East St. Louis, Illinois, black community, Teer received a degree in dance education from the University of Illinois, where she graduated with highest honors. She is the mother of two children. She did advanced studies in Germany, Switzerland and Paris, and began doing Broadway shows. Her first show was choreographed by Agnes DeMille, for whom she was DeMille's dance captain. The musical won a Tony Award. She studied drama with, among other leading directors, Lloyd Richards, director of the Yale School of Drama. A mastermind creative artist, she is an award-winning actress, director, producer, writer of stage, screen and television, a cultural leader in the Harlem community, a businesswoman, philosopher, entrepreneur, educator and real estate developer.

Teer's mounting desire to develop an art form which would address the immediate concerns of African American people, contributed to her founding the National Black Theatre in 1968. She has directed numerous productions, including the award-winning film *Rise: A Love Song for a Love People*, which was based on the life of Malcolm X. In 1972, she received a Ford Foundation Fellowship to visit seven African countries to further her research. She spent four months in Western Nigeria acquainting herself fully with the Yoruba culture and religion. She has visited Nigeria 14 times and considers it to be her "second home." She wanted to discover the science and secret behind the phenomenon of "Soul."

Teer has performed on Broadway and was cofounder, with actor Robert Hooks, of the Negro Ensemble Company, and has contributed drama articles to numerous publications, including the *New York Times* and *Black World*. She, along with her performing company of 35 people, continued their research in South America, the West Indies, Haiti, the Apollo Theatre, and numerous churches and bars in Harlem. The National Black Theatre has performed in Trinidad, Guyana, Western Nigeria, and throughout the United States. Because of the excellent cultural contributions to the city and state of New York, Mayor Koch and the governor of New York State proclaimed May 7, 1979 as "National Black Theatre Day."

Teer is the recipient of 30 awards and citations. She was included in *Who's Who in America*. She was a distinguished member of the Delta Sigma Theta Sorority's National Commission the Arts and the Uptown Chamber of Commerce in Harlem. As a real estate developer and entrepreneurial artist, she has lived and worked in Harlem for the past 22 years. She was the owner of three brownstones on "Strivers Row" in Harlem and it was through buying these brownstones to house the artists of the National Black Theatre staff that she developed her competency in the field of real estate. She had formulated an advisory committee of New York City's most masterful construction managers and developers.

In 1983, she purchased a city block-front of property on 125th Street and Fifth Avenue for NBT, and was completing the development of a new theatre in the Harlem community: the National Black Institute of Communication Through Theatre Arts. This facility was the first revenue-generating Black Arts Theatre complex in the country and was a blend of commercial, retail, and office space rentals with theatre arts activities.

Teer's awards and citations include: Legends in Our Time, honored in *Essence* magazine's Special Twentieth Anniversary Issue, May 1990; "Winner Award," Calvin's and Rocky's of 184 Lenox Avenue, "The Arts is something that people love with what you have found! We, the people present to the Arts"; the J. Raymond Jones Democratic Club Salutes — Barbara Ann Teer as a Gleaming Beacon Steadily Lighting a Progressive Direction for Harlem on Her 11th Anniversary; "Outstanding Achievement Award," East St. Louis Alumnae Chapter, Delta Sigma Theta Sorority Midwest Regional Conference; CEBA Award for merit, "In advertising and communications to black communities . . . and for continued pioneering efforts in the field"; AUDELCO (Audience Development Committee, Inc.) Special Achievement Award, "In recognition of her dedication, resourcefulness and perseverance in establishing the National Black Institute of Communication Through Theatre Arts in and for the Harlem Community"; Kwanzaa Expo '89 Award, "For exemplifying the spirit of KUJICHAGULIA: to define ourselves, name ourselves, create for ourselves and speak for ourselves instead of being defined, created for and spoken for by others."

In addition, she received the Certificate of Appreciation Award "For Outstanding and Dedicated Service," Marie Brooks Caribbean Dance Theatre; Harlem Week, "To the National Black Theatre in celebration and honor of their twenty years of excellence on cultural education development," the Directors of Harlem Week, Inc., 1988; Resilience Award, "For her determination to elicit, emancipate, embellish and preserve the culture through the ingenuity of her creative excellence and business management," presented by Extended Hands, 1987; Acknowledgment Award, "To National Black Theatre for a Commitment to Youth," Breakthrough Foundation New York

Youth at Risk; Sojourner Truth Award, "For contributions as an African-American Woman in Harlem Providing Social, Cultural or Economic Benefits to the Community," Harlem Women's Committee/New Future Foundations, Inc., The National Black Treasure Award, "For her outstanding contribution to Black American Theatre," presented by Hamilton Arts Center, Schenectady, New York; Monarch Merit Award, "For Outstanding Contribution to the Performing and Visual Arts," National Council for Culture and Art; and "For Contribution to the Field of Performing Arts," the Riverside Club, National Association of Negro and Professional Women's Clubs, Inc.

Teer has also received the following awards: "For Creative Excellence," Blackfrica Promotions, Harlem Week '80; Community Service Award, Reality House, Inc.; Universal Awareness Award, Toward a New Age, Inc.; Cultural Arts Service Award, Black Spectrum Theatre Company; Certificate of Participation, FESTAC, North American Region; Certificate of Participation, Lorton Voices, Lorton Penitentiary; Best Film, *Rise: A Love Song for a Love People*, National Association of Media Women's Black Film Festival; Female Artist of the Year Award, Blackfrica Promotions; Dedication and Achievement in Theatre, Mt. Morris Church; International Benin Award, New Dimensions Associates; Certificate of Achievement, Harlem Chamber of Commerce; First Annual AUDELCO Recognition Award in Theatre; "Token of Esteem," East St. Louis, Illinois Community Schools; "For Dedication and Efforts in the Field of Drama," New York Metropolitan Chapter of Alabama State University Alumni Association; "Distinguished Contribution," M.W. King Solomon Grand Lodge; "In Appreciation—Director of the Believers," Voices, Inc.; and the Vernon Rice Award, Best Actress.

THEUS, LUCIUS, was born on October 11, 1922, in Madison County, Tennessee. He married the former Gladys Marie Davis of Chicago, Illinois. He graduated from Community High School in Blue Island, Illinois. He has a B.S. degree from the University of Maryland, in 1956, a master's degree in business administration from George Washington University, 1957, and is a graduate of the Harvard Advanced Management Program, Harvard University Graduate School of Business Administration, 1969. During his Air Force career, Theus attended the Statistical Control Officers School at Lowry Air Force Base, Colorado, in 1948, and in 1966, he graduated with distinction from the Air War College at Maxwell Air Force Base, Alabama.

During World War II, Theus entered the Army Air Corps as a private in December 1942. After basic training, he attended the Army Administration School at Atlanta University. For the remainder of the war, he served as an administrative clerk, chief clerk, and first sergeant of pre-aviation cadet and basic training squadrons at Keesler Field, Mississippi. He entered Officer Candidate School, graduating second in his class with a commission as second lieutenant in January 1946. Following a one-year tour of duty as squadron adjutant at Tuskegee Army Air Field, Alabama, he went to Lockbourne Air Force Base, Ohio, as base statistical control officer. In August 1949, he was transferred to Erding Air Depot, Germany, where he served as the analysis and presentation officer, and later commander of the Statistical Control Flight and Depot Statistical Control Officer.

Theus was assigned in August 1952 to the office of the Deputy Chief of Staff, Comptroller, Headquarters United States Air Force, Washington, D.C., where he was chief of the Materiel Logistics Statistics Branch. In October 1957, he was assigned to Headquarters Central Air Materiel Forces, in Europe, Chateauroux Air

Base, France, as a statistical services staff officer. He was subsequently appointed Technical Statistical Advisor to the Comptroller, Headquarters Air Materiel Forces, in Europe. In January 1959, he was assigned duty as chief of Management Services Office in the Eastern Air Logistics Office, Athens, Greece. In February 1961, he was appointed chief of Management Analysis, Headquarters Spokane Air Defense Sector, Larson Air Force Base, Washington.

In December 1962, Theus was assigned as base comptroller at Kingsley Field, Oregon. His next assignment was as base comptroller of Cam Ranh Bay Air Base, Republic of Vietnam. For more than five months of this assignment, he also was acting deputy base commander of Cam Ranh Bay Air Base. Upon his return to the United States in July 1967, he was reassigned to Headquarters United States Air Force, Office of the Comptroller of the Air Force, as a data automation staff officer, in the Directorate of Data Automation. He served initially as chief, Technology and Standards Branch; chief, Plans, Policy and Technology Division; and later chief, Program Management Division. During that assignment, he also performed additional duty as chairman of the Inter-Service Task Force on Education in Race Relations, Office of the Secretary of Defense. The recommendations of the task force led to establishment of the Defense Race Relations Institute and the Department of Defense-wide education program in race relations.

In 1968, Theus attended the Department of Defense Computer Institute. In July 1971, he was assigned to the position of director of management analysis, Office of the Comptroller of the Air Force. In June 1972, he was appointed special assistant for social actions, Directorate of Personnel Plans, Deputy Chief of Staff, Personnel, Headquarters United States Air Force. On June 10, 1974, he was appointed

director of accounting and finance, Office of the Comptroller of the Air Force, Headquarters United States Air Force, and commander of the Air Force Accounting and Finance Center, Denver, Colorado.

General Theus was promoted to the two-star rank of major general, effective May 1, 1975, with date of rank July 1, 1972. His military decorations and awards include: the Distinguished Service Medal; Legion of Merit; the Bronze Star Medal; the Air Force Commendation Medal (with one oak leaf cluster); and the Air Force Outstanding Unit Award Ribbon.

THOMAS, CLARENCE, was born June 23, 1948, in Pin Point, Georgia. He is the second of three children born to Leola Williams and M. C. Thomas. His father left home when Clarence was 2, and at age 7 Clarence was sent to live with his grandfather in Savannah. In 1984, Clarence divorced his first wife, Kathryn Grace Ambush. In 1987, he married the former Virginia Bess Lamp, who was the senior legislative officer for Women's Bureau and Immigration Issues in the Labor Department's Office of Congressional Affairs. He has a son from his first marriage, Jamal Adeen Thomas. Thomas lives in Alexandria, Virginia.

Thomas attended Immaculate Conception Seminary, Conception Junction, Missouri, from September 1967 to May 1968. In 1971, he received a B.A. degree in English from Holy Cross College, Worcester, Massachusetts. In 1974, he received a law degree from Yale Law School. From 1974 to 1977, he served as an assistant attorney general of Missouri. From 1977 to 1979, he was an attorney with Monsanto Co. in St. Louis. From 1979 to 1981, he served as an legislative assistant to Sen. John C. Danforth (R–Missouri). In 1981, he was appointed the assistant secretary of education for civil rights. In 1982, he became chairman of the Equal Employment Opportunity Commission. In 1990, he was nominated and confirmed as a judge to the United States Court of Appeals in Washington, D.C. Then, on July 1, 1991, he was nominated by President Bush to the United States Supreme Court. Bush nominated him to succeed retiring Justice Thurgood Marshall on the nation's highest court, making Thomas only the second black to be nominated to the Supreme Court. On October 15, 1991, Clarence Thomas was confirmed to succeed retired Justice Thurgood Marshall and became only the second black person to sit on the Supreme Court.

On October 18, 1991, on the South Lawn of the White House, Thomas was sworn in as the 106th justice to serve on the United States Supreme Court. Justice Byron R. White administered the oath as President and Mrs. Bush watched. This grandson of a sharecropper declared at his oath taking, "There is joy, it is a time to move forward, a time to look for what is good in others, what is good in our country." On November 1, 1991, in a private swearing-in of the judicial oath at the Supreme Court, the newest justice joined the high court after being sworn in by Chief Justice William H. Rehnquist.

THOMAS, DEBI, was born March 25, 1967, in Poughkeepsie, New York, the daughter of Mckinley and Janice Thomas (divorced). She married Brian Vanden Hogen. She graduated from San Mateo High School in California, with a 3.5 grade point average. In 1989, she was a pre-med student at Stanford University. She took her first ice-skating lesson at age five, and won her first competition at age nine. Her mother at that time worked as a computer program analyst, paying for her skating fees on a modest salary and support check. By age 15, Thomas squeezed a normal day

at public school around six hours of practice while her skating peers took the easy education road paved with correspondence courses and tutors. By age 16, she became a World Class figure skater, performing in London for Live Aid; appearing at Celebration America on Ice in Indianapolis for the 25th Anniversary of the United States Figure Skating Association Memorial Fund; and special guest star "Stars on Ice."

In 1985, Thomas won the National Sport Festival, and was named the Athlete of the Year. She had two gold medal victories, one Skate America International, in Minneapolis, and at St. Ivel International, in Great Britain. She was United States Ladies Figure Skating Champion, 1986; and the World Champions in 1986. In late 1986, she began to train for the 1988 Olympic Games. At that time to train a champion skater, it took about $30,000 a year, and she had no sponsor other than her family. But after media attention she was able to get some offers from companies and organizations. In 1988, Thomas was the first black female athlete to try to win a medal in Winter Olympic Games in Calgary.

Thomas became the first black female athlete to win a medal in the Olympic Games by winning the Bronze Medal. She is a true pioneer; someone kids can look at and say, "Hey, here's a person who at the age of five took a sport that not many blacks took seriously, and at the age of 20 was the first black to make the world team, the first black to win a figure-skating gold medal, and the first black to win a medal for skating in the Olympic Games."

THOMAS, ISIAH LORD, III, was born April 30, 1961, in Chicago, Illinois, the seventh son and the youngest of nine children of Mary and Isiah Lord Thomas, II. When he was about three years old, his father left, leaving Mary Thomas with the job of raising their children. A formidable, strong-willed woman, she was determined to help her children by trying to shield them from the harsher realities of life in the tough, poverty-stricken West Side neighborhood known as "K-Town." Raised as a Baptist in the deep South, Mary Thomas converted to Roman Catholicism and, while Isiah was a pupil at Our Lady of Sorrows grade school, she worked there in the cafeteria and ran the youth center, where her son was a standout basketball player.

When Isiah was in the eighth grade, he applied for a basketball scholarship to Weber High School, a power in the city's Catholic basketball league, but the coach turned him down because he was "too small." Seeing the boy's disappointment, Isiah's brothers pleaded his case to Gene Pingatore, the coach at St. Joseph High School in Westchester, a Chicago suburb. In the meantime, Mary Thomas, by then working for Chicago's Department of Human Services, had fled the inner city, moving her family west, nearer to the city's white suburbs. Isiah had to leave home at six in the morning to commute to Westchester, traveling for 90 minutes on the elevated train and bus before reaching his final stop, from which he had to walk a mile and a half to St. Joseph High School.

Although his academic career began with a "D" average his freshman year, Isiah soon became an honor student. He led St. Joseph to a second place finish in the state championship tournament in his junior year, and as a senior he was one of the nation's most highly sought after college prospects. Recruited by more than 100 colleges, he chose to attend Indiana University, then coached by Bobby Knight. In his first season under Knight, he made the All-Big Ten Squad; and in his second, after having been named a consensus All-American, the 19-year-old Isiah led Indiana to the Final Four of the NCAA tournament. In the semifinal round, Indiana demolished Louisiana State University, setting up that decisive confrontation with the University of North Carolina. North Carolina was favored to win, then led by the star forwards James Worthy and Al Wood, but it was Isiah's two key steals in the second half that surged Indiana into a 63–50 rout. Finishing with a game-high 23 points, he was named the tournament's most valuable player.

In 1981, Thomas decided to leave school and turn pro. In the June 5, 1981, National Basketball Association draft, he was the second pick overall after his friend Mark Aguirre, the DePaul superstar who also hailed from K-Town. After signing with the Detroit Pistons, one of the first things Thomas did with his newfound wealth was buy his mother a ranch house in the largely white Chicago suburb of Clarendon Hills. During his rookie season, he was named to the Eastern Conference All-Star team, and he finished the 1981–1982 season with an average of 17 points per game. In the 1983–1984 season, he was once again named to the Eastern Conference All-Star team, and he was named the most valuable player in the All-Star game.

During the 1984–1985 season, Thomas set the NBA record for assists, 1,123, an average of 13.1 per game, and in 1986 he was once again named the All-Star game's most valuable player, as he led the Eastern Conference team to victory with 30 points, ten assists, and five steals. In 1989, he led the Pistons to their first-ever NBA championship, and then in 1990, after winning their second consecutive NBA championship, Thomas was named the 1990 NBA finals Most Valuable Player. In 1991, he was voted a starter in the NBA All-Star game, but didn't play because of an injury.

Throughout his career, Thomas has been celebrated as one of the NBA's unofficial ambassadors of goodwill, along with Julius Erving, Earvin "Magic" Johnson, and Larry Bird. He won the NBA's Walter Kennedy Award for civic responsibility for his work with inner-city children in his spare time. He is involved with the United Negro College Fund, the American Heart Association, the Michigan Special Olympics, United Way, the United Foundation, spokesperson against drunk driving for AAA auto clubs, spokesperson for Say No to Drugs campaigns and he has tried to make a difference to thousands of other young children, growing up facing the same perils he faced.

THOMAS, NATE, was born May 22, 1957, in Warren, Ohio, to the late Ace Thomas, and Rose Thomas. He holds a B.A. degree in theatre arts from St. Edward's University in Austin, Texas, and a master's degree in fine arts in cinema production from the University of Southern California, which he attended on a graduate fellowship from Warner Brothers Pictures. He has directed and produced numerous film projects ranging from award-winning PBS documentaries to television commercials, public service announcements, music videos, etc. He spent in-flight and ground travel time with 1988 presidential candidate Jesse Jackson and directed/produced "Under the Rainbow" for the campaign, a 23-minute promotional film narrated by Casey Kasem. In addi-

tion, Thomas produced several of Jackson's television commercials.

Thomas also spent time in Hawaii working on a 70mm imax film presentation for Expo '89, the Japanese World's Fair, and directed/produced a series of anti-alcohol public service announcements geared toward black women. The 35mm spots were sponsored by the California Department of Alcohol and Drug Programs which airs on television stations statewide. He produced the featurette and electronic press kit for Universal Pictures' *Ghost Dad* starring Bill Cosby.

In 1984, Thomas produced the nationally telecast PBS film *The Last of the One Night Stands*, a documentary on the surviving members of a traveling big band who had a reunion on the 30th anniversary of their last professional performance. The film won numerous awards including a Cine Golden Eagle, a 1984 Focus Award, honors at the San Francisco International Film Festival, and an award from the Black American Cinema Society. It had special screenings at the 15th Wellington Film Festival in New Zealand, and the Smithsonian Institution where it was contained in their film archives. Thomas is listed in *Who's Who Among Black Americans*, and is a professor of film at California State University, Northridge.

TIBBS, EDWARD A., was born April 12, 1940, in Pittsburgh, Pennsylvania. He attended Pittsburgh public schools; Community College of Allegheny County; University of Pittsburgh, and Wilson College, Chambersburg, Pennsylvania. He served in the U.S. Army in 1963 and received an honorable discharge. From 1982 to date, he serves as District Magistrate. His prior positions include: paymaster, Allegheny County, 1980–1982; telephone technician, Western Electric Co., 1963–1980; Executive Board member, Local 2596 Communications Workers of America and Committee on Ethnic Affairs, CWA, National Union.

Tibbs' professional memberships include the following associations: NAACP, life member; Elks, assistant to the Grand Exalted Ruler; Sixth Mt. Zion Baptist Church; board member, Lincoln, Lemington, Larimer, Belmar Development Corporation, Community Relations Board and Job Corps of Pittsburgh. He is the recipient of many awards which include: missileman of the month, U.S. Army, 1960; Community Service Award, Community Action, Pittsburgh, 1975; Mr. Elk, 1980; Meritorious Service Award, Chaplains Department, Pennsylvania State Association of Elks, 1981; Exalted Ruler Emeritus, Greater Pittsburgh Elks, 1982; and *Who's Who Among Black Americans*, 1986.

TILLMAN, EUGENE C. He is married to the former Vivian Vereen, and they have four children, Eugene, Jr., Thurmond, Emmanuel and Anita. He is a graduate of Howard University, Washington, D.C., College of Liberal Arts, 1946–1948, with a B.S. degree in psychology, and a master's degree in divinity, School of Religion, 1948–1951. He served in the United States Naval Reserve, 1944–1946, as a remedial school instructor assigned to Bainbridge, Maryland. He helped organize the Intra-Racial Ministerial Association of Halifax, Florida area, and served as its first vice-president and later as president and performed the same for the Glynn Brunswick Ministerial Association. He served as a member of the Florida Advisory Board of the U.S. Civil Rights Committee until leaving Florida, and was immediately appointed to the Georgia Advisory board on which he served 18 years.

Tillman has served as president of the Democratic Club of Glynn County; president of the Coastal Advancement Non-Profit Organization; chairman of the Urban Renewal Board of Brunswick, and was the former chairman of Glynn County Board of Education. In 1969, he was hired as the Human Resources Developer for the Coastal Area Planning and Development Commission. He held that position until April 15, 1981. In that position he was responsible in areas of community relationship with minority citizens upgrading employment, housing and community facilities within eight county areas in Georgia. He worked with minority groups on SBA and FHA 235J programs and employment and education opportunities. He served as acting director of the Comprehensive Area Wide Health Planning programs in coordinating the health care of all citizens of the six-county area. Tillman also encouraged active participation of all ethnic groups on the advisory council within the frame of this program.

Tillman assisted in the development of a Multi-Service Center Facility to assist minority groups in relationship with local government agencies, etc. He worked with day care centers, nursing homes and summer programs for the underprivileged youth. He served at the pleasure of Ellis MacDougal, former Director of Corrections, in the area of racial conflicts in prisons, and served on the monitoring team of the federal government for Reidsville Prison. He worked with 20th–Century Fox in the filming of a $2,500,000 movie in the Golden Isles of Georgia. He was appointed by the City and County Commission to a 22-man steering committee to decide the reuse of former Navy Glynco and later to a seven-man development authority to handle the assets of Glynco. On July 7, 1982, he was appointed to the newly formed Industrial Council for Glynn County.

Tillman is a former member of the Airport Commission at Glynco. He was appointed in 1975 by Governor George Busbee to the Board of Offender Rehabilitation. In 1980, he was appointed chairman of the board

and served in that position for approximately three years. He retired from the Board of Offender Rehabilitation in July of 1983. He was the former pastor of Mt. Bethel Baptist Church, Daytona Beach, Florida, where he served for nine years and is currently the pastor of the Shiloh Baptist Church, Brunswick, Georgia, where he has been for the past 26 years.

Tillman was the Democratic candidate for Georgia House seat 155, and is presently serving as vice chairman of the Glynn County Board of Commissioners. In 1985, he was appointed director of African Affairs for MAP International and made a trip to Africa inspecting cargo and refugee centers in Ethiopia, Nairobi, Kenya and Sudan and had an opportunity to visit Athens, Greece, and the Netherlands. He served as chairman of the Brunswick Job Corps Center Community Advisory Board for several years and was a life member of the NAACP. He was also an active member of Healthmasters Home Care of Georgia, Inc., the Kiwanis Club, the Golden Isles Chamber of Commerce, Brunswick College board of directors, and Youth Estate.

TONEY, ROBERT L., was born on August 30, 1934, in Monroe, Louisiana. He is married to the former Flora J. Wallace of San Diego, California. They have two daughters and one son. He attended Youngstown University in Youngstown, Ohio, from 1952 to 1954, and graduated in 1957 from California State University, Chico, with a B.A. degree. He was commissioned an ensign in the U.S. Navy Reserve on October 31, 1957. He completed the NATO Defense College in 1977. He is the director for Logistics and Security Assistance, U.S. Pacific Command, Camp H. M. Smith, Hawaii. He advises the Commander in Chief, U. S. Pacific Command, on all matters dealing with the defense of the United States through bilateral logistics agreements, cooperative funds, logistics planning, transportation, civil engineering, and security assistance.

Toney's early Navy tours included duty as the assistant communications officer aboard the USS *Bennington* (CVA-20); staff officer, commander, Training Command, U.S. Pacific Fleet; operations officer, USS *Guadalupe* (A-32); combat information officer, USS *Topeka* (CLG-8); senior projects officer at the Destroyer Development Group, Pacific Fleet; special projects officer for the Commander, Cruiser-Destroyer Group Pacific; executive officer, USS *Cowell* (DD-547); special assistant to the Chief of Naval Personnel, Washington, D.C.; commander, Navy Recruiting Command for Minority Affairs (Recruiting); and executive officer of USS *Wichita* (AOR-1), before assuming command of USS *Kiska* (AE-35).

Toney also served on the staff of the Commander, Allied Forces, Southern Europe from August 1977 to April 1979; and as chief staff officer, Commander Service Group One from April 1979 to March 1983. In August 1983, he became commanding officer of the USS *Roanoke* (AOR-7). After promotion to flag rank in August 1984, he assumed duties as Deputy Commander, Naval Surface Force, U.S. Pacific, in September 1984. In October 1985, he also assumed the additional duties as commander, Naval Surface Group Long Beach.

Adm. Toney assumed command of Naval Base San Francisco and Combat Logistic Group One in January 1986. In May 1988, he was selected for promotion to rear admiral (upper half). He assumed his present position in February 1989. His awards and decorations include: the Legion of Merit, Defense Meritorious Service Medal, Navy Meritorious Service Medal (second award), Navy Commendation Medal, Meritorious Unit Commendation, Armed Forces Expeditionary Medal, Vietnam Service Medal (fifth award), Republic of Vietnam Campaign Medal, and the National Defense Service Medal.

TOWLES-MOORE,   STACY MARIA, was born March 4, 1958, in Detroit, Michigan. She is married to David B. Moore, M.D., and they have

Medical Association; American Medical Association; Southern Medical Association and American College of Occupational Medicine.

TROTTER, DONNE E., was born on January 30, 1950, in Cairo, Illinois. He and his wife Rose have four children. He received a B.A. degree from the University of Arizona, and Chicago University. He serves as a hospital administrator at Cook County Hospital. He was first appointed and later elected as an Illinois State Representative, in 1988.

two children, David and Jordan. She attended the public school system and high school in Ft. Wayne, Indiana, and graduated with honors. She graduated from Northwestern University of Louisville School of Medicine with an M.D. degree, in 1980–1984, and completed her internship at the University of Louisville Department of Internal Medicine and Department of Pediatrics, 1984–1985. She completed her residency training in internal medicine at the Louisville Department of Internal Medicine, 1986–1988.

Towles-Moore has served as Divisional Medical Officer/U.S. Postal Service in the Atlanta Division since 1989. Prior positions include: staff physician, Autaugaville Health Clinic in Alabama. Honors received include: Honor Society, four years; Daughters of the American Revolution Citizenship Award; junior class president and senior class vice-president; *Who's Who Among American High School Students*, 1975–1976; and a four-year academic scholarship to Indiana University. She is affiliated with the following organizations: Student National

Since his election Trotter has served on numerous committees and commissions, which include: Transportation & Motor Vehicles; Human Services; Counties & Townships; Energy, Environment and Natural Resources and Appropriations I; Citizens Council on Children, Advisory Council for the Citizens Assembly; Legislative Reference Bureau, Co-Chair Speaker's Blue Ribbon Task Force on Foster Care; National Conference of State Legislatures (NCSL); Health Committee.

TRUMBO, GEORGE WILLIAM, was born September 24, 1926, in Newark, Ohio. He is the son of George Frank Trumbo and Beatrice Trumbo. He married Sara J. Harper and they have five children, Constance, James, Kimberlee, Karen, and Adam, and two grandchildren. He received his B.S. degree from Ohio State University and his LL.B. degree from Case Western Reserve Law School. He was admitted to practice law before the United States Supreme Court and United States Tax Court. From 1977 to 1982, he served as referee for the Court of Common Pleas in Cleveland. In 1982, he was appointed a judge to the Cleveland Municipal Court. In 1983, he was elected to a full term. In 1989, he was re-elected to another six-year term.

Judge Trumbo is a member of the National Bar Association, Greater Cleveland Bar Association, Ohio Bar Association, Cuyahoga County Bar Association, NAACP, and board of directors of the Judicial Council of the National Bar Association. He is past president of the Shaker Square Kiwanis Club, was a member of the Cleveland Public Library trustees board from 1977–1986, and president of the board from 1984 to 1986. He was also president of the Northern Ohio Municipal Judges Association in 1988. He has received awards from the Cuyahoga County Criminal Court Bar Associa-

tion in 1973 and the Ohio Supreme Court's Superior Judicial Service Award in 1982, 1984, and 1985.

TUCKER, WALTER, was born August 27, 1924, in Taft, Oklahoma. A twin, he was seventh of eight children. He is married to Martha Ann Hinton and they are the parents of four children, Keta, Walter, III, Kenneth and Camille. He attended Booker T. Washington High School in Haskell, Oklahoma; received a B.A. degree from Los Angeles State College, Los Angeles, California; graduated from the University of Southern California, Los Angeles, and Meharry Medical College School of Dentistry, Nashville, Tennessee, where he received his D.D.S. degree in 1955. He was elected to public office in 1967, and served three four-year terms as mayor of Compton. In April 1985, the people of Compton overwhelmingly returned him to office.

Tucker's total commitment and exceptional qualifications led him to be the first black person ever re-elected as mayor in Compton. In his political career, he maintained a full schedule, making appearances and representing the city. His charisma and concern for others led him to be well respected not only in his own community but throughout the state and across the nation for his skills and expertise in city government. In many instances, his presence also was enough to assure that Compton's best interest was not overlooked. He recognized the importance of Compton's participation in issues that reach beyond the city's borders. He was an avid supporter of the Compton community and, wanting to see it prosper, worked diligently toward that end.

Tucker was involved in ongoing negotiations and lobbying efforts to gain a higher ranking for the city in many federal and state programs, bringing much-needed funds to support city projects. He was instrumental in and supported the building of the first major hotel in the city through the long and difficult negotiation and construction periods. Among his priorities was his desire to see gun-control laws established. Also at the top of his list of priorities was the annexation of those properties within the sphere of influence of the city of Compton.

As a member of the board of directors of the National Conference of Black Mayors (NCBM) and a member of the World Conference of Mayors (WCM), the California Council of Criminal Justice Planning and many other such organizations, Tucker gained extensive knowledge and experience in dealing with the problems facing communities like Compton today. He adamantly promoted community involvement, recognizing that effective elimination of gang violence was a problem which requires a joint and concerted effort by communities at the local level as well as statewide. He took every opportunity to be among the residents of the community, not only as their mayor but as their family dentist, their neighbor and their friend. Mr.

Tucker held public office for more than 23 years, serving as a member of the Union High School Board of Trustees, the Unified School District Board of Trustees, as a city council member and, finally, as mayor.

———

TURNER, JOSEPH ELLIS, was born September 2, 1939, in Charleston, West Virginia, the son of Joseph Turner and Annetta Frances Malone Turner. He and his wife Norma Jean Turner have three children, Dr. Alan T., Brian D., and Joseph E., Jr. Upon completion of high school, he attended West Virginia State College, where he graduated and received his ROTC commission in 1961. Upon entering the Army, he attended the Signal Officer's Basic Course. Later he graduated from the Aviation Fixed and Rotary Wing Courses, the Signal Officer's Advanced Course, Army Aviation Safety Course, the Command and General Staff College, the Industrial College of the Armed Forces (National Security Manage-

ment Course) and the Air War College. He has completed the Federal Aviation Administration's Air Traffic Indoctrination Course, the University of Southern California's Aviation Safety and Management Course, and advanced studies in Human Resources Management at the University of Utah.

His active duty assignments include two tours in the Republic of Vietnam where he served as a Fixed Wing Aviator in the 17th Aviation Company, 1st Air Cavalry Division; signal officer, 17th Aviation Group; and commander of Headquarters Company, 210th Combat Aviation Battalion. He also served as a Fixed Wing Aviator for the Third United States Army, aviator and communications officer with the 187th Airplane Company, and as a signal platoon leader in the 1st Battle Group, 29th Infantry. He began his military career as a Reserve officer in January 1961, and was appointed as a regular Army officer in April 1966. His principal Reserve assignments have included serving as commander of the 335th Signal Group and the 3283rd United States Army Reserve Forces School.

In the 81st United States Army Reserve Command, Gen. Turner served as the Deputy Chief of Staff for Logistics, Deputy Chief of Staff for Resources Management, operations/training officer, aviation safety officer, and communication/electronics officer. In March 1988, he was promoted to the one-star rank of brigadier general and assigned to the 335th Signal Command, as deputy commander. He became the first black Georgia Reservist, and the first black in the 81st U.S. Army Reserve Command, to be promoted to the rank of general. In 1988, he was inducted into the Georgia Hall of Fame. He is employed by Delta Airlines where he serves as a first officer on the L1011 air craft. On September 7, 1991, he was named commander of the 335th Signal Command and is the first African American in the history of the 81st ARCOM to be nominated for the two-star grade of major general.

TYUS, WYOMIA, was born August 29, 1945, in Griffin, Georgia, the daughter of Will Tyus, a dairy farmer, and Maria Tyus. She married Duane Tillman and they have a daughter and a son. It was her father (who died when she was 15 years old) who encouraged her to participate in competitive sport. She participated in high school basketball and track. In 1963, she received an athletic scholarship to Tennessee State University and continued to train with Temple. From 1964 to 1966, she won three AAU 100-yard and 100-meter dash titles, and from 1966 to 1967, she won two AAU 200-yard dash crowns. In 1967, she won the Pan-American Games 200-meter title in Winnipeg. At the 1968 Mexico City Olympic Games, she won the 100 meters in a world record 11.0 seconds, finished sixth in the 200 meters, and collected another gold medal in the 4x100 meter relay, establishing a world record of 42.6 seconds. After the 1968 Olympiad, she retired from athletic participation as the world's premier female athlete.

From 1969 to 1970, she worked as a research assistant at UCLA's Afro-American Center; from 1970 to 1972, she taught physical education at Bret Harte Junior High School; from 1972 to 1973, she was a track coach at Beverly Hills High School; from 1973 to 1976, she worked as a public relations staffer for the International track Association; in 1976, she worked as a commentator for ABC-TV News coverage of the Olympic Games in Montreal.

VAUGHN, JACKIE, III, born November 17, 1930, in Birmingham, Alabama, is a graduate of Oxford University (England). He was a Fulbright Scholar and Fellow — one of the few Americans to receive the State Department's extension of the Fulbright Scholarship for three years. He received his master's degree from Oberlin College and his B.A. degree from Hillsdale College. Sen. Vaughn is associate president pro tempore of the Michigan Senate. During his illustrious career, he has authored such legislation as the 18-year-old Voting Rights Act and the Young Citizen Bill of Rights, the Dr. Martin Luther King, Jr. Holiday Bill, the Physician's Assistants Bill, the Prisoner's Bill of Rights, the Free College Tuition Bill, the Ethnic Studies Bill, the Peace Bill, Ratification of Statehood for Washington, D.C., the Free Tuition Bill for North American Indians, the High School Voter Registration Bill, the Free Community College Tuition for Senior Citizens Bill, the State Income Tax Exemption Bill for Vans and Buses Purchased by Churches and Religious Organizations, and the AIDS Education Act. Vaughn is one of the most respected legislators in the state, and one of the busiest.

Vaughn was a two-term past president of the Michigan Young Democrats, past president pro tempore of the Michigan Senate, past assistant president pro tempore of the Michigan Senate and Class Agent for both Hillsdale and Oberlin Colleges. He was an active member of the American Oxonian Society (Oxford, England), and served as a teacher at the University of Detroit and Wayne State University. He has received numerous honors, including gubernatorial appointment as statewide chairman of the Michigan Martin Luther King, Jr. Commission; the Hillsdale Alumni Achievement Award; and the Legislator or Senator of the Year in various years by the Detroit Medical Society, Wolverine Dental Society, Wolverine Medical Society, Michigan Osteopathic Society, Alpha Theta Chapter of Gamma Phi Delta Sorority, Rising Sun Grand Chapter of O.E.S., Scottish Rite Affiliation, Little

Rock Baptist Church, and the Michigan Chapter of the Southern Christian Leadership Conference.

Vaughn has also been adopted as an executive associate member of Detroit's oldest and most prestigious women's organization, the Rosa L. Gragg Educational and Civic Club, becoming the first male ever to receive this high honor. He was selected as "Outstanding and Model Legislator" by the *Michigan Chronicle* and was the recipient of the Distinguished Senator and Man of Peace Award from D'Etre University in Detroit. He has been listed in *Who's Who Among American College and University Students.* Among his many activities, Sen. Vaughn was a member of various organizations, and an active member and Sunday school instructor at Hartford Memorial Baptist Church in Detroit. He had been granted a private audience both with His Holiness Pope Paul VI and Pope John Paul II in the Vatican.

VINSON, PHYLLIS TUCKER, is the mother of five children, Nye, Amani Suna, Aisha, Bakari and Shasha. A graduate of California State University at Los Angeles, she earned a B.A. degree in child development. She is an executive producer for NBC Productions and has produced original children's programming for both Saturday morning and prime time television. She is currently involved in the development of a project she created with Bill Cosby entitled, "Wee People," and the producer of NBC's new Saturday morning program, "Rich Moranis in Gravedale High." She began as a secretary at NBC in 1972. Quickly rising through the ranks, she became the first African American female program executive when she was appointed manager of Variety Programs in 1977, where she was involved in the creative supervision of "Little House on the Prairie," "Chips" and "The Wonderful World of Disney."

Known for her creative success with programs directed toward young viewers, in 1979, Vinson was appointed to the position of director of Children's Programs. In 1981, she became the first African American woman to become a programming vice president in the history of network television. She was appointed vice president of Children's and Family Programming. Under her leadership, NBC achieved its "number one" position in the ratings for the Saturday morning line-up ahead of CBS and ABC. She was responsible for the development of shows such as "Smurfs," "Alvin and the Chipmunks," and "Mr. T." Her six-year winning streak was the longest consecutive run in the history of television, on any network.

Vinson is a member of the National Council of Family and Children, National Black Child development Institute, Jack and Jill of America, Inc., and the Hollywood Radio and Television Society. She was also on the board of directors of Crystal Stairs, a full child-care referral service. She has appeared in *Essence* magazine, on numerous occasions, for her outstanding contributions and achievements. She was also featured on the cover of the *Black Enterprise* 1986 Anniversary Issue honoring "The New Achievers, Young Black Men and Women Who Are Chang-

ing America." Some of her other awards include Career Woman of the Year by Zeta Phi Beta Sorority, NAACP Medgar Evers Community Service Award for Outstanding Achievement in Communications and Community Service, Newsmaker Award by the National Association of Media Women, Black Women of Achievement, special honoree by the NAACP Legal Defense, and she was saluted by *Dollars and Sense* magazine at the Delta Convention in 1985 as one of America's Top 100 Black Business and Professional Women.

VOORHEES, JOHN H., was born August 12, 1936, in New Brunswick, New Jersey. He married the former Jeanine Carter and they have two children, Melanie Shemyne and John Carter. He graduated from New Brunswick High School in 1954; received a B.S. degree in chemistry from Rutgers University in 1958; and a master's degree in management from the University of Southern California in 1967. He was designated as a senior executive fellow of Harvard University in 1981. He completed Squadron Officer School in 1962, and the National War College in 1973. He received his commission in 1958 as a distinguished military graduate of the Air Force Reserve Officer Training Corps program at Rutgers. He then completed navigator training at James Connally Air Force Base, Texas, and Mather Air Force Base, California.

From April 1960 to June 1966, Voorhees was a B-52 navigator with the 668th Bombardment Squadron at Griffiss Air Force Base, New York. He then entered the Air Force Institute of Technology program and completed his master's degree at the University of Southern California. In June 1968, the general joined the 14th Tactical Fighter Squadron at Udorn Royal Thai Air Force Base, Thailand, as an F-4 navigator systems operator. During this assignment he flew 176 combat missions, including 100 over North Vietnam. Upon returning to the United States in May 1969, he was assigned to the Space and Missile Systems Organization headquarters at Los Angeles Air Force Station, California, as chief of the Systems Effectiveness Branch and later as chief of the Test Support Division.

After graduation from the National War College in June 1973, he remained in Washington, D.C., as a research and development planner in the Organization of the Joint Chiefs of Staff. Moving to Wright-Patterson Air Force Base in July 1976, he was initially assigned as chief of the Strategic Plans Division and then as director of plans at Air Force Logistics Command headquarters. From July 1979 to May 1981, he was chief of the B-52 and Missile Systems Management Division for the Oklahoma City Air Logistics Center, Tinker Air Force Base, Oklahoma. He then became director of Materiel Management for the Sacramento Air Logistics Center, McClellan Air Force Base, California.

In August 1982, he took command of the Defense Contract Administration Services Region in Los Angeles. He was assigned as deputy director, Logistics and Security Assistance, J4/7, Headquarters European Command, Vaihingen, West Germany, in June 1984. In August 1986, he assumed command of the Defense Personnel Support Center, Defense Logistics Agency, Philadelphia. He was promoted to his two-star rank of major general on June 1, 1986. In January 1990, he assumed duties as deputy chief of staff for contracting and manufacturing, headquarters Air Force Logistics Command, Wright-Patterson Air Force Base, Ohio. His duties include management of an $11 billion contracting program in support of the command's logistics mission. Air Force Logistics Command completed almost 450,000 contracting actions annually that support the United States Air Force, as well as more than 70 friendly foreign air forces under the foreign military sales program. Gen. Voorhees is a Master Navigator with 3,800 flying hours in the B-52 and F-4C aircraft.

WALKER, ALICE MALSENIOR, was born on February 9, 1944, in Eatonton, Georgia, the youngest of eight children of Willie Lee and Minnie Tallulah (Grant) Walker. Her parents were storytellers, and at the age of eight, she began to record those stories and some poems of her own in a notebook, spending a great deal of time alone allowing her the quiet and solitude she needed to write. In 1952, she was accidentally wounded in the eye by a shot from a BB gun fired by one of her brothers. Owing to a week's delay in seeing a doctor, she was permanently blind in the eye.

After feeling like an outcast for so long, the scar tissue was removed at age 14 and Walker was voted most popular girl and queen of her senior class in addition to being honored as valedictorian. Because of the accident, she became eligible for a scholarship for handicapped students, which she used to attend Spelman College in Atlanta University Center, Atlanta, Georgia. Her neighbors raised the bus fare to Atlanta. At that time the Center included six black colleges and universities, the largest black educational center in the world. Most of the students were involved in the civil rights movement; she was already moved by it from what she had learned about it on television.

It was at this time that she met Staughton Lynds and Howard Zinn and soon became involved in civil rights demonstrations in downtown Atlanta. Zinn's dismissal in her sophomore year for being overly sympathetic to the demonstrators, and Spelman's restrictive rules in general led her to accept a scholarship offer from Sarah Lawrence, the exclusive but progressive women's college in Bronxville, New York. After receiving her B.A. degree from Sarah Lawrence in 1965, she canvassed voters in Liberty County, Georgia. Later she worked in New York City's Welfare Department by day and wrote by night.

When Walker won her first fellowship in 1966, she spent the summer in Mississippi to help with the voter registration. There she met Melvyn Rosenman Leventhal, a young Jewish civil rights lawyer; they were married on March 17, 1967, becoming the first legally married interracial couple in Jackson. There Leventhal sued racist real estate dealers and fought to desegregate the state's schools while his wife served briefly as a black history consultant to Friends of the Children of Mississippi (a Head Start Program), and as a writer-in-residence at Jackson State College in 1968–1969 and at Tougaloo College in 1970–1971.

During her stay in Jackson, Mississippi, Walker's literary career advanced considerably. Her first novel was written on a fellowship at the MacDowell Colony in New Hampshire in 1967 entitled *The Third Life of Grange Copeland*. Some of her other works are: "The Civil Rights Movement: What Good Was It?," her first published essay, an impassioned declaration of her commitment to the cause, "To Hell with Dying," her best-known and first published short story, and the famous novel *The Color Purple*.

WALKER, CHARLES W., was born in Burke County, Georgia. He is married to the former Sheila Davis and they have four children, Charles, Jr., Yolanda, Christopher and Kimberly. He is a graduate of Lucy Laney High School in Augusta, Georgia; a 1966 graduate of the Naval Training Center, Great Lakes, Illinois; received a B.A. in business administration from Augusta College in 1974; and is a graduate of Leadership Georgia. He attended Norfolk State College, Norfolk, Virginia. He is the president and chief executive officer of the Walker Group which represents a multi-faceted business operation and includes First Citizens Financial Services, Augusta *Focus* newspaper (of which he is publisher), Speedy Temporary Employment Agency, Speedy Courier Services, and Inner-City Development Corp.

Walker became a state legislator where he gained influence and stature in the Georgia General Assembly, filling the promises made during his campaign. He was re-elected to the House four consecutive times. The first time he had opposition he won with over 70 percent of the votes, and the second time, in 1988, when he had opposition, he won again by the same percentage of votes. After his second year in the General Assembly, he was elected chairman of the Georgia Legislative Black Caucus. When he had been elected chairman for the second time, it was a history-setting precedent: no other legislator had ever been elected chairman of the caucus for two consecutive terms. Under his leadership, the Georgia Legislative Black Caucus was incorporated and received the 501(C)(3) status to become a nonprofit organization.

Walker sponsored legislation that created an economic development corporation, because he believed that economic development was the key to economic and political parity in this county. Under the legislation he introduced, Georgia had for the first time an economic development corporation designed exclusively for small and minority businesses. In 1984, his second year in the General Assembly, he was primarily responsible for the complete reorganization of the city and county governments of Augusta and Richmond counties. When he took office in January 1983, he pledged he would bring parity and equity to the Richmond County Commission. The Commission had no minorities on it; he introduced legislation that completely revised the county commission and put it on a district basis so that the commission would have representation from all segments of the community.

Walker also introduced legislation that changed the City Council, reducing its membership from 16 to 8 and legislation that put the council on a ward-voting basis. He co-authored and introduced legislation which changed and reduced the Board of Education from 16 to 9 members and which put the board on legislative district so that it would contain representatives from all segments of the community. A strong advocate for senior citizens, he introduced legislation to remove sales tax from prescription medicines and drugs for them. In 1988, he introduced and created a commission for disadvantaged youths which provided jobs for young people, both black and white, throughout the Richmond County community.

Prior experience includes serving as chairman of the Georgia Association of Human Relations Commission; board of directors of the Greater Augusta Chamber of Commerce; on the OIC industrialization board; chairman of the Sickle Cell Anemia Advisory Board of Augusta; member of the executive committee of the Boy Scouts of America and CSRA Boy Scouts Council; executive board member of the Georgia-Carolina Boy Scouts of America, and a member of many more boards and authorities, and numerous other professional organizations. He has received many awards and recognition for his service, including being named one of the Outstanding Young Men of America. He has received two Businessman of the Year awards from the CSRA Involvement Council; Man of the Year and Citizen of the Year awards from the Lincoln League in Augusta; and in 1982 he received the Freedom Award from the Augusta Chapter of the NAACP.

WALLER, CALVIN AGUSTINE HOFFMAN, was born on December 17, 1937, in Baton Rouge, Louisiana. He received a B.S. degree in agriculture from Prairie View A&M University, and an M.S. degree in public administration from Shippensburg State University. He entered the United States Army in August 1959 as a student in the Infantry Officer Basic Course, United States Infantry School, Fort Benning, Georgia. In June 1961, he was assigned as the commander of the 247th Chemical Platoon, Fort Lewis, Washington. On July 30, 1962, he was promoted to the rank of first lieutenant. From August 1963 to December 1963, he was a student at the United States Army Chemical Center and School, Fort McClellan, Alabama. He was promoted to the rank of captain on July 29, 1963.

From December 1963 to June 1964, he served as the chief of the Chemical, Biological, Radiological Center, Office of the Assistant Chief of Staff G-2/G-3, 7th Logistics Command, Eighth United States Army, in Korea. From February 1965 to April 1967, he served as a chemical officer at Headquarters and Headquarters Company, later brigade chemical officer, 2nd Brigade, 82nd Airborne Division, Fort Bragg, North Carolina. He was promoted to the rank of major on September 5, 1967. From July 1968 to May 1969, he was a student at the United States Army Command and General Staff College, Fort Leavenworth, Kansas. From April 1971 to July 1972, he served as the training staff officer, Policy and Programs branch, Office of the Deputy Chief of Staff for Personnel, United States Army, Washington, D.C.

On June 1, 1975, Waller was promoted to the rank of lieutenant colonel. From August 1975 to May 1977, he was the commander of the 1st Battalion, 77th Armor, 4th Infantry Division (Mechanized), Fort Carson, Colorado. From August 1977 to June 1978, he was a student at the United States Army War College, Carlisle Barracks, Pennsylvania. From July 1980 to June 1981, he was the senior military assistant to the Assistant Secretary of Defense (Manpower, Reserve Affairs and Logistics), Washington, D.C. On August 1, 1980, he was promoted to the rank of colonel. From August 1983 to December 1983, he served as the chief of staff for the 24th Infantry Division (Mechanized), Fort Steward, Georgia.

From December 1983 to June 1984, he was the chief of staff, XVIII Airborne Corps, Fort Bragg, North Carolina. From June 1984 to July 1986, he served as the assistant division commander, 82nd Airborne Division, Fort Bragg. He was promoted to the one-star rank of brigadier general, on November 1, 1984. From July 1986 to July 1987, he served as the deputy commanding general, I Corps and Fort Lewis, Washington. From July 1987 to July 1989, he was the commanding general of the 8th Infantry Division (Mechanized), V Corps, United States Army in Europe and the Seventh Army.

On November 1, 1987, Gen. Waller was promoted to the two-star rank of major general. From August 1989 to November 1990, he was the commanding general of I Corps and Fort Lewis. He was promoted to the three-star rank of lieutenant general, August 3, 1989. In November 1990, he was named deputy commander in chief of the Central Command, in Saudi Arabia (Desert Storm).

WALTON, CHARLES D., a graduate from Shaw University in Raleigh, North Carolina, in 1971, with a B.A. degree in urban sociology and a minor in political science. During his educational studies at Shaw, he received a Shaw University Fellowship. In 1974, he received his M.Ed. in international studies from the University of Massachusetts School of Education in Amherst. While involved with his graduate studies he became a research assistant at the University of Nairobi and Zambia University, investigating the difference in African societies, secondary education versus the American system. He served as director of the Urban Educational Center of Rhode Island College, and is a Rhode Island State Senator from District 9.

The Urban Educational Center (UEC) is an adult learning center. As director, he was responsible for the day-to-day operation of the center which provided programs and services in the areas of general adult and continuing education, including high school equivalency preparation and testing, adult basic education, English as a Second Language (ESL), vocational classes and a tutoring and skills center program. He was also responsible for the Educational Opportunities Center Project which was an outreach organization designed to help low-income, minority and handicapped persons who wish to pursue college study or other types of postsecondary educational experiences. Under his leadership an Appraisal of Academic Skills and Assessment Program was developed.

Walton also strengthened the community advisory board and fostered relationships with postsecondary institutions statewide that assisted UEC students in continuing their education. As chief supervisor for a staff of 14 professionals and paraprofessionals and 40 to 50 part-time adjunct faculty for academic school services, his responsibility was to review and evaluate their employment needs, provide staff development and training, and direct curriculum development and implementation. He had served as research and planning specialist at UEC where his duties and responsibilities were to write project proposals from federal and local funding agencies for program development and expansion, developed currriculum courses for adult education and self-enrichment programs, implemented program evaluation on academic activities at the center, and conducted research and compiled data in adult education.

Prior to Walton's appointment as director of UEC he was acting director, Core-Facilitator/Curriculum developer at University Without Walls at Roger Williams College, and intern/teacher for the Providence School Department. He assumed this present position, as well as Deputy Majority Leader of the Senate, Secretary of the Finance Committee, member of the Health, Education and Welfare Committee, and the Joint Committee on Accounts and Claims.

Walton has sponsored many pieces of legislation, including legislation declaring Martin Luther King, Jr.'s birthday a state holiday, lowering medical costs for the elderly, highway safety legislation, and housing legislation. He is a member of the Rhode Island Adult Education Commission, Vocational Education Council, the NAACP, Rhode Island Black Heritage Society, American Association of Higher Education, African-American Institute for Afro-American Teachers/Professionals, and the Providence Community Action Program.

WALTON, ELBERT ARTHUR, JR., was born February 21, 1942, in St. Louis, Missouri, the son of Elbert A. Walton, Sr., and Luretta B. Ray Walton. He married Juanita Alberta Head (divorced), and he has five children, Rochelle, Angela, Elbert, III, Rhonda, and Johnathan. He graduated from Henry Elementary and Sumner High schools. In 1963, he received an A.A. degree from Harris Junior College; a B.A. degree in business from the University of Missouri in St. Louis, in 1968; an M.B.A. degree from the University of Washington, in 1970; and a J.D. degree from St. Louis University in 1974.

In 1969, he worked as a financial analyst for Continental Oil Corp., and from 1971 to 1978, he was an instructor of business law and accounting at University of Missouri at St. Louis.

In 1974, he became an attorney at law, and in 1977, was appointed a Municipal Court judge for the city of

St. Louis before being elected to the Missouri House of Representatives in 1979. Rep. Walton was honored during his first year in office by being selected by the Missouri Association of Public Employees to receive a certificate of recognition as an Outstanding Legislator. He is the recipient of the Outstanding Young Man of America Award (1976), Outstanding Achievement Award (1977), Distinguished Service Award (1975), and Man of the Year Award (1974). He was the national vice president of the National Association of Black Accountants from 1976 to 1977.

WARD, HORACE TALIAFERRO, was born in 1927, in LaGrange, Georgia, to Minnie Ward, a maid. He never knew his father, and because his mother lived with the white people for whom she worked, he lived his first nine years with his mother's parents. They rented two rooms in a community owned by Callaway Mills. His grandfather, Isaiah Ward, was a yardman and a Baptist Sunday school superintendent. Ward didn't start school until he was nine years old, reasons unknown. He advanced quickly, skipping fifth grade. He moved in with his mother and stepfather, a laundry worker, in a three-room house behind LaGrange College. He was valedictorian of East Depot Street High School in 1946. He received a freshman scholarship to Morehouse, majored in political science and graduated in three years, in 1949, with honors.

Ward played a saxophone in the Morehouse band and lived with his aunt across town to save money, riding Atlanta's trackless trolleys to class. He worked tirelessly to pay for his education, cleaning tables at a Peachtree Arcade Cafeteria at Five Points and delivering *The Atlanta Journal*. Upon graduation, he wanted to go to law school but didn't have enough money, so he accepted a scholarship to Atlanta University. He received a master's degree in political science the following year. In the summer of 1950, he applied to the University of Georgia Law School.

Ward initially thought he might be admitted without difficulty. Recent lawsuits had caused the integration of graduate schools in Texas, Oklahoma and Virginia, and blacks had been admitted to graduate schools in Arkansas, Louisiana and Tennessee. In 1952, after his application was rejected first by the registrar, then by the president and the chancellor, he filed suit charging a violation of the 14th Amendment. His attorneys were Atlantan A. T. Walden and the NAACP's then attorney Thurgood Marshall. Gov. Herman Talmadge vowed to fight the suit "to the bitter end" and put his personal attorney, B. D. Murphy, on the case. In 1953, one month before the case was to go to court, Ward was drafted. The case finally came to trial in December 1956, and in January 1957, the court handed down its decision upholding the university's refusal to admit Ward.

In 1959, he graduated from Northwestern and was admitted to the Georgia bar in 1960. He joined Hollowell's firm on Hunter Street (now Martin Luther King, Jr. Drive). In 1964, Ward won a state Senate seat in a majority-white district and became the second black man since Reconstruction to be elected to the General Assembly. Gov. Jimmy Carter appointed him to a judgeship on the Civil Court of Fulton County, making him the highest ranking black in the state judicial system. Then in 1977, he became the first black Superior Court judge in state history when Gov. George Busbee appointed him to an unexpired term in Fulton County.

In 1979, President Jimmy Carter nominated Judge Ward to a United States District Court judgeship. He was confirmed by the United States Senate, and the oath was administered by Chief Judge Charles A. Moye at the federal courthouse in Atlanta. He became the first black United States District Court judge in the state of Georgia.

WARREN, NAOMI WHITE, is a graduate of St. Paul the Apostle School, valedictorian, 1961; and salutatorian, St. Mary's Academy High School, 1965. She received a B.A. degree, Louisiana State University, New Orleans, 1968 and a J.D. degree, Texas Southern University, Houston, Texas, 1973 where she was voted Most Outstanding First Year Law Student, was on dean's list two years, and received two Jurisprudence awards: Contract and Property. She has served as State Representative for District 101 for two regular legislative sessions and two special legislative sessions, 1986–1987. She is a member of Standing Committees of the Louisiana House of Representatives: Civil Law and Procedure Committee, Education Committee, Retirement Committee and Subcommittee on oversight of the House Municipal, Parochial and Cultural Affairs Committee, and State Education Policy Seminar Program (SEPS) in Louisiana.

Warren's prior experience includes: trial lawyer for the United States Department of Justice, 1973–1979; assistant United States attorney in Sacramento, California, 1979; law clerk, Staff Judge Advocate General's Office (JAG), United States Marine Corps, 1972; law clerk, Office of the Inspector General, United States Department for Agriculture, 1971; and legislative advisor, for District 101. She was admitted to the Texas State Bar, 1974; District of Columbia Bar, 1975, and the United States Supreme Court Bar in 1977.

Warren is the recipient of many awards and honors: from the Louisiana Association of Educators: Legislative Honor Roll in 1989 and Outstanding Legislator Award in 1986; Louisiana Federation of Teachers, Golden Apple Award, 1986; Lowerlight Baptist Church, Elected Official Honoree, 1986; Christian Mission Baptist Church, Service Award, 1987; George Washington Carver Senior High School Athletic Program, Appreciation Award, 1987; George Washington Carver Senior High School, Distinguished Service Award, 1987; Department of Health and Human Resources, Appreciation Award, 1986; New Orleans Council on Aging, Appreciation Award, 1987; and Co-operative Participation Award, Black History Celebration (Alvar Center, 1987), New Orleans, Louisiana.

Additional awards include: Keynote Speaker Award Black Heritage Week Luncheon, 1987, Keesler Air Force Base, Biloxi, Mississippi; New Orleans East Democratic Association, Appreciation Award, 1986; Mu Sigma Chapter of Sigma Gamma Rho Sorority, Outstanding Contribution Award, 1986; *Who's Who Among Black Americans*, 1980–1981; University Service Award, Texas Southern University, 1973; Phi Alpha Delta Service Award, 1973, and Women's Law Caucus Book Award, 1973.

Warren's professional affiliations include: Governor's Conference for Persons with Disabilities Task Force, member, 1986; Sidney Collier Vo-Tech Advisory Committee, member, 1986; Community Education Advisory Committee, member, 1986; Another Chance, Inc., founding advisor, 1987; Desire Florida Business Association, founding advisor, 1987; Students for Human Advancement & Community (SHAC), president for two years; Desire Community Choir, member, 1969–1970; Desire Community Development Corporation, 2nd vice-president, 1969–1970; Desire Community Development Corporation board of directors, member, 1968–1969; "Desire" Community Newspaper, Editor, 1969–1970; NAACP-L.S.U.N.O. Chapter, vice president for one year; New Orleans Child Welfare Committee, member, 1969–1970; and New Orleans

City-Wide Youth Organization, vice president, 1969.

WASHINGTON, CLEO. He attended American University, 1984, Washington Semester Program; 1985, Wabash College, B.A. in political science; and 1988, received J.D. degree from the University of Missouri, Columbia School of Law. He was appointed as deputy public defender for St. Joseph County Superior Courts, State of Indiana in January 1990 to date. He has been in private practice since 1989 and is licensed to practice in the Indiana Supreme Court, Northern District Federal Court, Southern District Federal Court and all state courts. His areas of practice include: family law, personal injury litigator, banking, bankruptcy, Chapter 7 and 13, wills and estates, landlord/tenant disputes and contracts.

Washington's prior positions include: Family Children's Center, worked with emotionally disturbed male adolescents in the capacity as a Youth Treatment Specialist; Bethel Business Machines, Inc., an independent contractor; City Attorney's Office; Melvin Reed, professional corporation, law clerk; South Bend Community School Corporation (part-time substitute teacher); research assistant; Cleo Fellowship; head Democrat debater; Co-Trio Desk Director Lobbyist and Upward Bound counselor.

Washington is the recipient of many honors and awards, including: Mid-America Association of Educational Opportunity Program Personnel President's Award; Bertha Jones Award; Top Oralist in Moot Court Tournament (UMC, School of Law); honorary member of UMC Board of Advocates; YMCA Special Achievement Award. His professional affiliations include: Bible teacher at Ardmore LaSale Church of Christ; founding president of Leaders and Positive Role Models; Mayor's Minority Affairs Council; Big Brother in Big Brothers/Big Sisters Program; Minority Affairs Council (Ivy Tech); Redistricting Oversight Committee; Hansel Center board of directors; Community of Caring Speakers Staff Speakers (Memorial Family Practice).

Additional affiliations include: Minority Parenting Task Force; Urban Plunge Community Leaders speaker; Minority Advisory Board (Indiana University at South Bend); Community Minority Achievement Committee (South Bend Community School Corporation); St. Joseph County Local Coordinating Council for Governors Commission for a Drug-Free Indiana; Real Services Community Services Block Grant Advisory Council; UMC-Law School Minority Mentor Program; St. Joseph County Bar Association; Indiana Bar Association; and the American Bar Association.

WASHINGTON, CRAIG ANTHONY, is a native of Longview, Texas, and long-time resident of Houston. He is the father of five children, Craig, II, Chival, Alexander, Cydney and Christopher. He is a graduate of Prairie View A&M University and the Thurgood

Marshall School of Law at Texas Southern University. He is a criminal defense lawyer and a partner in the Houston law firm of Washington, Lampley, Evans & Braquet. Of special note among his many cases is his successful defense of Eroy Brown, a prison inmate charged with the murder of a prison warden and assistant warden in a series of three celebrated trials during the early 1980s. He served at various times as chairman of the Criminal Jurisprudence, Social Services, and Human Services Committees, as chairman of the Harris County Delegation and the Legislative Black Caucus, and as Speaker Pro Tempore.

Washington was elected to the Texas Senate from District 13, which includes portions of Harris and Fort Bend counties. In 1986, he was elected without opposition to a second term. As a member of the Senate, he served at various times on the Human Resources, Health & Human Services, Jurisprudence, Intergovernmental Relations, Criminal Justice, State Affairs, and Rules Committees, and the Subcommittees on Criminal Matters, Public Health, Health Services, Elections and Urban Affairs. In December 1989,

during the second Called Session of the 71st Legislature, he was elected president pro tempore of the Senate by his peers. As such, he served as the state's "Governor for a Day" on January 20, 1990.

Washington was elected to the U.S. House of Representatives to represent the 18th Congressional District following the tragic death of his friend Congressman Mickey Leland. He was sworn in as a member of the House of Representatives when the 101st Congress reconvened on January 23, 1990. He is well known for his consistent support of civil rights and civil liberties and for his efforts to increase the participation of women and minorities in Texas state government. Highlights of his legislative career include passage of bills creating the Texas Department on Aging, increasing monthly payments to recipients of Aid to Families with Dependent Children (AFDC), limiting state investments in businesses involved with South Africa, addressing the need of people with disabilities, and coordinating the Texas fight against AIDS.

---

†WASHINGTON, HAROLD, was born in Chicago, Illinois, on April 15, 1922, one of 11 children of Roy L. Washington and Bertha (Jones) Washington. A promising athlete, he won the city's high school championship in 120-meter high hurdles in 1939, and he also was an amateur middle weight boxer. He graduated from Du Sable High School, and received a B.A. degree from Roosevelt University in Chicago. He enrolled in Northwestern University Law School which granted him a J.D. degree in 1952. He served as an assistant city prosecutor from 1954 to 1958, and from 1960 to 1964 worked as an arbitrator for the Illinois Industrial Commission. From 1965 to 1976, Washington served for six terms in the Illinois House of Representatives and from 1977 through 1980, he was a member of the state Senate.

In 1980, Washington was elected to his first term in the U.S. House of Representatives. In 1983, he left the House to enter the Chicago mayoral contest, urged by the African American leaders who had supported his 1977 bid. He defeated former Mayor Jane Byrne in the Democratic primary and Republican Bernard Epton in a general election marked by racial divisiveness to become the city's first African American mayor. In 1987, Washington halted Byrne's comeback bid, beating her in the Democratic primary. He won re-election to his second term in April, defeating Republican Don Haidera. On November 25, 1987, he suffered a fatal heart attack in his City Hall office.

WASHINGTON, WALTER ED-WARD, was born on April 15, 1915, in Dawson, Georgia, the only child of William L. and Willie Mae Thornton Washington. He was reared in Jamestown, New York, where he graduated from high school in 1933. In 1938, he graduated from Howard University in Washington, D.C., with a B.A. degree in public administration and sociology. It was another ten years before he graduated from Howard's Law School. But during the interim period, he served as an administrative intern, a junior housing assistant, and finally housing manager of the National Capital Housing Authority. He continued to hold variety of executive positions until 1961, when he was appointed executive director of the National Capital Housing Authority.

In 1966, Washington was appointed chairman of the New York Public Housing Authority, a job he held for approximately one year before he returned to Washington as mayor in 1967, when he received a presidential appointment as mayor-commissioner of Washington. He was elected mayor of Washington in 1974 and served in that position until 1979. He was the first black mayor of Washington. His administration had to put down riots, and handle anti-war and welfare demonstrations.

WATERS, MAXINE, a native of St. Louis, Missouri, is married to Sidney Williams, and they have two children, Karen and Edward. A graduate of California State University at Los Angeles, she received a B.A. degree in sociology. She was the first woman in California history to be elected by her colleagues to chair the Assembly Democratic Caucus. Serving in the Legislature, her accomplishments have ranged from divestment of state pension funds from businesses involved in South Africa, to the creation of the nation's first statewide Child Abuse Prevention Training Program. As chair of the Assembly Ways and Means Subcommittee on State Administration, she had vigorously searched for ways to involve minorities and women in the allocation of state resources. To accomplish this she had passed legislation establishing minimum

goals for every state agency with regard to state contracts awarded to minority and women-owned businesses.

Waters also created the State Contracts Registry, a periodic publication of agencies seeking bidders on contracts. In addition, she successfully steered into law a bill preventing strip searches for nonviolent misdemeanors, and legislation to help prevent chemical catastrophes by requiring firms which store such materials to submit a list of the exact nature of the toxics to the local agency responsible for dealing with such emergencies. A legislative leader who was recognized nationally, she has received honorary doctorates from both Spelman College in Atlanta, Georgia, and North Carolina A&T State University.

Waters has been a delegate to the Democratic National Convention in every presidential election since 1972, and in 1984 she served on the Convention Rules Committee. She was also chair of the Joint Committee on Public Pension Fund Investments, and was a member of the key Joint Legislative Budget Committee, the Assembly Judiciary Committee, the Elections, Reapportionment, and Constitutional Amendments Committee, the Natural Resources Committee, the Joint Committee on Legislative Ethics, the Select Committee on Assistance to Victims of Sexual Assault, and the California Commission on the Status of Women.

WATKINS, LUEVENIA, was born November 6, 1934, in Hopkinsville, Kentucky. She is divorced and the mother of nine children. She attended Booker T. Washington Elementary School, Attucks High School, and Hughes Beauty College in Clarksville, Tennessee. She is the recipient of numerous awards: Pennyrile Allied Community Service Award (1979–1984); Durretts Avenue Community Service Award (1984); United Way

Volunteer Certificate (1985); NAACP the Rev. Cephas A. Stripling Volunteer Award for Time and Service in Promoting Human Relations (1986); Outstanding Leadership Award (1986); NAACP Magistrate Daniel Massie Award for NAACP Involvement Above and Beyond the Call of Duty; Gov. Martha Layne Collins and Chairman Edward M. Coleman Award for loyalty, dedication and leadership to the Democratic Party of Kentucky. She is a member of the Honorable Order of the Kentucky Colonels.

Watkins' community service includes: Democratic chairperson, Ward 9; Voter Registration Committee; volunteer U.S.D.A. Commodities Program; member, National Council of Negro Women; member, Pennyrile Allied Community Service and City Council Member, first black woman to serve on City Council, appointed July 7, 1987, elected January 1988 for a full two-year term; and re-elected in November 1989 for two years.

WATSON, DENNIS RAHIIM, was born May 14, 1953, in Hamilton, Bermuda. He is a graduate of Harlem Preparatory School; Fordham University, Bronx, New York; Pace University and New York University. He was a former high school drop-out who had succeeded against all odds. He has served as executive director of the National Black Youth Leadership Council (NBYLC) from 1984 to date. Prior positions include: executive director for the Theatre of Everyday Life and executive assistant for the New York City Council. He has lectured and conducted workshops at over 200 colleges and universities nationwide, including Harvard, Yale, Cornell, Howard and M.I.T. He has received over 100 awards for leadership, youth development, and community service, including three presidential citations.

Watson is one of the country's most dynamic motivational and inspirational

speakers. He has been honored by the Congressonal Black Caucus with its National Black Leadership Round-table/Avon Youth Award. He was named an outstanding young man of America in 1982, 1985 and 1987. *Dollars and Sense* magazine recently selected him as one of America's Best and Brightest Young Business and Professional Men. He has presented papers at over 100 conferences nationwide. He had addressed and conducted workshops for such groups as the National Alliance of Black School Educators, the NAACP, the Higher Education Opportunity Program, National Association for Equal Opportunity, Black Career Women's Association for Equal Opportunity, Black Career Women's Execucircle and Delta Sigma Theta Sorority.

WATSON, DIANE E., was born in Los Angeles, and is a graduate of Susan Miller Dorsey High School. She received an A.A. degree from Los Angeles City College, and earned her B.A. degree in education from the University of California, Los Angeles (UCLA). She received her M.S. degree

in school psychology from California State University, Los Angeles (CSULA). In addition to being an alumna of the Kennedy School of Government at Harvard University, she earned a Ph.D. degree in educational administration from the Claremont Graduate School in 1987. She made history in 1979, when she became the first black woman elected to the California Senate. In 1982, she was re-elected to the Senate by an overwhelming 75 percent of all votes cast, and in 1986, she received over 80 percent of all votes cast in the 28th Senatorial district.

In 1975, Watson served on the Board of Education for the Los Angeles Unified School District, thereby becoming the first elected black woman to serve in this capacity. Her foremost expertise was in the field of education and she was often remembered for her very dedicated attempt to desegregate the Los Angeles Unified School District during her tenure as a board member. She taught gifted children in Okinawa and France, and enrolled in the University of Maryland classes to study Japanese and French. She mastered several foreign languages and at one time spoke them fluently.

Watson's professional experience includes elementary school teacher, acting principal, assistant superintendent of child welfare and attendance, school psychologist and associate professor at both California State University, Los Angeles and Long Beach. She also served as director of the Secondary Schools Allied Health Professions Project at the University of California, Los Angeles (UCLA) and later became a health occupations specialist for the California Department of Education. She has co-authored instructional manuals in the field of health professions and occupations, which were published by Gregg/McGraw-Hill. In the Senate, she served as chairperson of the Health and Human Services Committee, including the Subcommittee on

Bioethics and the Subcommittee on Health Care Cost Management.

Watson has served on and chaired numerous legislative committees which include: Subcommittee No. 1 (Education), the Education Committee, the Judiciary Committee, including the Subcommittee on the Rights of the Disabled, the Public Employment and Retirement Committee, the Select Committee on AIDS, the Select Committee on Border Issues, Drug Trafficking and Contraband, the Select Committee on Citizen Participation in Government, the Select Committee on Substance Abuse, and the Select Committee on Children and Youth, the Senate Research Committee on Neighborhood Violence, and the Senate Special Committee on University of California Admissions.

In 1986–1987, Watson chaired the Senate Task Force on Laws Affecting Child and Student Abuse and Its Impact on the Public Schools, and the Senate Task Force on Psychotherapist/Patients Sexual Relations. In addition, she was the co-chairperson of the Joint Select Task Force on the Changing Family and was recently appointed to the newly created Joint Legislative Committee on Surrogate Parenting. In February 1983, she was elected chairperson of the California Legislative Black Caucus, a group of black elected officials representing their constituencies in the California State Legislature. In this capacity, she directs the efforts of the Caucus members in exerting greater influence on their colleagues and on the executive branch of government.

Watson was also the founder of the National Organization of Black Elected Legislators/Women (NOBEL/Women), a coalition of black women state legislators across the country, organized to address the challenges they face in the legislature. In addition, she was a member of the California Women Legislators Caucus, who collectively identify and take positions on legislation and issues concerning women. She is a recipient of several awards and honors, including the 1989 Outstanding Legislator by the California League of Conservation Voters; the 1988 Black Women of Achievement Award from the NAACP Legal Defense Fund; and honorary degree, Doctor of Medical Sciences, from the California School of Podiatric Medicine in 1987; the 1987 "Legislator of the Year Award" from the California Association for Health Services at Home; the 1983 "Senator of the Year" from the California State University at Los Angeles, the 1982 "Alumnus of the Year Award" from the University of California at Los Angeles; and named "Senator of the Year" by the California Trial Lawyers and "Legislator of the Year" by Los Angeles City College.

Watson is a member of numerous organizations including: the California Commission on the Status of Women, the Sammy Davis, Jr. National Liver Institute board of trustees, Black Agenda Inc., Friends of Golden State Minority Foundation, California Business and

Professional Women, NAACP, Urban League, Association of School Psychologists, National Education Association, United Teachers of Los Angeles, Alpha Kappa Alpha Sorority, the Steven's House board of trustees, the California Advisory Council on Vocational Education, the California Heritage Preservation Commission, the California Educational Innovation and Planning Commission, and the California Conservation Corps/Los Angeles Board.

Watson is a member of the California Democratic Party Executive Board and has served on the Democratic Policy Commission, 1985–1986, the Democratic Platform Commission for California, 1975–1976, Delegate to Democratic National Convention, 1980, 1984, and 1988. She is one of the most capable and hard working members of the California Legislature. She represents the 28th Senatorial District which encompasses the cities of Inglewood, Hawthorne and portions of Los Angeles. The district includes the communities of Venice, Marina Del Rey, Westchester, Los Angeles International Airport, Ladera Heights, View Park, Baldwin Hills, Hancock Park, Lawndale and Crenshaw.

WATSON, GEORGE T., was born in Harrison County, Mississippi, in 1925. He is married to the former Evelena Cook and they have two daughters and two grandchildren. His educational background includes graduation from Pass Christian High School, Alcorn State University, and a master's degree from the University of California, Los Angeles (magna cum laude). In 1973, he completed requirements for Ed.D at the University of Miami. After serving as a corporal in the United States Marine Corps from 1943 to 1946, he returned to Mississippi to teach in the public school system of Grenada. In 1961, he was elected principal of the

Pass Christian School, grades 1-12. From 1969 to 1986, he served as assistant superintendent of the Pass Christian School.

Prior to being named public service commissioner in February 1988, Watson was a member of the board of trustees for the Institution of Higher Learning for the State of Mississippi from 1980–1988. A Catholic, he serves as a lecturer and eucharistic minister at Our Mother of Mercy Catholic Church in Pass Christian. He is a past president of the Parish Council; Citizen of the Year for Pass Christian in 1978; WTAM Humanitarian of the Year in 1979; and received the United Way Distinguished Achievement Award in 1982. He is a member of the Omega Psi Phi fraternity and Alpha Kappa Mu National Honor Society.

WATSON, J. WARREN, was born February 20, 1923, in Pittsburgh, Pennsylvania. He is married to Carole Whedbee Watson and they have six children, James, Meredith, Wrenna, Robert, Kevin and Shiela. He attended Bennette Elementary School, 1929–1934; Baxter Junior High School, 1934–1937; Westinghouse High School, 1937–1940; Duquesne University, B.A.

degree in economics and political science, 1946–1949; and LL.B. degree from Duquesne School of Law, 1949–1953. He served in the United States Navy in 1943–1946. He was admitted to the bar in September 1954, and started his private practice with Thomas E. Barton, Esq., and Paul F. Jones, Esq. He entered into a partnership in 1960 to 1966 with Shields, Watson & Washington in Pittsburgh. He serves as judge, Court of Common Pleas of Allegheny County Orphans' Division.

Prior to serving as a judge, Watson worked with the Unemployment Compensation Bureau (presently Bureau of Employment Security), Department of Labor and Industry of Pennsylvania during the approximate period of 1953 to 1954; Bureau of Workmen's Compensation, Department of Labor and Industry of Pennsylvania, 1956–1962; City of Pittsburgh, Department of Law, Assistant City Solicitor, 1962–1966; and A.R.A. administrator, Duquesne University, associate professor administering training for minority entrepreneurs, 1965. Instructor for minority entrepreneurs primarily in business law for the following institutions: Penn State University, Robert Morris College, Pittsburgh Technical Institute and Business & Job Development Corporation.

Watson has received many awards: first black in the county to receive the "Man of the Year" award by the Disabled American Veterans, 1969; honorary member, Chiefs of Police; United Black Ward Chairman Achiever Award, Outstanding Community Service; Certificate of Merit, National Association of Negro Business, Professional, Civic and Cultural and Political Endeavors, 1972; service award, Political Education Committee; service award, Community Action Pittsburgh, Inc.; Court Service, initiating a program utilizing referees in Land Use cases, thereby eliminating backlog; Certificate of Merit, BALSA.

Watson's professional memberships include the following associations: Carlow College, President's Council; Community Action Pittsburgh, board of directors; Community Services of Pennsylvania, trustee; Health and Welfare Association of Allegheny County, board of directors; Health Research and Services Foundation, board of directors; Ile Elegba (drug program), board of directors; NAACP; Pittsburgh Blind Association, board of directors; WQED-WQEX (public television station), board of directors; American Federation of Musicians, honorary member and legal counsel; Boy Scouts of America, Institutional Representative for Crescent Elementary School; member, Organization and Extension Committee, Allegheny Council; Business and Job Development Corporation, board of directors; Cafe Theatre Society, parliamentarian and assistant musical director.

Additional memberships include: Catholic Social Services, board of directors; Central Avenue YMCA, board of directors and chairman of Athletic Committee; Cub Scouts; Health & Welfare Association Task Force on Service to Families and Children, chairman (one-year study); Homewood-Brushton Athletic Association, legal counsel and advisor; Homewood-Brushton Community Improvement Association, Legal Counsel and advisor; Iwawa Africa Education & Cultural Productions, Inc., board of directors; Kay-Shadyside Boys Clubs, board of directors; Leukemia Society, board of directors; Mendelssohn Choir, board of directors; Opportunities Industrialization Corporation, board of directors; Select Commission for Study of Method of School Board Selection (nine-month study, 1969); Teen Exposure, board of directors; Three Rivers Youth, board of directors; Vocational Rehabilitation Center, board of directors; YMCA Indian Guides; and American Wind Symphony. He still holds the longest term of service for a black judge in the Commonwealth of Pennsylvania.

WATSON, JOHN S., a native of Camden, and a widower, he was married to the late Marie Samuels Watson; he has four children, Bonnie, William, John, Jr., and Aaron Timothy, and he has seven grandchildren. He attended the American College of Life Underwriters and the Life Underwriters Training Council. First appointed to the Board of Freeholders in 1970, he became the first African American in New Jersey ever to be elected to the board in 1972. He subsequently became the first African American in New Jersey ever to serve as president of a Freeholder board. On January 1990, he was honored with his appointment as chairman of the Appropriations Committee, the first African American to hold this post. He formerly served as the Democratic Budget officer. He had always advocated pragmatic and responsive state spending.

As a member of the Appropriations Committee, Watson has authored resolutions which fund programs in the areas of education, human services, housing, health care and the arts. Most noteworthy he sponsored the New Jersey Pre-College Program, for high school students, and the Minority Opportunity Skills Training (MOST) Program. He was the sponsor of legislation (enacted in 1988) which transferred control of the War Memorial Building from an autonomous board to the state of New Jersey. He also sponsored legislation which permanently establishes the Martin Luther King, Jr. Commemorative Commission in the New Jersey statutes.

Watson formerly served as a member of the Appropriations Subcommittee on Government Operations, Public Investments and Finance. He served as a member of the Legislative Advisory Committee on Arts and Furnishings, and the New Jersey Commission on Capital Budgeting and Planning. He formerly served as vice-chairman of the Housing and Urban Policy Committee. He served as a member of the board of directors, Junior Achievement; member, Martin Luther King, Jr. Commission; board of directors, Carver Center; member, board of directors for the New Jersey State Museum; member, N.J. Commission to Study Benefits to Be Provided to Professional Boxers; member, N.J. Child Support Commission, and member, EOF Community Advisory Board, Trenton State College. Watson has served his fifth term in the New Jersey General Assembly. He also served ten years as a member of the Mercer County Board of Chosen Freeholders.

WATTLETON, ALYCE FAYE, was born July 8, 1943, in St. Louis, Missouri, the only child of George and Ozie Wattleton. She married Franklin Gordon and they have one child

Felicia. She skipped kindergarten and the first grade. She entered Ohio State University in Columbus, Ohio, at 16, and obtained her bachelor's degree in nursing in 1964. While in college she worked part-time at a children's hospital where she was exposed to battered children. After graduating from college, she taught at the Miami Valley Hospital School of Nursing in Dayton, Ohio, for two years. In 1966, she won a full scholarship to Columbia University's master's degree program in maternal and infant health care.

Specializing in midwifery during her year at Columbia, Wattleton trained at Harlem Hospital. There, she witnessed the hardship borne by women who tried to terminate their pregnancies during the days of illegal abortion. She remained in close contact with the victims of maladministered, illegal abortions as a public health nurse for two years following the receipt of her master's degree in 1967. As assistant director of the Montgomery County Combined Public Health District in Dayton, she worked to expand local prenatal health care services. Her success resulted in her appointment in 1970 as executive director of the local Planned Parenthood board, which she had been asked to join 18 months earlier.

During Wattleton's seven and a half years at the helm of Planned Parenthood in Dayton, she weathered criticism from all sides of the abortion and birth control debate during the 1970s. Shortly after, the Supreme Court decided in 1977 that states were not required to fund abortions for indigent women, two-thirds of the states enacted laws that deprived poor women of equal access to safe and legal abortions. In 1978, she was named president of Planned Parenthood. In January 1992, Wattleton announced that she would leave Planned Parenthood in April 1992 to host a daytime television talk show.

Wattleton has received numerous humanitarian awards and belongs to the board of the United States Committee for UNICEF, the Young Presidents' Organization, and the National Advisory Committee of the Tufts School of Public Service.

WEARY, BILLY RAY, JR., was born May 9, 1944, in Angie, Louisiana to Billy R. Weary, Sr., and Della R. Bridges Weary. He received a B.S. degree in criminal justice from American Technology University in Texas, and has also trained and was skilled through many other courses such as Law Enforcement, Military and Management. He has been a resident of Columbus, Georgia, since 1972, and is a retired chief warrant officer for the military with multiple assignments. He is a member of Wynnton Hill Baptist Church in Columbus, and an active member of various organizations. He was the founder and vice president of the Georgia Marshal's Association and N.O.B.L.E., where he presided over 23 counties.

Weary was the first black marshal of Muscogee County, Georgia, taking office on January 1, 1989. He realized that on a technical level he could not function as only a symbol of black political power, and that he would be different from what we call the "old heads" or "politics as usual" characterizations. He knew and proved that the only way to impact was to be organizationally sound, proficient in professionalism, high in integrity and loyal to the community's needs. His is the saga of a man who has used both brains and intuition, toughness and sensitivity, to achieve his ends.

WELLS, EVELYN M., was born October 16, 1946, in San Diego, California. She is married and the mother of three children. From 1976 to date, she has served in Lynwood Unified School District as financial supervisor for the Associated Student Body at Lynwood High School in Lynwood, California, controlling the financial functions pertaining to student body funds and collections authorized by the Board of Education. She operated the financial program of the student body in accordance with established policies; supervised and participated in the operation of the office, school activities, and the student store, ordering, selling, displaying and inventorying.

Wells' community involvement has been outstanding: member of Truevine Missionary Baptist Church; mayor of the city of Lynwood, January 1989; re-elected to Lynwood City Council, November 1989; Democratic Women's Study Group, June 2, 1989; Lynwood Lions Club, first vice president, April 21, 1989; California Elected Women's Association for Education and Research, April 1989; National Council of Negro Women, March 1989; National Women's Political Caucus, member, February 1989; St. Francis Medical Center Guild, member, 1988; councilwoman/mayor pro tem, city of Lynwood, November 1985; controller of California Democratic Council, 1988 to present; chair of 31st Congressional District Democratic Council, 1988 to present; founder of 31st Congressional District Democratic Headquarters, 1988 to present; board member of Lynwood Senior Advisory Board, 1988 to present; 4th vice-president, Minority Political Women, USA, 1988 to present; founder and vice president of Lynwood Democratic Club, 1987 to present; treasurer of 31st Congressional District Rainbow Coalition, 1987 to present.

Additional community activities include: member Martin Luther King, Jr. Democratic Club, 1987 to present; member South Gate Democratic Club, 1987 to present; member Gardena Valley Democratic Club, 1989; marched against drugs and gangs, 1986; member Association of Lynwood School Administrators, 1986 to present; delegate/board member So. Board of California Democratic Council, 1986 to present; member of Chamber of Commerce, 1985; member Lynwood Local Development, 1985; member of Committee on Wellness for Women at St. Francis Hospital, 1985; volunteer accountant UNCF Telethon, 1985 to 1987; delegate contract Cities Assoc., 1986 to present; treasurer/board member Lynwood Area Sheriffs Activities League, 1985 to present; board member/founder Official Miss Lynwood Scholarship Pageant, 1985 to present; president/co-founder Lynwood Sports Association, 1984 to present; member Black History Month Committee, 1985; marched with city employees against no salary increases, 1984.

Wells' further community activities include: marched against prostitution in Lynwood, 1984; protested against malathion spraying, 1984; Lynwood Unified School District Compensatory Education Advisory Council, 1984–1985; member Lynwood High School PTSA, 1986 to present; member

Hosler Junior High PTSA, 1984–1986; member Washington Elementary School PTSA, 1985–1986; Parent Booster Sports Club West, AAU Team, 1982–1986; member Mid-Cities Alliance of Black School Educators, 1983–1985; member California Association of School Business Officials, 1983 to present; vice-president of California School Employees Association, 1981–1982; member Concerned Citizens of Lynwood, 1981–1983; and basketball coach for girls at Lynwood Park, 1982, 1st place in the state of California Division C, 1982.

WELLS-DAVIS, MARGIE ELAINE, was born April 27, 1944. She is married and the mother of one child. A graduate of Fulton High School in Fulton, Missouri, in 1962, she received a B.A. degree in English/education from Simpson College, an M.A. degree in student personnel and administration in higher education from Syracuse University, and a Ph.D. degree in (interdisciplinary) educational psychology, community planning and social psychology from the University of Cincinnati. She has served as the Human Resources Department manager, Food and Olestra Products Division, Procter and Gamble Company since 1977. She has spent over 20 years as a successful line and staff manager in a variety of organizations (public, probate, education, and social welfare). Her specialty is organization effectiveness, making her strengths: program design, management consulting, group process, training design, delivery and counseling.

Wells-Davis' prior positions include: senior organizational analyst, Management Systems Division and Affirmative Coordinator, both positions held at Procter & Gamble; director of Staff and Organizational Development and supervisor, Medical Social Work, Medical Services Division, Cincinnati Health Department; sociologist, Division of Community Management Systems, Bureau of Community Environmental Management for the United States Public Health Service; educational coordinator for Narcotic Addiction Program of the Central Community Health Board; counselor, Supportive Services for Syracuse University; assistant to Dean of Students, assistant to Dean of Women, head resident counselor at the University of Cincinnati; assistant supervisor of residence for Job Corps Center for Women in Jersey City, New Jersey; teacher/counselor, Young Mothers Education Development Program for the Syracuse Board of Education, Syracuse, New York; and teacher for Beaumont High School in St. Louis, Missouri.

Wells-Davis is the recipient of many honors: Missouri Curators Scholarship, National Methodist Scholarship, Simpson College Honors Scholarship, Syracuse University Student Deanship, *Who's Who in American Colleges and Universities,* Epsilon Sigma (Phi Beta Kappa), Gold Key (Mortar Board), Resolution for Outstanding Service from city of Cincinnati (Health Department), Outstanding Young Women of America, *Who's Who Among Black Americans, Who's Who in the Midwest, Who's Who Among Women in the World* and YMCA Black Achiever.

WHEELER, ALBERT HAROLD, was born in 1915 in St. Louis, Missouri. He married Emma (Monteith) and they have three daughters, Mary, Alma and Nancy. A graduate of Sumner High School in St. Louis, he earned a B.S. degree in biology from Lincoln University in Pennsylvania; an M.A. degree in microbiology from Iowa State University in Ames in 1937; and an M.A. degree in public health from the University of Michigan in Ann Arbor in 1938. In 1944, he earned an M.D. degree in public health from the University of

Michigan. To date he is an associate professor of microbiology at the university.

Dr. Wheeler took office as the first black mayor of Ann Arbor on April 30, 1975, amid considerable controversy concerning an unusual election procedure that propelled him into office. In November 1974, Ann Arbor voters approved a city charter amendment providing for a preferential voting system that allows voters to indicate on ballots their first, second and third choices for mayor. In the April 7, 1975 mayoral election, he polled 40 percent of the first-choice votes, the incumbent drew 49 percent, and a third party candidate took 11 percent. Because neither won a majority of the votes, the third place candidate was removed from the race and her second-choice votes were tabulated and added to the other two candidates' totals, in accordance with local election procedures. Most of these second-choice votes went to Dr. Wheeler, putting him ahead of the incumbent by less than 1 percent. The 1975 election was the first political race he ever entered. The major issues of the campaign were fiscal responsibility, development of a city human services department, establishment of a rent control commission, and allocation of funds for a day care center.

WHIPPER, LUCILLE SIMMONS, is married to the Rev. Benjamin J. Whipper, Sr. She is pastor of St. Matthew and Charity Baptist Churches, a mother and grandmother. She is a graduate of Talladega College, Talladega, Alabama, with a B.S. degree in economics and sociology, an M.A. degree in political science from the University of Chicago, and a counseling education certification from South Carolina State College and the University of South Carolina. She held a teacher of social studies and high school counselor position at Charles-

ton Public Schools, from 1949 to 1972.

Whipper's prior positions include: assistant to the president and director of the Office of Human Relations, College of Charleston, Charleston, South Carolina, 1972–1976, 1978–1981; director of Project ESSA (Elementary and Secondary School Act), a $1.5 million Charleston County Schools Project, 1976–1978, and she retired from the College of Charleston in 1981.

Some of Whipper's elected offices were: Charleston School District 20 board, 1978–1982; vice chairman, Charleston County Democratic Party Convention, 1972, and representative, South Carolina House of Representatives House District 109, member of the South Carolina House Medical, Military, Public and Municipal Affairs Committee, 1987. Other appointed positions held include: S.C. Advisory Committee, International Women's Year; Mayors Committee on Human Relations; Charleston Commission on Women; S.C. Mental Health Commission; S.C. Advisory Committee for Technical and Vocational Education; S.C. Legislative Committee to Study Minimum Competency Testing and S.C. Human Affairs Commission.

Whipper is the recipient of many honors and awards, including: honoree, AKA Twenty-Four Distinguished Women; Gamma XI Omega Distinguished Service Award; South Atlantic Region, AKA Outstanding Soror Award, 1987; Omega Psi Phi Community Service Award; honoree, YWCA Tribute to Women; Federally Employed Women Distinguished Service Award (first to be given a non-federal employee); Charleston Chapter Links, Women of the Year, 1981, and honorary Doctorate of Humane Letters, Morris College, 1989.

WHITE, AUGUSTUS A., was born June 4, 1936, in Memphis, Tennessee, the son of Augustus White and Vivian Dandridge White. He is married to Anita Otteno, and they have three children, Alissa, Antina and Annica. He is a scientist who has distinguished himself on many fronts, most notably, orthopedics. He was Orthopaedic Surgeon-in-Chief at Beth Israel Hospital in Boston, Massachusetts, a major Harvard teaching hospital, and professor of Orthopaedic Surgery Technology. His career goals shifted from psychiatry to orthopaedics as a result of his experiences on the football team while an undergraduate at Brown University. A star athlete, as well as a scholar, he became fascinated by orthopaedic treatment of sports injuries and went on to specialize in orthopaedic surgery. While he was a medical student at Stanford University, he became interested in the complex problem of back pain.

Following graduation, White's skills were further noted at Yale Medical Center where he completed his orthopaedic residency and, subsequently at the Karolinska Institute in Sweden, where he earned his doctorate in medical science for his research on the biomechanics of the spine. He returned to Yale Medical School where he subsequently became a professor of orthopaedic surgery and director of the Engineering Laboratory for Musculoskeletal Disease, a currently active laboratory which he was instrumental in founding. In collaboration with a colleague at Beth Israel, he helped to institute that hospital's Orthopaedic Biomechanics Laboratory. This physician continues to concentrate much of his teaching, research and patient care on problems of the spine.

While his professional life has drawn him to the classroom, laboratory and lecture hall, White was most committed to direct patient care. However, stimulated by a desire to better meet the recent challenges in health care management, White completed the Advanced Management Program at the Harvard Business School where he was selected by his classmates to deliver the commencement address. He was an avid researcher whose major efforts were directed toward study of the spine and fracture healing. He has written and collaborated on more than 175 scientific publications including: chapters, books and articles. Most noted among them was the highly regarded, definitive work *The Clinical Biomechanics of the Spine*. This book, the first of its kind, was designed to present scientific material about spinal mechanics so as to provide direct application to the comprehensive care of patients with spine problems. An updated second edition of this publication is now in press.

White has also co-edited a book for scientists and physicians entitled *Symposium on Idiopathic Low Back Pain*. This work emanated from an international meeting chaired by White and designed specifically to review current knowledge and suggest future research on the scientific aspects of the cause of back pain. Convinced that patient education was a major factor in the successful resolution of back pain problems, he had completed a second edition of a book for patients entitled *Your Aching Back* published in 1990.

White is the recipient of numerous awards, including: the United States Jaycees "Ten Outstanding Young Men" Award, and the Martin Luther King, Jr. Medical Achievement Award. Among his credits are the Kappa Delta Award, a national honor granted for outstanding orthopaedic research, and the Eastern Orthopaedic Association's award for excellent spine research. He was a member of the Brown University Board of Fellows, and a past trustee at Northfield Mount Hermon School. He received a Bronze Star which he earned while stationed as a captain in the U.S. Army Medical Corps in Vietnam where he did extensive volunteer work in a leper colony. He was the recipient of the first William Rogers Award, an award given by the Associated Alumni of Brown University. This prize was in recognition of his contributions to society and carries the words of the Brown Charter "discharging the offices of life with usefulness and reputation."

In 1987, White was awarded an honorary Doctor of Humane Letters by the University of New Haven. He is listed in *Who's Who in America, Who's Who Among Black Americans,* and *American Men and Women in Science* and *Town and Country* magazine's *Directory of Best Medical Specialists in the U.S.A.* He is a member of the American Academy of Orthopaedic Surgeons, the American Orthopaedic Association, the Orthopaedic Research Society, the Scoliosis Research Society, the International Society for the Study of Lumbar Spine, and the American Orthopaedic Society for Sports Medicine, and was a founding member and past president of the Cervical Spine Research Society. Dr. White has served at the National Institutes of Health as a member of the advisory council of the National Institutes of Arthritis, Diabetes, and Digestive and Kidney Disease.

WHITE, JESSE C., JR., was born on June 23, 1934, in Alton, Illinois. He received a B.S. degree from Alabama State College in 1957. Jesse was a street fighter as a kid growing up in the Chicago ghetto. But there came a time in his 20s when he tired of the endless cycle of violence, the gang wars bloodying the summer nights, the hearses lined up outside the housing projects the morning after. A grade-school phys-ed. instructor, he resolved to fight back the only way he knew how, with his skills as an athlete and a teacher.

It was in 1959, when White launched the Jesse White Tumbling Team, draining his own savings account to purchase uniforms. His curriculum consisted of acrobatics and hope. His teaching style was drill-instructor tough; most of his kids came from fatherless homes, and he became the head of a vastly extended family. You don't get a tumble unless you play by his rules: no smoking, no drinking, no drugs, no gangs, no skipping school. Most obey; only 35 have washed out in 28 years. A total of 625 have stayed the course, 78 of them on the current team.

He likes to say he has outrecruited the gangs on his Near North Side turf. His kids put on 445 shows a year in Chicago and far beyond. About 3,600 kids are on a waiting list.

Athletics became White's form of activism because it is what he is best at. He was a baseball and basketball star at Alabama State University and signed a contract in 1956 with the Chicago Cubs. He was drafted into the Army before he could report to spring training. That delayed his baseball development and he never made it out of the minors.

White also serves as the state Representative for the 8th District, D-Chicago, where he chaired the Human Services Committee, which covers all state social programs. His district includes Cabrini-Green and the Gold Coast. Hollywood's Longbow Productions bought rights to his life story. It may become a two-hour television movie with the proceeds going to the tumbling team.

WHITE, KAREN L., is a graduate of Indiana State University, Terre Haute, with a B.S. degree in psychology/ social work, 1973; an M.S. degree in education/guidance and counseling

from Indiana University, Bloomington, 1979; and and an M.S. degree in public affairs candidate for 1993 from Indiana University at South Bend, with a major in management of public affairs. She has served as interim director of the University Division, Indiana University at South Bend since 1989. She is responsible for providing a comprehensive orientation and academic advising system for all entering freshman students. In addition, she has the responsibility for providing an ongoing counseling program for approximately 1,200 other students in the division who are returning freshmen and sophomores. These duties include the certification of students who qualify for admittance to upper divisions and the academic review of all students, which includes dismissals; also, a close working relationship with the faculty and other members of the Student Services professional staff.

White's prior positions include: affirmative action officer, Indiana University at South Bend, Chancellor's Office; project director, forums for youth self-sufficiency at Indiana University, School of Public and Environmental affairs; assistant director, University Division, Indiana University at South Bend; project director, Special Service Program at Indiana University; adjunct career planner, Center for Educational Opportunity, University of Notre Dame; and counselor/administrative assistant, Special Services, program counselor, Special Services Program, social worker/ counselor, South Bend Housing Authority, all at Indiana University at South Bend.

White was elected as a board of trustees member at South Bend Community School Corporation, in 1989. She is the recipient of many awards: LaSalle High School Black Culture Society's Outstanding Community Service Award, 1990; Community Service Award, Solidarity Day, 1989; featured in the *South Bend Tribune*'s "Accent" series, 1988; selected as a panel reviewer for the National Department of Health and Human Services, in 1988; Indiana Mid-American Educational Opportunity Personnel, Outstanding Service Award, 1979; and United Negro College Fund Distinguished Service Award Citation in 1977. Her professional affiliations are numerous.

WHITE, MICHAEL R., was born and raised in Glenville, Cleveland, and married Tamera Kay. He was educated in Cleveland Public Schools and graduated from Glenville High School in 1969. He earned a B.A. degree in education and a master's degree in public administration from Ohio State University. He served as a research associate, and later as a fellow, at the Academy for Contemporary Problems in Columbus, Ohio. There he created and codirected the Columbus Area Leadership Program. This program served as a model for Leadership in Cleveland and similar programs throughout the United States. He also

researched and wrote extensively on new strategies for saving older urban neighborhoods.

From 1975–1976, White served as special assistant to the mayor of Columbus, concentrating his efforts on housing programs. He wrote and directed the Columbus Urban Homesteading Program, a project designed to stem the tide of housing decay and abandonment in older parts of the city. He then moved back to Cleveland to work as the administrative assistant to the Cleveland City Council President. In 1977, he was elected to the City Council. He served for almost seven years as a member of the Finance Committee and three years as chairman of the Community Development Committee. He was a member of the 1979 Leadership Cleveland Class.

In 1984, he was appointed to the Ohio Senate for the 21st District to fill the unexpired term of Senator M. Morris Jackson. He was twice elected assistant minority whip. He served on the Judiciary, Ways and Means and Rules committees. In the Health and Human Services Committee he was the ranking minority leader. While in the Ohio Senate, he introduced legislation dealing with rape, home mortgages, foreclosure, pharmaceutical assistance for the elderly and drug abuse. His dedication to health and human service issues earned him an appointment as vice chairman of the Human Services Committee of the National Conference of State Legislators. Even with his statewise success, he remained committed to realize his lifelong dream of becoming mayor of the city of Cleveland.

White was considered a long shot in the mayoral election but captured second place in a field of five candidates in a nonpartisan primary and went on to win 56 percent of the vote in the general election. In a campaign with little money, but emphasizing unity, he focused on five issues: revitalization and preservation of neighborhoods;

economic development and job creation; improvement of public safety; better city-wide race relations and improvement of public education.

Inaugurated as the 54th mayor of the city of Cleveland on New Year's Day, January 1, 1990, at the age of 38, White became the second black mayor in the history of Cleveland. The inauguration ceremonies attracted more than 7,000 Clevelanders and included an interfaith ceremony at the Old Stone Church and an Inaugural Ball at the Cleveland Convention Center. In his inaugural address, "A Vision for a New Decade," he asserted, "we are here today to mark the coming of change and to welcome the birth of a new era. Let it be a new decade of hope, in a time of doubt, a new decade of commitment and courage for our entire community. I say let us join our voices today in a clarion call to action and justice. Confident that together we can meet any challenge and reclaim the dream of a greater Cleveland for our children, our neighborhood and ourselves."

In his first six months of office, White had already made great steps at achieving his goals. Putting safety and education as his first priorities, he has reorganized the police force to get more officers on the streets and has brought together educators, community, civic leaders and businessmen for a continuing dialogue on the state and future of our education system. In a new housing preservation policy more houses in Cleveland will be saved and renovated. Mayor White also led the campaign to pass an excise tax to partially fund a new baseball stadium and arena to house the Cleveland Indians and Cleveland Cavs. This project will create thousands of jobs and spawn new development in the Prospect-Ontario area.

_____

WHITE, VAN FREEMAN, was born August 2, 1924. He married Javarese Ewing and they have two children, Perri and Jovoni. He is a graduate of Patrick Henry High, 1943, audited classes at the University of Minneapolis, 1950, 1952, and attended the University of Minneapolis periodically, 1967, 1969 and 1970. He worked for Sally Distribution and the White House Restaurant at night. Later, he realized he needed more money and applied and started working for the Park Board, moving on to Public Works for the city of Minneapolis. In 1968, he worked for the Department of Economic Securities as an employment interviewer.

In 1979, White was elected as city councilman and served the people of Minneapolis for ten years. Much of his years had been spent serving his community on neighborhood boards and committees. He served on those boards strictly as a volunteer, and not a paid employee. His love for his ward and city took many hours of his evenings because he believed so strongly in his ward. His daughter, who was very young, had once asked him why he spent so many hours on a committee to build a park by Willard School when by the time it was built she would be too old to use it. His answer to her was, "I'm not working to build it for you but for those after you."

White's prior positions include: construction worker; shipping clerk at Minnesota Moccasin; shipping clerk at Earl Partridge, Inc.; city of Minneapolis Public Works, construction worker, acting assistant to supervisor on construction crew, record keeping, timekeeper; employment interviewer for Minnesota State Employment Services. He was appointed acting assistant office manager for the Northside Branch of the State Employment Services (now called Minnesota Department of Economic Security); Minneapolis City Council, 5th Ward council member, in 1980–1989; chair of Government Operations committee; chair of MCDA, Community Development, Claims, Licenses and Consumer Services.

White was the recipient of many awards: Achievement Award from State Employment Service; Commendation Award from City Council for Workable Program; Commendation from the National Alliance of Business Men, Award from the Committee on Urban Environment (CUE); letter of recognition from Senator Hubert H. Humphrey, community work; letter of recognition from Senator Walter Mondale, community work; and *Who's Who in Black America*.

WILDER, LAWRENCE DOUGLAS, was born January 17, 1931, in Richmond, Virginia. The grandson of slaves, he was named after Frederick Douglass and poet Paul Lawrence Dunbar. He was reared in the Church Hill section of Richmond. He is the father of three children, Lynn, Lawrence, Jr., and Loren. He is a graduate of Virginia Union University with a B.S. degree in chemistry, in 1951, and a J.D. degree from Howard University School of Law, 1959. He is a former founder and partner of the law firm of Wilder,

Gregory and Martin, 1959–1990. He served in the U.S. Army in Korea and was awarded the Bronze Star for heroism in ground combat. He was elected as governor of Virginia in November 1989, and inaugurated January 13, 1990.

Wilder previously was elected as Lieutenant Governor of Virginia. During his four-year term, he served as chairman of the National Democratic Lieutenant Governors' Association, and chairman of the National Conference of Lieutenant Governors' Drug Interdiction Task Force in 1985. Elected to the Virginia Senate by voters of Richmond in 1969 and re-elected in 1971, 1975, 1979 and 1983. He served as chairman of the Senate Committee on Transportation, chairman of the Senate Committee on Rehabilitation and Social Services, chairman of the Senate Committee on Privileges and Elections, chairman of the Virginia Advisory Legislative Council, and chairman of the Democratic Steering Committee.

Wilder was consistently named one of the most effective persons in state government in an annual survey by the *Norfolk Virginian-Pilot*. From 1971 to 1988, some major legislation included: prohibiting or regulating the possession, sale or distribution of drug paraphernalia; bringing sickle cell anemia under State Health Department regulations; requiring compulsory school attendance; establishing a state holiday for Martin Luther King, Jr., on January 15; requiring investigations and hearings of complaints about discriminatory housing practices by a licensed real estate agent or agency; increasing penalties for escape from prison or jail from a misdemeanor to a felony; eliminating parole eligibility for an inmate who escapes while serving a life sentence, and doubling the time capital murderers must spend behind bars before being eligible for parole.

Wilder's professional member-

ships include: American Bar Association; Virginia State Bar; Old Dominion Bar Association; American Trial Lawyers Association; Permanent Member of the Judicial Conference of the Fourth Circuit (federal); National Association of Criminal Defense Lawyers; Life Member of the National Bar Association.

WILKINS, ELMER V., was born in Roper, North Carolina. He is married to the former Elizabeth C. Witherspoon of Greensboro, North Carolina, and they have two daughters, Estelle and Corinne. He attended elementary and secondary school in Roper; received a B.S. degree in math and science, and an M.A. degree in secondary education from North Carolina Central University. He was elected mayor of Roper in 1975, 1977, 1979, 1981, 1983, 1985 and 1987.

Wilkins' prior positions include: elected town councilman of Roper, 1967, 1969, 1971 and 1973; principal of Washington County Union School, 1941–1975; and executive director of Eastern North Carolina Opportunities Industries of Eastern North Carolina, sponsored through a $75,000 venture grant from Weyerhaeuser Foundation.

He is the recipient of many awards, including: Mt. Eprew Baptist Church Citizen of the Year Award for Distinguished Service in Education, religion and Government, 1967; Community Service Award given by the Epsilon Chi Lambda Chapter of Alpha Phi Alpha Fraternity, Inc., 1972; Abundant Life Ministry Award for Services in Education, Religious and Civic Activities, 1975; class of 1950, J. J. Clemmons High School Award, Dedicated Services in Education as Principal of J. J. Clemmons High School and to the Community of Roper, 1975; Distinguished Citizen Award by N.C. Governor Jim Hunt, 1979; service award by N.C. Black Leadership Caucus, 1979; the Order of the Long Leaf Pine Award by Gov. Jim Hunt, January 1985; Booker T. Washington Foundation Award, a Tribute to the Nation's 244 Black Mayors Certificate for Outstanding Service, November 10, 1983, Washington, D.C.; N.C. Distinguished Ser-

vice Award, Lt. Gov. Jimmy Green, December 1, 1984; Ordained Deacon of Mt. Eprew Baptist Church; and life membership, NAACP.

WILLIAMS, AVON N., JR., was born December 22, 1921, Knoxville, Tennessee, to Avon Nyanza Williams, Sr., and Carrie Belle Williams, both deceased. He is married to the former Joan Marie Bontemps, and they have two children, Avon Nyanza Williams, III, and Wendy Janette Williams. He was educated in the public schools of Knoxville; received a B.A. degree in 1940 from Johnson C. Smith University, Charlotte, North Carolina, and an LL.B degree in 1947 and an LL.M. degree in 1948, from Boston University, Boston, Massachusetts. He was admitted to the Massachusetts Bar in April 1948, and to the Tennessee Bar in August 1948. He was admitted to practice in the United States Court of Appeals for the Sixth Circuit, 1953; United States Court of Military Appeals, 1956; and the Supreme Court of the United States, 1963. He was engaged in the general practice of law in Knoxville, Tennessee, from 1949–1953, and in general practice of law in association with the Hon. Z. Alexander Looby in Nashville, Tennessee, from 1953–1969. He has been in private practice of law in Nashville since 1969.

Williams was elected senator for the 19th District of Tennessee, and has served from 1968 to date. His prior positions include: delegate for the National Democratic Convention, 1972. He is the recipient of numerous citations and awards. His professional affiliations include: founding member, 1962, and general chairman, Tennessee Voters Council, 1966 to 1985; founding member, 1962, and former president, 1962–1966, for the Davidson County Independent Political Council; member, State Democratic Presidential Steering Committee, 1964; Omega Psi Phi Fraternity; Sigma Pi Phi Fraternity; and Lt. Col., JAGC, USAR (retired).

WILLIAMS, BILLY DEE, was born April 6, 1937, in New York, New York, the son of William December Williams, an immigrant from the West Indies, and Loretta Ann Williams. He has a twin sister. He married Teruko Nakagami and they have three children, Corey, Miyako, and Hanako. His mother, Loretta Ann Williams, was instrumental in launching his career. While working as an elevator operator at the Lyceum Theater in New York City, Kurt Weill and his wife, Lotte Lenya, were looking for someone to play a page boy. When they discovered Loretta Williams had a little boy, who was cute, they had him walk across the stage, and he has been in show business ever since. It was his mother's teaching that schooled him in the pitfalls of over-inflated egos and human values. When he was 11 years old he weighed 150 pounds, but his mother would always encourage him to pursue his dreams.

Williams doesn't have to do anything to arouse excitement, women just love him, whether it's in a photograph or on the silver screen. To his list of credits that includes TV appearances are *The Cool World*, *A Taste of Honey*, *Star Wars*, *Halleliyah Baby*, *Firebrand of Florence*, *Brian's Song*, *Lady Sings the Blues*, *Mahogany*, *I Have a Dream*, *Return of the Jedi*, *Night Hawks*, *Fear City*, *Deadly Illusion*, *The Glass House*, *The Hostage Tower*, *Time Bomb*, *Children of Divorce*, *Chiefs*, *Shooting Stars*, *King of Ragtime*, "The FBI," "Mission Impossible," "Mod Squad," "Police Woman," "Dynasty," "The Jeffersons," *The Empire Strikes Back*, *Batman* (movie), *Dangerous Passions* and *The Last Angry Man*.

WILLIAMS, CHARLOTTE L., was born May 28, 1928, in Flint, Michigan. She is married to Charles Clifford Williams, Sr., and they have three children, Charlita, Charles, Jr., and Cathryn. In November 1965, she was appointed to the Genesee County Board of Supervisors, representing the

9th Ward/4th District where she always lived. In 1967, she was appointed chairperson of the Welfare Committee and secretary of the Juvenile Home, Mental Health Services and Medical Service Committee. After she had served on a subcommittee and visited hospitals in Michigan and New York, recommendations were made for both of the county's hospitals to be governed by a single board. In June 1968, the county's Hospital Governing Board and the Board of County Institutions were established. (She was appointed for a two-year term and served as secretary-treasurer, and reappointed to a second three-year term. She served as vice president six years, and as president in 1979.)

Williams was the first black woman elected to public office in Genesee. She served as chairperson of the Social Welfare Committee under whose umbrella were the Department of Social Services, Community Mental Health and the County Health Department. She continued to serve on many committees relating to government operations. She has also served on special committees for Genesee County, Mott Foundation of the Flint Board of Education, Quinn Chapel, A.M.E., the Flint Branch of the NAACP, and numerous other organizations, along with receiving many honors and awards.

WILLIAMS, DOUGLAS LEE (DOUG), was born August 9, 1955, in Zachary, Louisiana, one of eight children of Robert Sr. and Laura Williams. Doug was a star in baseball, basketball and football in a rural, predominantly black Chaneyville High School. By his senior year, he was a major league baseball prospect. Williams overcame more than mediocrity while playing American Legion ball in Baton Rouge in 1971, the first year Legion teams were integrated. His brother Robert, Jr. was the league's only black coach, and his Central Sealtest team had the only black players— Doug, his brother Manzie and three others. In one American Legion game, he struck out 20 batters. However, he preferred football. Nicknamed the Rifleman because of his powerful arm, Williams passed for 1,800 yards and 22 touchdowns in his final season as Chaneyville High's quarterback.

Williams was also the Chaneyville Dragons' leading basketball scorer for three straight years. He wasn't regarded highly by college recruiters, mostly because there were only 25 students in his senior high school class and the level of Williams' competition couldn't be judged. Only Grambling, Southern University and Mississippi Valley State offered scholarships. After a telephone call from Eddie Robinson, the legendary football coach of the Grambling Tigers, Williams was off to Grambling. The first season he was red shirted. The next season he was the third-string quarterback until the fifth game. Then he got his chance and directed Grambling to a 21-0 victory over Tennessee State. He was the No. 1 quarterback for the rest of his Grambling career. In 1978, Williams was the first black selected as an All-American quarterback by the Associated Press.

In the same year, the Tampa Bay Buccaneers picked Williams as the first black quarterback ever to be chosen in the first round of the National Football League draft. Prior to his arrival, the

Bucs had finished 0–14 and 2–12. They made the playoffs three times during Williams' five seasons in town, but he remained the punchline of jokes that questioned everything from his efficiency to his intelligence. In 1979, he took the Bucs to the NFC Championship game against the L.A. Rams. His critics grew after he completed only 2 of 13 passes before he left the game in the third quarter with a torn biceps muscle. Never mind that his backup, Mike Rae, also completed only 2 of 13 passes, Williams was given much of the blame for the Bucs' 9–0 loss. Tampa's ownership closed its wallet when his contract expired following the 1982 season. He was hopelessly entangled in a contract dispute.

At the time Williams, one of the league's 28 starting quarterbacks, was earning a meager $125,000, making him 46th on the NFL quarterback salary list. He asked for $600,000 a year, but the Bucs offered $400,000. It was also in 1982, when he married Janice Goss, his best friend, soulmate and sweetheart he had met at his freshman year at Grambling, and dated for eight years. They had one child, Ashley Monique, who was born January 14, 1983. In the middle of negotiations Janice, his wife of less than a year, complained of headaches. Doctors discovered a brain tumor the size of a grapefruit, and she was dead a week later. Their daughter Ashley was less than three months old. "Suddenly, I didn't give a damn if I played another down of football or not," he said.

He finally left Tampa Bay in 1983 for the United States Football League and signed with the Oklahoma Outlaws. He was known as an oak in the pocket, a passer who stands back there and waits for the receiver to come upon, taking hits, to come open — and waits, and waits, he would take a lick. When the league folded in 1986, he got one phone call. It was from Joe Gibbs, the coach of the Washington Redskins.

He became a Redskin but in his first season he threw just one pass. Jay Schroeder was Washington's quarterback all the way to the Super Bowl. It was in 1987 that he met and married Lisa Robinson.

In the 1987 season, he became the first black quarterback to start in the Super Bowl. He passed for more yardage than any quarterback in Super Bowl history with 340; he led the Redskins to 35 second-quarter points, more points than were scored in any previous Super Bowl half; he threw four touchdown passes in the second quarter , as many as were ever thrown in a game, and including a record tying 80-yard touchdown pass; he engineered a comeback from a 10-0 deficit, the biggest comeback in Super Bowl history. Williams, playing less than 24 hours after root canal surgery, was named the game's Most Valuable Player.

It was through Williams' MVP-quality effort in Super Bowl XXII that the myth of the black quarterback not having the leadership qualities to take an NFL Team to the championship was finally laid to rest. The next day he returned to Reston, Virginia, his home during the football season. The following day, he received treatment on his strained left knee. The day after that he joined teammates to meet President Reagan at the White House and participate in a parade before an estimated 700,000 people in downtown Washington. Whatever the color of his skin, Williams now was golden, his name shining alongside those of Terry Bradshaw, Joe Montana, Johnny Unitas, and Joe Namath. "This is a tribute not only to a black quarterback, but to a very great quarterback." Williams stood in the bright TV lights of victory afterward and said, "I didn't come here with the Washington Redskins as a black quarterback, I came here as a quarterback with the Washington Redskins to play a football game."

WILLIAMS, EDDIE N., a graduate of the University of Illinois, he received a B.S. degree in 1954; a D.H.L. (honorary) degree from Bowie State University in 1980; an LL.B degree from the University of the District of Columbia, 1986. He has served as president for the Joint Center for Political and Economic Studies in Washington, D.C., since 1972. His prior positions include: vice president for Public Affairs for the University of Chicago, 1969–1972; director, Center for Policy Study, University of Chicago, 1970–1972, and Foreign Service Reserve Officer, U.S. Department of state, Washington, D.C., 1961–1968.

Williams is the recipient of many awards: Southern Christian Leadership Conference Award, 1989; Distinguished National Service and Leadership Award, 1989; Distinguished National Service and Leadership Award, Greater Memphis Minority Business Enterprise EEO Consortium, 1989; MacArthur Foundation Prize Fellows Award, 1988; University of Illinois at Urbana-Champaign Black Alumni Association Alumni Achievement Award, 1988; Liberty Award, National Black Caucus of Local Elected Officials, 1987; and Candace Award for Public Service, National Coalition of 100 Black Women, 1984.

Williams' professional affiliations include: National Coalition on Black Voter Participation (chairman); Substance Abuse Strategy Initiative (chairman); Children's Defense Fund; the Foundation Center; the Institute for Educational Leadership; Carnegie Council on Ethics and International Affairs; the Maxima Corporation; National Endowment for Democracy; WETA Television; Independent Sector; and the Riggs National Bank of Washington Board of Consultants; Black Leadership Forum; Council on Foreign Relations; the Kettering Foundation Associates Program; Visiting Committee, University of Maryland Afro-American Studies Program; Overseas Development Council; Kappa Tau Alpha Journalism Honor Society; Omega Psi Phi Fraternity; and Sigma Pi Phi fraternity.

WILLIAMS, ELYNOR A. She holds a B.S. degree from Spelman College in Atlanta, Georgia, and a master's degree from Cornell University in Ithaca, New York. She is vice-president of public responsibility for Sara Lee Corporation and is responsible for the development of strategies and plans for governing corporate and public responsibility programs and activities as these relate especially to key external corporate constituencies. She oversees the development of marketing-related public responsibility programs, and directs corporate activities that maintain productive working relationships with social, political and corporate leaders. She directs and manages the operations fund which makes corporate contributions to public interest groups and national and state organizations, and represents the corporation as official spokesperson on issues and causes relating to the public responsibility function.

Prior to joining Sara Lee Corporation, Williams held positions as public school teacher, editor and publicist, and as an executive and senior communications and public relations specialist with both nonprofit institutions and Fortune 500 companies. In 1983, she began her career with Sara Lee in the company's North Carolina office. She was promoted to the corporation's executive offices in 1986 and was elected by the board of directors to her current position in 1990. She was secretary of the board of trustees of the University of North Carolina at Greensboro; founding board member of the Executive Leadership Council; deacon of Chicago United and a member of the national corporate advisory boards of the NOW Legal Defense and Education Fund, League of Women Voters–U.S., and the National Women's Political Caucus. She was also a member of the National Technical Advisory Committee of OICs of America, Inc., a founding member of the Spelman College Corporate Women's Roundtable, a member of the Advisory Executive Committee for the National Women's Economic Alliance and a member of the board of directors of the National Coalition of 100 Black Women.

Williams is listed in several biographical publications, including the *World Who's Who of Women* and *Who's Who in Black America*. She has been inducted into the Black Women's Hall of Fame and was named a Distinguished Alumnae of the Year of the National Association of Equal Opportunity in Higher Education. In 1988, she was honored by *Dollars and Sense* magazine as one of America's top 100 Black Business and Professional Women. In 1989, she was named as one of 15 Women Who Make a Difference by *Minorities and Women in Business* magazine, and was selected by *Essence* magazine as one of the 10 top Black Women in Corporate America.

In 1988, *Ebony* magazine selected Williams as one of 100 "Best and Brightest Black Women in Corporate America," and in 1990, she was selected for participation in the Leadership America Program. The professional programs she had created won awards and recognition from many organizations, including the International Association of Business Communicators, National YWCA, Women in Communications, and the National Partnerships in Education.

WILLIAMS, JAMES R., has been married to Catherine for over thirty years, and they have two children. He is a graduate of the University of Akron, Akron, Ohio, with a B.A. degree, 1960, and a J.D. degree in law, 1965, and attended Ohio and National Judicial College. He serves as judge, Court of Common Pleas of Summit County (1989 to date); past presiding judge, Court of Common Pleas of Summit County; judge, Akron Municipal Court (1983–1989); past presiding/administrative judge, Akron Municipal Court; United States Attorney, Northern District of Ohio (1978–1982); attorney at law, formerly with firm of Parms, Purnell, Stubbs & Williams (1969–1978) and firm of Guren, Merritt, Feibel, Sogg & Cohen (1982–1983); city councilman, city of Akron, 1970 to March 1978; formerly taught in Akron Public Schools for four years and lectured in Senior Problems at the University of Akron. He served as senior staff member of Akron's Department of Planning and Urban Renewal (five years), and was in the United States Army 1953–1955.

Williams is the recipient of many awards: Outstanding Alumnus Award, University of Akron, June 10, 1978; "Outstanding Achievement" for Volunteer Service for the United Community Council of Summit County in 1968; Urban League's Outstanding Community Leadership Award in 1973; YMCA "Service Award" in 1974; YMCA "Pres-

idential Award" in April 1979; Honorary Doctor of Laws from Benedict College, May 1979; Appreciation for Dedicated Service Award by Greater Cleveland Crime Prevention Committee, June 1981; and Superior Judicial Service Award from Ohio Supreme Court for maintaining a current docket, 1984–1989.

Judge Williams' professional memberships include the following associations: member of American Bar Association; member of Ohio Bar Association; member of Akron Bar Association; fellow of Ohio State Bar Foundation; past treasurer and member of Executive Committee of Akron Area Bar Association; past chairman of Judicial Referendum Committee of Akron Bar Association; member of the Board of Advisors of the University of Akron School of Law; past president of Federal Bar Association (Cleveland Area); past president of Akron Barristers Club; past member of Executive Board of Municipal/County Judges Association of Ohio.

WILLIAMS, PAUL L., is a graduate of Lindbloom Technical High School, 1971, he received a B.A. degree in history education from Chicago State University, 1975, an M.A. degree in political science from Sangamon State University, 1979, a J.D. from DePaul University, School of Law, 1984, and was admitted to the Illinois Bar in 1984. He has served as State Representative for the 24th District and as a partner in the firm of Vaughn & Williams, attorneys at law, from 1987 to date.

Williams' prior positions include: a partnership with the law firm of Williams, Miller & Ferguson, attorneys at law; instructor of Business Law (two semesters) at Northeastern Illinois University Center for Inner City Studies; registered lobbyist and association executive for the Illinois Association of Realtors–Metropolitan Governmental Affairs Liaison (where he did research and bill analysis and worked with local real estate boards to develop local political affairs programs); legislative assistant with Senator Harold Washington and State Representative Lewis Caldwell; graduate assistant at Sangamon State University; and substitute teacher at Springfield School District #186.

His additional positions include: assistant in coordination of grants and contracts for the Public Affairs Department at Sangamon State University; legislative intern (graduate) under Senate President Cecil Partee for the Illinois State Senate Democratic Staff; administrative aide to State Representative Romie Palmer, Legislative Intern (undergraduate); security guard for Stanley Security Company; presplicer for Kodak Processing Lab; in the shipping department for Universal Metal Finishing; driver for Checker Taxi Company; and janitor for Chatham Avalon Nursery School.

Williams served with the Midwest Model United Nations as a delegate and staff member for four years, as head delegate and one year, and as legal counsel for the Counsel for the Economic and Social Council, and served as president of the General Assembly for the first year of the conference, and legal counsel the second for Chicago Model United Nations. His professional affiliations include: Phi Alpha Theta, member of the National History Honorary Society; NAACP, board of directors for the Chicago Southside Chapter of the NAACP. He was former chairman of Political Action Committee; Chicago Southside Branch NAACP; Liberty Baptist Church; Black American Law Student Association; Illinois State Bar Association; and Illinois House Black Caucus, secretary.

WILLIAMS, VANESSA, was born March 18, 1963, in New York, New York, the daughter of Milton and Helen Williams. She is married to Ramon Hervey II, and they have two daughters, Melanie and Jillian Kristin Hervey. When she was a year old her family moved to Millwood, a predominantly white and middle-class neighborhood. With her mother teaching singing in the public schools, and her father teaching music in the public schools, she and her brother Christopher studied music and other performing arts until the age of 15. She studied French horn for nine years, piano for five years, acting, melophone for 14 years, dancing for six years, modeling for six years and was in the marching band. On the strength of her obvious talents, she became a star performer at Horace Greeley High School in Chappaqua, New York.

Williams performed in plays and musicals, sang in the school choir, and played the French horn in both the school band and the orchestra. She joined the All-State Women's Choir and the All-County Orchestra and traveled with the orchestra on exchange trips. While still in high school she entered her first pageant, a talent program sponsored by the fraternal order of the Masons, finishing fourth in the national competition. She was also a drama finalist in the presidential scholars program.

In 1981, she enrolled at Syracuse University where she majored in musical theatre. One indication of her growing celebrity was the notation next to her picture in her high school yearbook which read, "See you on Broadway." Vanessa's interest in the Miss America pageant was aroused in the spring of 1983, when the executive director of the Miss America Greater Syracuse Pageant, who had seen her in a school show, approached her as a possible contestant. On the first night of the judging, in the Miss America Pageant held in Atlantic City, New Jersey, Wednesday, September 14, 1983, she won the swimsuit competition. On September 16, she ranked first in the talent competition, and on September 17, 1983, before a nationwide television audience, she was crowned Miss America, narrowly edging past Suzette Charles, who is also black, an occurrence that the eight-member all-white panel of judges dismissed as a mere coincidence.

That night Williams became the

first black woman to win the crown of Miss America in the 62-year history of the beauty pageant. The history-making pageant was witnessed by a record crowd of 22,600 crammed into Convention Hall, while more than 55 million television viewers caused the contest to rank No. 6 in the Nielsen survey of the top 66 TV programs. She went on to record an album which netted her four top 10 hits and three Grammy-award nominations off her gold debut album "The Right Stuff."

WILLIE, LOUIS J., was born in Fort Worth, Texas, and is married and the father of one son. He is a graduate of Lincoln High School, Dallas, Texas; Wiley College, Marshall, Texas, with a B.A. degree in economics; University of Michigan, Ann Arbor, with an M.B.A. degree; and American College of Life, Bryn Mawr, Pennsylvania, CLU degree (Chartered Life Underwriter). He serves as executive vice president of Booker T. Washington Insurance Company, and vice president and secretary of Citizens Federal Savings Bank. He has been the recipient of the Distinguished Citizens Award from Miles College. Willie, a black man who grew up in segregated Texas, found what seemed to be utopia in the late 1940s when he went north to the University of Michigan. After earning that coveted master's degree, however, reality set in. All the corporations were coming on campus at Michigan, and they were interviewing his classmates. They were not interviewing blacks. Willie took a couple of different jobs in Tennessee, neither of which was exactly what he wanted. Then came that day in 1952 when he sat down for a job interview with Birmingham's A. G. Gaston, who was already well on his way to becoming perhaps the most successful black businessman in Alabama's history. Willie had every intention of seizing the opportunity of work-

ing for Gaston. He told Gaston that "Nobody ever hired Louis Willie and regretted it." Confident that he had the job, he told his wife that night that he had the job. Two weeks later he received a letter from Gaston, who offered him the job and a salary of $5,000.

In the years since those early hesitant, tense efforts at interracial community cooperation, Willie has marked a broad spectrum of civic activities with his distinctive style. He has many professional business affiliations: former president and director of Federal Reserve Bank of Atlanta, Birmingham Branch; served on the board of directors for: Alabama Power Company, Alabama Association of Life Insurance Companies, AmSouth Bancorporation, United Way of Central Alabama, A. G. Gaston Boys Club, Alabama Shakespeare Festival, Birmingham Area Chamber of Commerce, Alabama Trust Fund, Meyer Foundation, Church of the Advent Day School, Health Services Foundation, UAB at Birmingham and Alabama Management Improvement Association; 1984, president, Birmingham Festival of Arts Salute to Nigeria, President's Council, University of Alabama at Birmingham and Advisory Board, and the Salvation Army. Among his citations are Distinguished Citizens awards from Miles College and Lawson State Jr. College; *Birmingham Post Herald's* Selection Award, and National Conference of Christians and Jews.

WILSON, JOHNNIE EDWARD, was born on February 4, 1944, in Baton Rouge, Louisiana. He received a B.S. degree in business administration from the University of Nebraska at Omaha, and an M.S. degree in logistics management from Florida Institute of Technology. He received an OCS commission to second lieutenant on May 31, 1967. From May 1967 to September

1969, he served as mechanical maintenance officer, later commander, of Company A, 782nd Maintenance Battalion, 82nd Airborne Division, Fort Bragg, North Carolina. On May 31, 1968, he was promoted to the rank of captain. From October 1969 to November 1970, he was the assistant brigade supply officer, later commander, of Company C, 173rd Support Battalion (Airborne), 173rd Airborne Brigade, United States Army in Vietnam.

From January 1971 to September 1971, Wilson was a student in the Ordnance Officer Advanced Course, United States Army Ordnance School, Aberdeen Proving Ground, Maryland. From December 1971 to December 1973, he was a student at the University of Nebraska, Omaha. From January 1974 to June 1976, he was the commander of Company B, later technical supply officer, of the 123rd Maintenance Battalion, 1st Armored Division, United States Army in Europe. He was promoted to the grade of major on June 9, 1976. From August 1976 to June 1977, he was a student at the United States Army Command and General Staff College, Fort Leavenworth, Kansas. From June 1977 to November 1977, he was a student at Florida Institute of Technology, Melbourne, Florida. From November 1977 to November 1980, he served as the professional development officer, later personnel management officer, and later chief of the Ordnance Assignment Branch, Combat Service Support Division, United States Army Military Personnel Center, Alexandria, Virginia.

From December 1980 to May 1983, Wilson was the commander of the 709th Maintenance Battalion, 9th Infantry Division, Fort Lewis, Washington. He was promoted to the grade of lieutenant colonel on July 13, 1980. From May 1983 to June 1984, he was a student at the Industrial College of the Armed Forces, Fort McNair, Washington, D.C. From August 1984 to December 1986, he was the commander of the Division Support Command, 1st Armored Division, United States Army in Europe. He was promoted to the grade of colonel on November 1, 1984. From December 1986 to July 1988, he was the commander of the 13th Support Command, Fort Hood, Texas.

From July 1988 to July 1990, Gen. Wilson was assigned as the deputy commanding general, 21st Theater Army Area Command, United States Army in Europe and the Seventh Army. On September 1, 1989, he was promoted to the grade of brigadier general. In July 1990, he was appointed commanding general of the United States Ordnance Center, Aberdeen Proving Ground. He has received numerous awards and decorations, including: the Distinguished Service Medal; the Legion of Merit; the Bronze Star Medal (with two oak leaf clusters); the Meritorious Service Medal (with two oak leaf clusters); the Army Commendation Medal; the Good Conduct Medal; the Master Parachutist Badge.

————————

WINFREY, OPRAH GAIL, was born January 29, 1954, in Kosciusko, Mississippi, the daughter of Vernita Lee and Vernon Winfrey. She learned to read at the age of two and a half, and when she was enrolled in kindergarten, she wrote a note that pointed out in no uncertain terms that she belonged in the first grade and her astonished teacher had her promoted. After completing that academic year, she skipped directly to the third grade. At the age of six, she was sent north to join her mother and two half-brothers in the Milwaukee ghetto. Her unmarried parents separated when she was very young, and she later moved to Nashville to live with her father and his wife Zelma.

Her father was a barber who became a member of the Nashville City

Council. He was a strict disciplinarian who provided her with guidance. He refused to let her have dinner unless she added five new words to her vocabulary every day, and he demanded a weekly book report. Under his stern regimen, she began to excel in school, both in and out of the classroom. She presided over the high school council, joined the drama club. When she was 16 she won an Elks Club oratorical contest that guaranteed her a full scholarship to Tennessee State University after her graduation, and in the following year she was invited to a White House Conference on Youth. While still in high school she was crowned Miss Fire Prevention by WVOL, a local radio station. In addition to awarding her the title and a Longines watch, the station hired her to read newscasts and for a few months before her high school graduation, she headed for work each day as soon as classes ended, to become, every half hour on the hour, the voice of WVOL.

During her freshman year at Tennessee State University, Winfrey became Miss Black Nashville and Miss Tennessee, and in 1971 she was also a contestant in the Miss Black America Pageant. When the local CBS television station offered her a job she turned it down twice, then a 19-year-old sophomore. When her speech teacher reminded her that job offers from CBS were the reason "people go to college," she accepted a position with WTVF-TV, becoming Nashville's first black woman to serve as coanchor on the evening news. After graduating in 1976, she accepted a job offer from WJZ-TV, the ABC affiliate in Baltimore, Maryland, as a reporter and coanchor on the six o'clock news. In 1977, the station switched her first to doing 7:25 a.m. "cut-ins"—updates on local news—on ABC's "Good Morning America."

Winfrey moved to Chicago in January 1984 to become an a.m. anchor for WLS-TV. One month after she arrived in the city, "A.M. Chicago"

drew even with Donahue in the ratings, and after three months it nosed ahead. By September 1985, the program had been expanded to an hour and had been renamed "The Oprah Winfrey Show." It was in 1985 that composer and producer Quincy Jones, on a six-hour visit to Chicago, "discovered" Winfrey as a potential motion picture actress after coming across her program while watching television in his hotel room. She was cast, through Quincy Jones, in a big-budget film adaptation of her favorite book, Alice Walker's The Color Purple.

When Warner Bros. released The Color Purple in December 1985, Winfrey was hailed for a debut that was called "shockingly good" by movie critic Gene Siskel in the Chicago Tribune (December 20, 1985). In addition to receiving Oscar and Golden Globe nominations for her performance, she was named a Woman of Achievement by the National Organization of Women in June 1986. But her mastery on television remained beyond dispute as her program, already drawing twice the size of the Chicago audience of the "Phil Donahue Show" in 1985, skyrocketed in popularity in the wake of her Color Purple Oscar nomination.

On September 8, 1986, King World put her show into syndication in a record 138 cities. In 1988, Winfrey was named the recipient of the International Radio and Television Society's "Broadcaster of the Year" award during a ceremony in New York. At 34, Winfrey was the youngest person to receive the honor in its 25-year history. She produced through her own company, Harpo Inc., The Women of Brewster Place, which she also starred in.

WOLFE, JOHN T., JR., was born in 1942, in Jackson, Mississippi. He was educated in Chicago, Illinois, where he attended elementary and secondary schools and earned a B.E. degree from Chicago Teachers College in 1964; an M.S. degree in English education and Ph.D. degree in linguistics, from Purdue University, in 1970. Between 1971 and 1977, while pursuing his degree, he worked and held full-time positions at Purdue University as a housing officer and employee relations manager. He immediately began teaching English in the Chicago Public Schools and worked with students in the Roosevelt University Upward Bound Program. It was because of this work with Upward Bound that he was subsequently offered a position with Upward Bound at Cuttington College in Liberia, West Africa, where he served for two and a half years.

While at Cuttington he taught linguistics and held a number of administrative positions including dean of men and chairman of the faculty senate. In 1977, Wolfe was offered a position as assistant professor of English at Fayetteville State University in North Carolina. During his time at the university, he moved through the administrative ranks from English head, Humanities and Fine Arts Division head to academic dean. He also won fellowships from the National Endowment for the Humanities and the American Council on Education.

Dr. Wolfe was recruited and offered the position of provost and vice president for Academic Affairs in 1985 at Bowie State University in Maryland, which he held from 1985 to 1990. While there he served on the Bowie New Town Center Minority Advisory Board, as chairman of the Advisory Board of the Prince George's County Entrepreneurial Development program, vice president of the middle Atlantic Writers Association, and is a member of the National Council of Teachers of English. He has had over 30 scholarly articles and presentations published. He was nominated and selected as the tenth president of Kentucky State University in March 1990. He assumed the position on July 1 and was actively giving new leadership to guiding the University into the 21st century.

WONDER, STEVIE, was born Steveland Judkins Morris on May 13, 1950, in Saginaw, Michigan. One of five children, his parents separated when he was very young. His mother moved the family to Detroit and subsequently remarried. Stevie was a premature baby who has been blind since birth. In 1960, when he was about ten years of age, a playmate's big brother, who was a member of the singing group, the Miracles, brought him to the studios of Motown Records, the fast-rising black record label then based in Detroit. He began to hang out at the recording studio every day after school, playing every instrument he could get his hands on and writing songs. People started calling him Little Stevie Wonder.

In 1963, he had his first big hit,

"Fingertips," a single which rose to the top of the charts during the summer of 1963 and sold over one million copies, earning him his first gold record. When Little Stevie Wonder became a recording artist for Motown, he became a member of the Motown "family." A court-appointed guardian was secured for him, and the money he earned was put in a trust to await his majority. For a time he continued to attend public school, but then he transferred to the Michigan School for the Blind in Lansing. While traveling, he studied for three or four hours a day with a private tutor. He received his diploma from the Michigan School for the Blind in 1969.

In 1971, Wonder decided to leave the Motown recording company. Taking the million dollars that had been held in trust for him, he used a quarter of the money to rent a recording studio in New York, where he taped his experiments on the musical ideas he had been storing up for years. Finally he came up with the album, "Music of My Mind." He returned to Motown with the album, released in 1972, and negotiated a new and more favorable contract that gave him more money and complete control over his music, production of his records, and bookings for his personal appearances. On February 7, 1973, he made a Carnegie Hall debut, and in January 1974, he was nominated for six Grammy awards, more than any other recording artist in the 16-year history of the awards.

That March he won five Grammies, including one for best pop vocal performance by a male singer. In 1974, he was also named best-selling male soul artist of the year. In 1976, he released "Songs in the Key of Life, which took more than two years to complete. In 1979, he released "Journey Through the Secret Life of Plants, which took three years to complete. One of his many hits of the 1980s was "Skeletons," from his "Characters" album, which followed his tradition of

mixing messages about the human condition with easygoing love songs.

Wonder also testified in Washington, D.C., before a Congressional committee considering a bill to make Dr. Martin Luther King's January 15th birthdate a national holiday. He had played an important role in the holiday proposal. Wonder's music has made him the reigning favorite of pop music critics and one of the most influential figures in black music.

WRIGHT, GEORGE C., JR., was born in Chesapeake City, Maryland, the son of Alice and George C. Wright, Sr. He has been married for more than thirty years to Mary. They have five children and seven grandchildren. He attended public schools in Chesapeake City and Elkton, Maryland. He attended Maryland State College, Princess Anne, Maryland; University of Delaware in Dover; Wesley College in Dover, and Wilmington College in Dover. He served on the Faculty of the Personnel Management School in Gunther AFS, Alabama, from 1982 to 1987.

Wright held membership in various organizations: chairman of the Steward Board of Bethel A.M.E. Church; president of the Delaware League of Local Governments; executive Committee of the Delaware League of Local Governments; member, Delaware Council on Police Training; St. John Lodge #7, 33 degree Mason; Morning State Chapter #7 Eastern Star; Atlas Post #9 American Legion.

Wright was elected mayor of Smyrna in 1981 and has been unopposed for four terms. He served on the town council 12 years prior to becoming mayor. He was named to *Who's Who Among Black Americans* and *Who's Who in Society* in 1987. He served with a six-member team that traveled to eight countries in Europe in 1971 to write a transportation movement plan for Europe. This plan is still in effect today and, in the first year alone, a savings of $10 million was realized. His greatest accomplishments were: "seven balanced budgets for the town of Smyrna with surpluses. To be a credit to my race; and to accomplish something that would make my mother, family and friends very proud to be associated with me."

WYATT-CUMMINGS, THELMA LAVERNE, was born July 6, 1945, in Amarillo, Texas. She is a middle child having two brothers, J. O., and Morris, and one sister Rose. She married Arthur B. Cummings, Sr. (now divorced), and is the mother of a son Khari, and daughter Ayanna. Her father, J. O. Wyatt, Sr., was a physician who established his own hospital when blacks were denied access to white hospitals. Her mother was a business woman. Thelma was educated in the public schools and at Palmer Institute before completing a B.A. degree at the University of California. After graduating from UCLA, she moved to Chicago where she taught school while continuing her educational pursuits at Chicago Teachers' College and the Illinois Institute of Technology.

Both of her brothers were in Atlanta, Georgia, her older brother James O. Wyatt, Jr., having graduated from Morehouse College and her younger brother Morris Wyatt, having graduated from Clark College in Atlanta. She became attracted to the potential of the power of politics in Atlanta. On moving there, she commenced the study of law at Emory University where her brother J. O. had already enrolled. They both graduated in 1971, she with highest honors. While at Emory, she was a member of the Order of the Coif (National Law Honor Society), the Bryan Society (Emory Law Honor Society), and a recipient of the Appellate Advocacy Award. She was also associate editor of the *Journal of Public Law.*

Shortly after graduation from Emory Law School, Wyatt-Cummings went into private practice with J. O., but soon moved out on her own and continued her private practice with Felker Ward, Jr. In 1976, she was appointed a special assistant to the State Attorney General's Office. She was appointed to the bench of the Municipal Court of Atlanta in 1977 by Mayor Maynard Jackson. At that time her husband Arthur Cummings was the purchasing director for the city of Atlanta, and her brother J. O. had been elected a Fulton County Commissioner and vice chairman of the Board of Commissioners, the first black American to hold either position.

Wyatt-Cummings was only the second black female to occupy the bench in Atlanta's Municipal Court. Her predecessor, Pruden Herndon, was appointed to the bench in 1965 by former Mayor Ivan Allen. In 1985, Gov. Joe Frank Harris appointed her as the first black woman in Georgia to serve on the State Court. Since her appointment, she has earned the respect of the legal profession by efficiently handling her caseload while tempering justice with mercy.

Among numerous honors, Wyatt-Cummings has received the 1990 Government Award from the Atlanta Business League; the National Conference of Black Mayors honored her in 1987; the Outstanding Jurist Award from the Gate City Bar Association in 1983; and the Outstanding Public Service Award from the Georgia Coalition of Black Women in 1984. She serves as chairperson of the Administrative Board of Cascade United Methodist Church and on the Advisory Board of Concerned Black Clergy.

---

†X, MALCOLM, was born Malcolm Little in 1925, in Omaha, Nebraska. He was the son of a Baptist preacher who had moved his family to Lansing, Michigan. When Malcolm was only six years old, his father was gruesomely murdered and he watched his mother slowly begin to lose her mind, until she was committed to a mental institution, leaving him and his seven siblings alone. He was sent to a foster home, then transferred to state institutions and boarding houses. In 1940, he left the Mason City, Iowa, school he attended and headed east, just after finishing the eighth grade. In Boston, Massachusetts, living with his sister, he held a variety of jobs, shoeshine boy, waiter, soda jerk. Three years later, in New York, he became involved in the underworld which resulted in a ten-year jail sentence in 1946.

It was in jail that Malcolm was introduced to the Lost-Found Nation of Islam, the Black Muslim religion led by Elijah Muhammad, with whom he began a correspondence. In 1952, on his parole from jail, he began speaking out in the idiom of his newly found philosophy. Soon a minister of the faith with the given name Malcolm X, he established a mosque in Philadelphia, Pennsylvania, and founded the newspaper *Muhammad Speaks* In 1954, Malcolm X went to Harlem in New York City to head the mosque there. His speeches in behalf of the movement helped spread the messages of racial separation, of black self-defense, of nonparticipation in white society or religion, and of western decadence and immorality.

During that time, the mere mention of his name was enough to strike fire. While Dr. Martin Luther King, Jr., preached the doctrine of nonviolence, Malcolm described white America as a racist beast and chastised black Americans for our slave ways, exhorting us to stand up, to meet force with force, and fight back. Using his compelling speaking skills, he articulated the frustrations and aspirations of blacks. He would time and again publicly express feelings of rage and contempt for white Americans, things that were normally only said when a black was speaking to another black. For this, white America branded him a hate-monger, as did some so-called Black Leaders. But most blacks said, "Malcolm said things that needed to be said but others were frightened to say." Many blacks did not like his methods, but the young blacks loved him for the things he said.

Malcolm was a revolutionary in that he understood the power structure in the country and knew it could not be depended upon to do justice to black people. He used the power of words to brand the white man "the devil" and to declare that economic power equals freedom, that freedom equals manhood and that black manhood resides in love and respect for blackness of one's skin. His popularity became a threat to the power of many Muslim leaders and finally, in 1963, after Malcolm X proposed that President John F. Kennedy's assassination was a case of the "chickens coming home to roost," he was suspended from the Black Muslim movement.

In 1964, his trips to Mecca, in

Saudi Arabia, and Ghana and Nigeria in West Africa broadened his knowledge about the Muslim religion. In Mecca, he found black and white Muslims who treated him as their equal. This gave him hope for blacks and whites in America. Returning to the United States, he resigned from the Nation of Islam and took the name El-Hajj Malik El-Shabazz. He formed the organization for Afro-American Unity to work for black unity and freedom in cooperation with other civil rights groups. And he modified his views to encompass the possibility that all white people were not evil and that progress in the black struggle could be made with the help of world organizations. He also projected a vision of black control of black communities.

While organizing his new vision, on February 21, 1965, Malcolm X was assassinated by members of a dissenting black group at the Audubon Ballroom in New York. His life, the gradual evolution of his world philosophy, and his violent end has had significant impact on the thinking of black Americans for many years. The state of New York Historic Preservation Office entered the ballrooms and the adjoining theater into the Register of Historical Places in 1986. Columbia University, which owns the land, plans to erect a biotechnology research park on the site of the Audubon and three adjacent blocks. Many had hoped to erect a memorial to Malcolm on the Audubon site, but in 1991, the building remains, like Malcolm himself in the minds of many in the mainstream, a forgotten symbol of what was, what could have been.

YOUNG, ANDREW JACKSON, JR., was born in New Orleans, Louisiana, on March 12, 1932. His father, Andrew J. Young, was a dentist and his mother, Daisy (Fuller) Young, a teacher. He married Jean Childs and they have four children, Andrea, Lisa, Paula and Andrew, III. he graduated from Gilbert Academy, a private high school, in 1947, and enrolled at Dillard University in New Orleans. The following year, he transferred to Howard University in Washington, D.C. He had intended to become a dentist but, after obtaining his B.S. degree in 1951, he had second thoughts about his career. He decided to enter the ministry. He entered Hartford Theological Seminary in Hartford, Connecticut, and graduated in 1955 with a B.D. degree. He was ordained a minister in the United Church of Christ.

In 1960, Young joined the Southern Christian Leadership Conference (SCLC), the civil rights organization founded by the late Dr. Martin Luther King, Jr. He served as executive director of that organization from 1964 to 1970. He was elected to the United States House of Representatives in 1972, becoming the first black ever elected to Congress from the South since 1901. On December 5, 1976, Rep. Young told a Jewish Men's Club that he had accepted a nomination by President Jimmy Carter as

United States Ambassador to the United Nations. Supreme Court Justice Thurgood Marshall administered the oath of office.

President Carter remarked, "Andy Young did not want or ask for this job, it was only with the greatest reluctance on his part that he finally agreed to accept this job for me, for our country." In May 1977, Sen. Barry Goldwater told Young to be "more diplomatic." But the outspoken ambassador drew criticism when he said, "Abraham Lincoln was a racist and it needs to be talked about, even if it gets me fired." He met with the Palestine Liberation Organization, without informing the president, on July 26, 1979 (U.N. Ambassador, Zehda Labib Terzi). It was this meeting that brought heavy criticism from Israel, U.N. Ambassador Yehuda Blum, and members of the United States House and Senate. On August 15, 1979, Young resigned as United States Ambassador to the United Nations. Taking sole responsibility for creating the incident which led to his resignation, he said "I made the decision that I should resign, I was not forced out, and I frankly think that I did it for my own tactical reasons."

In 1982, Young became the second black man to win the office of mayor in Atlanta, Georgia. As the mayor of Atlanta for eight years, he utilized his position to promote the city, its business, cultural contacts, and people with the international community, including the continent of Africa. After leaving the office of mayor in 1990, he made an unsuccessful bid to become Georgia's first and America's second black elected governor. Young has dedicated his life to the benefit of mankind as a civil rights leader, congressman, clergyman, former U.N. Ambassador, mayor and businessman.

YOUNG, ANTHONY L., is a graduate of Golden State University, San Francisco, California, graduating cum laude with a B.S. degree; has a J.D. degree from De Paul University College of Law, Chicago, Illinois, graduating in 1977; and was admitted to practice with the state of Illinois and the U.S. District Court for the Northern District of Illinois, 1977. He has served as State Representative since 1985, and in the general practice of law since 1977. He took the oath of office for the 17th District (Westside Chicago and South Oak Park) State Representative in January 1985. After a most successful first term, he was re-elected to a second two-year term receiving 79 percent of the vote, and was appointed a floor spokesman for the House Democrats. He won a third term with 77 percent of the vote and was appointed assistant House Majority Leader. He began a fourth term in January 1991.

Young has been a member of the Criminal Law Committee since 1985 and sponsor of the majority of legislation introduced on behalf of the public defender's office. From 1977 to 1982, he participated in a Cook County program that appointed private counsel to serve as public defender in cases with multiple defendants who could not afford an attorney. He represented one of the defendants in the Pontiac Prison riot case, wherein 16 men were accused of murdering three prison guards during the riot. The trial lasted two years and all defendants were acquitted.

Young is the recipient of the Christian Law Center Award for Pro Bono Legal Service. Prior positions include: adjunct professor for Central YMCA Community College, teaching classes in business law, economics and business administration. He served in the United States Air Force, 1970–1974, and received an honorable discharge. His organizations and awards are numerous.

YOUNG, COLEMAN A., was born in 1918 in Tuscaloosa, Alabama, the oldest of five children. He attended St. Mary's School, where he earned top grades. He graduated with honors from Detroit Eastern High School at the age of 16. A number of college scholarships were offered, but he had to seek employment in the auto industry. In 1937, he became an organizer for the Congress of Industrial Workers (CIO) in an automobile plant where he was an apprentice electrician. His union activities got him fired. He worked with the post office and began recruiting postal workers for the CIO, and again he was fired. It was during those early working years that he began a lifelong commitment to the civil rights movement.

Young organized picketing to end segregation in public housing, particularly Detroit's Sojourner Truth housing project. He has said he believed this was the first use of picket lines and demonstrations in the civil rights struggle, as well as the first time "respectable people" like ministers and black professionals had taken part in such protests. At the beginning of World War II, he entered the Army Air Corps and was commissioned a second lieutenant. His personal fight against discrimination did not end while he was in uniform. (He was the Air Corps' first black bombardier.) A group of young black officers waged a sit-in and succeeded in bringing an end to segregation in officers' clubs.

After the war, Young returned to Detroit and worked as a labor organizer, serving as director of organization for the Wayne County AFL-CIO. He also began his political career as an activist in the Michigan Democratic Party. Then came a period in his life which Young describes as "Hard Times." He headed the National Negro Labor Council from 1951 until it collapsed in 1955. Taking any job that came along, he worked as a cab driver, a meat handler and cleaning plant employee. Continuing his political ambitions, he made a bid for a Detroit City Council seat in 1959 and was defeated. His career took an upward turn in 1961 when he was elected a delegate to the Michigan Constitutional Convention.

In 1964, he was elected State Senator from Detroit's 4th District, after an unsuccessful run in 1962 for the State House of Representatives. He served as Senator until his election as mayor of Detroit in November 1973. During his Senate career, he exercised his leadership to: fight discrimination in state employment; worked for the establishment of low-income housing in Detroit, especially for citizens displaced by urban renewal; sponsored a law to give tax exemptions to senior citizen cooperative nonprofit housing; authored legislation to increase tenants' rights; wrote the Detroit School Decentralization Bill; served as key strategist in the passage of the Michigan Open Housing Law and introduced the first version of the no-fault auto insurance bill.

In his inaugural address in January 1974, Young said his primary goal would be to heal the wounds of racial polarization which had plagued the city of Detroit. "We can no longer afford the luxury of hatred and racial division," he said. In listing the major goals of his administration, he had promised a severe crackdown on crime and the drug traffic. He said he would build a new "people oriented" police department in which officers would earn the respect and cooperation of Detroiters by giving that same respect and cooperation to all citizens. The mayor's police Mini-Station Program had begun and had successfully brought the officer closer to citizens right in their own neighborhoods.

Mayor Young's other top-priority goals were to rehabilitate or demolish abandoned homes and buildings. To provide quality mass transit, to aid the community's business and industry and to improve services to the elderly. Programs have begun in all these areas, through the mayor's office. He summed up his hopes for the city in a post-election interview when he said: "I believe that we need to dream big dreams and propose grandiose schemes if we are to recapture the excitement, vibrancy and pride we once knew in Detroit."

YOUNG, JOE, SR., was born on July 15, 1927, in Milledgeville, Georgia. He is married to Ellen Young, and the proud father of five sons and one daughter, and has 12 grandchildren. He has an A.A. degree in business from Lansing Community College. He left Georgia at an early age to serve in the United States Army. He became active in the nativity of Our Lord Catholic Church and in the community through various civic organizations. He formerly served as chairman of the Black Police Recruitment Committee; chairman of the Detroit/Wayne County Criminal Justice Council; president of the Detroit Consumer Credit Union; as a committeeman of Local 101 AFSCME, and as staff representative of Council 23. He was appointed by Gov. Milliken to the Michigan Commission on Criminal Justice.

Young is a former member of the UAW and Teamsters unions and a lifetime member of the NAACP. His political career began by serving two

and a half terms as vice-chairman of the board of Wayne County Commissioners. While serving as a County Commissioner and as a State Representative, he was instrumental in bringing 4-H programs to urban areas. He was the only recipient of the 1986 Snyder-Kok Award from the Mental Health Association of Michigan, the 1987 Legislator of the Year Award from the Michigan Federation of Private Child and Family Agencies, and the 1988 Commissioners Award from the National Department of Health and Human Services.

Rep. Young was elected to his first term of office in the state legislature in 1974 in a special election, serving the 15th District of Detroit's east side. After a second term in 1976, he was assigned to the Committee on Appropriations. He completed his seventh term for the Michigan House of Representatives for the 14th District of Detroit. He was appointed to the House Appropriations Committee, where he chairs the Mental Health Subcommittee. Additional subcommittees include: Agriculture, General Government, Social Services, Corrections, School Aid and the Department of Education, Community Colleges, and Natural Resources and Environment.

YOUNG-CUMMINGS, MARY, was born in rural middle Georgia to Elder Matthew, Sr., and Ida Mae Moss; the 13th child of 16. She has two children, April and Demetrius. Her early education was received in the public schools of Ben Hill County, Georgia, where she graduated with honors. Her undergraduate work was completed at Savannah State College where she completed a major in mathematics and a minor in physics, earning a B.S. degree with honors. Thereafter she attended the Howard University School of law where she earned a J.D. degree, again with honors. She is presently self-employed since 1972 as Mary Young & Associates.

Young-Cummings' prior employment include: U.S. Department of Health, Education and Welfare as a compliance officer charged with monitoring school desegregation in the 1960s; the NAACP Legal Defense Fund in New York City; associate professor at Albany State College; legal intern with C. B. King and Associates. (Her political involvement includes service as a delegate to the 1972 through 1984 Democratic Conventions.) She spent 12 years on the County Democratic Committee and the State Democratic Committee for the state of Georgia; served as Congressional chairperson for the Democratic Women's Political Caucus and City Commissioner for the city of Albany for eight years.

Young-Cummings is presently serving as a state Representative to the Georgia House of General Assembly from District 134, having been elected in 1981; serves the Policy Committee of the Georgia Legislative Black Caucus and is the president of the Georgia Association of Black Elected Officials. She is the recipient of numerous citations, certificates and awards including: the Drum Major for Justice Award presented by the Southern Christian Leadership Conference, and the Outstanding Black Georgian in Politics Award presented by the Committee on the Life and History of Black Georgians. She has twice been invited to the White House to confer with Presidents Carter and Reagan. She also is a member of the Mount Pilgrim Baptist Church of Albany, Georgia, where she has served as a trustee and is an active member of the Senior Choir and the Ensemble.

ZIMMERMAN, MATTHEW AUGUSTUS, was born on December 9, 1941, in South Carolina. He received a B.S. degree in biology/chemistry from Benedict College, in 1962. He received an M.D.V degree in pastoral counseling from Duke University, in 1965, and a master's degree in education from Long Island University, in 1975. He received a commission, by direct appointment, to the rank of first lieutenant on March 21, 1967. From April 1967 to August 1967, he was a student at the Chaplain Officer Basic Course, United States Army Chaplain School, Fort Hamilton, New York. On April 3, 1967, he was promoted to the rank of captain. From August 1967 to January 1968, he served as chaplain, Headquarters Detachment 3rd Advanced Individual Training Bridge, United States Army Training Center (Infantry), Fort Gordon, Georgia.

From January 1968 to February 1969, he served as assistant IV Corps Tactical Zone Chaplain, Advisory Team 51, United States Military Assistance Command, in Vietnam. From February 1969 to September 1970, he was an assistant Support Command Chaplain, Headquarters and Headquarters Company and Band, Support Command, 1st Armored Division, Fort Hood, Texas. From March 1971 to August 1973, he served as Division Artillery Staff chaplain, 3rd Armored Division, United States Army in Europe and Seventh Army. From August 1974 to June 1975, he was a student at the Chaplain Officer Advanced Course, United States Army Chaplain Center and School, Fort Wadsworth, New Jersey.

On October 3, 1974, Zimmerman was promoted to the rank of major. From June 1975 to June 1976, he was the operations training staff officer, Office of the Chief of Chaplains, Washington, D.C. From June 1976 to June 1978, he served as staff parish development officer, Office of the Chief of Chaplains, Washington. From June 1978 to June 1979, he was a student at the United States Army Command and General Staff College, Fort Leavenworth, Kansas. From June 1979 to July 1980, he was the Deputy Corps Chaplain (Administrative), VII Corps, United States Army in Europe and Seventh Army. He was promoted to the rank of lieutenant colonel, on August 6, 1979.

From July 1980 to June 1982, he served as the division staff chaplain, 3rd Infantry Division, United States Army in Europe and Seventh Army. From June 1982 to June 1983, he was a student at the United States Army War College, Carlisle Barracks, in Pennsylvania. From June 1983 to June 1984, he was assistant command chaplain, United States Army Training and Doctrine Command, Fort Monroe, Virginia. He was promoted to the rank of colonel on July 1, 1984.

From December 1985 to August 1989, he served as a command staff chaplain at Forces Command, Fort McPherson, Atlanta, Georgia. From August 1989 to August 1990, he was the deputy chief of chaplains, Office of the Chief of Chaplains, United States Army, Washington. He was promoted to the one-star rank of brigadier general on October 1, 1989. On August 1, 1990, he was promoted to the two-star rank of major general. In August 1990, he was assigned as chief of chaplains, Office of the Chief of Chaplains, United States Army, Washington. His awards include: the Legion of Merit; the Bronze Star Medal; and the Meritorious Service Medal (with two oak leaf clusters).

Occupational Index

Activists (Civil/Social Rights)

Abernathy, Ralph David
Alexander, Avery C.
Ali, Muhammad
Barham, Sadie G.
Barnes, George H.
Belafonte, Harry
Brooks, Tyrone, Sr.
Brown, Ronald
Chisholm, Shirley Anita
Clayton, Xernona
Coggs-Jones, Elizabeth
Coleman, Eric D.
Collins, Cardiss
Crawford, William A.
Crockett, George W., Jr.
Dellums, Ronald
Dixon, Julian C.
Edelman, Marian Wright
Edwards, Al
Farrakhan, Louis
Fauntroy, Walter E.
Harris, Barbara Clementine
Hayes, Charles A.
Height, Dorothy Irene
Hooks, Benjamin Lawson
Hudson, Lizzan R.
Innis, Roy
Jackson, Jesse Louis
Jones, Roxanne H.
Jordan, Vernon Eulion, Jr.
Kelly, John Paul
Kilpatrick, Carolyn Cheeks
King, Coretta Scott
King, Robert Lewis, Sr.
Langford, Arthur, Jr.
Lee, Bernard Scott
Lewis, John
Lowery, Joseph E.
McKissick, Floyd
Mitchell, Parren J.
Morial, Ernest N.

Norton, Eleanor Holmes
Parks, Rosa Louise
Pierce, Lawrence W.
Rangel, Charles B.
Shackelford, Lottie H.
Smith, Ada L.
Sutton, Percy E.
Walker, Alice Malsenior
Ward, Horace Taliaferro
Wattleton, Alyce Faye
X, Malcolm
Young, Andrew Jackson, Jr.
Young, Coleman A.

Air Force

Edmonds, Albert J.
Gregory, Frederick D.
James, Daniel, Jr.
Jordan, Kenneth U.
Kelly, John Paul, Jr.
Phillips, John F.
Price, Albert J.
Randolph, Bernard P.
Theus, Lucius
Voorhees, John H.

Army

Adams-Ender, Clara Leach
Alexander, Clifford Leopold, Jr.
Allen, Robert Lee
Arnold, Wallace Cornelius
Barnes, Thomas V.
Becton, Julius W., Jr.
Brailsford, Marvin Delano
Byrd, Melvin Leon
Cadoria, Sherian Grace
Chandler, Allen E.
Coffey, Vernon Cornelius, Jr.
Cowings, John Sherman
Cromartie, Eugene Rufus
Davis, Benjamin Oliver, Jr.

Thomas, Debi
White, Jessie C.

Attorneys

Adrine, Ronald B.
Alexander, Clifford L., Jr.
Allen, Carolyn W.
Allen, Niathan
Allen, Roy L., II
Arrington, Marvin S.
Barnes, Thomas V.
Benham, Robert
Bradley, Tom
Brandveen, Antonio I.
Brown, Robert L.
Brown, Willie L., Jr.
Bryant, Wayne R.
Burke, Yvonne Brathwaite
Bush, Stephanie R.
Cannon, James F.
Coleman, Eric D.
Cousins, William, Jr.
Crockett, George W., Jr.
Davis, L. Clifford
Davis, Phillip Samuel
Deiz, Mercedes F.
Demerson, Elisha L.
Dinkins, David N.
Dixon, Sharon Pratt
Early, Norman S., Jr.
Figures, Michael Anthony
Finney, James Nathaniel
Fleming, Charles W.
Floyd, Donald J.
Galiber, Joseph L.
Gammage, Andre
Gordon, Levan
Grant, Edith Ingram
Green, Melvia B.
Grimes, Hubert L.
Harris, Barbara Ann
Harris, Patricia Robert
Hatcher, Richard Gordon
Haynes, Charles A.
Haynes, Lloyd R., Sr.
Hicks, Maryellen Whitlock
Higginbotham, A. Leon, Jr.
Hilliard, Earl F.
Hills, Carla Anderson
Holden, Melvin Lee
Hooks, Benjamin Lawson
Hudson, Samuel W., III
Jackson, Janet E.

Jackson, Maynard Holbrook
Jasmin, Ernest A.
Jasper, Mabel M.
Jimison, Z. Mae
Johnson, Leroy R.
Jones, Leonade Diane
Jones, Stephanie Tubbs
Jordan, Vernon Eulion J.
Joyner, Gordon L.
Kearse, Amalya Lyle
Keith, Damon J.
Lafontant-Mankarious, Jewel
Lane, Bensonetta Tipton
Leonard-Dent, Marva J.
Lewis, Delano E.
McCollum, Alice O.
McKissick, Floyd Bixler, Sr.
Marshall, Thurgood
Miller, Stanley A.
Morial, Ernest N.
Norton, Eleanor Holmes
Owens, Darryl T.
Penn, Robert W.
Phillips, Wilbur L.
Pierce, Lawrence W.
Powell, Romae Turner
Saffold, Shirley Strickland
Schmoke, Kurt L.
Sears-Collins, Leah J.
Shakoor, Adam A.
Shaw, Leander J., Jr.
Smith, Charles Z.
Smith, Virgil C., Jr.
Smitherman, Carole Catlin
Stamper, Russell
Stokes, Carl
Stokes, Louis
Strayhorn, Earl E.
Sutton, Percy E.
Thomas, Clarence
Tibbs, Edward A.
Trumbo, George William
Walton, Elbert Arthur, Jr.
Ward, Horace Taliaferro
Warren, Naomi White
Washington, Cleo
Washington, Craig Anthony
Washington, Harold
Watson, J. Warren
Williams, Avon N., Jr.
Williams, James R.
Williams, Paul L.
Wyatt-Cummings, Thelma L.
Young, Anthony L.

Obi, James E.
Procope, Ernesta Gertrude
Stone, Jim
Willie, Louis, Jr.

Public Utilities

Davis, James K.
Hill, Robert L.
Lewis, Delano E.
Morrow, Charles, III

Civil Rights *see* Activists

Clergy

Abernathy, Ralph David
Alexander, Avery C.
Barnes, George H., Sr.
Bishop, Louise Williams
Bronson, Oswald P., Sr.
Brown, Leo C., Jr.
Cary, William Sterling
Cleaver, Emanuel, II
Farrakhan, Louis
Fauntroy, Walter E.
Flemming, Timothy
Foreman, George
Gray, William H.
Harris, Barbara Clementine
Hooks, Benjamin Lawson
Jackson, Jesse Louis
King, Barbara Lewis
King, Martin Luther, Jr.
Lee, Bernard Scott
Lowery, Joseph E.
Moore, Farney
Richardson, Luns C.
Summers, William E., III
Tillman, Eugene C.
Watson, George T.
X, Malcolm
Young, Andrew
Zimmerman, Matthew Augustus

Communications

Executives

Black, Don G.
Brown, William Anthony (Tony)
Brunson, Dorothy E.
Clayton, Xernona
Conley, Karyne Jones
Eller, Carl

Graves, Earl G.
Gray, Robert Earl
Hall, Arsenio
Holden, Melvin Lee
Hooks, Benjamin
Johnson, John Harold
Lee, Spike
McNair, Ronald
Morse, Mildred S.
Paige, Emmett, Jr.
Rice, Condoleezza
Rogers, Johnathan Arlin
Short, Alonzo E.
Smith, Joshua Isaac
Taylor, Kristin Clark
Turner, Joseph Ellis
Vinson, Phyllis Tucker
Winfrey, Oprah Gail

Telephone

Edmonds, Albert J.
Gray, Robert Earl
Paige, Emmett, Jr.
Turner, Joseph Ellis

Television and Radio

Allen, Deborah
Bather, Paul
Bishop, Louis Williams
Bogle, Dick
Bradley, Edward
Brown, William Anthony (Tony)
Carter, Vic
Clayton, Xernona
Edwards, Linda A.
Gumbel, Bryant Charles
Hall, Arsenio
Hall, Robert
Holden, Melvin Lee
Hughes, Catherine Liggins
Jacob, Tracie D.
Kaufman, Monica
Morse, Mildred S.
Rice, Norman B.
Rodgers, Johnathan Arlin
Rosenthal, Robert E.
Russell, William Felton
Simpson, Donnie
Smith, Charles Z.
Stokes, Carl
Summers, William E.
Sutton, Percy E.
Vinson, Phyllis Tucker

Doctors *see* Medical Doctors

Educators

Hughes, Teresa P.
James, Sharpe
Johnson, Gloria Tapscott
Johnson-Brown, Hazel
Jones, Clara Stanton
Jones, Herbert C.
Jones, Stephanie Tubbs
Jordan, Barbara Charline
Joyner, Gordon
Lomax, Michael L.
McCollum, Alice O.
Miller, Yvonne Bond
Milliones, Jake
Moore, Gwen
Norton, Eleanor Holmes
Peay, Francis
Phillips, Wilbur L.
Reese, Mamie Bynes
Rice, Condoleezza
Sanderson, Walter H.
Shakoor, Adam A.
Smith, Charles Z.
Smitherman, Carole Catlin
Strayhorn, Earl
Stringer, C. Vivian
Walton, Elbert Arthur, Jr.
Watson, Dennis Rahiim
Watson, J. Warren
Wheeler, Albert Harold
White, Augustus A.
Williams, Eddie N.
Williams, Paul
Vaughn, Jackie, III
Wyatt-Cummings, Thelma Laverne
Young, Anthony L.
Young-Cummings, Mary

Teachers

Amos, Archie L.
Atkins, Fredd Glossie
Barham, Sadie G.
Bethea, Julianne
Birckhead, Fannie
Black, Charlie J.
Bradley, Donald
Brown, Charlie
Bryan, Curtis Eugene
Dymally, Mervyn M.
Foster, Shirley M.
Hunter, Teola P.
Kelly, John Paul, Jr.
Lee, George L.
McCullough, George W. J.
Matthews, Virginia

Moore, Farney
Morrow, Charles, III
Paramore, Gwen
Rogers, Earline Smith
Tillman, Eugene C.
Whipper, Lucille Simmons
White, Jesse C., Jr.

Engineers

Bell, William V.
Berry, Eugene Dwight
Brown, Constance
Demerson, Elisha L.
Gaston, Mack Charles
Gibson, Kenneth Allen
Goodall, Hurley Charles
Harrell, Ernest James
Henderson, Henry F., Jr.
Hurley, Samuel W., Jr.
Lawson, Lawyer
McNair, Ronald
Patin, Jude Wilmot Paul
Patrick, Jennie R.
Randolph, Bernard P.
Sanderson, Walter H., Jr.

Entertainers

Comedians

Cosby, William Henry, Jr.
Hall, Arsenio
Murphy, Eddie

Composers

Butler, Jerry
Charles, Ray
Hines, Gregory Oliver
Jackson, Michael Joseph
Jones, Quincy Delight, Jr.
Richie, Lionel
Wonder, Stevie

Dancers

Allen, Deborah
Hines, Gregory Oliver
Jackson, Janet
Jackson, Michael Joseph
Teer, Barbara

Directors and Producers

Allen, Deborah
Cosby, William Henry, Jr.

Films *see* **Entertainers**

Government

Judges (Appointed and Elected)

Law Enforcement
(*see also* **Judges**)

Geographical Index

Alabama

Aaron, Henry Louis
Abernathy, Ralph David
Arrington, Richard, Jr.
Austin, Richard H.
Black, Don G.
Brown, Robert L.
Buskey, James E.
Carter, Annette
Cottrell, Comer J., Jr.
Escott-Russell, Sundra E.
Figures, Michael Anthony
Gaston, Arthur G., Sr.
Gibson, Kenneth Allen
Gordon, Fred Augustus
Hall, James Reginald, Jr.
Harrell, Ernest James
Hilliard, Earl F.
Holmes, Arthur, Jr.
Holyfield, Evander
Horn, William Fred
Jones, Herbert C.
King, Coretta Scott
Lewis, Brenda J. Early
Lewis, John
Lowery, Joseph E.
Marbury, Carl Harris
Owens, James Cleveland (Jesse)
Paige, Leroy Robert (Satchel)
Parks, Rosa Louise
Patrick, Jennie R.
Penn, Robert W.
Petersen, Frank E., Jr.
Rattley, Jessie Menifield
Rice, Condoleezza
Richie, Lionel
Sears-Collins, Leah J.
Smitherman, Carole Catlin
Vaughn, Jackie, III
Willie, Louis J.
Young, Coleman A.

Arizona

Fletcher, Arthur A.
Paige, Emmett, Jr.

Arkansas

Barnes, George H.
Brock, Louis
Davis, L. Clifford
English, Clarence R.
Johnson, John Harold
Ross, Carson
Shackelford, Lottie H.

California

Abdul-Jabbar, Kareem
Bradley, Tom
Brown, Willie L., Jr.
Burke, William A.
Burke, Yvonne Brathwaite
Carey, Howard H.
Charles, Ray
Cottrell, Comer J., Jr.
Craig, Roger
Cunningham, Randall
Davie, Frank
Dellums, Ronald
Dixon, Julian C.
Dymally, Mervyn M.
Ferguson, Lloyd N.
Gordy, Berry, Jr.
Green, Dianna
Greene, Bill
Griffey, Dick
Guiton, Bonnie
Hacker, Benjamin T.
Hall, Arsenio
Hawkins, Augustus F. (Gus)
Henderson, Rickey
Hills, Carla Anderson
Hines, Gregory Oliver
Hughes, Teresa P.

Illinois

Indiana

490   Geographical Index

About the Author

Walter Lee Hawkins was born in Atlanta, Georgia,
on January 17, 1949, to Walter and Helen Johnson Hawkins.
He is married to the former Carol V. Hooks, and
they have three children: Winter LaDonna, Michael Donta
and Whitney LeAnn. He graduated from South Fulton High
School in East Point, Georgia, in 1967, and began work
for the Atlanta police department. From 1968 to 1970
he served in the U.S. Army (14 months in Korea);
he is a reserve sergeant major in the signal corps.
In 1971 Hawkins rejoined the Atlanta police;
in 1975, he and two others became the first black
officers ever in the Fulton County police department
and in 1976, he became its first black sergeant.
In 1982, Hawkins opened "The Wiz" hair salon in Atlanta.
In 1985, he joined the Fulton County sheriff's department
and in 1987, accepted a law enforcement job with the
U.S. Postal Service. Hawkins attended Dekalb College,
Decatur, and the University of Georgia in Athens.